MW01641211

Disclosure: This study guide is intended for educational purposes only and does not guarantee success on any examination. The content provided is based on general information available at the time of creation and may not reflect the most current exam format, content, or requirements.
Users of this study guide acknowledge that:

Exam formats, content, and requirements may change without notice.

This guide is not a substitute for official exam materials or courses provided by authorized examination bodies.
The creators and distributors of this guide are not responsible for any errors, omissions, or outdated information.

Success on any examination depends on multiple factors, including individual preparation, understanding of the subject matter, and test-taking skills.
This guide does not replace professional advice or guidance from qualified instructors or institutions.

By using this study guide, you agree that the creators and distributors shall not be held liable for any damages or losses resulting from its use. Users are encouraged to verify information with official sources and seek additional resources as needed.

TABLE OF CONTENTS

INTRODUCTION

The alert came at 2:43 AM. Sarah Chen, Chief Information Security Officer at Regional Healthcare Network, was jolted awake by an urgent notification: unusual encrypted traffic patterns detected across multiple hospital systems. Within minutes, she was remote connecting to the security operations center, her CISSP training immediately kicking in as she assessed the situation.

The signs were clear – an active ransomware attack targeting patient records and medical devices. But unlike many organizations that discover breaches too late, Sarah's team was catching this one in its early stages. Her mind quickly cycled through the CISSP domains she'd mastered: identifying the threat vectors, assessing business impact, implementing incident response procedures, all while considering legal and regulatory requirements unique to healthcare.

Drawing on her security architecture expertise, Sarah directed her team to isolate affected systems while maintaining critical patient care services. She coordinated with hospital administrators, legal counsel, and public relations – skills she'd developed through the CISSP's comprehensive management approach. Within hours, the attack was contained, patient data secured, and hospital operations stabilized. What could have been a catastrophic breach became a testament to the power of proper security leadership.

This is the reality of modern cybersecurity leadership. Every day, professionals like Sarah stand between critical assets and those who would compromise them. Whether protecting patient data in healthcare, financial transactions in banking, or industrial control systems in critical infrastructure, security leaders must be ready to make split-second decisions that balance security, business operations, and regulatory compliance.

You've taken an important step by picking up this guide. The journey to CISSP certification is more than exam preparation – it's your pathway to joining an elite community of security leaders. The certification's eight domains will transform your understanding of security from tactical to strategic, technical to managerial. You'll learn to speak the language of business while maintaining deep technical expertise.

Consider how CISSP knowledge applies across industries: In healthcare, it helps protect sensitive patient data and medical devices. In financial services, it secures transaction systems and prevents fraud. In manufacturing, it safeguards intellectual property and operational technology. The common thread is the comprehensive, risk-based approach that CISSP champions.

This isn't just about passing an exam. It's about developing the expertise to protect organizations, their assets, and ultimately, people's lives in our interconnected world. Whether responding to incidents like Sarah, designing secure systems, or building security programs, the knowledge you'll gain here forms the foundation of effective security leadership.

This guide will systematically prepare you for success, breaking down complex concepts into digestible components while maintaining the strategic perspective that CISSP demands. Each chapter builds upon the last, creating a comprehensive understanding of security principles and their practical application.

Your journey to joining the ranks of distinguished security professionals starts here. Let's begin.

Understanding the CISSP Certification: A Comprehensive Overview

The CISSP (Certified Information Systems Security Professional) represents the gold standard in cybersecurity certifications. This section will provide you with a clear understanding of what lies ahead in your certification journey, from exam structure to career impact.

Exam Structure and Format The CISSP exam employs a sophisticated Computer Adaptive Testing (CAT) format that dynamically adjusts to your performance. You'll face between 100 to 150 questions during a three-hour testing period. Each response influences the difficulty of subsequent questions, ensuring a precise assessment of your knowledge depth. The passing score is 700 out of 1000 points, but remember – it's the pattern of your responses, not just the number of correct answers, that determines your success.

Domain Coverage and Weights The exam tests your knowledge across eight critical domains:

- Security and Risk Management (15%): Governance, compliance, and risk management
- Asset Security (10%): Protecting security of assets
- Security Architecture and Engineering (13%): Design principles and fundamentals
- Communication and Network Security (13%): Managing secure networks

- Identity and Access Management (13%): Controlling access and managing identity
- Security Assessment and Testing (12%): Testing security and conducting assessments
- Security Operations (13%): Day-to-day security operations
- Software Development Security (11%): Understanding secure software development

Each domain interlinks with the others, forming a comprehensive security management framework. This isn't just about memorizing facts – you'll need to understand how these domains interact in real-world scenarios.

Eligibility Requirements To qualify for CISSP certification, you must demonstrate:

- Five years of cumulative paid work experience in two or more of the eight domains
- Or four years of experience plus a college degree or approved certification
- Endorsement from a current (ISC)² certified professional
- Commitment to the (ISC)² Code of Ethics
- Ongoing professional education (120 CPE credits every three years)

Industry Recognition and Career Impact The CISSP certification carries significant weight in the industry:

- Average salary increase of 15-20% post-certification
- Recognition by organizations worldwide
- Mandatory requirement for many senior security positions
- DOD 8570 compliance for specific roles
- Enhanced credibility in security leadership positions

Recent Updates and Current Focus The exam has evolved to address modern security challenges:

- Expanded coverage of cloud security architectures
- Integration of zero trust principles
- Enhanced privacy regulation content (GDPR, CCPA)
- Focus on emerging technologies (IoT, AI/ML)
- Updated incident response frameworks

Question Format and Testing Approach CISSP questions test both technical knowledge and management acumen through:

- Scenario-based questions requiring analysis and judgment
- Management-focused decision-making scenarios
- Technical concept application
- Risk assessment and mitigation strategies
- Policy and procedure evaluation

This guide aligns perfectly with these requirements, providing:

- Comprehensive coverage of all domains
- Real-world examples and case studies
- Practice questions matching exam style
- Strategy tips for exam success
- Focus on management-level thinking

Your journey through this guide will systematically build your knowledge and confidence, preparing you not just for the exam, but for real-world security leadership roles. Each chapter integrates technical details with management principles, reflecting the exam's dual focus on operational and strategic security management.

Remember, CISSP certification isn't just about passing an exam – it's about developing the mindset and knowledge base of a security leader. This guide will help you achieve both objectives, providing the foundation for your success in the exam and your career advancement in information security.

Mastering the CISSP Exam: Strategies for Success

Understanding the CAT Format and Its Impact The CISSP's Computer Adaptive Testing (CAT) format is crucial to your success. Unlike traditional exams, each question's difficulty adapts based on your previous answers. Get a question right, and the next one becomes more challenging. Get it wrong, and you'll receive an easier question. This means every answer significantly impacts your score, especially early in the exam. The key is maintaining consistent performance rather than aiming for perfection.

Question Analysis Techniques When approaching CISSP questions, remember you're being tested as a security manager, not just a technician. Follow these steps:

1. Read the entire question twice before looking at answers
2. Identify the key question elements: Who, What, When, Where, Why
3. Look for qualifier words: MOST, BEST, LEAST, FIRST
4. Eliminate obviously incorrect answers
5. Compare remaining options from a management perspective
6. Select the most comprehensive, risk-aware solution

Time Management Strategy With 3 hours for 100-150 questions, time management is critical:

- Spend 1-2 minutes maximum per question
- Don't get stuck – flag challenging questions for review
- Reserve 15 minutes for reviewing flagged questions
- Account for varying question complexity
- Remember you can't return to previous questions

Study Planning and Execution Develop a structured study approach:

- Conduct initial knowledge assessment across all domains
- Create a study schedule based on domain weights
- Focus on weak areas while maintaining strong ones
- Use varied learning methods (reading, practice tests, videos)
- Schedule regular review sessions
- Join study groups or find a study partner

Memory Techniques for Complex Material Master complex information through:

- Mnemonic devices for frameworks and standards
- Mind mapping for connecting concepts
- Visualization techniques for processes
- Real-world examples to anchor abstract concepts
- Regular review and reinforcement
- Teaching concepts to others

Test Day Preparation Physical and Mental Readiness:

- Get adequate sleep the night before
- Arrive early to reduce stress
- Bring required identification
- Eat a light, energizing meal
- Practice relaxation techniques
- Review key concepts briefly, not intensively
- Wear comfortable, layered clothing

During the Exam:

- Take deep breaths before starting
- Read instructions carefully
- Maintain steady pacing
- Stay focused on current question
- Trust your preparation
- Use breaks if needed
- Monitor time regularly

Success Stories and Strategies Successful candidates consistently report:

- Regular practice with scenario-based questions

- Focus on understanding "why" rather than memorization
- Active participation in study groups
- Teaching concepts to strengthen understanding
- Regular self-assessment and adjustment
- Strong focus on management perspectives

Final Exam Day Checklist

The Night Before:

□ Review light summary materials
□ Prepare identification documents
□ Set multiple alarms
□ Plan route to test center
□ Pack water and snacks
□ Get adequate sleep

Morning Of:

□ Eat a balanced breakfast
□ Arrive 30 minutes early
□ Review test center rules
□ Use relaxation techniques
□ Focus on confidence building
□ Brief review of key concepts

Remember, CISSP success comes from demonstrating security management expertise, not just technical knowledge. Approach each question as a security leader making risk-based decisions. Your preparation, combined with these strategies, will position you for success in achieving this prestigious certification.

Security and Risk Management

SECURITY GOVERNANCE AND ENTERPRISE RISK MANAGEMENT INTEGRATION

Board directors shape organizational security through their oversight responsibilities. They set the tone for security culture while ensuring adequate resource allocation and risk oversight. Directors evaluate security strategies, approve policies, and monitor program effectiveness through regular reporting and metrics review. They maintain fiduciary responsibility for protecting shareholder value through proper security governance.

Security programs must align precisely with business goals and objectives. This alignment occurs through strategic planning processes that map security initiatives to business outcomes. For example, a financial institution's security program might prioritize payment system protection to support the business objective of maintaining customer trust. The security team works with business units to understand their objectives, risks, and requirements.

The reporting structure places the CISO in a position to effectively communicate security needs to executive leadership. Most organizations position the CISO reporting to the CIO, CEO, or board, depending on organizational size and industry. The security team typically includes:

- Security Operations Center (SOC) analysts
- Security architects
- Identity and access management specialists
- Governance, risk and compliance personnel
- Security engineers

Key performance indicators measure security program effectiveness:

Technical Metrics:

- Mean time to detect (MTTD) incidents
- Mean time to respond (MTTR)
- Patch implementation times
- Security control coverage
- Vulnerability remediation rates

Business Metrics:

- Security program ROI
- Risk reduction measurements
- Audit findings closure rates
- Security awareness participation
- Budget variance analysis

Daily security governance integration requires:

- Regular risk assessments
- Policy compliance monitoring
- Security working groups
- Change management processes
- Incident response procedures
- Vendor security reviews
- Asset management practices
- Access certification reviews

The organization implements governance through:

Policy Framework:

Level 1: Security Policy
↓
Level 2: Standards
↓
Level 3: Procedures
↓
Level 4: Guidelines

Control Implementation:

- Administrative controls (policies, training)
- Technical controls (firewalls, encryption)
- Physical controls (badges, cameras)

Security committees meet regularly to:

- Review metrics and KPIs
- Assess emerging threats
- Evaluate control effectiveness
- Approve policy exceptions
- Prioritize security initiatives
- Allocate resources
- Address audit findings

Program assessment occurs through:

- Internal audits
- External audits
- Penetration testing
- Control validation
- Metrics analysis
- Maturity assessments

Security governance requires continuous monitoring and improvement based on:

- Changes in threat landscape
- Business environment shifts
- Regulatory updates
- Technological advances
- Organizational changes
- Risk appetite adjustments

MAJOR SECURITY CONTROL FRAMEWORKS: ISO 27001, NIST CSF, AND COBIT

Security control frameworks guide organizations in managing risks, protecting assets, and ensuring compliance. ISO 27001, NIST Cybersecurity Framework (CSF), and COBIT represent three major frameworks with distinct purposes yet significant overlaps. Organizations need to understand the relationships between these frameworks, implementation considerations, and integration challenges to choose the best fit for their needs.

Mapping Relationships Between ISO 27001, NIST CSF, and COBIT

ISO 27001 provides a formal structure for implementing an Information Security Management System (ISMS), focusing on risk management and operational controls. It includes 114 security controls divided into 14 domains, such as physical security, access control, and incident management. Its global certification is a key differentiator, particularly for industries needing compliance demonstration, like healthcare or finance.

The NIST CSF, on the other hand, focuses on cybersecurity risk management. It is built around five core functions—Identify, Protect, Detect, Respond, and Recover—and is particularly suited for critical infrastructure sectors. Unlike ISO 27001, it is not certifiable but provides a flexible, practical approach to managing cyber threats.

COBIT (Control Objectives for Information and Related Technologies) emphasizes IT governance, process optimization, and aligning IT with business goals. While its scope is broader than ISO 27001 or NIST CSF, COBIT shares key areas, such as risk assessment, incident management, and access control.

ISO 27001 and NIST CSF frequently overlap in security controls, particularly in areas like risk management and incident response. COBIT complements both by offering governance and process monitoring, making it ideal for organizations prioritizing IT strategy alignment.

Aspect	ISO 27001	NIST CSF	COBIT
Primary Focus	ISMS and risk management	Cybersecurity management	IT governance
Certification Available	Yes	No	No
Key Structure	14 domains, 114 controls	5 core functions	40 governance processes
Industry Applicability	Broad, all sectors	Critical infrastructure	IT-intensive organizations

Implementation Considerations

ISO 27001 implementation begins with establishing an ISMS. This requires identifying the organization's scope, performing a risk assessment, and defining security controls to mitigate identified risks. One challenge is ensuring alignment across departments and addressing resource constraints. For example, a multinational company may struggle to apply a uniform approach to compliance while managing jurisdiction-specific regulations.

NIST CSF is more flexible and adaptable. It can be customized for organizations of any size, making it especially useful for small and medium-sized businesses. However, its lack of certification can make demonstrating compliance difficult, especially in highly regulated sectors. An example would be a healthcare provider balancing NIST CSF with HIPAA compliance requirements.

COBIT implementation requires organizations to map their IT processes against COBIT's governance and management objectives. It involves establishing performance metrics, identifying critical processes, and ensuring alignment with broader business goals. A typical challenge involves integrating COBIT into an existing cybersecurity program, such as one built on ISO 27001, without creating redundancies.

Framework Selection Criteria Based on Organization Type

ISO 27001 is particularly well-suited for organizations seeking certification to demonstrate compliance with international standards. Financial institutions, for instance, frequently adopt ISO 27001 to meet client and regulatory expectations.

NIST CSF is ideal for organizations that prioritize adaptability and need a lightweight, scalable framework. It is particularly favored in the U.S., where it aligns with federal and state regulations for critical infrastructure.

COBIT is best for organizations seeking a governance-focused approach that connects IT processes with broader strategic goals. A global technology company, for instance, may choose COBIT to integrate IT risk management with its corporate governance model.

A small retail company looking to improve cybersecurity without the complexity of certification might choose NIST CSF, while a global bank operating under stringent regulatory environments might select ISO 27001 for its formalized and certifiable structure.

Integration Challenges and Solutions

Integrating multiple frameworks often creates challenges, such as overlapping requirements, redundant controls, and misalignment between technical and governance-focused objectives. For instance, combining ISO 27001's detailed control requirements with COBIT's governance processes may lead to conflicting priorities.

One solution is to create a unified risk management program that consolidates the requirements of all frameworks. Tools like GRC (Governance, Risk, and Compliance) platforms can help centralize risk assessment, monitoring, and reporting. Published crosswalks, such as ISO 27001-to-NIST mappings, can also simplify integration by identifying areas of overlap.

For example, a critical infrastructure operator might adopt NIST CSF for operational cybersecurity, ISO 27001 for formal risk management and certification, and COBIT for governance oversight. Integrating these frameworks could involve using NIST CSF to address daily operations, while ISO 27001 ensures audit readiness, and COBIT provides governance dashboards for senior executives.

Compliance Mapping Between Frameworks

Frameworks often share foundational concepts, such as risk management, incident response, and asset security. Mapping compliance helps organizations meet requirements without duplicating efforts. For example, ISO 27001's risk assessment and treatment plan align closely with NIST CSF's Identify function and COBIT's risk governance processes.

Using such mappings, an organization can demonstrate compliance with multiple frameworks simultaneously. For instance, a healthcare provider using ISO 27001 to comply with HIPAA can leverage NIST CSF's guidance to strengthen incident response processes while using COBIT for IT performance management.

ISO 27001 Control	NIST CSF Function	COBIT Process
A.5: Information Security Policy	Identify	APO12: Manage Risk
A.9: Access Control	Protect	DSS05: Manage Security
A.16: Incident Management	Respond	DSS02: Incident Response
A.17: Business Continuity	Recover	APO10: Manage Configuration

BUSINESS ALIGNMENT STRATEGIES

Aligning a security program with business objectives requires integrating measurable outcomes, optimizing resources, and fostering clear communication with stakeholders. The process involves leveraging financial metrics, prioritization frameworks, and performance evaluations to ensure security supports broader organizational goals while mitigating risks effectively.

SECURITY PROGRAM ROI CALCULATION METHODS

Quantifying the return on investment (ROI) for a security program demonstrates its financial and operational value to stakeholders. Unlike traditional ROI models, security ROI focuses on cost avoidance rather than direct revenue generation.

1. **Annualized Loss Expectancy (ALE):** This method evaluates the potential annual cost of specific risks by assessing the single loss expectancy (SLE) and its annualized rate of occurrence (ARO).
    - Formula: ALE = SLE × ARO
    - Example: A ransomware attack could cost $300,000 per incident (SLE) and is likely to occur 25% of the time annually (ARO = 0.25). This leads to an ALE of $75,000. A $40,000 solution that mitigates this risk provides a clear ROI.
2. **Cost of Controls vs. Risk Mitigation:** By comparing the cost of implementing a security measure against the monetary value of the risks it reduces, organizations can determine investment effectiveness. For example, a $25,000 firewall upgrade preventing $150,000 in potential damages highlights a strong ROI.
3. **Business Impact Analysis (BIA):** BIA identifies critical processes and quantifies the financial and operational impact of disruptions, forming the foundation for calculating ROI by linking security investments to uninterrupted business functions.

COST-BENEFIT ANALYSIS TECHNIQUES

Cost-benefit analysis (CBA) is a decision-making tool that balances the financial and operational trade-offs of security investments. It includes both tangible and intangible elements.

1. **Tangible Costs and Benefits:**
    - Costs: Implementation expenses, ongoing maintenance, operational impacts, and training requirements.
    - Benefits: Avoided downtime, minimized compliance penalties, and reduced recovery costs.
    - Example: A data encryption tool costing $50,000 annually could prevent a $400,000 breach, offering significant cost savings.
2. **Intangible Benefits:** Consider less quantifiable advantages such as enhanced brand reputation, customer trust, and employee morale. For example, a highly secure payment gateway builds customer loyalty in competitive markets.
3. **Net Present Value (NPV) and Return Periods:** NPV calculates the long-term financial value of security investments by discounting future benefits to present terms. Payback periods measure how quickly investments recover their costs.
4. **Scenario Analysis:** This approach models potential outcomes of different investment decisions, allowing decision-makers to visualize risk reduction trade-offs and financial impacts across a range of conditions.

SECURITY INVESTMENT PRIORITIZATION

Given finite resources, prioritizing security investments ensures the most critical risks are addressed first.

1. **Risk-Based Prioritization:** Investments are ranked based on their ability to mitigate high-likelihood, high-impact risks. For instance, securing privileged accounts may take precedence over endpoint hardening in environments where insider threats are prevalent.

2. **Regulatory and Compliance Obligations:** Organizations prioritize measures required by law or regulations, such as PCI-DSS for payment processing or GDPR for personal data protection, to avoid significant penalties.
3. **Strategic Alignment:** Using frameworks like the NIST Cybersecurity Framework, security initiatives can be directly mapped to the organization's objectives and risk appetite, ensuring resources are allocated to areas most relevant to business operations.
4. **Business Case Development:** Priorities are established by building detailed business cases for investments, demonstrating their impact on operational continuity, financial health, and customer satisfaction.
5. **Pareto Principle (80/20 Rule):** Allocating resources to mitigate the top 20% of risks, which account for 80% of overall exposure, ensures efficiency while addressing critical vulnerabilities.

STAKEHOLDER COMMUNICATION STRATEGIES

Clear communication is crucial for obtaining buy-in and ensuring alignment between security teams and business stakeholders. Translating technical details into business value fosters mutual understanding and support.

1. **Business-Oriented Language:** Replace technical jargon with relatable concepts. Instead of discussing "malware signature updates," emphasize "reducing operational downtime by minimizing attack vectors."
2. **Visual Representations:** Dashboards, heatmaps, and infographics convey complex information effectively. For example, a risk heatmap showing critical systems at higher risk helps stakeholders visualize vulnerabilities at a glance.
3. **Tailored Communication:** Present information based on the audience:
   - Executives need high-level summaries tied to business impact and ROI.
   - Operational teams require actionable, technical instructions for implementation.
4. **Regular Updates and Feedback:** Quarterly reviews of security metrics, including incident response times, risk reductions, and regulatory compliance, keep stakeholders informed of progress.
5. **Storytelling:** Relating security measures to real-world events resonates with non-technical stakeholders. For example, referencing a high-profile data breach reinforces the importance of investments in security.

PERFORMANCE MEASUREMENT METHODOLOGIES

Effective performance measurement ensures a security program remains aligned with business objectives and continues to deliver measurable benefits.

1. **Key Performance Indicators (KPIs):** KPIs track critical security outcomes such as reduced incident response times, compliance rates, and the percentage of patched systems. For example, reducing mean time to detect (MTTD) a breach from 72 hours to 24 hours could demonstrate significant progress.
2. **Key Risk Indicators (KRIs):** KRIs assess potential exposures, such as the number of open vulnerabilities or unpatched systems, to guide proactive actions before incidents occur.
3. **Maturity Models:** Frameworks like the Capability Maturity Model Integration (CMMI) measure the effectiveness of security processes on a scale from initial (ad hoc processes) to optimized (continuously improving).
4. **Benchmarking:** Comparing the organization's security metrics to industry peers identifies performance gaps and improvement opportunities. For instance, an organization with slower incident response times than its competitors might prioritize investments in SOC tools and training.
5. **Balanced Scorecards:** Evaluating security performance across dimensions such as financial impact, operational effectiveness, customer satisfaction, and innovation ensures a holistic understanding of a program's value.
6. **Automated Monitoring:** Tools like SIEMs (Security Information and Event Management) and SOARs (Security Orchestration, Automation, and Response) provide continuous visibility into program performance, helping teams adapt to evolving threats in real time.

Integrating these strategies and measurement techniques creates a dynamic security program that supports organizational objectives, drives efficiency, and communicates value effectively across all levels of the business.

COMPREHENSIVE RISK ASSESSMENT METHODOLOGIES

Risk identification integrates multiple techniques to uncover potential threats and vulnerabilities. Business impact analysis examines critical processes and their dependencies. Threat modeling applies frameworks like STRIDE (Spoofing, Tampering, Repudiation, Information disclosure, Denial of service, Elevation of privilege) to identify potential attack vectors. Asset inventory analysis maps data flows and system interconnections to reveal exposure points.

Asset valuation incorporates both quantitative and qualitative methods:

Quantitative Valuation:

Asset Value = Initial Cost + (Maintenance Cost × Expected Life) + (Revenue Impact × Time) + Replacement Cost

Qualitative Factors:

- Regulatory requirements
- Intellectual property value
- Customer trust impact
- Market share effects
- Brand reputation damage
- Operational disruption

Threat and vulnerability analysis examines:

External Threats:

- Advanced persistent threats (APTs)
- Cybercriminal organizations
- Hacktivists
- Nation-state actors
- Industrial competitors

Internal Threats:

- Privileged users
- Contractors
- Disgruntled employees
- Human error
- System misconfigurations

Vulnerability Assessment Methods:

- Automated scanning
- Manual testing
- Code review
- Configuration analysis
- Architecture review
- Penetration testing

Impact assessment evaluates potential losses through:

Financial Impact:

- Direct costs
- Legal expenses
- Recovery costs
- Lost revenue
- Regulatory fines
- Insurance premiums

Operational Impact:

- Service disruption
- Productivity loss
- Customer attrition
- Market share decline
- Reputation damage
- Strategic setbacks

Risk Register Structure:

Risk ID	Description	Assets	Threats	Vulnerabilities	Controls	Likelihood	Impact	Risk Score
R1	Data breach	Customer DB	Hackers	SQL injection	WAF, encryption	High	High	Critical
R2	Power outage	Data center	Natural disaster	Single power grid	UPS, generator	Low	High	Medium

Risk appetite determination examines:

Organizational Factors:

- Industry standards
- Competitive position
- Growth objectives
- Innovation goals
- Investment capacity
- Stakeholder expectations

Market Conditions:

- Economic climate
- Industry trends
- Technology changes
- Regulatory environment
- Customer expectations
- Competitive pressure

Risk assessment tools integrate:

- Automated risk scoring
- Threat intelligence feeds
- Vulnerability databases
- Asset management systems
- Control frameworks
- Compliance requirements

Organizations document findings through:

- Risk treatment plans
- Mitigation strategies
- Control implementation
- Monitoring procedures
- Review schedules
- Escalation paths

Risk metrics track:

- Control effectiveness
- Incident frequency
- Loss magnitude
- Recovery time
- Mitigation costs
- Residual risk levels

Regular assessment updates reflect:

- New threats
- System changes

- Business evolution
- Control modifications
- Performance data
- Incident lessons

COMPREHENSIVE THREAT MODELING APPROACH

Threat modeling is a systematic approach to identifying, understanding, and mitigating potential threats within a system, application, or network. By focusing on vulnerabilities and anticipating possible attack vectors, organizations can proactively enhance their security posture. Incorporating methodologies like STRIDE, attack tree development, data flow diagrams, trust boundary identification, and control validation ensures a thorough assessment of risks.

STRIDE Methodology Application

STRIDE, developed by Microsoft, is a framework for identifying six categories of threats: **Spoofing, Tampering, Repudiation, Information Disclosure, Denial of Service (DoS), and Elevation of Privilege**. It helps security teams evaluate potential threats during the design and development phases of a system.

The process involves analyzing system components (e.g., user interfaces, APIs, databases) and determining how each STRIDE category might manifest. For example:

- **Spoofing**: An attacker impersonates a legitimate user or service (e.g., credential theft or forged JWT tokens).
- **Tampering**: Modification of data during transmission (e.g., altering a configuration file).
- **Repudiation**: The inability to track actions (e.g., lack of proper logging or auditing).
- **Information Disclosure**: Unauthorized access to sensitive data (e.g., exposed S3 buckets or SQL injection).
- **Denial of Service**: Overwhelming a resource to disrupt availability (e.g., volumetric DDoS attacks).
- **Elevation of Privilege**: Gaining unauthorized higher-level access (e.g., privilege escalation due to misconfigured IAM policies).

To apply STRIDE effectively, begin with a high-level view of the system and break it into smaller components, mapping each one to its potential vulnerabilities. For instance, when evaluating a web application, STRIDE might reveal the need for multifactor authentication (to prevent spoofing) or database encryption (to counter information disclosure).

Attack Tree Development

An attack tree provides a visual and hierarchical representation of how an attacker might achieve a malicious goal. The root node represents the ultimate objective (e.g., stealing customer data), while child nodes outline various attack paths and sub-objectives.

Developing an attack tree involves the following steps:

1. **Define the Root Node**: Identify the attacker's ultimate goal, such as gaining administrative access to a system.
2. **Enumerate Attack Paths**: Break down the goal into all possible means to achieve it. For example, administrative access might be gained by credential theft, exploiting a vulnerability, or social engineering.
3. **Assign Details to Nodes**: For each path, identify required conditions, tools, or dependencies (e.g., exploiting a specific CVE or gaining access to a phishing target).
4. **Evaluate Node Likelihood**: Assign probabilities or difficulty levels to each node to prioritize mitigations.

For example, an attack tree for stealing data might include:

- Root Node: Exfiltrate sensitive customer data.
    - Path 1: Compromise a database.
        - Subpath: Exploit SQL injection.
        - Subpath: Exploit misconfigured database permissions.
    - Path 2: Access a backup system.
        - Subpath: Steal unencrypted backup files.

Attack trees help security teams visualize the full scope of potential threats, prioritize defenses for high-probability paths, and simulate "what if" scenarios to gauge their preparedness.

Data Flow Diagram Creation

Data Flow Diagrams (DFDs) depict how information moves through a system, identifying potential vulnerabilities at each stage. A DFD typically includes entities (users, systems), processes (applications, APIs), data stores (databases, files), and data flows (arrows indicating movement of information).

To create a DFD:

1. **Define the Scope**: Determine the system or process to be analyzed.
2. **Identify Components**: Map out users, applications, data sources, and endpoints.
3. **Outline Data Flows**: Draw arrows to represent how data travels between components.
4. **Label Sensitivity**: Annotate flows with the type of data involved (e.g., PII, payment details) and its sensitivity.

For example, a web application DFD might include:

- Users entering credentials (data flow to an authentication server).
- An authentication server verifying the credentials against a database.
- The server sending a session token back to the user.

Using DFDs, you can pinpoint vulnerabilities, such as unencrypted transmission of sensitive data, and assess areas requiring additional security measures. They are also critical for mapping out trust boundaries, described below.

Trust Boundary Identification

Trust boundaries are demarcations in a system where the trust level changes, such as between a user and a server or between internal and external networks. Identifying trust boundaries is essential for ensuring that data crossing these boundaries is properly validated, authenticated, and secured.

To identify trust boundaries:

1. **Review Data Flows**: Examine the DFD to locate points where data transitions from one system or entity to another.
2. **Analyze Control Changes**: Identify where responsibility shifts, such as from a third-party service to an internal application.
3. **Evaluate Security Requirements**: For each boundary, consider mechanisms like input validation, encryption, authentication, and monitoring.

Common examples of trust boundaries include:

- Between a client and a web server (user input validation and TLS encryption).
- Between internal APIs and external third-party services (API keys, rate limiting).
- Between a public network and a corporate intranet (firewall and VPN enforcement).

Trust boundaries often reveal areas requiring enhanced controls, such as robust authentication for external APIs or hardened configurations for public-facing servers.

Control Validation Techniques

Control validation ensures that implemented security measures are functioning as intended and effectively mitigating threats. Techniques for control validation include:

1. **Penetration Testing**: Simulate real-world attacks to identify exploitable vulnerabilities. For example, testing a web application might uncover improper access control or injection vulnerabilities.
2. **Vulnerability Scanning**: Use automated tools (e.g., Nessus, Qualys) to identify outdated software, configuration issues, or missing patches.
3. **Red Team/Blue Team Exercises**: Conduct adversarial simulations where a red team attacks the system and a blue team defends it, enabling identification of both technical and procedural gaps.
4. **Code Reviews**: Analyze application code for security flaws, such as hardcoded credentials or weak cryptographic implementations.
5. **Threat Simulations**: Use frameworks like MITRE ATT&CK to simulate specific attack tactics and techniques, validating defensive measures against them.
6. **Policy Compliance Audits**: Ensure that configurations and operational procedures align with organizational policies and standards (e.g., ensuring encryption is consistently applied to all sensitive data flows).

For example, a penetration test might validate that rate limiting successfully prevents brute force attacks on login endpoints, while a code review could reveal overlooked input validation vulnerabilities. Regular control validation ensures that security defenses remain effective against emerging threats.

Integrated Threat Modeling in Practice
A comprehensive threat modeling approach combines these techniques to create a dynamic, iterative process. For instance, after using STRIDE to identify potential spoofing and tampering threats, you can develop an attack tree to understand how attackers might exploit these threats. From there, a DFD can be used to visualize the data flow and identify trust boundaries where these vulnerabilities are most likely to manifest. Finally, control validation techniques can be applied to test the effectiveness of implemented defenses and address gaps.

SUPPLY CHAIN RISK MANAGEMENT DEEP DIVE

Managing supply chain risks requires a proactive, structured approach to identify, evaluate, and mitigate vulnerabilities introduced by third-party vendors, suppliers, and partners. In an interconnected world where a single weak link can compromise an entire organization, supply chain risk management (SCRM) has become a cornerstone of cybersecurity.

VENDOR ASSESSMENT FRAMEWORKS

Evaluating vendors involves a structured process to ensure third parties meet the organization's security, compliance, and operational standards. Effective frameworks combine qualitative and quantitative measures to provide a comprehensive risk profile.

1. **NIST Cyber Supply Chain Risk Management (C-SCRM):**
   The NIST C-SCRM framework provides a methodology for identifying and managing supply chain risks. Key steps include:
   - Mapping the supply chain to understand dependencies and critical paths.
   - Evaluating the cybersecurity posture of each vendor against NIST standards.
   - Establishing contractual requirements for security controls.
2. **Shared Assessments Standardized Information Gathering (SIG):**
   This industry-standard questionnaire evaluates a vendor's security practices across multiple domains, including data protection, access control, and incident response readiness. The SIG framework ensures consistency in vendor evaluations.
3. **ISO 27036:**
   Part of the ISO 27000 series, this standard focuses on information security in supplier relationships. It emphasizes risk identification, requirements setting, and monitoring of third-party agreements.
4. **Customized Scoring Models:**
   Many organizations develop scoring systems tailored to their risk appetite. Vendors are rated on factors such as:
   - Historical performance and reputation.
   - Technical controls (e.g., endpoint security, encryption).
   - Regulatory compliance (e.g., GDPR, HIPAA).

Vendor assessment frameworks provide a repeatable, scalable process for vetting and approving new suppliers while maintaining accountability across the supply chain.

THIRD-PARTY RISK METRICS

Quantifying third-party risks helps prioritize mitigation efforts and ensures data-driven decisions. Common third-party risk metrics include:

1. **Risk Ratings:**
   Assigning numerical risk scores to vendors based on their security posture and the criticality of their services. Tools like BitSight and SecurityScorecard automate this process, providing real-time ratings based on external scans and reported incidents.
2. **Time to Patch (TTP):**
   Measuring the time vendors take to patch known vulnerabilities is critical for assessing their responsiveness. Vendors with excessive TTP windows may introduce unnecessary risk.
3. **Data Sensitivity Tiering:**
   Vendors are categorized based on the type and sensitivity of data they process or access. For example, a payroll processing vendor handling employee PII would be placed in a high-risk tier compared to a vendor delivering non-sensitive office supplies.

4. **SLAs for Security Incident Response:**
   Monitoring adherence to service-level agreements (SLAs) related to incident response, such as response time, notification protocols, and reporting requirements, provides insight into a vendor's preparedness.
5. **Compliance Audits:**
   Regular audits of vendor compliance with industry standards (e.g., SOC 2, ISO 27001) and regulatory requirements help assess their overall risk profile and adherence to security best practices.

Using these metrics, organizations can continuously evaluate and compare vendors, ensuring high-risk entities are addressed promptly.

CONTINUOUS MONITORING STRATEGIES

Vendor risks evolve over time, making static assessments insufficient. Continuous monitoring ensures organizations remain aware of changing threats, vulnerabilities, and compliance gaps within their supply chain.

1. **Third-Party Risk Monitoring Platforms:**
   Tools like RiskRecon or Prevalent provide real-time insights into vendors' security postures by monitoring public data, breach reports, and dark web activity. For example, these tools can alert organizations when a vendor's IP addresses are involved in suspicious activity.
2. **Attack Surface Monitoring:**
   Continuous monitoring of exposed endpoints, vulnerable software, and open ports ensures that vendors' external-facing systems are secure. Security testing services, such as penetration tests or vulnerability scans, can supplement this effort.
3. **Behavioral Analytics:**
   Monitoring network behavior and access patterns for anomalies in vendor activity can uncover potential insider threats or compromised vendor accounts. For instance, unusual access attempts to critical systems after business hours could indicate malicious intent.
4. **Risk Reassessment Frequency:**
   While high-risk vendors should be reviewed quarterly, lower-risk vendors may only need annual or semi-annual reassessments. Regular updates to questionnaires and reassessments ensure new risks are accounted for.
5. **Threat Intelligence Integration:**
   Incorporating threat intelligence feeds into vendor monitoring provides early warnings about cybercriminal campaigns targeting supply chain vulnerabilities. This allows preemptive mitigation efforts.

Continuous monitoring strengthens an organization's ability to detect and address risks before they escalate into major incidents.

CONTRACT SECURITY REQUIREMENTS

Well-drafted contracts establish clear expectations for vendor security practices and create enforceable obligations to maintain compliance and risk mitigation. Key components of contract security requirements include:

1. **Minimum Security Standards:**
   Contracts should specify baseline security measures, such as:
   - Data encryption in transit and at rest.
   - Multi-factor authentication (MFA) for privileged accounts.
   - Endpoint protection and monitoring.
2. **Right-to-Audit Clauses:**
   Granting the organization the ability to audit vendors' security practices ensures ongoing compliance and transparency. Audits may include site visits, policy reviews, and technical assessments.
3. **Breach Notification Requirements:**
   Vendors must commit to notifying the organization of security incidents within a specified timeframe (e.g., 24–72 hours). The notification process should include details of the breach, affected systems, and remediation plans.
4. **Subcontractor Management:**
   Vendors often rely on subcontractors, which introduces additional risks. Contracts should:
   - Require vendors to impose equivalent security standards on subcontractors.
   - Mandate pre-approval of subcontractor use.

5. **Termination and Data Handling:**
   Define security requirements for contract termination, such as secure deletion of sensitive data or return of proprietary information. Provisions should specify timelines and verification processes for data destruction.

Strong contract terms help enforce accountability and ensure vendors prioritize cybersecurity as part of their relationship with the organization.

INCIDENT RESPONSE INTEGRATION

Supply chain incident response (IR) plans must incorporate vendors to address breaches originating from third-party systems or services. Coordination ensures rapid containment and minimizes operational disruption.

1. **Shared Incident Response Plans:**
   Vendors should be required to provide their IR plans for review. Plans must align with the organization's overall incident response strategy, ensuring seamless coordination.
2. **Communication Protocols:**
   Establishing predefined communication channels and escalation paths reduces response times. Vendors must identify points of contact for incident reporting and remediation.
3. **Joint Tabletop Exercises:**
   Conducting simulated attack scenarios with vendors evaluates their readiness and identifies gaps in collaborative response efforts. For example, a ransomware simulation may reveal delays in data restoration processes that need to be addressed.
4. **Forensic Collaboration:**
   Vendors should cooperate with forensic investigations, providing access to logs, system images, and other relevant data. Clear contractual obligations ensure compliance with forensic requirements.
5. **Post-Incident Reviews:**
   After resolving a supply chain incident, both the organization and the vendor should conduct a joint review to identify root causes, improve defenses, and update response plans.

By fully integrating vendors into incident response strategies, organizations can minimize the impact of supply chain attacks and maintain operational resilience.

GLOBAL PRIVACY REGULATIONS AND COMPLIANCE IMPLEMENTATION

GDPR establishes foundational privacy requirements across EU member states and affects organizations worldwide that process EU resident data. Organizations must implement privacy by design principles through their data processing activities:

Data Processing Requirements:

- Legal basis for processing
- Purpose limitation
- Data minimization
- Storage limitations
- Accuracy maintenance
- Integrity and confidentiality

CCPA Implementation Framework:

Data Inventory → Notice Requirements → Consumer Rights → Vendor Management → Training → Documentation

Privacy Impact Assessment Components:

Assessment Phase	**Key Activities**	**Deliverables**
Scoping	System identification, data flow mapping	Process diagram
Risk Analysis	Threat modeling, vulnerability assessment	Risk matrix
Control Review	Security measure evaluation, gap analysis	Control catalog
Recommendations	Mitigation strategies, implementation plan	Action items

Data Subject Rights Management:

Access Rights Process:

1. Request intake

2. Identity verification
3. Scope determination
4. Data collection
5. Format preparation
6. Response delivery

Deletion Rights Workflow:

1. Request validation
2. Data identification
3. Impact assessment
4. Execution planning
5. Deletion verification
6. Documentation

Cross-border Data Transfer Mechanisms:

Standard Contractual Clauses (SCCs):

- EU-approved contract terms
- Legally binding obligations
- Privacy safeguards
- Enforcement provisions
- Liability allocation
- Audit requirements

Binding Corporate Rules:

- Internal privacy policies
- Training requirements
- Audit procedures
- Complaint handling
- Enforcement mechanisms
- Update processes

Privacy Shield Replacement:

- Adequacy determinations
- Essential equivalence
- Redress mechanisms
- Oversight requirements
- Transparency obligations
- Review procedures

Technical Controls:

- Encryption standards
- Access controls
- Monitoring systems
- Data classification
- Retention policies
- Incident response

Documentation Requirements:

- Processing records
- Impact assessments
- Consent management
- Rights requests
- Transfer mechanisms
- Security measures

Training Programs:

- Privacy principles
- Handling procedures
- Incident response
- Rights management
- Transfer requirements
- Documentation practices

Organizations monitor compliance through:

- Regular assessments
- Internal audits
- External reviews
- Incident analysis
- Metrics tracking
- Process improvement

Privacy program integration requires:

- Policy frameworks
- Operational procedures
- Technical controls
- Training programs
- Monitoring systems
- Review processes

CONTRACTUAL OBLIGATIONS

Contractual obligations are critical in defining responsibilities, expectations, and accountability between parties in any business relationship. For organizations, especially in the context of outsourcing, vendor management, or cloud service engagements, contracts must establish clear guidelines for security, performance, compliance, and liability. Well-structured contracts mitigate risks, ensure alignment with legal requirements, and provide recourse in case of disputes or breaches.

Service Level Agreement Components

Service Level Agreements (SLAs) define the performance and availability expectations between service providers and their clients. SLAs must be explicit and measurable, as they form the foundation for evaluating service delivery and resolving disputes.

Key components include:

- **Performance Metrics**: Clearly defined criteria such as uptime (e.g., 99.9% availability), response time for resolving issues, and transaction processing speeds.
- **Monitoring and Reporting**: Specifications for how performance will be tracked, such as through monitoring tools or dashboards, and how results will be communicated (e.g., weekly reports or real-time access).
- **Remediation and Penalties**: Actions to be taken if service levels are not met, such as issuing service credits, escalating incidents, or applying financial penalties.
- **Maintenance and Downtime**: Planned maintenance schedules and notification requirements, ensuring minimal disruption to operations.
- **Disaster Recovery Provisions**: Details on recovery time objectives (RTOs) and recovery point objectives (RPOs) in the event of an outage.

For example, a cloud service provider might include an SLA guaranteeing 99.99% availability for critical services, with a penalty clause providing prorated service credits for downtime exceeding 0.01% per month. Organizations must verify that SLAs align with their operational needs and assess whether penalties adequately compensate for potential losses due to service disruptions.

Security Requirements in Contracts

Contracts must include detailed security requirements to ensure that third parties maintain the organization's desired level of protection for sensitive data and systems. Security requirements often include both technical and procedural obligations, such as:

- **Access Controls**: Restrictions on who can access systems or data, often based on least privilege and role-based access models.
- **Data Encryption**: Mandates for encrypting data in transit (e.g., TLS 1.2 or higher) and at rest (e.g., AES-256).
- **Incident Response**: Requirements for how the service provider will detect, report, and remediate security incidents.
- **Audits and Assessments**: Rights for the organization to conduct audits of the vendor's security controls or review third-party audit reports, such as SOC 2 Type II reports.
- **Secure Development Practices**: If applicable, obligations to follow secure coding guidelines (e.g., OWASP Top 10) and conduct vulnerability scans or penetration tests.

For instance, a data processing agreement (DPA) might specify that the vendor implements multifactor authentication (MFA) for administrative access and performs annual penetration testing. Organizations should carefully review contracts to ensure these requirements align with internal security policies and applicable regulations.

Liability and Indemnification Clauses

Liability and indemnification clauses allocate responsibility for potential losses, damages, or legal claims that may arise during the business relationship. These clauses protect parties from financial risks and disputes.

- **Liability Limitation**: Caps the amount a party can be held financially responsible for, often expressed as a multiple of the contract value (e.g., "liability limited to 2x the total contract value").
- **Exclusions**: Specifies types of damages excluded from liability limits, such as indirect, incidental, or consequential damages.
- **Indemnification**: Obligates one party to compensate the other for specific losses or claims. For example, the vendor may indemnify the client for losses caused by data breaches due to the vendor's negligence.

For example, a cloud provider might include a liability cap limiting compensation for service outages to the total fees paid in the preceding 12 months, but exclude liability for consequential losses like lost business revenue. Clients should negotiate terms to balance liability exposure, especially in high-risk areas like data breaches.

Breach Notification Requirements

Contracts often include provisions outlining breach notification requirements to ensure timely reporting and effective incident management. These requirements are particularly important when sensitive data is involved.

- **Notification Timeline**: Specifies how quickly the vendor must notify the client after discovering a breach, often within 24–72 hours.
- **Information to Be Provided**: Details about the breach, such as the nature of the incident, affected data or systems, and steps taken to mitigate the impact.
- **Coordination Obligations**: Specifies collaboration on breach response, including forensic investigations, remediation plans, and public communication strategies.
- **Costs and Responsibilities**: Clarifies which party bears the costs of notification, remediation, and any regulatory fines or penalties.

For instance, a contract with a payment processor might mandate notification within 48 hours of detecting unauthorized access to credit card data, along with forensic reports and a timeline for corrective action. Failure to include clear breach notification clauses can lead to delays, regulatory penalties, and reputational harm.

Regulatory Compliance Obligations

Organizations must ensure that their contracts with third parties explicitly address compliance with relevant laws and regulations. These obligations vary depending on the industry, geographic location, and type of data involved. Examples include:

- **Data Protection Regulations**: Compliance with laws like the GDPR, which mandates specific protections for personal data, including data minimization, encryption, and breach notification within 72 hours.
- **Sector-Specific Regulations**: Adherence to standards such as HIPAA (for healthcare data), PCI DSS (for payment card data), or FINRA (for financial services).

- **Cross-Border Data Transfers**: Requirements for ensuring lawful data transfers across jurisdictions, such as using standard contractual clauses (SCCs) under the GDPR.
- **Audit Rights**: Allowing organizations to verify compliance through audits or certifications like ISO 27001 or SOC 2.

For example, a SaaS vendor storing personal data of EU residents might include contract provisions addressing GDPR compliance, such as appointing a Data Protection Officer (DPO), supporting Data Subject Access Requests (DSARs), and using SCCs for cross-border transfers. Without explicit compliance obligations, organizations risk fines and legal disputes.

Contracts that clearly define regulatory responsibilities, audit rights, and data protection obligations provide assurance that vendors meet compliance requirements. Organizations should involve legal and compliance teams in reviewing and negotiating these terms.

BUSINESS CONTINUITY PLANNING (BIA METHODOLOGY OUTLINE)

A Business Impact Analysis (BIA) identifies the critical functions, resources, and interdependencies necessary for an organization to maintain or rapidly restore operations after a disruption. A structured BIA methodology serves as the cornerstone for effective business continuity planning by prioritizing recovery efforts and aligning them with organizational objectives. Below is a comprehensive outline of the essential steps in a BIA methodology.

CRITICAL FUNCTION IDENTIFICATION

The first step in a BIA is to determine the core functions and processes essential for the organization's operations. These functions are evaluated based on their contribution to revenue, compliance, and overall business objectives.

1. **Key Questions for Identification:**
    - Which functions are directly tied to delivering critical products or services?
    - What processes, if interrupted, would severely disrupt operations or customer satisfaction?
    - What regulatory or compliance obligations depend on specific processes?
2. **Categorization of Functions:**
   Functions are typically grouped into tiers based on their criticality:
    - *Tier 1:* Vital functions requiring immediate recovery (e.g., payment processing, customer support systems).
    - *Tier 2:* Important functions tolerating short-term disruption (e.g., HR payroll processing).
    - *Tier 3:* Non-critical functions that can resume after longer delays (e.g., routine internal reporting).
3. **Stakeholder Input:**
   Collaboration with department heads and process owners ensures accurate identification of critical functions and captures organization-wide perspectives.

RECOVERY TIME OBJECTIVE (RTO) DETERMINATION

The Recovery Time Objective (RTO) specifies the maximum acceptable downtime for a critical function before significant operational, financial, or reputational damage occurs.

1. **RTO Classification:**
   RTOs vary based on the nature of the process:
    - *Immediate (0–4 hours):* Critical operations like IT infrastructure restoration.
    - *Short-term (4–24 hours):* High-priority systems such as customer-facing platforms.
    - *Extended (1–5 days):* Less urgent but necessary business processes.
2. **RTO Prioritization Factors:**
    - Business impact of downtime (e.g., revenue loss per hour).
    - Regulatory and contractual obligations tied to uptime.
    - Dependencies on external stakeholders (e.g., vendors, customers).
3. **Scenario Testing:**
   Validating RTOs through disaster recovery drills and simulations helps ensure realistic expectations for recovery timelines.

RECOVERY POINT OBJECTIVE (RPO) SETTING

The Recovery Point Objective (RPO) defines the maximum allowable data loss in terms of time, measured from the last successful data backup to the disruption event. RPO directly affects the frequency and scope of data backup processes.

1. **RPO and Data Sensitivity:**
   - Critical customer data may require near-zero RPOs, necessitating real-time replication or continuous backups.
   - Less sensitive data, such as archived records, may tolerate RPOs of hours or even days.
2. **Backup Strategies:**
   - *High-Frequency Backups:* Automated replication and snapshot technologies reduce RPOs to seconds or minutes.
   - *Scheduled Backups:* Nightly or periodic backups may suffice for non-critical systems.
3. **Trade-Offs:**
   Setting RPOs balances recovery capabilities with associated costs. For instance, maintaining real-time replication for all systems can be resource-intensive, so organizations must align RPOs with business needs and risk tolerances.

RESOURCE REQUIREMENTS ANALYSIS

Determining the resources needed to restore critical functions ensures the organization can meet RTOs and RPOs effectively. Resource analysis spans personnel, technology, physical infrastructure, and vendor support.

1. **Resource Types:**
   - *Human Resources:* Essential staff for recovery efforts, such as IT, customer support, and incident management teams.
   - *Technological Resources:* Backup systems, data recovery platforms, alternate servers, and communication tools.
   - *Physical Resources:* Alternate workspaces, critical supplies, or on-premises equipment replacements.
2. **Key Resource Questions:**
   - What is the minimum required infrastructure to restore operations?
   - Are there redundancies in place for key resources?
   - Which resources rely on third-party vendors, and what SLAs are in place?
3. **Resource Gaps:**
   Identifying gaps during resource analysis enables organizations to implement measures such as procuring backup systems, engaging managed service providers, or developing cross-training programs for critical roles.

IMPACT ASSESSMENT CRITERIA

Impact assessments quantify the effects of disruptions to critical functions. These assessments are multi-dimensional, covering financial, operational, reputational, and compliance impacts.

1. **Financial Impact Metrics:**
   - Revenue loss per hour/day of downtime.
   - Cost of penalties for SLA or compliance violations.
   - Expense of recovery operations, including overtime pay or expedited vendor services.
2. **Operational Impact Metrics:**
   - Loss of productivity due to unavailable systems or processes.
   - Disruption of supply chains or customer service functions.
3. **Reputational Impact Metrics:**
   - Loss of customer trust due to missed deadlines, poor communication, or service outages.
   - Negative media or social media attention.
4. **Compliance Impact Metrics:**
   - Fines and penalties for failure to meet regulatory deadlines or data protection requirements.
5. **Prioritization via Weighting Systems:**
   Applying weighting systems (e.g., assigning higher weights to financial and compliance impacts) helps quantify and prioritize recovery efforts.

DEPENDENCY MAPPING TECHNIQUES

Mapping dependencies ensures all interconnected systems, processes, and external parties are accounted for during recovery planning. This prevents critical oversights that could disrupt continuity efforts.

1. **Process Dependencies:**
    - Identify upstream and downstream processes that rely on or support each critical function. For example, payroll processing may depend on IT systems, HR databases, and bank integrations.
2. **System Interdependencies:**
    - Document relationships between systems, such as shared databases, APIs, or network connections. Dependency maps should show how failures in one system cascade to others.
3. **Third-Party Dependencies:**
    - Evaluate reliance on vendors, suppliers, and partners for key functions. Examples include cloud service providers, logistics partners, or outsourced IT teams.
4. **Mapping Techniques:**
    - *Flowcharts:* Illustrate workflows and interconnections between processes.
    - *Dependency Matrices:* Chart dependencies in a tabular format, showing which functions rely on which systems or vendors.
    - *Visualization Tools:* Software like Visio, Lucidchart, or business continuity platforms can create dynamic, updatable maps.
5. **Risk-Based Dependency Mapping:**
    - Highlight dependencies that represent high risks due to single points of failure, lack of redundancy, or poor vendor reliability. Addressing these vulnerabilities should be prioritized.

A well-defined BIA methodology creates the foundation for actionable business continuity plans, ensuring organizations can sustain operations and minimize losses during disruptions.

DISASTER RECOVERY STRATEGY SELECTION AND IMPLEMENTATION

Recovery site selection depends on system criticality, recovery time objectives (RTOs), and budget constraints. A comparative analysis reveals:

Hot Sites:

- Fully configured data centers
- Real-time data replication
- Immediate cutover capability
- High operational readiness
- 24/7 staff availability
- Monthly testing capability
- Recovery time: Minutes to hours
- Annual cost: $1-2M+

Warm Sites:

- Partially configured systems
- Periodic data synchronization
- Hardware/software installation required
- Limited staff presence
- Quarterly testing capability
- Recovery time: Hours to days
- Annual cost: $500K-1M

Cold Sites:

- Basic infrastructure only
- Manual data restoration
- Full system configuration needed
- No permanent staff
- Annual testing capability
- Recovery time: Days to weeks
- Annual cost: $100-500K

Cloud Recovery Architecture:

Component	Primary Setup	Recovery Configuration
Compute	Auto-scaling groups	Cross-region replication
Storage	Multi-AZ deployment	Automated snapshots
Database	Multi-region clusters	Point-in-time recovery
Network	Redundant connections	Region failover

Data Backup Implementation:
Full Backups:

- Weekly execution
- Complete system image
- Offsite storage rotation
- Encryption requirements
- Retention periods
- Recovery testing

Incremental Backups:

- Daily execution
- Changed data only
- Local/cloud storage
- Compression ratios
- Verification processes
- Chain integrity

Personnel Recovery Planning:
Remote Work Capabilities:

- VPN infrastructure
- Collaboration tools
- Security controls
- Resource access
- Performance monitoring
- Support processes

Alternate Work Locations:

- Office space agreements
- Equipment availability
- Network connectivity
- Security measures
- Support services
- Access controls

Communication Framework:
Emergency Notification System:

- Contact databases
- Message templates
- Delivery methods
- Response tracking
- Escalation procedures
- Update frequency

Stakeholder Communication:

- Customers

- Employees
- Vendors
- Regulators
- Media
- Executives

Recovery teams maintain:

- Current procedures
- Contact information
- Role assignments
- Resource access
- Technical documentation
- Testing schedules

Regular testing validates:

- Recovery procedures
- System restoration
- Data integrity
- Team readiness
- Communication flows
- Support processes

Recovery metrics track:

- System availability
- Data currency
- Recovery times
- Cost effectiveness
- Team performance
- Process improvements

Asset Security

DATA CLASSIFICATION FRAMEWORKS AND IMPLEMENTATION METHODOLOGIES

Government classification levels form the foundation of modern data protection schemes. Top Secret information requires the highest protection, applied to information that would cause exceptionally grave damage to national security if disclosed. Secret classification protects data whose disclosure would cause serious national security damage. Confidential designation safeguards information that could cause damage to national security. Unclassified information requires basic protection measures.

Commercial organizations typically implement four-tier classification:

Level	Description	Examples	Controls
Restricted	Business-critical data	Trade secrets, M&A plans	Encryption, access logging
Confidential	Internal sensitive data	Employee records, contracts	Role-based access
Internal	General business data	Procedures, policies	Basic authentication
Public	Open information	Marketing materials, press releases	Content verification

Military classification incorporates additional handling caveats:

- NOFORN (No Foreign Nationals)
- SCI (Sensitive Compartmented Information)
- SAP (Special Access Programs)
- ORCON (Originator Controlled)

Healthcare data classification aligns with HIPAA requirements:

Protected Health Information (PHI):

- Patient medical records
- Treatment information
- Payment details
- Healthcare operations data
- Genetic information
- Biometric identifiers

Personal Identifiable Information (PII):

- Names and addresses
- Social security numbers
- Medical record numbers
- Account information
- Device identifiers
- Biometric data

Financial sector classifications follow regulatory frameworks:

Category	Examples	Requirements
Customer Data	Account numbers, PINs	Encryption at rest/transit
Transaction Data	Payment records, transfers	Audit logging, integrity checks
Market Data	Trading algorithms, positions	Access controls, monitoring
Corporate Data	Strategic plans, risk assessments	Data loss prevention

Data labeling methodologies incorporate:

Visual Markings:

- Header/footer tags
- Watermarks
- Color coding

- Classification banners
- Digital signatures
- Metadata tags

Automated Classification:

- Pattern matching
- Content analysis
- Context evaluation
- User behavior
- Access patterns
- Data flows

Classification inheritance follows:

- Parent-child relationships
- Container assignments
- Aggregation rules
- Derived classifications
- Trust boundaries
- Security domains

Data owners determine:

- Initial classification
- Reclassification criteria
- Access requirements
- Protection measures
- Review schedules
- Declassification procedures

Systems enforce classification through:

- Access control lists
- Security labels
- Data loss prevention
- Encryption requirements
- Monitoring systems
- Audit trails

DATA HANDLING REQUIREMENTS DEEP DIVE

Managing sensitive data requires adherence to specific handling, storage, and transmission standards to ensure confidentiality, integrity, and availability. This involves implementing structured processes such as chain of custody procedures, access controls, classification-based storage and transmission protocols, and incident response measures for events like data spills. Each of these components plays a unique role in ensuring the secure lifecycle of data within an organization.

CHAIN OF CUSTODY PROCEDURES

Chain of custody ensures the integrity and accountability of data during its collection, handling, transfer, and storage. This process is especially important for legal, regulatory, or forensic purposes, where evidence must remain tamper-proof and its authenticity verifiable.

1. **Documentation Requirements:** Every individual who accesses or transfers the data must be logged. This includes the date, time, location, and purpose of access. Digital logs should include metadata, such as user IDs and system event logs, while physical documentation can include signatures.
2. **Secure Handoffs:** Transfers between custodians must occur in a controlled manner. Physical media (e.g., USB drives) should use tamper-evident seals, while digital files should leverage encrypted transmission methods.

3. **Storage Controls:** Data awaiting transfer or analysis should be stored in secure environments such as locked containers, access-controlled server rooms, or encrypted storage volumes.
4. **Preservation of Integrity:** Hashing algorithms, such as SHA-256, can verify data has not been altered. For instance, forensic files should be hashed at the point of collection and re-hashed after each transfer to confirm integrity.

DATA ACCESS CONTROLS BASED ON CLASSIFICATION

Data classification determines how information is accessed, shared, and protected based on its sensitivity and importance to the organization. Access controls must align with the classification to prevent unauthorized exposure or modification.

1. **Classification Levels:**
    - *Public Data:* Accessible by anyone with minimal restrictions (e.g., company press releases).
    - *Internal Data:* Restricted to employees or authorized personnel for internal use only.
    - *Confidential Data:* Sensitive information accessible to a limited group (e.g., HR records, financial reports).
    - *Restricted/Highly Sensitive Data:* Requires the highest level of security, such as encryption, and is accessible only on a strict need-to-know basis (e.g., trade secrets, classified government data).
2. **Role-Based Access Control (RBAC):** Access rights are granted based on job responsibilities. For example, a finance department employee may access payroll data, while an IT administrator handles database configurations without viewing specific content.
3. **Least Privilege Principle:** Users and systems are given the minimum permissions required to perform their duties. If an employee does not need access to customer credit card data, their access permissions should explicitly exclude it.
4. **Access Logging and Monitoring:** Access events must be logged, and abnormal patterns, such as attempts to access unauthorized files, should trigger alerts. Logs should include timestamps, user IDs, and accessed data identifiers.

STORAGE REQUIREMENTS PER CLASSIFICATION LEVEL

Secure storage practices differ depending on the classification of the data being stored. The goal is to maintain security while complying with legal and regulatory standards.

1. **Encrypted Storage:**
    - Highly sensitive data should be stored using encryption algorithms such as AES-256.
    - Encryption keys must be stored securely, often using hardware security modules (HSMs) or key management systems.
2. **Physical Security for Media:**
    - Hard drives and backup tapes storing classified information should be kept in locked safes or access-controlled data centers with physical surveillance.
    - Data centers should include additional safeguards like biometric access controls and 24/7 monitoring.
3. **Data Backup Protocols:**
    - Regular backups should be created for all classification levels, but sensitive data backups should be encrypted and stored in separate, secure locations to ensure recovery options during incidents like ransomware attacks.
    - Replication for highly sensitive data may occur across geographically dispersed data centers to improve disaster recovery capabilities.
4. **Retention Policies:**
    - Each classification level should have defined retention periods. For example, public records might be stored indefinitely, while restricted data is securely deleted after a defined legal retention period ends.

TRANSMISSION SECURITY REQUIREMENTS

Secure data transmission ensures that information remains protected from interception, tampering, or unauthorized access during transit between systems or endpoints.

1. **Encryption in Transit:** Protocols like TLS (Transport Layer Security) must be used to encrypt sensitive data during transmission. For highly sensitive communication, end-to-end encryption should be implemented to prevent unauthorized decryption at intermediate points.
2. **VPN and Private Networks:** Confidential or restricted data transmitted between locations should use VPNs or private networks rather than public internet connections.
3. **Email Security:** Sensitive files shared via email should be encrypted with additional protections like password-protected attachments or secure email gateways (SEGs). Alternatively, file-sharing platforms with built-in security controls can replace email-based sharing.
4. **Integrity Checks:** Transmission protocols, such as HTTPS, include message integrity features. Additionally, hash verification ensures files are not altered during transit.

DATA SANITIZATION STANDARDS

Sanitization is the process of securely erasing data to ensure it cannot be reconstructed or recovered after deletion, whether it's stored on digital media or physical documents.

1. **Methods of Data Sanitization:**
   - *Clearing:* Overwriting storage media with random data multiple times. For example, NIST SP 800-88 recommends overwriting magnetic drives with at least three passes of random data.
   - *Purging:* Degaussing magnetic storage devices to render them unreadable.
   - *Physical Destruction:* Shredding, crushing, or incinerating hard drives and storage media. Shredders for physical documents should reduce paper to particles no larger than $1mm^2$ for highly sensitive material.
2. **Sanitization Policies by Classification:** Public data may be cleared using simple deletion, while highly sensitive data requires physical destruction or certified purging methods.
3. **Verification:** Post-sanitization audits ensure compliance. For instance, IT administrators may use forensic tools to confirm no data remnants remain on sanitized storage devices.

CROSS-DOMAIN SOLUTIONS

Cross-domain solutions (CDS) enable secure data transfer between systems operating at different security levels, such as unclassified and classified networks, without risking data leakage.

1. **One-Way Data Transfers:** Implementing diode-based systems allows data to flow in one direction (e.g., from unclassified to classified systems) while preventing reverse flows, minimizing leakage risks.
2. **Content Filtering:** Data is automatically inspected and sanitized before being transferred between domains. For example, email attachments may be scanned for malware and redacted to remove sensitive metadata.
3. **Policy Enforcement Engines:** These systems ensure that transfer requests comply with pre-defined security policies. A policy engine might block transfers that contain sensitive keywords or violate classification boundaries.
4. **High-Assurance Gateways:** Cryptographic separation mechanisms isolate high-security domains while facilitating necessary exchanges of pre-approved data.

DATA SPILLAGE HANDLING

Data spillage occurs when information is inadvertently transferred to a system or environment with insufficient security controls. Proper handling mitigates potential exposure and restores compliance.

1. **Immediate Containment:** Isolate the affected system or environment to prevent further unauthorized access. For instance, disconnecting the system from the network or disabling access privileges.
2. **Data Classification Review:** Determine the sensitivity of the spilled data and assess the potential impact of exposure. This includes identifying affected files, users, and systems.
3. **Forensic Analysis:** Analyze logs, access history, and transfer records to understand how the spillage occurred. This might reveal whether it resulted from misconfigured access controls, user error, or a system breach.
4. **Data Remediation:** For digital spills, remove sensitive information from the affected environment using sanitization techniques. Physical spills, such as printed documents left in unsecured areas, require secure collection and shredding.
5. **Reporting and Notification:** Inform relevant stakeholders, including regulatory authorities if required. For example, under GDPR, data breaches affecting personal information must be reported within 72 hours.

6. **Policy Updates:** Revise policies and implement additional controls to prevent similar incidents. Training programs may be necessary for users if human error contributed to the spillage.

DATA LIFECYCLE MANAGEMENT

Data lifecycle management (DLM) encompasses the processes, policies, and technologies governing data from its creation to its secure destruction. Effective management ensures data integrity, security, and compliance throughout its lifecycle, aligning with organizational goals and regulatory requirements. The lifecycle can be broken into several key stages: creation, storage, usage, archival, retention, and destruction, with controls and safeguards applied to maintain security during data state transitions (at rest, in motion, and in use).

Creation and Collection Controls

The first stage of the data lifecycle involves the creation or collection of data. Controls at this phase focus on ensuring data accuracy, integrity, and proper classification based on sensitivity and value.

- **Data Classification**: As data is created or collected, it must be tagged with appropriate classifications such as confidential, sensitive, or public. Classification frameworks (e.g., NIST SP 800-60) guide organizations in determining handling requirements for each category.
- **Access Control Implementation**: During creation or collection, access permissions should be defined using role-based or attribute-based access control (RBAC/ABAC) principles to restrict access based on users' roles or attributes.
- **Input Validation**: To prevent injection attacks or errors during data collection, input validation mechanisms should sanitize and verify data before it enters the system.
- **Consent and Transparency**: When collecting personal or sensitive information, organizations must implement mechanisms to obtain consent and provide clear information about how the data will be used, as required under laws such as GDPR or CCPA.

For example, an online retailer collecting customer data during checkout might use TLS encryption to secure form submissions and ensure that sensitive fields (like credit card numbers) are validated to prevent malicious inputs.

Storage and Maintenance Procedures

Data storage and maintenance require robust procedures to ensure confidentiality, integrity, and availability throughout the data's active lifecycle. Storage methods must account for physical, logical, and regulatory considerations.

- **Encryption**: Data at rest should be encrypted using strong algorithms (e.g., AES-256) to protect against unauthorized access in the event of storage media theft or compromise.
- **Redundancy**: Mechanisms like RAID, backups, and replication help ensure availability by mitigating risks of hardware failures or data corruption.
- **Access Logs**: Logs should record all access to stored data, including who accessed it, what changes were made, and when, enabling auditability.
- **Patch Management**: Storage systems must be regularly updated with patches to mitigate vulnerabilities that could expose data to attackers.

For instance, in a cloud storage environment, policies might specify that sensitive data be encrypted with a unique key per tenant and stored across multiple geographic regions for disaster recovery purposes.

Usage Monitoring and Auditing

The usage stage involves active interaction with data, such as querying, processing, or analyzing it. Monitoring and auditing ensure appropriate use and protect against unauthorized access or breaches.

- **Real-Time Monitoring**: Systems such as Security Information and Event Management (SIEM) platforms can monitor data usage in real time to detect unusual activity, such as anomalous queries or unauthorized downloads.
- **Audit Trails**: Usage logs should include detailed records of who accessed or modified data, along with timestamps and the specific actions performed. These logs support forensic investigations in case of incidents.
- **Behavioral Analytics**: Advanced tools can analyze user behavior patterns to identify insider threats or compromised accounts attempting to misuse data.

For example, a financial institution using customer transaction data might rely on behavioral analytics to detect fraudulent activities, flagging unusual withdrawals that deviate from a customer's normal patterns.

Archive Requirements

Archiving moves inactive data to lower-cost, long-term storage systems while preserving accessibility for compliance or historical reference. Proper archiving ensures that data remains intact and retrievable even years after its active use ends.

- **Data Compression and Deduplication**: Archived data is often compressed to save storage space, and deduplication ensures that only unique copies are retained.
- **Access Controls**: Even archived data must remain secure, with strict access permissions to prevent unauthorized retrieval.
- **Immutability**: To maintain integrity, archived data should be stored on systems that prevent tampering, such as write-once, read-many (WORM) storage technologies.
- **Regulatory Retention**: Industry standards or regulations often dictate how long archived data must be kept. For instance, the SEC requires financial records to be retained for six years, while healthcare organizations may need to store patient records for a decade or more.

An organization archiving email records for compliance purposes might use a specialized solution that indexes messages for easy search and retrieval while ensuring they remain immutable for the required retention period.

Retention Period Determination

Retention policies determine how long data must be stored before it can be securely destroyed. These periods are often dictated by legal, regulatory, or operational requirements.

- **Regulatory Requirements**: Compliance laws such as GDPR, HIPAA, and Sarbanes-Oxley specify retention requirements for certain types of data.
- **Operational Needs**: Data with ongoing business value, such as historical sales figures, may be retained beyond the regulatory minimum for analysis or forecasting.
- **Retention Schedules**: Organizations should establish clear schedules categorizing data by type, sensitivity, and applicable retention period. Automating this process can reduce human error.

For example, tax records in the United States are typically retained for seven years to comply with IRS guidelines, while marketing data might be purged sooner if it no longer serves business purposes.

Secure Destruction Methods

Secure destruction ensures data is irrecoverable once its retention period expires, preventing unauthorized access to sensitive information. Different methods are used depending on the storage medium and data sensitivity.

- **Physical Destruction**: For hardware such as hard drives or backup tapes, methods like shredding, pulverizing, or incineration render the media unusable.
- **Logical Destruction**: Digital data can be securely erased using tools that overwrite the storage medium multiple times with random data, following standards like NIST SP 800-88 (Guidelines for Media Sanitization).
- **Certificate of Destruction**: For outsourced destruction services, obtaining a certificate of destruction ensures accountability and verifies compliance with organizational policies.

A hospital decommissioning old servers containing patient records might physically shred hard drives and maintain documentation confirming that destruction was completed according to HIPAA standards.

Data State Transitions (At Rest, In Motion, In Use)

Data exists in three states—at rest, in motion, and in use—each requiring distinct security measures to maintain confidentiality, integrity, and availability during transitions.

- **At Rest**: Encryption is critical for stored data, whether on local drives, cloud storage, or backup media. Access controls should limit exposure.
- **In Motion**: Data in transit should be protected with encryption protocols like TLS or IPsec to prevent interception during transmission over networks.
- **In Use**: While being processed by applications, data must be protected against unauthorized memory access or side-channel attacks. Techniques like memory encryption and secure enclaves (e.g., Intel SGX) can enhance protection.

For example, an e-commerce platform might encrypt customer payment data at rest using AES-256, secure it in motion using TLS 1.3, and protect it during use by isolating it in a secure processing environment within its payment gateway.

REGULATORY DATA CLASSIFICATION AND COMPLIANCE MAPPING

The GDPR classifies personal data based on processing risk levels and sensitivity. Special categories include:
Processing Risk Levels:
High Risk
- Genetic data
- Biometric data
- Criminal records
- Political opinions
- Religious beliefs

Medium Risk
- Financial information
- Location data
- Online identifiers
- Employment details
- Educational records

Standard Risk
- Basic contact details
- Professional life
- Public records
- Device information
- Preferences

HIPAA establishes specific data categories:

Category	Examples	Protection Requirements
ePHI	Electronic health records	Encryption, access controls
Treatment	Medical procedures	Role-based access
Payment	Billing records	Transaction logging
Operations	Administrative data	Basic security controls

PCI DSS categorizes cardholder data:
Primary Account Data:

- Full PAN (Primary Account Number)
- Cardholder name
- Expiration date
- Service code

Sensitive Authentication Data:

- Full track data
- CAV2/CVC2/CVV2/CID
- PINs/PIN blocks

SOX compliance requires classification of:
Financial Records:

- General ledger entries
- Journal records
- Transaction data
- Account reconciliations
- Financial statements

- Audit documentation

Control Documentation:

- Process narratives
- Risk assessments
- Control matrices
- Test results
- Remediation plans
- Management reports

Industry-specific classification examples:

Manufacturing:

- Product designs
- Process controls
- Quality data
- Supply chain
- Production metrics
- Research data

Energy Sector:

- Grid operations
- SCADA systems
- Customer usage
- Infrastructure maps
- Maintenance records
- Emergency plans

Cross-border considerations address:

Data Transfer Requirements:

- Adequacy decisions
- Standard contractual clauses
- Binding corporate rules
- Privacy shield mechanisms
- Local storage requirements
- Transfer impact assessments

Classification mapping strategies:

Regulation	**High**	**Medium**	**Low**
GDPR	Special Categories	Personal Data	Public
HIPAA	ePHI	Operations	Marketing
PCI DSS	SAD	PAN	Public
SOX	Financial	Operations	Public

Implementation methods include:

- Automated classification tools
- Data discovery systems
- Content analyzers
- Policy engines
- Access controls
- Monitoring systems

Documentation maintains:

- Classification policies

- Mapping procedures
- Review schedules
- Audit trails
- Training records
- Compliance reports

ASSET INVENTORY CONTROL SYSTEMS

Effectively managing an organization's assets requires robust inventory control systems that provide comprehensive visibility into hardware, software, and virtual resources. These systems ensure accurate tracking, classification, and management of assets throughout their lifecycle while supporting security and operational goals. By employing discovery tools, inventory databases, tagging protocols, and reconciliation procedures, organizations can minimize risks, optimize resource allocation, and maintain compliance with industry regulations.

ASSET DISCOVERY METHODS

Asset discovery identifies all physical and virtual assets connected to an organization's environment, including devices, applications, and network components.

1. **Active Discovery:**
   - Scanning tools actively probe the network to identify connected assets, using methods like ICMP (ping sweeps), SNMP queries, or port scans. Tools like Nmap, Nessus, or SolarWinds can detect devices, services, and operating systems.
   - Active methods can also uncover unauthorized devices, such as rogue access points or shadow IT.
2. **Passive Discovery:**
   - Passive methods monitor network traffic to identify assets without initiating direct queries. Packet capture tools (e.g., Wireshark) analyze communication patterns to infer the presence of devices.
   - Passive discovery minimizes disruptions but may miss devices that are not actively communicating.
3. **Cloud Asset Discovery:**
   - Cloud-specific tools like AWS Config, Azure Resource Graph, or Google Cloud Asset Inventory provide visibility into virtual machines, storage buckets, databases, and other cloud-native resources.
4. **Endpoint Detection Tools:**
   - Endpoint detection and response (EDR) solutions, such as CrowdStrike or Microsoft Defender, help identify workstations, laptops, and mobile devices deployed across the organization.

INVENTORY DATABASE MANAGEMENT

An inventory database serves as a centralized repository for storing information about all discovered assets. Proper database management ensures accurate tracking, quick retrieval of data, and simplified compliance reporting.

1. **Fields in an Inventory Database:**
   - Asset ID, type, and classification (e.g., server, endpoint, network device).
   - Serial number, model, and manufacturer details.
   - Software version, patch level, and configuration status.
   - Asset location (physical or virtual) and assigned owner.
   - Purchase date, cost, and depreciation schedule.
2. **Database Platforms:**
   - Relational databases like MySQL or PostgreSQL are often used for inventory systems. Specialized asset management platforms, such as ServiceNow, Lansweeper, or Ivanti, provide prebuilt solutions tailored for IT environments.
3. **Integrations:**
   - Integration with CMDBs, ticketing systems, and monitoring tools ensures that asset data remains current and actionable. For example, linking the inventory database to a vulnerability scanner can help prioritize patching based on asset criticality.

4. **Data Validation:**
   - Periodic audits of database entries prevent errors, duplicates, or outdated information. Automated checks, such as comparing database entries to real-time discovery scans, ensure consistency.

ASSET TAGGING PROTOCOLS

Asset tagging involves assigning unique identifiers to each asset to enable tracking and management throughout its lifecycle.

1. **Tagging Methods:**
   - *Barcodes:* Simple and cost-effective, used for physical assets like laptops and printers.
   - *RFID Tags:* Radio frequency identification enables fast scanning of multiple assets, ideal for inventory-heavy environments like warehouses.
   - *Digital Tags:* Software-based identifiers (e.g., UUIDs or IP addresses) are used for virtual resources such as virtual machines or cloud storage.
2. **Tagging Standards:**
   - Tags should follow consistent naming conventions, incorporating attributes like department, asset type, and acquisition date. For example, a laptop assigned to IT purchased in 2023 might have the tag "IT-LAP-2023-001."
   - Adhering to ISO/IEC 19762 standards for automatic identification ensures global compatibility for tagged items.
3. **Tagging Workflow:**
   - Assets should be tagged at the time of acquisition or upon first deployment. Maintenance events, upgrades, or reassignments should be logged under the same asset tag to maintain continuity.

AUTOMATED VS. MANUAL TRACKING

Choosing between automated and manual tracking depends on the complexity of the organization's asset ecosystem, resource availability, and desired accuracy.

1. **Automated Tracking:**
   - Uses discovery tools, sensors, and integrations to continuously monitor asset status. Tools like SCCM (System Center Configuration Manager) and Qualys automate tracking by gathering real-time information on configurations, software installations, and compliance.
   - Pros: Real-time updates, scalability, and reduced human error.
   - Cons: High implementation costs and dependency on tool configuration.
2. **Manual Tracking:**
   - Relies on spreadsheets, physical checklists, or manual entries in asset databases.
   - Pros: Low cost and minimal technology overhead.
   - Cons: Prone to inaccuracies, resource-intensive, and difficult to scale for large or dynamic environments.
3. **Hybrid Approaches:**
   - Combining automated and manual methods ensures gaps in automated systems (e.g., non-networked devices) are addressed while reducing the burden of fully manual tracking.

CONFIGURATION MANAGEMENT DATABASE (CMDB)

A CMDB provides a comprehensive view of the organization's IT infrastructure by mapping the relationships and dependencies between assets.

1. **Key Features of a CMDB:**
   - Stores detailed information about hardware, software, networks, and configurations.
   - Tracks interdependencies, such as a server's relationship with applications, databases, and network interfaces.
   - Provides change management capabilities to ensure system updates are logged and their impact on related assets is understood.
2. **Use Cases for CMDBs:**
   - Incident management: When a server fails, the CMDB helps identify all systems and applications affected by the outage.

- Compliance: Automates evidence collection for audits, such as tracking patch levels or encryption configurations.
- Capacity planning: Insights from the CMDB support resource allocation and future growth strategies.

3. **Popular CMDB Tools:**
   - ServiceNow CMDB, BMC Helix, and Freshservice CMDB are commonly used in enterprise environments.

ASSET OWNERSHIP ASSIGNMENT

Assigning ownership ensures accountability for the use, security, and maintenance of assets. Ownership tracking is especially important for enforcing policies and streamlining incident response.

1. **Types of Ownership:**
   - *Individual Ownership:* Specific employees are responsible for assets like laptops or mobile devices.
   - *Departmental Ownership:* Shared resources like printers, servers, or specialized equipment are assigned to departments or teams.
2. **Responsibility Tracking:**
   - Owners must ensure compliance with organizational policies, such as updating software or reporting loss.
   - Changes in ownership, such as transfers between departments, should be documented in the asset inventory.
3. **Integration with HR Systems:**
   - HR systems can be linked to the asset inventory to automatically update ownership records during employee onboarding, offboarding, or role changes.

INVENTORY RECONCILIATION PROCEDURES

Reconciliation verifies the accuracy of the asset inventory by comparing records against physical or digital asset discoveries.

1. **Reconciliation Frequency:**
   - Quarterly or annual audits are common for most organizations, while high-risk environments may require monthly checks.
2. **Reconciliation Steps:**
   - Perform a complete discovery scan using automated tools or manual inspections.
   - Compare discovered assets to the inventory database, identifying discrepancies such as missing entries, duplicates, or outdated records.
   - Investigate discrepancies to determine causes, such as decommissioned devices not removed from the database.
3. **Discrepancy Resolution:**
   - Missing or untracked assets should be tagged and added to the database.
   - Stale entries for decommissioned or lost assets should be archived, with documentation retained for audit purposes.
4. **Reporting:**
   - Reconciliation reports should include the total number of assets, discrepancies found, corrective actions taken, and recommendations for improving future tracking processes.

A well-maintained asset inventory system, leveraging both automated tools and structured processes, ensures accurate visibility, efficient management, and long-term operational stability.

MEDIA MANAGEMENT STRATEGIES

Effective media management ensures the confidentiality, integrity, and availability of data across physical and digital media throughout its lifecycle. Media encompasses physical devices like hard drives, USBs, backup tapes, and digital storage, including cloud-based systems. Strategies must address physical and digital protection, secure transportation, controlled access, and appropriate reuse and storage procedures.

Physical Media Controls

Physical media refers to tangible storage devices such as hard drives, CDs, USB drives, and backup tapes. Proper controls help prevent unauthorized access, damage, or theft.

- **Inventory Management**: Maintain an up-to-date inventory of all physical media, including unique identifiers, serial numbers, and assigned custodians. This facilitates tracking and accountability.
- **Labeling**: Sensitive media should be clearly labeled with classification levels (e.g., "Confidential," "Restricted") to guide handling procedures.
- **Tamper-Evident Seals**: Use tamper-evident seals on media containers to deter unauthorized access and ensure evidence of tampering if it occurs.
- **Regular Audits**: Conduct routine audits of stored media to confirm its presence and condition, ensuring it matches the inventory records.

For example, a financial institution storing backup tapes in an off-site facility would maintain a detailed inventory of the tapes and ensure they are labeled with retention dates and encryption requirements.

Digital Media Protection

Digital media includes files and storage hosted on electronic devices or cloud systems. Protecting digital media requires controls to prevent unauthorized access, modification, or exposure.

- **Encryption**: Encrypt all sensitive digital data, both at rest and in transit, using strong encryption protocols such as AES-256. For example, external drives and USBs should be hardware-encrypted to prevent data breaches if lost or stolen.
- **Endpoint Security**: Devices storing digital media should be protected with antivirus, firewalls, and data loss prevention (DLP) tools to block unauthorized data exfiltration or malware infections.
- **Secure Disposal**: Ensure proper deletion of data before disposing of digital media, using tools like Secure Erase or BitRaser to overwrite storage multiple times in compliance with NIST SP 800-88 guidelines.

For instance, a healthcare organization using portable drives for patient records must ensure that all data is encrypted and set to auto-lock after a period of inactivity to reduce the risk of unauthorized access.

Media Transportation Security

The transportation of media, whether physical or digital, introduces risks of loss, theft, or tampering. Secure transportation protocols mitigate these risks.

- **Physical Transport**: Use locked, tamper-proof containers for transporting physical media. Choose secure courier services with tracking capabilities and consider requiring chain-of-custody documentation to track possession at every stage.
- **Digital Transfers**: For digital data transmission, use secure channels such as TLS-encrypted connections or virtual private networks (VPNs). Avoid public networks and unencrypted transfers.
- **Personnel Vetting**: Only authorize trusted, background-checked personnel to transport or transmit sensitive media. For physical media, dual-control policies can reduce the risk of insider threats by requiring two authorized individuals to accompany sensitive items.

For example, a government agency transferring encrypted backup tapes to an off-site data center might use a secure courier service with real-time GPS tracking and obtain a signed receipt upon delivery.

Environmental Controls

Environmental risks, such as fire, flooding, extreme temperatures, or humidity, can damage both physical and digital media. Environmental controls ensure storage locations are designed to mitigate these risks.

- **Climate Control**: Storage environments should maintain temperature and humidity within acceptable ranges for media types (e.g., 60–75°F and 35–50% humidity for magnetic tapes).
- **Fire Suppression Systems**: Use non-damaging fire suppression systems, such as inert gas-based systems, in media storage areas to protect against fire without causing water damage.
- **Physical Protection**: Store media in areas with reinforced structures to withstand natural disasters or physical attacks.
- **Clean Environments**: Ensure media storage areas are free from dust, static electricity, and other contaminants that could damage sensitive devices.

For instance, an organization storing long-term backup tapes might use temperature-controlled vaults with inert gas fire suppression to protect tapes from both environmental and physical threats.

Access Control Mechanisms

Access to media must be restricted to authorized personnel and tracked to prevent unauthorized use or exposure.

- **Role-Based Access Control (RBAC)**: Grant access based on roles and responsibilities. For example, system administrators may have access to backup media, while general users do not.
- **Logging and Monitoring**: Record all access attempts to physical and digital media. Use audit logs to track access events, including user IDs, timestamps, and actions performed.
- **Authentication Mechanisms**: Implement multifactor authentication (MFA) for accessing digital media and secure physical storage areas with keycards, PINs, or biometric locks.
- **Separation of Duties**: Prevent conflicts of interest by dividing responsibilities for media handling and access across multiple personnel. For example, the individual who encrypts a backup file should not be the same person who transports it.

A data center might implement badge access systems with video surveillance for physical media storage areas while logging all badge entries for compliance purposes.

Media Reuse Procedures

When reusing media, organizations must ensure that residual data from previous use is securely erased to prevent unauthorized recovery. Media reuse procedures depend on the sensitivity of the previously stored data.

- **Data Sanitization**: Use tools that meet recognized standards, such as NIST SP 800-88 or DoD 5220.22-M, to securely overwrite existing data multiple times. Tools like DBAN or Blancco provide automated solutions.
- **Reformatting vs. Overwriting**: Simply reformatting media is insufficient for secure reuse, as data can often be recovered. Overwriting with random data is required for sensitive media.
- **Verification**: After sanitization, verify that the data has been completely erased using data recovery tools to confirm no recoverable data remains.

For example, before reassigning laptops to new employees, a company might overwrite the storage drives three times using an approved tool to ensure no residual data is accessible.

Secure Media Storage

Storing media securely protects it from physical theft, environmental damage, or unauthorized access during periods of inactivity.

- **Locked Cabinets or Safes**: Store physical media in locked cabinets or safes located within restricted areas, such as data centers or secure rooms.
- **Off-Site Storage**: For backup or archival purposes, use reputable third-party storage providers with robust security controls, such as video surveillance, 24/7 guards, and climate-controlled environments.
- **Segmentation**: Separate storage areas for media with different classification levels to prevent accidental exposure or mixing of data.
- **Periodic Inspections**: Conduct regular inspections of storage areas to ensure compliance with policies and to identify any signs of tampering, degradation, or environmental risks.

An enterprise managing sensitive client data might contract with a third-party vault provider to store encrypted backup tapes in a climate-controlled facility, ensuring compliance with regulatory and operational requirements.

ASSET RETIREMENT AND SECURE DISPOSAL MANAGEMENT

End-of-life determination follows asset evaluation criteria:

Factor	**Evaluation Metrics**	**Decision Triggers**
Age	Years in service	Manufacturer EOL
Performance	Speed/capacity	System requirements
Maintenance	Repair frequency	Support availability
Security	Patch status	Vulnerability risk
Cost	TCO analysis	Replacement ROI

Data sanitization standards align with NIST SP 800-88:

Clear Operations:

- Standard delete commands
- Factory reset functions

- Disk reformatting
- File system wiping

Purge Methods:

- Secure erase command
- Degaussing for magnetic media
- Cryptographic erasure
- Block overwriting

Destruction Techniques:

- Physical shredding
- Pulverization
- Disintegration
- Melting
- Chemical dissolution
- Incineration

Hardware disposal procedures incorporate:

Preparation Steps:

1. Asset identification
2. Data classification review
3. Sanitization method selection
4. Removal from network
5. Component inventory
6. Documentation initiation

Chain of custody documentation tracks:

Asset Movement:

- Current location
- Transfer dates
- Handler identification
- Security measures
- Transport methods
- Storage conditions

Required Documentation:

- Asset tags
- Serial numbers
- Model information
- Department ownership
- Sanitization status
- Disposal approval

Environmental considerations include:

Regulatory Compliance:

- E-waste regulations
- Hazardous materials
- Recycling requirements
- Export restrictions
- Local ordinances
- Industry standards

Verification procedures ensure:

Data Removal:

- Visual inspection

- Tool verification
- Sample testing
- Log review
- Security scan
- Documentation check

Certificates of destruction contain:

Element	Details Required	Verification Method
Asset Information	Serial numbers, asset tags	Physical inspection
Sanitization Method	Tools, standards used	Process documentation
Date and Location	Disposal facility, timing	Site certification
Technician Details	Name, certification	Credential verification
Witness Information	Observer credentials	Signature verification
Environmental Compliance	Regulation adherence	Audit documentation

Quality control measures include:

- Process audits
- Random sampling
- Tool calibration
- Staff certification
- Documentation review
- Compliance verification

CASE STUDY: DATA BREACH DUE TO IMPROPER CLASSIFICATION

An international financial services company suffered a significant data breach that exposed sensitive customer information. The root cause was traced back to improper data classification, where confidential customer data was stored and handled as if it were general business information. This lapse allowed the compromised system to be insufficiently protected, leading to unauthorized access by a threat actor.

The customer data, including personally identifiable information (PII) such as names, Social Security numbers, and financial records, had been mislabeled as "internal-use" instead of "confidential." As a result, critical controls—such as encryption, enhanced access controls, and robust monitoring—were not implemented on the affected systems.

Following the breach, the company faced regulatory penalties totaling $4.5 million under GDPR and similar regional privacy regulations, along with reputational damage that caused a 15% decline in its stock value. Remediation included implementing a stricter data classification framework, enhanced staff training, and automated tools to label and enforce policies based on data sensitivity.

CASE STUDY: ASSET TRACKING SYSTEM IMPLEMENTATION

A medium-sized healthcare organization faced challenges tracking medical devices, IT equipment, and software licenses across multiple facilities. With no centralized asset tracking system in place, the organization experienced frequent issues such as lost assets, redundant purchases, and expired software licenses, leading to inefficiencies and compliance risks under HIPAA.

To address these issues, the organization implemented an automated asset tracking system leveraging RFID tags and integration with a Configuration Management Database (CMDB). The new system provided real-time visibility into asset locations, usage status, and maintenance schedules.

Within six months, the implementation reduced asset loss by 40%, eliminated $250,000 in redundant equipment purchases, and ensured compliance by flagging unlicensed or unpatched systems. The project also introduced ownership assignment protocols and quarterly reconciliation audits, enabling the organization to maintain an up-to-date and accurate inventory.

CASE STUDY: MEDIA DISPOSAL INCIDENT ANALYSIS

A government contractor specializing in defense projects experienced an incident where sensitive information stored on decommissioned hard drives was improperly disposed of. Instead of following established media sanitization standards (e.g., NIST 800-88), an employee sold the hard drives to a third-party vendor without ensuring the data had been securely erased.

The vendor discovered the issue after accessing classified project files during routine refurbishment of the hard drives. Although the vendor reported the incident, the delay in containment resulted in potential exposure of national security data.

The contractor faced a suspension of its government contracts and launched an internal investigation, which revealed gaps in media disposal policies and employee training. Remediation measures included mandatory staff education on sanitization protocols, implementing automated data destruction systems, and introducing a chain-of-custody process to track decommissioned media.

CASE STUDY: CLASSIFICATION SYSTEM MIGRATION

A multinational technology firm initiated a migration of its legacy data classification system to align with a new framework based on ISO 27001 standards. The previous system lacked granularity, leading to overclassification of some data and underclassification of sensitive customer records, which created inefficiencies in resource allocation and elevated compliance risks.

The migration project involved reclassifying all existing data into four tiers—Public, Internal, Confidential, and Restricted—using automated classification tools. The process also included stakeholder workshops to align business and security priorities, as well as pilot testing in two departments before full-scale rollout.

During the migration, the firm encountered challenges such as inconsistent labeling practices, resistance from users accustomed to the old system, and technical hurdles with integrating the new classification framework into legacy systems. To resolve these issues, the firm conducted targeted employee training and implemented API-based connectors to bridge legacy applications with the new classification schema.

The migration reduced compliance violations by 30% and improved resource allocation by ensuring restricted data received the highest level of protection, while public and internal data required fewer safeguards.

CASE STUDY: CROSS-BORDER DATA TRANSFER CHALLENGES

An e-commerce company operating in the U.S., EU, and APAC regions faced compliance challenges in transferring customer data across borders due to varying regulatory requirements, such as GDPR, CCPA, and local data residency laws in APAC countries. The company's initial approach relied on generic data transfer agreements and standard contractual clauses (SCCs), but inconsistent enforcement and lack of visibility into data flows exposed the organization to non-compliance risks.

During a GDPR audit, regulators flagged the company for transferring EU citizens' data to the U.S. without adequate safeguards, resulting in a €2 million fine. Additionally, a breach in an APAC data center revealed data that should have been stored only in the EU due to residency restrictions.

The company implemented a multi-faceted solution, including:

- Establishing regional data centers to comply with residency laws.
- Encrypting all data transfers with key management restricted to the originating region.
- Deploying Data Loss Prevention (DLP) tools to monitor cross-border transfers and flag unauthorized movements.
- Revising vendor contracts to include specific data handling requirements for international operations.

These measures enabled the organization to meet regional compliance standards, reduce legal risks, and maintain customer trust across its global operations.

CASE STUDY: ASSET INVENTORY RECONCILIATION PROJECT

A global manufacturing company with operations across five continents initiated a reconciliation project to address inconsistencies in its asset inventory. The organization's previous manual tracking approach resulted in outdated records, duplicate entries, and $1.2 million in unidentified hardware assets over the past year.

The project involved implementing an automated discovery tool integrated with the company's CMDB to reconcile physical, virtual, and cloud-based assets. This process began with a network-wide discovery scan that identified all active devices, followed by a physical audit to validate unconnected or legacy assets.

Key challenges included identifying shadow IT systems (e.g., unauthorized SaaS applications) and reconciling discrepancies between regional inventories. To address this, the company created regional reconciliation teams, standardized asset naming conventions, and introduced real-time dashboards for tracking inventory updates.

Within 12 months, the project identified and documented 98% of all assets, resulting in a 25% reduction in unnecessary procurement costs and improved visibility into hardware and software compliance status. The reconciliation also supported the company's security team by providing accurate data for risk assessments and patch management prioritization.

PRACTICE QUESTIONS FOR DATA AND ASSET MANAGEMENT

Examining practical scenarios and decision-making processes enhances understanding of data and asset management concepts. Practice questions should focus on applying theoretical principles to realistic situations involving classification, handling, lifecycle management, regulatory compliance, risk assessment, and disposal. These questions test the ability to recognize risks, implement policies, and navigate complex organizational and regulatory environments.

Data Classification Decision-Making

Scenario 1: A financial institution has customer data that includes names, account numbers, and transaction histories. The organization uses a classification framework with categories of Public, Internal, Confidential, and Restricted. How should this data be classified, and why? What additional context might change the classification?

- **Key Considerations:** Evaluate the sensitivity of customer data, the impact of unauthorized access, and any regulatory requirements (e.g., PCI DSS). Discuss how factors like encryption or de-identification might lower risk.

Scenario 2: An employee drafts a report summarizing internal performance metrics, including customer feedback trends, but no personal or sensitive data. Would this document qualify as Confidential or Internal? Why?

- **Key Considerations:** Discuss how access restrictions are determined based on the business need and classification framework.

Handling Procedures for Various Classifications

Scenario 1: An organization's classification policy states that "Restricted" data must be encrypted in transit and at rest, with access limited to a select group of employees. If an email containing Restricted data is sent unencrypted outside the organization, what procedures should be followed?

- **Key Considerations:** Evaluate incident response steps, notification protocols, and potential remediation actions such as retraining employees or updating policies.

Scenario 2: A developer stores an unencrypted database backup on a shared network drive accessible to multiple teams. The backup contains Confidential customer information. What immediate actions should the organization take to handle this mishandling of data?

- **Key Considerations:** Examine the need for data removal, access logging review, encryption, and disciplinary actions if policy violations occurred.

Asset Lifecycle Management

Scenario 1: A company is transitioning to new laptops and needs to retire older devices. What steps should be taken to ensure proper management of the old devices through the asset lifecycle?

- **Key Considerations:** Address inventory tracking, data migration, secure data erasure, and physical disposal or repurposing of the devices.

Scenario 2: During an internal audit, it is discovered that some company-owned mobile devices are no longer accounted for in the asset inventory. How should the organization handle this situation, and what process improvements could prevent recurrence?

- **Key Considerations:** Highlight asset tracking, loss investigation, and policy updates for managing mobile devices.

Media Protection Requirements

Scenario 1: An organization plans to transport backup tapes containing critical financial records to an off-site storage facility. What media protection controls should be implemented during transportation to ensure security?

- **Key Considerations:** Discuss the use of tamper-evident seals, secure courier services, encryption, and chain-of-custody documentation.

Scenario 2: USB drives containing marketing materials are distributed at a conference. Should these drives have any security controls? If so, why?

- **Key Considerations:** Consider risks such as unauthorized access to corporate files or malware infections and discuss mitigations like read-only configurations or pre-scanning for threats.

Disposal Procedures

Scenario 1: A company retires a server containing sensitive financial data. The server is scheduled for physical destruction. What specific steps should be taken to securely dispose of this asset?

- **Key Considerations:** Examine data sanitization methods, physical destruction techniques (e.g., shredding, incineration), and chain-of-custody tracking.

Scenario 2: An employee disposes of printed documents labeled as Confidential by placing them in a standard trash bin. What procedural gaps exist in this scenario, and what corrective actions should be implemented?

- **Key Considerations:** Analyze the need for secure shredding policies and employee awareness training.

Regulatory Compliance Scenarios

Scenario 1: A company operating in the European Union collects customer data through an e-commerce platform. The data includes email addresses, purchase histories, and billing information. How should the company manage this data to remain GDPR-compliant?

- **Key Considerations:** Address data minimization, encryption, data subject rights (e.g., access and deletion), and lawful processing bases.

Scenario 2: A U.S.-based healthcare provider needs to share patient records with a third-party vendor for billing purposes. What steps must be taken to comply with HIPAA requirements?

- **Key Considerations:** Discuss the importance of Business Associate Agreements (BAAs), secure data transmission methods, and audit trails.

Risk Assessment in Asset Management

Scenario 1: An organization identifies a risk that mobile devices containing corporate email may be lost or stolen. What steps should be taken to assess and mitigate this risk?

- **Key Considerations:** Analyze the use of encryption, remote wipe capabilities, mobile device management (MDM) solutions, and employee training programs.

Scenario 2: A company's risk assessment identifies an outdated storage system with known vulnerabilities. What steps should the company take to address this risk, and how should the storage system's role in the organization's operations influence prioritization?

- **Key Considerations:** Discuss patching, replacement, or migration strategies, as well as operational dependencies and cost-benefit analysis.

Classification Inheritance Scenarios

Scenario 1: An organization classifies its financial databases as Restricted. A monthly financial report is generated from this data and shared with department heads via email. Should the classification of the report match the database, or can it be downgraded to Confidential? Why?

- **Key Considerations:** Examine the principle of classification inheritance, the sensitivity of aggregated data, and controls applied during data transformation or transfer.

Scenario 2: A project summary document is derived from classified research data but does not include sensitive details. Should the classification of the summary be inherited from the source data? Why or why not?

- **Key Considerations:** Analyze how data context and exposure risks affect classification adjustments.

Security Architecture and Engineering

SECURITY MODEL ARCHITECTURES AND FOUNDATIONAL COMPONENTS

State machine models represent system security through finite states and transitions. Each state captures the current security configuration, including subject access rights, object security levels, and active security policies. Transitions between states occur through authorized operations that maintain security invariants.

Security state components include:

State Definition:

- Current access matrix
- Security level mappings
- Active processes
- Resource states
- System configurations
- Policy conditions

Reference monitors enforce security policies through:

Component	Function	Implementation
Policy Engine	Rule evaluation	Access control lists
Interceptor	Request capture	System calls, API hooks
Validator	Permission check	Security attributes
Logger	Activity recording	Audit trails
Enforcer	Decision execution	Resource controls

Security kernel architecture layers:

Hardware Layer:

- Memory management
- Process isolation
- I/O controls
- Interrupt handling
- Hardware security

Kernel Layer:

- Process management
- Resource allocation
- Security enforcement
- System calls
- Event handling

Security Layer:

- Access control
- Authentication
- Audit logging
- Encryption
- Policy enforcement

Formal security models establish mathematical frameworks:

Bell-LaPadula Model:

- Simple security property
- *-property
- Discretionary security
- Security levels
- Access modes

Biba Integrity Model:

- Simple integrity
- Integrity *-property
- Subject integrity
- Object integrity
- Invocation property

Trust Computing Base components:
Protection Mechanisms:

- Memory protection
- Process isolation
- Access control
- Security policies
- Audit functions

TCB Boundary defines:

- Security perimeter
- Trust relationships
- Interface controls
- Data flows
- Resource access

Security evaluation methods:
Common Criteria:

- Protection profiles
- Security targets
- Assurance levels
- Evaluation methods
- Certification process

TCSEC Requirements:

- Security policy
- Identification
- Labels
- Accountability
- Assurance

System architects implement:

- Layered protection
- Least privilege
- Complete mediation
- Open design
- Economy of mechanism

ACCESS CONTROL MODELS DEEP DIVE

The Bell-LaPadula (BLP) model, designed to enforce data confidentiality in government and military systems, is a foundational access control model that uses formal mathematical rules to manage security levels and prevent unauthorized access. The model operates on a mandatory access control (MAC) framework, assigning security levels to both subjects (users, processes) and objects (files, databases) to regulate interactions based on hierarchical clearance. Implementing Bell-LaPadula in practice requires adherence to its core principles: the simple security property, *-property, strong star property, and security level relationships.

BELL-LAPADULA MODEL IMPLEMENTATION

SIMPLE SECURITY PROPERTY

The simple security property ("no read up" or NRU) dictates that a subject at a given security level cannot read data classified at a higher security level. This prevents unauthorized disclosure of sensitive information by ensuring that lower-clearance entities cannot access more sensitive data.

For example, in a military context, a user with a "Confidential" clearance cannot read files labeled "Secret" or "Top Secret." This is enforced by comparing the clearance level of the subject to the classification level of the object. The system checks if the subject's clearance is equal to or higher than the object's classification before granting read access.

In practice, this rule is implemented through labeling mechanisms. Operating systems using Bell-LaPadula principles, such as SELinux (Security-Enhanced Linux), enforce labels on both users and files. The system kernel evaluates access requests against the simple security property, rejecting any that violate "no read up."

***-PROPERTY (STAR PROPERTY)**

The *-property ("no write down" or NWD) ensures that a subject at a given security level cannot write to objects at a lower security level. This prevents unauthorized downgrading of sensitive information to less secure classifications, maintaining confidentiality throughout the system.

For instance, a user with "Top Secret" clearance cannot write data into a file classified as "Confidential." If this rule were not enforced, users could unintentionally or maliciously leak sensitive information to a less secure environment. Implementing the *-property requires strict checks during write operations. For databases or file systems, each transaction is evaluated to ensure that the target object's classification is not below the subject's clearance. In systems designed for multilevel security (MLS), write operations are rejected outright if they violate this rule.

STRONG STAR PROPERTY

The strong star property refines the *-property by adding an additional restriction: a subject may only read and write at the same security level. While the simple security and *-properties control read and write operations independently, the strong star property enforces symmetry, ensuring that users interact exclusively within their clearance level.

For example, if a user is assigned a "Secret" clearance, they can only read from and write to files labeled "Secret." This eliminates the risk of mixed interactions where a subject could read at one level and write at another, creating potential vectors for data leaks.

This property is particularly useful in environments with strict compartmentalization requirements, such as intelligence agencies or defense contractors. It ensures that data stays strictly within its designated classification level, minimizing exposure to external threats.

SECURITY LEVEL RELATIONSHIPS

Security level relationships define how subjects and objects interact based on their assigned classifications and clearances. The Bell-LaPadula model uses these relationships to create a hierarchical structure, commonly represented as a lattice. The lattice defines dominance relationships between security levels, where:

- A security level is a combination of a *classification* (e.g., Confidential, Secret, Top Secret) and a *compartment* (e.g., a project code or department).
- A subject's clearance dominates an object's classification if the subject's classification is equal to or higher, and the subject has the necessary compartment access.

For example, consider the following security levels:

1. **Top Secret {Project X}**
2. **Secret {Project X, Project Y}**
3. **Confidential {Project Y}**

A user with "Secret {Project X, Project Y}" clearance can:

- Read data labeled "Secret {Project X}" or "Confidential {Project Y}" under the simple security property.
- Write to objects classified "Secret {Project X, Project Y}" under the *-property.

These relationships enable precise control over data flow while maintaining the integrity of the classification hierarchy. For implementation, access control matrices or rules are defined to map subject clearances to object classifications, with automated systems evaluating access requests in real time.

The Bell-LaPadula model's primary focus on confidentiality makes it well-suited for environments where information leaks must be prevented at all costs, although it is often complemented by other models (e.g., Biba) to address integrity concerns.

BIBA MODEL AND CLARK-WILSON MODEL

The Biba and Clark-Wilson models focus on maintaining data integrity in security systems but approach it from distinct perspectives. The Biba model emphasizes preventing unauthorized modification of data by using integrity levels, while the Clark-Wilson model ensures integrity through structured processes, well-formed transactions, and strict enforcement of separation of duties. Together, they provide frameworks for safeguarding information systems against corruption and unauthorized changes.

Biba Model Components

The Biba Integrity Model, introduced in 1977, establishes rules to prevent the corruption of data by unauthorized or untrusted entities. It enforces a strict hierarchical structure of integrity levels and is particularly effective in environments where the integrity of information is more important than confidentiality.

Integrity Levels

The Biba model assigns integrity levels to both subjects (users or processes) and objects (data or resources). These levels dictate which subjects can access and modify which objects. Integrity levels are hierarchical, with higher levels representing greater trustworthiness or accuracy. For example:

- **High Integrity Level**: Critical financial data or system configuration files.
- **Medium Integrity Level**: Internal reports or moderately sensitive data.
- **Low Integrity Level**: Public-facing web content or temporary files.

Subjects with a high integrity level should only interact with objects of equal or higher integrity to prevent the contamination of trusted data by less trustworthy entities.

Simple Integrity Axiom

The simple integrity axiom (also known as the "no read down" rule) prohibits subjects from reading data at a lower integrity level. This ensures that high-trust processes do not become contaminated by potentially corrupt or less trustworthy information. For example, a high-level financial auditing application cannot access logs generated by a less-trusted application running at a lower integrity level to avoid introducing errors or biases.

Integrity Star Property

The integrity star property (also known as the "no write up" rule) prevents subjects at a lower integrity level from modifying or writing to objects at a higher integrity level. This ensures that less trustworthy processes cannot corrupt data or resources that require greater accuracy or reliability. For example, a standard user account cannot write changes to a database containing sensitive configuration settings used by administrators.

The Biba model's combined "no read down" and "no write up" rules are ideal for environments like financial or healthcare systems, where preserving the accuracy and reliability of data is paramount.

Clark-Wilson Model

The Clark-Wilson model focuses on ensuring integrity through well-defined processes and the proper enforcement of roles and responsibilities. It was designed to address the limitations of earlier integrity models like Biba by incorporating real-world business requirements and workflows. The Clark-Wilson model is process-oriented, emphasizing proper use of data through controlled mechanisms rather than hierarchical trust levels.

Well-Formed Transactions

Well-formed transactions are structured processes that transform data from one valid state to another in a secure and predictable way. These transactions are implemented through controlled interfaces that enforce business rules and security policies. For example, in an e-commerce system:

- A customer placing an order may trigger a transaction that validates the order details, processes payment, and updates inventory.
- Each step in the transaction ensures that data integrity is maintained, such as verifying payment details to prevent fraudulent activity.

The model uses Transformation Procedures (TPs) to define these processes and ensure that only authorized changes can be made to the system. For example, a TP might enforce rules requiring multiple approvals for high-value transactions, ensuring accuracy and accountability.

Separation of Duties

Separation of duties prevents a single individual from having complete control over a sensitive process. By dividing responsibilities among multiple parties, the risk of fraud or unauthorized changes is minimized. For example:

- In a financial institution, one employee may initiate a wire transfer (e.g., create the transaction), while another employee must approve it (e.g., authorize the transaction).
- The use of independent roles enforces oversight and reduces the likelihood of intentional or accidental violations of system integrity.

Clark-Wilson achieves separation of duties by assigning specific roles to subjects and enforcing constraints on what actions they can perform. Access Control Lists (ACLs) and role-based access control (RBAC) are often used to implement these restrictions.

Constrained Data Items

Constrained Data Items (CDIs) are the data objects within a system that require integrity protection. CDIs are only modified through the use of well-formed transactions, ensuring that all changes are subject to proper validation and controls. For example:

- A company's payroll database might be classified as a CDI, with strict policies requiring all modifications to go through predefined procedures, such as approval workflows or automated scripts.
- Unconstrained Data Items (UDIs), by contrast, are less sensitive and do not require the same level of protection. However, UDIs can only be converted into CDIs through the application of a certified transaction.

By carefully categorizing data as constrained or unconstrained and controlling how it is accessed or transformed, the Clark-Wilson model provides strong protection against unauthorized or erroneous modifications.

SECURITY ARCHITECTURE PRINCIPLES AND IMPLEMENTATION STRATEGIES

Defense in depth implements multiple security layers:

Layer	Controls	Purpose
Physical	Guards, locks, cameras	Facility protection
Network	Firewalls, IPS, segmentation	Traffic control
Host	Hardening, AV, EDR	System security
Application	Input validation, encryption	Software protection
Data	Access controls, encryption	Information security

Least privilege enforcement requires:

Implementation Steps:

1. Role definition
2. Access mapping
3. Permission assignment
4. Account review
5. Elevation processes
6. Monitoring setup

Separation of duties matrices:

Function	Initiator	Approver	Executor	Auditor
Change Mgmt	Developer	Manager	Operator	Security
Finance	Accountant	Controller	Treasurer	Auditor
Security	Admin	Manager	Engineer	Analyst

Fail-secure mechanisms:

- Access denial on failure
- System shutdown procedures
- Resource isolation
- State preservation
- Recovery processes

Fail-safe operations:

- Safety prioritization
- Emergency access
- Backup systems
- Manual overrides
- Degraded modes

Complete mediation ensures:

- Access verification
- Request validation
- Policy enforcement
- Session tracking
- Audit logging

Economy of mechanism through:

- Simple designs
- Clear interfaces
- Minimal components
- Standard protocols
- Proven algorithms

Open design principles incorporate:

- Published standards
- Peer review
- Documentation
- Source availability
- Testing frameworks

Zero trust architecture components:
Network Implementation:

- Micro-segmentation
- Identity-based access
- Continuous verification
- Encryption everywhere
- Asset visibility

Access Controls:

- Identity verification
- Device validation
- Context evaluation
- Risk assessment
- Policy enforcement

Resource Protection:

- Application segmentation
- API security

- Data classification
- Monitoring systems
- Response automation

Security architects design:

- Control frameworks
- Protection layers
- Trust boundaries
- Access paths
- Recovery methods

Verification methods include:

- Architecture review
- Control testing
- Penetration testing
- Configuration analysis
- Performance monitoring

Documentation maintains:

- Design principles
- Control objectives
- Implementation guides
- Test procedures
- Review findings

SYMMETRIC CRYPTOGRAPHY

Symmetric cryptography uses the same key for both encryption and decryption, making it a fast and efficient method for securing data. It plays a key role in modern information security systems, especially in scenarios requiring high-speed encryption, such as securing communications, file encryption, and database encryption. Implementing symmetric cryptography effectively requires understanding block and stream cipher operations, key management, modes of operation, algorithm selection, and the potential challenges associated with its use.

BLOCK CIPHER OPERATIONS

Block ciphers process data in fixed-size blocks, typically 64 or 128 bits. Plaintext is divided into blocks, and each block undergoes encryption independently using a specific encryption algorithm and key. Popular block ciphers include AES (Advanced Encryption Standard) and 3DES (Triple Data Encryption Standard).

1. **Substitution-Permutation Networks (SPNs):** Most modern block ciphers rely on SPNs, which involve a series of substitution (S-box) and permutation steps to provide confusion and diffusion, enhancing security. For instance, AES employs multiple rounds of substitutions, row shifts, and column mixes to transform plaintext into ciphertext.
2. **Padding:** If the plaintext's size is not a multiple of the block size, padding schemes like PKCS#7 are used to fill the final block with extra bytes. Proper padding is critical, as improper handling may result in vulnerabilities such as padding oracle attacks.

STREAM CIPHER IMPLEMENTATION

Stream ciphers encrypt data one bit or byte at a time, making them suitable for scenarios with variable-length data or real-time applications like video streaming. Instead of processing fixed blocks, stream ciphers generate a keystream (a sequence of pseudorandom bits) that is XORed with plaintext to produce ciphertext.

1. **Synchronous Stream Ciphers:** Keystreams are generated independently of the plaintext or ciphertext. Popular algorithms include RC4 and modern stream ciphers like ChaCha20. Synchronous ciphers require precise synchronization between sender and receiver to avoid decryption errors.
2. **Self-Synchronizing Stream Ciphers:** Keystreams are derived from previously processed ciphertext, ensuring that the system can recover from minor data losses or synchronization issues. For example, Cipher Feedback Mode (CFB) implements stream cipher functionality using a block cipher in a self-synchronizing manner.

3. **Security Considerations:** Stream ciphers are sensitive to keystream reuse. Re-encrypting data with the same key and initialization vector (IV) can lead to ciphertext XOR attacks, exposing plaintext relationships.

KEY MANAGEMENT PROCEDURES

Effective key management is fundamental to the security of symmetric cryptography. The strength of the system lies in keeping the symmetric key confidential, as its compromise can allow an adversary to decrypt all encrypted data.

1. **Key Generation:** Keys must be generated using secure random number generators (RNGs) to ensure unpredictability. Hardware-based RNGs or software RNGs like those conforming to NIST SP 800-90 standards are typically used.
2. **Key Storage:** Keys should be stored in a secure environment, such as a Hardware Security Module (HSM) or a Trusted Platform Module (TPM). Keys stored in memory should be protected using operating system-level protections to prevent leakage.
3. **Key Distribution:** Symmetric keys are shared between parties using secure channels. Methods like pre-shared keys (PSKs), Diffie-Hellman key exchange, or encrypted transport protocols (e.g., TLS) are used to distribute keys securely.
4. **Key Rotation and Lifespan:** Keys should have a defined lifespan to minimize exposure. Rotating keys periodically ensures that compromised keys have limited usefulness. This is particularly important in environments like database encryption, where long-term keys are more vulnerable to attacks.

MODE OF OPERATIONS

Block ciphers cannot securely encrypt plaintext by themselves when used repeatedly. Modes of operation define how plaintext blocks are encrypted and chained to ensure security and flexibility in different scenarios.

1. **Electronic Codebook (ECB):**
   - Each plaintext block is encrypted independently.
   - *Weaknesses:* ECB reveals patterns in the plaintext, making it insecure for most applications. For instance, encrypting an image with ECB would still show discernible outlines.
   - *Use Case:* Encrypting small, independent data segments like unique keys.

2. **Cipher Block Chaining (CBC):**
   - Each plaintext block is XORed with the previous ciphertext block before encryption. An IV ensures unique outputs for identical plaintexts.
   - *Advantages:* Conceals patterns in plaintext, ensuring security.
   - *Use Case:* File encryption, where the entire plaintext is known before encryption.
3. **Cipher Feedback Mode (CFB):**
   - Operates as a stream cipher by encrypting an IV and feeding the ciphertext back to the encryption process.
   - *Use Case:* Real-time communication or applications requiring incremental encryption.
4. **Output Feedback Mode (OFB):**
   - Generates a keystream by encrypting an IV repeatedly. The keystream is XORed with plaintext for encryption.
   - *Use Case:* Scenarios where error propagation must be minimized, such as satellite communication.

5. **Counter Mode (CTR):**
   - Uses a counter combined with an IV to produce unique keystream blocks for encryption.
   - *Advantages:* Supports parallel processing and random access to encrypted data.
   - *Use Case:* Database encryption or high-performance applications.

ALGORITHM SELECTION CRITERIA

Selecting a symmetric encryption algorithm involves balancing security, performance, and compliance requirements.

1. **Security Strength:** AES is widely regarded as the standard due to its proven resistance against known attacks and its approval by NIST and FIPS 197 standards. Algorithms like 3DES are deprecated because of their limited key length (effective 112 bits) and susceptibility to brute-force attacks.
2. **Key Length:** A larger key size, such as 256 bits in AES, provides stronger security but may incur higher computational overhead. For most applications, AES-128 or AES-192 strikes a balance between security and performance.

3. **Regulatory Compliance:** Ensure the chosen algorithm meets industry-specific compliance standards, such as PCI-DSS or HIPAA, which mandate specific cryptographic techniques for data protection.
4. **Use Case Fit:** For low-power IoT devices, lightweight encryption algorithms like AES-GCM-SIV or ChaCha20-Poly1305 may be more suitable due to their reduced resource requirements.

PERFORMANCE CONSIDERATIONS

Symmetric cryptography is generally faster than asymmetric cryptography due to its simpler mathematical operations, but performance depends on several factors:

1. **Hardware Acceleration:** Modern CPUs include hardware instruction sets like Intel AES-NI or ARM Cryptography Extensions to accelerate AES encryption and decryption.
2. **Parallelization:** Modes like CTR and GCM allow blocks to be encrypted in parallel, significantly improving performance on multicore systems.
3. **Resource Constraints:** Embedded systems or mobile devices may require lightweight algorithms optimized for constrained environments.

IMPLEMENTATION CHALLENGES

Implementing symmetric cryptography comes with potential pitfalls that can compromise its security if not addressed properly.

1. **Key Management Errors:** Inadequate protection of keys, such as hardcoding them into source code or storing them unencrypted, is a common vulnerability. Key management systems (KMS) like AWS KMS or Azure Key Vault mitigate these risks.
2. **Improper IV Usage:** Reusing an IV in modes like CBC or CTR can lead to ciphertext compromise. Best practices dictate that IVs should be randomly generated and never reused.
3. **Padding Oracle Attacks:** Incorrect padding validation in block ciphers can allow attackers to exploit error messages and decrypt data. Libraries like OpenSSL include padding countermeasures to mitigate these attacks.
4. **Side-Channel Attacks:** Timing or power consumption analysis can leak information about encryption keys. Constant-time algorithms and hardware countermeasures help defend against such attacks.

Careful attention to proper implementation and ongoing management is necessary to ensure symmetric cryptography provides the intended security benefits.

ASYMMETRIC CRYPTOGRAPHY

Asymmetric cryptography, also called public-key cryptography, uses a pair of mathematically related keys: a public key for encryption or signature verification and a private key for decryption or signature generation. This approach enables secure communication over untrusted channels and underpins key technologies like digital signatures, key exchanges, and secure certificate systems. It plays a critical role in ensuring confidentiality, integrity, authentication, and non-repudiation.

Public Key Infrastructure

Public Key Infrastructure (PKI) is a framework for managing public and private keys, enabling secure communication and authentication across systems. PKI ensures that a user's public key is valid and belongs to the correct individual or entity through the use of digital certificates issued by trusted Certificate Authorities (CAs).

- **Components**: PKI includes several key components:
  - **Certificate Authorities (CAs)**: Issue and manage digital certificates, such as X.509 certificates.
  - **Registration Authorities (RAs)**: Verify the identities of entities requesting certificates.
  - **Certificate Repositories**: Store and distribute issued certificates and public keys.
  - **Certificate Revocation Lists (CRLs)** or **Online Certificate Status Protocol (OCSP)**: Ensure expired or compromised certificates are invalidated in real time.

For example, PKI is the backbone of HTTPS, enabling secure communication between a browser and a website by validating the server's identity and encrypting data using the server's public key.

Digital Signature Systems

Digital signatures provide authentication, integrity, and non-repudiation by allowing a sender to sign a message with their private key. The recipient can then verify the authenticity of the message using the sender's public key.

- **How It Works**:
    - A hash of the message is created using a cryptographic hashing algorithm (e.g., SHA-256).
    - The hash is encrypted with the sender's private key to create the digital signature.
    - The recipient decrypts the signature using the sender's public key and compares the hash to the message's calculated hash. A match confirms authenticity and integrity.

For instance, software developers use digital signatures to certify the authenticity of distributed software packages, ensuring users that the code has not been tampered with.

Key Exchange Protocols

Key exchange protocols facilitate the secure sharing of cryptographic keys between parties over an insecure channel. Asymmetric cryptography plays a central role in these protocols, which are often used to exchange symmetric keys for subsequent encryption.

- **Diffie-Hellman (DH)**: One of the earliest key exchange protocols, DH allows two parties to generate a shared secret without transmitting it directly. DH is vulnerable to man-in-the-middle attacks if authentication is not integrated.
- **Elliptic Curve Diffie-Hellman (ECDH)**: A more efficient variation of DH that uses elliptic curve cryptography to generate the shared secret. ECDH is preferred in systems with limited computational resources, such as IoT devices.
- **RSA-Based Exchange**: RSA can be used for key exchange by encrypting a symmetric session key with the recipient's public key and having the recipient decrypt it with their private key.

For example, TLS protocols use a combination of ECDH or RSA for key exchange to establish secure communication channels over the internet.

Algorithm Characteristics

Asymmetric algorithms differ from symmetric ones in terms of operation, key management, and use cases. Key characteristics include:

- **Key Pairs**: Public and private keys are mathematically linked, but the private key cannot be derived from the public key (assuming secure parameters).
- **Computational Complexity**: Asymmetric encryption is computationally more expensive than symmetric encryption, making it better suited for tasks like authentication or key exchange rather than bulk data encryption.
- **Key Length**: Asymmetric keys are much longer than symmetric keys for equivalent security. For example, RSA requires 2048 bits or more for strong security, while AES achieves the same level of security with just 256 bits.
- **Use Cases**: Asymmetric algorithms are primarily used in scenarios requiring key distribution, digital signatures, and encryption of small amounts of data.

RSA Operations

RSA (Rivest-Shamir-Adleman) is one of the most widely used asymmetric algorithms. It relies on the mathematical difficulty of factoring large composite numbers into their prime factors.

- **Key Generation**:
    1. Select two large prime numbers, ppp and qqq.
    2. Compute n=p×qn = p \times qn=p×q (the modulus) and ϕ(n)=(p−1)(q−1)\phi(n) = (p-1)(q-1)ϕ(n)=(p−1)(q−1).
    3. Select a public exponent eee, typically 65537, which is a commonly used value for efficiency.
    4. Compute the private key ddd such that (e⋅d)mod ϕ(n)=1(e \cdot d) \mod \phi(n) = 1(e⋅d)modϕ(n)=1.
- **Encryption**: The sender encrypts the plaintext MMM as C=Memod nC = M^e \mod nC=Memodn.
- **Decryption**: The recipient decrypts the ciphertext CCC as M=Cdmod nM = C^d \mod nM=Cdmodn.

For example, RSA is often used in TLS to encrypt session keys that are then used for faster symmetric encryption.

Elliptic Curve Cryptography

Elliptic Curve Cryptography (ECC) is a highly efficient form of public-key cryptography based on the algebraic structure of elliptic curves over finite fields. ECC provides the same security as RSA with much shorter key lengths, making it ideal for environments with limited resources.

- **How It Works**: ECC relies on the difficulty of the Elliptic Curve Discrete Logarithm Problem (ECDLP), where computing the scalar multiple of a point on the curve is easy, but reversing the operation is computationally infeasible.
- **Efficiency**: A 256-bit ECC key provides equivalent security to a 3072-bit RSA key.
- **Applications**: ECC is widely used in ECDH for key exchange, ECDSA (Elliptic Curve Digital Signature Algorithm) for signatures, and secure protocols like TLS and SSH.

For instance, ECC is used in modern devices like smartphones and IoT devices due to its low power consumption and speed.

Quantum Cryptography Considerations

Quantum computing poses a significant threat to traditional asymmetric algorithms, as quantum algorithms like Shor's algorithm can efficiently factor large integers (breaking RSA) and solve discrete logarithm problems (breaking ECC).

- **Post-Quantum Cryptography**: To mitigate this risk, researchers are developing quantum-resistant algorithms, such as lattice-based, hash-based, and code-based cryptography.
- **Quantum Key Distribution (QKD)**: QKD, such as the BB84 protocol, uses quantum mechanics to securely exchange keys. It provides unconditional security based on the laws of physics rather than computational complexity.
- **Current Implications**: While large-scale quantum computers are not yet available, organizations handling long-term sensitive data (e.g., government agencies) are already exploring quantum-resistant solutions.

For example, NIST is conducting a standardization process for post-quantum cryptography, with algorithms like CRYSTALS-Kyber emerging as promising candidates for secure communications in a quantum-capable future.

PUBLIC KEY INFRASTRUCTURE COMPONENTS AND OPERATIONAL FRAMEWORKS

Certificate Authority hierarchy establishes:

Root CA:

- Self-signed certificate
- Offline storage
- Maximum security
- Policy definition
- Trust anchor
- Key ceremony

Intermediate CAs:

Level 1: Policy CA

↓

Level 2: Issuing CA

↓

Level 3: Operating CA

Registration Authority functions:

Function	Process	Verification
Identity Verification	Document review	Multi-factor
Request Validation	Policy check	Compliance
Key Generation	Secure creation	Standards
Certificate Request	Format check	Completeness
Approval Process	Authority review	Authorization

Certificate lifecycle management:
Generation Phase:

- Key pair creation
- CSR formatting
- Policy validation
- Authority approval
- Certificate issuance

Distribution Methods:

- Manual delivery
- Automated push
- Pull mechanisms
- Directory services
- Email delivery

Revocation mechanisms include:
CRL Implementation:

- Distribution points
- Update frequency
- Size management
- Delta CRLs
- Access methods

OCSP Services:

- Real-time status
- Response signing
- Cache control
- Load balancing
- High availability

Trust models support:
Hierarchical:

- Single root
- Clear path
- Simple validation
- Central control
- Easy management

Mesh:

- Peer relationships
- Multiple paths
- Complex validation
- Distributed control
- Flexible structure

Bridge:

- Central connector
- Multiple domains
- Efficient paths
- Simplified trust
- Scale management

Certificate policies define:
Usage Requirements:

- Key usage
- Extended usage
- Validation level
- Subscriber obligations
- Relying party duties

Operational Procedures:

- Key generation
- Certificate issuance
- Directory services
- Revocation handling
- Archive management

Cross-certification enables:
Trust Establishment:

- Policy mapping
- Path discovery
- Validation rules
- Name constraints
- Policy constraints

Technical Implementation:

- Certificate extensions
- Name spaces
- Trust paths
- Validation methods
- Revocation handling

CRYPTOGRAPHIC ATTACK METHODS

Cryptographic systems aim to secure data by employing mathematical algorithms and implementation techniques designed to resist a wide range of attacks. However, attackers leverage various methods to compromise encryption schemes, ranging from brute-force attempts to advanced side-channel and protocol exploits. Understanding these attack methods is critical to designing, implementing, and maintaining secure cryptographic solutions.

BRUTE FORCE TECHNIQUES

Brute force attacks systematically try every possible key or password combination to decrypt a message. While conceptually simple, their feasibility depends on the length and complexity of the key or password.

1. **Keyspace Size:** The time required for a brute force attack is directly proportional to the size of the keyspace. For example:
    - A 128-bit key (as in AES-128) has 21282^{128}2128 possible combinations, which is computationally infeasible for modern hardware.
    - Weak keys, such as those in DES (56-bit keyspace), are susceptible to brute force and can be cracked in hours using modern computing clusters.
2. **Distributed Brute Force (Botnets and Cloud Attacks):** Attackers may leverage distributed computing power, such as botnets or cloud GPU clusters, to accelerate brute force attempts. Tools like Hashcat and John the Ripper are often used for such attacks.
3. **Defenses:** Increasing key lengths (e.g., using AES-256) and implementing mechanisms like account lockouts and rate-limiting for authentication systems effectively mitigate brute force attacks.

MATHEMATICAL ATTACKS

Mathematical attacks exploit vulnerabilities in the underlying cryptographic algorithms rather than their implementation. These attacks often rely on theoretical breakthroughs or advances in computational techniques.

1. **Factoring-Based Attacks:** Cryptographic schemes like RSA depend on the difficulty of factoring large composite numbers into their prime components. Algorithms like the General Number Field Sieve (GNFS) are used to perform factoring attacks.
   - RSA with keys smaller than 2048 bits is now considered vulnerable to such attacks.
2. **Discrete Logarithm Attacks:** Algorithms such as Diffie-Hellman and DSA rely on the difficulty of solving discrete logarithm problems. Index calculus and its variants have been used to reduce the complexity of solving these problems in some finite fields.
   - Elliptic Curve Cryptography (ECC) is often preferred as it offers higher security with smaller keys, making discrete log attacks computationally infeasible.
3. **Cryptanalysis of Symmetric Ciphers:** Techniques like differential cryptanalysis and linear cryptanalysis target block ciphers by finding statistical patterns in ciphertext. These attacks have been effective against older ciphers like DES but are ineffective against modern designs like AES.
4. **Defenses:** Robust algorithm design, large key sizes, and frequent updates to cryptographic standards reduce the effectiveness of mathematical attacks.

SIDE-CHANNEL ANALYSIS

Side-channel attacks exploit physical characteristics of a cryptographic system rather than its algorithm. These attacks gather indirect information from the system's behavior, such as power consumption, electromagnetic radiation, or timing variations.

1. **Timing Attacks:** Measure the time taken by cryptographic operations to infer secret information. For example, the time taken to compare password hashes could reveal where a comparison fails, allowing attackers to reconstruct the input step by step.
   - Defenses: Use constant-time algorithms, which ensure that execution time does not depend on input values.
2. **Power Analysis:** Observe the power consumption of a device during cryptographic operations to extract secrets.
   - *Simple Power Analysis (SPA):* Directly correlates power traces to operations.
   - *Differential Power Analysis (DPA):* Uses statistical analysis of multiple power traces to identify key-related patterns.
   - Defenses: Use power-randomizing techniques, decoupling power traces from operations.
3. **Electromagnetic Analysis:** Monitor electromagnetic radiation emitted during cryptographic operations to extract secret information.
   - Defenses: Shielding and noise injection mitigate this attack vector.
4. **Fault Injection Attacks:** Deliberately introduce faults (e.g., voltage spikes, temperature fluctuations, or laser pulses) into hardware systems to disrupt cryptographic computations, potentially exposing keys or plaintext.
   - Example: Differential Fault Analysis (DFA) on AES has been used to deduce key material by observing faulty ciphertexts.
   - Defenses: Hardware error-checking, redundancy, and fault detection mechanisms.

IMPLEMENTATION VULNERABILITIES

Cryptographic systems can be compromised by implementation flaws, even if the underlying algorithms are secure. Common implementation vulnerabilities include:

1. **Padding Oracle Attacks:** Exploit improper error handling in padding schemes for block ciphers like AES in CBC mode. Attackers use padding error messages to incrementally decrypt ciphertext.
   - Defenses: Use authenticated encryption modes like AES-GCM or AES-CCM to eliminate the need for padding.
2. **Improper Random Number Generation:** Weak or predictable random number generators can lead to the compromise of cryptographic keys. For instance, weak randomness in RSA key generation has previously been exploited to recover private keys.
   - Defenses: Use secure random number generators like those compliant with NIST SP 800-90A.
3. **Side-Channel Leakage in Libraries:** Cryptographic libraries like OpenSSL may introduce timing or memory vulnerabilities.

- Example: The Heartbleed vulnerability allowed attackers to extract sensitive data from server memory due to improper bounds checking.

4. **Defenses:** Regular code reviews, fuzz testing, and adopting well-tested cryptographic libraries reduce the risk of implementation vulnerabilities.

PROTOCOL ATTACKS

Protocol-level attacks target the design or implementation of cryptographic communication protocols.

1. **Replay Attacks:** Intercepted messages are replayed by attackers to mimic legitimate communication. For example, an attacker might replay an encrypted payment authorization message.
   - Defenses: Use timestamps or sequence numbers to ensure message freshness.
2. **Man-in-the-Middle (MITM) Attacks:** Intercept communication between two parties to read or modify data. For example, attackers may exploit weak or absent authentication during key exchange protocols like Diffie-Hellman.
   - Defenses: Use certificates for mutual authentication (e.g., in TLS) and ensure public keys are verified by trusted authorities.
3. **Downgrade Attacks:** Force communication to fall back to a weaker encryption protocol or version. For example, attackers may exploit vulnerabilities like POODLE, which downgraded HTTPS connections to SSL 3.0.
   - Defenses: Disable legacy protocols and enforce modern standards like TLS 1.3.
4. **Cryptographic Oracle Attacks:** Protocol errors or side-channel information allows attackers to act as "oracles," providing feedback that helps decrypt messages or forge signatures. For instance, Bleichenbacher's attack exploited RSA's PKCS#1 padding to decrypt ciphertexts without knowing the private key.
   - Defenses: Harden protocols against error-specific feedback and ensure robust padding validation.

PERFORMANCE CONSIDERATIONS

Many of these attack methods exploit performance trade-offs in cryptographic systems. For example, optimizing algorithms for speed or hardware efficiency may inadvertently expose timing or power side channels. Balancing security, usability, and efficiency is a key challenge for cryptographic designers.

Attackers are constantly innovating techniques, necessitating continual updates to cryptographic algorithms, libraries, and protocols. Advances in quantum computing, for instance, may render many of today's asymmetric cryptographic methods obsolete, further highlighting the need for forward-thinking defenses and cryptographic agility.

CRYPTOGRAPHIC IMPLEMENTATION

Implementing cryptography effectively requires precise adherence to best practices across key generation, random number usage, key storage, and secure hardware mechanisms. Proper algorithm selection, protocol design, performance optimization, and compliance with established security standards ensure that cryptographic implementations remain robust and reliable under real-world conditions. Missteps at any stage can lead to vulnerabilities that compromise data confidentiality, integrity, and availability.

Key Generation Requirements

Key generation is a cornerstone of cryptographic security. Cryptographic keys must be randomly generated, sufficiently long, and unpredictable to withstand attacks such as brute force or key derivation attempts. Key generation must follow these principles:

- **Key Length**: Select a key length appropriate to the algorithm and the desired level of security. For example, AES keys should be 128, 192, or 256 bits, while RSA keys should be at least 2048 bits.
- **Entropy Source**: Use a high-entropy source for key generation to ensure randomness. Sources like hardware-based entropy generators are preferred over software-based pseudo-random number generators (PRNGs).
- **Key Lifespan**: Define key rotation policies to replace keys periodically, reducing the risk of compromise. For instance, symmetric keys used for session encryption should be replaced more frequently than long-term signing keys.

An example is the generation of ephemeral keys for Transport Layer Security (TLS) sessions, which ensures forward secrecy even if long-term keys are compromised.

Random Number Generation
Cryptographic systems rely heavily on randomness to generate keys, initialization vectors (IVs), nonces, and salts. A weak or predictable random number generator (RNG) undermines the entire security system.

- **True Random Number Generators (TRNGs)**: TRNGs use physical phenomena like thermal noise or electrical signal variations to produce truly random numbers. These are ideal for generating cryptographic keys.
- **Cryptographically Secure Pseudo-Random Number Generators (CSPRNGs)**: When true randomness is not feasible, CSPRNGs like those based on NIST SP 800-90A (e.g., Hash_DRBG or HMAC_DRBG) ensure pseudo-random numbers are computationally infeasible to predict.
- **Seed Management**: RNGs require a high-quality seed to produce secure output. Seeding must be done with data from entropy sources to ensure unpredictability.

For example, predictable random numbers in the Debian OpenSSL vulnerability (2008) compromised the generation of private keys, exposing millions of systems to attack.

Key Storage Protection
Proper protection of cryptographic keys is critical to ensuring they are not exposed to unauthorized access, which would negate the security of the cryptosystem.

- **Hardware Security Modules (HSMs)**: Store and manage cryptographic keys in tamper-proof hardware devices. HSMs are designed to resist physical and logical attacks and provide key management functions like encryption, signing, and key rotation.
- **Secure Key Wrapping**: Encrypt keys using other keys (key-encryption keys) before storing them to add a layer of protection. Algorithms like AES Key Wrap (RFC 3394) are commonly used.
- **Memory Protection**: Avoid storing plaintext keys in memory for prolonged periods. Use secure memory management functions that clear sensitive data immediately after use.
- **Access Control**: Implement strict access controls to limit who or what can retrieve keys. Use multifactor authentication (MFA) or hardware tokens for additional security.

An example is storing private keys in an HSM for signing SSL/TLS certificates, ensuring that the key cannot be extracted even by privileged users.

Hardware Security Modules
HSMs are dedicated devices designed to securely manage, store, and process cryptographic keys. They are essential for high-assurance environments, such as payment systems, digital signatures, and government encryption.

- **Tamper Resistance**: HSMs include tamper-detection and tamper-response mechanisms. For example, if the device detects a physical breach attempt, it can zeroize stored keys.
- **Performance**: HSMs are optimized for high-throughput cryptographic operations, making them suitable for environments like secure transaction processing.
- **Compliance**: HSMs often meet certifications like FIPS 140-2 Level 3, ensuring their design and implementation adhere to stringent security standards.

For instance, HSMs are widely used in securing the private keys for Certificate Authorities (CAs) in PKI systems.

Cryptographic Protocols
Cryptographic protocols define how cryptographic algorithms are applied to achieve secure communication, authentication, or data protection. Protocols must be carefully designed to prevent implementation errors and attacks.

- **TLS (Transport Layer Security)**: Provides secure communication over the internet, combining asymmetric key exchange (e.g., ECDHE), symmetric encryption (e.g., AES), and message authentication (e.g., HMAC).
- **IPsec (Internet Protocol Security)**: Protects IP communication by encrypting and authenticating data packets, often used in VPNs.
- **Secure/Multipurpose Internet Mail Extensions (S/MIME)**: Enables encryption and digital signatures for email.

Weaknesses in cryptographic protocol implementations, such as failing to verify digital certificate chains in TLS, can lead to exploits like man-in-the-middle attacks.

Algorithm Selection

Choosing the right cryptographic algorithm involves balancing security, performance, and compatibility. Commonly used algorithms include:

- **Symmetric Encryption**: AES is the industry standard for encryption due to its speed and security. Block modes like GCM (Galois/Counter Mode) provide both encryption and integrity checks.
- **Asymmetric Encryption**: RSA and ECC are widely used for digital signatures and key exchanges. ECC is favored for environments with limited resources due to its shorter key lengths.
- **Hash Functions**: SHA-2 (e.g., SHA-256) and SHA-3 are the preferred cryptographic hashing algorithms, replacing older, weaker algorithms like MD5 and SHA-1.
- **Message Authentication Codes (MACs)**: HMAC (Hash-based Message Authentication Code) ensures message integrity and authenticity.

For example, AES-256-GCM is often chosen for secure data transmission because it provides both strong encryption and integrity in a single operation.

Performance Optimization

Cryptographic operations can be computationally expensive, particularly in environments with high transaction volumes or limited processing resources.

- **Hardware Acceleration**: Modern CPUs include instructions like AES-NI (Intel and AMD) or ARMv8 Cryptographic Extensions to optimize symmetric encryption. Dedicated accelerators like HSMs or FPGA cards can also offload cryptographic tasks.
- **Ephemeral Keys**: Use ephemeral keys for short-term encryption tasks, such as during a TLS session, to reduce computational overhead and improve scalability.
- **Load Balancing**: Distribute cryptographic workloads across multiple servers to handle large-scale operations, such as signing transactions in blockchain networks.

For instance, high-performance web servers often leverage AES-NI to accelerate HTTPS encryption and reduce latency for end users.

Security Standards Compliance

Cryptographic implementations must comply with established standards to ensure interoperability and reliability. Key standards include:

- **FIPS 140-2/3**: Specifies security requirements for cryptographic modules used in government systems.
- **NIST Recommendations**: Guidelines like SP 800-38A (block cipher modes) and SP 800-56A (key establishment schemes) provide best practices for cryptographic implementations.
- **ISO/IEC 19790**: An international standard for cryptographic module security, similar to FIPS 140-2.

For example, FIPS 140-2 compliance is mandatory for cryptographic modules used in U.S. federal systems, ensuring that implementations meet rigorous security requirements.

PKI AND CRYPTOGRAPHIC SYSTEM CASE STUDIES

Global Bank PKI Deployment Project:

Initial State:

- Multiple legacy systems
- Manual certificate processes
- Inconsistent key management
- Limited visibility
- No central authority

Implementation Phases:

Phase 1: Infrastructure Setup

- Root CA establishment
- Hardware security modules
- Directory services
- Backup systems

Phase 2: Process Development
- Certificate policies
- Operating procedures
- Validation methods
- Audit controls

Phase 3: Integration
- Application updates
- User enrollment
- System testing
- Training delivery

Healthcare Provider Cryptographic Breach:

Incident Timeline:

Time	Event	Response
Day 0	Key exposure detected	Incident declared
Day 1	Impact assessment	System isolation
Day 2	Certificate revocation	New key generation
Day 3	System reconfiguration	Service restoration
Day 4	Root cause analysis	Control updates

Zero Trust Migration Project:

Assessment Framework:

- Asset inventory
- Network mapping
- Access patterns
- Trust relationships
- Security controls

Implementation Strategy:

- Identity foundation
- Network segmentation
- Access policies
- Monitoring systems
- Automation tools

Manufacturing Firm Key Compromise:

Detection Methods:

- Anomaly detection
- Access monitoring
- System logs
- User reports
- Security alerts

Response Actions:

- Key revocation
- System isolation
- Evidence collection
- Impact analysis
- Recovery planning

Algorithm Obsolescence Management:
Risk Assessment:

- Algorithm strength
- Threat landscape
- Usage context
- Migration impact
- Resource requirements

Migration Framework:

- Inventory affected systems
- Select replacement algorithms
- Test compatibility
- Phase implementation
- Verify security

Security teams maintain:

- Incident playbooks
- Recovery procedures
- Test scenarios
- Documentation updates
- Lesson repositories

SECURITY MODEL APPLICATION

Security models provide formal frameworks for implementing and analyzing the security of systems. Models like Bell-LaPadula, Biba, and Clark-Wilson are applied based on the organization's priorities, such as confidentiality, integrity, or both. For example, Bell-LaPadula is used in environments like government systems where confidentiality is paramount, while Biba enforces data integrity in industrial systems to prevent unauthorized changes. Applying the Clark-Wilson model in financial systems ensures integrity by enforcing well-formed transactions through separation of duties and access constraints.

ACCESS CONTROL IMPLEMENTATION

Access control systems enforce who can interact with specific data or resources based on predefined rules. Role-Based Access Control (RBAC) is commonly implemented in enterprises to ensure employees access only the resources required for their roles, such as an HR manager accessing payroll data but not server configurations. In highly secure environments, Attribute-Based Access Control (ABAC) may be used, considering multiple attributes like user location, device type, and time of access. Implementation also involves integrating access controls with centralized directories (e.g., Active Directory) and monitoring tools to audit and enforce compliance with organizational policies.

ARCHITECTURE PRINCIPLE SCENARIOS

Security architecture principles are applied to ensure the design of systems aligns with organizational goals while addressing risk. For example:

- **Defense-in-Depth:** A web application implements multiple layers of security, such as firewalls, web application firewalls (WAFs), intrusion detection systems (IDS), and endpoint protection, to prevent and detect threats at various levels.
- **Least Privilege:** An IoT device management system grants administrators minimal permissions, such as access to logs and firmware updates, without allowing direct control of other systems.
- **Zero Trust:** A financial institution designs a network where all devices, users, and applications must continuously authenticate and validate their trustworthiness before accessing sensitive systems.

CRYPTOGRAPHIC PROTOCOL SELECTION

Choosing cryptographic protocols requires balancing security, performance, and compliance with industry standards.

- **TLS 1.3** is the preferred protocol for secure communications over networks, offering enhanced security features like encrypted handshake messages and forward secrecy.
- **IPsec** is selected for securing VPN connections at the network layer, ensuring encrypted and authenticated communication between remote sites.
- **S/MIME** or **PGP** is chosen for encrypting email communication, depending on the organization's preference for centralized certificate management versus user-specific encryption keys.
- **AES-GCM** is commonly selected for symmetric encryption due to its combination of confidentiality and authenticated encryption properties, making it suitable for both data storage and transmission.

ATTACK MITIGATION STRATEGIES

Effective mitigation strategies address specific attack vectors to strengthen security postures.

- **Phishing Attacks:** Implementing multi-factor authentication (MFA), email filtering solutions, and user training programs reduces the likelihood of successful phishing.
- **SQL Injection:** Using prepared statements and parameterized queries in application code ensures malicious input cannot manipulate database commands.
- **Ransomware Attacks:** Regularly backing up critical data, implementing endpoint detection and response (EDR) tools, and restricting privileged access prevents ransomware proliferation.
- **Distributed Denial of Service (DDoS):** Leveraging content delivery networks (CDNs), rate limiting, and dedicated anti-DDoS services minimizes the impact of high-volume traffic attacks.

PKI TROUBLESHOOTING

Public Key Infrastructure (PKI) troubleshooting typically involves addressing issues related to certificate issuance, revocation, and validation.

- **Certificate Trust Errors:** Often caused by missing or improperly installed root/intermediate CA certificates in the trusted store. Resolving this involves ensuring all required certificates are installed correctly and the certificate chain is valid.
- **CRL/OCSP Failures:** If certificate revocation checks fail due to unreachable CRL or OCSP endpoints, network connectivity to those services must be verified. Transitioning to OCSP stapling can also reduce dependency on external checks.
- **Expired Certificates:** Periodic audits of certificate expiration dates and implementing automated renewal processes through tools like Let's Encrypt can address expired certificates proactively.
- **Key Usage Misconfigurations:** Certificates with incorrect usage flags (e.g., a signing certificate used for encryption) may fail validation during operations like document signing or VPN connections. Ensuring proper certificate profiles during issuance can prevent this.

IMPLEMENTATION DECISIONS

Implementation decisions revolve around aligning security measures with business objectives and technical constraints. For example:

- **Cloud vs. On-Premises:** A company handling sensitive health records may opt for on-premises solutions to retain full control over its infrastructure, while a start-up may prioritize a cloud-first approach for scalability.
- **Encryption vs. Tokenization:** In payment processing, tokenization is often preferred for securing cardholder data as it replaces sensitive data with non-sensitive tokens, simplifying compliance with PCI DSS.
- **IDS/IPS Placement:** An intrusion detection system (IDS) may be deployed in monitor mode on internal segments to detect threats, while an intrusion prevention system (IPS) is placed inline at network boundaries to block malicious traffic.

STANDARDS COMPLIANCE

Compliance ensures systems meet regulatory and industry-specific requirements.

- **HIPAA (Healthcare):** Implementing encryption for electronic protected health information (ePHI), logging access to patient records, and ensuring regular risk assessments meet HIPAA requirements.
- **PCI DSS (Payments):** Encrypting cardholder data, masking PANs (Primary Account Numbers), and segmenting payment systems from general IT systems are common practices for meeting PCI DSS compliance.
- **ISO 27001 (Information Security):** Defining a robust Information Security Management System (ISMS), performing risk assessments, and implementing continuous monitoring meet the standard's framework for managing risks to information security.
- **GDPR (Privacy):** Data pseudonymization, encryption, and mechanisms for user data access requests are required to comply with GDPR's privacy mandates.

Standards compliance is often achieved through automated compliance tools, ongoing audits, and mapping controls to specific frameworks, such as NIST CSF or CIS Controls.

Communication and Network Security

NETWORK DEFENSE ARCHITECTURE AND LAYERED SECURITY IMPLEMENTATION

OSI model security controls align with specific layer protections:

Physical Layer:

- Cable shielding
- Physical access controls
- Electromagnetic shielding
- Tamper detection
- Power protection

Data Link Layer:

- MAC filtering
- Port security
- VLAN segmentation
- Switch hardening
- ARP inspection

Network Layer:

Protection Mechanisms:

- Routing security
- Network ACLs
- Packet filtering
- IPSec implementation
- Anti-spoofing

Transport Layer:

Control	Purpose	Implementation
TLS	Encryption	Protocol v1.3+
Connection control	Flow management	TCP hardening
Port filtering	Access control	Service restriction
Session management	State tracking	Timeout enforcement

TCP/IP security measures incorporate:

Network Access:

- Interface security
- Media controls
- Physical protection
- Link encryption
- Access management

Internet Layer:

- IP filtering
- ICMP controls
- Route protection
- Fragment handling
- Protocol security

Security zone design establishes:

External Zone:

- DMZ systems
- Proxy servers
- VPN endpoints

- Public services
- Edge protection

Internal Zones:

- User segments
- Server farms
- Management networks
- Backup systems
- Development environments

Control layering implements:

Prevention Controls:

- Access restrictions
- Authentication systems
- Encryption services
- Input validation
- Configuration management

Detection Controls:

- IDS/IPS systems
- Log monitoring
- Traffic analysis
- Behavior monitoring
- Anomaly detection

Microsegmentation architecture:

Workload Isolation:

- Application groups
- Service clusters
- Data classifications
- User populations
- Resource types

Policy Implementation:

- Fine-grained rules
- Context awareness
- Dynamic adaptation
- State monitoring
- Response automation

Effectiveness metrics track:

- Control coverage
- Alert accuracy
- Response times
- System uptime
- Incident rates
- Recovery speed

Security teams establish:

- Monitoring systems
- Update processes
- Testing procedures
- Documentation standards
- Review cycles

NETWORK SEGMENTATION DEEP DIVE

Network segmentation involves dividing a network into smaller, logically isolated sections to improve security, performance, and manageability. Proper segmentation minimizes the risk of lateral movement by attackers and optimizes traffic flows between different parts of the network. This requires a combination of VLANs, subnets, DMZs, traffic management strategies, and software-defined technologies tailored to the organization's needs.

VLAN IMPLEMENTATION STRATEGIES

Virtual Local Area Networks (VLANs) create logical groupings of devices on the same physical network to control broadcast domains and isolate traffic.

1. **Department-Based VLANs:**
   VLANs can be configured based on organizational units, such as separating Finance, HR, and IT departments. This isolates sensitive resources while allowing inter-department communication through Layer 3 routing.
2. **Application-Based VLANs:**
   VLANs can group devices running the same application or service, such as web servers or database servers, regardless of their physical location. For instance, a VLAN dedicated to VoIP traffic ensures call quality by segregating it from general data traffic.
3. **Access VLANs and Native VLANs:**
   Access VLANs assign devices like workstations to specific VLANs, while the native VLAN on trunk links is used for untagged traffic. Best practices include not using VLAN 1 as the native VLAN to avoid potential VLAN hopping attacks.
4. **Trunking and Tagging:**
   VLAN tagging with protocols like IEEE 802.1Q ensures that traffic from multiple VLANs can travel over a single trunk link between switches. Proper trunk configuration prevents unnecessary VLAN propagation.
5. **Segmentation Enforcement:**
   VLANs should be paired with Access Control Lists (ACLs) or Layer 3 firewalls to restrict communication between VLANs, ensuring that sensitive traffic stays within its designated VLAN.

SUBNET DESIGN AND PLANNING

Subnetting divides IP address spaces into smaller, manageable segments that support efficient routing, security, and resource allocation.

1. **Subnetting by Function:**
   Assign subnets to specific functions, such as user workstations, servers, and printers, ensuring that each group has its own IP address range. For example, allocate 192.168.10.0/24 to workstations and 192.168.20.0/24 to servers.
2. **CIDR Blocks:**
   Use Classless Inter-Domain Routing (CIDR) to define subnets. Smaller CIDR blocks (e.g., /28) conserve address space for smaller subnets, while larger blocks (e.g., /22) accommodate resource-heavy segments.
3. **Private vs. Public IP Ranges:**
   Internal networks should use private IP ranges (e.g., 10.0.0.0/8, 192.168.0.0/16) to avoid conflicts with public addresses and secure internal traffic. Public IPs should be reserved for internet-facing services only.
4. **Broadcast Domains:**
   Subnets confine broadcast traffic to their domain, reducing congestion. Proper subnetting prevents broadcast traffic from overwhelming large segments of the network.
5. **Hierarchical Addressing:**
   Design subnets in a hierarchical structure to reflect organizational or geographic divisions, simplifying routing. For example, regional offices may have unique subnet ranges (e.g., 10.1.0.0/16 for North America and 10.2.0.0/16 for Europe).

DMZ ARCHITECTURE

A Demilitarized Zone (DMZ) isolates public-facing systems from internal networks, providing a buffer against external threats.

1. **Three-Legged Firewall Design:**
   A single firewall is configured with three interfaces: one for the external network (internet), one for the

internal network, and one for the DMZ. Public-facing services, such as web and email servers, reside in the DMZ.

2. **Dual Firewall Design:**
   Two firewalls are deployed, with the DMZ sandwiched between them. The external firewall protects the DMZ from the internet, while the internal firewall secures internal networks from the DMZ.
3. **Service Placement:**
   Servers in the DMZ are typically limited to those requiring public access, such as DNS, web servers, and reverse proxies. Internal databases and sensitive systems remain within the internal network.
4. **Traffic Control:**
   Firewall rules should enforce strict traffic flow, such as:
   - Internet → DMZ: Allow HTTP/HTTPS traffic to web servers.
   - DMZ → Internal: Block direct access unless required (e.g., web servers querying internal databases via specific ports).

NETWORK ISOLATION TECHNIQUES

Isolation ensures that systems or devices with differing trust levels cannot communicate unless explicitly allowed.

1. **Physical Isolation:**
   High-security environments, such as SCADA systems, may use air-gapped networks with no physical connection to external or internal networks.
2. **Logical Isolation:**
   Technologies like VLANs, subnets, and SDN can isolate networks logically without requiring separate physical infrastructure.
3. **MAC Address Filtering:**
   Configure switches to restrict communication between devices based on MAC addresses. This prevents unauthorized devices from connecting to isolated network segments.
4. **Host-Based Isolation:**
   Host firewalls or endpoint protection tools can enforce communication restrictions at the device level. For example, laptops on a guest network may be isolated from internal corporate resources.

EAST-WEST TRAFFIC CONTROL

East-west traffic refers to communication within a data center or between devices on the same network. Controlling it limits the lateral movement of attackers.

1. **Microsegmentation:**
   Break down east-west communication into smaller segments using software-defined networking (SDN) or virtual firewalls. Each segment has its own policies to enforce isolation between workloads.
2. **Zero Trust Enforcement:**
   Authenticate and authorize all east-west traffic at every communication point. For instance, implement mutual TLS between application workloads to validate traffic.
3. **Internal Firewalls:**
   Deploy firewalls within the network to inspect and control east-west traffic between VLANs, subnets, or even individual hosts.

NORTH-SOUTH TRAFFIC MANAGEMENT

North-south traffic describes communication between internal systems and external networks, such as the internet. Proper management ensures secure and efficient traffic flow.

1. **Perimeter Firewalls:**
   Deploy firewalls at the edge of the network to enforce access controls and protect internal systems from external threats.
2. **Load Balancers:**
   Use load balancers to distribute north-south traffic across multiple servers, ensuring availability and scalability for external-facing applications.
3. **DDoS Protection:**
   Integrate DDoS mitigation solutions, such as cloud-based scrubbing centers or rate-limiting on ingress traffic, to safeguard against volumetric attacks.

SOFTWARE-DEFINED SEGMENTATION

Software-defined segmentation uses SDN to dynamically control traffic flows and enforce segmentation across the network.

1. **Policy-Based Segmentation:**
   Centralized SDN controllers define traffic policies based on attributes such as user identity, application, or device type. For example, employees accessing a finance application may be routed through a secure segment with additional monitoring.
2. **Dynamic Updates:**
   Segmentation policies adapt automatically to changes in the environment, such as new workloads or device connections.
3. **Integration with Security Tools:**
   SDN integrates with firewalls, intrusion detection systems (IDS), and endpoint detection and response (EDR) tools to enhance visibility and control over network flows.

CONTAINER NETWORK ISOLATION

Containerized environments, like Kubernetes and Docker, require isolation to protect workloads running on shared infrastructure.

1. **Namespace Isolation:**
   Kubernetes namespaces logically separate resources, ensuring containers in one namespace cannot access those in another unless explicitly permitted.
2. **Network Policies:**
   Kubernetes Network Policies define ingress and egress rules for container communication. For instance, web containers may only allow traffic from application containers on specific ports.
3. **Service Mesh:**
   Tools like Istio or Linkerd add a layer of security by managing container-to-container communication with mutual TLS and access controls.
4. **CNI Plugins:**
   Container Network Interface (CNI) plugins, such as Calico or Flannel, provide advanced isolation features like network segmentation, IP filtering, and policy enforcement for container traffic.

PROTOCOL SECURITY ANALYSIS

Analyzing and securing protocols involves evaluating their implementation, assessing vulnerabilities, and ensuring they meet encryption, authentication, and security standards. Protocols such as IPSec, TLS/SSL, SSH, and DNSSEC are essential for modern communication, but their security depends on correct configuration, robust encryption, and mitigations against potential attacks.

Secure Protocol Implementation

Proper implementation of protocols is fundamental for protecting communications and data. Misconfigurations or the use of outdated versions often result in vulnerabilities that can be exploited by attackers.

IPSec Configuration

IPSec secures communication at the network layer, providing encryption, authentication, and integrity for IP packets. It operates in two modes:

- **Transport Mode**: Secures only the payload of the packet, commonly used for host-to-host communication.
- **Tunnel Mode**: Encrypts the entire packet, often used for VPNs.

A secure IPSec configuration involves:

- **Encryption**: Use strong encryption algorithms like AES-256 for data confidentiality.
- **Authentication**: Implement HMAC-SHA-256 or higher for message integrity and authentication.
- **Key Exchange**: Use IKEv2 (Internet Key Exchange version 2), which provides better security and performance compared to IKEv1.
- **Perfect Forward Secrecy (PFS)**: Enable PFS to ensure that session keys are not compromised if the server's private key is exposed.

For example, a site-to-site VPN between corporate offices might use IPSec in tunnel mode with AES-256 encryption and PFS enabled to protect traffic from interception.

TLS/SSL Deployment

TLS (and its predecessor SSL) ensures secure communication over application-layer protocols such as HTTP, SMTP, and FTP. A secure deployment involves:

- **Protocol Version**: Use TLS 1.2 or TLS 1.3, as older versions (SSL 3.0, TLS 1.0, TLS 1.1) are considered insecure due to vulnerabilities like POODLE and BEAST.
- **Certificate Management**: Obtain certificates from trusted Certificate Authorities (CAs) and use strong key pairs (e.g., 2048-bit RSA or ECDSA with a 256-bit curve).
- **Cipher Suites**: Disable weak cipher suites like RC4 and 3DES. Use secure suites with forward secrecy, such as those combining AES-GCM and ECDHE.
- **HSTS (HTTP Strict Transport Security)**: Enforce HTTPS connections to prevent protocol downgrade attacks.

For example, a secure e-commerce website would use TLS 1.3 with an ECDSA certificate, AES-GCM encryption, and HSTS to protect customer data during transactions.

SSH Implementation

SSH secures remote login and command execution by encrypting data and authenticating users. A secure implementation includes:

- **Key-Based Authentication**: Use public-private key pairs instead of password-based authentication to reduce the risk of brute force attacks.
- **Protocol Version**: Disable SSH version 1, as it contains design flaws. Use SSH version 2 exclusively.
- **Strong Ciphers**: Configure the server to use ciphers like AES-256 and HMAC-SHA-2 for message integrity.
- **Access Restrictions**: Limit access by defining allowed users and restricting SSH to specific IP addresses or networks using firewalls and /etc/hosts.allow or /etc/hosts.deny.
- **Port Configuration**: Change the default SSH port (22) to a non-standard port to reduce automated scanning attempts.

For example, a cloud-hosted server accessed by administrators might use key-based SSH authentication with only approved IPs allowed via a security group.

DNSSEC Setup

DNSSEC (Domain Name System Security Extensions) secures DNS by enabling authentication of DNS responses and mitigating risks like cache poisoning. Key steps for secure DNSSEC setup include:

- **Key Signing**: Generate a Key Signing Key (KSK) and a Zone Signing Key (ZSK) to authenticate the DNS records.
- **Chain of Trust**: Establish a chain of trust by signing the DNS records and registering the KSK with the parent zone.
- **Signature Updates**: Regularly rotate keys and update signatures to maintain security.
- **Validation**: Enable DNSSEC validation on resolvers to verify the authenticity of responses.

For example, a registrar setting up DNSSEC for a domain would sign the zone with the ZSK, use the KSK for validation, and update the parent zone's delegation signer (DS) record.

Protocol Vulnerability Assessment

Assessing protocol vulnerabilities involves identifying weaknesses that could be exploited, such as outdated versions, weak configurations, or implementation flaws. Common methods include:

- **Automated Scanning**: Use tools like Nessus, Nmap, or Qualys to detect insecure protocols, deprecated versions, or weak cipher suites.
- **Man-in-the-Middle (MitM) Simulation**: Test resilience to MitM attacks by intercepting protocol communications.
- **Configuration Analysis**: Review server and network configurations to identify gaps, such as missing HSTS headers in HTTPS implementations or weak SSH access controls.

An example of a protocol vulnerability is the Heartbleed flaw in OpenSSL, which allowed attackers to extract private keys and sensitive data from servers.

Encryption Requirements

Encryption ensures confidentiality and protects data in transit or at rest. Protocols must enforce robust encryption standards:

- **Algorithm Strength**: Use algorithms like AES-256, ChaCha20-Poly1305 (TLS 1.3), or ECC-based algorithms for modern security needs.
- **Key Management**: Protect private keys using HSMs or secure key stores. Rotate session keys frequently for short-term use cases.
- **Randomness**: Ensure encryption relies on cryptographically secure random number generation for keys, IVs, and nonces.

For example, a VPN using IPSec should encrypt packets with AES-256 in GCM mode and rotate session keys periodically using IKEv2.

Authentication Mechanisms

Protocols must incorporate robust authentication mechanisms to verify identities and prevent unauthorized access:

- **Mutual Authentication**: Use two-way authentication, such as client and server certificates in TLS, to ensure both entities are trusted.
- **Multifactor Authentication (MFA)**: Add an additional layer of security by requiring something the user knows (password), has (token), or is (biometrics).
- **Passwordless Authentication**: Leverage public-key cryptography for authentication, as seen in SSH key-based access or WebAuthn for web applications.

For instance, a banking API might implement mutual TLS to authenticate both the client and the server before any data is exchanged.

Protocol Attack Mitigation

Mitigating protocol attacks involves addressing known weaknesses and ensuring configurations are resilient to exploitation. Examples include:

- **Replay Attacks**: Use timestamps or nonces to ensure messages cannot be reused maliciously.
- **Downgrade Attacks**: Disable older protocol versions and insecure cipher suites to prevent attackers from forcing weaker encryption (e.g., disabling SSL 3.0 in favor of TLS 1.2+).
- **DNS Spoofing**: Deploy DNSSEC to authenticate DNS responses and mitigate cache poisoning.
- **Session Hijacking**: Use strong session management practices, such as encrypting session tokens and enabling HTTP-only and secure flags for cookies.

For example, enabling TLS 1.3 in web servers mitigates attacks like ROBOT (Return of Bleichenbacher's Oracle Threat), which exploit vulnerabilities in earlier versions of TLS.

NETWORK SECURITY CONTROL IMPLEMENTATION AND MANAGEMENT

Next-generation firewall capabilities extend beyond traditional packet filtering:

Application Control:

Layer 7 Functions:

- Deep packet inspection
- Protocol validation
- Application identification
- User awareness
- Content filtering

Advanced Features:

Feature	Purpose	Implementation
SSL Inspection	Encrypted traffic analysis	Certificate management
Threat Prevention	Malware blocking	Signature matching
URL Filtering	Web access control	Category databases
Identity Integration	User-based policies	Directory services

IDS/IPS deployment incorporates:

Sensor Placement:

- Network ingress/egress

- Segment boundaries
- Critical asset protection
- Data center monitoring
- Cloud environments

Detection Methods:

- Signature-based
- Anomaly detection
- Protocol analysis
- Behavior monitoring
- Heuristic analysis

Rule base management follows:

Policy Framework:

- Base policies
- Custom rules
- Exception handling
- Change control
- Review cycles

Optimization Process:

- Rule cleanup
- Hit count analysis
- Redundancy removal
- Order optimization
- Performance tuning

Signature development includes:

Pattern Creation:

- Threat analysis
- Pattern extraction
- Regular expressions
- Protocol elements
- Byte sequences

Testing Framework:

- False positive checking
- Performance impact
- Coverage validation
- Tuning procedures
- Documentation

Anomaly detection utilizes:

Statistical Analysis:

- Baseline establishment
- Deviation tracking
- Threshold setting
- Alert correlation
- Pattern recognition

Machine Learning:

- Training data
- Model development
- Classification rules

- Behavior profiling
- Continuous learning

SIEM integration enables:

Data Collection:

- Log aggregation
- Alert forwarding
- Context enrichment
- Asset mapping
- Threat intelligence

Analysis Capabilities:

- Event correlation
- Pattern matching
- Risk scoring
- Impact assessment
- Response automation

Performance metrics monitor:

- Throughput rates
- Latency impact
- CPU utilization
- Memory usage
- Rule processing

Security operations include:

- Daily monitoring
- Rule updates
- Incident response
- Threat hunting
- System maintenance

VPN AND REMOTE ACCESS SECURITY

Virtual Private Networks (VPNs) and remote access solutions are critical for securing communication between remote users and organizational resources over untrusted networks. A secure and effective implementation depends on selecting the right protocols, designing a robust architecture, and ensuring proper authentication and access control mechanisms. This also involves addressing split tunneling risks, managing certificates, and monitoring performance to maintain security and usability.

VPN PROTOCOL SELECTION

The choice of a VPN protocol depends on security requirements, performance, and compatibility with organizational systems.

1. **IPsec (Internet Protocol Security):**
    - Provides encryption, authentication, and data integrity at the network layer.
    - Suitable for site-to-site VPNs and remote access solutions.
    - Supported by protocols like IKEv2 for efficient key exchange and NAT traversal.
2. **SSL/TLS (Secure Sockets Layer/Transport Layer Security):**
    - Operates at the application layer and is widely used for client-to-site VPNs.
    - SSL VPNs provide easier deployment as they work through web browsers, avoiding firewall and NAT traversal issues.
    - OpenVPN and TLS-based VPNs like AnyConnect are common implementations.
3. **WireGuard:**
    - A lightweight, modern protocol offering fast performance and simpler configuration compared to IPsec or OpenVPN.

- Uses modern cryptographic primitives like ChaCha20 for encryption and Curve25519 for key exchange.

4. **L2TP/IPsec (Layer 2 Tunneling Protocol over IPsec):**
   - Combines L2TP for tunneling and IPsec for encryption.
   - Provides strong security but is slower than newer protocols like WireGuard.
5. **PPTP (Point-to-Point Tunneling Protocol):**
   - An outdated protocol with known security vulnerabilities and weak encryption. It is no longer recommended.

REMOTE ACCESS ARCHITECTURE

Remote access architecture ensures secure connectivity between remote users and internal resources, tailored to the organization's structure and requirements.

1. **Client-to-Site VPN:**
   - Enables individual users to securely connect to internal networks. Common for employees working remotely.
   - Deployed using VPN clients like OpenVPN or Cisco AnyConnect.
2. **Site-to-Site VPN:**
   - Connects entire remote offices or branches to the central corporate network.
   - Uses dedicated hardware like routers or firewalls with built-in IPsec support.
3. **Zero Trust Network Access (ZTNA):**
   - An alternative to traditional VPNs, ZTNA verifies user identity and device security at every access point. It provides access only to authorized applications rather than the entire network.
4. **Cloud-Integrated Remote Access:**
   - Combines VPNs with cloud-based solutions to securely connect remote users to hybrid or fully cloud environments. Platforms like AWS Client VPN and Azure VPN Gateway enable cloud integration.
5. **VPN Gateways:**
   - Positioned at the perimeter of the corporate network to terminate encrypted traffic from remote clients. Firewalls, such as FortiGate or Palo Alto, often provide integrated VPN gateway features.

AUTHENTICATION METHODS

Authentication mechanisms validate users and devices attempting to connect via VPN or remote access solutions.

1. **Single-Factor Authentication (SFA):**
   - Basic authentication using usernames and passwords.
   - Weak against phishing and brute force attacks and should not be used alone for VPN access.
2. **Multi-Factor Authentication (MFA):**
   - Combines multiple factors, such as:
     - *Something you know:* Passwords or PINs.
     - *Something you have:* Hardware tokens (e.g., YubiKeys), soft tokens, or mobile authenticators (e.g., Google Authenticator).
     - *Something you are:* Biometric verification like fingerprints or facial recognition.
   - MFA significantly reduces the risk of unauthorized access.
3. **Certificate-Based Authentication:**
   - Uses client certificates issued by a trusted Certificate Authority (CA) to authenticate devices.
   - Offers strong authentication for managed endpoints and eliminates reliance on passwords.
4. **RADIUS and LDAP Integration:**
   - Remote Authentication Dial-In User Service (RADIUS) and Lightweight Directory Access Protocol (LDAP) integrate VPN authentication with centralized user directories like Active Directory for streamlined user management.

SPLIT TUNNELING CONSIDERATIONS

Split tunneling allows remote users to route specific traffic through the VPN while other traffic goes directly to the internet.

1. **Advantages:**
   - Reduces VPN bandwidth usage by excluding non-business traffic, such as video streaming.

   - Improves user performance for non-critical traffic by avoiding the corporate network.
2. **Risks:**
   - Creates a potential attack vector if malicious traffic bypasses corporate security controls.
   - Sensitive data may accidentally traverse unencrypted channels if improperly configured.
3. **Best Practices:**
   - Enforce split tunneling policies selectively for non-sensitive users or tasks.
   - Use domain-based routing to send only business-critical domains through the VPN. For example, limit VPN routing to specific internal IP ranges or SaaS applications.

MOBILE VPN DEPLOYMENT

Mobile VPNs are designed to maintain secure connectivity for users on mobile devices or moving between networks.

1. **Session Persistence:**
   - Unlike traditional VPNs, mobile VPNs maintain connections even as users switch between Wi-Fi, cellular networks, or experience brief signal drops. Protocols like IKEv2 and proprietary solutions (e.g., NetMotion) support session persistence.
2. **Device Authentication:**
   - Enforce device-level authentication to ensure only registered mobile devices can connect. Use mobile device management (MDM) tools to push configurations and certificates.
3. **VPN Clients for Mobile Platforms:**
   - Native clients (e.g., iOS and Android's built-in IKEv2/IPsec clients) or third-party clients like OpenVPN and AnyConnect are widely used.
4. **Data Usage Optimization:**
   - Compress traffic to reduce mobile data consumption. For example, enabling GZIP compression on the VPN server can optimize traffic for mobile devices.

CERTIFICATE MANAGEMENT

Certificate management is a core component of securing VPN implementations, especially those relying on SSL/TLS or certificate-based authentication.

1. **Certificate Authorities (CAs):**
   - Use a trusted internal or external CA to issue certificates for users and devices. Internal PKI systems, such as Microsoft CA or EJBCA, enable better control over certificate issuance.
2. **Certificate Revocation:**
   - Implement Certificate Revocation Lists (CRLs) or Online Certificate Status Protocol (OCSP) to revoke compromised or expired certificates.
3. **Automation Tools:**
   - Use tools like Let's Encrypt or enterprise PKI management systems to automate certificate issuance and renewal, reducing manual errors.
4. **Certificate Expiration Monitoring:**
   - Monitor certificate lifecycles to prevent connection failures caused by expired certificates.

ACCESS CONTROL POLICIES

Access control policies define how and when remote users can connect to the network, minimizing exposure to unauthorized access.

1. **Role-Based Access Control (RBAC):**
   - Assign permissions based on user roles. For example, IT administrators may access network management tools, while sales teams only access CRM systems.
2. **Context-Aware Policies:**
   - Restrict access based on factors like location, time of day, or device type. For example, block connections from regions with high cybercrime activity or untrusted devices.
3. **Quarantine Networks:**
   - Place non-compliant devices in a restricted quarantine zone until they meet security requirements, such as installing patches or updating antivirus software.

PERFORMANCE MONITORING

Performance monitoring ensures the VPN infrastructure supports reliable and efficient remote access while identifying bottlenecks or issues.

1. **Traffic Monitoring:**
    - Tools like SolarWinds or Zabbix monitor VPN bandwidth usage to ensure sufficient capacity for user traffic. Overloaded VPN gateways can lead to dropped connections or slow performance.
2. **Latency and Jitter Analysis:**
    - Measure latency and jitter to identify performance issues affecting real-time applications like VoIP or video conferencing.
3. **Endpoint Health Checks:**
    - Ensure that remote user devices are not contributing to performance issues. This includes verifying that VPN clients are up-to-date and not misconfigured.
4. **Logging and Analytics:**
    - Collect logs from VPN gateways for insights into authentication errors, connection drops, or unusual traffic patterns. Analyze trends to proactively identify and resolve performance issues.

VPN and remote access security combines robust protocol selection, well-architected infrastructures, and strict policy enforcement to enable secure and efficient connectivity. Performance monitoring and consistent policy refinement further ensure reliability and long-term scalability.

CLOUD NETWORK SECURITY

Securing cloud networks involves designing robust architectures, ensuring secure connectivity, leveraging advanced networking technologies, and maintaining visibility across cloud environments. The complexity of cloud ecosystems, particularly with multi-cloud and hybrid deployments, necessitates strategies that integrate technologies like virtual private clouds (VPCs), software-defined networking (SDN), and monitoring tools while addressing the unique challenges posed by containers and serverless applications.

Virtual Private Cloud Design

A Virtual Private Cloud (VPC) is an isolated, logically defined segment within a public cloud that provides the flexibility of public cloud resources with the control and security of a private network. Key design considerations for a secure VPC include:

- **Subnet Segmentation**: Separate subnets for different tiers of an application (e.g., web, application, and database) to reduce the attack surface. Public-facing resources like web servers should reside in public subnets, while sensitive components like databases should be in private subnets with no direct internet access.
- **Network Access Control**: Use security groups and network access control lists (ACLs) to enforce least privilege access at both instance and subnet levels. For example, a database instance should only accept traffic from the application server's security group.
- **Peering and Inter-VPC Connectivity**: Use VPC peering or transit gateways for secure communication between VPCs. Ensure traffic between VPCs is encrypted, especially in multi-region architectures.

For example, an organization hosting a multi-tier web application on AWS might design a VPC with an internet-facing load balancer in the public subnet, EC2 instances in a private subnet, and a database in an isolated private subnet. Routing rules and security groups ensure controlled traffic flow.

Cloud Connectivity Options

Cloud connectivity options enable secure communication between on-premises networks and cloud environments or across multiple cloud providers:

- **VPN Connections**: Virtual private network (VPN) connections provide encrypted tunnels between on-premises data centers and cloud environments. They are cost-effective but may introduce latency, making them suitable for low-bandwidth or backup connections.
- **Dedicated Connections**: Services like AWS Direct Connect or Azure ExpressRoute offer dedicated, private links between on-premises networks and cloud providers, bypassing the public internet. These connections are ideal for latency-sensitive or high-bandwidth applications.
- **Hybrid Connectivity**: Combine VPN and dedicated connections for redundancy and failover, ensuring high availability.
- **Multi-Cloud Interconnect**: Solutions like Google Cloud Interconnect or third-party providers such as Equinix Fabric facilitate private and secure connections across multiple cloud platforms.

For instance, a financial institution might use a combination of Direct Connect for high-bandwidth workloads and VPN tunnels for branch offices needing intermittent cloud access.

Software-Defined Networking

Software-Defined Networking (SDN) centralizes network control by decoupling the control plane from the data plane. In cloud environments, SDN allows for dynamic configuration, automation, and scalability of network resources:

- **Centralized Control**: SDN controllers provide a single point for managing network policies and traffic flows across virtual and physical devices.
- **Microsegmentation**: SDN enables granular segmentation at the workload level, isolating applications or containers within the same subnet to prevent lateral movement of threats.
- **Policy Enforcement**: Policies based on attributes like application identity or tags can be dynamically applied to workloads regardless of their physical location.

For example, VMware NSX is an SDN solution that provides microsegmentation and application-level controls for virtualized environments, helping to reduce the risk of lateral attacks.

Cloud Access Security Brokers

Cloud Access Security Brokers (CASBs) act as intermediaries between users and cloud services, providing visibility and control over data and security policies. CASBs are critical for enforcing governance and preventing data leakage:

- **Data Loss Prevention (DLP)**: Monitor and block sensitive data from being uploaded to unauthorized cloud services or shared externally.
- **Shadow IT Discovery**: Identify unsanctioned cloud applications used within an organization, which may bypass security controls.
- **Access Management**: Enforce policies like multi-factor authentication (MFA), device trust, and location-based access.
- **Threat Protection**: Detect and mitigate malware or anomalous behavior within cloud applications.

For example, a CASB might prevent employees from uploading sensitive customer data to personal cloud storage accounts like Dropbox or Google Drive by enforcing corporate DLP policies.

Container Networking Security

Containers introduce unique networking challenges due to their dynamic, short-lived nature and reliance on orchestration platforms like Kubernetes. Securing container networks involves:

- **Network Segmentation**: Use Kubernetes network policies to enforce communication rules between pods, namespaces, or external services. For instance, only allow pods within the "frontend" namespace to communicate with pods in the "backend" namespace.
- **Ingress/Egress Controls**: Secure container ingress points (e.g., API gateways, load balancers) with encryption and authentication. Limit egress traffic to prevent malicious containers from accessing unauthorized external endpoints.
- **Service Mesh**: Deploy service meshes like Istio or Linkerd to provide secure, encrypted communication between containerized services using mutual TLS (mTLS).

For example, in a Kubernetes cluster, Istio can be used to enforce mTLS between microservices, ensuring that traffic is encrypted and services authenticate each other.

Serverless Security

Serverless computing introduces unique challenges because traditional security controls like host-based firewalls and intrusion detection cannot be applied. Securing serverless functions requires:

- **Least Privilege Permissions**: Grant serverless functions only the permissions they need using granular IAM roles. For example, an AWS Lambda function should only access specific S3 buckets or databases it needs to interact with.
- **Environment Variables**: Store sensitive data like API keys or credentials in secure services like AWS Secrets Manager or Azure Key Vault rather than embedding them in the code or configuration files.
- **Input Validation**: Prevent injection attacks by validating all user inputs passed to serverless functions.

For instance, a serverless application processing user-uploaded images might validate the file type and size before processing to mitigate risks like code injection or resource exhaustion.

Multi-Cloud Networking

Multi-cloud architectures require secure and consistent networking across multiple cloud providers, which can introduce complexity due to differing native controls and APIs. Strategies for multi-cloud networking include:

- **Unified Management**: Use tools like Aviatrix or Cisco Cloud ACI to manage networking across cloud platforms through a single pane of glass. These tools abstract the complexity of platform-specific networking.
- **Consistent Security Policies**: Standardize security controls, such as firewall rules and access policies, across clouds to ensure consistent protection.
- **Traffic Encryption**: Encrypt data in transit between cloud providers using protocols like IPSec or TLS.

An example would be a global enterprise using Azure and AWS for different workloads, with unified routing and policy enforcement provided by Aviatrix for inter-cloud communication.

Cloud Network Monitoring

Continuous monitoring is essential for detecting threats, ensuring compliance, and maintaining visibility into cloud networks. Key monitoring practices include:

- **Flow Logs**: Enable VPC flow logs or equivalent services (e.g., AWS VPC Flow Logs, Google Cloud VPC Flow Logs) to capture metadata about network traffic, helping identify anomalous activity.
- **Network IDS/IPS**: Deploy network intrusion detection and prevention systems to detect malicious traffic patterns or intrusions.
- **Cloud-Native Tools**: Leverage native monitoring tools like AWS CloudWatch, Azure Monitor, or Google Cloud Operations Suite for real-time performance and security insights.
- **Threat Intelligence**: Integrate threat intelligence feeds to correlate network events with known attack signatures or indicators of compromise (IOCs).

For instance, a retail company might use AWS VPC Flow Logs and CloudWatch Insights to detect suspicious outbound traffic from an EC2 instance that may indicate compromise.

EMERGING NETWORK SECURITY TECHNOLOGIES AND FRAMEWORKS

SD-WAN security architecture implements:

Network Segmentation:

Overlay Design:

- Virtual WAN segments
- Traffic isolation
- Path selection
- QoS enforcement
- Security policy

Control Mechanisms:

Function	Implementation	Purpose
Encryption	IPSec/TLS	Data protection
Authentication	Zero trust	Access control
Monitoring	Telemetry	Visibility
Orchestration	Automation	Management

5G network security incorporates:

Architecture Protection:

- Network slicing
- Security edge protection
- Service authentication
- Subscriber privacy
- Core security

IoT security framework:
Device Protection:

- Identity management
- Firmware security
- Communication encryption
- Access control
- Update mechanisms

Network Segmentation:

- Micro-segmentation
- Traffic isolation
- Policy enforcement
- Monitoring systems
- Response automation

Zero trust network access requires:
Identity Verification:

- User authentication
- Device validation
- Location checking
- Risk assessment
- Context evaluation

Access Control:

- Policy enforcement
- Session management
- Resource protection
- Activity monitoring
- Response automation

Network function virtualization implements:
Security Services:

- Virtual firewalls
- IDS/IPS systems
- VPN endpoints
- Load balancers
- Security gateways

Edge computing protection includes:
Security Controls:

- Local processing
- Data filtering
- Access management
- Threat detection
- Incident response

Quantum networking considerations:
Cryptographic Impact:

- Algorithm selection
- Key distribution
- Encryption methods
- Protocol design
- Migration planning

AI/ML security applications:
Threat Detection:

- Pattern recognition
- Anomaly detection
- Behavior analysis
- Risk prediction
- Response automation

Security teams monitor:

- Performance metrics
- Security events
- System health
- User behavior
- Network traffic

CASE STUDY: NETWORK SEGMENTATION PROJECT

A global manufacturing company decided to segment its flat network after a ransomware attack impacted all its business-critical systems, halting production for two days. The lack of segmentation allowed the malware to spread laterally across the network, exploiting shared resources and open communication between devices.

The segmentation project involved dividing the network into zones based on functional groups, such as production systems, corporate IT, and guest networks. VLANs were used for logical separation, and firewalls enforced strict access control policies between segments. For example, the production VLAN was isolated from the corporate VLAN except for specific database queries.

Microsegmentation was implemented for the data center using software-defined networking (SDN) tools like VMware NSX. This limited east-west traffic between servers and ensured each application had tailored security policies. The project reduced the attack surface and contained potential threats to individual segments, minimizing the risk of future incidents.

CASE STUDY: CLOUD MIGRATION SECURITY

A financial services firm migrated its on-premises infrastructure to a hybrid cloud environment to reduce costs and improve scalability. Security challenges arose, including ensuring regulatory compliance, securing data in transit, and protecting workloads across cloud providers.

The firm adopted a multi-layered approach to secure the migration:

- **Data Encryption:** All sensitive data was encrypted both at rest and in transit using AES-256. Customer PII in the cloud was tokenized to reduce exposure.
- **Cloud Security Posture Management (CSPM):** Tools like Prisma Cloud were deployed to monitor and enforce compliance with GDPR and PCI DSS.
- **Zero Trust Integration:** Conditional access policies were applied to cloud resources, requiring multi-factor authentication (MFA) and verifying device security posture before granting access.
- **Workload Protection:** A cloud workload protection platform (CWPP) was used to scan containers and virtual machines for vulnerabilities.

The migration improved operational flexibility while maintaining a strong security posture, with regular audits ensuring continued compliance.

CASE STUDY: IDS/IPS DEPLOYMENT

A regional healthcare provider implemented an intrusion detection and prevention system (IDS/IPS) after experiencing multiple attempts to breach its network through phishing and malicious traffic. The goal was to enhance visibility into network activity and actively block threats.

The IDS/IPS was deployed inline at key network boundaries using a next-generation firewall (NGFW) with integrated IDS/IPS functionality. Signature-based detection identified known threats, while anomaly-based detection flagged unusual behavior, such as a sudden spike in outbound traffic from a compromised endpoint.

To reduce false positives, the system was fine-tuned by excluding legitimate traffic patterns for medical devices and telemedicine applications. Additionally, Security Information and Event Management (SIEM) integration centralized alerts for incident response. Within three months, the provider detected and blocked several malware delivery attempts, preventing further compromise.

CASE STUDY: VPN INFRASTRUCTURE UPGRADE

A multinational corporation faced performance and security issues with its aging VPN infrastructure, especially as remote work surged. The existing VPN relied on PPTP and lacked the scalability needed for a growing workforce. The upgrade introduced modern VPN protocols like IKEv2 and WireGuard, offering better encryption and faster performance. A new cloud-based VPN gateway was deployed to reduce latency for remote workers in different regions, while split tunneling ensured non-business traffic bypassed the VPN to conserve bandwidth.

Multi-factor authentication was mandated for all VPN users, and certificate-based authentication was implemented for managed devices. Additionally, real-time monitoring tools provided insights into connection health and flagged anomalies, such as connections from unexpected locations. The upgraded infrastructure supported a 40% increase in remote users while improving reliability and security.

CASE STUDY: ZERO TRUST IMPLEMENTATION

An e-commerce company implemented a Zero Trust security model after suffering a data breach caused by compromised employee credentials. The attack highlighted the risks of relying on perimeter-based security, as once inside, the attackers had unfettered access to sensitive customer and payment data.

The Zero Trust architecture was built on three pillars:

- **Verify Every User:** Multi-factor authentication was enforced for all users, and identity providers like Okta were used to validate users before granting access.
- **Verify Every Device:** All devices were assessed for compliance with security policies, such as running updated operating systems and endpoint protection software. Non-compliant devices were quarantined.
- **Least Privilege Access:** A software-defined perimeter (SDP) segmented applications, ensuring users accessed only the resources necessary for their roles. Sensitive databases were further restricted to access via bastion hosts.

Microsegmentation limited east-west traffic within the company's data center, and user activity was continuously monitored for anomalies using behavior analytics. The implementation resulted in stronger protection for sensitive data and significantly reduced the risk of lateral movement during potential breaches.

CASE STUDY: SECURITY INCIDENT RESPONSE

A SaaS provider experienced a distributed denial-of-service (DDoS) attack targeting its customer-facing web applications. The attack overwhelmed its servers, causing downtime and impacting hundreds of clients.

The incident response team immediately activated the response plan, which included:

- **Traffic Diversion:** Routing traffic through a DDoS protection service (e.g., Cloudflare or Akamai) to filter malicious traffic and prioritize legitimate requests.
- **Network Analysis:** Using NetFlow and packet capture tools to identify attack patterns, such as source IPs and botnet characteristics.
- **Internal System Checks:** Ensuring no secondary attacks, such as data breaches, occurred during the DDoS.

Post-incident, the team performed a root cause analysis, revealing that the attack exploited an unprotected API endpoint. The API was secured by requiring authentication and rate-limiting requests. Additionally, the provider implemented an improved incident response workflow, including real-time alerting and biannual tabletop exercises to prepare for future attacks.

PRACTICE QUESTIONS FOR CLOUD NETWORK SECURITY

Practice questions designed to reinforce knowledge in cloud network security should focus on real-world scenarios involving architecture design, protocol selection, security control placement, and troubleshooting. By applying critical thinking to these areas, candidates can gain practical insights into balancing performance, security, compliance, and risk management across complex cloud environments.

Architecture Design Decisions

Scenario 1: A company plans to deploy a multi-tier web application on a public cloud platform. The design requires an internet-facing load balancer, application servers, and a database. How should the network architecture be structured to maximize security?

- **Key Considerations:** Design the architecture using subnets for segmentation, with public subnets hosting the load balancer and private subnets for the application servers and database. Include access controls like security groups, NAT gateways for outbound access, and VPC peering if the database spans multiple VPCs.

Scenario 2: An organization is migrating its on-premises workloads to a hybrid cloud environment. What factors should be considered when designing connectivity between the cloud VPC and on-premises data center?

- **Key Considerations:** Compare VPN and dedicated connections (e.g., AWS Direct Connect or Azure ExpressRoute), evaluate bandwidth and latency requirements, configure route tables to prioritize private connectivity, and ensure encryption is used for all communication.

Protocol Selection Scenarios

Scenario 1: A healthcare provider needs to securely transmit patient records between on-premises servers and a cloud-hosted application to comply with HIPAA. Which protocol should be used for secure data transmission, and why?

- **Key Considerations:** Evaluate TLS for application-layer encryption and IPSec VPN for network-layer security. Consider the encryption strength, overhead, and compatibility with HIPAA's encryption requirements.

Scenario 2: An organization is implementing secure remote access to cloud-hosted development environments. Should they use SSH, RDP over TLS, or a VPN?

- **Key Considerations:** Assess the use case for each protocol, including ease of management (e.g., SSH key-based access), encryption requirements, and risk mitigation (e.g., VPN for enhanced traffic protection across multiple environments).

Security Control Placement

Scenario 1: A retail company wants to protect its e-commerce application hosted on a public cloud from DDoS attacks. Where should security controls like Web Application Firewalls (WAFs) and DDoS mitigation services be placed within the architecture?

- **Key Considerations:** Place the WAF in front of the application at the edge (e.g., AWS WAF with CloudFront or Azure Front Door). Ensure that DDoS mitigation is integrated into the CDN or cloud provider's edge services.

Scenario 2: A development team uses a Kubernetes cluster for a microservices-based application. How should network policies be configured to limit communication between pods?

- **Key Considerations:** Use Kubernetes network policies to restrict pod-to-pod traffic based on namespaces, labels, or application roles. For example, limit database pod access to only the application pods requiring database queries.

Incident Response Procedures

Scenario 1: A financial organization detects unauthorized outbound traffic from one of its cloud VMs. What steps should the incident response team take?

- **Key Considerations:** Isolate the VM by modifying security group rules or shutting down the instance, review VPC flow logs to trace the source of the traffic, capture forensic data from the compromised VM, and determine whether the incident was caused by malware or credential compromise.

Scenario 2: An employee accidentally exposes an AWS S3 bucket containing sensitive customer data to the public. What should the organization do to contain the breach and respond?

- **Key Considerations:** Remove public access immediately by adjusting the bucket policy, enable access logging to identify potential data downloads, notify affected customers as required by regulations, and review IAM roles and policies to prevent recurrence.

Performance vs. Security Tradeoffs

Scenario 1: A streaming service needs to optimize performance for users worldwide while ensuring data is encrypted during transit. Should they use TLS for all connections, or balance encryption with performance by encrypting only certain segments of traffic?

- **Key Considerations:** Weigh the performance cost of end-to-end TLS against the need to protect customer data from interception, especially on public networks. Consider TLS offloading at edge locations (e.g., a CDN) to optimize performance without sacrificing security.

Scenario 2: A database hosting customer data requires low-latency access for a high-frequency trading application. Would encrypting data at rest impact performance, and how can performance be maintained while meeting encryption requirements?

- **Key Considerations:** Evaluate the performance impact of disk encryption technologies provided by the cloud provider (e.g., AWS KMS, Azure Disk Encryption). Use dedicated encryption hardware (e.g., Nitro instances in AWS) to offload the processing overhead.

Compliance Requirements

Scenario 1: A government agency is deploying workloads in a cloud environment and must comply with FedRAMP. What specific network security controls should be implemented to meet compliance?

- **Key Considerations:** Ensure data encryption in transit and at rest, enforce multi-factor authentication, implement continuous monitoring, and leverage the cloud provider's FedRAMP-certified services.

Scenario 2: A retail organization operating in the EU must meet GDPR requirements for customer data. What network security measures are required to ensure compliance?

- **Key Considerations:** Use encryption to protect personal data in transit, implement strict access controls, ensure secure data transfers across regions, and maintain audit trails to demonstrate accountability for data handling.

Troubleshooting Scenarios

Scenario 1: A user reports connectivity issues when trying to access a cloud-hosted application. How should the issue be investigated and resolved?

- **Key Considerations:** Check security group rules, VPC route tables, and access control policies. Use tools like traceroute or cloud-native diagnostics (e.g., AWS VPC Reachability Analyzer or Azure Network Watcher) to identify routing or firewall misconfigurations.

Scenario 2: An application hosted on a Kubernetes cluster experiences intermittent connectivity issues between pods. How can the root cause be identified?

- **Key Considerations:** Review Kubernetes network policies, inspect pod logs, check the health of the cluster's network plugin (e.g., Calico or Flannel), and ensure DNS resolution is functioning properly within the cluster.

Risk Assessment

Scenario 1: An organization allows third-party vendors to connect to its cloud-hosted resources for maintenance tasks. What risks are introduced, and how can they be mitigated?

- **Key Considerations:** Identify risks such as unauthorized access, lateral movement, and exposure of sensitive data. Mitigate with least privilege access, role-based IAM policies, logging vendor activity, and requiring MFA for all connections.

Scenario 2: A company uses a multi-cloud architecture to host its workloads. What risks should be assessed, and how can they ensure consistent security across clouds?

- **Key Considerations:** Assess risks such as inconsistent policies, misconfigured security controls, and lack of visibility. Use centralized tools like CASBs or multi-cloud networking platforms to enforce uniform policies and monitor traffic across all environments.

Identity and Access Management

AUTHENTICATION MECHANISMS AND ADAPTIVE SECURITY FRAMEWORKS

Authentication factors align with specific security requirements through layered validation approaches. Knowledge factors incorporate passwords, PINs, security questions, and cognitive patterns. Possession factors include smart cards, hardware tokens, mobile devices, and digital certificates. Inherence factors validate biometric elements such as fingerprints, retinal patterns, facial geometry, and voice characteristics.

Authentication Strength Matrix:

Factor Type	Strength	Attack Resistance	User Impact
Knowledge	Medium	Medium	Low
Possession	High	High	Medium
Inherence	Very High	Very High	Medium
Location	Medium	Medium	Low
Behavioral	High	High	Low

Behavioral analysis examines:

User Patterns:

- Keystroke dynamics
- Mouse movements
- Touch screen gestures
- Application usage
- Navigation patterns

Location-based authentication utilizes:

- GPS coordinates
- Network location
- IP geolocation
- Device proximity
- Time zone correlation

Risk-based authentication implements:

Risk Scoring:

- Device reputation
- Network analysis
- Behavior patterns
- Transaction value
- Resource sensitivity

Authentication strength metrics measure:

Effectiveness:

- False acceptance rates
- False rejection rates
- Account takeover attempts
- Recovery procedures
- Session anomalies

Adaptive authentication adjusts:

- Factor requirements
- Authentication methods
- Session duration
- Access permissions
- Monitoring intensity

Password alternatives include:

- Passkeys
- Biometric tokens
- Hardware authenticators
- Mobile push notifications
- QR code validation

Zero trust authentication requires:
Continuous Verification:

- Session monitoring
- Context validation
- Risk assessment
- Policy enforcement
- Response automation

Implementation strategies incorporate:

- Identity federation
- Access management
- Directory services
- Policy frameworks
- Audit mechanisms

Organizations monitor:

- Authentication attempts
- Failure patterns
- System performance
- User experience
- Security events

MULTI-FACTOR AUTHENTICATION IMPLEMENTATION

Multi-factor authentication (MFA) adds layers of security by requiring users to present two or more forms of evidence to verify their identity before granting access to systems or resources. The effectiveness of MFA depends on its deployment strategy, the selection of appropriate factors, seamless integration with existing systems, and usability considerations. Implementation also involves managing tokens, addressing mobile device concerns, and ensuring secure recovery mechanisms.

MFA DEPLOYMENT STRATEGIES

1. **Perimeter-Based Deployment:**
   MFA is applied to access points at the network edge, such as VPNs, web applications, or gateways. Users attempting to connect from external networks must authenticate with MFA before entering the internal network.
2. **Application-Specific Deployment:**
   MFA is enforced at the application layer for specific services or resources, such as email, financial systems, or sensitive databases. This approach is suitable for environments where not all applications require the same level of protection.
3. **Role-Based Deployment:**
   MFA is selectively applied to high-risk roles, such as administrators, privileged users, or finance staff. For instance, IT administrators accessing server configurations must authenticate with MFA, while non-privileged users may only require single-factor authentication.
4. **Phased Rollout:**
   Large organizations often implement MFA in phases to minimize disruptions. Deployment starts with high-priority groups, such as executives or IT staff, and gradually expands to include all users. Training and communication plans accompany each phase to ensure smooth adoption.

5. **Geofencing and Conditional Access:**
   Conditional MFA policies enforce MFA only when access attempts deviate from predefined conditions, such as connections from unknown locations, new devices, or during non-business hours. Geofencing blocks access from high-risk regions and triggers MFA when users connect from untrusted IPs.

FACTOR SELECTION CRITERIA

MFA relies on three primary categories of authentication factors:

- *Something you know* (e.g., passwords, PINs).
- *Something you have* (e.g., hardware tokens, smartphone apps).
- *Something you are* (e.g., biometric data like fingerprints or facial recognition).

1. **Security Level:**
   Factors with low susceptibility to compromise should be prioritized. Hardware tokens or biometric authentication are stronger than SMS-based codes, which can be intercepted via SIM-swapping attacks.
2. **Usability:**
   MFA must balance security with user convenience. Push notifications via mobile apps are intuitive and faster than typing a code. High-friction methods, like hardware tokens, may be reserved for critical systems.
3. **Accessibility:**
   Consider the user base and their environment. Employees in remote areas may not reliably receive SMS-based codes, and hardware tokens may be impractical for large-scale distributed teams.
4. **Compliance Requirements:**
   Regulatory standards like PCI DSS or NIST SP 800-63B may dictate acceptable factors. For example, SMS-based authentication is no longer recommended for sensitive systems under NIST guidelines due to its vulnerabilities.
5. **Cost and Scalability:**
   Evaluate the cost of deploying and maintaining factors like hardware tokens versus mobile apps. App-based MFA scales more easily for large organizations compared to distributing physical devices.

INTEGRATION CHALLENGES

1. **Legacy Systems:**
   Many older applications lack native MFA support, requiring additional tools like Single Sign-On (SSO) platforms or reverse proxies to enable MFA. Middleware solutions such as Duo or Okta can extend MFA to legacy systems without modifying the source code.
2. **Multiple Identity Providers:**
   Organizations using multiple identity providers (e.g., Azure AD, LDAP, or Google Workspace) may encounter compatibility issues. Integrating MFA requires a unified identity and access management (IAM) strategy to synchronize user credentials and enforce MFA policies consistently.
3. **Custom Applications:**
   Homegrown applications may require custom development to integrate MFA APIs. Developers can use frameworks like OAuth 2.0 or OpenID Connect (OIDC) to incorporate MFA functionality.
4. **User Experience:**
   Poor integration may result in repeated authentication prompts, frustrating users. Single Sign-On (SSO) integration with MFA reduces authentication fatigue by allowing users to log in once and gain access to multiple systems securely.

PUSH NOTIFICATION SECURITY

Push notifications provide a seamless MFA experience, but their implementation must guard against risks like social engineering or unauthorized approvals.

1. **Authorization Prompt Design:**
   Push notifications must clearly display contextual details, such as the location, device type, and time of the access request. This enables users to recognize and reject unauthorized attempts.
2. **Attack Mitigation:**
   Address "push fatigue" attacks where users may approve repeated notifications out of annoyance or carelessness. Limit the number of MFA attempts within a specific time frame and lock the account after multiple failed approvals.

3. **Device Trust:**
   Push notifications should only be sent to trusted, registered devices. Require device registration during initial MFA setup and use mobile device management (MDM) tools to monitor device compliance.
4. **Encryption:**
   Ensure push notification data is encrypted end-to-end, preventing interception by attackers during transit.

TOKEN MANAGEMENT

Token-based MFA uses physical or virtual devices to generate one-time passcodes (OTPs) or provide authentication approval.

1. **Hardware Tokens:**
   Physical tokens, like YubiKeys or RSA SecurID, are robust and operate independently of internet connectivity. They are well-suited for high-security environments but require logistical planning for distribution and replacement.
2. **Soft Tokens:**
   Mobile apps like Google Authenticator, Microsoft Authenticator, or Duo generate OTPs. These are easier to deploy but depend on device integrity. Secure app deployment and regular updates minimize risks.
3. **Token Expiration:**
   OTPs typically expire within 30–60 seconds to reduce their usability if intercepted. Expired tokens should immediately invalidate authentication attempts.
4. **Token Replacement:**
   Implement policies for replacing lost, stolen, or damaged tokens. Require identity verification before issuing replacements to prevent misuse.

RECOVERY PROCEDURES

Lost or unavailable authentication factors can lock users out of their accounts, making robust recovery procedures necessary.

1. **Backup Authentication Methods:**
   Allow users to register multiple authentication methods, such as a backup hardware token or alternate mobile device, during initial MFA setup.
2. **Recovery Codes:**
   Provide one-time-use recovery codes that users can securely store offline. These codes allow users to regain access if their primary factor is unavailable.
3. **Help Desk Support:**
   Set up identity verification procedures for help desk teams to assist with factor resets. This may include verifying government-issued IDs, answering security questions, or confirming employment details.
4. **Self-Service Portals:**
   Deploy self-service portals where users can reset or update their MFA settings after passing identity verification.

MOBILE DEVICE CONSIDERATIONS

Mobile devices are the most commonly used factor in MFA but come with unique challenges.

1. **Device Registration:**
   Require users to register their mobile devices during the initial MFA setup. Device registration ensures MFA factors are tied to known devices and prevents unauthorized enrollment.
2. **Device Security:**
   Enforce policies requiring users to enable lock screens, biometric authentication, and encryption on mobile devices. Use MDM solutions to ensure compliance and remotely wipe data from lost or stolen devices.
3. **App Updates:**
   Mandate regular updates to mobile MFA apps to address security vulnerabilities and improve compatibility with authentication systems.
4. **Lost or Replaced Devices:**
   Develop a workflow for securely unregistering old devices and registering new ones. Automated alerts should notify IT when users attempt to add a new device.

BIOMETRIC IMPLEMENTATION

Biometrics leverage unique physical or behavioral traits for authentication, such as fingerprints, facial recognition, or voice patterns.

1. **Hardware Compatibility:**
   Ensure biometric systems are compatible with devices used in the organization. For example, facial recognition may require cameras with specific resolution capabilities.
2. **Data Security:**
   Store biometric templates in secure environments, such as on-device storage or within secure enclaves. Avoid storing raw biometric data to minimize privacy risks.
3. **Spoofing Defenses:**
   Implement anti-spoofing measures, such as liveness detection for facial recognition or pressure-sensitive touchpads for fingerprint readers. These defenses reduce the risk of attackers using replicas or synthetic data.
4. **Fallback Options:**
   Provide fallback authentication methods, such as OTPs, for scenarios where biometrics fail, such as injuries or poor environmental conditions.

SINGLE SIGN-ON AND FEDERATION

Single Sign-On (SSO) and federation simplify authentication by enabling users to access multiple systems or applications with a single set of credentials. SSO focuses on centralizing authentication within a domain or organization, while federation extends authentication across multiple domains, often involving trust relationships between separate organizations. Implementations rely on secure architectures, protocols like SAML, OAuth, and OpenID Connect, and robust session management to ensure both convenience and security.

SSO Architectures

Enterprise SSO

Enterprise SSO centralizes authentication within an organization, allowing employees to access internal resources, such as email, file shares, and enterprise applications, with one set of credentials. It relies on centralized identity providers (IdPs) like Microsoft Active Directory (AD) or third-party solutions like Okta or Ping Identity.

- **Architecture**: Enterprise SSO typically integrates with an organization's existing directory service, such as AD or LDAP, to authenticate users and manage their access to internal systems. Kerberos is a commonly used protocol in enterprise SSO environments.
- **Advantages**: Reduces the burden on users by eliminating the need to remember multiple passwords. Enhances security by centralizing credential storage and enabling strong authentication methods like smart cards or biometrics.
- **Challenges**: Legacy applications that do not support modern authentication standards often require workarounds like password vaulting, which can introduce security risks.

For example, an enterprise using Microsoft AD with Kerberos enables employees to authenticate once to access systems like SharePoint, email, and internal databases without additional logins.

Web SSO

Web SSO focuses on providing seamless access to web-based applications through a centralized authentication mechanism. Web SSO solutions often rely on protocols like SAML, OAuth, or OpenID Connect to enable secure single authentication for multiple applications.

- **Architecture**: In web SSO, an IdP authenticates the user and provides a token (e.g., SAML assertion, OAuth token) that is passed to the relying party (service provider or application). The application validates the token and grants access.
- **Use Case**: Web SSO is commonly used by organizations to manage access to SaaS applications like Salesforce, Google Workspace, and Microsoft 365.

For example, a user logs into Okta (the IdP) once, and Okta generates SAML tokens to authenticate the user to various applications like Box, Zoom, or Slack without additional credentials.

Federated SSO

Federated SSO extends SSO functionality beyond a single organization, enabling users to authenticate once and access resources across multiple domains or trust boundaries. Federated SSO establishes trust relationships between IdPs and service providers in separate organizations.

- **Architecture**: Federation relies on identity federation protocols like SAML, OAuth, or OpenID Connect to share authentication information between organizations. Each entity manages its own users and credentials while trusting the other entity's authentication assertions.
- **Use Case**: Federated SSO is widely used in B2B and B2C scenarios, such as enabling a contractor to use their company credentials to access a client's systems or a user signing into a third-party service with their Google or Facebook account.

For example, a university using Federated SSO might allow students to access research journals hosted by external academic institutions through a Shibboleth-based federation.

Identity Federation Protocols

SAML (Security Assertion Markup Language)

SAML is an XML-based protocol that allows IdPs to authenticate users and send assertions to service providers. It is widely used in enterprise and federated SSO implementations for web-based applications.

- **Components**:
  - **IdP**: Authenticates users and issues SAML assertions (e.g., user identity and attributes).
  - **Service Provider (SP)**: Consumes SAML assertions to grant access to the application.
- **Workflow**:

1. A user attempts to access an SP.
2. The SP redirects the user to the IdP for authentication.
3. The IdP authenticates the user and generates a SAML assertion.
4. The assertion is sent back to the SP, which validates it and grants access.

For example, SAML is commonly used for enabling SSO between a corporate IdP and SaaS platforms like Salesforce or Workday.

OAuth (Open Authorization)

OAuth is an open standard for authorization, allowing users to grant applications limited access to their resources without sharing credentials. OAuth is often used in combination with OpenID Connect for authentication.

- **Components**:
  - **Resource Owner**: The user who owns the data or resource.
  - **Client**: The application requesting access to the resource.
  - **Authorization Server**: Authenticates the user and issues tokens.
  - **Resource Server**: Hosts the resource and validates tokens.

For example, OAuth enables a user to authorize a third-party app like a social media management tool to post on their behalf without sharing their account password.

OpenID Connect (OIDC)

OIDC builds on OAuth 2.0 to provide authentication capabilities. It introduces an ID token to convey user identity information to relying parties, making it suitable for SSO scenarios.

- **Components**:
  - **ID Token**: Contains information about the authenticated user, such as their username and email address, encoded in a JSON Web Token (JWT).
  - **Endpoints**: OIDC defines discovery and metadata endpoints to simplify integration for developers.

For example, OIDC is widely used for enabling social logins, such as signing into an e-commerce site with a Google or Facebook account.

Trust Relationships

Trust relationships are the foundation of SSO and federation. They define how entities like IdPs and SPs authenticate and exchange information securely.

- **Certificates**: Trust is often established through the exchange of digital certificates, which are used to sign and encrypt authentication tokens or assertions.

- **Metadata**: Federation protocols like SAML rely on metadata files to describe the endpoints, keys, and attributes of participating entities. Metadata is exchanged during the setup of the trust relationship.
- **Mutual Trust**: Federated SSO requires a bidirectional trust relationship between the IdP and SP, where each entity validates the other's identity and assertions.

For example, in a SAML-based federation, the IdP and SP exchange metadata and certificates to establish trust, ensuring that assertions are only accepted from the trusted IdP.

Session Management

Session management ensures that authenticated users maintain access to applications during a session while providing controls to mitigate risks like session hijacking.

- **Session Tokens**: Tokens like SAML assertions, OAuth access tokens, or OIDC ID tokens are issued after authentication to maintain the session. Tokens often have expiration times to limit exposure.
- **Single Logout (SLO)**: In SSO, SLO ensures that when a user logs out of one application, their session is terminated across all connected applications. For instance, logging out of an IdP (e.g., Okta) logs the user out of all connected SaaS apps.
- **Session Hardening**: Protect tokens and sessions using secure transmission (e.g., HTTPS), secure and HTTP-only cookies, and anti-CSRF tokens to prevent misuse.

For example, an OIDC session might issue a short-lived access token and a refresh token to balance security and usability, with the refresh token enabling the client to obtain a new access token without requiring reauthentication.

IDENTITY LIFECYCLE AND ACCESS MANAGEMENT FRAMEWORKS

User provisioning workflows establish systematic identity creation and management:

Onboarding Process:

Request → Approval → Creation → Access Grant → Notification → Validation

Access Management Matrix:

Stage	Actions	Systems	Validation
Request	HR initiation	HRIS	Manager approval
Creation	Account setup	IAM	Directory sync
Access	Role assignment	PAM	Security review
Validation	Access check	Audit	Compliance

Access certification implements:

Review Cycles:

- Quarterly user reviews
- Monthly privilege audits
- Weekly service account checks
- Daily administrative access
- On-demand certifications

Account termination procedures:

Immediate Actions:

- Access revocation
- System lockouts
- Key deactivation
- Certificate revocation
- Token collection

Identity reconciliation includes:

- Account mapping
- Attribute synchronization
- Orphan detection

- Duplicate resolution
- Conflict management

Identity repositories maintain:
Data Elements:

- User attributes
- Group memberships
- Role assignments
- Access history
- Security markers

Directory services configuration:
Architecture Design:

- Multi-master replication
- Site topology
- Trust relationships
- Schema extensions
- Backup systems

Identity synchronization establishes:
Sync Mechanisms:

- Real-time updates
- Scheduled jobs
- Delta synchronization
- Conflict resolution
- Error handling

Emergency access procedures:
Break Glass Process:

- Request validation
- Temporary access
- Usage monitoring
- Time limitations
- Activity logging

Technical implementation includes:

- Automated workflows
- Policy enforcement
- Audit logging
- Recovery procedures
- Security controls

System maintenance requires:

- Regular backups
- Performance monitoring
- Security updates
- Health checks
- Capacity planning

ROLE ENGINEERING AND MANAGEMENT

Role engineering and management are foundational components of access control strategies, particularly in environments leveraging Role-Based Access Control (RBAC). Defining, maintaining, and refining roles ensures that users have appropriate access to systems and data based on their job responsibilities. This involves methodologies for role creation, techniques for discovering access patterns, designing hierarchies, enforcing separation of duties (SoD), and using tools to automate and streamline management processes.

ROLE DEFINITION METHODOLOGIES

1. **Top-Down Approach:**
   - In this method, roles are defined based on organizational structures, job descriptions, and security policies. For example, a "Finance Manager" role might include access to payroll systems, financial reports, and budgeting tools.
   - Benefits include alignment with business functions and easy integration with compliance requirements.
   - Challenges arise when predefined roles fail to match actual access needs, leading to over-permissioned or under-permissioned roles.
2. **Bottom-Up Approach:**
   - Access patterns are analyzed to determine the permissions users currently utilize, and roles are created to reflect these real-world needs.
   - This method is data-driven, typically using role mining techniques to analyze access logs.
   - A challenge with this approach is that it may perpetuate existing access redundancies or conflicts if not properly validated against policies.
3. **Hybrid Approach:**
   - Combines the strengths of top-down and bottom-up methods. Initial roles are defined using business functions, then refined based on usage data.
4. **Task-Based Role Creation:**
   - Roles are defined based on specific tasks users perform, such as "Process Payroll" or "Generate Reports." This approach works well in task-oriented environments.

ROLE MINING TECHNIQUES

Role mining identifies patterns in user permissions and groups them into logical roles.

1. **Clustering Techniques:**
   - Clustering algorithms, such as k-means or hierarchical clustering, group users with similar access permissions. These clusters inform the creation of roles that match user needs.
2. **Frequent Permission Set Analysis:**
   - Analyzes access logs to find permission sets that are frequently used together. For instance, if most users in a department access the same five applications, this combination can be defined as a role.
3. **Attribute-Based Analysis:**
   - User attributes, such as department, location, or job title, are mapped to permissions. This can uncover discrepancies, such as a user in HR with access to IT systems.
4. **Machine Learning Models:**
   - Supervised and unsupervised learning algorithms analyze historical access patterns and create suggested roles. AI-based tools like Saviynt and SailPoint offer advanced role mining capabilities.

ROLE HIERARCHY DESIGN

Role hierarchies organize roles in a structured, parent-child relationship, allowing permissions to be inherited across different levels.

1. **Flat Role Structures:**
   - Roles are independent of one another and do not inherit permissions. This works well in simple environments but becomes cumbersome in large organizations with overlapping access needs.
2. **Hierarchical Structures:**
   - Higher-level roles inherit permissions from lower-level roles. For example, a "Senior Developer" role inherits all permissions from a "Developer" role but adds access to additional tools like code deployment platforms.
   - Hierarchical designs reduce redundancy by reusing lower-level roles.
3. **Permission Inheritance Control:**
   - Restrict inheritance in certain scenarios to enforce least privilege. For instance, a manager in IT inherits access to administrative tools but does not inherit access to HR systems.

4. **Graph-Based Models:**
    - Modern access control tools use graph-based models to design complex hierarchies with interdependent roles and relationships, enabling more flexible permission assignments.

SEPARATION OF DUTIES

Separation of duties (SoD) prevents conflicts of interest and reduces the risk of fraud or misuse by ensuring that no single user has complete control over critical processes.

1. **Key Principles:**
    - Split responsibilities across multiple roles. For example, in financial systems, the role responsible for approving payments should not also initiate them.
2. **SoD Policy Definition:**
    - Policies define specific access combinations that are prohibited. For instance, "a user with access to payroll processing cannot have access to payment approval systems."
3. **Conflict Detection:**
    - Role mining tools and governance systems identify users or roles with conflicting access privileges, flagging SoD violations.
4. **Compensating Controls:**
    - In scenarios where SoD cannot be enforced due to operational constraints, compensating controls like increased monitoring, logging, and audits are used.

ROLE REVIEW PROCESSES

Role reviews ensure roles remain relevant, secure, and aligned with business needs as the organization evolves.

1. **Periodic Reviews:**
    - Conduct quarterly or annual reviews to validate role definitions and permissions. This identifies redundant, outdated, or over-permissioned roles.
2. **Access Recertification:**
    - Managers or role owners validate that users assigned to specific roles still require those permissions. For example, an employee who has changed departments should not retain access to their previous department's systems.
3. **Policy Alignment:**
    - Roles are reviewed against compliance policies like PCI DSS or GDPR to ensure they meet regulatory standards.
4. **Tool-Based Automation:**
    - Role governance tools, such as SailPoint or RSA Identity Governance, automate role review processes, sending alerts and reports to stakeholders.

ROLE-BASED ACCESS CONTROL

RBAC simplifies access management by assigning users to predefined roles instead of managing individual permissions.

1. **Role Assignment:**
    - Users are assigned to roles based on their job responsibilities. For example, a "Marketing Manager" role grants access to campaign management tools, analytics platforms, and marketing databases.
2. **Role Enforcement:**
    - RBAC systems enforce access rules at the application, database, and file system levels, ensuring users can only access resources allowed by their roles.
3. **Advantages:**
    - Simplifies access control by grouping permissions.
    - Enhances security by enforcing least privilege.
    - Streamlines audits and compliance reporting.
4. **Limitations:**
    - Static roles may not adapt well to dynamic environments or temporary access needs, requiring additional mechanisms like dynamic roles.

DYNAMIC ROLE ASSIGNMENT

Dynamic roles adapt to contextual factors such as user attributes or environmental conditions, enabling flexible access control.

1. **Attribute-Based Role Assignment:**
   - Attributes like department, location, and project assignment dynamically determine role membership. For example, a contractor working in IT for a specific project may receive access to specific systems during the project's duration.
2. **Time-Based Roles:**
   - Temporary roles grant access for a specific duration, such as during onboarding or project execution. After the time expires, the role is automatically revoked.
3. **Context-Aware Roles:**
   - Roles adjust based on real-time factors like device security posture or login location. For instance, if a user logs in from an untrusted device, their role may restrict access to sensitive resources.

ROLE MANAGEMENT TOOLS

Role management tools automate and streamline the creation, assignment, and review of roles across the organization.

1. **Identity Governance and Administration (IGA) Tools:**
   - Platforms like SailPoint, Okta, and One Identity provide role mining, access certification, and policy enforcement features.
   - These tools integrate with directories like Active Directory or Azure AD to centralize role management.
2. **Access Analytics:**
   - Tools like Saviynt analyze access trends and flag deviations, enabling continuous role refinement.
3. **Audit and Reporting:**
   - Role management platforms generate compliance reports, highlighting role assignments, SoD conflicts, and access violations.
4. **Integration with ITSM Systems:**
   - Integration with IT Service Management (ITSM) platforms like ServiceNow automates role assignment workflows. For instance, when a new hire request is logged, the system assigns the relevant roles automatically.

PRIVILEGED ACCESS MANAGEMENT

Privileged Access Management (PAM) focuses on securing, controlling, and monitoring access to privileged accounts, which have elevated permissions within an organization's IT environment. These accounts are prime targets for attackers due to their ability to alter critical systems, access sensitive data, and bypass security controls. Proper implementation of PAM minimizes the risk of misuse or compromise by ensuring that privileged accounts are strictly managed, monitored, and audited.

Privileged Account Inventory

Maintaining an accurate inventory of privileged accounts is a foundational step in PAM. These accounts often include administrative accounts, service accounts, domain administrators, and accounts with elevated access to critical applications or infrastructure.

- **Identification**: Identify all privileged accounts across systems, including operating systems, databases, applications, cloud environments, and network devices. This includes shared accounts, non-human accounts (e.g., service accounts), and hardcoded credentials in scripts or applications.
- **Classification**: Categorize accounts based on their access scope and risk level. For example:
  - **Domain Administrator**: Full control over the Active Directory environment.
  - **Database Administrator**: Access to sensitive database information and schema.
  - **Cloud Root Accounts**: Unrestricted control over cloud environments.
- **Validation**: Regularly review the inventory to detect orphaned or unused accounts that could be exploited if left unmanaged.

For example, an organization conducting a privileged account audit might discover unused service accounts for legacy applications and disable or delete them to reduce the attack surface.

Password Vaulting

Password vaulting involves storing privileged credentials in a secure, centralized repository that restricts direct access and enforces strong password management practices.

- **Secure Storage**: Vaults encrypt passwords using strong encryption algorithms like AES-256. Access to the vault itself is tightly controlled through multi-factor authentication (MFA) and role-based access.
- **Randomized Passwords**: Automatically generate unique, complex passwords for each privileged account and rotate them regularly, often after every use.
- **Credential Access**: Limit access to passwords to authorized users only and ensure passwords are not visible in plaintext. Temporary passwords or one-time passwords (OTPs) can be issued to reduce long-term exposure.
- **Integration**: Integrate vaulting solutions with Single Sign-On (SSO) or API-based automation for seamless access without revealing passwords to users.

For example, a PAM solution like CyberArk or BeyondTrust may automatically rotate the password for a privileged database account after each session, ensuring credentials remain secure.

Session Recording

Session recording captures and logs the actions performed during privileged access sessions, providing accountability and forensic data for incident response.

- **Keystroke and Screen Recording**: PAM solutions record keystrokes, commands, and screen activity during administrative sessions to create a comprehensive audit trail.
- **Real-Time Monitoring**: Allow security teams to monitor privileged sessions in real time, providing the ability to terminate a session if suspicious behavior is detected.
- **Replay Capability**: Stored session recordings can be replayed for forensic analysis or compliance audits to verify that actions performed align with organizational policies.

For example, session recording can capture a system administrator's activities while making configuration changes on a firewall, enabling review to ensure no unauthorized modifications were made.

Just-in-Time Access

Just-in-Time (JIT) access grants privileged access temporarily, limiting the window of exposure to security risks. Instead of providing standing privileges, JIT ensures that access is granted only when required and revoked automatically after the task is completed.

- **Workflow**: Users must request access, which is reviewed and approved based on predefined policies. Access is provisioned for a specific duration or task.
- **Ephemeral Accounts**: PAM solutions can create temporary privileged accounts that are deleted once the task is completed, ensuring no lingering permissions.
- **Use Cases**: JIT access is ideal for third-party contractors or administrators who need short-term access to critical systems.

For example, an IT admin needing to troubleshoot a server issue might request JIT access through a PAM solution, which creates a temporary account with elevated permissions that expires after one hour.

Emergency Access

Emergency access, also known as "break-glass" access, is used in critical situations where immediate privileged access is required, bypassing the standard approval workflow.

- **Control Mechanisms**: Emergency accounts are preconfigured with restricted privileges and must be used only in well-documented scenarios.
- **Audit Logs**: Every instance of emergency access must be logged and reviewed to ensure it was used appropriately.
- **Multi-Factor Authentication**: Enforce MFA to prevent unauthorized access to emergency accounts.

For example, if an organization experiences a major outage affecting the primary authentication system, an administrator may use an emergency account stored securely in a PAM vault to restore operations.

Privilege Escalation

Privilege escalation occurs when a user or process gains higher privileges than originally granted, often through exploitation of vulnerabilities, misconfigurations, or abuse of legitimate workflows. PAM minimizes the risks of privilege escalation through:

- **Least Privilege Principle**: Assign only the minimum permissions needed for a role or task. For example, a developer should not have administrative access to production servers.
- **Control Elevation**: Require explicit approval and logging for privilege elevation. Use PAM workflows to manage elevation requests securely.
- **Patch Management**: Regularly update systems to address vulnerabilities that could allow privilege escalation attacks, such as unpatched operating system or software flaws.

For instance, a PAM solution may detect a non-administrative user attempting to execute a command requiring root privileges and block the action unless authorized.

Monitoring and Auditing

Continuous monitoring and auditing ensure that privileged access activities are tracked and anomalies are identified.

- **Activity Logs**: PAM solutions record all privileged account activities, including login times, executed commands, accessed resources, and changes made.
- **Anomaly Detection**: Use behavior analytics to detect unusual patterns, such as an administrator accessing systems outside normal hours or from unrecognized locations.
- **Compliance Reporting**: Generate reports to demonstrate compliance with regulations like PCI DSS, GDPR, and HIPAA, which require detailed logging of privileged activities.

For example, a PAM system might generate an alert if an administrator account is used to log in from a foreign IP address for the first time.

Access Reconciliation

Access reconciliation involves comparing granted access permissions with organizational policies and removing excess privileges or inactive accounts.

- **Review Processes**: Conduct regular reviews of privileged accounts and their permissions to identify discrepancies or violations of the least privilege principle.
- **Orphaned Account Detection**: Identify and remove accounts left behind when employees leave or roles change, as these can pose significant security risks.
- **Remediation**: Use automated workflows to revoke unnecessary access, ensuring that permissions are always aligned with current roles.

For example, access reconciliation may reveal that a former database administrator still has root-level permissions to production databases, prompting immediate removal to prevent unauthorized access.

ACCESS CONTROL ARCHITECTURES AND IMPLEMENTATION FRAMEWORKS

DAC implementation establishes granular ownership-based controls:

Resource Ownership Matrix:

Owner Privileges:

- Read/Write/Execute
- Modify permissions
- Grant access
- Delegate control
- Revoke rights

Delegation Framework:

Action	**Permission**	**Inheritance**	**Limits**
Grant	Full/Partial	Yes/No	Time/Scope
Transfer	Ownership	Complete	Permanent
Share	Specific	Limited	Temporary

Access Matrix Design:

- Subject identification
- Object classification
- Permission sets
- Inheritance rules
- Constraint mapping

MAC deployment structures:
Security Level Hierarchy:

- Top Secret
- Secret
- Confidential
- Restricted
- Unclassified

Category Implementation:

- Department codes
- Project identifiers
- Geographic locations
- Data classifications
- Function groups

Label Management:

- Format standards
- Assignment procedures
- Validation rules
- Update processes
- Audit requirements

ABAC framework incorporates:
Attribute Categories:

- Subject attributes
- Object attributes
- Action attributes
- Environment attributes
- Context attributes

Policy Structure:

- Attribute combinations
- Boolean logic
- Decision trees
- Conflict resolution
- Default handling

Rule Development:

- Condition definition
- Action specification
- Exception handling
- Override procedures
- Review cycles

Rule-based systems implement:
Policy Components:

- Condition sets

- Action definitions
- Target specifications
- Effect determinations
- Combining algorithms

Enforcement Mechanisms:

- Request evaluation
- Policy application
- Decision logging
- Response generation
- Audit recording

Exception Management:

- Request validation
- Approval workflow
- Time limitations
- Usage monitoring
- Documentation requirements

Organizations maintain:

- Policy repositories
- Rule databases
- Audit trails
- Review schedules
- Change controls

CASE STUDY: MFA DEPLOYMENT PROJECT

A large retail organization initiated an MFA deployment project after a phishing attack compromised multiple employee credentials, leading to unauthorized access to sensitive customer data. The goal of the project was to enhance security by adding a second layer of authentication for all users, with a focus on balancing security, usability, and scalability.

The deployment involved selecting a multi-factor authentication platform, with Microsoft Authenticator and YubiKey chosen to support both soft and hardware token options. Employees were categorized into groups based on risk profiles. For instance, administrative and IT staff were prioritized for immediate rollout, while store-level employees were included in the second phase.

Integration challenges were addressed by using Azure AD to implement conditional access policies, ensuring that MFA was enforced only for high-risk scenarios such as external logins or access to critical systems. During the rollout, a training program was implemented to educate employees on how to use the new authentication methods, supported by a self-service portal for device registration and recovery.

Within three months, the organization achieved a 95% adoption rate and reported a significant reduction in account compromise incidents. The rollout was completed with minimal disruptions to business operations, and ongoing monitoring highlighted no major usability issues.

CASE STUDY: FEDERATION IMPLEMENTATION

A healthcare provider implemented a federation solution to enable secure single sign-on (SSO) across its partner network of hospitals, labs, and insurance providers. Prior to this, each partner managed separate credentials, creating inefficiencies and increasing security risks due to repeated password reuse.

The organization adopted SAML (Security Assertion Markup Language) as the federation standard, allowing users to authenticate once within their home organization's identity provider (IdP) and access partner services without requiring additional credentials. Azure AD was configured as the central IdP, while SP (Service Provider) configurations were established with key partners using SAML integration.

Integration challenges arose with legacy applications that lacked SAML support. These were addressed using a reverse proxy with SSO capabilities to provide federated access. The organization also faced trust model complexities, as each partner had its own set of security policies and requirements. A common baseline for identity verification and secure authentication was established to address these inconsistencies.

The federation implementation reduced login friction for end users and allowed seamless access to critical systems across partners. It also improved visibility into authentication events and reduced the administrative burden of managing credentials across organizations.

CASE STUDY: PAM SYSTEM BREACH

A financial services company experienced a breach of its Privileged Access Management (PAM) system due to improperly configured security controls. Attackers exploited a vulnerable administrative account, which had not been enrolled in multi-factor authentication, to gain access to the PAM console. Once inside, they escalated privileges and accessed sensitive credentials stored in the system, which were used to compromise critical infrastructure.

A forensic investigation revealed several issues, including:

- Lack of MFA enforcement for administrative accounts.
- Overly permissive access policies allowing unnecessary PAM access.
- Inadequate monitoring and alerting for unusual PAM activities, such as bulk credential retrieval.

The company responded by immediately revoking compromised credentials, isolating affected systems, and enforcing emergency access controls. As part of the remediation process, the PAM platform was reconfigured with stricter access policies, enforced MFA for all users, and implemented just-in-time (JIT) privilege escalation to minimize standing privileges. Additionally, SIEM integration was established to monitor PAM activity and alert on anomalous behavior.

Lessons from the breach informed a broader security strategy, including enhanced employee training, regular PAM audits, and a zero-trust approach to privileged access.

CASE STUDY: ROLE MINING EXERCISE

A manufacturing firm conducted a role mining exercise as part of an initiative to improve access management and prepare for RBAC implementation. The legacy access control system relied on direct assignment of permissions, resulting in significant over-permissioning and compliance risks during audits.

Role mining was performed using a hybrid approach:

- Top-down analysis began by defining roles based on organizational hierarchy and job descriptions. For example, "Plant Supervisor" and "Maintenance Technician" were identified as distinct roles based on their responsibilities.
- Bottom-up analysis used a role mining tool to analyze actual permission usage. Clustering techniques grouped users with similar access patterns, revealing discrepancies such as employees with unused permissions or conflicting access rights.

The exercise identified redundant permissions and opportunities for consolidation. For example, 80% of employees in the maintenance department used the same subset of permissions, allowing the creation of a unified "Maintenance Worker" role. Outliers, such as employees with unique responsibilities, were assigned individual overrides.

By the end of the exercise, the company had established 25 well-defined roles, reducing permission sprawl and improving compliance with industry standards like ISO 27001. The exercise also highlighted a need for periodic role reviews to maintain alignment with evolving business needs.

CASE STUDY: ACCESS MODEL MIGRATION

A global energy company migrated from a discretionary access control (DAC) model to a role-based access control (RBAC) model to improve scalability and meet compliance requirements. Under the DAC model, individual managers assigned permissions to employees, resulting in inconsistent access patterns and difficulty enforcing policies like separation of duties (SoD).

The migration process began with role definition, leveraging input from business units and an analysis of existing access patterns. Using role mining tools, common permission sets were grouped into roles such as "Field Engineer" and "Operations Manager."

To minimize disruptions, the migration was conducted in phases. The first phase targeted low-risk environments, allowing the team to refine role definitions and identify gaps. Subsequent phases expanded the implementation to high-risk environments, such as operational technology (OT) systems. SoD policies were enforced by restricting conflicting roles, such as those that could initiate and approve critical changes.

The company also integrated the new RBAC model with its identity governance platform, automating role assignments for new hires based on department and job title. Post-migration audits showed a 35% reduction in excessive permissions and improved compliance with industry regulations, including NERC CIP and GDPR.

CASE STUDY: IDENTITY GOVERNANCE IMPLEMENTATION

A global pharmaceutical company implemented an identity governance and administration (IGA) platform to address challenges related to managing user identities across its subsidiaries and ensuring compliance with HIPAA and GDPR. The existing identity management process relied on manual workflows, resulting in delays in onboarding, offboarding, and access certification.

The IGA platform, SailPoint IdentityNow, was selected for its ability to automate identity lifecycle management, streamline access certification, and integrate with existing systems like Active Directory and HR software.

The implementation involved:

- Automating provisioning and deprovisioning workflows. For instance, when a new hire was added to the HR system, their account was automatically created in Active Directory with role-appropriate permissions.
- Conducting access reviews to ensure users retained only the permissions necessary for their current roles. This addressed compliance gaps, such as employees retaining access to patient records after changing departments.
- Establishing risk-based policies to flag high-risk access requests, such as those involving sensitive research data or financial systems, for additional approval.

The IGA implementation improved operational efficiency by reducing onboarding times from two weeks to two days and ensuring consistent enforcement of compliance requirements across all subsidiaries. It also provided detailed audit logs and reports, simplifying regulatory audits.

PRACTICE QUESTIONS FOR IDENTITY AND ACCESS MANAGEMENT

Practice questions for identity and access management (IAM) should emphasize real-world scenarios to test decision-making, troubleshooting, and implementation skills. They should focus on evaluating various authentication mechanisms, managing identities and privileged access, ensuring compliance, selecting appropriate security models, and addressing implementation challenges. These questions help candidates apply theoretical knowledge to complex situations.

Authentication Scenarios

Scenario 1: An organization wants to implement multi-factor authentication (MFA) for remote employees accessing sensitive systems. Which combination of authentication factors should be chosen to maximize security without causing significant usability issues?

- **Key Considerations:** Evaluate knowledge-based factors (passwords), possession-based factors (hardware tokens or mobile authenticator apps), and inherence factors (biometrics). Assess the security, convenience, and risk of phishing or token theft.

Scenario 2: A developer sets up a web application that requires users to authenticate via social login (e.g., Google or Facebook). How can OpenID Connect be used to enable this functionality, and what security considerations should be addressed?

- **Key Considerations:** Explain the OpenID Connect authentication flow, secure handling of ID tokens, redirect URIs, and CSRF protection for login redirection.

Federation Troubleshooting

Scenario 1: A user is unable to log in to a federated application using Single Sign-On (SSO) via SAML. The identity provider (IdP) authentication succeeds, but the service provider (SP) denies access. What troubleshooting steps should be taken?

- **Key Considerations:** Check for mismatched configurations, such as invalid SAML metadata, certificate expiration, incorrect audience in the assertion, or missing user attributes required by the SP.

Scenario 2: A company uses a federated SSO system for contractors to access internal resources. A contractor reports they are redirected to the IdP login page repeatedly. What might cause this issue?

- **Key Considerations:** Review session cookies, clock synchronization between IdP and SP, misconfigured session timeout policies, or issues with the contractor's IdP account.

Access Control Decisions

Scenario 1: An organization implements Role-Based Access Control (RBAC) for a cloud environment. A user requests temporary access to resources outside their assigned role. Should the organization grant the request, and what measures should be in place?

- **Key Considerations:** Evaluate the use of Just-in-Time (JIT) access, role exceptions, and approval workflows. Consider auditing and automatic revocation to ensure temporary access is monitored and does not persist unnecessarily.

Scenario 2: A healthcare provider must ensure that only authorized personnel can access patient records. Which access control model (Discretionary Access Control, Mandatory Access Control, or Attribute-Based Access Control) is best suited for this use case, and why?

- **Key Considerations:** Compare the models in terms of granularity, regulatory compliance (e.g., HIPAA), and the need for context-based policies (e.g., location or time of access).

Identity Lifecycle Management

Scenario 1: An employee moves from the marketing department to the finance department. How should their identity and access permissions be updated to reflect the role change?

- **Key Considerations:** Address deprovisioning of marketing-related access, granting of finance-related access, and ensuring no orphaned privileges remain. Highlight the importance of automated identity lifecycle management tools like IAM systems or HR-integrated workflows.

Scenario 2: A contractor's account was not deactivated after their project ended, leaving their access credentials active for an extended period. What processes should be implemented to prevent this oversight?

- **Key Considerations:** Discuss role expiration policies, automated deprovisioning workflows tied to contract end dates, and regular access reviews to identify dormant accounts.

Privileged Access Scenarios

Scenario 1: An administrator needs to perform maintenance on a critical production database. How can privileged access be securely granted for this task while minimizing risk?

- **Key Considerations:** Implement Just-in-Time access through a Privileged Access Management (PAM) system, enforce session monitoring and recording, and ensure privileges are automatically revoked after the task is completed.

Scenario 2: A privileged account for a network device is shared among several administrators. What are the risks of this practice, and how can shared accounts be managed securely?

- **Key Considerations:** Highlight risks like lack of accountability and password compromise. Recommend password vaulting, session logging, and unique accounts for each administrator with role-based privileges.

Compliance Requirements

Scenario 1: A retail company handles payment card information and must comply with PCI DSS. What IAM-related controls should be implemented to meet compliance requirements?

- **Key Considerations:** Address password policies (e.g., complexity, rotation), MFA for administrative access, logging and monitoring of privileged access, and least privilege enforcement.

Scenario 2: An organization operating in the EU must ensure compliance with GDPR when managing employee identities. What IAM practices should be implemented to protect personal data?

- **Key Considerations:** Include data minimization, strong access controls, encryption of sensitive information, and audit logs to track identity-related actions.

Security Model Selection

Scenario 1: A research institution processes highly classified data and needs a security model that prevents unauthorized disclosure while allowing authorized users to access data based on their clearance level. Which model (e.g., Bell-LaPadula or Biba) should be selected, and why?

- **Key Considerations:** Discuss the Bell-LaPadula model for confidentiality enforcement, its "no read up" and "no write down" rules, and its suitability for classified environments.

Scenario 2: A financial institution must prevent the corruption of transaction data. Which security model is most appropriate for ensuring data integrity?

- **Key Considerations:** Analyze the Biba model's focus on integrity and explain how the "no read down" and "no write up" rules mitigate risks of data tampering.

Implementation Challenges

Scenario 1: An organization deploys an enterprise IAM system but experiences resistance from employees due to changes in authentication methods (e.g., enforcing MFA). How can the organization address these challenges?

- **Key Considerations:** Emphasize user education, seamless integration with existing workflows, MFA options like push notifications or biometric authentication for ease of use, and phased rollouts.

Scenario 2: A company implements SSO for its internal applications but struggles with legacy systems that do not support modern authentication protocols like SAML or OAuth. How can these systems be integrated securely?

- **Key Considerations:** Discuss solutions like password vaulting, reverse proxies, or using middleware to translate modern authentication methods into credentials compatible with legacy applications. Address the risks of maintaining older systems and suggest prioritizing upgrades where feasible.

Security Assessment and Testing

VULNERABILITY ASSESSMENT METHODOLOGY AND IMPLEMENTATION

Assessment frameworks establish structured approaches to security evaluation through comprehensive scanning and analysis. The planning phase determines assessment boundaries, objectives, timelines, and resource requirements. Scope definition identifies target systems, applications, networks, and data stores while considering business impact and regulatory requirements.

Assessment Planning Matrix:

Phase	Activities	Deliverables	Timeline
Preparation	Asset inventory, Risk analysis	Scope document	Week 1
Discovery	Network mapping, System identification	Asset list	Week 2
Assessment	Vulnerability scanning, Analysis	Findings report	Week 3
Reporting	Result compilation, Recommendations	Final report	Week 4

Network scanning implementations:

Scan Types:

- Port scanning
- Service enumeration
- OS fingerprinting
- Protocol analysis
- Configuration review

Web application assessment includes:

Static Analysis:

- Source code review
- Configuration checks
- Framework assessment
- Library evaluation
- Security controls

Dynamic Testing:

- Input validation
- Authentication bypass
- Session management
- Authorization controls
- Business logic

Database scanning examines:

Configuration Review:

- Version assessment
- Patch status
- Access controls
- Encryption settings
- Audit configurations

Security Testing:

- Authentication mechanisms
- Authorization schemes
- Data encryption
- Backup procedures
- Monitoring systems

Cloud infrastructure scanning incorporates:
Service Assessment:
- Instance configuration
- Network security
- Storage protection
- Identity management
- Access controls

Compliance Validation:
- Security standards
- Industry regulations
- Best practices
- Corporate policies
- Technical baselines

Scanning tools utilize:
- Automated discovery
- Credential validation
- Policy verification
- Compliance checking
- Risk scoring

Organizations implement:
- Scanning schedules
- Tool management
- Result analysis
- Remediation tracking
- Progress monitoring

TOOL SELECTION CRITERIA

Selecting the right tools for security, operational, or compliance needs involves evaluating several factors, including the choice between commercial and open-source solutions, the ability to meet specific compliance requirements, and the coverage capabilities of the tool in addressing organizational needs. A structured approach to tool selection ensures compatibility with technical and regulatory frameworks while balancing cost, scalability, and functionality.

COMMERCIAL VS. OPEN-SOURCE

The decision between commercial and open-source tools hinges on organizational priorities, budget, and resource availability for maintenance and support.

1. **Commercial Tools:**
    - **Advantages:**
        - Typically include vendor support for setup, troubleshooting, and updates.
        - Offer polished user interfaces and extensive documentation, making them easier to implement for teams with less technical expertise.
        - Provide enhanced security features like automated patching, dedicated threat intelligence feeds, and integrations with third-party platforms.
    - **Drawbacks:**
        - Often have high upfront licensing or subscription costs.
        - May lock organizations into proprietary ecosystems, making it difficult to switch to alternative solutions later.
    - **Examples:**
        - Palo Alto's Cortex XDR for threat detection and response.
        - ServiceNow for ITSM and workflow automation.

2. **Open-Source Tools:**
   - **Advantages:**
     - Cost-effective, with no licensing fees.
     - Provides flexibility to customize or extend functionality to suit specific use cases.
     - Active community support often leads to quick identification of bugs and vulnerabilities.
   - **Drawbacks:**
     - Requires in-house expertise to implement, maintain, and secure.
     - Support is often limited to online forums or paid third-party consultants.
   - **Examples:**
     - OpenVAS for vulnerability scanning.
     - OSSEC for host-based intrusion detection.
3. **Hybrid Approach:**
   - Many organizations adopt a hybrid model, combining open-source tools for specific tasks (e.g., ELK stack for log analysis) with commercial solutions for enterprise-scale features (e.g., Splunk for security information and event management).

COMPLIANCE REQUIREMENTS

The ability of a tool to meet regulatory or industry compliance standards is a major factor in its selection, particularly in industries like healthcare, finance, and government.

1. **Regulatory Standards:**
   - Tools must align with specific compliance frameworks, such as:
     - **HIPAA:** Healthcare organizations require tools that encrypt data in transit and at rest, log access to patient records, and provide detailed audit trails.
     - **GDPR:** Solutions must support data subject access requests (DSARs), data anonymization, and secure cross-border data transfers.
     - **PCI DSS:** Tools like vulnerability scanners (e.g., Nessus) must support regular scans of cardholder environments and enforce multi-factor authentication for administrative access.
2. **Certification Requirements:**
   - Vendors often obtain certifications like SOC 2, ISO 27001, or FedRAMP for their tools, signaling alignment with industry best practices.
3. **Audit and Reporting Features:**
   - Tools should provide automated audit logs, compliance reports, and alerts for policy violations. For example, a cloud security posture management (CSPM) tool like Prisma Cloud provides continuous monitoring for misconfigurations against frameworks like CIS Benchmarks or NIST.
4. **Customization for Compliance Needs:**
   - Tools should allow users to tailor settings to unique organizational policies. For instance, an Identity Governance platform like SailPoint allows granular access review workflows based on regional data privacy laws.

COVERAGE CAPABILITIES

Coverage capabilities define the scope and depth of a tool's ability to address organizational needs, such as scalability, integration, and functionality across diverse environments.

1. **Breadth of Functionality:**
   - A tool that offers multi-functional capabilities may reduce the need for multiple point solutions. For example, SentinelOne provides endpoint protection, detection, and response in one package.
2. **Scalability:**
   - Consider how well the tool can grow with the organization. A small business might adopt a cost-effective, lightweight solution initially, but as the organization grows, the tool must handle increased workloads without performance degradation. Cloud-native solutions like CrowdStrike Falcon are often chosen for their scalability and ability to handle global operations.

3. **Environment Coverage:**
   - Tools must support diverse environments, such as on-premises, hybrid, or multi-cloud setups. For instance, a cloud security tool should integrate seamlessly with AWS, Azure, and Google Cloud while monitoring on-premises data centers.
4. **Threat Landscape Adaptation:**
   - Tools must be capable of addressing evolving threats. Threat detection tools like Darktrace leverage AI to adapt to new attack techniques, ensuring ongoing relevance.
5. **Integration with Existing Systems:**
   - The tool should easily integrate with current infrastructure, including identity management systems, ticketing platforms, and data lakes. For example, a SIEM tool like Splunk should be able to ingest logs from firewalls, endpoint protection systems, and cloud platforms.
6. **Automation and Orchestration:**
   - Evaluate the automation capabilities of the tool to reduce manual workload. Security Orchestration, Automation, and Response (SOAR) platforms like Palo Alto Cortex XSOAR automate repetitive tasks, such as threat investigation and response workflows.
7. **User Base and Use Case Fit:**
   - Tools should be selected based on the audience (e.g., security teams, IT administrators, or compliance managers). A vulnerability scanner like Qualys offers granular options for expert users, while simpler tools like Rapid7 Nexpose cater to IT teams with less experience.
8. **Performance Benchmarks:**
   - Tools should meet performance benchmarks, such as low latency in VPN solutions, high throughput in firewalls, or minimal resource usage for endpoint security. Evaluating these metrics during proof-of-concept (PoC) testing ensures the tool will meet operational needs without impacting productivity.

Tool selection requires carefully weighing organizational needs, compliance obligations, and operational constraints. A thorough evaluation process often includes conducting a PoC, consulting with relevant stakeholders, and assessing the total cost of ownership (TCO) over time.

RESULTS ANALYSIS METHODOLOGY

Analyzing the results of security assessments, vulnerability scans, and monitoring activities involves a structured approach to interpreting data, prioritizing risks, and planning remediation. Effective results analysis identifies actionable insights while filtering out noise such as false positives. Incorporating methods like risk prioritization, remediation planning, and trend analysis ensures vulnerabilities are addressed systematically and improvements are measurable over time.

False Positive Identification

False positives occur when a security tool or assessment flags an issue that is not a genuine vulnerability or threat. Identifying and eliminating false positives is essential to avoid wasting resources and ensure accurate reporting.

- **Validation Process**: Compare flagged findings against known baselines, configurations, and system behaviors to determine if the issue is real. For example, if a scanner flags an outdated software version as vulnerable, confirm whether compensating controls, such as access restrictions or virtual patching, mitigate the risk.
- **Cross-Verification**: Use multiple tools or methods to verify findings. For instance, a vulnerability flagged by a web application scanner can be cross-checked manually or with another scanner to confirm its validity.
- **Configuration Context**: False positives often arise due to misinterpretation of system configurations. For example, a flagged open port might be used legitimately for a secure service like HTTPS, making it non-threatening.
- **Continuous Feedback Loop**: Adjust detection thresholds and refine tool settings over time to minimize false positives. For instance, exclude specific findings from future scans if they are repeatedly identified as non-issues.

An example of false positive identification is reviewing a security information and event management (SIEM) alert that indicates suspicious login activity. If the activity is verified as legitimate user behavior, the alert can be tuned out to prevent recurrence.

Risk Prioritization

Not all findings represent the same level of risk, and effective prioritization ensures that resources are allocated to address the most critical issues first. This involves evaluating vulnerabilities based on their potential impact, likelihood of exploitation, and relevance to the organization's specific environment.

- **Severity Scoring**: Use established scoring systems such as the Common Vulnerability Scoring System (CVSS) to rate vulnerabilities. A CVSS score of 9.0 or higher, for example, would typically indicate a critical issue requiring immediate attention.
- **Business Context**: Align risk prioritization with the organization's operational and strategic objectives. A vulnerability in a public-facing application that processes customer data may take precedence over one in an internal development server.
- **Exploitability**: Assess the likelihood of exploitation by considering factors like whether proof-of-concept exploits exist or if the vulnerability is actively being exploited in the wild.
- **Asset Criticality**: Assign higher priority to vulnerabilities affecting critical systems, such as those handling sensitive financial data, customer information, or operational technology (OT).

For example, a high-severity vulnerability in a web application with internet exposure may be prioritized over a medium-severity issue in an internal server. Risk prioritization should balance immediate threats with long-term security posture improvements.

Remediation Planning

Remediation planning involves developing a strategy to address identified risks effectively, ensuring fixes are implemented without disrupting business operations.

- **Root Cause Analysis**: Identify the underlying cause of the vulnerability, such as misconfigurations, unpatched software, or coding errors, to ensure the issue is resolved comprehensively.
- **Action Plans**: Define specific actions for remediation, such as applying patches, reconfiguring security controls, updating firewall rules, or deploying additional safeguards. For instance, a vulnerable database might require patching, encrypting stored data, and implementing stronger authentication.
- **Ownership Assignment**: Assign responsibility for each remediation action to specific teams or individuals. For example, patch management may fall under the IT operations team, while application vulnerabilities may be addressed by development teams.
- **Prioritized Timelines**: Establish realistic timelines based on the criticality of the issue. For critical vulnerabilities, set immediate remediation deadlines, while low-risk issues can be scheduled during routine maintenance windows.
- **Testing and Validation**: Verify that remediation actions have successfully mitigated the vulnerability. This may involve rescanning systems, conducting penetration tests, or reviewing logs for suspicious activity.

An example of remediation planning is responding to a zero-day vulnerability affecting an enterprise's VPN gateway. The organization may implement compensating controls, such as tightening firewall rules, while the vendor works on an official patch.

Trend Analysis

Trend analysis provides insight into recurring patterns, emerging risks, and the effectiveness of previous remediation efforts by reviewing historical data over time.

- **Recurring Issues**: Identify vulnerabilities or misconfigurations that frequently reappear. For example, repeated findings of weak passwords may indicate the need for stronger password policies or enforcement mechanisms like MFA.
- **Emerging Threats**: Detect trends related to new attack vectors or vulnerabilities. For instance, analyzing scan data may reveal an increase in unpatched IoT devices on the network, signaling the need for targeted remediation.

- **Effectiveness of Controls**: Evaluate whether implemented controls are reducing vulnerabilities and incidents over time. Metrics like the reduction in high-severity findings between consecutive assessments can indicate progress.
- **Incident Trends**: Examine security incidents to identify trends in attack patterns, such as a rise in phishing-related breaches. This analysis can inform adjustments to security awareness programs or technical controls.

For example, a financial institution may review six months of vulnerability scan results to identify that most high-risk findings involve third-party software dependencies. This insight might prompt the organization to implement stricter vendor management practices.

ADVANCED VULNERABILITY SCANNING METHODOLOGIES AND IMPLEMENTATION

Scanning approaches differ based on authentication levels and access permissions. Unauthenticated scans identify externally visible vulnerabilities through network enumeration, service detection, and basic vulnerability checks. Authenticated scanning provides deeper system access, enabling thorough configuration reviews and internal vulnerability assessment.

Authentication Methods:

Local Access:

- System accounts
- Domain credentials
- Service accounts
- Privileged access
- Temporary credentials

Remote Access:

- SSH keys
- API tokens
- Certificate auth
- VPN credentials
- Agent deployment

Configuration Assessment Matrix:

Component	Check Type	Validation Method
OS Settings	Baseline comparison	CIS benchmarks
Services	Running processes	Service configs
Network	Port analysis	Protocol review
Storage	Permission check	Access control
Security	Control validation	Policy compliance

Custom signature development:

Pattern Creation:

- Vulnerability analysis
- Exploit research
- Pattern extraction
- Testing validation
- Documentation

Performance optimization includes:

Scan Windows:

- Off-peak hours
- Maintenance periods
- Load distribution
- Parallel scanning

- Sequential execution

Coverage validation implements:
Verification Methods:

- Asset discovery
- Scope confirmation
- Result validation
- Gap analysis
- Control testing

Tool configurations optimize:

- Thread count
- Timeout settings
- Retry attempts
- Bandwidth limits
- Resource allocation

Scanning frameworks incorporate:

- Policy templates
- Custom checks
- Exception handling
- Result filtering
- Report generation

Organizations manage:

- Scanning schedules
- Credential rotation
- Access controls
- Performance monitoring
- Result analysis

RED TEAM OPERATIONS

Red team operations simulate real-world cyberattacks to assess an organization's detection, response, and resilience against advanced threats. These operations are conducted by skilled adversaries, who replicate tactics, techniques, and procedures (TTPs) of malicious actors. Success requires meticulous planning, alignment with frameworks like MITRE ATT&CK, effective exploitation and post-exploitation activities, and rigorous documentation to provide actionable insights to the organization.

ENGAGEMENT PLANNING

1. **Defining Scope and Rules of Engagement (RoE):**
    - Scope includes systems, networks, and applications to be tested. For example, the scope may cover external-facing assets like web servers or internal corporate networks.
    - Rules of engagement define constraints, such as which techniques are prohibited (e.g., destructive payloads) or specific systems excluded from the test (e.g., production databases).
    - Include clear agreements on acceptable risk levels, communication protocols, and response escalation procedures during testing.
2. **Threat Modeling:**
    - Threat modeling helps identify high-value assets (crown jewels) and likely attack paths. For instance, critical targets in a financial institution may include payment processing systems or customer databases.
    - Tools like threat intelligence feeds and risk assessments provide insight into attacker motivations and likely methods.

3. **Operational Timing:**
    - Define time windows for testing to minimize disruptions. Red team exercises can be conducted during normal business hours for realism or off-hours to reduce impact.
4. **Team Structure:**
    - Assign roles such as operators (offensive specialists), support personnel, and engagement managers. Ensure the blue team (defenders) is unaware of red team operations unless it's a collaborative purple team exercise.

MITRE ATT&CK FRAMEWORK APPLICATION

The MITRE ATT&CK framework provides a comprehensive library of adversary TTPs, categorized into tactics such as Initial Access, Privilege Escalation, and Data Exfiltration.

1. **Initial Access:**
    - Techniques like spear phishing (T1566) or exploiting public-facing applications (T1190) are mapped to gain entry into the target environment.
    - For example, a phishing email containing a malicious Excel macro (T1203) can simulate a common entry vector.
2. **Privilege Escalation:**
    - Red teams use techniques like bypassing User Account Control (T1548.002) or exploiting kernel vulnerabilities to escalate privileges.
    - Mapping these steps ensures coverage of key attack paths and aligns activities with known adversarial behaviors.
3. **Post-Exploitation:**
    - Framework categories like Lateral Movement and Persistence guide operators in testing an organization's ability to detect adversary actions beyond initial compromise.
4. **Customization:**
    - Tailor the framework to match the organization's threat landscape. For instance, industries like healthcare may emphasize techniques used by ransomware operators.

EXPLOITATION TECHNIQUES

1. **Vulnerability Exploitation:**
    - Leverage unpatched vulnerabilities, such as CVEs, to compromise systems. For instance, exploiting a known vulnerability in Apache Log4j (CVE-2021-44228) provides attackers with remote code execution capabilities.
2. **Credential Harvesting:**
    - Techniques include phishing, keylogging, or stealing credentials from memory (e.g., dumping LSASS using Mimikatz).
3. **Custom Payloads:**
    - Red teams develop tailored payloads to bypass endpoint detection and response (EDR) solutions. Payloads are often obfuscated or encrypted to avoid signature-based detection.
4. **Social Engineering:**
    - Techniques such as impersonating IT support to convince employees to share credentials or install malicious software.

POST-EXPLOITATION ACTIVITIES

1. **Lateral Movement:**
    - Tools like PsExec or PowerShell Remoting enable movement across systems. Techniques like Pass-the-Hash (T1550.002) or Kerberoasting (T1558.003) are common for accessing additional resources.
    - Simulate attempts to pivot to high-value targets, such as domain controllers.
2. **Persistence Mechanisms:**
    - Techniques include creating scheduled tasks (T1053) or backdooring startup scripts to maintain access even after detection or remediation.
3. **Data Discovery:**
    - Search for sensitive data, such as files containing customer PII, intellectual property, or internal credentials. File types and directory structures often hint at valuable targets.

4. **Privilege Escalation:**
   - Identify ways to escalate privileges further to access restricted areas. Examples include abusing misconfigured Group Policy Objects or exploiting sudo misconfigurations in Linux environments.

COMMAND AND CONTROL

1. **C2 Channels:**
   - Establish secure command-and-control (C2) communication channels to maintain connectivity with compromised hosts. C2 traffic may use HTTP(S), DNS tunneling, or custom protocols to simulate real-world attacker behavior.
2. **Beaconing:**
   - Implement low-and-slow beaconing techniques to avoid detection. Tools like Cobalt Strike or Sliver can emulate adversary-controlled implants.
3. **Redundancy:**
   - Use multiple C2 servers or fallback mechanisms to maintain resilience during testing. For instance, if the primary C2 server is blocked, a secondary DNS-based channel can maintain access.

DATA EXFILTRATION TESTING

1. **Simulated Exfiltration Techniques:**
   - Use common methods such as transferring data over HTTP(S), SMTP, or FTP. For example, simulate sending sensitive files via email to an external domain.
   - For stealthier testing, exfiltrate data over covert channels like DNS queries (T1071.004) or cloud storage services (e.g., AWS S3 buckets).
2. **Data Types:**
   - Focus on high-value data, such as financial records, employee PII, or system configuration files. Encrypt test files during exfiltration to avoid actual exposure of sensitive information.
3. **Detection Validation:**
   - Test whether security tools flag or block exfiltration attempts. For example, observe if DLP systems detect large outbound transfers.

EVASION TECHNIQUES

1. **Anti-Detection Techniques:**
   - Employ obfuscation methods such as encoding scripts, packing payloads, or altering file headers to evade antivirus solutions.
2. **Log Manipulation:**
   - Delete or alter event logs to hide malicious activity. For example, use PowerShell's Clear-EventLog cmdlet to erase evidence on Windows systems.
3. **Process Injection:**
   - Inject malicious code into legitimate processes, such as explorer.exe, to bypass process-based monitoring.
4. **Living-Off-the-Land (LOTL):**
   - Use built-in tools like PowerShell or WMI for malicious activity, minimizing the use of external tools that may trigger alarms.

DOCUMENTATION REQUIREMENTS

1. **Attack Plan:**
   - Include detailed pre-engagement planning documentation, such as the scope, objectives, TTPs, and tools to be used.
2. **Activity Logs:**
   - Maintain logs of all executed commands, payloads used, and systems accessed. These logs help demonstrate what actions were taken during the operation.
3. **Findings Report:**
   - Document vulnerabilities exploited, attack paths taken, and critical gaps discovered in the environment. Include screenshots, log snippets, and timelines to support findings.
4. **Recommendations:**
   - Provide actionable remediation steps, such as patching vulnerabilities, improving monitoring capabilities, and enforcing least privilege access.

5. **Lessons Learned:**
    - Highlight areas where defenses performed well and areas requiring improvement. These insights inform future defensive strategies and security investment priorities.

BLUE TEAM OPERATIONS

Blue team operations focus on defending an organization's infrastructure by developing proactive security strategies, detecting malicious activity, and responding to incidents. These activities involve continuous monitoring, improving detection capabilities, analyzing logs, hunting threats, and ensuring that defensive tools and procedures are effectively implemented. A strong blue team ensures coordinated efforts to prevent, detect, and mitigate attacks, aligning all activities to the organization's overall security posture.

Defense Strategy Development

Developing a robust defense strategy involves aligning security policies, tools, and processes to protect against the most relevant threats. This requires an understanding of the organization's assets, threat landscape, and business goals.

- **Asset Identification and Classification**: Inventory critical assets, such as sensitive databases, public-facing applications, and endpoints. Classify them based on their value, sensitivity, and exposure to threats.
- **Risk Assessment**: Perform regular risk assessments to identify vulnerabilities, misconfigurations, and high-risk areas. Use frameworks like NIST CSF or ISO 27001 to guide risk prioritization.
- **Layered Security (Defense in Depth)**: Build multiple layers of defense to reduce reliance on any single control. For example, combine perimeter defenses (e.g., firewalls), endpoint protection (e.g., EDR tools), and user awareness training.
- **Adaptive Strategy**: Incorporate threat intelligence and lessons from past incidents to evolve defenses against emerging attack techniques.

For example, a blue team at a financial institution might focus its defense strategy on ransomware prevention by strengthening email filters, deploying backup systems, and implementing network segmentation to limit lateral movement.

Detection Capabilities

Effective detection capabilities are critical for identifying suspicious activity before attackers can achieve their objectives. Detection is achieved by deploying tools, defining triggers, and continuously refining rules to reduce false positives.

- **Endpoint Detection and Response (EDR)**: Use tools like CrowdStrike or Carbon Black to monitor endpoint activity for signs of compromise, such as unauthorized access or execution of suspicious processes.
- **Network Traffic Analysis (NTA)**: Analyze traffic patterns with tools like Zeek or Suricata to identify anomalies such as unexpected data exfiltration or unusual port usage.
- **Behavioral Analytics**: Implement User and Entity Behavior Analytics (UEBA) tools to detect deviations from normal behavior, such as account logins from unusual geolocations or access attempts outside working hours.
- **Threat Intelligence Integration**: Leverage feeds and platforms like MISP or Recorded Future to detect indicators of compromise (IOCs) associated with known threats.

For example, an organization might detect brute force login attempts on its VPN by monitoring authentication logs for repeated failed login attempts originating from the same IP address.

Incident Response Procedures

Incident response (IR) involves a systematic approach to addressing security incidents to minimize damage and prevent recurrence. IR teams rely on predefined playbooks and workflows tailored to specific incident types.

- **Preparation**: Develop and test incident response plans, ensuring all stakeholders understand their roles. Use tabletop exercises to simulate potential attacks, such as ransomware infections or phishing campaigns.
- **Detection and Analysis**: Investigate alerts to determine whether an event constitutes a legitimate incident. This may involve correlating data from logs, SIEMs, and forensic tools.
- **Containment**: Implement measures to stop the attack's progression, such as isolating affected systems, revoking compromised credentials, or blocking malicious IPs.

- **Eradication and Recovery**: Remove the threat from the environment, such as cleaning malware or patching exploited vulnerabilities. Restore operations using clean backups, ensuring that systems are fully secured before reconnecting to the network.
- **Post-Incident Review**: Analyze the root cause, evaluate the effectiveness of the response, and implement changes to prevent similar incidents.

For instance, after containing a phishing-related breach, the blue team might strengthen email filtering, implement additional MFA requirements, and deliver targeted user training.

Threat Hunting

Threat hunting involves proactively searching for signs of malicious activity that may have bypassed automated defenses. It requires expertise, hypothesis-driven investigation, and the ability to correlate disparate data sources.

- **Hypothesis Creation**: Develop hypotheses based on threat intelligence or known adversary tactics. For example, investigate whether advanced attackers are leveraging living-off-the-land techniques like PowerShell scripts for lateral movement.
- **Data Collection**: Collect and analyze data from endpoints, network logs, memory dumps, and cloud environments. Use tools like Sysmon for detailed system telemetry or Zeek for network insights.
- **Behavioral Indicators**: Search for suspicious behaviors, such as unusual persistence mechanisms (e.g., registry modifications or scheduled tasks) or long-running processes consuming high memory.
- **Threat Emulation**: Use red team or adversary emulation exercises to test for potential gaps in detection and defenses.

For example, a threat hunting exercise might reveal unauthorized PowerShell usage on an endpoint, indicating possible malware execution or attacker reconnaissance.

Log Analysis

Log analysis allows teams to identify suspicious activity by reviewing audit logs, security alerts, and system records. This process forms the foundation of detection and forensic investigations.

- **Log Sources**: Aggregate logs from diverse sources, including firewalls, application servers, EDR tools, DNS queries, and cloud management consoles.
- **Correlation**: Use SIEMs or custom tools to correlate log data, identifying patterns that may indicate coordinated attacks. For instance, failed authentication attempts followed by successful access might suggest brute force.
- **Search Queries**: Use advanced search techniques to identify anomalies. For example, in Splunk, a query like index=auth user=* | stats count by user might reveal accounts with unusually high login attempts.
- **Retention and Analysis**: Retain logs for long enough to conduct retrospective investigations, aligning with regulatory or organizational requirements (e.g., GDPR mandates retaining access logs for specific periods).

For example, an analysis of DNS logs might reveal domain name queries to known malicious domains, pointing to possible malware command-and-control (C2) activity.

SIEM Integration

Security Information and Event Management (SIEM) platforms provide centralized visibility and correlation of security events across an organization's infrastructure. Effective SIEM integration involves configuring, optimizing, and tuning the platform to align with the organization's detection and response goals.

- **Data Sources**: Configure the SIEM to collect data from critical sources such as firewalls, intrusion detection systems (IDS), endpoints, cloud services, and directory services.
- **Use Cases and Rules**: Define and implement detection rules for high-priority scenarios, such as privilege escalation attempts, data exfiltration, or unusual network traffic patterns.
- **Alert Management**: Tune alerts to reduce false positives while maintaining sensitivity to legitimate threats. Group related alerts to simplify investigation.
- **Dashboards**: Create visualizations and dashboards for real-time monitoring of key metrics, such as user authentication trends, suspicious IP activity, or system performance anomalies.

For instance, a SIEM might trigger an alert if it detects simultaneous logins to a user account from two geographically distant locations, indicating potential credential compromise.

Tool Effectiveness Evaluation

Regular evaluation of defensive tools ensures they are providing the intended security benefits. Tools must be tested for accuracy, relevance, and performance under real-world conditions.

- **Coverage**: Assess whether tools are protecting all critical assets and systems. For example, ensure EDR tools are deployed on all endpoints, not just workstations.
- **Performance**: Monitor tool efficiency, ensuring minimal impact on system performance. For example, ensure that security scanning tools do not disrupt operations or overload network bandwidth.
- **Accuracy**: Evaluate the tool's detection capabilities by simulating real-world attacks. Use tools like Atomic Red Team or MITRE Caldera to test detection against common adversary tactics.
- **Cost vs. Value**: Ensure that each tool's value aligns with its cost and overlaps with other solutions. For example, evaluate whether overlapping network and endpoint tools can be consolidated.

For example, regular testing of an intrusion prevention system (IPS) can ensure its rules are updated to detect new exploit signatures.

Team Coordination

Coordination between team members and other security functions (e.g., red teams, IT operations) is critical for effective blue team operations.

- **Roles and Responsibilities**: Clearly define roles within the blue team, such as incident responders, threat hunters, and analysts, to avoid gaps or overlaps.
- **Collaboration Tools**: Use platforms like Slack or Microsoft Teams with dedicated incident response channels for rapid communication during incidents.
- **Knowledge Sharing**: Share insights and findings from incidents, threat hunts, or simulations across team members. Maintain a knowledge base of lessons learned and documented playbooks.
- **Cross-Functional Coordination**: Collaborate with other teams, such as red teams, to identify blind spots in defenses, or IT teams to implement remediation actions efficiently.

For instance, during a simulated phishing attack conducted by the red team, the blue team might coordinate with IT operations to block the malicious domain and reset affected users' credentials while simultaneously investigating logs for further indicators of compromise.

PURPLE TEAM SECURITY ASSESSMENT AND COLLABORATION FRAMEWORK

Purple team exercises combine red team attacks with blue team defense through structured collaboration. Team integration enables real-time attack simulation, defense validation, and immediate feedback loops for security control enhancement.

Exercise Structure:

Planning Phase:

- Scope definition
- Target selection
- Tool preparation
- Team assignments
- Timeline development

Execution Phase:

- Attack simulation
- Defense monitoring
- Real-time analysis
- Control adjustment
- Documentation

Knowledge Transfer Matrix:

Activity	Red Team	Blue Team	Outcome
Attack Review	Technique sharing	Detection methods	Coverage gaps
Defense Analysis	Evasion methods	Response procedures	Control updates
Tool Assessment	Attack tools	Defense systems	Integration points

Tool validation examines:
Offensive Tools:

- Exploit effectiveness
- Evasion capabilities
- Detection rates
- Performance impact
- False positive rates

Defensive Systems:

- Detection accuracy
- Response times
- Alert fidelity
- System coverage
- Integration effectiveness

Process improvement focuses:
Attack Workflows:

- Technique selection
- Execution methods
- Documentation quality
- Success rates
- Lessons learned

Defense Procedures:

- Alert handling
- Response actions
- Recovery steps
- Communication flows
- Team coordination

Metrics track:
Performance Indicators:

- Detection rates
- Response times
- Recovery speed
- Control effectiveness
- Team efficiency

Effectiveness Measures:

- Attack success
- Defense coverage
- Gap identification
- Control validation
- Process improvements

Teams implement:

- Joint planning
- Shared toolsets
- Combined analysis
- Unified reporting
- Collaborative review

Organizations maintain:

- Exercise schedules

- Tool inventories
- Process documentation
- Metrics tracking
- Improvement plans

AUDIT PROCESS DEVELOPMENT

Developing an effective audit process requires a structured approach to ensure thoroughness, compliance, and alignment with organizational goals. This involves creating a clear audit charter, defining the scope, allocating resources, establishing timelines, and developing evidence collection and documentation methodologies. Quality assurance and stakeholder communication must also be integrated into the process to ensure transparency and actionable outcomes.

AUDIT CHARTER DEVELOPMENT

1. **Purpose and Objectives:**
    - The audit charter defines the purpose, authority, and responsibilities of the audit function. For example, a charter for an IT audit may include objectives such as evaluating cybersecurity controls, compliance with regulations, and effectiveness of risk management practices.
2. **Governance Structure:**
    - Establish reporting relationships and accountability. For instance, internal auditors may report directly to the Audit Committee to ensure independence.
3. **Authorization of Access:**
    - Clearly state the authority to access records, systems, and personnel. Include provisions for accessing sensitive information, ensuring confidentiality and compliance with legal requirements like GDPR or HIPAA.
4. **Approval and Review:**
    - The charter should be approved by senior management and periodically reviewed to ensure alignment with organizational changes and evolving risks.

SCOPE DEFINITION

1. **Risk-Based Approach:**
    - Focus on high-risk areas based on prior incidents, risk assessments, or regulatory priorities. For instance, a financial audit might emphasize areas prone to fraud, such as accounts payable or procurement.
2. **Operational and Compliance Audits:**
    - Define whether the audit will focus on operational efficiency, regulatory compliance, or both. For example, an operational audit may assess the performance of IT systems, while a compliance audit evaluates adherence to PCI DSS standards.
3. **Inclusion and Exclusion Criteria:**
    - Specify the boundaries of the audit. For instance, an IT audit may exclude systems that are already undergoing a separate compliance review.
4. **Stakeholder Input:**
    - Consult stakeholders to identify critical areas of concern, such as data privacy compliance for legal teams or system uptime for IT departments.

RESOURCE ALLOCATION

1. **Audit Team Composition:**
    - Assign team members based on expertise. For example, a cybersecurity audit may require Certified Information Systems Auditors (CISA), while a financial audit may need Certified Public Accountants (CPA).
2. **Budget Planning:**
    - Allocate budgets for tools, travel, training, and external consultants if required. For instance, a cloud security audit may require specialized tools to analyze configurations in AWS or Azure.

3. **Technology Support:**
   - Identify tools required for the audit, such as audit management software (e.g., AuditBoard or Galvanize), data analytics platforms (e.g., Tableau), or compliance scanning tools (e.g., Nessus).
4. **Third-Party Resources:**
   - If expertise is unavailable internally, engage third-party auditors or consultants. Ensure contracts define clear deliverables and confidentiality agreements.

TIMELINE PLANNING

1. **Milestone Identification:**
   - Break down the audit into phases, such as planning, fieldwork, reporting, and follow-up. For instance, the planning phase may take two weeks, while fieldwork may span four weeks.
2. **Deadlines:**
   - Establish deadlines for each phase. Include buffer time to accommodate unforeseen delays, such as unresponsive stakeholders or additional testing requirements.
3. **Dependencies:**
   - Account for dependencies, such as waiting for system logs, access approvals, or data from third-party vendors.
4. **Critical Events:**
   - Plan audits around critical organizational events. For example, financial audits should be scheduled after year-end reporting to ensure data accuracy.

EVIDENCE COLLECTION METHODS

1. **Interviews:**
   - Conduct interviews with key personnel to understand processes, identify risks, and validate control implementations. For example, speak with system administrators to verify backup procedures.
2. **Document Reviews:**
   - Examine policies, procedures, and records. For instance, review access control policies to ensure they align with least privilege principles.
3. **System Logs and Data:**
   - Collect and analyze system logs for anomalies, such as unauthorized access attempts or unusual traffic patterns. Use tools like Splunk or ELK for log analysis.
4. **Observations:**
   - Observe operations in real-time to verify compliance. For example, during a physical security audit, observe if visitors are properly logged and escorted.
5. **Sampling Techniques:**
   - Use statistical sampling to select records for testing, such as randomly reviewing 10% of transactions for fraud indicators.
6. **Testing Controls:**
   - Perform control testing, such as attempting to bypass user authentication mechanisms or simulating a phishing attack to evaluate email filtering effectiveness.

DOCUMENTATION STANDARDS

1. **Standardized Templates:**
   - Use templates for audit plans, checklists, workpapers, and reports. This ensures consistency and reduces the risk of missing key information.
2. **Traceability:**
   - Maintain clear links between audit objectives, evidence collected, and findings. For example, a finding related to weak password policies should reference the specific control tested and evidence obtained.
3. **Version Control:**
   - Use document management systems to track revisions and maintain an audit trail.
4. **Retention Policies:**
   - Define how long audit documentation will be retained, such as retaining financial audit records for seven years to meet legal requirements.

QUALITY ASSURANCE

1. **Peer Review:**
   - Conduct peer reviews to validate findings and ensure that evidence supports conclusions. For example, an IT audit's findings on firewall misconfigurations should be reviewed by another cybersecurity specialist.
2. **Internal Audit Standards:**
   - Follow established standards, such as those from the Institute of Internal Auditors (IIA) or ISACA, to ensure high-quality audits.
3. **Continuous Improvement:**
   - After each audit, collect feedback to identify areas for improvement. For instance, auditors may suggest refining scope definition processes to better target high-risk areas.
4. **Error Correction:**
   - Address discrepancies or errors in audit reports through formalized review procedures.

STAKEHOLDER COMMUNICATION

1. **Pre-Audit Communication:**
   - Notify stakeholders about the audit objectives, scope, and schedule in advance. Provide clear instructions for providing access to systems, personnel, and data.
2. **Status Updates:**
   - Share progress updates during the audit, especially for long engagements. For instance, weekly meetings with the IT team may address pending evidence requests or clarify processes.
3. **Exit Meeting:**
   - Present preliminary findings to stakeholders, allowing them to provide additional context or dispute incorrect assumptions.
4. **Final Reporting:**
   - Deliver comprehensive reports that include findings, evidence, risk assessments, and recommendations. Tailor the content for different audiences; for example, provide high-level summaries for executives and technical details for IT teams.
5. **Follow-Up:**
   - Establish a timeline for addressing findings and schedule follow-up audits to verify corrective actions. Share updates with stakeholders to maintain accountability.

EVIDENCE MANAGEMENT

Effective evidence management ensures the integrity, security, and admissibility of data during and after investigations. This process encompasses maintaining a clear chain of custody, proper evidence storage, adherence to legal and organizational requirements, and thorough documentation. Secure handling and storage procedures prevent evidence tampering or loss, while compliance with legal and regulatory standards ensures admissibility in court or during audits.

Chain of Custody

The chain of custody is the documented and unbroken record of how evidence is collected, handled, transferred, stored, and eventually disposed of. Maintaining this chain ensures evidence integrity and credibility.

- **Documentation**: Record every individual who handles the evidence, the date and time of transfer, the purpose of handling, and the location where it is stored. For example, a chain of custody log may document the forensic investigator collecting a hard drive, transferring it to an evidence storage facility, and later delivering it to legal counsel.
- **Tamper Evident**: Use tamper-evident packaging, such as seals, tags, or secure containers, to detect unauthorized access.
- **Transfer Protocols**: Minimize the number of handoffs and ensure that each transfer is documented and acknowledged by both the sender and the recipient.
- **Automation**: Use digital chain of custody systems to automate tracking, reducing human error and maintaining a comprehensive record.

For example, during a cyber forensic investigation, a USB drive containing malware evidence must have its collection, analysis, and storage steps fully documented, ensuring that no unauthorized person accessed or altered the contents.

Evidence Storage

Proper storage of evidence prevents unauthorized access, environmental damage, and contamination. Both physical and digital evidence require secure and controlled environments.

- **Physical Evidence**: Store physical items (e.g., hard drives, devices) in locked evidence rooms or cabinets with restricted access. Environmental controls such as temperature regulation and anti-static packaging prevent degradation of hardware.
- **Digital Evidence**: Secure digital evidence using encrypted storage solutions with redundant backups. Store evidence on write-protected media or in read-only formats to preserve the original data.
- **Inventory Management**: Maintain a clear inventory of stored evidence with unique identifiers, such as barcodes or serial numbers, to track each item's location.
- **Access Logging**: Log every access to the storage location, whether physical (e.g., keycard access logs) or digital (e.g., file access logs), to ensure accountability.

For instance, digital evidence collected from a compromised server might be stored on an encrypted external drive and kept in a fireproof safe with access granted only to authorized personnel.

Data Classification

Data classification ensures that evidence is handled according to its sensitivity, value, and regulatory requirements.

- **Classification Categories**: Classify evidence as confidential, restricted, public, or sensitive based on its potential impact if exposed. For example, personal information collected during an investigation may be classified as highly sensitive due to privacy regulations.
- **Handling Protocols**: Develop specific handling protocols for each classification level. Highly classified evidence may require encryption, additional logging, or physical transport under armed escort.
- **Tagging and Labeling**: Clearly label evidence with classification tags to guide handling. For example, an email archive flagged as confidential should include a tag indicating that it contains personally identifiable information (PII).

For example, evidence containing medical data would require HIPAA-compliant handling processes, including encryption in storage and restricted access.

Access Controls

Access controls protect evidence from unauthorized access or tampering, ensuring only authorized personnel can retrieve or handle it.

- **Role-Based Access**: Grant access based on roles and responsibilities. For example, forensic analysts may require read-only access to evidence, while investigators may need full access to conduct analyses.
- **Multi-Factor Authentication (MFA)**: Implement MFA for accessing digital evidence storage systems, adding an extra layer of security beyond usernames and passwords.
- **Physical Access Restrictions**: Use measures like biometric scanners, keycard systems, or pin-protected safes to secure physical storage locations.
- **Logging**: Record all access attempts, whether successful or unsuccessful, to detect potential unauthorized access or anomalies.

For example, a forensic analysis team may store case evidence in a network folder protected by RBAC and MFA, ensuring only assigned team members can access it.

Retention Requirements

Retention policies specify how long evidence must be stored to comply with organizational, legal, or regulatory obligations. These policies vary based on the type of evidence and applicable laws.

- **Legal Requirements**: Comply with jurisdictional mandates. For example, certain laws may require retaining evidence related to financial crimes for seven years.
- **Case-Specific Retention**: Retain evidence until the conclusion of legal proceedings or investigations, plus any additional time required by organizational policy.
- **Archival Solutions**: Use archival systems designed for long-term storage, such as WORM (write once, read many) media, to ensure evidence cannot be altered or deleted during retention.

- **Destruction Policies**: Define clear retention expiration dates and follow standardized processes for securely disposing of evidence once retention requirements are met.

For instance, evidence collected during a GDPR-related investigation must be securely deleted after the retention period to comply with data minimization principles.

Disposal Procedures

Securely disposing of evidence once it is no longer needed ensures that sensitive data cannot be recovered or misused.

- **Digital Evidence**: Use data sanitization tools that comply with standards such as NIST SP 800-88 (Guidelines for Media Sanitization) to overwrite or destroy data. Shredding or physically destroying storage media may also be required.
- **Physical Evidence**: Physically destroy hardware using industrial shredders, incinerators, or degaussing devices to render it inoperable and unreadable.
- **Documentation**: Maintain disposal logs that record what was disposed of, the method used, and the individuals involved in the process. Include certificates of destruction when using third-party disposal services.

For example, at the end of a cybercrime investigation, old storage devices containing evidence may be shredded and incinerated to ensure complete destruction.

Legal Considerations

Legal considerations guide evidence handling to ensure it remains admissible in court and complies with relevant laws and regulations.

- **Admissibility**: Preserve evidence in its original form to ensure it is admissible. Courts often require a clear chain of custody and proof that the evidence was not tampered with.
- **Jurisdictional Requirements**: Follow local and international laws governing evidence handling, such as GDPR in Europe or the Federal Rules of Evidence in the U.S.
- **Privacy Protections**: Protect sensitive information during investigations to comply with laws like HIPAA, GDPR, or CCPA. For instance, redact personal information when sharing evidence outside authorized entities.
- **Third-Party Access**: Ensure appropriate non-disclosure agreements (NDAs) are in place when third parties (e.g., forensic consultants or legal teams) handle evidence.

For example, evidence collected during an investigation into financial fraud must comply with both local data protection laws and financial regulatory requirements to remain admissible in court.

Documentation Standards

Comprehensive documentation is critical for tracking evidence throughout its lifecycle and demonstrating compliance with policies and regulations.

- **Collection Reports**: Document how, when, and where evidence was collected, including details about the tools and methods used.
- **Storage Logs**: Maintain records of where evidence is stored, who has accessed it, and any modifications made.
- **Analysis Records**: Record all forensic analysis processes and results, ensuring repeatability and transparency.
- **Chain of Custody Logs**: Include timestamps, signatures, and reasons for transfers, ensuring every action taken with the evidence is accounted for.

For instance, during a digital forensics investigation, the team may use standardized templates to document evidence collection (e.g., photographing the crime scene, logging the device serial numbers) and ensure that all actions are traceable.

STATIC CODE ANALYSIS AND SECURITY TESTING FRAMEWORK

Static analysis tools examine source code for security vulnerabilities and quality issues without execution. Tool configuration establishes scanning parameters, rule sets, and analysis depth based on programming languages and frameworks.

Tool Configuration Matrix:
Scanner Settings:
- Language support
- Framework plugins
- Custom rules
- Scan depth
- Performance limits

Rule Implementation:

Category	Check Type	Severity	Examples
Security	Input validation	High	SQL injection
Quality	Code complexity	Medium	Cyclomatic metrics
Style	Format standards	Low	Naming conventions
Performance	Resource usage	Medium	Memory leaks

False positive management includes:
Filtering Process:

- Result review
- Pattern analysis
- Context evaluation
- Rule adjustment
- Baseline updates

CI/CD integration implements:
Pipeline Steps:

- Pre-commit hooks
- Build scanning
- Result analysis
- Status reporting
- Gate enforcement

Code metrics measure:
Quality Indicators:

- Complexity scores
- Duplication rates
- Test coverage
- Documentation level
- Maintainability index

Security standards enforce:
Coding Requirements:

- Input sanitization
- Output encoding
- Authentication checks
- Authorization controls
- Error handling

Compliance validation examines:
Standard Requirements:

- PCI DSS
- HIPAA
- SOX
- GDPR

- Industry standards

Results prioritization considers:

Risk Factors:

- Vulnerability severity
- Exposure level
- Exploit likelihood
- Business impact
- Remediation effort

Teams implement:

- Scan scheduling
- Result analysis
- Issue tracking
- Fix verification
- Progress monitoring

Organizations maintain:

- Tool configurations
- Rule repositories
- Exception lists
- Metrics dashboards
- Improvement plans

DYNAMIC ANALYSIS

Dynamic analysis involves testing and evaluating software, systems, or applications during runtime to assess their behavior, identify vulnerabilities, validate security controls, and measure performance. Unlike static analysis, which evaluates code without execution, dynamic analysis observes systems in real-world execution contexts. Effective implementation of dynamic analysis requires careful setup of environments, management of test data, and correlation of results to derive actionable insights.

RUNTIME TESTING

1. **Execution Monitoring:**
    - Assess applications during runtime to identify unexpected behaviors, crashes, memory leaks, or misconfigurations. For instance, runtime testing of a web application may involve simulating user interactions like login attempts, data submissions, and session navigation.
2. **Dynamic Application Security Testing (DAST):**
    - Tools like Burp Suite or OWASP ZAP test for vulnerabilities in running applications by simulating attacks, such as injection (SQL or command), cross-site scripting (XSS), and authentication bypass.
    - DAST can uncover issues that static code analysis might miss, such as vulnerabilities introduced by runtime dependencies or configurations.
3. **Error and Exception Handling Validation:**
    - Test how the system responds to invalid inputs or edge cases. For example, observe whether the application exposes stack traces or other sensitive information when errors occur.

BEHAVIORAL ANALYSIS

1. **Behavioral Profiling:**
    - Examine how the system behaves under specific conditions, such as increased user load or unusual input. Behavioral analysis can identify malicious patterns or unintended system responses.
2. **Malware Dynamic Analysis:**
    - Analyze suspicious executables or files in a sandbox environment. Tools like Cuckoo Sandbox and Any.Run monitor malware behavior, such as network connections, file creation, and process manipulation, to understand its capabilities and intent.

3. **Indicators of Compromise (IOCs):**
    - Detect behavioral signs that indicate security risks, such as outbound communication to known malicious IPs, file changes in protected directories, or suspicious memory usage.
4. **Automated Behavior Logging:**
    - Use runtime monitoring tools to log system calls, API interactions, and changes in system state. For example, strace on Linux or Procmon on Windows captures low-level system behaviors for deeper analysis.

PERFORMANCE IMPACT

1. **Load and Stress Testing:**
    - Assess application performance under normal and peak loads to determine scalability and stability. For example, simulate 10,000 concurrent users on a web application to evaluate response times and system resource usage.
    - Identify bottlenecks in processing, database queries, or I/O operations.
2. **Resource Utilization Monitoring:**
    - Monitor CPU, memory, disk, and network usage during dynamic testing to identify performance hotspots. Tools like JMeter or Apache Bench evaluate resource impact under various test conditions.
3. **Impact of Security Features:**
    - Measure the performance trade-offs introduced by security controls, such as encryption, logging, or access validation mechanisms. For example, determine if enabling HTTPS significantly increases response times in a web application.
4. **Baseline Establishment:**
    - Compare results with established baselines to measure deviations caused by updates, new configurations, or external factors.

SECURITY CONTROL VALIDATION

1. **Real-World Attack Simulation:**
    - Validate security mechanisms by simulating real-world attacks. For instance, test if an application properly enforces authentication when accessing restricted resources or handles invalid credentials securely.
2. **Access Control Testing:**
    - Validate that users cannot exceed their privileges, such as accessing administrative functions with non-administrative accounts. This may involve testing role-based access controls and session management mechanisms.
3. **Encryption Validation:**
    - Test cryptographic controls to ensure data is encrypted during transmission (e.g., TLS configuration testing) and storage (e.g., disk encryption validation). Tools like SSL Labs test the strength and configuration of encryption protocols.
4. **Logging and Alerting Validation:**
    - Confirm that security events, such as failed logins or unauthorized access attempts, are logged and generate alerts. SIEM systems should flag anomalies in test environments as they occur.

INTEGRATION TESTING

1. **System Compatibility:**
    - Test how the application interacts with other systems, APIs, or databases during runtime. Integration testing ensures smooth communication and error-free data exchange between components.
2. **Inter-System Dependencies:**
    - Evaluate whether dependent services, such as third-party APIs or authentication servers, respond as expected. For example, simulate failure conditions like an unavailable API endpoint and observe the application's response.

3. **Cross-Platform Testing:**
   - Validate application behavior across different operating systems, browsers, or devices. For example, test a mobile app's functionality on Android and iOS platforms to confirm consistent behavior.
4. **Third-Party Component Testing:**
   - Test third-party libraries or plug-ins integrated into the application to ensure they function correctly and securely during runtime.

ENVIRONMENT SETUP

1. **Isolated Test Environment:**
   - Create a controlled, isolated environment (e.g., virtual machines, containers, or sandboxes) to conduct testing without impacting production systems. For example, set up a staging environment that mirrors the production environment.
2. **Replica Data and Configurations:**
   - Ensure the test environment replicates the production configuration, including network settings, database connections, and authentication mechanisms. Misaligned environments may lead to false test results.
3. **Network Traffic Capture:**
   - Deploy network monitoring tools, such as Wireshark or tcpdump, to capture traffic for analysis. This helps identify vulnerabilities like plaintext credentials or unauthorized data exfiltration attempts.
4. **Scalability Testing in Cloud Environments:**
   - Use scalable cloud resources for performance and stress testing. For instance, deploy a test application in AWS or Azure with auto-scaling enabled to evaluate how well it handles fluctuating demand.

TEST DATA MANAGEMENT

1. **Synthetic Data Generation:**
   - Use tools like Mockaroo or Faker to generate realistic but non-sensitive test data, such as randomized names, addresses, and account numbers. This prevents the use of real production data, reducing privacy risks.
2. **Data Masking:**
   - Mask sensitive fields, such as customer PII, in production data before importing it into test environments. Masked data ensures compliance with regulations like GDPR or CCPA.
3. **Database Rollbacks:**
   - Ensure test environments support database rollbacks after tests to maintain consistency and prevent data corruption.
4. **Edge Case Testing:**
   - Design test cases to validate application behavior under edge conditions, such as null values, empty inputs, or extremely large datasets.

RESULTS CORRELATION

1. **Cross-Tool Analysis:**
   - Correlate results from multiple tools to build a comprehensive view of system behavior. For instance, compare results from a DAST tool (e.g., Burp Suite) with logs from a runtime monitoring tool (e.g., ELK stack).
2. **Anomaly Identification:**
   - Analyze deviations in behavior during runtime testing to identify vulnerabilities or performance bottlenecks. For example, unusual spikes in memory usage during a specific workflow may indicate a memory leak.
3. **Trend Analysis:**
   - Compare current test results with historical data to identify regressions, such as degraded performance or newly introduced vulnerabilities.

4. **Prioritization of Findings:**
   - Categorize findings based on severity, likelihood, and impact. For instance, a SQL injection vulnerability (critical severity) should take precedence over a minor CSS rendering issue.
5. **Visualization:**
   - Use dashboards and visualization tools, such as Kibana or Grafana, to present correlated results and trends for easier interpretation by stakeholders.

Dynamic analysis delivers actionable insights by revealing vulnerabilities, performance issues, and misconfigurations under runtime conditions. It combines behavioral evaluation, security validation, and performance monitoring to provide a comprehensive understanding of system resilience and functionality.

CASE STUDY TOPICS

Examining case studies across various cybersecurity and IT disciplines provides insights into real-world challenges, strategies, and solutions. Topics like enterprise vulnerability assessments, red team engagements, and testing automation projects illustrate how to approach complex problems and implement effective security controls. By analyzing these scenarios, practitioners can understand decision-making processes, risks, and outcomes.

Enterprise Vulnerability Assessment

A healthcare organization with a hybrid infrastructure—including on-premises servers, cloud services, and medical IoT devices—faces increased cyber threats due to industry-targeted ransomware campaigns. The organization initiates a comprehensive enterprise vulnerability assessment to identify weaknesses across its environment.

- **Scope Definition**: The assessment focuses on critical assets, including electronic health record (EHR) systems, network infrastructure, IoT-connected medical devices, and third-party cloud storage.
- **Tool Selection**: The organization employs vulnerability scanners like Nessus for network devices, Qualys for cloud assets, and specialized tools for IoT systems. It also leverages manual assessments for high-value systems.
- **Findings**: The scan reveals several vulnerabilities:
  - Unpatched software on IoT devices.
  - Misconfigured S3 buckets with public access enabled.
  - High-risk CVEs affecting an unpatched on-premises database server.
  - Excessive user permissions across critical applications.
- **Action Plan**:
  - Implement an IoT device management solution to apply firmware updates and monitor device behavior.
  - Reconfigure S3 buckets to enforce least privilege access and enable logging for compliance purposes.
  - Patch the database server and implement an automated patch management process.
  - Perform a permissions audit to align access with the principle of least privilege.

This assessment highlights the importance of addressing vulnerabilities specific to unique environments, such as IoT devices and cloud resources.

Red Team Engagement

A financial services firm contracts a red team to simulate an advanced persistent threat (APT) attack targeting its internal network and customer data. The engagement aims to test the organization's defenses, identify gaps, and measure incident response readiness.

- **Scenario Design**: The red team creates a scenario where attackers attempt to compromise customer data by gaining access to the firm's customer relationship management (CRM) system.
  - **Initial Access**: The red team simulates a phishing attack with a malicious payload, targeting employees in the HR department.
  - **Lateral Movement**: Once inside the network, they escalate privileges and use tools like Mimikatz to obtain credentials.
  - **Data Exfiltration**: They simulate the exfiltration of customer data by transferring it over an encrypted channel to mimic real-world techniques.

- **Key Observations**:
  - The phishing email bypasses email filtering due to insufficient keyword and attachment scanning.
  - The blue team detects lateral movement too late, only after significant access is gained.
  - Weak segmentation between corporate and CRM networks allows unrestricted access to the CRM system.
- **Recommendations**:
  - Enhance phishing defenses with advanced email filtering, user training, and MFA enforcement for email access.
  - Strengthen network segmentation and implement monitoring on high-value systems like the CRM.
  - Deploy real-time detection tools like EDR or NDR to identify suspicious behavior earlier in the attack chain.

The red team's findings enable the organization to fortify its defenses against targeted attacks and refine its incident response processes.

Audit Finding Remediation

An internal audit of a manufacturing company's IT systems reveals multiple compliance violations and gaps in its cybersecurity program. The audit focuses on adherence to ISO 27001 and local data protection laws.

- **Findings**:
  - Lack of a formal incident response plan.
  - Absence of encryption on laptops storing sensitive customer data.
  - Inadequate logging and monitoring of administrative account activity.
  - Noncompliance with data retention policies for customer records.
- **Remediation Efforts**:
  - **Incident Response**: The company develops an incident response plan, conducts tabletop exercises, and trains employees on their roles during incidents.
  - **Encryption**: Deploys full-disk encryption on all employee laptops using BitLocker and enables policies for encryption enforcement.
  - **Logging and Monitoring**: Implements centralized log management with Splunk to monitor administrative actions and configure alerts for anomalous behavior.
  - **Data Retention**: Automates data deletion processes based on retention policies, ensuring compliance with both ISO 27001 and GDPR.
- **Outcome**: The company passes its follow-up audit and improves its cybersecurity posture by addressing the gaps.

This case highlights the importance of integrating audit remediation with security and compliance objectives to achieve measurable improvements.

Code Review Implementation

A software development company discovers several security vulnerabilities, such as injection flaws and authentication bypasses, in production applications. In response, it implements a formal code review process to improve software security.

- **Goals**:
  - Detect and mitigate security flaws during development.
  - Ensure compliance with secure coding standards, such as OWASP Top 10 and CIS benchmarks.
  - Integrate code review into the CI/CD pipeline.
- **Process**:
  - **Automated Code Scanning**: Tools like SonarQube and Checkmarx are integrated into the pipeline to automatically identify coding issues in pull requests.
  - **Manual Reviews**: Peer reviews focus on sensitive application components, such as authentication logic and database queries.
  - **Developer Training**: Developers receive training on secure coding practices, including how to avoid common issues like SQL injection and insecure deserialization.

- **Results**:
  - The number of security bugs detected post-deployment drops significantly.
  - Development teams improve their awareness of secure coding, reducing the recurrence of vulnerabilities.

By integrating automated tools and manual reviews, the company ensures that security becomes an integral part of its software development lifecycle.

Purple Team Exercise

A retail company conducts a purple team exercise to improve collaboration between its red and blue teams and strengthen defenses against credential theft attacks. The exercise simulates an attacker leveraging compromised credentials to access sensitive customer data.

- **Red Team Role**:
  - Exploits weak password policies to gain initial access through brute force.
  - Uses tools like BloodHound to map Active Directory and escalate privileges.
  - Simulates data exfiltration through a compromised account.
- **Blue Team Role**:
  - Monitors alerts from the SIEM and EDR systems to detect suspicious login attempts.
  - Deploys threat-hunting techniques to identify the red team's lateral movement paths.
  - Tests containment strategies, such as disabling compromised accounts and applying network segmentation.
- **Outcome**:
  - The red team successfully identifies and exploits several gaps, including the use of shared passwords and insufficient monitoring of lateral movement.
  - The blue team improves its detection rules for unusual authentication activity and strengthens the response playbook for compromised credentials.

The purple team exercise fosters knowledge-sharing and results in actionable changes to prevent real-world credential theft attacks.

Testing Automation Project

An e-commerce company faces challenges with scaling manual testing efforts for its growing product portfolio. To streamline testing and improve security coverage, the company launches a testing automation project.

- **Objectives**:
  - Automate functional and security testing for web applications, APIs, and mobile apps.
  - Ensure compliance with PCI DSS requirements by integrating automated scans for payment-related components.
- **Implementation**:
  - **Tool Selection**: Choose tools like Selenium for functional testing, OWASP ZAP for security scanning, and Postman for API testing.
  - **CI/CD Integration**: Configure the automation suite to run tests during every build and deployment cycle, with results fed into a centralized dashboard.
  - **Custom Scripts**: Develop scripts for edge cases, such as testing rate-limiting mechanisms or handling unexpected inputs.
- **Results**:
  - The automated suite identifies regressions and vulnerabilities earlier in the development process, reducing time-to-remediation.
  - Manual testers focus on exploratory testing and complex scenarios, improving overall quality assurance efforts.

The project demonstrates how automation enhances efficiency, improves security, and reduces costs in fast-paced development environments.

SECURITY ASSESSMENT AND AUDIT PRACTICE SCENARIOS

Sample Question

1: During a web application security assessment, the scanning tool reports SQL injection vulnerabilities with varying severity levels. Which factors should the security team consider when prioritizing remediation?

A. Number of affected endpoints, authentication requirements, data sensitivity, exploit complexity

B. Development team size, server location, network topology, application version

C. User interface design, database vendor, operating system type, backup schedule

D. Application language, development framework, server hardware, network bandwidth

Correct Answer: A Analysis: Remediation prioritization examines risk impact, exploit potential, and data exposure. Authentication boundaries and endpoint exposure directly affect vulnerability exploitation likelihood.

Sample Question 2:

Phase	**Evidence Type**	**Retention**	**Access**
Planning	Scope docs	1 year	Team
Testing	Raw results	3 years	Limited
Reports	Final analysis	7 years	Restricted

Which audit evidence handling practice violates standard requirements?

A. Storing raw results for 3 years

B. Team access to scope documents

C. Limited access to testing data

D. Restricted report distribution

Correct Answer: A Explanation: Raw testing data should maintain the same retention period as final reports for audit trail completeness and investigation support.

Sample Question 3: A security team implements automated vulnerability scanning. Which configuration ensures optimal coverage while minimizing business impact?

Scanner Settings:

1. Scan window: 2200-0400
2. Bandwidth limit: 100Mbps
3. Authentication: Local accounts
4. Target segments: Production

A. Configuration achieves balance

B. Bandwidth limit too restrictive

C. Authentication insufficient

D. Scan window too broad

Correct Answer: C Analysis: Local account usage limits scan depth. Implementation should use domain credentials with appropriate privileges for comprehensive assessment.

Additional Testing Areas:

Methodology Selection:

- Risk-based approach
- Resource availability
- Technical requirements
- Business constraints
- Regulatory needs

Tool Configuration:

- Performance tuning
- Credential management
- Exception handling
- Alert thresholds
- Reporting formats

Team Coordination:

- Role assignments
- Communication plans
- Escalation procedures
- Status reporting
- Review meetings

Compliance Validation:

- Control mapping
- Evidence collection
- Documentation requirements
- Finding classification
- Remediation tracking

Security Operations

INCIDENT RESPONSE STRUCTURE AND OPERATIONAL FRAMEWORK

Incident response plans establish structured approaches for handling security events through defined teams, processes, and procedures. The response framework builds on team organization, clear communication channels, and documented escalation paths.

Response Team Structure:

Leadership:

- Incident Commander
- Technical Lead
- Communications Lead
- Legal Advisor
- Executive Sponsor

Operations:

- Security Analysts
- System Administrators
- Network Engineers
- Forensics Specialists
- Business Liaisons

Communication Protocols Matrix:

Level	Recipients	Method	Timing
Initial	First responders	Alert system	Immediate
Tactical	Technical teams	Secure chat	< 15 min
Management	Leadership	Phone/Email	< 30 min
Executive	C-suite/Board	Briefing	< 1 hour

Detection mechanisms implement:

Alert Correlation:

- Log aggregation
- Pattern matching
- Threshold monitoring
- Behavioral analysis
- Anomaly detection

Indicator Analysis:

- IOC processing
- Threat intelligence
- Historical comparison
- Risk assessment
- Impact evaluation

Incident Classification Criteria:

- Data impact
- System compromise
- Service disruption
- Regulatory exposure
- Reputation risk

Response Priority Framework:

Priority 1:

- Active breaches

- Data exfiltration
- System compromise
- Service outages
- Regulatory violations

Priority 2:

- Attempted intrusions
- Suspicious activity
- Policy violations
- System anomalies
- Performance issues

Legal Considerations:

- Evidence preservation
- Chain of custody
- Notification requirements
- Regulatory compliance
- Investigation support

Organizations maintain:

- Response procedures
- Communication plans
- Documentation standards
- Training programs
- Review processes

INCIDENT HANDLING DEEP DIVE

Effective incident handling ensures security events are managed with minimal disruption to business operations while mitigating damage, preserving evidence, and improving future response capabilities. This process involves containment, eradication, recovery, and post-incident activities, each with specific techniques tailored to the nature and scope of the incident.

CONTAINMENT STRATEGIES

Containment limits the scope of an incident, prevents further damage, and isolates affected systems while maintaining the integrity of evidence for later analysis.

1. **Short-Term Containment:**
   - Immediate actions are taken to stop the incident from spreading or escalating. Examples include disconnecting compromised systems from the network, blocking malicious IP addresses, or disabling user accounts suspected of being compromised.
   - Use firewall rules or intrusion prevention systems (IPS) to block malicious traffic in real time. For instance, if ransomware is detected, block the command-and-control (C2) servers used by the malware to prevent further encryption of files.
   - Quarantine infected devices while ensuring critical business processes remain operational.
2. **Long-Term Containment:**
   - Stabilize the environment to support investigative efforts and remediation. This may involve applying temporary patches, deploying virtual LAN (VLAN) isolation for affected segments, or redirecting traffic through a sandboxed environment for monitoring.
   - For example, if a database server is compromised, implement long-term containment by migrating essential services to a backup server while forensic analysis is conducted on the original system.
   - Use segmented backups to isolate clean data from potentially compromised systems, ensuring the integrity of recovery resources.
3. **Evidence Preservation:**

- Maintain the chain of custody for all collected evidence to support legal or forensic investigations. Evidence includes system logs, volatile memory (RAM) snapshots, disk images, and network packet captures.
- Use tools like FTK Imager or EnCase to create forensic disk images, ensuring no data is altered during the acquisition process.
- Avoid making unnecessary changes to compromised systems to preserve volatile data such as running processes, network connections, and active memory.

ERADICATION PROCEDURES

Eradication focuses on eliminating the root cause of the incident and preventing its recurrence.

1. **Root Cause Analysis:**
    - Identify the origin of the compromise by analyzing forensic evidence, log files, and attack indicators.
    - Tools like SIEM platforms (e.g., Splunk or QRadar) and threat intelligence feeds help correlate events and detect attack vectors. For example, analyze how attackers exploited a vulnerability in an unpatched application to gain access.
2. **Malware Removal:**
    - Use endpoint detection and response (EDR) tools like CrowdStrike or Carbon Black to detect and remove malware from affected systems.
    - If malware persists or evades detection, perform a full system wipe and reinstallation to ensure complete eradication.
    - Scan connected systems to identify lateral movement or secondary infections, ensuring all instances of the malware are removed.
3. **System Hardening:**
    - Address vulnerabilities exploited during the incident by applying patches, reconfiguring settings, or disabling unused services. For example, if attackers exploited weak SSH passwords, enforce strong password policies, and enable two-factor authentication.
    - Conduct penetration testing to verify that remediated vulnerabilities are no longer exploitable.

RECOVERY PROCESSES

Recovery restores systems, data, and services to normal operation while verifying that the environment is secure and functional.

1. **System Restoration:**
    - Rebuild affected systems using clean backups or images. Ensure restored systems are up-to-date with patches and security configurations before reconnecting them to the production environment.
    - Validate that all critical services, such as web servers, databases, and file shares, are functional after restoration.
2. **Data Recovery:**
    - Recover lost or corrupted data from secure backups. Use backup integrity checks to ensure restored files are complete and unmodified. For example, test the recovery of financial transaction data from the previous week to ensure consistency.
    - If backups are unavailable or incomplete, data recovery tools like Recuva or R-Studio may be used to retrieve lost files from affected systems.
3. **Service Validation:**
    - Test systems under typical workloads to ensure performance and functionality have been fully restored. For instance, verify that a database server can handle queries and updates as expected.
    - Perform security scans and vulnerability assessments to confirm that the environment is free of malicious artifacts and misconfigurations.

POST-INCIDENT ACTIVITIES

Post-incident activities focus on learning from the event to improve future response efforts and prevent similar incidents.

1. **Lessons Learned:**
   - Conduct a post-incident review to analyze the incident timeline, identify gaps in detection or response, and evaluate decision-making during the event.
   - Gather input from all involved teams, including IT, security, management, and any third-party vendors, to ensure a comprehensive understanding of the incident.
   - Create a detailed incident timeline, noting key events, decisions, and actions taken.
2. **Process Improvement:**
   - Identify areas for improvement in existing policies, procedures, and controls. For example, if phishing emails bypassed spam filters, enhance email security configurations and user training programs.
   - Develop playbooks for similar incidents, outlining response steps for specific scenarios like ransomware attacks, insider threats, or data breaches.
3. **Documentation Updates:**
   - Update incident response plans (IRPs), playbooks, and other documentation to incorporate lessons learned. Ensure these updates reflect new tools, techniques, or procedures implemented during or after the incident.
   - For example, if the incident highlighted delays due to incomplete contact information for stakeholders, update contact lists and escalation matrices in the IRP.
   - Document and store all evidence, findings, and recommendations securely for future reference or regulatory compliance.

Dynamic and continuous improvement of the incident handling process ensures that the organization is better prepared for future security events and reduces the likelihood of repeated compromises.

SIEM IMPLEMENTATION

Implementing a Security Information and Event Management (SIEM) system involves designing a scalable architecture, integrating log sources, developing actionable use cases, and ensuring compliance with organizational and regulatory standards. Proper tuning, correlation, and storage management are critical to optimizing performance and reducing false positives, enabling organizations to identify and respond to threats effectively.

Architecture Design

SIEM architecture design starts with identifying the infrastructure's scale, security requirements, and operational goals. The architecture must account for data ingestion, processing, analysis, and storage while ensuring high availability and performance.

- **Deployment Models**: Choose between on-premises, cloud-based, or hybrid SIEM solutions. For instance:
  - On-premises solutions like Splunk or QRadar are ideal for environments requiring tight control over data storage and processing.
  - Cloud-based SIEMs, such as Azure Sentinel or Sumo Logic, simplify scaling and maintenance.
- **Components**: A typical SIEM architecture includes:
  - **Data Collectors/Forwarders**: Agents or appliances deployed across endpoints, servers, and network devices to collect and forward logs.
  - **Ingestion Layer**: Processes raw logs, applies parsing rules, and normalizes data into a unified format.
  - **Processing Engine**: Analyzes events, applies correlation rules, and generates alerts.
  - **Storage**: Handles both short-term (hot) and long-term (cold) storage for raw logs and analyzed data.
  - **Dashboard and Reporting Interface**: Provides real-time monitoring, visualization, and reporting for analysts.
- **Scalability**: Design for scalability by considering data volume, growth rate, and peak event loads. Use clustering, distributed architectures, or horizontal scaling to handle increasing demands.
- **Network Placement**: Ensure log collectors and SIEM components are strategically placed to capture all relevant traffic without overloading network segments. Secure communication between components using encryption protocols like TLS.

For example, a hybrid deployment might use on-premises collectors for sensitive data and forward logs to a cloud-based SIEM for analysis and storage.

Log Source Integration

Integrating log sources is a foundational step in SIEM implementation. The SIEM must collect logs from diverse systems and normalize them to ensure consistency across sources.

- **Log Source Categories**:
  - **Operating Systems**: Windows Event Logs, Linux Syslogs.
  - **Network Devices**: Firewalls, routers, IDS/IPS systems.
  - **Applications**: Web servers, databases, email servers.
  - **Cloud Platforms**: AWS CloudTrail, Azure Activity Logs.
  - **Endpoints**: Antivirus and Endpoint Detection and Response (EDR) solutions like CrowdStrike or Carbon Black.
- **Log Formats**: Support common formats such as Syslog, JSON, CEF (Common Event Format), and LEEF (Log Event Extended Format). For proprietary formats, custom parsers may be required.
- **Agent-Based vs. Agentless**: Use agent-based collection for environments requiring advanced filtering or encrypted log transmission. In contrast, agentless methods like SNMP traps or API integration are suitable for lightweight scenarios.
- **Validation**: Perform tests to ensure logs are being collected correctly and parsed accurately. Missing fields or unstructured logs can lead to incomplete event analysis.

For instance, integrating a firewall might involve configuring Syslog exports to forward logs to the SIEM, mapping fields like source IP, destination IP, and action (allow/deny) for correlation and monitoring.

Correlation Rule Development

Correlation rules identify relationships between different events, enabling the detection of suspicious patterns and advanced threats that might otherwise go unnoticed.

- **Rule Logic**: Define conditions that link multiple events or attributes. For example:
  - A brute force login detection rule might correlate multiple failed login attempts within a short timeframe from the same IP address.
  - Lateral movement detection might combine logs of a user authenticating to multiple systems with elevated privileges in a short period.
- **Prebuilt Rules**: Many SIEMs come with out-of-the-box rules for common threats, such as failed logins, privilege escalation, or suspicious file modifications. Customize these rules to fit the organization's environment.
- **Custom Rules**: Create rules for specific organizational use cases or risks, such as detecting unauthorized access to critical servers or anomalies in financial transaction logs.
- **Enrichment**: Enhance rules with contextual data, such as user roles, asset criticality, or threat intelligence feeds, to improve accuracy and relevance.
- **Testing**: Validate new rules in a test environment or with historical data to ensure they trigger appropriately and do not generate false positives.

For example, a correlation rule might flag potential ransomware activity by linking logs indicating unusual file write operations, high CPU usage, and network connections to known malicious IPs.

Alert Tuning

Tuning alerts ensures the SIEM generates actionable notifications while minimizing noise from false positives or irrelevant events.

- **Threshold Adjustments**: Modify default thresholds to better reflect the organization's environment. For instance, increase failed login thresholds in environments with high authentication activity, such as call centers.
- **Whitelist Known Behavior**: Suppress alerts for expected or approved actions, such as authorized system scans or maintenance activities.
- **Dynamic Alerting**: Implement behavioral baselines to account for variations in normal activity. For example, flag login attempts from unusual locations while ignoring activity from regular user regions.

- **Severity Levels**: Categorize alerts by severity (e.g., low, medium, high, critical) to prioritize responses. Assign higher severity to events involving critical assets or known threat signatures.
- **Feedback Loop**: Regularly review alert performance metrics (e.g., false positive rates) and update rules based on analyst feedback.

For instance, if an alert for excessive file access triggers frequently during scheduled backup jobs, tuning the alert to exclude backup operations reduces unnecessary noise.

Use Case Development

Use cases define the specific threats, behaviors, or scenarios the SIEM is designed to detect, aligning monitoring capabilities with organizational priorities.

- **Threat-Based Use Cases**: Focus on detecting common attack techniques, such as phishing, credential stuffing, or privilege escalation.
- **Compliance Use Cases**: Develop use cases to meet regulatory requirements, such as detecting unauthorized access to financial records for SOX compliance or monitoring access to healthcare data for HIPAA.
- **Industry-Specific Use Cases**: Tailor use cases to the organization's industry. For example, detect insider threats in financial institutions or unusual traffic patterns in industrial control systems.
- **Operational Use Cases**: Include scenarios like server downtime, misconfigured systems, or failed backups to identify non-malicious issues that impact operations.
- **Iterative Development**: Review use case performance regularly, retire outdated cases, and create new ones to address emerging threats.

For example, a retail company might create a use case to detect cardholder data exfiltration by correlating outbound traffic logs with file access logs from the payment processing system.

Performance Optimization

Performance optimization ensures the SIEM processes high volumes of data efficiently while maintaining low latency for alerting and reporting.

- **Ingestion Limits**: Monitor log ingestion rates to prevent bottlenecks. Configure rate limits or filters to drop low-value logs (e.g., debug messages) to prioritize critical data.
- **Load Balancing**: Distribute workloads across multiple collectors, processors, or nodes to prevent single points of failure and improve scalability.
- **Query Performance**: Optimize frequently used queries by indexing relevant fields or precomputing aggregate metrics.
- **Retention Tiers**: Use tiered storage to maintain high-speed access to recent data while archiving older logs for compliance or forensic purposes.

For example, indexing fields like "IP Address" and "Event Type" can speed up searches for threat hunting or incident investigations.

Storage Management

Efficient storage management ensures that logs are retained in compliance with regulations while balancing costs and performance.

- **Retention Policies**: Define retention periods based on the criticality of the log source and compliance requirements. For example, PCI DSS mandates storing certain logs for at least one year.
- **Compression**: Use data compression to reduce storage requirements, particularly for archived logs.
- **Hot vs. Cold Storage**: Store frequently accessed data (hot storage) on high-performance drives while archiving older logs (cold storage) on cheaper, slower media like object storage or tape backups.
- **Data Purging**: Automatically delete logs that exceed retention periods to save space and comply with privacy regulations.

For instance, an organization might retain firewall logs in hot storage for three months for active monitoring, then archive them in cold storage for one year to satisfy regulatory requirements.

Compliance Requirements

SIEM implementations must align with applicable regulatory frameworks, industry standards, and internal policies.

- **Regulations**: Meet requirements like PCI DSS (log retention and monitoring), GDPR (privacy protections for stored logs), and SOX (audit trail transparency).

- **Auditing and Reporting**: Generate compliance-specific reports, such as failed login trends for SOX or data access violations for HIPAA.
- **Log Anonymization**: Anonymize sensitive data, such as user PII, before storing logs to align with GDPR and similar regulations.
- **Third-Party Audits**: Configure the SIEM to facilitate audits by external assessors, ensuring clear visibility into log collection, analysis, and retention practices.

For example, healthcare organizations using a SIEM must demonstrate that access logs for patient data are reviewed regularly and retained securely to comply with HIPAA.

ADVANCED SECURITY MONITORING AND THREAT DETECTION FRAMEWORKS

Threat hunting methodologies follow structured approaches to proactively identify security threats. Hunters use systematic techniques combining data analysis, behavioral patterns, and threat intelligence.

Hunting Framework:

Process Flow:

1. Hypothesis Formation
   - Threat analysis
   - Intel correlation
   - Pattern identification
2. Data Collection
   - Log aggregation
   - Network captures
   - System telemetry
3. Investigation
   - Pattern matching
   - Behavior analysis
   - Anomaly detection
4. Validation
   - Evidence collection
   - Finding confirmation
   - Impact assessment

Behavioral Analysis Matrix:

Behavior Type	Indicators	Detection Method	Response
User Activity	Access patterns, Resource usage	Profile matching	Alert/Block
Network Traffic	Flow analysis, Protocol usage	Baseline deviation	Investigation
System Events	Process behavior, File access	Pattern recognition	Containment

Machine Learning Implementation:

Model Types:

- Supervised classification
- Unsupervised clustering
- Anomaly detection
- Pattern recognition
- Predictive analytics

Indicator Management:

- Collection methods
- Validation processes
- Storage systems
- Distribution mechanisms
- Lifecycle tracking

Intelligence Integration:

- Threat feeds
- OSINT sources
- Industry sharing
- Partner networks
- Internal telemetry

Attribution Analysis:

- TTP correlation
- Actor profiling
- Campaign tracking
- Infrastructure mapping
- Motivation assessment

Response Automation:

- Playbook execution
- Containment actions
- Evidence collection
- Alert enrichment
- Incident documentation

Security teams implement:

- Detection rules
- Analysis workflows
- Response procedures
- Documentation standards
- Performance metrics

DR STRATEGY DEVELOPMENT

Disaster Recovery (DR) strategy development ensures business continuity by preparing systems, processes, and personnel to respond to disruptive incidents such as cyberattacks, natural disasters, or hardware failures. A comprehensive DR strategy includes recovery site selection, defining recovery objectives, calculating resource requirements, and establishing testing procedures. Effective planning minimizes downtime and data loss while optimizing resource use and cost.

RECOVERY SITE SELECTION

Recovery sites serve as backup locations to restore operations in the event of a disaster. The choice of a recovery site depends on factors such as organizational needs, criticality of systems, and budget constraints.

1. **Hot Site Implementation:**
    - A hot site is a fully operational facility equipped with real-time replication of production systems, allowing near-instantaneous recovery.
    - Data synchronization occurs continuously, using technologies such as storage replication (e.g., VMware Site Recovery) or cloud-based replication services like AWS Elastic Disaster Recovery.
    - Hot sites are ideal for organizations with low recovery time objectives (RTOs) and high business continuity requirements, such as financial institutions or healthcare providers.
    - Example: A bank implements a hot site in a geographically distant region, replicating all customer transaction data in real time to prevent data loss during outages.
2. **Warm Site Setup:**
    - A warm site includes pre-configured hardware and software but requires additional setup before it becomes fully operational. For example, systems may need to load recent backups or sync databases upon activation.
    - Warm sites provide a middle ground between cost and recovery speed, typically achieving RTOs of several hours.

- These sites are commonly used by organizations where full redundancy is not cost-effective but moderate recovery speeds are acceptable, such as mid-sized enterprises.

3. **Cold Site Planning:**
   - A cold site is a basic facility with physical infrastructure but no active IT systems or pre-installed software. Cold sites rely on transporting and installing hardware, restoring data from backups, and manually configuring systems, which may take days to weeks.
   - Cold sites are cost-effective but unsuitable for organizations requiring rapid recovery. They are typically used by businesses with non-critical workloads.
   - Example: A manufacturing firm may opt for a cold site to restore production scheduling systems after a disaster but can operate manually in the interim.

RECOVERY TIME OBJECTIVES (RTOs)

1. **Definition and Importance:**
   - RTO defines the maximum acceptable downtime for a system or service before it impacts business operations. For instance, a CRM system used by a sales team may have an RTO of four hours, while a mission-critical payment processing system may require an RTO of minutes.
2. **RTO Categories:**
   - **Critical Systems:** Require the shortest RTOs, typically near-zero, to maintain business continuity. Examples include online transaction processing (OLTP) systems or emergency communication platforms.
   - **Moderate-Criticality Systems:** Allow downtime of several hours, such as HR or payroll systems.
   - **Non-Critical Systems:** Can remain offline for extended periods, such as archival databases or test environments.
3. **Alignment with Business Impact Analysis (BIA):**
   - RTOs are determined during the BIA phase, where the impact of downtime is evaluated for each system.

RECOVERY POINT OBJECTIVES (RPOs)

1. **Definition and Considerations:**
   - RPO defines the maximum amount of data loss acceptable during a disaster, measured as the time between the last backup and the incident. An RPO of zero indicates no data loss, achieved through continuous replication.
2. **RPO Classification:**
   - **Zero RPO:** Continuous replication ensures no data is lost. Used for systems like financial transactions or patient health records.
   - **Short RPO (1-4 Hours):** Periodic snapshots or backups, suitable for email or database systems.
   - **Long RPO (Daily or More):** Used for non-critical systems like archival logs.
3. **Backup Strategies for RPOs:**
   - **Incremental Backups:** Capture only changes since the last backup, reducing storage use and meeting short RPOs.
   - **Continuous Data Protection (CDP):** Provides real-time replication, enabling near-zero RPOs.

RESOURCE REQUIREMENTS

1. **Infrastructure Requirements:**
   - Define hardware, software, and networking needs for recovery. For example, recovering a database server may require equivalent computing power, storage, and network bandwidth at the recovery site.
2. **Personnel and Expertise:**
   - Assign trained personnel to manage the recovery process. Roles include IT administrators for system restoration, business continuity managers for coordination, and security teams for post-incident monitoring.
3. **Third-Party Services:**
   - Include third-party cloud providers, managed service providers (MSPs), or disaster recovery as a service (DRaaS) vendors in the resource plan.

4. **Dependencies:**
    - Map dependencies between systems to ensure all necessary resources are available for full recovery. For example, restoring an e-commerce website requires both the web servers and backend databases.

COST-BENEFIT ANALYSIS

1. **Cost Estimation:**
    - Factor in capital expenditures (e.g., hardware purchases, data center setup) and operational expenditures (e.g., ongoing replication, staff training, and maintenance).
    - Example: A hot site with continuous replication incurs higher costs but minimizes downtime. A cold site costs less but significantly increases recovery time.
2. **Business Impact Analysis (BIA):**
    - Quantify potential financial losses due to downtime or data loss. For example, calculate lost revenue for an e-commerce platform experiencing downtime during peak hours.
3. **Optimization:**
    - Balance cost and risk by categorizing systems into tiers based on criticality. Allocate resources to critical systems while using lower-cost options (e.g., cold sites or periodic backups) for non-critical workloads.
4. **ROI Considerations:**
    - Evaluate long-term benefits, such as improved resilience, regulatory compliance, and customer trust, against the upfront and ongoing costs.

TESTING PROCEDURES

1. **Test Planning:**
    - Develop test plans outlining objectives, systems to be tested, and success criteria. For example, a DR test for a database system may aim to verify that recovery can occur within the defined RTO and RPO.
2. **Types of DR Testing:**
    - **Tabletop Exercises:** Simulate disaster scenarios with team discussions and process walkthroughs.
    - **Functional Tests:** Conduct actual failover to a recovery site or restore data from backups to validate processes. For example, failover a web application to a warm site and confirm its availability.
    - **Full-Scale Tests:** Simulate real-world disasters by shutting down production systems and activating recovery sites.
3. **Environment Setup:**
    - Create isolated test environments to avoid impacting production systems. Ensure all dependencies are included, such as applications, databases, and network configurations.
4. **Performance Metrics:**
    - Measure recovery times, data integrity, and system performance during testing. Compare results against RTO and RPO goals to identify gaps.
5. **Frequency of Testing:**
    - Conduct regular tests, such as quarterly or biannual exercises, to account for changes in systems, personnel, or infrastructure.
6. **Lessons Learned:**
    - Document findings from tests, such as bottlenecks or process gaps. Update the DR strategy based on test results to ensure continuous improvement.

BCP IMPLEMENTATION

Business Continuity Plan (BCP) implementation ensures that an organization can maintain or quickly restore critical operations during and after a disruption. This process requires a thorough understanding of business functions, structured recovery teams, effective communication plans, and regular testing to keep the plan relevant. BCPs also depend on strong vendor relationships and adaptable maintenance practices to address evolving risks.

Business Impact Analysis

A Business Impact Analysis (BIA) identifies the potential consequences of a disruption and helps prioritize recovery efforts. It serves as the foundation for developing a BCP by assessing the criticality of processes and estimating the financial, operational, and reputational impact of downtime.

- **Key Metrics**:
    - **Maximum Tolerable Downtime (MTD)**: The maximum period a business function can be disrupted without causing severe damage.
    - **Recovery Time Objective (RTO)**: The target time to restore a business function after a disruption.
    - **Recovery Point Objective (RPO)**: The acceptable amount of data loss, measured as the time between the last backup and the disruption.
- **Data Collection**: Use surveys, interviews, and workshops with business units to understand dependencies, processes, and resource requirements.
- **Analysis of Dependencies**: Map interdependencies between systems, applications, and teams to identify cascading impacts. For instance, the failure of an order-processing system might also disrupt logistics and invoicing.

An example BIA for an e-commerce platform might reveal that the payment gateway has an RTO of 30 minutes and an RPO of zero, indicating that it must be restored immediately without any loss of transaction data.

Critical Function Identification

Identifying critical functions is essential for prioritizing recovery efforts during a disruption. These functions typically have the greatest impact on the organization's ability to operate.

- **Criteria for Criticality**:
    - Functions that generate revenue, such as sales and order processing.
    - Processes required for regulatory compliance, such as financial reporting.
    - Activities tied to customer satisfaction, such as help desk services.
- **Tiered Prioritization**:
    - **Tier 1**: Functions requiring immediate recovery (e.g., payroll, payment processing).
    - **Tier 2**: Functions recoverable within a short time window (e.g., HR operations).
    - **Tier 3**: Non-critical functions that can wait until normal operations resume (e.g., marketing campaigns).

For example, a hospital's critical functions might include patient care systems, pharmacy services, and emergency department operations, all of which require near-instantaneous recovery.

Recovery Team Structure

A well-defined recovery team structure assigns clear roles and responsibilities, ensuring efficient coordination during a disruption. Teams should include representatives from all critical business areas and technical teams.

- **Core Teams**:
    - **Incident Management Team**: Oversees the entire recovery process, makes key decisions, and coordinates across teams.
    - **IT Recovery Team**: Restores systems, applications, and networks, ensuring the functionality of technical resources.
    - **Business Unit Recovery Teams**: Restore specific business processes, such as customer support or supply chain operations.
- **Role Assignments**:
    - Assign leaders, alternates, and specialists for each team to ensure continuity if primary team members are unavailable.
    - Define escalation paths for decision-making.
- **Third-Party Coordination**: Include representatives from key vendors or service providers in the recovery team for rapid resolution of external dependencies.

For instance, during a ransomware attack, the IT Recovery Team might isolate affected systems, while the Incident Management Team coordinates communication with legal counsel and stakeholders.

Communication Plans

Communication plans ensure timely and accurate information is shared with employees, customers, vendors, and other stakeholders during a disruption.

- **Internal Communication**:
  - Define primary and backup communication channels, such as email, messaging platforms (e.g., Slack), or emergency hotlines.
  - Use pre-approved templates for notifications about operational status, safety instructions, or changes to recovery timelines.
- **External Communication**:
  - Establish protocols for customer notifications, such as issuing service updates or outage advisories on social media.
  - Coordinate with vendors to confirm service availability or alternative support.
  - Assign a spokesperson to handle media inquiries and ensure consistent messaging.
- **Crisis Communication Teams**: Train designated teams to manage sensitive communications and maintain composure under pressure.

For example, during a data breach, the communication plan may outline immediate notification of affected customers, delivery of breach details to regulators, and regular updates to employees.

Training Requirements

BCP training ensures that all stakeholders understand their roles and can act effectively during a disruption. Training should be tailored to specific teams and responsibilities.

- **Employee Awareness**:
  - Conduct general training for employees to ensure they understand the organization's BCP, including evacuation routes, communication channels, and reporting procedures.
- **Role-Specific Training**:
  - Provide specialized training for recovery teams, focusing on their specific responsibilities and the tools they will use during a disruption.
- **Technical Training**:
  - Train IT staff on system recovery procedures, such as restoring backups, implementing failover systems, or configuring alternate networks.
- **Ongoing Updates**:
  - Deliver refresher courses and update training materials whenever the BCP is revised or new threats emerge.

For example, an organization might conduct quarterly tabletop exercises where the IT recovery team practices restoring cloud services after a simulated failure.

Exercise Scenarios

Regular testing of the BCP through realistic scenarios identifies gaps and ensures the plan works as intended. Exercises should vary in scope and complexity to simulate a range of possible disruptions.

- **Tabletop Exercises**: Walk through a hypothetical disruption in a low-stress environment. For instance, simulate a cyberattack to discuss decision-making, communication, and recovery priorities.
- **Functional Exercises**: Test specific recovery actions, such as restoring critical systems, switching to backup data centers, or implementing failover for a network outage.
- **Full-Scale Drills**: Conduct comprehensive simulations that involve all recovery teams, critical business units, and external partners.
- **Common Scenarios**:
  - Natural disasters: Simulate power outages, floods, or fires affecting physical locations.
  - Cyberattacks: Practice responses to ransomware, DDoS attacks, or data breaches.
  - Supply chain disruptions: Test vendor dependency plans and alternative sourcing strategies.

An example full-scale drill for a retail chain might involve simulating a regional data center outage and testing failover to a secondary site, complete with employee communication and vendor coordination.

Plan Maintenance
BCPs must be continuously updated to reflect organizational changes, emerging threats, and lessons from exercises or real disruptions.

- **Scheduled Reviews**:
  - Review the BCP annually or whenever there are significant changes, such as mergers, new systems, or updated regulations.
- **Post-Incident Updates**:
  - Revise the plan after real incidents to address gaps identified during response efforts.
- **Ownership**:
  - Assign a dedicated BCP coordinator or team to manage updates, track changes, and ensure stakeholder participation.
- **Document Versioning**:
  - Use version control to maintain a history of plan revisions, ensuring that everyone references the latest version.

For example, after experiencing a supply chain disruption, a manufacturer might update its BCP to include alternate shipping providers and emergency stockpiles.

Vendor Management
Vendors play a key role in maintaining business continuity, especially when critical functions depend on third-party services. Vendor management ensures that these dependencies are accounted for in the BCP.

- **Vendor Risk Assessments**:
  - Assess the business continuity capabilities of critical vendors, such as cloud providers, logistics partners, or software vendors. Request their BCP documentation or certifications, like ISO 22301.
- **Service Level Agreements (SLAs)**:
  - Define SLAs that include recovery time objectives (RTOs) and recovery point objectives (RPOs) for vendor-provided services.
- **Redundancy**:
  - Establish relationships with backup vendors to mitigate risks from a single point of failure.
- **Communication Protocols**:
  - Include vendors in communication plans and testing exercises to ensure seamless coordination during disruptions.

For instance, a SaaS provider might include its cloud hosting vendor in disaster recovery drills to verify the vendor's failover capabilities.

CHANGE MANAGEMENT AND CONTROL PROCESS IMPLEMENTATION

Change request procedures establish structured workflows for system modifications, updates, and configuration changes. The process begins with formal request submission containing detailed change descriptions, business justification, and technical requirements.

Change Management Flow:
Request → Assessment → Planning → Approval → Testing → Implementation → Review

Risk Assessment Matrix:

Risk Factor	Impact Level	Mitigation	Validation
Service Disruption	High/Med/Low	Redundancy	Testing
Data Loss	Critical/High	Backups	Verification
Performance Impact	Med/Low	Monitoring	Benchmarks
Security Risk	High/Med	Controls	Assessment

Impact Analysis Components:

- System dependencies
- User impact

- Resource requirements
- Schedule constraints
- Cost implications

Testing Framework:

- Unit testing
- Integration testing
- User acceptance
- Performance validation
- Security assessment

Implementation Planning:

- Resource allocation
- Schedule development
- Communication plan
- Backup procedures
- Monitoring setup

Rollback Procedures:

- System snapshots
- Configuration backups
- Data preservation
- Recovery scripts
- Validation checks

Emergency Change Protocol:

- Expedited approval
- Risk acceptance
- Limited testing
- Enhanced monitoring
- Post-implementation review

Documentation Requirements:

- Change details
- Risk assessment
- Approval records
- Test results
- Implementation logs
- Review findings

Teams maintain:

- Change calendar
- Request tracking
- Status reporting
- Metrics collection
- Process improvement

PHYSICAL SECURITY ARCHITECTURE

Physical security architecture encompasses the design, implementation, and management of measures to protect facilities, assets, and personnel from physical threats. A comprehensive strategy integrates facility design, access control, environmental monitoring, and emergency response mechanisms. Each component must work together to minimize risk and maintain a secure environment while ensuring business operations are not disrupted.

FACILITY DESIGN PRINCIPLES

1. **Crime Prevention Through Environmental Design (CPTED):**
   - Use CPTED principles to design facilities that deter unauthorized access and reduce opportunities for crime. For example, position entrances in well-lit areas and design landscapes that minimize blind spots.
2. **Layered Defense:**
   - Implement concentric layers of security, starting from the perimeter and moving inward to critical zones. For example, a data center's security architecture might consist of perimeter fences, controlled entry gates, security checkpoints, and biometric access to server rooms.
3. **Single Entry Points:**
   - Design facilities with controlled, limited access points for personnel and vehicles to monitor and manage traffic effectively. Emergency exits should remain locked from the outside and comply with safety regulations.
4. **Traffic Flow and Partitioning:**
   - Separate public, restricted, and sensitive zones. For example, in a corporate building, visitor areas should be partitioned from employee-only areas, with physical barriers such as turnstiles or locked doors.

SECURITY ZONE IMPLEMENTATION

1. **Public Zone:**
   - Areas accessible to the general public, such as reception areas or lobbies. Physical security measures include surveillance cameras, on-site security personnel, and controlled entry points.
2. **Restricted Zone:**
   - Areas where only authorized personnel are allowed. Examples include employee workspaces and storage rooms. These zones require keycards, PINs, or biometric credentials for access.
3. **Sensitive Zone:**
   - High-security areas containing critical assets, such as data centers, server rooms, or laboratories. Additional controls include two-factor authentication, airlock entry systems, and mantraps to prevent piggybacking or tailgating.
4. **Custom Security Levels:**
   - Some industries, such as healthcare and financial services, require custom zones to comply with regulations like HIPAA or PCI DSS. For instance, patient data storage rooms or payment processing systems may be categorized as sensitive zones.

ACCESS CONTROL SYSTEMS

1. **Credential-Based Access:**
   - Deploy systems that require keycards, PINs, or biometrics to validate personnel identity. RFID-based cards are commonly used for proximity access, while biometric systems like fingerprint or facial recognition provide enhanced authentication.
2. **Role-Based Access:**
   - Assign access permissions based on job roles. For example, IT administrators may have access to data centers, while general employees are restricted to workspaces.
3. **Physical Access Logs:**
   - Maintain detailed logs of all access attempts, including timestamps, user credentials, and entry points. Use these logs for auditing and forensic analysis in case of an incident.
4. **Anti-Tailgating Mechanisms:**
   - Implement mantraps, turnstiles, or interlocking doors to prevent unauthorized personnel from following authorized users into secure areas.
5. **Integration with IT Systems:**
   - Integrate physical access control systems with identity management solutions, such as Active Directory, to synchronize access permissions across physical and logical systems.

ENVIRONMENTAL MONITORING

1. **Temperature and Humidity Control:**
   - Data centers and critical infrastructure require precise environmental conditions. Use sensors to monitor temperature and humidity levels, ensuring they remain within acceptable thresholds. Deviation alerts can prevent equipment failure or downtime.
2. **Fire Detection and Suppression Systems:**
   - Equip facilities with smoke detectors, heat sensors, and gas-based fire suppression systems (e.g., FM-200 or inert gases) to protect sensitive equipment without causing water damage.
3. **Flood and Leak Monitoring:**
   - Deploy water leak detection systems near HVAC units, data center floors, or plumbing to mitigate flood risks. Sensors placed under raised floors or near water pipes can send alerts when leaks are detected.
4. **Power Monitoring:**
   - Implement uninterruptible power supplies (UPS) and backup generators to ensure continuous operations during power failures. Monitor voltage, load, and capacity to identify issues before they cause downtime.

VIDEO SURVEILLANCE

1. **Camera Placement:**
   - Position cameras to cover entry points, critical assets, and high-traffic areas. Avoid blind spots and ensure that cameras are tamper-proof.
   - Use wide-angle or 360-degree cameras for lobbies and open spaces, while narrow-angle cameras can monitor specific doors or corridors.
2. **Live Monitoring and Recording:**
   - Integrate cameras with a central control room where security personnel can monitor live feeds. Store recorded footage in a secure location, with retention policies aligned to compliance requirements (e.g., 90-day retention for financial institutions).
3. **Video Analytics:**
   - Use AI-powered systems to analyze footage for anomalies, such as loitering, unauthorized access attempts, or unattended bags. Real-time alerts can improve response times.
4. **Remote Access:**
   - Allow authorized personnel to access live or recorded feeds from remote devices. Secure access with strong authentication, such as VPNs or MFA.

PERIMETER SECURITY

1. **Fencing and Barriers:**
   - Install perimeter fencing with anti-climbing features and clear signage to deter unauthorized entry. For higher security, consider electric fences or intrusion detection systems integrated into the fence.
2. **Vehicle Access Control:**
   - Deploy barriers such as bollards, gates, or retractable barricades to prevent unauthorized vehicles from entering. High-security facilities may use vehicle scanners or undercarriage inspection systems.
3. **Lighting:**
   - Install motion-activated lighting to eliminate dark areas around the perimeter. Bright and even lighting deters intruders and enhances camera visibility during nighttime.
4. **Patrols:**
   - Combine electronic surveillance with physical patrols by security personnel to provide active monitoring of the perimeter.

ASSET PROTECTION

1. **Secure Storage:**
   - Use locked cabinets, safes, or vaults for high-value physical assets, such as hard drives, sensitive documents, or prototypes. Multi-layered authentication may be required for access.

2. **Asset Tracking Systems:**
   - Tag and track assets with RFID, barcodes, or GPS systems to monitor their location in real time. Alerts can be triggered if an asset is moved without authorization.
3. **Theft Prevention Measures:**
   - Equip portable devices, such as laptops or tablets, with cable locks or motion sensors to deter theft. Implement screen locks and encryption to secure stolen devices.

EMERGENCY RESPONSE

1. **Emergency Plans:**
   - Develop and document detailed emergency response plans for events such as fire, natural disasters, or active shooter situations. Plans should include evacuation routes, muster points, and communication protocols.
2. **Alarm Systems:**
   - Install alarms for fire, unauthorized entry, or environmental hazards. Ensure alarms are integrated with centralized systems to provide immediate notifications to security personnel and emergency services.
3. **Personnel Training:**
   - Train employees on emergency procedures, including evacuation protocols, first aid, and how to report incidents. Conduct regular drills to ensure preparedness.
4. **Incident Communication:**
   - Establish communication channels for emergencies, such as loudspeakers, SMS alerts, or mobile apps. Ensure messages reach all affected personnel quickly and clearly.
5. **Backup Power for Security Systems:**
   - Ensure that access controls, surveillance cameras, and alarm systems remain operational during power outages by connecting them to backup power sources like UPS or generators.

CASE STUDY TOPICS

Analyzing case studies across various cybersecurity domains provides practical insights into challenges, decision-making, and remediation strategies. Topics like incident response, SIEM deployment, and disaster recovery testing highlight the importance of proactive planning, effective execution, and lessons learned from failures or successes. Each case reflects the complexities of maintaining operational resilience and securing organizational assets.

Major Incident Response

An e-commerce company experiences a widespread ransomware attack that encrypts critical databases and disables customer-facing applications during a peak sales period. The company activates its incident response (IR) plan to contain and recover from the attack.

- **Incident Timeline**:
  - **Initial Detection**: The Security Operations Center (SOC) detects unusual file encryption activity on multiple servers and elevated CPU usage on endpoints. Alerts are triggered in the SIEM for abnormal outbound traffic.
  - **Containment**: The IR team isolates infected systems by disabling network access and implementing firewall blocks to prevent lateral movement.
  - **Communication**: Executive leadership is notified, and internal and external communication plans are activated, including notifying affected customers and stakeholders.
  - **Root Cause Analysis**: Forensic investigators identify the attack vector as a phishing email with a malicious macro attachment that led to the deployment of ransomware.
- **Outcome**:
  - The company restores services using clean backups stored in an air-gapped environment.
  - The IR team implements new controls, including phishing-resistant MFA, endpoint detection and response (EDR), and enhanced email filters.
  - The organization updates its ransomware playbook to address gaps identified during the response.

This case highlights the importance of rapid containment, effective communication, and pre-established backups in mitigating the damage caused by ransomware attacks.

SIEM Deployment

A multinational organization implements a Security Information and Event Management (SIEM) platform to centralize log management and improve threat detection across its global IT environment.

- **Deployment Objectives**:
  - Centralize log collection from diverse sources, including cloud services, on-premises infrastructure, and third-party SaaS applications.
  - Enhance detection capabilities with correlation rules for advanced threats like privilege escalation, lateral movement, and data exfiltration.
  - Meet compliance requirements for GDPR, PCI DSS, and SOX.
- **Implementation Steps**:
  - **Architecture Design**: Deploy a hybrid SIEM with on-premises log collectors forwarding logs to a cloud-based analysis platform.
  - **Log Source Integration**: Integrate 50+ log sources, including firewalls, Active Directory, EDR tools, and cloud platforms (e.g., AWS CloudTrail).
  - **Rule Tuning**: Customize out-of-the-box rules to reduce false positives, such as excluding scheduled vulnerability scans from triggering alerts.
  - **Dashboards**: Create custom dashboards to monitor key metrics like failed logins, firewall activity, and outbound traffic anomalies.
- **Outcome**:
  - The SIEM identifies multiple unauthorized login attempts originating from known malicious IPs within the first week of deployment.
  - Over time, the SOC reduces its mean time to detect (MTTD) and mean time to respond (MTTR) through better visibility and refined alerts.

This case emphasizes the importance of tailoring a SIEM deployment to organizational needs, refining detection rules, and prioritizing actionable alerts.

DR Test Execution

A financial institution conducts a disaster recovery (DR) test to simulate a major outage of its primary data center and assess its ability to restore critical operations.

- **Test Objectives**:
  - Validate the effectiveness of the DR plan and recovery time objectives (RTOs).
  - Ensure critical applications and databases can fail over to the secondary data center.
  - Test coordination between IT teams, business units, and external partners.
- **Test Execution**:
  - **Simulated Scenario**: A simulated power outage causes the primary data center to go offline. DR teams initiate failover procedures.
  - **Recovery Process**: Key applications are restored on backup servers, and customer-facing services are rerouted to the secondary data center.
  - **Team Involvement**: Business continuity, IT, and application support teams collaborate to verify system functionality and resolve issues.
- **Findings**:
  - The failover process for the core banking application took 30 minutes longer than the defined RTO due to an overlooked database dependency.
  - A third-party vendor was not reachable during the test, delaying the restoration of their integrated system.
- **Improvements**:
  - Update the DR plan to include all system dependencies and verify vendor participation in future tests.
  - Automate parts of the failover process to reduce manual steps.

This case demonstrates the value of regular DR testing to identify gaps and refine recovery procedures.

Change Management Failure

A technology company experiences a major outage after a routine configuration change disrupts a production environment, leading to significant downtime and financial loss.

- **Incident Details**:
  - **Change Request**: A network engineer submits a change request to update routing rules on core switches to optimize performance.
  - **Implementation Issue**: The changes are applied during business hours without proper validation in a staging environment. A configuration error causes network instability, disconnecting critical systems.
  - **Impact**: The outage lasts four hours, affecting internal applications, customer-facing services, and third-party integrations.
- **Post-Mortem Findings**:
  - The change management process was bypassed, and no peer review or approval was conducted.
  - Monitoring alerts were ignored during the change window, delaying incident detection.
  - Documentation for the affected systems was outdated, further slowing recovery.
- **Remediation**:
  - Enforce strict adherence to the change management process, requiring peer reviews and approvals for all production changes.
  - Update system documentation to reflect current configurations.
  - Schedule all changes during approved maintenance windows and test them in a staging environment before production deployment.

This case highlights the consequences of poorly managed changes and the importance of robust change management controls.

Physical Security Breach

A pharmaceutical company experiences a physical security breach when unauthorized personnel gain access to a restricted area containing sensitive research data.

- **Breach Details**:
  - **Entry Method**: The intruders use stolen employee access badges to bypass physical security controls.
  - **Target**: The attackers access a server room containing proprietary research and attempt to exfiltrate data using USB drives.
  - **Detection**: Security personnel identify the breach via surveillance footage and an alert from the access control system about unusual after-hours activity.
- **Response**:
  - The facility is locked down, and the intruders are detained by on-site security.
  - Forensic analysis determines that while the attackers accessed servers, encryption and USB restrictions prevented data exfiltration.
- **Post-Breach Actions**:
  - Reissue access badges with enhanced security features, such as embedded biometric authentication.
  - Implement stricter access controls, including role-based restrictions and dual authentication for sensitive areas.
  - Enhance surveillance systems with AI-powered behavior analytics to detect unusual activity in real time.

This case illustrates the importance of layered physical security controls and rapid response to mitigate potential data theft.

Monitor Tuning Project

A retail organization undertakes a project to tune its monitoring tools after a significant increase in false positives overwhelms its SOC analysts, delaying the response to genuine threats.

- **Challenges**:
    - The EDR solution generates frequent alerts for routine software updates and internal system scans.
    - The SIEM produces repetitive alerts for failed login attempts due to password spray attempts on non-critical systems.
    - Analysts are unable to focus on high-priority threats due to the alert volume.
- **Tuning Activities**:
    - **Whitelisting**: Suppress alerts for approved activities, such as scheduled vulnerability scans, routine software updates, and known safe applications.
    - **Threshold Adjustments**: Modify alert thresholds to reflect typical activity patterns. For example, increase the threshold for failed logins on public-facing systems to reduce noise from low-risk attempts.
    - **Anomaly-Based Alerts**: Implement behavioral baselines to detect deviations from normal activity, such as unusual login locations or file access patterns.
    - **Severity Classification**: Categorize alerts based on criticality, focusing SOC attention on high-priority events.
- **Outcome**:
    - False positives are reduced by 40%, enabling analysts to focus on actionable threats.
    - Time-to-respond (TTR) for critical alerts decreases, improving overall threat management.

This case highlights how tuning monitoring tools improves SOC efficiency, reduces alert fatigue, and strengthens an organization's security posture.

SECURITY OPERATIONS PRACTICE SCENARIOS AND ASSESSMENTS

Scenario 1: Incident Response Your organization detects unauthorized access to customer data systems. Initial analysis shows:

- Multiple failed login attempts
- Successful credential use
- Data access patterns
- File downloads
- External connections

What immediate actions align with incident response procedures?
A. Shut down all systems
B. Notify law enforcement
C. Isolate affected systems, preserve evidence, initiate response plan
D. Contact customers about breach
Correct Answer: C Analysis: Follow established IR procedures, preserve evidence, contain impact.
Monitoring Configuration Example:
SIEM Implementation:
- Log sources configured
- Correlation rules active
- Alerts defined
- Dashboards created
- Reports scheduled

Which configuration gap creates the highest risk?
A. Missing network logs
B. Weekly report schedule
C. Basic correlation rules
D. Standard dashboards
Correct Answer: A Explanation: Network visibility gaps prevent comprehensive threat detection.

DR Strategy Matrix:

Component	RTO	RPO	Strategy	Cost
Core Apps	4hrs	15min	Hot site	High
Email	8hrs	1hr	Warm site	Med
File shares	24hrs	24hrs	Cold site	Low

Which strategy misalignment creates recovery risk?
A. Core Apps RTO/RPO
B. Email recovery strategy
C. File share timing
D. Cost allocation
Correct Answer: B Analysis: Email warm site strategy doesn't meet stated RTO/RPO requirements.
Change Impact Scenario: Planning system upgrade:

- Core database migration
- Authentication changes
- Network reconfiguration
- Application updates

Which impact analysis element requires highest priority?
A. Performance testing
B. User communication
C. Service dependencies
D. Cost analysis
Correct Answer: C Explanation: Service dependency mapping prevents cascade failures during changes.
Physical Security Design Question: Designing data center security:
Layers:
1. Perimeter controls
2. Building access
3. Floor access
4. Rack access
5. Asset tracking

Which design element creates vulnerability?
A. Single authentication
B. Camera placement
C. Guard rotation
D. Access logs
Correct Answer: A Analysis: Single authentication violates defense-in-depth principles.
Organizations implement:

- Testing programs
- Documentation standards
- Review processes
- Improvement tracking
- Performance metrics

PHYSICAL SECURITY ARCHITECTURE

Physical security architecture encompasses the design, implementation, and management of measures to protect facilities, assets, and personnel from physical threats. A comprehensive strategy integrates facility design, access control, environmental monitoring, and emergency response mechanisms. Each component must work together to minimize risk and maintain a secure environment while ensuring business operations are not disrupted.

FACILITY DESIGN PRINCIPLES

1. **Crime Prevention Through Environmental Design (CPTED):**
   - Use CPTED principles to design facilities that deter unauthorized access and reduce opportunities for crime. For example, position entrances in well-lit areas and design landscapes that minimize blind spots.
2. **Layered Defense:**
   - Implement concentric layers of security, starting from the perimeter and moving inward to critical zones. For example, a data center's security architecture might consist of perimeter fences, controlled entry gates, security checkpoints, and biometric access to server rooms.
3. **Single Entry Points:**
   - Design facilities with controlled, limited access points for personnel and vehicles to monitor and manage traffic effectively. Emergency exits should remain locked from the outside and comply with safety regulations.
4. **Traffic Flow and Partitioning:**
   - Separate public, restricted, and sensitive zones. For example, in a corporate building, visitor areas should be partitioned from employee-only areas, with physical barriers such as turnstiles or locked doors.

SECURITY ZONE IMPLEMENTATION

1. **Public Zone:**
   - Areas accessible to the general public, such as reception areas or lobbies. Physical security measures include surveillance cameras, on-site security personnel, and controlled entry points.
2. **Restricted Zone:**
   - Areas where only authorized personnel are allowed. Examples include employee workspaces and storage rooms. These zones require keycards, PINs, or biometric credentials for access.
3. **Sensitive Zone:**
   - High-security areas containing critical assets, such as data centers, server rooms, or laboratories. Additional controls include two-factor authentication, airlock entry systems, and mantraps to prevent piggybacking or tailgating.
4. **Custom Security Levels:**
   - Some industries, such as healthcare and financial services, require custom zones to comply with regulations like HIPAA or PCI DSS. For instance, patient data storage rooms or payment processing systems may be categorized as sensitive zones.

ACCESS CONTROL SYSTEMS

1. **Credential-Based Access:**
   - Deploy systems that require keycards, PINs, or biometrics to validate personnel identity. RFID-based cards are commonly used for proximity access, while biometric systems like fingerprint or facial recognition provide enhanced authentication.
2. **Role-Based Access:**
   - Assign access permissions based on job roles. For example, IT administrators may have access to data centers, while general employees are restricted to workspaces.
3. **Physical Access Logs:**
   - Maintain detailed logs of all access attempts, including timestamps, user credentials, and entry points. Use these logs for auditing and forensic analysis in case of an incident.
4. **Anti-Tailgating Mechanisms:**
   - Implement mantraps, turnstiles, or interlocking doors to prevent unauthorized personnel from following authorized users into secure areas.
5. **Integration with IT Systems:**
   - Integrate physical access control systems with identity management solutions, such as Active Directory, to synchronize access permissions across physical and logical systems.

ENVIRONMENTAL MONITORING

1. **Temperature and Humidity Control:**
   - Data centers and critical infrastructure require precise environmental conditions. Use sensors to monitor temperature and humidity levels, ensuring they remain within acceptable thresholds. Deviation alerts can prevent equipment failure or downtime.
2. **Fire Detection and Suppression Systems:**
   - Equip facilities with smoke detectors, heat sensors, and gas-based fire suppression systems (e.g., FM-200 or inert gases) to protect sensitive equipment without causing water damage.
3. **Flood and Leak Monitoring:**
   - Deploy water leak detection systems near HVAC units, data center floors, or plumbing to mitigate flood risks. Sensors placed under raised floors or near water pipes can send alerts when leaks are detected.
4. **Power Monitoring:**
   - Implement uninterruptible power supplies (UPS) and backup generators to ensure continuous operations during power failures. Monitor voltage, load, and capacity to identify issues before they cause downtime.

VIDEO SURVEILLANCE

1. **Camera Placement:**
   - Position cameras to cover entry points, critical assets, and high-traffic areas. Avoid blind spots and ensure that cameras are tamper-proof.
   - Use wide-angle or 360-degree cameras for lobbies and open spaces, while narrow-angle cameras can monitor specific doors or corridors.
2. **Live Monitoring and Recording:**
   - Integrate cameras with a central control room where security personnel can monitor live feeds. Store recorded footage in a secure location, with retention policies aligned to compliance requirements (e.g., 90-day retention for financial institutions).
3. **Video Analytics:**
   - Use AI-powered systems to analyze footage for anomalies, such as loitering, unauthorized access attempts, or unattended bags. Real-time alerts can improve response times.
4. **Remote Access:**
   - Allow authorized personnel to access live or recorded feeds from remote devices. Secure access with strong authentication, such as VPNs or MFA.

PERIMETER SECURITY

1. **Fencing and Barriers:**
   - Install perimeter fencing with anti-climbing features and clear signage to deter unauthorized entry. For higher security, consider electric fences or intrusion detection systems integrated into the fence.
2. **Vehicle Access Control:**
   - Deploy barriers such as bollards, gates, or retractable barricades to prevent unauthorized vehicles from entering. High-security facilities may use vehicle scanners or undercarriage inspection systems.
3. **Lighting:**
   - Install motion-activated lighting to eliminate dark areas around the perimeter. Bright and even lighting deters intruders and enhances camera visibility during nighttime.
4. **Patrols:**
   - Combine electronic surveillance with physical patrols by security personnel to provide active monitoring of the perimeter.

ASSET PROTECTION

1. **Secure Storage:**
   - Use locked cabinets, safes, or vaults for high-value physical assets, such as hard drives, sensitive documents, or prototypes. Multi-layered authentication may be required for access.

2. **Asset Tracking Systems:**
   - Tag and track assets with RFID, barcodes, or GPS systems to monitor their location in real time. Alerts can be triggered if an asset is moved without authorization.
3. **Theft Prevention Measures:**
   - Equip portable devices, such as laptops or tablets, with cable locks or motion sensors to deter theft. Implement screen locks and encryption to secure stolen devices.

EMERGENCY RESPONSE

1. **Emergency Plans:**
   - Develop and document detailed emergency response plans for events such as fire, natural disasters, or active shooter situations. Plans should include evacuation routes, muster points, and communication protocols.
2. **Alarm Systems:**
   - Install alarms for fire, unauthorized entry, or environmental hazards. Ensure alarms are integrated with centralized systems to provide immediate notifications to security personnel and emergency services.
3. **Personnel Training:**
   - Train employees on emergency procedures, including evacuation protocols, first aid, and how to report incidents. Conduct regular drills to ensure preparedness.
4. **Incident Communication:**
   - Establish communication channels for emergencies, such as loudspeakers, SMS alerts, or mobile apps. Ensure messages reach all affected personnel quickly and clearly.
5. **Backup Power for Security Systems:**
   - Ensure that access controls, surveillance cameras, and alarm systems remain operational during power outages by connecting them to backup power sources like UPS or generators.

Software Development Security

SECURITY REQUIREMENTS AND THREAT MODELING IMPLEMENTATION

Security requirement gathering integrates business objectives, technical constraints, and compliance needs into the software development lifecycle. Requirements flow from risk assessments, compliance mandates, and security testing outcomes.

Requirements Framework:

Source Hierarchy:

1. Regulatory mandates
   - Industry standards
   - Legal requirements
   - Privacy regulations
2. Business requirements
   - Data protection
   - Service availability
   - User authentication
3. Technical specifications
   - Security controls
   - Architecture design
   - Implementation details

STRIDE Threat Model Matrix:

Threat Type	Attack Examples	Controls	Validation
Spoofing	Identity theft, Impersonation	Strong auth	Identity verification
Tampering	Data modification, Code injection	Integrity checks	Hash validation
Repudiation	Transaction denial, Log alteration	Digital signatures	Audit trails
Info Disclosure	Data leaks, Unauthorized access	Encryption	Access control
Denial of Service	Resource exhaustion, Flooding	Rate limiting	Availability monitoring
Elevation	Privilege escalation, Access bypass	Least privilege	Permission checks

Attack Tree Development:

- Root goal identification
- Attack vector analysis
- Mitigation mapping
- Cost/complexity assessment
- Success probability

Data Flow Analysis:

- Trust boundaries
- Entry points
- Exit points
- Process flows
- Data storage
- Authentication points

Control Mapping Process:

- Requirement identification
- Control selection
- Implementation planning
- Testing procedures
- Validation methods

Architecture Review Components:

- Design patterns
- Security controls
- Integration points
- Trust relationships
- Data handling

Design Validation:

- Threat assessment
- Control effectiveness
- Implementation feasibility
- Performance impact
- Maintenance requirements

Security teams maintain:

- Requirements database
- Threat models
- Control documentation
- Testing procedures
- Validation results

SECURITY TESTING STRATEGY

A security testing strategy ensures that software and systems are evaluated for vulnerabilities, misconfigurations, and flaws throughout the development lifecycle. A robust approach includes careful test planning, applying multiple testing types, developing comprehensive test cases, and measuring progress with security metrics. It integrates defect management workflows, structured code reviews, and defined release criteria to deliver secure, reliable systems.

TEST PLANNING AND COVERAGE

1. **Scope Definition:**
   - Define the scope of the testing effort by identifying critical components, sensitive data, and potential attack surfaces. For example, in a web application, focus on APIs, user authentication modules, and input fields.
   - Include third-party components and dependencies in the scope, as vulnerabilities in these areas can impact overall security.
2. **Risk-Based Prioritization:**
   - Prioritize testing activities based on risk assessments. High-risk areas, such as payment gateways or admin interfaces, should receive more intensive scrutiny.
   - Use threat modeling tools like STRIDE or DREAD to identify and rank threats.
3. **Test Environment Setup:**
   - Mirror the production environment to ensure accurate results. Include representative hardware, network configurations, and datasets to replicate real-world scenarios. For example, if the production environment uses a load balancer and CDN, include these components in the test setup.
4. **Test Coverage Goals:**
   - Define the desired coverage metrics, such as testing all application endpoints, achieving 100% code coverage for critical modules, or ensuring compliance with OWASP Top 10 standards.

SECURITY TESTING TYPES

1. **Unit Testing:**
   - Evaluate individual functions or modules for secure coding practices. For example, test input validation functions to ensure they properly sanitize user inputs and prevent injection attacks.
   - Automate unit tests using frameworks like JUnit (Java), NUnit (.NET), or pytest (Python) to ensure consistency.

2. **Integration Testing:**
   - Verify the security of interfaces and data exchange between integrated components. For instance, test API endpoints to ensure they enforce authentication and restrict access based on user roles.
   - Conduct negative testing to validate how the system handles invalid or malicious inputs, such as sending malformed JSON payloads to an API.
3. **System Testing:**
   - Assess the end-to-end security of the entire system under realistic conditions. For example, simulate an attacker attempting to exploit a misconfigured firewall or a privilege escalation vulnerability in the application.
   - Include load testing to ensure security controls, such as rate limiting or intrusion detection, perform under stress.

TEST CASE DEVELOPMENT

1. **Threat-Specific Test Cases:**
   - Develop test cases targeting specific threats, such as SQL injection, cross-site scripting (XSS), and cross-site request forgery (CSRF). For example, test whether input fields accept malicious SQL queries designed to extract database records.
2. **Functional Security Test Cases:**
   - Test features such as login mechanisms, multi-factor authentication (MFA), and role-based access control (RBAC). For example, verify that users with "viewer" roles cannot access administrative functions.
3. **Boundary and Edge Cases:**
   - Create test cases that push the system to its limits, such as entering extremely large inputs, sending unexpected data formats, or attempting simultaneous login attempts from multiple IPs.
4. **Compliance Test Cases:**
   - Ensure test cases validate compliance with regulatory requirements such as GDPR, HIPAA, or PCI DSS. For example, test whether PII is encrypted both in transit and at rest.

SECURITY METRICS

1. **Coverage Metrics:**
   - Track the percentage of tested attack surfaces, APIs, or lines of code. For example, achieve 95% code coverage for modules handling sensitive data.
2. **Defect Metrics:**
   - Monitor the number, severity, and type of vulnerabilities identified. Break these into categories such as injection vulnerabilities, misconfigurations, or broken authentication.
3. **Time-to-Remediate:**
   - Measure the average time taken to fix security issues from detection to resolution. For example, aim to resolve high-severity issues within 48 hours of discovery.
4. **False Positive Rate:**
   - Track the percentage of reported issues that are false positives, especially for automated tools, to measure testing efficiency and reduce unnecessary manual effort.
5. **Regression Metrics:**
   - Monitor the rate of recurring vulnerabilities to evaluate the effectiveness of past remediations and whether the same issues reappear in later builds.

CODE REVIEW PROCESS

1. **Automated Code Scanning:**
   - Use static application security testing (SAST) tools such as SonarQube, Checkmarx, or Veracode to identify insecure coding practices, such as hardcoded credentials or improper error handling.
   - Set thresholds to prevent builds with critical vulnerabilities from progressing to deployment.
2. **Manual Reviews:**
   - Conduct peer or senior developer reviews of critical code sections. Focus on areas such as cryptographic implementations, access controls, and data handling routines.
   - Include checklists to ensure all security aspects are considered. For example, confirm that functions use parameterized queries to prevent SQL injection.

3. **Secure Coding Standards:**
    - Enforce adherence to secure coding frameworks such as OWASP Secure Coding Practices or CERT coding standards.
4. **Integrated Development Pipelines:**
    - Integrate code review tools into CI/CD pipelines to ensure all commits pass security checks before deployment.

DEFECT MANAGEMENT

1. **Vulnerability Categorization:**
    - Classify identified defects based on severity (critical, high, medium, low) and type (e.g., input validation errors, cryptographic weaknesses). Use frameworks like CVSS to calculate severity scores.
2. **Remediation Workflow:**
    - Assign vulnerabilities to responsible developers with clear timelines and resolution steps. For example, critical vulnerabilities may require immediate attention and resolution within 24 hours.
    - Use tools like Jira or ServiceNow to track remediation progress and maintain transparency across teams.
3. **Testing Post-Fixes:**
    - Retest resolved vulnerabilities to ensure they have been adequately addressed without introducing new issues. For instance, test if a patched SQL injection flaw is still vulnerable to alternate attack vectors.
4. **Root Cause Analysis:**
    - Conduct root cause analyses for recurring defects to identify underlying issues, such as gaps in training, insufficient security controls, or inadequate test coverage.

RELEASE CRITERIA

1. **Defect Thresholds:**
    - Define acceptable thresholds for unresolved vulnerabilities. For example, only low-severity defects with documented mitigations may remain open before release.
2. **Compliance Certification:**
    - Ensure the system meets all relevant compliance requirements, such as PCI DSS certification for payment systems or SOC 2 certification for SaaS platforms.
3. **Performance of Security Controls:**
    - Validate the effectiveness of critical controls, such as firewalls, encryption, and intrusion detection systems, under operational conditions.
4. **Security Test Completion:**
    - Ensure all planned security tests, including functional, regression, and penetration tests, have been executed and results have been reviewed.
5. **Approval Process:**
    - Obtain sign-off from security teams, QA leads, and relevant stakeholders to confirm the system is ready for release. Include a detailed report summarizing test results, resolved defects, and remaining risks.

INPUT VALIDATION IMPLEMENTATION

Implementing robust input validation ensures that user-provided data is properly vetted before processing, reducing the risk of common security vulnerabilities like SQL injection, cross-site scripting (XSS), and command injection. A combination of validation strategies, sanitization techniques, and secure coding practices enables applications to handle inputs securely and consistently across all layers.

Validation Strategies

Whitelist vs. Blacklist

- **Whitelist Validation**: Specifies acceptable input formats or values, rejecting everything that does not conform. This approach is more secure because it explicitly defines what is allowed. For instance, a field accepting a U.S. zip code can enforce a pattern of five digits (^\d{5}$).

- **Blacklist Validation**: Identifies and blocks known bad patterns or characters (e.g., <script>, DROP TABLE, or ../). Blacklisting is less reliable as attackers can use variations to bypass it. For example, encoding or obfuscating malicious inputs often defeats blacklist-based defenses.

A best practice is to favor whitelisting over blacklisting whenever possible, as it provides stricter control over acceptable inputs.

Regular Expressions

Regular expressions are powerful tools for defining patterns to validate input. They are useful for enforcing specific formats, such as email addresses, phone numbers, or dates.

- **Example Use Case**:
  - Email Validation: ^[a-zA-Z0-9._%+-]+@[a-zA-Z0-9.-]+\.[a-zA-Z]{2,}$
  - Date Validation (YYYY-MM-DD): ^\d{4}-\d{2}-\d{2}$
  - IP Address Validation: ^(25[0-5]|2[0-4][0-9]|[0-1]?[0-9][0-9]?)\.([...]

While regular expressions are effective, overly complex patterns can become error-prone and introduce performance issues. Testing and optimization are essential for efficient implementation.

Schema Validation

Schema validation ensures that input adheres to a predefined structure or format. This is particularly useful when dealing with structured data, such as JSON or XML, and can be implemented using tools or libraries.

- **JSON Schema Validation**:
  - Example Schema for User Input

```
{
  "type": "object",
  "properties": {
    "username": { "type": "string", "maxLength": 50 },
    "age": { "type": "integer", "minimum": 18 },
    "email": { "type": "string", "format": "email" }
  },
  "required": ["username", "email"]
}
```

  - This schema enforces that username is a string with a maximum of 50 characters, age is a number greater than or equal to 18, and email is a valid email address.
- **XML Validation**: Use XSD (XML Schema Definition) to enforce data structures in XML documents.

Schema validation automates much of the validation process while ensuring consistency and readability.

Sanitization Techniques

Sanitization cleans potentially dangerous data by removing or encoding unsafe characters. It complements validation by ensuring that even unexpected inputs are rendered harmless.

- **HTML Encoding**: Encode special characters like <, >, &, and " to their HTML entity equivalents (<, >, &, "). For example, an input like <script> becomes harmless when displayed as <script> in a web page.
- **Escaping**: Use escaping techniques appropriate to the context, such as escaping quotes in SQL queries or backslashes in file paths.
- **Output Encoding**: Sanitize data at the output stage to neutralize potentially dangerous inputs. For example, encode untrusted input when rendering HTML, generating SQL queries, or passing data to APIs.

Sanitization ensures that even if malicious data bypasses validation, it cannot cause harm when processed.

Parameter Binding

Parameter binding prevents injection attacks by separating user input from code logic. It works by using placeholders for variables in database queries or commands, binding actual values to these placeholders at runtime.

- **SQL Example**:
  - Vulnerable Query

    SELECT * FROM users WHERE username = '" + userInput + "';

    If userInput is admin' --, the query becomes SELECT * FROM users WHERE username = 'admin' --, allowing an attacker to bypass authentication.

- ○ Secure Query (Using Parameter Binding):
  SELECT * FROM users WHERE username = ?;
  The parameterized query ensures that userInput is treated as a literal value, not executable code.
- **Implementation**: Use libraries that support parameterized queries, such as PreparedStatement in Java, PDO in PHP, or pg_query_params in PostgreSQL

Parameter binding effectively mitigates SQL, LDAP, and command injection risks.

Cross-Site Scripting (XSS) Prevention

XSS attacks occur when malicious scripts are injected into web pages viewed by other users. Proper input validation and output encoding prevent these attacks.

- **Validation**: Reject inputs containing scripts, event handlers, or JavaScript keywords. For example, disallow <script> or onmouseover.
- **Output Encoding**: Use a library like OWASP's Java Encoder or a framework's built-in encoding functions. Ensure all untrusted data is encoded before being rendered in the browser.
- **Content Security Policy (CSP)**: Configure CSP headers to restrict the execution of scripts to trusted sources:
  Content-Security-Policy: default-src 'self'; script-src 'self' https://trusted-cdn.com;
  CSP significantly reduces the impact of XSS by preventing execution of unauthorized scripts.

For example, input <img src=x onerror=alert(1)> would be rendered as a harmless string if HTML encoding (<img src=x onerror=alert(1)>) is applied.

SQL Injection Mitigation

SQL injection attacks exploit vulnerabilities in database queries to execute unauthorized SQL commands. Prevention relies on strict input validation and secure query practices.

- **Parameterized Queries**: Always use parameterized statements for database interactions.
- **Stored Procedures**: Use database-stored procedures that isolate SQL logic and prevent dynamic query construction.
- **Input Length Limits**: Define maximum lengths for input fields to restrict payload size.
- **Database Permissions**: Use the principle of least privilege to restrict database accounts. For example, an application user account should only have permissions for required queries, not schema modifications.

For instance, a vulnerable query like SELECT * FROM users WHERE id = " + userInput can be exploited with an input like 1; DROP TABLE users. Using parameterized queries prevents this.

Command Injection Protection

Command injection vulnerabilities occur when untrusted input is passed to system commands or shell scripts. Mitigation focuses on avoiding dynamic command construction.

- **Avoid Direct Command Execution**: Use APIs or libraries instead of shell commands. For example, in Python, use os.listdir() instead of subprocess.run("ls").
- **Sanitize Inputs**: Validate and escape input strings to prevent malicious commands. For example, reject special characters like ;, &&, or |.
- **Whitelisting Commands**: Explicitly define acceptable commands or inputs. For example, allow only predefined options for a ping utility.
- **Environment Isolation**: Use containerized environments to limit the impact of a successful injection attempt.

For instance, a web application that executes a system command to compress files should explicitly validate filenames and use APIs like Python's shutil.make_archive() rather than os.system().

Deserialization Controls

Deserialization vulnerabilities arise when untrusted data is deserialized into objects, potentially allowing attackers to execute malicious code or manipulate object states.

- **Validation**: Validate serialized input before deserialization. Ensure it matches the expected structure and format.

- **Avoid Insecure Libraries**: Use libraries that enforce strict validation of deserialized objects. For example, in Java, prefer JsonObjectMapper over default deserialization mechanisms.
- **Signed Data**: Use digital signatures to verify the integrity of serialized objects. For example, serialize and sign data with HMAC to prevent tampering.
- **Restrict Classes**: In languages like Java, limit the classes that can be deserialized using techniques like whitelisting allowed classes with an ObjectInputFilter.

An example of a deserialization vulnerability is using Java's ObjectInputStream to deserialize untrusted data, allowing attackers to exploit class constructors for malicious actions. Restricting class types and validating input can mitigate this.

SECURITY CONTROL AND SESSION MANAGEMENT FRAMEWORK

Session management establishes secure methods for maintaining user state and tracking interactions. Token implementation follows cryptographic standards while ensuring proper lifecycle management.

Token Generation Framework:

Implementation Requirements:

- Cryptographic randomness
- Sufficient entropy
- Length requirements
- Format standards
- Transmission security

Session Control Matrix:

Control Type	Implementation	Validation	Monitoring
Token Creation	Secure random	Entropy check	Generation logs
Timeout	Inactivity limit	Session track	Expiration events
State Control	Server storage	Validation	Access checks

Session Timeout Implementation:

- Absolute timeouts
- Idle timeouts
- Sliding windows
- Grace periods
- Re-authentication

State Management:

- Server-side storage
- Client-state validation
- Synchronization checks
- Race condition prevention
- Concurrent access control

Error Handling Standards:

- Exception capture
- Error classification
- Message sanitization
- User notification
- System recovery

Exception Management:

- Try-catch blocks
- Error hierarchies
- Recovery procedures

- Cleanup operations
- Resource release

Error Message Controls:

- Generic messages
- Detail suppression
- Status codes
- User guidance
- Support references

Logging Requirements:

- Event types
- Data elements
- Timestamp format
- Source identification
- Severity levels

Security teams implement:

- Token validators
- Session monitors
- Error analyzers
- Log collectors
- Audit trails

CRYPTOGRAPHIC CONTROLS

Cryptographic controls safeguard data confidentiality, integrity, and authenticity by implementing secure algorithms, robust key management, and proper storage techniques. Effective cryptographic controls ensure the protection of sensitive information against unauthorized access and tampering while aligning with industry standards and regulatory requirements.

ALGORITHM SELECTION

1. **Symmetric Algorithms:**
    - Use symmetric encryption for fast and efficient data protection when the same key is used for both encryption and decryption.
    - Common algorithms:
        - **AES (Advanced Encryption Standard):** Widely used in applications like disk encryption, VPNs, and secure file storage. AES-256 offers strong security and is the standard for most use cases.
        - **ChaCha20:** Often used in mobile and low-power environments due to its high performance and efficiency. Examples include its use in TLS and messaging apps like WhatsApp.
    - Considerations: Select AES-GCM (Galois/Counter Mode) for authenticated encryption, combining confidentiality and integrity. Avoid outdated algorithms like DES and 3DES due to known vulnerabilities.
2. **Asymmetric Algorithms:**
    - Use asymmetric encryption for key exchange, digital signatures, and secure communications where a public-private key pair is involved.
    - Common algorithms:
        - **RSA:** Suitable for secure key exchange and digital signatures. RSA keys should be at least 2048 bits to ensure adequate security.
        - **Elliptic Curve Cryptography (ECC):** Offers equivalent security with smaller key sizes, making it more efficient. Algorithms like ECDSA and ECDH are widely used in TLS and secure messaging protocols.

- Considerations: Transition from RSA to ECC for better performance and security, particularly as computing power grows.

3. **Hashing Algorithms:**
   - Use cryptographic hashing to ensure data integrity by generating fixed-length outputs from input data.
   - Common algorithms:
     - **SHA-256 and SHA-3:** Reliable and secure hashing algorithms for most use cases.
     - **HMAC (Hash-Based Message Authentication Code):** Combines hashing with a secret key for message authentication, ensuring both integrity and authenticity.
   - Considerations: Avoid MD5 and SHA-1 due to collision vulnerabilities, which can allow attackers to generate duplicate hashes for malicious data.
4. **Post-Quantum Cryptography (PQC):**
   - As quantum computing progresses, traditional algorithms like RSA and ECC may become vulnerable. Evaluate post-quantum algorithms such as CRYSTALS-Dilithium (for signatures) and Kyber (for key exchange), which are emerging as leading candidates in NIST's PQC standardization process.

KEY MANAGEMENT

1. **Key Generation:**
   - Use hardware-based random number generators (RNGs) or cryptographic modules to generate strong and unpredictable keys. Software RNGs should comply with standards like NIST SP 800-90A.
   - Avoid manually generated keys or weak key derivation practices, which can introduce predictability.
2. **Key Distribution:**
   - For symmetric encryption, securely exchange keys using asymmetric encryption methods like RSA or Diffie-Hellman.
   - Use secure channels such as TLS 1.3 or hardware security modules (HSMs) to distribute keys.
3. **Key Storage:**
   - Protect keys using secure storage mechanisms, such as hardware security modules, trusted platform modules (TPMs), or encrypted key vaults.
   - Use Key Management Services (KMS) provided by cloud providers (e.g., AWS KMS, Azure Key Vault) to securely store and manage keys with minimal exposure risk.
4. **Key Rotation:**
   - Regularly rotate cryptographic keys to limit their exposure over time. Key rotation intervals can follow recommendations like every 1–3 years for symmetric keys and shorter intervals for high-risk environments.
   - Automate rotation processes to prevent delays or errors using tools like HashiCorp Vault or cloud KMS solutions.
5. **Key Revocation:**
   - Implement mechanisms to revoke compromised or outdated keys promptly. Use Certificate Revocation Lists (CRLs) or Online Certificate Status Protocol (OCSP) for revoking asymmetric keys and certificates.
   - Ensure systems automatically reject revoked keys to prevent unauthorized access.
6. **Access Control for Keys:**
   - Limit access to cryptographic keys to authorized users or systems based on the principle of least privilege.
   - Use role-based access control (RBAC) to enforce granular permissions and audit key usage.
7. **Secure Key Backup:**
   - Back up keys in encrypted formats and store them in physically secure, geographically diverse locations to ensure availability during recovery scenarios.

8. **Key Lifecycle Management:**
    - Manage the entire lifecycle of keys, from generation and distribution to retirement. This includes securely destroying keys when they are no longer needed, using zeroization methods to prevent recovery.

SECURE STORAGE

1. **Encryption of Sensitive Data:**
    - Use strong encryption to protect sensitive data at rest. For example, encrypt customer PII, financial records, or intellectual property stored in databases or file systems.
    - For disk encryption, implement full-disk encryption (e.g., BitLocker, dm-crypt) with AES-256. For databases, enable Transparent Data Encryption (TDE) or application-layer encryption.
2. **Tokenization:**
    - Replace sensitive data with non-sensitive tokens that retain the format of the original data but hold no exploitable value. For example, tokenize credit card numbers in payment systems to reduce the impact of a breach.
3. **Secure Credential Storage:**
    - Store authentication credentials, such as passwords, using strong hashing algorithms like bcrypt, Argon2, or PBKDF2, with a high iteration count.
    - Avoid storing plaintext passwords, and ensure salt values are unique for each password to mitigate rainbow table attacks.
4. **Hardware Security Modules (HSMs):**
    - Use HSMs to securely store cryptographic keys, certificates, and sensitive credentials. These hardware devices provide tamper resistance and limit exposure of cryptographic operations. Examples include AWS CloudHSM and on-premises devices from Thales or Utimaco.
5. **Secure Storage for Mobile Devices:**
    - Leverage secure enclaves or hardware-backed key storage features provided by mobile platforms, such as Apple's Secure Enclave or Android's Trusted Execution Environment (TEE). These features protect sensitive data like biometric credentials or app-specific secrets.
6. **Cloud-Based Secure Storage:**
    - Use encrypted storage options provided by cloud services. For example, enable server-side encryption (SSE) for AWS S3 buckets, or use Azure Storage Service Encryption. Ensure encryption keys are managed securely, either using customer-managed keys (CMKs) or key management services (KMS).
7. **Data Masking:**
    - Mask sensitive data when stored in development or testing environments to reduce exposure. For example, mask the last four digits of a credit card number in non-production databases.
8. **Secure Backup Storage:**
    - Encrypt backup files to protect sensitive data during storage and transit. Ensure that backup encryption keys are stored separately from the backup data itself to prevent unauthorized decryption in the event of compromise.

Proper implementation of cryptographic controls minimizes vulnerabilities in sensitive systems, ensuring secure communication, data protection, and key management while addressing potential risks at every stage of the cryptographic lifecycle.

TESTING TOOLS AND INTEGRATION

Integrating static, dynamic, and interactive application security testing (SAST, DAST, and IAST) into the software development lifecycle (SDLC) enhances the identification and remediation of vulnerabilities during different phases of application development. Proper tool selection, configuration, and validation ensure efficient detection while minimizing false positives and operational disruptions.

SAST Implementation

Static Application Security Testing (SAST) analyzes source code, bytecode, or binaries to identify vulnerabilities early in the development process. SAST is often integrated into CI/CD pipelines to ensure continuous security validation.

Tool Selection

Selecting the right SAST tool depends on the organization's development environment, supported languages, and integration requirements.

- **Language and Framework Support**: Ensure the tool supports the programming languages, frameworks, and libraries used by the development teams. For instance, tools like Checkmarx, Fortify, and SonarQube offer broad language compatibility.
- **Integration Capabilities**: Verify that the tool integrates with version control systems (e.g., GitHub, GitLab), CI/CD tools (e.g., Jenkins, Azure DevOps), and IDEs (e.g., Visual Studio, Eclipse) to streamline developer workflows.
- **Custom Rule Support**: Evaluate whether the tool allows custom rules to address unique security policies or application-specific risks.
- **Scalability**: Assess the tool's ability to handle large codebases and simultaneous scans across multiple projects without significant performance degradation.

For example, a DevSecOps team might choose SonarQube for its seamless integration with Jenkins and support for multiple programming languages like Java, Python, and JavaScript.

Rule Configuration

Proper rule configuration ensures that scans are tailored to the organization's risk profile, reducing unnecessary findings.

- **Baseline Rules**: Start with industry-standard rule sets, such as OWASP Top 10, CWE/SANS Top 25, and PCI DSS requirements.
- **Custom Rules**: Develop custom rules for application-specific risks, such as enforcing input validation for critical modules or prohibiting unsafe APIs.
- **Language-Specific Adjustments**: Enable or disable rules based on the language being scanned. For example, SQL injection rules might be more relevant for a Java web application than for a Python-based API.
- **Prioritization**: Assign severity levels to rules based on potential business impact, ensuring high-risk vulnerabilities (e.g., hardcoded credentials) are addressed first.

False Positive Management

Reducing false positives ensures that developers focus on actionable findings rather than spending time triaging irrelevant results.

- **Contextual Analysis**: Use the tool's contextual capabilities to differentiate between actual vulnerabilities and safe code patterns. For instance, if a query uses parameter binding, it may not need to trigger SQL injection alerts.
- **Suppressions**: Configure the tool to suppress alerts for known safe code or accepted risks using annotations, inline comments, or configuration files.
- **Feedback Loops**: Establish a process for developers and security teams to provide feedback on false positives, which can be used to refine rules over time.

For example, a SAST tool might incorrectly flag a dynamically generated SQL query as vulnerable. By marking the instance as a false positive, future scans can suppress similar findings.

DAST Deployment

Dynamic Application Security Testing (DAST) evaluates running applications by simulating external attacks to identify vulnerabilities like XSS, SQL injection, and misconfigurations. It is particularly effective for uncovering runtime issues that static analysis may miss.

Scan Configuration

Configuring DAST scans ensures comprehensive coverage of the application while minimizing performance impact.

- **Crawl Settings**: Define the depth and scope of crawling to ensure all application pages and endpoints are covered. Use sitemaps or API specifications (e.g., OpenAPI) to guide crawlers.
- **Scan Profiles**: Select scan types based on the environment (e.g., full scans for staging environments or targeted scans for specific vulnerabilities like XSS).
- **Rate Limiting**: Configure request throttling to prevent overwhelming the application or triggering rate-limiting mechanisms, especially in production-like environments.

- **Exclusions**: Exclude non-critical endpoints (e.g., logout pages, admin-only areas) to focus scans on high-value targets and avoid disrupting services.

For example, a DAST scan on an e-commerce site might prioritize pages handling payment transactions, such as the checkout flow, while excluding static resources like image galleries.

Authentication Handling

Proper authentication handling ensures the DAST tool can access restricted areas of the application.

- **Authentication Methods**: Configure the tool to use session cookies, bearer tokens, or OAuth flows to authenticate and maintain session continuity during scans.
- **Multi-Factor Authentication (MFA)**: For applications using MFA, use pre-generated session tokens or integrate with tools that support MFA workflows.
- **Dynamic Tokens**: Handle applications with dynamically generated CSRF tokens by configuring the scanner to recognize and include them in requests.

For instance, scanning a banking application requires the DAST tool to handle secure login with session cookies and refresh tokens to access protected user dashboards.

Result Validation

Validating DAST results ensures the reported vulnerabilities are reproducible and relevant.

- **Manual Validation**: Cross-check critical findings, such as SQL injection or authentication bypass, by replicating the attack manually or with another tool.
- **False Positive Filtering**: Review findings to eliminate false positives, such as XSS alerts triggered by harmless user input that is not rendered back in the browser.
- **Contextual Analysis**: Correlate results with application logs and monitoring tools to confirm the existence and potential impact of reported vulnerabilities.

For example, if a DAST tool reports an open redirect vulnerability, the team might verify it by manually crafting a redirect URL to confirm that it can be abused.

IAST Setup

Interactive Application Security Testing (IAST) combines elements of SAST and DAST by monitoring applications in real-time as they run. IAST tools provide deeper insights into runtime vulnerabilities by analyzing code execution, user inputs, and application behavior.

Agent Deployment

IAST tools rely on agents deployed within the application runtime to monitor and analyze code execution paths.

- **Supported Runtimes**: Ensure the tool supports the application's runtime environment (e.g., JVM for Java, .NET CLR for C#, or Node.js for JavaScript).
- **Deployment Locations**: Install agents on staging or development servers to monitor traffic during functional testing, CI/CD pipelines, or pre-production environments.
- **Configuration**: Configure the agent to track specific classes, functions, or methods, particularly in high-risk modules such as authentication or data access layers.

For example, deploying an IAST agent on a QA server allows it to monitor how input fields in a login page interact with the authentication backend.

Runtime Monitoring

IAST tools analyze application behavior during execution to detect vulnerabilities in real-time.

- **Instrumentation**: The agent instruments the application's code, monitoring function calls, database queries, and data flows to detect issues like injection vulnerabilities or insecure object deserialization.
- **Input-Output Correlation**: Track how user inputs are processed and whether proper validation and sanitization occur before data is used in sensitive operations.
- **Risk Scoring**: Use dynamic risk scoring to prioritize vulnerabilities based on runtime conditions, such as whether a vulnerable function is executed frequently.

For instance, an IAST tool might flag a vulnerable deserialization method in a Java app and provide stack traces showing how untrusted user input flows into the method.

Performance Impact

Minimizing the performance impact of IAST ensures it can operate seamlessly within development and testing environments.

- **Resource Management**: Limit resource consumption by adjusting the level of instrumentation or focusing monitoring on specific components or flows.
- **Non-Intrusive Testing**: Deploy IAST in non-production environments to avoid latency or performance degradation in customer-facing systems.
- **Scalability**: Evaluate the tool's scalability to handle large or distributed systems, especially for microservices architectures.

For example, an IAST tool might be configured to monitor only high-risk functions, such as user authentication, rather than instrumenting the entire application, reducing overhead without sacrificing coverage.

Integrating SAST, DAST, and IAST into the SDLC provides a comprehensive security testing approach that addresses vulnerabilities at different stages of development and runtime. This layered approach enhances overall security while reducing remediation costs and improving application quality.

DEVOPS PIPELINE AND CONTAINER SECURITY IMPLEMENTATION

CI/CD security integrates security controls throughout the development and deployment pipeline. Build processes incorporate code analysis, dependency scanning, and security validation at each stage.

Pipeline Security Framework:

Stage Controls:

1. Code Commit
   - Secret detection
   - Code scanning
   - Policy validation
2. Build Process
   - Dependency check
   - Artifact signing
   - Security testing
3. Deployment
   - Configuration validation
   - Security baseline
   - Compliance checks

Infrastructure as Code Matrix:

Component	Security Control	Validation	Monitoring
Templates	Hardening rules	Syntax check	Version control
Policies	Access controls	Compliance	Audit logs
Resources	Security groups	Configuration	State tracking

Container Security Implementation:

Image Security:

- Base image validation
- Layer analysis
- Vulnerability scanning
- Signature verification
- Policy enforcement

Runtime Protection:

- Resource limits
- Privilege controls
- Network policies

- Volume security
- Behavior monitoring

Registry Controls:

- Access management
- Image signing
- Vulnerability scanning
- Policy enforcement
- Audit logging

Security Policy Framework:

- Resource configurations
- Network controls
- Access management
- Compliance rules
- Monitoring requirements

Validation Methods:

- Static analysis
- Dynamic testing
- Configuration review
- Compliance scanning
- Security baselines

Teams implement:

- Pipeline monitors
- Security scanners
- Policy enforcers
- Audit systems
- Response procedures

CLOUD-NATIVE SECURITY

Cloud-native security encompasses strategies, tools, and practices to secure applications and infrastructure built and deployed using cloud-native technologies. This includes addressing the unique security challenges of serverless architectures, APIs, microservices, service meshes, and other components of modern cloud environments. Robust identity management, secrets protection, and automated compliance processes ensure that security is embedded into the development lifecycle and operations.

SERVERLESS SECURITY

1. **Minimal Attack Surface:**
    - Serverless functions, such as AWS Lambda, Azure Functions, or Google Cloud Functions, have no exposed underlying infrastructure, reducing the attack surface. However, focus is needed on application-level security, such as input validation and secure code practices.
2. **Role-Based Access Control (RBAC):**
    - Apply the principle of least privilege by assigning minimal permissions to serverless functions. For example, configure AWS IAM policies to restrict a Lambda function to only the S3 bucket or DynamoDB table it needs to access.
3. **Dependency Management:**
    - Functions often rely on third-party libraries, which may introduce vulnerabilities. Use tools like Snyk or Dependabot to identify and patch known issues in dependencies.
4. **Event Injection Attacks:**
    - Validate and sanitize all event input to avoid injection attacks. For example, if a Lambda function processes events from an SQS queue, ensure malicious payloads cannot exploit deserialization flaws.

5. **Function Isolation:**
    - Deploy functions in separate accounts, containers, or virtual private clouds (VPCs) to isolate workloads and prevent lateral movement.
6. **Execution Time Monitoring:**
    - Monitor runtime execution with tools like AWS Lambda Powertools or Datadog. Configure alarms to detect unusual function execution patterns, such as increased memory usage, anomalous API calls, or extended execution times.

API SECURITY

1. **Authentication and Authorization:**
    - Use secure API authentication mechanisms, such as OAuth 2.0 and OpenID Connect, to validate user or application identity. For example, protect sensitive API endpoints with token-based authentication.
2. **Rate Limiting and Throttling:**
    - Apply rate limiting to protect APIs from abuse, such as denial-of-service (DoS) attacks. Tools like AWS API Gateway or Azure API Management allow you to throttle excessive traffic from specific IPs or users.
3. **Input Validation:**
    - Validate all incoming API parameters to ensure they conform to expected formats, lengths, and types. For instance, reject API requests with SQL injection payloads in query strings or JSON fields.
4. **TLS Enforcement:**
    - Enforce HTTPS for all API traffic, ensuring data is encrypted in transit. Use certificates from trusted certificate authorities, such as Let's Encrypt or AWS Certificate Manager.
5. **API Gateway Security:**
    - Use API gateways to centralize security controls. For example, AWS API Gateway can enforce authentication, validate requests, log traffic, and throttle excessive calls.
6. **Monitoring and Logging:**
    - Log all API activity, including requests, responses, and error codes. Tools like Splunk, Elastic Stack, or Datadog provide visibility into API usage and anomalies.

MICROSERVICES PROTECTION

1. **Network Segmentation:**
    - Isolate microservices using network policies. For example, use Kubernetes NetworkPolicies or AWS Security Groups to restrict inter-service communication to only the required paths.
2. **Service-to-Service Authentication:**
    - Require mutual TLS (mTLS) for communication between microservices to ensure both services authenticate each other. Tools like Istio or Linkerd enable mTLS in Kubernetes-based environments.
3. **Data Protection:**
    - Encrypt data in transit and at rest for all microservices. Use managed encryption services provided by cloud providers, such as AWS KMS or Azure Key Vault, to simplify key management.
4. **Granular RBAC:**
    - Assign roles at the microservice level. For example, configure Kubernetes RoleBindings to grant specific pods or namespaces the permissions required for their tasks.
5. **Dependency Vulnerability Management:**
    - Continuously scan microservice containers and dependencies for vulnerabilities. Use tools like Aqua Security or Trivy to identify outdated or vulnerable images.

SERVICE MESH SECURITY

1. **Zero Trust Networking:**
    - Implement service mesh solutions, such as Istio, Consul, or Linkerd, to enforce zero trust principles. Services must authenticate and authorize each communication request before exchanging data.

2. **mTLS for Secure Communication:**
   - Enable mutual TLS for all inter-service traffic to ensure encryption and authentication. Service mesh tools automate the certificate lifecycle, reducing administrative overhead.
3. **Traffic Control Policies:**
   - Define traffic policies to limit communication between services. For example, only allow a frontend service to talk to a backend service, blocking all other paths.
4. **Observability:**
   - Use service mesh telemetry features to gain visibility into traffic flows and detect abnormal patterns, such as unexpected data transfers or high-latency paths. Tools like Grafana or Prometheus integrate with service mesh for monitoring.
5. **Rate Limiting and Fault Injection:**
   - Protect services from abuse using rate limiting. Simulate failure conditions (e.g., latency injection) to test resilience and validate fallback mechanisms.

IDENTITY MANAGEMENT

1. **Centralized Identity Providers:**
   - Use cloud-based identity providers, such as AWS IAM, Azure AD, or Okta, to manage user and application identities.
   - Integrate federated identity standards like SAML or OpenID Connect to allow single sign-on (SSO) across multiple services.
2. **Granular Role Assignment:**
   - Assign roles and permissions based on the principle of least privilege. For instance, developers should have read-only access to production environments unless elevated access is explicitly required.
3. **Identity Federation:**
   - Federate identities between on-premises and cloud environments. Azure AD Connect or AWS Single Sign-On (SSO) can synchronize Active Directory users with cloud services.
4. **Auditing and Monitoring:**
   - Monitor identity-related activities, such as failed login attempts or unauthorized permission changes. Integrate IAM logs into a SIEM system for threat detection and compliance reporting.

SECRETS MANAGEMENT

1. **Centralized Secrets Management Tools:**
   - Use secrets management platforms like AWS Secrets Manager, HashiCorp Vault, or Azure Key Vault to securely store and retrieve sensitive data, such as API keys, database credentials, or encryption keys.
2. **Secrets Rotation:**
   - Automate the rotation of secrets to reduce the impact of potential leaks. For example, AWS Secrets Manager can rotate database credentials automatically.
3. **Avoid Secrets in Code:**
   - Ensure secrets are not hardcoded into source code or configuration files. Use environment variables or centralized secrets management APIs to access secrets securely.
4. **Access Control for Secrets:**
   - Limit access to secrets based on roles. For example, only the application process should access the database password, not developers or other systems.
5. **Audit Trails:**
   - Maintain detailed logs of secret access to identify potential misuse or unauthorized access.

COMPLIANCE AUTOMATION

1. **Policy-as-Code:**
   - Use tools like Terraform or AWS Config to codify compliance policies, ensuring consistent enforcement across cloud environments. For instance, define a policy that ensures all S3 buckets must have encryption enabled.

2. **Continuous Compliance Monitoring:**
   - Implement compliance monitoring tools, such as AWS Security Hub, Azure Policy, or Prisma Cloud, to detect and remediate misconfigurations automatically.
3. **Audit-Ready Reporting:**
   - Automate the generation of compliance reports for standards like GDPR, HIPAA, or PCI DSS using tools like CloudHealth or Dome9.
4. **Configuration Drift Detection:**
   - Detect and resolve configuration drifts in real time. For example, use AWS Config Rules to identify non-compliant resources, such as an unencrypted RDS instance.
5. **Integrating CI/CD Pipelines:**
   - Embed compliance checks into CI/CD pipelines using tools like Checkov or Snyk. This ensures that code or configurations violating policies are flagged and remediated before deployment.

CASE STUDY TOPICS

Examining case studies across areas such as SDLC security integration, secure coding, and cloud or container security provides insight into addressing real-world security challenges. These scenarios focus on integrating security into processes, responding to incidents, and leveraging tools effectively to minimize risks.

SDLC Security Integration

A global financial services company sought to integrate security into its software development lifecycle (SDLC) to prevent vulnerabilities from reaching production. The organization adopted a shift-left approach, embedding security practices into the early stages of development.

- **Key Actions**:
  - Introduced **threat modeling** during the requirements phase to identify potential risks for critical components, such as payment APIs and user authentication workflows.
  - Implemented **SAST tools** (e.g., Checkmarx) in the coding phase to detect vulnerabilities such as hardcoded secrets and SQL injection risks.
  - Added **DAST scanning** for staging environments to uncover runtime vulnerabilities, such as XSS in login pages.
  - Trained developers on secure coding practices and incentivized remediation by integrating vulnerability metrics into performance reviews.
- **Outcome**:
  - Reduced the number of vulnerabilities in production deployments by 45%.
  - Improved collaboration between development, security, and operations teams through cross-functional security champions.

This case demonstrates how early and continuous integration of security in the SDLC can prevent costly post-deployment remediations.

Secure Coding Implementation

An e-commerce company faced repeated XSS and SQL injection incidents due to insecure development practices. To address the issue, the company rolled out a secure coding initiative.

- **Steps Taken**:
  - **Policy Development**: Created coding standards aligned with OWASP secure coding guidelines, requiring input validation, output encoding, and parameterized queries.
  - **Tool Integration**: Integrated code review tools like SonarQube into the CI/CD pipeline to enforce compliance with secure coding standards.
  - **Training Programs**: Delivered mandatory training sessions for developers on secure coding techniques, including live demos of exploiting and fixing common vulnerabilities.
  - **Code Review Enhancements**: Established peer code reviews with a security focus, ensuring that no critical code changes bypass review.
- **Results**:
  - SQL injection incidents dropped to zero within six months.

    - The development team became more aware of security issues, proactively flagging risks during planning sessions.

By implementing secure coding practices and providing developers with the necessary training and tools, the organization enhanced its overall security posture and reduced vulnerability recurrence.

Testing Tool Deployment

A logistics company needed to deploy security testing tools to identify vulnerabilities in its complex, microservices-based architecture. The initiative aimed to combine SAST, DAST, and IAST tools for comprehensive security coverage.

- **Deployment Process**:
    - Selected **SAST tools** like Fortify for early detection of insecure code, particularly focusing on service-to-service communication vulnerabilities.
    - Deployed **DAST scanners** in staging environments to test APIs for runtime issues such as insecure authentication mechanisms and improper error handling.
    - Used **IAST tools** like Contrast Security during QA to analyze real-time application behavior, identifying vulnerabilities like insecure object deserialization.
    - Configured these tools to generate findings in a centralized vulnerability management platform (e.g., DefectDojo) to streamline triage and remediation.
- **Challenges**:
    - Addressed false positives from the SAST tool by fine-tuning rules based on feedback from developers.
    - Overcame scanning delays in DAST by optimizing crawl configurations to focus on critical endpoints first.
- **Outcomes**:
    - Detected and remediated over 300 vulnerabilities in the first six months, including high-severity issues like exposed admin endpoints.
    - Reduced time-to-remediate vulnerabilities by integrating results directly into the issue-tracking system (e.g., Jira).

This case highlights the value of deploying complementary testing tools to address vulnerabilities across the development and runtime spectrum.

Pipeline Security Breach

A software company suffered a breach when attackers compromised its CI/CD pipeline to inject malicious code into a popular open-source library. This incident exposed thousands of downstream users to potential threats.

- **Incident Details**:
    - Attackers exploited weak SSH keys on a build server to gain unauthorized access to the pipeline.
    - The pipeline lacked controls to verify the integrity of third-party dependencies, allowing the attackers to introduce a malicious payload into the build artifacts.
    - The malicious code was pushed to production and included in downstream projects, compromising multiple organizations.
- **Remediation Efforts**:
    - Implemented **stronger authentication mechanisms**, such as SSH key rotation and MFA for accessing build servers.
    - Added **code signing** to verify the integrity of build artifacts before deployment.
    - Introduced **dependency scanning tools** like Snyk to detect and block malicious or vulnerable libraries in the build process.
    - Conducted a post-incident review and improved pipeline security by enforcing least privilege access and deploying an internal bug bounty program.
- **Outcome**:
    - No further compromise of the pipeline was observed, and all affected downstream users were notified within 48 hours.
    - The company adopted a zero-trust approach to its pipeline security, including immutable builds and enhanced audit logging.

This case illustrates the risks associated with insecure pipelines and the importance of securing every stage of the CI/CD process.

Cloud Migration Security

A retail company migrating its infrastructure to AWS needed to ensure security during the transition from on-premises systems to the cloud. The migration introduced risks related to misconfigurations and data exposure.

- **Approach**:
  - Conducted a **risk assessment** to identify assets requiring extra protection, such as customer databases and payment processing systems.
  - Leveraged **AWS native security tools** like AWS Config, CloudTrail, and GuardDuty to monitor and enforce secure configurations.
  - Used **infrastructure-as-code (IaC)** tools (e.g., Terraform) to define secure baseline configurations, including VPC segmentation, security group restrictions, and encryption settings.
  - Implemented **IAM policies** enforcing least privilege, preventing users or services from accessing resources unnecessarily.
- **Challenges**:
  - Addressed data exposure risks by enabling server-side encryption for all S3 buckets and enforcing bucket policies.
  - Resolved misconfigurations detected during deployment by using automated IaC scans with tools like Checkov and AWS IAM Access Analyzer.
- **Results**:
  - Prevented a potential data breach by detecting and remediating public S3 buckets before production deployment.
  - Enhanced monitoring capabilities to detect anomalous activity in real-time, such as unauthorized access attempts.

This case demonstrates how proactive security measures during cloud migration can prevent misconfigurations and protect sensitive data.

Container Security Incident

A media streaming company experienced a container security incident when attackers exploited a misconfigured Kubernetes cluster to deploy cryptocurrency mining workloads.

- **Incident Details**:
  - A publicly accessible Kubernetes API server allowed unauthenticated access to cluster resources.
  - Attackers deployed malicious pods configured to mine cryptocurrency, consuming significant compute resources and degrading performance for legitimate workloads.
  - Logs revealed that the attackers accessed the cluster via an exposed kubectl dashboard with no authentication required.
- **Response**:
  - Isolated the affected cluster and terminated all unauthorized pods.
  - Rotated all secrets and tokens stored within the cluster to prevent further exploitation.
  - Hardened the Kubernetes environment by:
    - Enforcing **role-based access control (RBAC)** policies to limit permissions.
    - Securing the API server with network policies and authentication requirements.
    - Deploying tools like **Kube-bench** and **Kubernetes Audit Logs** to detect configuration issues and suspicious activity.
- **Lessons Learned**:
  - Conducted regular vulnerability scans of container images with tools like Trivy and Aqua Security.
  - Established a secure container pipeline, including image signing and runtime monitoring with Falco.
  - Created automated alerts for unusual Kubernetes activity, such as high CPU usage or unexpected pod creation.

- **Outcomes**:
    - Prevented further exploitation of Kubernetes resources by enforcing strict security policies and monitoring practices.
    - Developed a hardened container security strategy, reducing misconfigurations and runtime risks.

This case highlights the importance of securing Kubernetes environments and implementing runtime protections to prevent abuse of containerized infrastructure.

SOFTWARE SECURITY AND IMPLEMENTATION PRACTICE SCENARIOS

Scenario 1: Security Requirements Analysis A financial application processes credit card transactions. Review the requirements:

Application Features:
- Payment processing
- Transaction history
- User authentication
- Account management
- Reporting functions

Which security requirement creates highest risk if omitted?
A. Input validation
B. Session management
C. Encryption at rest
D. Error logging

Correct Answer: C Analysis: PCI DSS mandates encryption for card data, making this requirement foundational.

Code Vulnerability Example:

```
def process_payment(user_input):
    query = "SELECT * FROM transactions WHERE id = " + user_input
    cursor.execute(query)
    return cursor.fetchall()
```

What security vulnerability exists?
A. Input validation
B. SQL injection
C. Authentication bypass
D. Error handling

Correct Answer: B Analysis: Direct string concatenation enables SQL injection attacks.

Tool Selection Matrix:

Tool Type	Purpose	Integration	Coverage
SAST	Code analysis	Build pipeline	Source code
DAST	Runtime testing	Test environment	Running app
SCA	Dependency check	Package manager	Libraries

Which tool selection creates coverage gap?
A. SAST only
B. DAST missing
C. No container scanning
D. Limited SCA

Correct Answer: C Analysis: Container deployments require specific security scanning.

Pipeline Implementation:

Which control point requires enhancement?

A. Pre-commit hooks B. Build validation C. Production monitoring D. Test coverage

Correct Answer: A Analysis: Early detection through pre-commit security checks prevents downstream issues.

Security teams maintain:

- Testing frameworks
- Validation procedures
- Documentation standards
- Monitoring systems
- Response processes

Advanced Topics and Emerging Trends

CLOUD SERVICE SECURITY ARCHITECTURES AND IMPLEMENTATION

Cloud service models define security responsibility boundaries between providers and customers. Each model presents unique security requirements and control implementations based on the service level.

IaaS Security Framework:

Customer Controls:

- Operating systems
- Applications
- Data encryption
- Network security
- Access management

Provider Controls:

- Physical security
- Hypervisor
- Infrastructure
- Core networking
- Storage systems

Service Model Matrix:

Component	IaaS	PaaS	SaaS
Application	Customer	Customer	Provider
Data	Customer	Customer	Shared
Runtime	Customer	Provider	Provider
Middleware	Customer	Provider	Provider
OS	Customer	Provider	Provider
Infrastructure	Provider	Provider	Provider

PaaS Security Implementation:

- Application security
- API protection
- Container security
- Service integration
- Platform hardening

SaaS Control Requirements:

- Data classification
- Access controls
- User management
- Activity monitoring
- Compliance tracking

Identity Management:

- Federation services
- SSO implementation
- MFA requirements
- Role management
- Access reviews

Data Protection Strategies:

- Encryption methods
- Key management

- Data lifecycle
- Backup systems
- Recovery procedures

Compliance Framework:

- Regulatory mapping
- Control validation
- Audit procedures
- Evidence collection
- Reporting methods

Teams implement:

- Security baselines
- Control monitoring
- Risk assessments
- Incident response
- Change management

Organizations maintain:

- Security policies
- Technical standards
- Audit programs
- Training materials
- Process documentation

MULTI-CLOUD SECURITY

Multi-cloud environments require a comprehensive security approach that addresses the complexities of managing resources, identities, and data across multiple cloud service providers (CSPs). Designing a secure multi-cloud architecture involves standardizing controls, integrating monitoring and response capabilities, ensuring data sovereignty, and maintaining compliance with regulatory and business requirements. Risk management practices are essential to continuously assess and mitigate threats across diverse platforms.

SECURITY ARCHITECTURE DESIGN

1. **Unified Security Framework:**
    - Design a security framework that spans all CSPs, ensuring consistent application of security policies. For example, enforce encryption for all storage services, whether in AWS, Azure, or Google Cloud. Use centralized identity and access management (IAM) systems and apply uniform logging and monitoring practices across environments.
2. **Zero Trust Model:**
    - Adopt a Zero Trust architecture where no implicit trust is granted to users, devices, or applications, regardless of their location. Implement strong identity verification, least-privilege access, and continuous monitoring across all cloud providers.
3. **Segmentation and Isolation:**
    - Use network segmentation to isolate workloads across clouds. For example, deploy virtual private clouds (VPCs) in AWS, virtual networks (VNets) in Azure, and similar structures in other CSPs to isolate sensitive applications or data. Use firewalls and service-specific policies to control traffic between segments.
4. **Cloud-Native Security Features:**
    - Leverage security tools and features offered by each CSP. For instance, use AWS Security Groups, Azure Network Security Groups, and Google Cloud Firewall Rules to manage access control at the network level. Ensure these configurations align with overall security policies.

5. **Encryption Across Layers:**
   - Encrypt data at rest and in transit using native tools such as AWS KMS, Azure Key Vault, or Google Cloud KMS. Use strong encryption algorithms like AES-256 for storage and TLS 1.3 for data transmission.

CONTROL STANDARDIZATION

1. **Policy Uniformity:**
   - Standardize access control, logging, and encryption policies across CSPs to eliminate inconsistencies that could lead to vulnerabilities. For example, enforce multi-factor authentication (MFA) for administrative access in all clouds, regardless of platform.
2. **Automation with IaC (Infrastructure as Code):**
   - Use tools like Terraform or Ansible to codify and enforce consistent security controls. This ensures that resource configurations, such as security groups or IAM policies, are deployed uniformly across cloud platforms.
3. **Configuration Management:**
   - Monitor configurations using tools like AWS Config, Azure Policy, or third-party solutions like HashiCorp Sentinel. These tools detect and remediate non-compliant resources, such as open storage buckets or improperly configured firewalls.
4. **Standardized Logging Format:**
   - Normalize logs across CSPs to enable centralized analysis. Use tools like Fluentd or Logstash to transform logs into a consistent format before sending them to a Security Information and Event Management (SIEM) platform.

IDENTITY FEDERATION

1. **Centralized Identity Providers:**
   - Integrate multi-cloud environments with a centralized identity provider, such as Azure AD, Okta, or Ping Identity, to simplify user authentication and access management across platforms.
2. **Cross-Cloud Role Mapping:**
   - Map roles and permissions consistently across CSPs. For example, a "Cloud Admin" in AWS should have equivalent permissions to a "Cloud Administrator" in Azure, ensuring a uniform approach to privilege assignments.
3. **Federated Authentication:**
   - Use standards like SAML, OAuth 2.0, or OpenID Connect to enable federated authentication across clouds. This ensures users can access resources in multiple environments without requiring separate credentials for each.
4. **Conditional Access Policies:**
   - Implement conditional access policies based on context, such as user location, device compliance, or risk levels. For instance, restrict high-privilege operations from untrusted locations or devices.

DATA SOVEREIGNTY

1. **Geographic Data Residency:**
   - Ensure sensitive data remains within designated geographic boundaries to comply with data sovereignty laws such as GDPR or the CLOUD Act. Use CSP-specific tools like AWS Regions, Azure Geographies, and Google Cloud Locations to control data residency.
2. **Cross-Border Data Transfers:**
   - Minimize unnecessary data transfers across regions. For example, replicate data between regions only if it is essential for redundancy or disaster recovery.
3. **Encryption to Protect Data Jurisdiction:**
   - Encrypt sensitive data using keys managed within the required jurisdiction. For example, use customer-managed keys (CMKs) stored in a specific region's key management service to prevent unauthorized decryption outside the intended jurisdiction.
4. **Data Classification:**
   - Classify data based on sensitivity and residency requirements, using CSP tagging features to track and enforce compliance.

MONITORING INTEGRATION

1. **Centralized Log Aggregation:**
   - Aggregate logs from all CSPs into a single monitoring system for analysis. Use tools like Splunk, Datadog, or Elastic Stack to collect and analyze logs from AWS CloudWatch, Azure Monitor, and Google Cloud Operations.
2. **Unified Alerts:**
   - Configure alerts for critical events, such as unauthorized access, failed login attempts, or data exfiltration. Consolidate these alerts into a central dashboard to streamline incident response.
3. **Cloud-Native SIEM Integration:**
   - Use native SIEM integrations, such as AWS Security Hub, Microsoft Sentinel, or Chronicle Security, to correlate security events across cloud providers.
4. **Continuous Monitoring with CSP Tools:**
   - Enable native security monitoring tools like AWS GuardDuty, Azure Security Center, and Google Cloud Security Command Center to detect and respond to threats within each CSP.

INCIDENT RESPONSE

1. **Cross-Cloud Incident Playbooks:**
   - Develop unified incident response playbooks for scenarios like credential leaks, ransomware attacks, or resource misconfigurations. Include specific steps for each CSP, ensuring all teams follow a consistent approach.
2. **Automated Containment:**
   - Implement automated response workflows, such as isolating compromised instances or disabling compromised credentials, using tools like AWS Lambda, Azure Logic Apps, or Google Cloud Functions.
3. **Forensic Data Collection:**
   - Ensure each CSP has tools for forensic data collection, such as retrieving instance snapshots, preserving logs, and capturing network traffic.
4. **Post-Incident Reviews:**
   - After resolving incidents, conduct reviews to identify gaps and update response plans. Ensure lessons learned are shared across teams and applied to all environments.

COMPLIANCE MAPPING

1. **Regulatory Framework Alignment:**
   - Map CSP-specific controls to compliance frameworks like GDPR, HIPAA, PCI DSS, or ISO 27001. Use tools like AWS Artifact, Azure Compliance Manager, or Google Cloud Compliance Reports to validate compliance.
2. **Automated Compliance Checks:**
   - Use tools like Prisma Cloud or CloudCheckr to perform continuous compliance checks and generate audit-ready reports.
3. **Tagging for Compliance Tracking:**
   - Use resource tagging to track compliance status. For example, tag storage resources by compliance categories such as "PCI-DSS Compliant" or "GDPR Zone."
4. **Shared Responsibility Clarity:**
   - Clearly document which compliance requirements are managed by the organization versus the CSP, as outlined in each provider's shared responsibility model.

RISK MANAGEMENT

1. **Risk Assessments Across CSPs:**
   - Conduct regular risk assessments to identify vulnerabilities, misconfigurations, and gaps in the multi-cloud environment. Tools like AWS Well-Architected Framework or Azure Advisor provide insights into risk factors.
2. **Third-Party Risk Management:**
   - Assess risks introduced by third-party services or integrations in the cloud. Ensure third-party applications comply with organizational security policies and standards.

3. **Threat Intelligence Integration:**
    - Integrate threat intelligence feeds into your security tools to detect emerging threats across CSPs.
4. **Risk Prioritization and Mitigation:**
    - Rank identified risks based on impact and likelihood, then implement mitigation measures such as patching vulnerabilities, hardening configurations, or reducing unnecessary permissions.

Multi-cloud security strategies must account for platform-specific features and differences while maintaining centralized visibility, control, and compliance to ensure comprehensive protection across all environments.

IOT SECURITY ARCHITECTURE

Securing Internet of Things (IoT) devices requires a robust architecture that addresses the unique challenges of limited computational resources, diverse device ecosystems, and complex network environments. A comprehensive IoT security architecture includes stringent device security measures, secure network design, strong authentication and encryption mechanisms, proactive vulnerability management, and monitoring systems to detect and respond to threats in real-time.

Device Security Requirements

Ensuring the security of IoT devices involves implementing protective measures at the hardware, firmware, and software levels.

- **Secure Boot**: Devices should use secure boot mechanisms to verify the integrity of firmware and ensure only trusted code executes during startup. This can be achieved using cryptographic signatures.
- **Hardware Root of Trust**: Include dedicated hardware elements such as Trusted Platform Modules (TPMs) or secure enclaves to store cryptographic keys and enforce secure operations.
- **Access Controls**: Limit device functionality to authorized users and processes. For example, administrative interfaces should require strong authentication mechanisms and should not be accessible over unencrypted channels.
- **Device Identity**: Assign each device a unique immutable identity, such as a secure cryptographic key pair, for authentication and lifecycle management.
- **Attack Surface Reduction**: Minimize installed software, open ports, and unnecessary services to reduce exploitable vulnerabilities. For instance, a sensor device used for monitoring temperatures should not have unnecessary web server components.

Devices deployed in critical industries like healthcare or manufacturing should have physical tamper resistance to prevent attackers from extracting sensitive information or modifying device operations.

Network Segmentation

IoT networks must be segmented from other parts of the IT environment to limit the impact of device compromise and reduce lateral movement risks.

- **Dedicated VLANs**: Place IoT devices on separate virtual LANs (VLANs) to isolate them from sensitive corporate assets, such as databases or administrative systems.
- **Microsegmentation**: Use software-defined networking (SDN) or zero-trust principles to enforce granular access control policies between individual devices and services. For example, a smart thermostat should only communicate with its designated cloud service and not other devices on the network.
- **Firewalls and Gateways**: Deploy IoT gateways with built-in firewalls to filter traffic and enforce policies for devices with limited capabilities. This includes blocking outgoing traffic to unauthorized domains or IPs.
- **Deny by Default**: Use default-deny rules at the network level, allowing communication only on explicitly authorized ports, protocols, and destinations.
- **Anomaly Detection**: Implement network-based intrusion detection or behavioral monitoring tools to identify deviations in device communication patterns.

For instance, in a smart home environment, security cameras should operate on an isolated segment separate from user devices like smartphones and laptops.

Authentication Methods

Strong authentication mechanisms prevent unauthorized access to IoT devices and their associated services.

- **Mutual Authentication**: Use mutual authentication protocols, such as TLS with client certificates, to ensure both the device and server authenticate each other during communication.
- **PKI (Public Key Infrastructure)**: Leverage PKI to issue device certificates, ensuring unique and secure identities for IoT devices. For example, IoT devices in an industrial environment could use PKI to authenticate with control systems.
- **OAuth 2.0 and Token-Based Authentication**: When devices need access to APIs, use OAuth 2.0 with short-lived tokens to restrict unauthorized API calls.
- **Multi-Factor Authentication (MFA)**: For administrative access to IoT management platforms or interfaces, enforce MFA to prevent credential theft or misuse.
- **Default Credentials Elimination**: Prohibit the use of default or weak passwords. Require devices to enforce strong passwords during setup, and ensure credentials are never hardcoded into the firmware.

Authentication should also account for constrained devices by using lightweight authentication protocols such as EAP-TLS or DTLS for resource-constrained environments like IoT sensor networks.

Encryption Implementation

Encrypting data in transit and at rest prevents attackers from intercepting or tampering with sensitive information.

- **Encryption in Transit**: Use strong encryption protocols such as TLS 1.3 to secure communication between devices, gateways, and cloud services. For example, ensure data streams from security cameras are encrypted to protect against interception.
- **Encryption at Rest**: Encrypt sensitive data stored on devices using AES-256 or similar algorithms. Sensitive information, such as device configuration or user credentials, should be stored in encrypted format.
- **Key Management**: Securely generate, distribute, and store cryptographic keys using hardware security modules (HSMs) or secure key management services. Rotate encryption keys periodically to minimize risks from key compromise.
- **End-to-End Encryption (E2EE)**: Implement E2EE for IoT communication to ensure data is encrypted from the source device to the final recipient. This is especially critical for applications like healthcare IoT, where patient data requires the highest level of protection.

Properly implemented encryption ensures that even if an attacker gains access to IoT traffic or device storage, they cannot extract meaningful information.

Update Management

Effective update mechanisms are necessary to address newly discovered vulnerabilities and enhance device functionality.

- **Secure Firmware Updates**: Use signed and verified updates to ensure that only authenticated and untampered firmware is installed. Devices should validate signatures before applying updates.
- **Over-the-Air (OTA) Updates**: Implement OTA capabilities to streamline updates across large-scale IoT deployments without requiring physical access to devices.
- **Update Rollback**: Provide rollback mechanisms to revert to previous versions if an update introduces issues or fails to complete.
- **Version Control**: Maintain version tracking for firmware updates and monitor deployment status to ensure all devices are running the latest secure version.

For example, smart home devices like smart locks must have mechanisms to apply critical patches securely and automatically to mitigate vulnerabilities in real time.

Vulnerability Management

Proactive vulnerability management is essential for addressing weaknesses in both devices and IoT ecosystems.

- **Vulnerability Scanning**: Regularly scan IoT devices and their ecosystems for known vulnerabilities using tools like Nessus or custom scripts tailored to IoT protocols.
- **Threat Intelligence**: Integrate threat intelligence feeds to stay informed about new vulnerabilities or exploits targeting IoT platforms, such as Mirai or Mozi botnets.
- **Patch Management**: Prioritize patches for high-risk vulnerabilities and test them before deployment to avoid introducing instability.

- **Bug Bounty Programs**: Collaborate with security researchers by offering incentives for reporting vulnerabilities in IoT devices or services.

For example, vulnerability scanning might detect an outdated software library used in an IoT medical device, prompting the manufacturer to deploy a patch before the issue is exploited.

Security Monitoring

Continuous monitoring ensures visibility into the behavior of IoT devices and their ecosystems.

- **Log Aggregation**: Collect logs from IoT devices, gateways, and networks into a central SIEM platform for analysis and correlation. Include logs such as authentication attempts, device configuration changes, and communication patterns.
- **Behavioral Analytics**: Use machine learning or anomaly detection tools to establish baseline behavior for IoT devices. Flag unusual activities, such as an unexpected surge in data transmission or a device communicating with an unapproved IP.
- **Real-Time Alerts**: Configure alerts for critical events, such as failed authentication attempts, firmware tampering, or communication with known malicious domains.

For example, monitoring traffic patterns from a smart grid might reveal unexpected data transfers to external IPs, indicating a possible compromise.

Incident Response

Incident response plans for IoT environments must account for the unique nature of connected devices and their ecosystems.

- **Isolation Protocols**: Define procedures to isolate compromised devices, such as dynamically applying network segmentation or disconnecting the device from the network.
- **Forensic Analysis**: Ensure devices and gateways can provide forensic data, such as logs and configuration states, to investigate incidents effectively.
- **Recovery Procedures**: Maintain backup configurations for IoT devices to facilitate rapid restoration after incidents. In the event of a compromise, ensure that devices can be securely reset to factory defaults.
- **Coordination**: Collaborate with device vendors and cloud service providers during incidents to deploy hotfixes or patches quickly.

For instance, during a botnet attack leveraging IoT cameras, an organization could isolate all affected devices and work with the vendor to apply emergency patches while analyzing traffic logs for malicious patterns.

IOT DATA SECURITY AND PRIVACY PROTECTION FRAMEWORK

IoT data collection implements granular controls at device and gateway levels. Edge processing filters sensitive information before transmission, while maintaining data integrity and authenticity.

Data Collection Matrix:

Control Layers:

1. Device Level
   - Sensor validation
   - Data filtering
   - Local processing
   - Buffer management
2. Gateway Level
   - Aggregation rules
   - Protocol conversion
   - Security enforcement
   - Edge analytics

Privacy Implementation:

Data Type	Classification	Protection	Access
Personal	Restricted	Encryption	Limited
Telemetry	Internal	Integrity	Monitored
Status	Public	Authentication	Controlled

Storage Security Requirements:

- Encryption standards
- Key management
- Access controls
- Audit logging
- Backup procedures

Transmission Protection:

- Protocol security
- Channel encryption
- Certificate management
- Message integrity
- Authentication methods

Access Control Framework:

- Identity verification
- Role assignments
- Permission sets
- Session management
- Activity monitoring

Data Lifecycle Stages:

- Collection rules
- Processing methods
- Storage duration
- Usage limitations
- Disposal procedures

Compliance Requirements:

- Privacy regulations
- Industry standards
- Data sovereignty
- Audit procedures
- Documentation needs

Risk Assessment Components:

- Threat modeling
- Vulnerability assessment
- Impact analysis
- Control evaluation
- Mitigation planning

Security teams implement:

- Monitoring systems
- Incident response
- Change management
- Audit procedures
- Training programs

ZERO TRUST IMPLEMENTATION

Zero Trust is a security model based on the principle of "never trust, always verify." It assumes that threats exist both outside and inside the network, requiring continuous verification of identity, strict access control, segmentation, and policy enforcement for every user, device, and application. Implementing Zero Trust requires integrating advanced security technologies and practices to ensure that resources are accessed securely and only by those with legitimate, verified needs.

ARCHITECTURE PRINCIPLES

1. **Verify Every Access Request:**
   - Authenticate and authorize every user, device, and application attempting to access resources, regardless of location. Use contextual signals such as device health, geolocation, and user behavior as part of the verification process.
2. **Least Privilege Access:**
   - Limit access to only what is necessary for a user's role or task. For example, an HR employee should access HR databases but not financial systems.
3. **Microsegmentation:**
   - Break down the network into smaller, isolated zones to limit lateral movement of attackers. For instance, segment an organization's development and production environments into separate zones with tightly controlled communication.
4. **Continuous Verification:**
   - Trust should be dynamic and constantly evaluated. Use real-time monitoring and risk assessments to determine whether to allow, deny, or reauthenticate a request.
5. **Assume Breach Mentality:**
   - Design systems with the assumption that breaches can occur. Build defenses that can limit the damage, detect malicious activity quickly, and facilitate rapid recovery.

IDENTITY VERIFICATION

1. **Multi-Factor Authentication (MFA):**
   - Enforce MFA for all users, including employees, contractors, and third-party partners. For example, combine something the user knows (password) with something they have (mobile push notification or hardware token).
2. **Single Sign-On (SSO):**
   - Implement SSO to simplify access while maintaining strong authentication policies. For example, use Azure AD, Okta, or Ping Identity to centralize identity management across applications and services.
3. **Adaptive Authentication:**
   - Use contextual factors like device reputation, geolocation, or historical behavior patterns to dynamically adjust authentication requirements. For example, flag login attempts from unusual locations for additional verification.
4. **Identity Federation:**
   - Integrate identity providers (IdPs) across different environments to enable seamless authentication. For example, federate on-premises Active Directory accounts with cloud-based services using SAML or OpenID Connect.

ACCESS CONTROL

1. **Role-Based Access Control (RBAC):**
   - Assign permissions based on user roles to enforce least privilege. For instance, a "Developer" role might have read-only access to production logs but write access to development resources.
2. **Attribute-Based Access Control (ABAC):**
   - Enforce access policies based on user attributes (e.g., department, clearance level) and contextual data (e.g., device health, location).
3. **Just-In-Time (JIT) Access:**
   - Provide temporary, time-limited access for sensitive tasks. For example, grant an administrator elevated permissions only for a specific maintenance activity, with permissions revoked automatically after the task.
4. **Device Trust:**
   - Verify that devices accessing the network are compliant with security policies. For example, ensure that endpoint protection is active and updated before granting access.

5. **Policy-Based Access Control:**
    - Implement centralized access policies using tools like AWS Identity and Access Management (IAM), Azure AD Conditional Access, or Google BeyondCorp.

NETWORK SEGMENTATION

1. **Logical Segmentation:**
    - Divide the network into zones based on sensitivity and purpose. For example, create separate zones for finance, HR, production, and guest access.
2. **Software-Defined Networking (SDN):**
    - Use SDN technologies like VMware NSX or Cisco ACI to define segmentation policies programmatically, enabling flexibility and dynamic enforcement.
3. **Zero Trust Network Access (ZTNA):**
    - Replace VPNs with ZTNA solutions to limit access to specific applications rather than providing full network access. Solutions like Zscaler Private Access or Palo Alto Prisma Access enable granular control.
4. **Microsegmentation:**
    - Implement fine-grained segmentation at the workload level. For example, use Kubernetes NetworkPolicies to isolate containers in a microservices architecture, ensuring only authorized communication between components.
5. **East-West Traffic Control:**
    - Monitor and control lateral (east-west) traffic within the network using tools like host-based firewalls or cloud-native network security policies.

RESOURCE PROTECTION

1. **Encryption:**
    - Encrypt sensitive data at rest and in transit. For example, use TLS 1.3 for securing communication and AES-256 for database encryption.
2. **Endpoint Protection:**
    - Deploy endpoint detection and response (EDR) tools like CrowdStrike or SentinelOne to monitor and protect devices accessing resources.
3. **Application Whitelisting:**
    - Restrict applications to only those explicitly approved to run on servers, endpoints, or containers.
4. **Data Loss Prevention (DLP):**
    - Implement DLP solutions to monitor and prevent unauthorized transfer of sensitive data. For example, block users from sending unencrypted emails containing customer PII.
5. **Backup and Recovery:**
    - Ensure resources are backed up regularly and test recovery processes. Secure backups to prevent attackers from tampering with or deleting them.

MONITORING REQUIREMENTS

1. **Real-Time Monitoring:**
    - Use tools like SIEMs (e.g., Splunk, Microsoft Sentinel) or cloud-native monitoring services (e.g., AWS CloudWatch) to analyze logs and detect anomalies.
2. **Behavioral Analytics:**
    - Leverage user and entity behavior analytics (UEBA) to detect suspicious activity, such as unusual login times or data transfer patterns.
3. **Endpoint Monitoring:**
    - Monitor endpoints for malware, unauthorized software, or misconfigurations. Integrate endpoint telemetry into centralized monitoring systems for better visibility.
4. **Full Packet Capture:**
    - Use tools like Zeek (formerly Bro) to capture and analyze network packets in sensitive segments for detailed forensic analysis.

POLICY ENFORCEMENT

1. **Dynamic Policy Enforcement:**
    - Automate enforcement of policies that adapt to changing contexts, such as user behavior, device health, or threat intelligence. For example, block access from devices that fail a compliance check.
2. **Centralized Policy Management:**
    - Manage access and security policies from a single pane of glass using tools like Cisco Identity Services Engine (ISE), Azure Conditional Access, or HashiCorp Sentinel.
3. **Auditable Policies:**
    - Ensure all policies are documented, versioned, and traceable for regulatory and compliance audits.
4. **Integration with CI/CD Pipelines:**
    - Embed policy checks into CI/CD pipelines to block deployments that violate security or compliance rules. For example, prevent deployment of container images with critical vulnerabilities.

SECURITY ORCHESTRATION

1. **Security Orchestration, Automation, and Response (SOAR):**
    - Automate repetitive security tasks like incident triage and response using SOAR platforms like Cortex XSOAR or Splunk Phantom.
2. **Incident Playbooks:**
    - Develop automated playbooks to handle specific scenarios, such as blocking a compromised account or isolating an infected device.
3. **API-Driven Integrations:**
    - Integrate security tools via APIs to enable seamless sharing of data and coordinated actions. For example, integrate SIEM tools with firewalls to block malicious IPs automatically.
4. **Threat Intelligence:**
    - Use threat intelligence feeds to enrich monitoring and incident response capabilities. Automatically block known malicious domains or IP addresses.

A Zero Trust implementation unifies these elements into a security ecosystem that continuously evaluates risks, restricts access, and dynamically adapts to evolving threats.

MICRO-SEGMENTATION STRATEGY

Micro-segmentation enhances network security by dividing environments into smaller, isolated zones, controlling traffic at a granular level, and applying security policies tailored to each segment. Unlike traditional perimeter defenses, this strategy provides east-west traffic control, minimizes attack surfaces, and prevents lateral movement by attackers.

Segmentation Design

Effective micro-segmentation begins with a detailed understanding of the network, applications, and data flows. Segmentation design ensures that workloads, devices, and applications are organized logically to reduce risk and enforce least privilege access.

- **Asset Mapping**: Identify all assets within the environment, including servers, virtual machines, containers, endpoints, and IoT devices. Group them based on their function, sensitivity, and communication patterns.
- **Workload Classification**:
    - Segment workloads by type (e.g., development, staging, production).
    - Separate workloads handling sensitive data (e.g., customer records, payment information) from less critical systems.
- **Zone Definition**: Define segmentation zones based on risk and function. Examples include:
    - User workstations in a corporate zone.
    - Databases in a secure, isolated zone.
    - Third-party systems in a demilitarized zone (DMZ).
- **Traffic Flow Mapping**: Document how traffic flows between assets to identify dependencies and essential communication paths. Use tools like network flow analyzers or SIEM systems to capture detailed traffic data.

For example, in a financial organization, an internal payroll database might be placed in a restricted zone that only communicates with specific HR systems, while preventing access from other parts of the network.

Policy Development

Policies define the rules that govern access between segments and workloads. Micro-segmentation policies enforce least privilege and ensure only authorized communications occur.

- **Zero-Trust Principles**: Assume no trust between zones or assets. Require explicit policy definitions for every allowed communication.
- **Allowlist Policies**: Use allowlists to specify permitted traffic paths. For instance, allow database servers to communicate only with application servers and block all other traffic.
- **Granular Policies**: Create policies at a fine-grained level, such as application-layer protocols, users, or specific processes. For example:
    - Permit HTTP traffic on port 443 between a web server and an external API.
    - Block SSH access except from designated administrative systems.
- **Identity-Based Policies**: Use workload identities, such as tags or labels in cloud environments, to dynamically apply policies. For example, workloads labeled "production" can communicate with each other but are isolated from "development" workloads.
- **Compliance Requirements**: Align policies with regulatory frameworks like PCI DSS, HIPAA, or GDPR. For example, ensure cardholder data environments (CDE) are fully isolated and restricted to authorized users.

Policies should be iteratively refined based on observed traffic and business needs.

Enforcement Methods

Enforcing micro-segmentation policies involves deploying controls at different layers of the network and application stack.

- **Host-Based Controls**: Implement policies directly on workloads using host firewalls (e.g., iptables on Linux) or agents installed on endpoints. These controls ensure policies remain effective regardless of network topology changes.
- **Network-Level Enforcement**:
    - Use software-defined networking (SDN) solutions, such as VMware NSX or Cisco ACI, to enforce segmentation policies at the virtual network level.
    - In cloud environments, leverage native controls like AWS Security Groups, Azure NSGs, or GCP Firewall Rules.
- **Microservices and Containers**: Use service mesh technologies like Istio or Linkerd to enforce communication policies between containerized workloads. These tools provide identity-based traffic controls and encryption for microservices.
- **Physical Segmentation**: For environments with legacy systems or IoT devices, implement segmentation using VLANs, access control lists (ACLs), and hardware firewalls.

For instance, a containerized e-commerce application can enforce policies via a service mesh to restrict payment processing services to interact only with the payment gateway API.

Traffic Control

Controlling traffic within a micro-segmented network involves defining and enforcing rules at multiple levels to ensure authorized traffic flows seamlessly while blocking unauthorized access.

- **East-West Traffic**: Monitor and control lateral traffic between workloads within the same network segment. Use deep packet inspection (DPI) or next-generation firewalls to enforce application-layer controls.
- **Protocol Restrictions**: Limit traffic to specific protocols and ports. For example, allow database traffic (TCP port 3306) only between the application server and the database server.
- **Application-Aware Policies**: Use tools capable of understanding application-specific behaviors, such as user agents or API calls, to enforce granular policies. For example, restrict an API endpoint to accept requests only from a specific application and deny requests from unknown origins.
- **Rate Limiting**: Prevent abuse of resources by implementing rate limits on connections or requests between segments.

In a healthcare IoT environment, traffic control can be used to limit medical devices like MRI machines to communicate only with hospital management systems.

Application Security

Integrating application-level security into micro-segmentation ensures that vulnerabilities within applications cannot be exploited to compromise other parts of the network.

- **Secure Application Interfaces**: Validate that APIs and services between micro-segments are secured with strong authentication (e.g., OAuth 2.0) and encrypted communication (e.g., TLS).
- **WAF Deployment**: Place web application firewalls (WAFs) at the boundary of micro-segments handling HTTP/S traffic to inspect for threats like SQL injection or XSS.
- **Input Validation**: Enforce strict input validation for inter-segment communication to prevent injection attacks.
- **Service Hardening**: Disable unnecessary application features, remove debug interfaces, and ensure proper configuration of application services to reduce exposure.

For example, in a segmented environment for a cloud-hosted SaaS platform, application-layer controls ensure that only authorized requests with valid API keys reach critical backend services.

Monitoring Implementation

Monitoring within a micro-segmented architecture ensures visibility into traffic flows, policy compliance, and potential security events.

- **Flow Monitoring**: Use network traffic analyzers like SolarWinds or open-source tools like Zeek to monitor and visualize traffic patterns within and across segments.
- **Log Collection**: Aggregate logs from firewalls, hosts, and enforcement points into a central logging system or SIEM for correlation and analysis.
- **Anomaly Detection**: Implement behavior-based detection to identify unusual traffic patterns, such as unexpected spikes in connections between micro-segments or unauthorized communication attempts.
- **Policy Audits**: Regularly review and audit segmentation policies to verify compliance with organizational standards and regulatory requirements.

For instance, monitoring might reveal an abnormal volume of SSH traffic between a web server and a database, prompting further investigation into potential misuse.

Incident Detection

Detecting incidents in a micro-segmented network requires tools and processes to identify malicious activity within tightly controlled zones.

- **Intrusion Detection Systems (IDS)**: Deploy IDS solutions tailored to segmented traffic, such as host-based IDS for individual workloads or network-based IDS at segment boundaries.
- **Threat Intelligence Integration**: Correlate events with threat intelligence feeds to identify traffic associated with known malicious IPs, domains, or signatures.
- **Decoy Systems**: Use honeypots within segments to detect attackers attempting lateral movement or reconnaissance activities.
- **Behavioral Analytics**: Leverage machine learning tools to establish baselines and detect deviations indicating compromised assets or insider threats.

For example, an IDS deployed in a database segment might detect repeated unauthorized access attempts, indicating a potential brute force attack.

Response Automation

Automating responses within a micro-segmented architecture enables rapid containment of threats while minimizing manual intervention.

- **Quarantine Automation**: Use orchestration tools to automatically isolate compromised workloads by applying updated policies to block all non-essential traffic.
- **Real-Time Policy Updates**: Integrate security tools like SOAR (Security Orchestration, Automation, and Response) platforms to dynamically adjust policies based on detected threats.
- **Workflow Integration**: Trigger alerts and response playbooks in collaboration platforms like PagerDuty or Slack for incident resolution.

- **Rollback Mechanisms**: Automate rollback of policy changes if unintended consequences are detected, such as service outages caused by over-restrictive rules.

For instance, when malware is detected on a server in a micro-segment, an automated response might block all external connections from the server, notify the SOC, and begin remediation workflows.

SECURITY IMPLEMENTATION AND PRACTICAL LAB EXERCISES

Cloud Security Lab Implementation:

Exercise Flow:

1. Environment Setup
   - VPC configuration
   - Security groups
   - IAM policies
   - Network ACLs
2. Security Testing
   - Access validation
   - Control verification
   - Monitoring checks
   - Incident response

IoT Device Hardening Matrix:

Component	Hardening Steps	Validation	Testing
Firmware	Updates, Security patches	Version check	Vulnerability scan
Network	Segmentation, Filtering	Connection test	Protocol analysis
Access	Authentication, Authorization	Login testing	Penetration test

Zero Trust Deployment Lab:

Access Workflow:

- Identity verification
- Device validation
- Resource authorization
- Activity monitoring
- Session management

Security Monitoring:

- Log collection
- Alert configuration
- Dashboard setup
- Response procedures
- Performance tracking

Incident Response Simulation:

Scenario Types:

- Data breach
- Malware infection
- Service outage
- Insider threat
- Physical security

Risk Assessment Exercise:

Assessment Components:

- Asset inventory
- Threat identification
- Vulnerability analysis

- Impact evaluation
- Control effectiveness

Lab Documentation:

- Setup guides
- Test procedures
- Validation steps
- Results analysis
- Improvement recommendations

Teams practice:

- Implementation procedures
- Response protocols
- Recovery methods
- Documentation standards
- Review processes

ADVANCED TEST STRATEGIES

Success in exams often requires more than just subject knowledge; it demands strategic approaches to analyzing questions, managing time, and applying knowledge effectively. Advanced test strategies combine methods for dissecting questions, making informed choices, and optimizing performance under pressure. By integrating these techniques, candidates can approach exams with confidence and precision, ensuring their preparation is reflected in their results.

QUESTION ANALYSIS TECHNIQUES

1. **Identify Key Terms:**
   - Highlight critical words or phrases in the question stem, such as "best," "most likely," "first step," or "not." For example, in a security certification exam, a question asking for the "most effective mitigation" requires prioritization, whereas "initial action" focuses on sequence.
2. **Break Down Multi-Part Questions:**
   - Separate compound questions into smaller components. For instance, a question like "Which access control model ensures confidentiality and is commonly used in military applications?" combines requirements (confidentiality) and context (military), pointing to the Bell-LaPadula model.
3. **Focus on Context Clues:**
   - Use information within the question to infer the correct answer. For example, a scenario involving sensitive data stored in the cloud may hint at encryption as a primary solution.
4. **Understand the Question Format:**
   - Determine whether the question is straightforward, scenario-based, or tricky. For example, "Which of the following is NOT true?" requires carefully identifying the exception.
5. **Clarify Ambiguities:**
   - If a question appears vague or confusing, reread it and rephrase it in your own words to ensure you understand what is being asked.

TIME MANAGEMENT SKILLS

1. **Pace Yourself:**
   - Allocate a set amount of time per question based on the total time available. For instance, in a 120-minute exam with 60 questions, spend an average of two minutes per question.
2. **Prioritize Easy Questions:**
   - Answer straightforward questions first to build momentum and save time for more challenging ones. Use the “mark and move” strategy to flag difficult questions for later review.
3. **Use the Two-Pass Method:**
   - In the first pass, answer questions you’re confident about. In the second pass, return to flagged questions to make more calculated choices.

4. **Monitor the Clock:**
    - Check your progress at regular intervals. For example, if the exam is divided into sections, ensure you finish each section with enough time for review.
5. **Avoid Overthinking:**
    - Spending too much time on a single question can eat into your time for others. If unsure, eliminate options and make an educated guess.

ANSWER ELIMINATION METHODS

1. **Rule Out Incorrect Options:**
    - Eliminate options that are clearly wrong. For example, in a multiple-choice question about encryption, if an answer mentions outdated protocols like DES, you can confidently disregard it.
2. **Look for Opposites:**
    - If two answers are opposites, one is often correct. For instance, “encrypt sensitive data” and “do not encrypt sensitive data” likely indicate a clear preference for encryption in most contexts.
3. **Identify Distractors:**
    - Exam questions often include plausible-sounding distractors. Focus on whether each option fully aligns with the question. For example, an option that partially addresses the scenario might still be incorrect.
4. **Evaluate Absolute Language:**
    - Be cautious of options with absolute terms like “always” or “never,” which are often incorrect unless clearly supported by the scenario.
5. **Match Terminology:**
    - Pay attention to terms in the question and match them with those in the answers. For example, a question on “confidentiality” likely rules out answers focused solely on “availability.”

KNOWLEDGE APPLICATION

1. **Map Concepts to Scenarios:**
    - Relate theoretical concepts to practical scenarios. For example, when asked how to secure data in transit, consider applying encryption protocols like TLS.
2. **Leverage Real-World Experience:**
    - Draw from practical knowledge or examples, especially for scenario-based questions. For instance, think of common misconfigurations in firewalls when troubleshooting access control issues.
3. **Integrate Key Frameworks:**
    - Use industry frameworks and models to guide your answers. For example, if the question involves risk management, apply elements from frameworks like NIST or ISO 27001.
4. **Focus on Best Practices:**
    - When in doubt, choose the answer aligned with widely accepted best practices. For instance, multi-factor authentication (MFA) is generally the preferred answer for securing accounts.

SCENARIO EVALUATION

1. **Assess the Problem:**
    - Identify the key issue or challenge in the scenario. For example, if a question describes a data breach caused by phishing, focus on email security and employee awareness solutions.
2. **Consider Stakeholders:**
    - Think about who is impacted and what their goals are. For instance, a question about disaster recovery might involve minimizing downtime for critical business functions.
3. **Sequence of Actions:**
    - Determine the logical order of operations. For example, in incident response, containment typically precedes eradication and recovery.
4. **Context-Specific Prioritization:**
    - Tailor your answer to the context provided in the scenario. For example, protecting customer data in a healthcare environment might prioritize compliance with HIPAA.

PERFORMANCE OPTIMIZATION

1. **Pre-Exam Preparation:**
   - Practice with timed mock exams to improve speed and familiarity with the question format. Identify and address weak areas during preparation.
2. **Mental Sharpening:**
   - Use memory aids, such as mnemonics, to recall key frameworks and concepts. For instance, remember the CIA triad (Confidentiality, Integrity, Availability) for security principles.
3. **Answer with Confidence:**
   - Avoid second-guessing yourself unless new information arises. Your first instinct is often correct if you've prepared thoroughly.
4. **Simulate the Testing Environment:**
   - Replicate exam conditions during practice sessions, including timed settings and minimal distractions, to reduce anxiety and improve focus.

STRESS MANAGEMENT

1. **Controlled Breathing:**
   - Practice deep breathing techniques to stay calm and focused during the exam. For example, inhale for four seconds, hold for four seconds, and exhale for four seconds.
2. **Mental Reset:**
   - If you feel overwhelmed, take a brief mental pause and refocus. Shift your attention to a simpler question to regain momentum.
3. **Pre-Exam Routines:**
   - Get adequate rest the night before and eat a balanced meal before the exam. Avoid excessive caffeine, which can heighten anxiety.
4. **Confidence Building:**
   - Remind yourself of your preparation efforts and focus on solving one question at a time rather than worrying about the entire exam.

REVIEW TECHNIQUES

1. **Flag for Review:**
   - Use exam tools to mark questions you are unsure about, and revisit them after completing the others.
2. **Reassess Assumptions:**
   - Reread flagged questions carefully and verify that your initial interpretation aligns with the information provided.
3. **Check for Misreads:**
   - Look for common mistakes like misreading "not" or overlooking qualifiers such as "most effective."
4. **Avoid Overchanging Answers:**
   - Only change an answer if you identify clear evidence that your initial choice was incorrect.
5. **Final Walkthrough:**
   - Use any remaining time to quickly scan for skipped questions, missing answers, or overlooked details.

By applying these advanced test strategies, candidates can effectively tackle challenging exams, optimize performance, and make the best use of their preparation efforts.

CASE STUDY TOPICS

Real-world scenarios in areas such as cloud migration, IoT security, and zero trust demonstrate how organizations address complex challenges, balance operational needs, and implement proactive security measures. These case studies provide actionable insights into deploying effective solutions and responding to incidents.

Cloud Migration Security

A pharmaceutical company migrating its critical data and workloads from on-premises data centers to Microsoft Azure encountered unique security challenges. The migration included patient data, intellectual property, and research workloads.

- **Challenges**:
    - Protecting sensitive data during the transition and in the cloud.
    - Ensuring compliance with HIPAA and GDPR for patient records.
    - Implementing robust access controls for distributed teams.
- **Security Measures**:
    - **Data Encryption**: Implemented AES-256 encryption for data in transit and at rest, ensuring that all patient records and research data were encrypted before and after migration.
    - **Identity Management**: Leveraged Azure Active Directory (AAD) for centralized identity management. Implemented conditional access policies requiring multi-factor authentication (MFA) for high-risk activities.
    - **Configuration Validation**: Used Azure Security Center to validate secure configurations, including ensuring that all resources had network security groups (NSGs) with strict inbound/outbound traffic controls.
    - **Zero Trust Architecture**: Applied zero trust principles by segmenting workloads into dedicated Azure VNets, isolating critical research environments from general employee access.
    - **Continuous Monitoring**: Deployed Azure Sentinel for security monitoring and alerting during and after the migration process, providing real-time visibility into access attempts and anomalous activity.
- **Outcome**:
    - Migration was completed without data loss or unauthorized access incidents.
    - Regular audits confirmed compliance with HIPAA and GDPR.
    - Post-migration monitoring identified and resolved a misconfigured blob storage bucket that temporarily allowed public access.

This case highlights how layered security measures can mitigate risks during cloud migration, ensuring compliance and operational continuity.

IoT Security Breach

A manufacturing company experienced a security breach when attackers exploited vulnerabilities in IoT devices used for predictive maintenance of industrial equipment. The attackers used compromised devices as an entry point to pivot into the company's corporate network.

- **Incident Details**:
    - Attackers gained access by exploiting default credentials on IoT devices.
    - Lateral movement allowed them to exfiltrate sensitive operational data, including intellectual property related to manufacturing processes.
    - Malware was deployed on compromised devices to participate in a botnet for a DDoS attack.
- **Remediation Steps**:
    - **Device Hardening**: Replaced default credentials with unique, complex passwords and disabled unused services on all IoT devices.
    - **Network Segmentation**: Isolated IoT devices into a separate VLAN with strict firewall rules preventing communication with corporate systems.
    - **Firmware Updates**: Rolled out critical security patches to address known vulnerabilities in device firmware.
    - **Continuous Monitoring**: Implemented network traffic monitoring with anomaly detection to identify unusual device behavior, such as high data transfer rates or unexpected outbound traffic.
    - **Zero Trust Policies**: Enforced mutual TLS authentication between IoT devices and the backend servers to prevent unauthorized communication.
- **Lessons Learned**:
    - Established a vulnerability management program specific to IoT devices, including regular patching and vendor security assessments.
    - Improved onboarding processes to include secure configuration requirements for all IoT devices.

The breach revealed the importance of securing IoT devices through proper segmentation, access controls, and continuous monitoring to prevent lateral movement and malicious activities.

Zero Trust Implementation

A financial institution adopted zero trust principles to secure its hybrid environment, which included on-premises systems, cloud services, and a remote workforce. The organization faced increasing threats from phishing attacks and insider threats.

- **Steps Taken**:
  - **Identity-Centric Access Control**: Migrated to a zero trust framework using Microsoft AAD with conditional access policies. Users were granted access based on contextual factors, such as device compliance, geolocation, and risk level.
  - **Micro-Segmentation**: Divided the internal network into micro-segments, ensuring critical financial systems and customer databases could only communicate with authorized applications and users.
  - **Endpoint Security**: Deployed endpoint detection and response (EDR) tools like CrowdStrike to monitor and secure employee devices, requiring devices to meet compliance baselines before connecting to the network.
  - **Secure Access for Third-Party Vendors**: Enabled temporary just-in-time (JIT) access for external contractors using privileged access management (PAM) tools.
  - **Logging and Analytics**: Leveraged a SIEM (Splunk) to monitor all access requests, flagging anomalous behavior such as repeated failed login attempts or unauthorized data access.
- **Benefits**:
  - Reduced the attack surface by applying least-privilege principles across all user accounts and workloads.
  - Successfully prevented a credential-stuffing attack when the zero trust system flagged unusual login attempts from multiple geolocations.

This example demonstrates how zero trust architecture can significantly improve security by eliminating implicit trust and enforcing granular, context-based access controls.

Multi-Cloud Integration

An e-commerce company operating on both AWS and Google Cloud sought to integrate security and monitoring tools across its multi-cloud environment. The challenge was maintaining consistent policies and visibility while ensuring compliance with PCI DSS.

- **Integration Strategies**:
  - **Unified Identity Management**: Implemented a centralized identity provider (Okta) to manage user and service accounts across both cloud environments. Enabled MFA and adaptive authentication for all privileged users.
  - **Infrastructure as Code (IaC)**: Used Terraform to enforce consistent security configurations, such as enabling encryption for all storage buckets, across AWS S3 and Google Cloud Storage.
  - **Cross-Cloud Monitoring**: Deployed Datadog to aggregate logs and metrics from both clouds, providing a unified view of application performance and security events.
  - **Traffic Control**: Configured cloud-native firewalls (AWS Security Groups and Google VPC Firewalls) to enforce least-privilege access between microservices running in different clouds.
  - **Encryption Key Management**: Centralized key management using AWS KMS and Google Cloud KMS to simplify encryption and decryption processes while maintaining separate keys for each environment.
- **Outcomes**:
  - PCI DSS compliance was achieved through consistent encryption, access control, and monitoring policies.
  - Unified visibility enabled the rapid identification of a misconfigured Google Cloud Storage bucket that exposed sensitive order details.

This case highlights the importance of standardizing policies and tools in multi-cloud environments to achieve security and operational consistency.

Security Monitoring Deployment

A healthcare organization needed to deploy a centralized security monitoring system to protect patient data and meet HIPAA compliance requirements. The IT environment included on-premises servers, cloud-hosted applications, and IoT medical devices.

- **Deployment Approach**:
  - **Log Aggregation**: Deployed a SIEM (Splunk) to collect logs from on-premises servers, cloud platforms (AWS CloudTrail), and IoT device gateways.
  - **Endpoint Monitoring**: Integrated EDR tools to monitor endpoints for suspicious activity, such as unauthorized file access or malware execution.
  - **Behavioral Analytics**: Used UEBA (User and Entity Behavior Analytics) tools to detect anomalies, such as unusual access to patient records outside of standard working hours.
  - **Real-Time Alerts**: Configured alerting for high-risk activities, such as access to sensitive patient data from unregistered devices or external IPs.
  - **Threat Intelligence Integration**: Leveraged threat intelligence feeds to correlate events with known malicious IPs or attack patterns.
- **Results**:
  - Detected and mitigated a phishing attack targeting administrative staff within hours, preventing unauthorized access to patient records.
  - Improved compliance audit readiness by automating log collection and retention for HIPAA requirements.

This deployment provided the organization with the visibility and real-time alerting needed to protect sensitive data in a complex environment.

Compliance Validation

A retail organization underwent compliance validation to ensure its payment systems adhered to PCI DSS standards after migrating to a hybrid cloud environment.

- **Validation Process**:
  - **Asset Inventory**: Conducted a detailed inventory of all systems in scope for PCI DSS, including payment processing servers, databases, and network components.
  - **Encryption Audits**: Verified that all cardholder data was encrypted at rest and in transit using AES-256 and TLS 1.3.
  - **Access Controls**: Reviewed access policies to ensure that only authorized personnel could access systems storing cardholder data, with MFA enforced for all privileged accounts.
  - **Vulnerability Scanning**: Performed quarterly scans using Qualys to identify and remediate vulnerabilities in payment systems.
  - **Logging and Monitoring**: Validated that all security logs were aggregated and retained for at least one year, meeting PCI DSS requirements.
- **Outcome**:
  - Passed the PCI DSS compliance audit without any critical findings.
  - Implemented automated compliance checks using IaC to ensure ongoing adherence to PCI DSS in the hybrid cloud.

This case demonstrates how proactive compliance validation ensures adherence to regulatory standards and prevents disruptions during audits.

ADVANCED SECURITY IMPLEMENTATION PRACTICE SCENARIOS

Scenario 1: Cloud Architecture A global organization plans multi-region cloud deployment:

Requirements:

- Data sovereignty
- High availability
- Security controls
- Compliance tracking
- Performance monitoring

What creates a security weakness?
A. Authentication step
B. Device validation
C. Static risk score
D. Session tracking
Correct Answer: C Analysis: Static risk scoring fails to adapt to changing threat conditions.
Multi-cloud Management:

- Resource inventory
- Policy enforcement
- Security controls
- Compliance validation
- Cost optimization

Which management aspect requires enhancement?
A. Resource tracking
B. Identity federation
C. Security standardization
D. Compliance mapping
Correct Answer: C Analysis: Inconsistent security controls across clouds increase risk exposure.
Security teams implement:

- Testing programs
- Response procedures
- Documentation standards
- Review processes
- Improvement tracking

PRACTICE TEST QUESTIONS

Welcome to the practice test section of the CISSP Exam Preparation Study Guide. This comprehensive collection of questions has been carefully designed to help you master the material and build confidence before your exam.

To maximize the effectiveness of your study sessions, we've structured this section with answers and detailed explanations immediately following each question. This intentional design offers several key benefits:

Instant Feedback When you answer a question, you want to know right away if your understanding is correct. Rather than flipping to the back of the book to check your answer, you'll find it right below the question. This immediate feedback loop helps you quickly identify areas where you're strong and where you need more focus.

We recommend covering the answer section with a blank piece of paper or notecard as you work through each question. This allows you to simulate exam conditions while still having quick access to explanations when you need them.

Enhanced Learning and Retention Research consistently shows that immediate feedback significantly improves knowledge retention and understanding. When you can immediately connect your thought process with the correct answer and thorough explanation, you're more likely to remember the concept and apply it correctly in the future.

Multiple Perspectives on Key Topics You'll notice that certain critical concepts appear multiple times throughout this section, presented from different angles and contexts. This repetition is intentional – the CISSP exam tests your ability to apply security concepts across various scenarios, so practicing with diverse question types will strengthen your grasp of these fundamental ideas.

Comprehensive Coverage We've invested significant effort in creating high-quality questions that reflect both the depth and breadth of the CISSP exam domains. Each question is accompanied by a detailed explanation that not only provides the correct answer but also explains the underlying concepts and their practical applications in information security.

Practice Makes Progress Studies have consistently shown a strong correlation between the number of practice questions completed and exam success rates. This is why we've included an extensive collection of questions in this section. Each one has been carefully crafted to match the style, difficulty, and format you'll encounter on the actual exam.

Take your time with these questions. Use them not just to test your knowledge, but as learning opportunities to deepen your understanding of information security concepts. Whether you're answering correctly or incorrectly, each question is a chance to reinforce your knowledge and identify areas that may need additional review.

Let's begin your journey toward CISSP certification with our first practice question...

1. A healthcare organization is adopting the NIST Risk Management Framework (RMF) to comply with federal regulations. During the "Categorize Information System" step, which key activity must the organization prioritize to ensure accurate system categorization?
a. Identifying the security control baseline based on FIPS 199
b. Assigning risk tolerance levels for information systems
c. Identifying the information types processed by the system
d. Implementing monitoring tools to detect vulnerabilities

Answer: c. Identifying the information types processed by the system. Explanation: The "Categorize Information System" step in the NIST RMF requires organizations to identify and document the information types processed, stored, or transmitted by the system to determine its security impact level using FIPS 199 guidelines. Option a is incorrect because determining the security control baseline occurs later in the "Select Security Controls" step. Option b is incorrect because risk tolerance levels are part of the governance policy, not system categorization. Option d is incorrect as monitoring tools are implemented in the "Monitor Security Controls" step.

2. An organization using the quantitative Annual Loss Expectancy (ALE) method identifies a critical server with an Annual Rate of Occurrence (ARO) of 0.5 and a Single Loss Expectancy (SLE) of $50,000. What is the ALE for this server?
a. $25,000

b. $50,000
c. $75,000
d. $100,000

Answer: a. $25,000. Explanation: ALE is calculated as SLE × ARO. In this case, $50,000 (SLE) × 0.5 (ARO) = $25,000. Option b is incorrect because it incorrectly assumes an ARO of 1. Option c is incorrect because it adds instead of multiplying SLE and ARO. Option d is incorrect as it doubles the SLE without considering the correct ARO.

3. In the FAIR™ (Factor Analysis of Information Risk) taxonomy, what is the most appropriate way to assess the "Loss Event Frequency" for a specific threat scenario?
a. Identify the number of detected vulnerabilities in the system.
b. Calculate the probability of a threat actor exploiting the vulnerability.
c. Determine the frequency of relevant threat actions and control strength.
d. Analyze the estimated financial loss if the event occurs.

Answer: c. Determine the frequency of relevant threat actions and control strength. Explanation: Loss Event Frequency in FAIR™ is calculated based on the frequency of threat actions and the effectiveness of existing controls. Option a is incorrect because vulnerabilities alone do not determine event frequency. Option b is incomplete, as it ignores control strength. Option d focuses on financial impact, which relates to "Loss Magnitude" in FAIR™, not frequency.

4. Which of the following best describes the purpose of Residual Risk Acceptance Criteria (RRAC) in an organization's risk governance strategy?
a. Define a framework for assigning resources to security controls.
b. Set thresholds for determining acceptable levels of remaining risk.
c. Establish a methodology for quantitative risk assessment.
d. Specify guidelines for periodic risk reassessment.

Answer: b. Set thresholds for determining acceptable levels of remaining risk. Explanation: RRAC establishes what levels of residual risk an organization is willing to accept after implementing security controls. Option a is incorrect as RRAC does not focus on resource allocation. Option c is incorrect because RRAC does not involve a specific risk assessment methodology. Option d relates to ongoing monitoring, which is separate from RRAC.

5. Under the COBIT framework, what is the primary role of "Governance" processes in information security risk management?
a. Ensuring the alignment of IT and business objectives.
b. Managing the day-to-day implementation of security controls.
c. Developing policies and procedures for incident response.
d. Monitoring and measuring the effectiveness of deployed controls.

Answer: a. Ensuring the alignment of IT and business objectives. Explanation: Governance in COBIT ensures that IT initiatives support business objectives, particularly in security and risk management. Option b relates to management, not governance. Option c is incorrect because incident response is operational, not governance-related. Option d pertains to monitoring, which supports governance but is not its primary focus.

6. A retail organization using the NIST RMF has reached the "Select Security Controls" step. What is the first task the organization must complete in this step?
a. Define the minimum assurance levels for the controls.
b. Tailor baseline security controls to the system's needs.
c. Identify all applicable organizational and system-level controls.
d. Document the security control implementation plan.

Answer: b. Tailor baseline security controls to the system's needs. Explanation: The "Select Security Controls" step begins with tailoring the baseline controls based on the system's categorization and organizational policies. Option a occurs later during control assurance. Option c is incorrect because identifying controls is part of the tailoring process. Option d happens in the "Implement Security Controls" step.

7. During a risk assessment process, which metric is critical for determining the overall Exposure Factor (EF) in a quantitative risk analysis?
a. Asset value
b. Annualized Loss Expectancy (ALE)
c. Percentage of asset loss if a threat materializes
d. Probability of the threat occurring

Answer: c. Percentage of asset loss if a threat materializes. Explanation: EF measures the percentage of asset value expected to be lost due to a specific threat event. Option a is incorrect as EF is a percentage of asset value, not the value itself. Option b is calculated after determining EF. Option d is incorrect because probability affects ARO, not EF.

8. In FAIR™, which of the following factors directly contributes to calculating "Vulnerability"?
a. Control strength relative to threat capability
b. Frequency of external threat actions
c. Asset value and criticality
d. Probability of technical failure

Answer: a. Control strength relative to threat capability. Explanation: Vulnerability in FAIR™ depends on the strength of controls compared to the capability of potential threat actors. Option b influences Threat Event Frequency, not Vulnerability. Option c relates to impact, not Vulnerability. Option d concerns technical failures, which are outside FAIR™'s scope for Vulnerability.

9. What is the primary goal of integrating the COBIT framework into an organization's information security risk management strategy?
a. Align IT processes with ISO 27001 standards.
b. Ensure regulatory compliance for IT operations.
c. Provide a governance framework linking IT goals with business objectives.
d. Develop a risk assessment methodology specific to IT.

Answer: c. Provide a governance framework linking IT goals with business objectives. Explanation: COBIT integrates IT and business governance to optimize alignment. Option a is incorrect as COBIT is not specifically tied to ISO 27001. Option b addresses compliance but not COBIT's core purpose. Option d is incorrect because COBIT does not focus solely on risk assessment methodology.

10. An organization is developing a Residual Risk Acceptance Criteria (RRAC) policy. What key factor must be included to ensure the policy aligns with business objectives?
a. Technical feasibility of control implementations
b. Tolerance thresholds for operational disruptions
c. Cost-benefit analysis of proposed security measures
d. Classification levels of the organization's assets

Answer: b. Tolerance thresholds for operational disruptions. Explanation: RRAC policies require defining acceptable levels of risk, which include tolerance for operational disruptions. Option a supports the policy but is not the primary focus. Option c is used during risk analysis but is not exclusive to RRAC. Option d is essential for risk categorization but not RRAC directly.

11. An organization plans to implement Zero Trust Network Access (ZTNA) to enhance security for its cloud-based applications. What is the primary principle of ZTNA that distinguishes it from traditional perimeter-based security models?
a. Continuous user authentication and device validation
b. Limiting access based on predefined network zones
c. Relying on a centralized firewall for traffic inspection
d. Using a virtual private network (VPN) to secure remote connections

Answer: a. Continuous user authentication and device validation. Explanation: ZTNA operates on the principle of "never trust, always verify," requiring continuous verification of both users and devices to ensure access security. Option b describes traditional network segmentation, not ZTNA. Option c refers to perimeter-based security, which ZTNA aims to replace. Option d is a feature of VPNs but does not encompass ZTNA's core principle.

12. In an East-West traffic microsegmentation strategy, what is the primary objective of using granular security policies?
a. Preventing unauthorized access to resources in the demilitarized zone (DMZ)
b. Minimizing the attack surface within the internal network
c. Blocking inbound threats from external sources
d. Prioritizing bandwidth for critical applications

Answer: b. Minimizing the attack surface within the internal network. Explanation: Microsegmentation focuses on controlling lateral movement by applying granular policies, which reduce the attack surface within the internal network. Option a is unrelated, as the DMZ typically concerns North-South traffic. Option c deals with external threats, which are managed differently. Option d is about network optimization, not security.

13. A company deploying a Software-Defined Perimeter (SDP) solution wants to ensure secure access for external contractors. Which feature of SDP best addresses this requirement?
a. Dynamic creation of encrypted microtunnels per user session
b. Continuous monitoring of border firewalls for suspicious activity
c. Centralized management of user credentials and tokens
d. Implementation of static IP whitelisting for user devices

Answer: a. Dynamic creation of encrypted microtunnels per user session. Explanation: SDP creates microtunnels that are session-specific and encrypted, ensuring secure and isolated access for each user. Option b is a traditional perimeter control not specific to SDP. Option c is a supportive feature but does not uniquely address the access model. Option d is static and inflexible, contrary to SDP's dynamic nature.

14. Which of the following is a critical security concern when implementing split-tunnel VPN configurations?
a. Increased latency for remote connections
b. Unencrypted traffic bypassing corporate security controls
c. Limited scalability for multiple remote users
d. Dependency on specific VPN client software versions

Answer: b. Unencrypted traffic bypassing corporate security controls. Explanation: Split-tunneling routes some traffic directly to the internet, potentially bypassing encryption and corporate security measures, increasing exposure to risks. Option a is incorrect as split-tunneling reduces latency. Option c relates to VPN infrastructure scalability, not a direct security issue. Option d is a minor operational concern, not a critical risk.

15. An enterprise is concerned about securing Border Gateway Protocol (BGP) sessions against hijacking attacks. What is the most effective control to mitigate this risk?
a. Configuring route redistribution policies
b. Implementing BGP prefix filtering

c. Enabling BGP route flap dampening
d. Deploying BGP route origin validation (ROV) using RPKI

Answer: d. Deploying BGP route origin validation (ROV) using RPKI. Explanation: ROV using Resource Public Key Infrastructure (RPKI) verifies the legitimacy of BGP route announcements, mitigating hijacking risks. Option a is a general routing practice, not specific to hijacking prevention. Option b reduces exposure to incorrect prefixes but lacks cryptographic validation. Option c mitigates route instability, not hijacking.

16. A company is designing a Zero Trust architecture for its hybrid cloud environment. What key component ensures secure access to resources across both on-premises and cloud environments?
a. Identity provider (IdP) with single sign-on (SSO) support
b. Centralized firewall with deep packet inspection (DPI)
c. Secure email gateway with advanced phishing detection
d. Hardware security module (HSM) for key management

Answer: a. Identity provider (IdP) with single sign-on (SSO) support. Explanation: An IdP with SSO ensures secure and seamless authentication across multiple environments, a cornerstone of Zero Trust. Option b is limited to traditional perimeter defenses. Option c focuses on email security, not resource access. Option d handles cryptographic keys but does not address resource access control.

17. In an environment with microsegmentation, which type of security control is essential to enforce East-West traffic policies?
a. Stateful firewalls at the network perimeter
b. Application-layer firewalls between workloads
c. Intrusion detection systems (IDS) for external traffic
d. VPN tunnels for all user connections

Answer: b. Application-layer firewalls between workloads. Explanation: Application-layer firewalls enforce granular policies between workloads, a key aspect of microsegmentation. Option a targets North-South traffic. Option c detects threats but does not enforce policies. Option d applies to user connections, not workload communication.

18. Which of the following scenarios best demonstrates a security benefit of a Software-Defined Perimeter (SDP)?
a. A user can access only assigned cloud applications without visibility into the broader network.
b. All employees' devices are monitored continuously for potential malware infections.
c. Sensitive emails are encrypted end-to-end before delivery to recipients.
d. Network routers are configured with static access control lists (ACLs).

Answer: a. A user can access only assigned cloud applications without visibility into the broader network. Explanation: SDP provides application-specific access rather than network-wide visibility, improving security. Option b is endpoint protection, not SDP. Option c concerns email encryption, not network access control. Option d reflects a static approach, contrary to SDP's dynamic nature.

19. What is a primary advantage of implementing East-West traffic microsegmentation in a virtualized data center?
a. Enhanced performance for high-bandwidth applications
b. Improved detection of encrypted traffic anomalies
c. Mitigation of lateral movement by compromised workloads
d. Simplified compliance reporting for regulatory audits

Answer: c. Mitigation of lateral movement by compromised workloads. Explanation: Microsegmentation limits East-West traffic pathways, reducing an attacker's ability to move laterally within a network. Option a relates to performance, not security. Option b addresses detection but not prevention. Option d concerns compliance, which is a secondary benefit.

20. A remote access solution combines split-tunneling with endpoint security tools. What key measure should be implemented to reduce risks associated with this configuration?
a. Use certificate-based authentication for user sessions.
b. Ensure endpoints route DNS queries through the corporate network.
c. Configure IP whitelisting for trusted client devices.
d. Block all outbound connections to public IP addresses.

Answer: b. Ensure endpoints route DNS queries through the corporate network. Explanation: Routing DNS queries through the corporate network ensures security policies apply to split-tunneled traffic. Option a secures sessions but does not address traffic routing. Option c increases device trust but does not mitigate DNS risks. Option d is impractical for many use cases.

21. A cloud service provider supports single sign-on (SSO) using SAML 2.0. Which assertion is responsible for specifying the user's permissions within the service?
a. Authentication assertion
b. Authorization assertion
c. Attribute assertion
d. Access control assertion

Answer: b. Authorization assertion. Explanation: Authorization assertions in SAML specify what actions a user is permitted to perform within the service. Option a is incorrect because authentication assertions validate the user's identity but do not define permissions. Option c is wrong as attribute assertions provide additional information about the user but do not specify permissions. Option d is a distractor as there is no "access control assertion" in the SAML standard.

22. In an OAuth 2.0 implementation, which grant type is most suitable for server-to-server communication where no user interaction is required?
a. Authorization code grant
b. Implicit grant
c. Client credentials grant
d. Resource owner password credentials grant

Answer: c. Client credentials grant. Explanation: The client credentials grant is specifically designed for server-to-server interactions where the client acts on its own behalf. Option a is incorrect because the authorization code grant is user-interactive. Option b is wrong because the implicit grant is typically used for browser-based clients. Option d is incorrect as resource owner password credentials require user credentials, which are not applicable in server-to-server communication.

23. Which feature of Just-In-Time (JIT) provisioning helps reduce the administrative burden of identity management in federated systems?
a. Automatically assigning access based on predefined roles
b. Requiring manual approval for user account creation
c. Validating all permissions against an external database
d. Generating periodic reports for compliance audits

Answer: a. Automatically assigning access based on predefined roles. Explanation: JIT provisioning creates user accounts dynamically during login, assigning access based on predefined roles, reducing administrative overhead. Option b is incorrect because manual approval negates the benefit of automation. Option c is wrong as validating permissions against an external database is unrelated to JIT provisioning. Option d is irrelevant since generating reports does not directly reduce identity management burdens.

24. What is the primary advantage of implementing Privileged Access Management (PAM) in a zero-trust architecture?
a. Eliminates the need for multi-factor authentication for privileged accounts
b. Centralizes control and auditing of privileged account activities
c. Allows direct login to sensitive systems without intermediary tools
d. Enables the sharing of administrative credentials across multiple teams

Answer: b. Centralizes control and auditing of privileged account activities. Explanation: PAM centralizes management of privileged accounts, ensuring compliance with zero-trust principles by limiting and auditing access. Option a is incorrect as multi-factor authentication is a cornerstone of zero-trust security. Option c is wrong because direct logins without intermediary tools contradict PAM principles. Option d is incorrect as PAM minimizes credential sharing to enhance security.

25. Risk-Adaptive Access Control (RAdAC) differs from traditional access control models by:
a. Enforcing access based solely on a user's role within the organization
b. Dynamically adjusting access permissions based on real-time risk analysis
c. Relying exclusively on static rules defined in an access control matrix
d. Allowing access requests without identity verification

Answer: b. Dynamically adjusting access permissions based on real-time risk analysis. Explanation: RAdAC adapts access permissions dynamically using context-aware risk assessments. Option a is incorrect because traditional role-based access control (RBAC) enforces static permissions. Option c is wrong as static rules are not flexible or dynamic. Option d is incorrect because identity verification is essential for access control in RAdAC.

26. Which OAuth 2.0 flow is designed to support browser-based applications with no secure backend?
a. Authorization code flow
b. Implicit flow
c. Client credentials flow
d. Device authorization flow

Answer: b. Implicit flow. Explanation: The implicit flow is suitable for browser-based apps that lack a secure backend because it allows tokens to be issued directly to the client. Option a is incorrect because the authorization code flow is intended for apps with secure backends. Option c is wrong as the client credentials flow is for server-to-server communication. Option d is unrelated as it is used for devices without user input capabilities.

27. A user in a federated identity system attempts to access a service provider but receives an error indicating an expired session token. What is the most likely cause of the issue?
a. The identity provider failed to validate the user's authentication request
b. The service provider's metadata was not updated in the identity provider
c. The session timeout value configured by the identity provider was exceeded
d. The user's permissions are not mapped correctly within the service provider

Answer: c. The session timeout value configured by the identity provider was exceeded. Explanation: Session tokens expire based on timeout configurations, preventing unauthorized reuse. Option a is incorrect because the user was already authenticated. Option b is wrong as metadata mismatches typically result in immediate errors, not timeouts. Option d is unrelated because permission mapping does not affect token expiration.

28. What is the purpose of an OAuth 2.0 refresh token in the context of authorization?
a. Enables immediate revocation of access tokens
b. Allows clients to obtain new access tokens without user interaction
c. Increases the expiration time of the original access token
d. Encrypts access tokens for secure transmission

Answer: b. Allows clients to obtain new access tokens without user interaction. Explanation: Refresh tokens are issued to reauthorize clients without requiring the user to reauthenticate. Option a is incorrect as refresh tokens do not directly revoke access tokens. Option c is wrong as refresh tokens generate new tokens rather than extending the old token's validity. Option d is unrelated since token encryption occurs independently of refresh tokens.

29. How does SAML 2.0 ensure security when transferring authentication information between the identity provider (IdP) and service provider (SP)?
a. By encrypting all assertion responses
b. By digitally signing assertions to prevent tampering
c. By mandating multi-factor authentication during login
d. By using short-lived access tokens for authentication

Answer: b. By digitally signing assertions to prevent tampering. Explanation: Digital signatures on assertions ensure their integrity and authenticity. Option a is incorrect because encryption is optional and focuses on confidentiality rather than tamper prevention. Option c is unrelated to how SAML secures assertion transfers. Option d is incorrect because SAML does not use access tokens as OAuth does.

30. A financial services firm is adopting Cloud Security Posture Management (CSPM) to automate compliance monitoring across its multi-cloud environment. Which of the following is a primary benefit of CSPM tools?
a. Continuous monitoring for misconfigurations and policy violations
b. Automated patch management for virtual machines in the cloud
c. Centralized management of cloud encryption keys
d. Real-time mitigation of distributed denial-of-service (DDoS) attacks

Answer: a. Continuous monitoring for misconfigurations and policy violations. Explanation: CSPM tools are designed to identify and alert on cloud misconfigurations and policy violations, ensuring compliance with regulatory and security standards. Option b is incorrect as patch management is typically handled by other tools like CWPP. Option c is a function of key management services (KMS), not CSPM. Option d relates to DDoS protection, which CSPM does not provide.

31. During the deployment of a Cloud Workload Protection Platform (CWPP), what is the most critical security feature to prioritize for protecting containerized applications?
a. Stateful packet inspection on container host systems
b. Runtime protection to detect anomalous behavior in containers
c. Pre-deployment vulnerability scans of container images
d. Multi-factor authentication for developers accessing the CI/CD pipeline

Answer: b. Runtime protection to detect anomalous behavior in containers. Explanation: CWPPs provide runtime protection to detect and respond to anomalous behaviors in containerized applications, which is crucial in a dynamic cloud environment. Option a focuses on network security, not workload protection. Option c is important but does not address runtime threats. Option d enhances access security but is not specific to workload protection.

32. A global enterprise plans to integrate a Cloud Access Security Broker (CASB) into its cloud security architecture. What is a core functionality of a CASB?
a. Encrypting traffic between on-premises users and the cloud
b. Providing visibility and control over shadow IT usage
c. Managing secure connections to hybrid cloud environments
d. Monitoring performance metrics of cloud-hosted applications

Answer: b. Providing visibility and control over shadow IT usage. Explanation: CASBs offer visibility into unauthorized cloud services (shadow IT) and enforce policies for their usage. Option a is incorrect, as CASBs primarily focus on access and policy enforcement, not encryption of traffic. Option c relates to hybrid connectivity, not CASB functionality. Option d concerns application performance monitoring, not security enforcement.

33. An organization is implementing the Shared Responsibility Model for its Infrastructure as a Service (IaaS) environment. Which responsibility remains entirely with the cloud provider?
a. Securing the hypervisor layer that hosts virtual machines
b. Managing the access control policies for virtual machines
c. Encrypting data stored within virtual disks
d. Monitoring compliance with internal security policies

Answer: a. Securing the hypervisor layer that hosts virtual machines. Explanation: In the Shared Responsibility Model for IaaS, the cloud provider manages and secures the infrastructure, including the hypervisor. Option b is the customer's responsibility. Option c may be jointly shared, but encryption key management often falls to the customer. Option d is the responsibility of the customer to enforce internal policies.

34. When securing a Kubernetes environment, which control is most effective in preventing unauthorized lateral movement between containers?
a. Implementing pod-level network policies using namespaces
b. Encrypting container images with symmetric keys
c. Restricting access to the kubelet API server
d. Deploying an intrusion prevention system (IPS) at the network perimeter

Answer: a. Implementing pod-level network policies using namespaces. Explanation: Pod-level network policies enforce isolation and limit lateral movement within Kubernetes clusters. Option b secures container images but does not address lateral movement. Option c protects the kubelet API but is unrelated to container communication. Option d addresses perimeter security, not intra-cluster threats.

35. An organization uses Cloud Security Posture Management (CSPM) tools to assess its cloud environment. What critical task should the organization automate to enhance its security posture?
a. Real-time identification of public-facing storage buckets
b. Automated scaling of virtual machine instances
c. Configuration of firewall rules for edge devices
d. Routine updates to cloud-native applications

Answer: a. Real-time identification of public-facing storage buckets. Explanation: CSPM tools automate the discovery of misconfigured storage buckets that are publicly accessible, a common risk in cloud environments. Option b relates to scalability, not security posture. Option c is typically handled through other network security tools. Option d involves application management, not a CSPM focus.

36. Which of the following is a key advantage of integrating a Cloud Workload Protection Platform (CWPP) with serverless architectures?
a. Reducing costs associated with deploying traditional virtual machines
b. Enabling visibility into ephemeral workloads and ensuring their security
c. Improving latency and response times for application requests
d. Providing centralized logging for compliance purposes

Answer: b. Enabling visibility into ephemeral workloads and ensuring their security. Explanation: CWPPs provide security for ephemeral workloads, such as those in serverless environments, by monitoring and protecting against runtime threats. Option a is a cost consideration, not a CWPP feature. Option c pertains to performance, not security. Option d is a feature of centralized logging systems, not specific to CWPP.

37. A company migrating to containers in the cloud is concerned about securing its images. Which action is most critical to ensure container image security before deployment?
a. Implementing user access reviews for container registries
b. Conducting vulnerability scanning for container images
c. Encrypting all images stored in the container registry
d. Restricting container image pull requests to internal users

Answer: b. Conducting vulnerability scanning for container images. Explanation: Vulnerability scanning ensures that container images do not contain exploitable software before deployment. Option a supports access management but does not address image integrity. Option c secures image data but does not verify its security posture. Option d limits access but does not validate the security of images.

38. Which of the following best illustrates a limitation of the Shared Responsibility Model in cloud environments?
a. Customers have full control over encryption key management.
b. Providers do not monitor customer compliance with regulations.
c. Providers are solely responsible for physical data center security.
d. Customers cannot implement their own identity management systems.

Answer: b. Providers do not monitor customer compliance with regulations. Explanation: Under the Shared Responsibility Model, compliance with regulations remains the customer's responsibility, as providers focus on infrastructure-level controls. Option a is a feature, not a limitation. Option c is a provider responsibility, not a limitation. Option d is incorrect, as customers retain control over identity management.

39. During the implementation of a Security Orchestration, Automation, and Response (SOAR) platform, a key goal is reducing analyst response time to phishing incidents. Which capability of SOAR is most critical to achieving this goal?
a. Automated ticket generation and routing
b. Preconfigured playbooks for repetitive incident types
c. User behavior analytics (UBA) integration
d. Real-time collaboration tools for incident teams

Answer: b. Preconfigured playbooks for repetitive incident types. Explanation: Preconfigured playbooks enable SOAR to automate responses to common incidents like phishing, significantly reducing manual effort and response time. Option a is incorrect as ticket routing, while useful, does not directly automate incident response. Option c is wrong because UBA focuses on detecting anomalous behavior, not automating response. Option d is irrelevant as collaboration tools improve teamwork but do not directly reduce response time.

40. Which type of Indicator of Compromise (IoC) is least likely to produce false positives in a SIEM environment?
a. File hash values from known malware samples
b. IP addresses associated with suspicious activities
c. Domain names flagged for phishing
d. Behavioral anomalies in user logins

Answer: a. File hash values from known malware samples. Explanation: File hashes are specific and unchanging, making them highly reliable indicators. Option b is incorrect because IP addresses can frequently change or be reused. Option c is wrong because domain names may be flagged incorrectly due to overlap with benign domains. Option d is incorrect as behavioral anomalies are context-dependent and prone to false positives.

41. A security team using a SIEM has noticed an overwhelming number of alerts, leading to alert fatigue. Which strategy is the most effective for reducing noise while maintaining detection accuracy?
a. Disabling rules that generate the most alerts
b. Adjusting correlation rule thresholds based on historical data
c. Increasing the time window for log aggregation

d. Relying solely on machine learning to filter alerts

Answer: b. Adjusting correlation rule thresholds based on historical data. Explanation: Fine-tuning correlation rules to align with normal patterns reduces noise without sacrificing detection accuracy. Option a is incorrect because disabling rules risks missing genuine threats. Option c is wrong as increasing log aggregation time windows may delay detection. Option d is incorrect as machine learning alone may still produce false positives without proper tuning.

42. A Network Detection and Response (NDR) solution has detected a high volume of DNS queries to a suspicious domain. What is the most appropriate next step?
a. Block all DNS traffic across the network immediately
b. Perform a reverse DNS lookup to confirm the domain's ownership
c. Use threat intelligence to verify the domain's reputation
d. Investigate endpoint activity associated with the queries

Answer: c. Use threat intelligence to verify the domain's reputation. Explanation: Verifying the domain's reputation helps determine if the activity is malicious. Option a is incorrect because blocking all DNS traffic is overly disruptive. Option b is wrong as ownership confirmation does not assess malicious intent. Option d is insufficient as it delays addressing the suspicious activity at the network level.

43. What is the primary goal of measuring Mean Time to Detect (MTTD) in a SOC?
a. To evaluate the effectiveness of containment strategies
b. To measure how quickly security incidents are identified
c. To track the overall efficiency of ticket resolution
d. To assess the reliability of detection technologies

Answer: b. To measure how quickly security incidents are identified. Explanation: MTTD tracks the time it takes to detect an incident, reflecting the SOC's monitoring effectiveness. Option a is incorrect because containment is measured by response time. Option c is wrong as ticket resolution pertains to operational workflows. Option d is unrelated because detection reliability is not directly measured by MTTD.

44. An organization implements a new SIEM system but finds it difficult to tune correlation rules effectively. What is the best approach to improve rule accuracy?
a. Enable all default rules provided by the SIEM vendor
b. Map rules to the MITRE ATT&CK framework for better coverage
c. Disable any rules that generate more than 50 alerts per day
d. Rely on third-party managed services to tune the SIEM

Answer: b. Map rules to the MITRE ATT&CK framework for better coverage. Explanation: Mapping rules to the MITRE ATT&CK framework ensures that the rules address known adversary techniques and improves accuracy. Option a is incorrect because default rules often require customization. Option c is wrong as disabling rules based on volume risks missing critical alerts. Option d is suboptimal because reliance on third parties may limit the organization's ability to adapt rules dynamically.

45. In a SOC focused on reducing Mean Time to Respond (MTTR), which tool or approach is most effective for containing lateral movement during an incident?
a. Endpoint detection and response (EDR) isolation features
b. Network segmentation using VLANs
c. Manual firewall rule updates during incidents
d. Real-time threat intelligence feeds

Answer: a. Endpoint detection and response (EDR) isolation features. Explanation: EDR solutions can isolate compromised endpoints quickly, preventing lateral movement. Option b, while useful, is a preventive measure, not an immediate response. Option c is incorrect because manual updates are too slow for effective containment. Option d is wrong as threat intelligence feeds aid detection but not immediate containment.

46. A SOC analyst reviews a playbook for ransomware response. Which step is most critical to execute first after confirming ransomware activity?
a. Identifying the ransomware strain using forensic tools
b. Initiating containment by isolating infected systems
c. Restoring encrypted files from the latest backups
d. Notifying law enforcement about the ransomware attack

Answer: b. Initiating containment by isolating infected systems. Explanation: Containment is the priority to prevent further spread of the ransomware. Option a is secondary to containment. Option c is incorrect because restoring files before containment risks re-encryption. Option d, while necessary, does not address the immediate need to stop the spread.

47. During a review of SOC metrics, it is observed that MTTD has decreased but MTTR remains high. What is the most likely explanation for this discrepancy?
a. The SOC is effectively detecting threats but lacks adequate response processes
b. False positives are inflating the detection metrics
c. Correlation rules are improperly tuned, leading to delayed escalations
d. The organization is overly reliant on manual detection methods

Answer: a. The SOC is effectively detecting threats but lacks adequate response processes. Explanation: A low MTTD indicates timely detection, but a high MTTR suggests delays in response processes. Option b is incorrect because false positives would likely increase MTTD. Option c is wrong as improper tuning would also affect MTTD. Option d is unrelated because manual detection impacts detection speed, not response time.

48. A financial organization is deploying Dynamic Application Security Testing (DAST) to identify vulnerabilities in its web applications. What is a primary limitation of DAST that must be addressed to ensure comprehensive application security?
a. Inability to detect issues in runtime environments
b. Limited capability to identify vulnerabilities in backend APIs
c. Dependency on access to the source code for effective scanning
d. Insufficient coverage for identifying vulnerabilities in third-party libraries

Answer: b. Limited capability to identify vulnerabilities in backend APIs. Explanation: DAST primarily focuses on web-facing components, often missing vulnerabilities in APIs and backend systems. Option a is incorrect because DAST specifically assesses runtime behavior. Option c is a limitation of SAST, not DAST. Option d relates to Software Composition Analysis (SCA), not DAST.

49. During a Static Application Security Testing (SAST) scan, Abstract Syntax Tree (AST) analysis is used. What is the main benefit of this technique in identifying vulnerabilities?
a. Simulating runtime interactions to uncover logic flaws
b. Performing semantic analysis of code to detect structural flaws
c. Mapping external API calls to detect insecure dependencies
d. Tracking real-time data flows to identify injection vulnerabilities

Answer: b. Performing semantic analysis of code to detect structural flaws. Explanation: AST analysis builds a hierarchical representation of code to detect structural vulnerabilities at compile time. Option a describes DAST, not SAST. Option c relates to SCA for dependency analysis. Option d is associated with dynamic or runtime testing, not SAST.

50. A development team wants to address third-party library risks in their applications. Which tool or method should they prioritize to effectively manage this risk?
a. Conducting regular DAST scans on deployed applications
b. Performing Software Composition Analysis (SCA) during builds
c. Utilizing SAST tools to assess source code vulnerabilities
d. Deploying IAST tools in pre-production environments

Answer: b. Performing Software Composition Analysis (SCA) during builds. Explanation: SCA identifies known vulnerabilities in third-party libraries by analyzing their metadata and versions. Option a does not address third-party risks directly. Option c focuses on source code, not external libraries. Option d is used for runtime testing, not dependency analysis.

51. An organization deploying an Interactive Application Security Testing (IAST) tool aims to maximize its effectiveness. What condition is essential for IAST tools to identify vulnerabilities accurately?
a. Execution of the application in an active testing environment
b. Integration of IAST with existing bug tracking systems
c. Availability of the application's source code during scanning
d. Exclusive use of automated test cases during assessments

Answer: a. Execution of the application in an active testing environment. Explanation: IAST relies on real-time analysis of an actively running application to detect vulnerabilities. Option b enhances workflow but is not essential for vulnerability detection. Option c applies to SAST tools, not IAST. Option d limits effectiveness, as manual testing often uncovers additional issues.

52. Which of the following is a common misstep in implementing Cross-Site Request Forgery (CSRF) token protection?
a. Using the same token across multiple user sessions
b. Generating tokens dynamically for each user session
c. Validating the token on the server side for every request
d. Including the CSRF token in a hidden field within forms

Answer: a. Using the same token across multiple user sessions. Explanation: Reusing the same token across sessions increases the risk of CSRF attacks, as it compromises uniqueness. Option b is correct practice, ensuring session-specific tokens. Option c is essential for CSRF defense. Option d is a common and effective implementation strategy.

53. A team is conducting Dynamic Application Security Testing (DAST) to detect vulnerabilities in a public-facing web application. Which vulnerability is DAST most likely to identify?
a. Insecure deserialization in backend systems
b. SQL injection flaws in dynamic form inputs
c. Usage of outdated third-party libraries
d. Hardcoded credentials in source code

Answer: b. SQL injection flaws in dynamic form inputs. Explanation: DAST is effective at detecting runtime vulnerabilities, such as SQL injection. Option a is challenging to detect without access to source code. Option c is better addressed using SCA. Option d is identified by SAST, not DAST.

54. During a Software Composition Analysis (SCA) scan, a critical vulnerability is discovered in a widely used third-party library. What is the most effective immediate response to mitigate this risk?
a. Replace the library with an alternative from a different vendor
b. Remove the library from the application's dependency tree
c. Patch the library to the latest secure version
d. Implement runtime monitoring to detect potential exploitation

Answer: c. Patch the library to the latest secure version. Explanation: Updating the library to a secure version is the most effective immediate mitigation. Option a may introduce new risks and is time-consuming. Option b may not be feasible due to dependencies. Option d mitigates the impact but does not resolve the vulnerability.

55. Which feature makes IAST tools uniquely suited for identifying application vulnerabilities during QA testing?
a. Real-time analysis of runtime data flows and interactions
b. Comprehensive static analysis of the entire codebase
c. Integration with cloud-based security posture tools
d. Dynamic analysis of network-layer traffic patterns

Answer: a. Real-time analysis of runtime data flows and interactions. Explanation: IAST works within the application during runtime, offering detailed insights into vulnerabilities. Option b describes SAST. Option c pertains to cloud security tools. Option d is a feature of network monitoring, not IAST.

56. A retail company plans to implement CSRF protection in its payment application. How should they ensure the CSRF token remains effective in mitigating attacks?
a. Include the token in a session cookie sent to the browser
b. Encrypt the token before including it in forms
c. Generate a unique token for each user session
d. Store the token on the client side for improved performance

Answer: c. Generate a unique token for each user session. Explanation: Unique session tokens ensure that attackers cannot reuse them across sessions. Option a is insecure, as CSRF tokens should not be stored in cookies. Option b is unnecessary; token uniqueness is the priority. Option d exposes the token to manipulation, undermining security.

57. During an incident response involving advanced persistent threat (APT) activity, which phase of the MITRE ATT&CK framework is most likely associated with lateral movement using SMB protocol exploitation?
a. Reconnaissance
b. Privilege escalation
c. Lateral movement
d. Command and control

Answer: c. Lateral movement. Explanation: Lateral movement in the MITRE ATT&CK framework involves techniques such as SMB protocol exploitation to navigate within a network. Option a is incorrect because reconnaissance focuses on gathering information outside the network. Option b is wrong because privilege escalation typically involves acquiring higher-level credentials rather than network traversal. Option d is incorrect as command and control pertains to maintaining communication with a compromised system.

58. In a digital forensics investigation, which of the following steps is critical to ensure the admissibility of evidence in legal proceedings?
a. Imaging the drive without hash verification
b. Maintaining a proper chain of custody document
c. Analyzing evidence directly on the suspect's original system
d. Storing all evidence on a shared network drive for easy access

Answer: b. Maintaining a proper chain of custody document. Explanation: A chain of custody ensures evidence integrity by documenting its handling. Option a is incorrect because imaging without hash verification may compromise evidence integrity. Option c is wrong as analyzing evidence on the original system risks contamination. Option d is incorrect because storing evidence on a shared drive increases the risk of unauthorized access or modification.

59. When mapping an incident to the Cyber Kill Chain, what is the primary focus of the "delivery" phase?
a. Exploiting a vulnerability in a target system
b. Transmitting malicious payloads to the intended victim
c. Establishing persistent access to the target environment
d. Exfiltrating sensitive data from the compromised system

Answer: b. Transmitting malicious payloads to the intended victim. Explanation: The delivery phase in the Cyber Kill Chain involves delivering the malicious payload to the victim. Option a is incorrect as exploitation occurs in the subsequent phase. Option c is wrong because establishing persistence is part of later phases. Option d is incorrect because data exfiltration occurs much later in the attack lifecycle.

60. What is the primary role of the Incident Commander within the Incident Command System (ICS) during a major cybersecurity incident?
a. Directing the technical response team's remediation activities
b. Ensuring communication between stakeholders and management
c. Coordinating all incident response activities and resources
d. Leading post-incident forensic analysis and reporting

Answer: c. Coordinating all incident response activities and resources. Explanation: The Incident Commander oversees and directs the entire incident response process, ensuring cohesive coordination. Option a is incorrect because technical tasks are delegated to specialized team leads. Option b, while important, is a subset of the Incident Commander's broader responsibilities. Option d is unrelated to the Incident Commander's primary role during active response.

61. A ransomware attack has encrypted critical systems, and the organization needs to determine its initial entry point. Which technique is most effective for identifying how the attack began?
a. Reviewing endpoint detection and response (EDR) logs
b. Conducting a retrospective analysis of firewall rules
c. Scanning all encrypted files for malware signatures
d. Restoring from the most recent known-good backup

Answer: a. Reviewing endpoint detection and response (EDR) logs. Explanation: EDR logs can reveal the initial compromise point by tracking system activity and intrusion indicators. Option b is incorrect as firewall rules alone may not reveal entry methods. Option c is wrong because scanning encrypted files cannot uncover the attack's origin. Option d is irrelevant to identifying the entry point, as it focuses on recovery.

62. Which component of the Digital Forensics and Incident Response (DFIR) process is most critical during evidence acquisition?
a. Ensuring evidence is encrypted before imaging
b. Avoiding duplication of evidence to reduce storage overhead
c. Verifying that imaging tools produce bit-by-bit copies
d. Conducting a live analysis of volatile data without preservation

Answer: c. Verifying that imaging tools produce bit-by-bit copies. Explanation: Bit-by-bit imaging ensures the integrity of evidence, making it admissible in legal proceedings. Option a is incorrect because encryption is optional and secondary to accurate imaging. Option b is wrong as duplication is necessary for analysis and backups. Option d is incorrect because volatile data must be preserved before analysis to maintain integrity.

63. When using the Cyber Kill Chain to respond to a phishing attack, which phase should focus on identifying malicious URLs or email attachments?
a. Weaponization
b. Delivery

c. Exploitation
d. Reconnaissance

Answer: b. Delivery. Explanation: The delivery phase involves the transmission of malicious payloads such as phishing emails with harmful URLs or attachments. Option a is incorrect as weaponization pertains to creating the malicious payload. Option c is wrong because exploitation occurs after the payload is executed. Option d is unrelated since reconnaissance involves gathering information before an attack.

64. An organization wants to integrate the MITRE ATT&CK framework into its incident response playbooks. What is the primary benefit of this integration?
a. Enhancing log retention policies for better compliance
b. Standardizing technical terminology across global teams
c. Mapping adversary techniques to improve detection and response
d. Reducing the complexity of post-incident reporting

Answer: c. Mapping adversary techniques to improve detection and response. Explanation: The MITRE ATT&CK framework enables teams to identify and address adversary tactics and techniques systematically. Option a is incorrect because log retention is unrelated to MITRE ATT&CK. Option b is wrong as standardization is a secondary benefit, not the primary purpose. Option d is irrelevant since post-incident reporting complexity is not directly affected.

65. During the containment phase of a critical incident, why is isolating affected systems essential?
a. It prevents data exfiltration by halting attacker communication.
b. It eliminates the need for follow-up forensic analysis.
c. It enables faster recovery by bypassing compromised systems.
d. It ensures that backups remain unaffected by the incident.

Answer: a. It prevents data exfiltration by halting attacker communication. Explanation: Isolation interrupts communication between the attacker and compromised systems, reducing the risk of data theft. Option b is incorrect because forensic analysis is still required post-isolation. Option c is wrong because bypassing systems does not ensure containment. Option d, while important, is a secondary benefit of isolation.

66. A financial institution has determined that a core transaction processing system has an RTO of 4 hours. What does this metric represent in the context of the organization's business continuity plan?
a. The maximum acceptable data loss during a disruption
b. The time required to fully restore data backups
c. The maximum time the system can be offline without significant impact
d. The target duration for recovery of dependent systems

Answer: c. The maximum time the system can be offline without significant impact. Explanation: The RTO defines the maximum allowable downtime for a system before significant business consequences occur. Option a describes the Recovery Point Objective (RPO). Option b is related to recovery actions but does not define downtime tolerance. Option d pertains to interdependencies but does not describe RTO specifically.

67. During a Business Impact Analysis (BIA), a team calculates that a key application has an MTD of 6 hours. Which of the following strategies best aligns with this requirement?
a. Deploying a cold site with a 24-hour activation window
b. Implementing a hot site with immediate failover capability
c. Establishing a warm site with an 8-hour recovery SLA
d. Relying on nightly backups stored in an offsite facility

Answer: b. Implementing a hot site with immediate failover capability. Explanation: A hot site ensures the system can recover within the 6-hour MTD. Option a exceeds the MTD. Option c does not meet the requirement, as the recovery SLA is too long. Option d does not guarantee rapid recovery due to dependency on backup restoration.

68. A company is optimizing its Recovery Point Objective (RPO) for a high-frequency trading platform. Which measure is most appropriate to minimize potential data loss?
a. Enabling hourly incremental backups to a local storage array
b. Deploying synchronous replication to a geographically separate data center
c. Utilizing asynchronous replication with a 30-minute lag time
d. Scheduling database snapshots every 6 hours

Answer: b. Deploying synchronous replication to a geographically separate data center. Explanation: Synchronous replication ensures no data loss by simultaneously writing data to primary and secondary locations. Option a does not eliminate potential loss due to its hourly schedule. Option c introduces a 30-minute lag, violating a low RPO. Option d provides infrequent snapshots, increasing potential loss.

69. Which metric is most critical when evaluating the effectiveness of a Business Impact Analysis (BIA)?
a. The total cost of disaster recovery solutions
b. The alignment of RTO and RPO with business priorities
c. The number of identified single points of failure
d. The speed at which recovery teams are deployed

Answer: b. The alignment of RTO and RPO with business priorities. Explanation: Effective BIAs ensure that RTOs and RPOs reflect the organization's operational priorities and tolerance for downtime or data loss. Option a focuses on costs, not alignment with priorities. Option c addresses risk identification but is secondary. Option d measures response efficiency, not the BIA's core purpose.

70. An organization must implement a disaster recovery site for its ERP system, with a requirement to resume operations within 2 hours. Which solution best meets this requirement?
a. Cold site with daily tape backups shipped offsite
b. Warm site with pre-configured servers and 4-hour SLA
c. Hot site with real-time data synchronization and full redundancy
d. Co-location facility with weekly infrastructure checks

Answer: c. Hot site with real-time data synchronization and full redundancy. Explanation: A hot site provides immediate failover and ensures minimal disruption, meeting the 2-hour RTO. Option a cannot meet the RTO due to the time required for tape restoration. Option b exceeds the RTO. Option d is insufficient for rapid recovery.

71. A manufacturing firm uses BIA metrics to prioritize applications for recovery during a disruption. Which application should receive the highest priority based on these metrics?
a. Inventory management system with an MTD of 3 days and RTO of 12 hours
b. Payroll system with an MTD of 5 days and RTO of 24 hours
c. Production line control system with an MTD of 4 hours and RTO of 30 minutes
d. Email communication platform with an MTD of 2 days and RTO of 8 hours

Answer: c. Production line control system with an MTD of 4 hours and RTO of 30 minutes. Explanation: The production line control system has the most critical metrics, with the shortest MTD and RTO, indicating the highest business impact from downtime. Options a, b, and d have longer MTDs, making them less urgent.

72. A retail chain is deploying a warm site for disaster recovery. Which characteristic most accurately describes this strategy?
a. Fully operational with real-time data synchronization

b. Equipped with basic infrastructure but requires data restoration
c. Completely offline until infrastructure is provisioned
d. Designed for testing and development rather than production

Answer: b. Equipped with basic infrastructure but requires data restoration. Explanation: A warm site includes pre-configured hardware and some software but requires restoration of data to become operational. Option a describes a hot site. Option c refers to a cold site. Option d is unrelated to disaster recovery.

73. Which of the following directly influences the Maximum Tolerable Downtime (MTD) for a mission-critical system?
a. Regulatory requirements for uptime
b. The cost of implementing redundancy
c. The frequency of hardware failures
d. The organization's tolerance for financial and operational losses

Answer: d. The organization's tolerance for financial and operational losses. Explanation: MTD is based on how long a business can tolerate the impact of system unavailability. Option a indirectly influences MTD through compliance. Option b relates to mitigation strategies, not MTD determination. Option c pertains to reliability but not directly to MTD.

74. An organization with limited budget resources must choose between a hot site and a warm site for disaster recovery. Which criterion should most strongly influence the decision?
a. Total cost of ownership for each solution
b. MTD for the organization's most critical systems
c. Geographic location of the disaster recovery sites
d. Availability of vendor support for hardware replacement

Answer: b. MTD for the organization's most critical systems. Explanation: The choice of recovery site depends on whether the MTD can be met. A hot site is needed for short MTDs, while a warm site suffices for longer MTDs. Option a is a consideration but secondary to business impact. Option c affects accessibility but is not decisive. Option d is a minor factor.

75. A multinational organization is conducting a Data Protection Impact Assessment (DPIA) for a new marketing analytics platform that uses customer behavior data. Which step is most critical during the risk identification phase of the DPIA?
a. Identifying the marketing team's specific data requirements
b. Evaluating vendor compliance with international privacy standards
c. Determining how data processing could impact individuals' rights and freedoms
d. Assessing the compatibility of the platform with existing security tools

Answer: c. Determining how data processing could impact individuals' rights and freedoms. Explanation: The DPIA focuses on identifying risks to individuals' rights and freedoms, which is the cornerstone of data privacy regulations. Option a is incorrect because the focus is on individuals' risks, not internal team needs. Option b is a part of the broader compliance check, not the specific risk identification phase. Option d is irrelevant to the DPIA's primary purpose of assessing privacy risks.

76. When designing systems under Privacy by Design (PbD), which principle requires embedding privacy measures as default settings in the system?
a. Privacy as the default setting
b. End-to-end security
c. Visibility and transparency
d. User-centric privacy controls

Answer: a. Privacy as the default setting. Explanation: The principle of privacy as the default setting ensures that personal data is protected without requiring user intervention. Option b focuses on securing data throughout its lifecycle but not default privacy settings. Option c is wrong because visibility and transparency pertain to providing clarity on privacy measures, not default configurations. Option d, while important, emphasizes user control rather than automatic privacy protection.

77. A company receives a Data Subject Access Request (DSAR) from an individual requesting all personal data processed about them. What is the company's primary responsibility under the General Data Protection Regulation (GDPR)?
a. Confirm the identity of the requester before taking further action
b. Provide access to the data only after receiving a processing fee
c. Disclose data processing records only with explicit supervisory authority approval
d. Destroy the individual's data immediately to ensure privacy

Answer: a. Confirm the identity of the requester before taking further action. Explanation: Confirming the identity of the requester ensures that data is disclosed to the rightful owner, preventing unauthorized access. Option b is incorrect because GDPR prohibits charging fees unless requests are excessive or repetitive. Option c is wrong as supervisory authority approval is not required to fulfill a DSAR. Option d is incorrect because destruction of data without lawful justification violates GDPR.

78. What is the primary advantage of Privacy-Preserving Record Linkage (PPRL) in healthcare data sharing?
a. Ensures full anonymization of all shared records
b. Allows for secure linking of datasets without exposing personally identifiable information (PII)
c. Automatically encrypts all data to prevent misuse
d. Complies with all international data privacy regulations

Answer: b. Allows for secure linking of datasets without exposing personally identifiable information (PII). Explanation: PPRL facilitates collaboration by linking records securely while maintaining privacy. Option a is incorrect because PPRL typically uses pseudonymization rather than full anonymization. Option c is wrong because encryption is a tool, not the primary feature of PPRL. Option d is overly broad as PPRL itself does not guarantee compliance with all regulations.

79. An organization transferring personal data from the EU to a US-based cloud provider plans to use standard contractual clauses (SCCs). What additional step must the organization take to ensure compliance with GDPR?
a. Obtain explicit consent from each data subject
b. Perform a data transfer impact assessment (DTIA)
c. Encrypt all transferred data at rest and in transit
d. Register the SCCs with the relevant data protection authority

Answer: b. Perform a data transfer impact assessment (DTIA). Explanation: A DTIA evaluates the receiving country's data protection laws to ensure the SCCs provide adequate safeguards. Option a is incorrect because SCCs do not require individual consent. Option c, while a good practice, is not specific to SCC compliance. Option d is wrong because SCCs do not need to be registered with authorities.

80. When handling Data Subject Access Requests (DSARs), which action could violate data privacy regulations?
a. Providing a copy of personal data in a machine-readable format
b. Informing the requester of the purposes for data processing
c. Retaining the requester's data indefinitely for future inquiries
d. Correcting inaccuracies in the data upon the requester's request

Answer: c. Retaining the requester's data indefinitely for future inquiries. Explanation: Indefinite retention without a lawful basis violates privacy regulations like GDPR. Option a complies with data portability requirements. Option b aligns with transparency principles. Option d fulfills the right to rectification, making it compliant.

81. Which of the following best describes the principle of "visibility and transparency" in Privacy by Design (PbD)?
a. Ensuring only authorized individuals can view personal data
b. Demonstrating compliance with privacy practices to users and regulators
c. Encrypting data to prevent unauthorized access during processing
d. Allowing users to delete their data without administrative approval

Answer: b. Demonstrating compliance with privacy practices to users and regulators. Explanation: Visibility and transparency emphasize clear communication of privacy measures to stakeholders. Option a is incorrect as it pertains to access control. Option c focuses on security, not transparency. Option d is unrelated, as it refers to user control rather than visibility.

82. In the context of cross-border data transfers, what is the purpose of binding corporate rules (BCRs)?
a. To provide a legal basis for transferring data within multinational organizations
b. To standardize contractual terms for third-party data processors
c. To ensure compliance with US federal privacy regulations
d. To enforce encryption of all data during international transmission

Answer: a. To provide a legal basis for transferring data within multinational organizations. Explanation: BCRs are internal policies approved by regulators for lawful intra-group transfers. Option b is incorrect as standard contractual clauses, not BCRs, are used for third parties. Option c is irrelevant as BCRs are primarily for GDPR compliance. Option d misrepresents BCRs, which do not mandate encryption.

83. A privacy engineer designs a system that collects minimal data required to achieve its purpose. Which Privacy by Design principle does this approach exemplify?
a. Full functionality
b. End-to-end lifecycle protection
c. Data minimization
d. Proactive not reactive

Answer: c. Data minimization. Explanation: Data minimization ensures only necessary data is collected, reducing privacy risks. Option a is unrelated to limiting data collection. Option b focuses on securing data throughout its lifecycle, not minimizing collection. Option d refers to addressing privacy risks proactively, not reducing data scope.

84. A healthcare organization is evaluating recovery strategies for its electronic medical records (EMR) system. The system has an RTO of 1 hour and an RPO of 15 minutes. Which solution is the most suitable to meet these requirements?
a. Warm site with database backups every 30 minutes
b. Hot site with synchronous replication and automated failover
c. Cold site with tape backups stored offsite and a 24-hour restoration SLA
d. Co-location facility with weekly system snapshots

Answer: b. Hot site with synchronous replication and automated failover. Explanation: A hot site with synchronous replication ensures near-zero data loss and immediate recovery, meeting both the 1-hour RTO and 15-minute RPO. Option a fails the RPO due to 30-minute backup intervals. Option c cannot meet either the RTO or RPO. Option d is too infrequent and unsuitable for critical systems.

85. During a Business Impact Analysis (BIA), which of the following would be the most significant indicator of a high-priority system?
a. High regulatory penalties for non-compliance due to downtime
b. Low operational dependency on other systems
c. Long recovery time objectives relative to other systems
d. Low cost of system replacement and restoration

Answer: a. High regulatory penalties for non-compliance due to downtime. Explanation: Systems with high penalties for downtime due to regulatory requirements are typically high-priority for recovery. Option b describes a less critical system. Option c implies the system is less time-sensitive. Option d indicates a low-priority system due to minimal financial impact.

86. A logistics company is considering a cold site for disaster recovery to minimize costs. What is a significant disadvantage of this approach?
a. Requires real-time data replication to maintain system availability
b. Recovery time depends on provisioning hardware and restoring backups
c. Maintenance costs are higher than alternative recovery sites
d. Cannot store backup data due to compliance restrictions

Answer: b. Recovery time depends on provisioning hardware and restoring backups. Explanation: A cold site lacks pre-configured infrastructure, leading to longer recovery times. Option a is incorrect because cold sites do not involve real-time replication. Option c is false as cold sites are cost-effective. Option d is unrelated, as data storage depends on the backup solution, not the site type.

87. An organization is reviewing its disaster recovery plan and finds that it lacks clear RPOs for critical databases. What risk does this pose to the organization?
a. Increased operational costs due to over-provisioning resources
b. Loss of data that exceeds the organization's tolerance threshold
c. Inability to maintain compliance with data encryption standards
d. Delayed detection of unauthorized access to backup systems

Answer: b. Loss of data that exceeds the organization's tolerance threshold. Explanation: Without defined RPOs, the organization risks exceeding its data loss tolerance during a disruption. Option a relates to resource planning, not RPOs. Option c concerns encryption, which is unrelated to RPO. Option d pertains to security monitoring, not recovery objectives.

88. Which statement about the relationship between RTO and MTD is correct?
a. The RTO must always be longer than the MTD to ensure adequate recovery time.
b. The RTO defines the point beyond which data loss becomes unacceptable.
c. The RTO must be shorter than the MTD to avoid exceeding business tolerance.
d. The RTO is irrelevant when MTD is based on financial thresholds.

Answer: c. The RTO must be shorter than the MTD to avoid exceeding business tolerance. Explanation: RTO represents the time allowed to recover a system and must fit within the MTD to prevent unacceptable business impact. Option a is incorrect as RTO must be shorter, not longer. Option b describes RPO, not RTO. Option d is false because RTO is always relevant to MTD.

89. A company performs nightly backups for its email server and stores the data at an offsite location. What is the most likely RPO for this setup?
a. 24 hours
b. 4 hours

c. 15 minutes
d. Zero data loss

Answer: a. 24 hours. Explanation: Nightly backups result in an RPO of 24 hours since any disruption would cause a loss of data generated since the last backup. Option b is incorrect because the RPO is based on the frequency of backups. Option c requires more frequent backups or replication. Option d implies synchronous replication, which is not the case here.

90. A business continuity manager is tasked with evaluating alternate sites for disaster recovery. Which factor is the most critical when selecting a hot site?
a. Distance from the primary site to reduce latency
b. The ability to perform regular maintenance testing
c. Full duplication of IT infrastructure and data
d. Minimal cost to the organization during normal operations

Answer: c. Full duplication of IT infrastructure and data. Explanation: A hot site requires full infrastructure and data replication to ensure immediate failover capability. Option a is secondary unless latency affects operations. Option b is useful but not the primary consideration. Option d is typically higher for hot sites, making it a less critical factor.

91. A company is implementing a Software Bill of Materials (SBOM) to improve supply chain transparency. Which of the following is the most critical feature to include in an SBOM?
a. List of suppliers' physical locations
b. Version numbers of all components used in the software
c. Documentation of third-party licensing agreements
d. Policies for retiring obsolete software components

Answer: b. Version numbers of all components used in the software. Explanation: Including version numbers ensures traceability and helps identify vulnerabilities tied to specific components. Option a is incorrect because physical supplier locations are not critical to SBOM functionality. Option c is wrong as licensing agreements, while important, are secondary to tracking component details. Option d focuses on lifecycle management but does not define an SBOM's core purpose.

92. During a Vendor Security Assessment Process (VSAP), which measure is most effective for evaluating a vendor's ability to handle sensitive data?
a. Reviewing the vendor's financial stability
b. Analyzing the vendor's incident response policy
c. Verifying the vendor's compliance with local labor laws
d. Conducting a physical inspection of the vendor's facilities

Answer: b. Analyzing the vendor's incident response policy. Explanation: A robust incident response policy demonstrates a vendor's readiness to handle sensitive data securely. Option a is incorrect because financial stability does not directly measure data protection capabilities. Option c is irrelevant to data security. Option d, while useful for other assessments, does not address sensitive data management.

93. What is the primary goal of Third-Party Risk Management (TPRM) frameworks in supply chain security?
a. Reducing costs associated with vendor operations
b. Ensuring third-party compliance with ethical labor standards
c. Identifying and mitigating risks posed by external partners
d. Enforcing penalties for non-compliance with contracts

Answer: c. Identifying and mitigating risks posed by external partners. Explanation: TPRM focuses on assessing and reducing risks from third-party entities in the supply chain. Option a is incorrect as cost reduction is not its primary purpose. Option b, while important, is tangential to TPRM's goal of addressing security risks. Option d is wrong because enforcement is a contractual issue, not a risk management strategy.

94. Which best describes the role of Silicon Root of Trust in hardware security?
a. Enforcing application-level encryption keys
b. Providing a hardware-based cryptographic foundation for system integrity
c. Verifying the identity of end users before granting access
d. Automating firmware updates for improved security

Answer: b. Providing a hardware-based cryptographic foundation for system integrity. Explanation: The Silicon Root of Trust establishes a secure foundation at the hardware level, ensuring the integrity of the boot process. Option a is incorrect because encryption key enforcement is not specific to silicon-level security. Option c pertains to user authentication, not hardware integrity. Option d, while beneficial, is unrelated to the concept of a root of trust.

95. During an N-tier supplier risk assessment, which factor presents the highest level of risk for a critical software project?
a. Tier 2 supplier's reliance on a single Tier 3 provider
b. Tier 1 supplier's use of open-source components
c. Tier 3 supplier's financial insolvency risk
d. Tier 2 supplier's lack of regular cybersecurity audits

Answer: c. Tier 3 supplier's financial insolvency risk. Explanation: A financially unstable Tier 3 supplier can disrupt the supply chain, causing significant downstream impact. Option a, while a concern, is less critical than insolvency. Option b is incorrect because open-source components are manageable with proper oversight. Option d is important but less critical than financial stability.

96. What is the main advantage of using SBOMs to mitigate supply chain risks in software development?
a. Accelerates software release cycles by streamlining approvals
b. Reduces software licensing costs by identifying duplicate components
c. Identifies vulnerabilities in software components before deployment
d. Ensures compliance with international shipping regulations

Answer: c. Identifies vulnerabilities in software components before deployment. Explanation: SBOMs provide visibility into software dependencies, enabling pre-deployment vulnerability assessments. Option a is incorrect because SBOMs are not directly tied to approval processes. Option b is wrong as SBOMs are not designed for cost reduction. Option d is unrelated to software development.

97. A company evaluating a third-party vendor discovers that the vendor has minimal disaster recovery planning. What is the best mitigation strategy for this risk?
a. Require the vendor to implement a Silicon Root of Trust
b. Establish contractual penalties for downtime events
c. Implement redundancy within the organization to reduce dependency
d. Migrate all critical processes to a different vendor immediately

Answer: c. Implement redundancy within the organization to reduce dependency. Explanation: Redundancy minimizes reliance on vendors with insufficient disaster recovery measures. Option a is irrelevant as Silicon Root of Trust pertains to hardware security. Option b addresses accountability but does not mitigate operational risk. Option d is overly disruptive and impractical as a first response.

98. In supply chain security, which key consideration is addressed by implementing a formal TPRM framework?
a. Standardizing contract lengths with all third parties
b. Managing access control for internal staff
c. Identifying vulnerabilities within subcontractor relationships
d. Ensuring product delivery timelines are met

Answer: c. Identifying vulnerabilities within subcontractor relationships. Explanation: TPRM frameworks focus on evaluating risks, including those within subcontractor relationships. Option a is unrelated to risk management. Option b pertains to internal security, not third-party risk. Option d is a logistics concern, not directly addressed by TPRM.

99. Why is Silicon Root of Trust critical in detecting hardware tampering?
a. It stores tamper-proof logs of user activities
b. It verifies the authenticity of firmware before execution
c. It enables automatic hardware replacement in case of failure
d. It encrypts all data stored on the device

Answer: b. It verifies the authenticity of firmware before execution. Explanation: Silicon Root of Trust validates firmware integrity, preventing hardware tampering. Option a is incorrect because activity logs are not its function. Option c is wrong because hardware replacement is not automated through this technology. Option d, while important, is not specific to the Silicon Root of Trust.

100. An organization is updating its Configuration Management Database (CMDB) to improve asset tracking. Which practice is essential to ensure the CMDB remains accurate and reliable?
a. Conducting quarterly vulnerability scans on network devices
b. Automatically synchronizing asset data from discovery tools
c. Restricting access to CMDB entries to IT administrators only
d. Archiving historical asset records after six months

Answer: b. Automatically synchronizing asset data from discovery tools. Explanation: Synchronizing data from discovery tools ensures the CMDB reflects the current state of the organization's assets, minimizing inaccuracies. Option a is important for security but does not directly address CMDB accuracy. Option c improves security but does not ensure up-to-date information. Option d risks losing valuable historical data for analysis.

101. A retail company is implementing Data Loss Prevention (DLP) tools to classify sensitive customer data. What is the most effective approach for creating classification schemes?
a. Assigning sensitivity levels based on the data owner's discretion
b. Using predefined templates for regulatory compliance mandates
c. Classifying data based on its origin and business criticality
d. Labeling all data as sensitive to maximize protection

Answer: c. Classifying data based on its origin and business criticality. Explanation: Classification based on origin and criticality ensures that DLP policies align with business needs and compliance requirements. Option a introduces inconsistency due to subjective decisions. Option b may not fully address organizational needs. Option d is inefficient and leads to overprotection, reducing system usability.

102. An asset inventory reconciliation process reveals several discrepancies in the records of IT equipment. Which action is most effective in resolving these issues?
a. Conducting a physical audit of all inventoried assets
b. Comparing current inventory to procurement records
c. Removing all unverified assets from the inventory
d. Disabling network access for assets with missing records

Answer: a. Conducting a physical audit of all inventoried assets. Explanation: A physical audit provides the most reliable method for resolving discrepancies by verifying the actual existence and location of assets. Option b addresses procurement but does not confirm the presence of assets. Option c risks removing legitimate assets. Option d is disruptive and may affect operational continuity.

103. An organization is decommissioning hardware that has reached its end of life (EOL). What is the most critical step to ensure security during the decommissioning process?
a. Releasing the hardware to a certified recycling vendor
b. Ensuring all data is securely erased or destroyed
c. Updating the CMDB to reflect the decommissioned status
d. Archiving the device configuration files for future reference

Answer: b. Ensuring all data is securely erased or destroyed. Explanation: Secure data destruction is essential to prevent unauthorized access to sensitive information on decommissioned devices. Option a supports environmental compliance but does not guarantee data security. Option c maintains inventory accuracy but does not address security. Option d is useful for troubleshooting but not critical for security.

104. A manufacturing firm wants to enhance its Hardware Asset Management (HAM) program to prevent asset theft. Which control should they prioritize?
a. Implementing asset tagging with GPS tracking
b. Installing biometric access controls in asset storage areas
c. Requiring managerial approval for asset relocations
d. Enforcing regular user access reviews for IT systems

Answer: a. Implementing asset tagging with GPS tracking. Explanation: GPS tracking provides real-time location data, making it easier to detect and prevent asset theft. Option b enhances physical security but does not address asset tracking. Option c reduces unauthorized movement but may not prevent theft. Option d is unrelated to physical asset theft.

105. Which statement best describes the role of a Configuration Management Database (CMDB) in supporting asset management security?
a. It serves as a centralized repository for patch management workflows.
b. It tracks relationships between assets and their dependencies.
c. It monitors real-time performance metrics of IT systems.
d. It generates encryption keys for hardware devices.

Answer: b. It tracks relationships between assets and their dependencies. Explanation: The CMDB supports asset management by documenting dependencies, ensuring that changes or failures are effectively managed. Option a relates to patch management, not asset tracking. Option c is a function of performance monitoring tools. Option d pertains to encryption management, not CMDB functions.

106. An organization discovers unauthorized devices connected to its network during a hardware inventory review. What immediate action should be taken to mitigate this risk?
a. Isolate the unauthorized devices from the network
b. Document the devices in the CMDB for future reference
c. Apply standard security patches to the devices
d. Perform a vulnerability scan on the unauthorized devices

Answer: a. Isolate the unauthorized devices from the network. Explanation: Isolating unauthorized devices prevents potential threats to the network while further investigation occurs. Option b delays mitigation. Option c assumes the devices are authorized, which is not confirmed. Option d provides useful information but does not immediately mitigate risk.

107. A company needs to implement a secure process for tracking IT assets in high-turnover environments. Which control is most effective for achieving this?
a. Conducting monthly asset inventory reviews
b. Integrating RFID tags with asset tracking systems
c. Assigning asset ownership to department managers
d. Performing quarterly audits with external vendors

Answer: b. Integrating RFID tags with asset tracking systems. Explanation: RFID tags provide continuous tracking, improving accuracy in high-turnover environments. Option a offers periodic updates but lacks real-time tracking. Option c supports accountability but is not sufficient for detailed tracking. Option d is useful but less effective than RFID for real-time needs.

108. When designing a Data Loss Prevention (DLP) policy, which consideration is most critical to ensure its effectiveness?
a. Selecting tools that offer customizable reporting features
b. Defining clear rules for detecting and blocking sensitive data transfers
c. Ensuring that the policy is reviewed annually for updates
d. Restricting access to the DLP management console to IT staff

Answer: b. Defining clear rules for detecting and blocking sensitive data transfers. Explanation: Effective DLP policies depend on well-defined rules that align with organizational goals and regulatory requirements. Option a improves visibility but does not impact the policy's core function. Option c is important for maintenance, not initial effectiveness. Option d ensures security but does not directly impact policy success.

109. A data center uses multi-factor authentication (MFA) for physical access control. Which factor would provide the strongest second layer of authentication after a proximity card?
a. A personal identification number (PIN)
b. A biometric fingerprint scan
c. A one-time passcode sent via email
d. A security question answer

Answer: b. A biometric fingerprint scan. Explanation: Biometrics provides a unique, non-transferable authentication factor, strengthening physical security. Option a is incorrect because a PIN is knowledge-based and can be shared. Option c is wrong as email-based one-time passcodes are vulnerable to interception. Option d is the weakest because security questions are easily compromised or guessed.

110. Which configuration ensures the effectiveness of a mantrap in high-security environments?
a. Allowing simultaneous entry and exit through both doors
b. Requiring both doors to be closed before either can be opened
c. Using transparent doors to improve visibility inside the mantrap
d. Locking both doors only during emergency evacuations

Answer: b. Requiring both doors to be closed before either can be opened. Explanation: This configuration prevents tailgating and ensures controlled access. Option a undermines security by allowing simultaneous access. Option c improves visibility but does not ensure controlled entry. Option d is incorrect because locking during emergencies could hinder evacuation.

111. HVAC systems in secure facilities must be monitored primarily to prevent which risk?
a. Excessive humidity causing data corruption
b. Unauthorized access to network switches housed in server rooms
c. Overheating of equipment leading to operational downtime
d. Physical theft of sensitive equipment from server racks

Answer: c. Overheating of equipment leading to operational downtime. Explanation: Proper HVAC monitoring ensures temperature control, preventing hardware failures. Option a is incorrect because excessive humidity rarely causes direct data corruption. Option b is unrelated to HVAC and pertains to access control. Option d is unrelated, as HVAC systems do not address theft risks.

112. An environmental monitoring system detects fluctuations in server room humidity. What is the most appropriate immediate action?
a. Increase the airflow to normalize temperature levels
b. Deactivate non-essential systems to reduce energy consumption
c. Investigate the root cause of the fluctuations and address it
d. Schedule routine maintenance for the HVAC system

Answer: c. Investigate the root cause of the fluctuations and address it. Explanation: Identifying and resolving the root cause prevents further environmental instability. Option a may help with temperature but does not address humidity. Option b is unrelated to humidity control. Option d delays action and could exacerbate the issue.

113. Which measure best supports a physical security zone approach in a data center?
a. Placing motion detectors at all main building entrances
b. Implementing a zoning system with increasing security levels toward the core
c. Deploying surveillance cameras at high-traffic areas only
d. Allowing universal access to all personnel within the building

Answer: b. Implementing a zoning system with increasing security levels toward the core. Explanation: This ensures that access becomes more restricted as one approaches sensitive areas. Option a is inadequate for internal zoning. Option c provides surveillance but lacks layered access controls. Option d contradicts the principle of limiting access based on necessity.

114. During a physical security audit, it is discovered that a server room has no humidity controls. Which risk does this most likely pose?
a. Condensation causing electrical shorts
b. Increased frequency of network outages
c. Elevated risk of malware infiltration
d. Unauthorized access due to lax environmental security

Answer: a. Condensation causing electrical shorts. Explanation: Uncontrolled humidity can lead to condensation, damaging hardware. Option b is incorrect because network outages are not directly caused by humidity. Option c is unrelated to environmental factors. Option d is a distraction, as humidity control does not affect physical access.

115. What is the primary security purpose of implementing raised flooring in data centers?
a. Protecting equipment from accidental spills
b. Facilitating efficient cable management and airflow
c. Preventing unauthorized physical access to cabling
d. Improving structural stability during earthquakes

Answer: b. Facilitating efficient cable management and airflow. Explanation: Raised flooring supports optimal cooling and organized cabling, enhancing security by reducing heat-related failures. Option a is secondary. Option c is incorrect, as raised flooring does not inherently secure cables. Option d is not a primary design objective for raised floors.

116. Which control is most critical to ensure the security of a biometric MFA system for physical access?
a. Periodic calibration of biometric sensors
b. Storing biometric templates in plaintext for quick retrieval

c. Allowing fallback to PINs when biometrics fail
d. Using third-party cloud storage for template backups

Answer: a. Periodic calibration of biometric sensors. Explanation: Calibration ensures accuracy, preventing unauthorized access due to faulty readings. Option b is incorrect as plaintext storage compromises security. Option c weakens MFA by relying on less secure factors. Option d introduces risks related to third-party breaches.

117. What role does physical security zoning play in mitigating insider threats?
a. Prevents unauthorized use of external email systems
b. Limits access to sensitive areas based on role and need-to-know
c. Eliminates the need for surveillance in high-traffic zones
d. Detects malware propagation within internal networks

Answer: b. Limits access to sensitive areas based on role and need-to-know. Explanation: Zoning restricts access, minimizing insider threats. Option a is irrelevant to physical zones. Option c is incorrect because surveillance complements zoning. Option d pertains to cybersecurity, not physical security.

118. What HVAC feature is most important for a Tier IV data center?
a. Automated vent sealing during fire suppression events
b. Variable airflow rates to accommodate fluctuating temperatures
c. Energy efficiency to minimize operational costs
d. Redundant cooling systems to ensure continuous operation

Answer: d. Redundant cooling systems to ensure continuous operation. Explanation: Tier IV data centers require continuous availability, necessitating redundant systems. Option a is useful but secondary. Option b is insufficient for Tier IV standards. Option c, while desirable, is not critical for Tier IV reliability.

119. A financial organization deploys a Database Activity Monitoring (DAM) solution to enhance security. Which of the following is the primary function of DAM?
a. Encrypting sensitive data stored in the database
b. Logging and analyzing database transactions in real-time
c. Establishing a secure baseline configuration for the database
d. Scanning the database for misconfigurations and vulnerabilities

Answer: b. Logging and analyzing database transactions in real-time. Explanation: DAM tools monitor database transactions in real-time to detect unauthorized access or suspicious behavior. Option a describes Transparent Data Encryption (TDE). Option c pertains to baseline security configurations. Option d is performed by database security scanners, not DAM.

120. An e-commerce company wants to implement Row-Level Security (RLS) to restrict access to sensitive customer records. What is the primary advantage of RLS over traditional access control mechanisms?
a. Provides automated data encryption at rest and in transit
b. Applies granular policies that control access to individual rows based on user attributes
c. Monitors database queries for malicious activity in real-time
d. Enhances system performance by caching frequently queried rows

Answer: b. Applies granular policies that control access to individual rows based on user attributes. Explanation: RLS allows access to specific rows based on user-defined attributes, enabling fine-grained control. Option a describes encryption, not access control. Option c relates to DAM, not RLS. Option d addresses performance, not security.

121. Which of the following best illustrates the primary benefit of Transparent Data Encryption (TDE) in a database environment?
a. Protecting data in use by authorized applications
b. Encrypting data backups to prevent unauthorized access
c. Securing sensitive data against SQL injection attacks
d. Ensuring all database transactions are logged and auditable

Answer: b. Encrypting data backups to prevent unauthorized access. Explanation: TDE encrypts database files and backups to protect against physical theft or unauthorized access. Option a refers to application-level encryption. Option c addresses input sanitization, not TDE. Option d relates to database logging, not encryption.

122. During a database security scan, a misconfiguration is detected that allows unauthorized users to view schema metadata. Which immediate corrective action should be taken?
a. Implement Row-Level Security (RLS) to restrict access
b. Revoke public access privileges to metadata tables
c. Enable Transparent Data Encryption (TDE) for all sensitive tables
d. Configure a DAM tool to log metadata access attempts

Answer: b. Revoke public access privileges to metadata tables. Explanation: Revoking public access ensures that unauthorized users cannot view schema metadata. Option a is inappropriate because RLS targets row-level data, not metadata. Option c encrypts data but does not resolve access issues. Option d monitors access but does not address the root cause.

123. A healthcare organization is establishing a secure configuration baseline for its patient records database. Which of the following is the most critical step in this process?
a. Performing a full backup before applying configuration changes
b. Disabling unused default accounts and privileges
c. Implementing multi-factor authentication (MFA) for database users
d. Encrypting all stored records using Transparent Data Encryption (TDE)

Answer: b. Disabling unused default accounts and privileges. Explanation: Default accounts and privileges are common attack vectors, making their removal critical for baseline security. Option a ensures recoverability but does not directly enhance security. Option c improves authentication but is not part of configuration baselines. Option d protects data but does not address baseline misconfigurations.

124. A manufacturing firm implements Transparent Data Encryption (TDE) for its supply chain database. What is a potential limitation of TDE?
a. It requires significant application modifications to integrate encryption.
b. It does not protect data during transmission between systems.
c. It increases the risk of database fragmentation, reducing performance.
d. It restricts access to sensitive data to authorized users only.

Answer: b. It does not protect data during transmission between systems. Explanation: TDE encrypts data at rest but does not secure data in transit, which requires additional encryption protocols like TLS. Option a is incorrect because TDE is typically transparent to applications. Option c is a misconception, as TDE has minimal impact on fragmentation. Option d describes access control, not encryption.

125. Which scenario best demonstrates the role of Database Activity Monitoring (DAM) in enhancing security?
a. Encrypting sensitive data stored in a production database
b. Blocking unauthorized queries from unapproved applications
c. Auditing and reporting on failed login attempts in real-time
d. Restricting access to database tables based on user roles

Answer: c. Auditing and reporting on failed login attempts in real-time. Explanation: DAM tools excel at monitoring and reporting suspicious activities, such as failed login attempts. Option a is handled by TDE. Option b describes intrusion prevention, not DAM. Option d is related to access control mechanisms, not DAM.

126. An organization plans to implement a secure configuration baseline for its databases. Which of the following should be prioritized to prevent privilege abuse?
a. Restricting database administrators' access to metadata
b. Limiting the use of shared accounts for administrative tasks
c. Encrypting all database backups using hardware security modules
d. Performing daily snapshots of database configuration changes

Answer: b. Limiting the use of shared accounts for administrative tasks. Explanation: Shared accounts complicate accountability and increase the risk of privilege abuse. Option a is unnecessary as administrators typically require access to metadata. Option c secures backups but does not address privilege abuse. Option d is helpful for monitoring but not directly related to privilege abuse prevention.

127. Which practice is essential when performing a database security scan to identify vulnerabilities?
a. Excluding high-priority databases to reduce scan times
b. Updating database management software to the latest version
c. Running scans in a non-production environment to avoid disruptions
d. Disabling all user accounts during the scanning process

Answer: c. Running scans in a non-production environment to avoid disruptions. Explanation: Scans in a non-production environment prevent performance impacts and potential downtime. Option a compromises security by ignoring critical assets. Option b is a general best practice but does not replace scanning. Option d is disruptive and impractical.

128. A financial institution uses Row-Level Security (RLS) to restrict access to sensitive transaction data. Which scenario demonstrates a potential misconfiguration of RLS?
a. Authorized users can access all rows of data without filtering.
b. Unauthorized users can see metadata but not row-level data.
c. RLS policies are applied dynamically based on user roles.
d. Users are restricted to viewing data for which they are explicitly authorized.

Answer: a. Authorized users can access all rows of data without filtering. Explanation: If authorized users bypass RLS policies and access all rows, it indicates a misconfiguration or missing enforcement. Option b is not a violation since metadata access is separate from RLS. Option c describes correct dynamic application of RLS policies. Option d aligns with proper RLS implementation.

129. An organization deploying Transparent Data Encryption (TDE) for its database systems needs to securely manage encryption keys. Which approach is most effective?
a. Storing encryption keys in the same database instance as the encrypted data
b. Using a hardware security module (HSM) for key management and storage
c. Backing up encryption keys to an external drive stored in a secure vault
d. Generating encryption keys dynamically during database initialization

Answer: b. Using a hardware security module (HSM) for key management and storage. Explanation: HSMs provide secure key storage and management, reducing the risk of key compromise. Option a introduces risk by co-locating keys with encrypted data. Option c lacks real-time key protection and relies on physical security. Option d is impractical for operational environments requiring persistent keys.

130. A database security team discovers a high-severity vulnerability in a widely used database engine. Which immediate action is most effective in mitigating the risk while maintaining operational continuity?
a. Apply the latest security patch provided by the vendor immediately.
b. Block external access to the database until the patch can be tested and deployed.
c. Restrict database queries to read-only operations temporarily.
d. Update database configuration files to disable unnecessary services.

Answer: b. Block external access to the database until the patch can be tested and deployed. Explanation: Blocking external access reduces exposure to the vulnerability while testing the patch. Option a risks introducing untested changes into production. Option c may not address the specific vulnerability. Option d enhances security but may not mitigate the identified vulnerability.

131. During a database audit, it is discovered that multiple applications use a shared database account for authentication. What is the most critical risk associated with this practice?
a. Increased complexity in monitoring query performance
b. Limited accountability for database access and actions
c. Reduced efficiency in database connection pooling
d. Higher risk of data corruption due to conflicting queries

Answer: b. Limited accountability for database access and actions. Explanation: Shared accounts obscure individual user actions, complicating audits and increasing the risk of undetected abuse. Option a is unrelated to security. Option c pertains to performance optimization, not security. Option d may occur in specific scenarios but is not the primary concern.

132. A retail company is implementing a Database Activity Monitoring (DAM) solution. To maximize its effectiveness, where should the DAM tool be positioned in the database architecture?
a. At the network perimeter to capture all traffic entering the database
b. Integrated with the database engine to monitor internal activities
c. Between the database and the application layer to filter SQL queries
d. Within the application code to log interactions with the database

Answer: b. Integrated with the database engine to monitor internal activities. Explanation: Integrating DAM with the database engine allows it to monitor both internal and external activities comprehensively. Option a captures only incoming traffic, missing internal actions. Option c focuses on filtering but lacks comprehensive monitoring. Option d addresses application interactions but cannot monitor database-level operations.

133. A security analyst is reviewing database configuration baselines and identifies that auditing is disabled. Which risk does this pose to the organization?
a. Increased potential for SQL injection attacks
b. Reduced ability to detect unauthorized access or activity
c. Greater likelihood of database fragmentation and slow queries
d. Inability to enforce row-level access control policies

Answer: b. Reduced ability to detect unauthorized access or activity. Explanation: Without auditing, the organization lacks visibility into unauthorized actions or policy violations. Option a relates to input sanitization, not auditing. Option c pertains to performance issues, not security. Option d involves access controls, which auditing does not enforce.

134. An organization implements row-level security (RLS) to ensure compliance with data privacy regulations. How does RLS help enforce these regulations?
a. Encrypts sensitive rows to prevent unauthorized access
b. Restricts access to specific rows based on user roles or attributes

c. Prevents SQL injection attacks from modifying sensitive rows
d. Logs all access attempts to rows containing sensitive data

Answer: b. Restricts access to specific rows based on user roles or attributes. Explanation: RLS enforces compliance by allowing access to only the rows that a user is authorized to view. Option a involves encryption, not access control. Option c addresses input validation, not RLS. Option d relates to logging, which RLS does not inherently provide.

135. During a review of network security, an organization decides to enforce Transport Layer Security (TLS) 1.3. Which feature of TLS 1.3 improves its security posture compared to TLS 1.2?
a. Use of the RC4 cipher suite for faster encryption
b. Removal of support for weak and outdated algorithms
c. Mandatory mutual authentication between client and server
d. Introduction of static Diffie-Hellman key exchanges

Answer: b. Removal of support for weak and outdated algorithms. Explanation: TLS 1.3 eliminates insecure ciphers and algorithms, enhancing overall security. Option a is incorrect because RC4 is deprecated. Option c is wrong because mutual authentication is optional in TLS 1.3. Option d is incorrect as TLS 1.3 uses ephemeral Diffie-Hellman key exchanges to ensure forward secrecy.

136. In an IPSec implementation, which scenario most justifies the use of transport mode over tunnel mode?
a. Securing end-to-end communication between two devices on the same network
b. Encrypting all traffic between two gateway routers
c. Providing confidentiality for multicast traffic within a VPN
d. Preventing IP header visibility during external routing

Answer: a. Securing end-to-end communication between two devices on the same network. Explanation: Transport mode encrypts only the payload, making it suitable for end-to-end communication within the same network. Option b is incorrect because tunnel mode is used for gateway-to-gateway communication. Option c is wrong as IPSec transport mode does not natively support multicast traffic. Option d is incorrect because transport mode does not hide IP headers.

137. Which SNMPv3 feature provides message integrity and protection against replay attacks?
a. Authentication and encryption using MD5
b. User-based Security Model (USM) with time synchronization
c. Community strings for secure device management
d. Trap forwarding with access control lists (ACLs)

Answer: b. User-based Security Model (USM) with time synchronization. Explanation: USM provides integrity, confidentiality, and protection against replay attacks using authentication and encryption. Option a is partially correct but outdated, as MD5 is weak. Option c is incorrect because community strings lack robust security. Option d is irrelevant to message integrity or replay protection.

138. What is the primary advantage of the Secure Remote Password (SRP) protocol over traditional password authentication mechanisms?
a. It encrypts passwords using symmetric algorithms during transmission
b. It prevents password exposure by relying on zero-knowledge proofs
c. It requires fewer computational resources than public key cryptography
d. It enforces two-factor authentication without additional hardware

Answer: b. It prevents password exposure by relying on zero-knowledge proofs. Explanation: SRP uses zero-knowledge proofs to authenticate without transmitting passwords, enhancing security. Option a is incorrect because SRP does not transmit passwords at all. Option c is wrong as computational efficiency is not its primary benefit. Option d is irrelevant because SRP is not a two-factor authentication method.

139. In an IEEE 802.1X deployment, which component acts as the intermediary between the supplicant and the authentication server?
a. Authenticator
b. Radius server
c. EAP module
d. VLAN controller

Answer: a. Authenticator. Explanation: The authenticator forwards authentication requests from the supplicant to the server, enforcing access control. Option b is incorrect because the Radius server performs authentication, not mediation. Option c is a protocol, not a component. Option d is irrelevant to 802.1X authentication.

140. Which enhancement in TLS 1.3 improves connection speed while maintaining security?
a. Pre-shared keys (PSK) for session resumption
b. Support for the RSA key exchange mechanism
c. Static session keys for repeated connections
d. Compression algorithms for smaller data packets

Answer: a. Pre-shared keys (PSK) for session resumption. Explanation: PSKs allow secure resumption of previous sessions without renegotiation, improving speed. Option b is incorrect as TLS 1.3 removed RSA key exchanges. Option c is wrong because static keys do not provide forward secrecy. Option d is irrelevant since TLS 1.3 does not use compression due to security risks.

141. When configuring IPSec for securing communication between branch offices, which consideration favors tunnel mode over transport mode?
a. The need to secure communication between individual devices within each office
b. The requirement to encrypt both IP headers and payloads
c. The need for faster communication with lower processing overhead
d. The ability to use community strings for traffic authentication

Answer: b. The requirement to encrypt both IP headers and payloads. Explanation: Tunnel mode encrypts the entire packet, including headers, making it ideal for inter-office communication. Option a describes transport mode. Option c is incorrect because tunnel mode may increase processing overhead. Option d is unrelated to IPSec configurations.

142. What is a key limitation of SNMPv3 in high-security environments?
a. Lack of support for encryption during data transmission
b. Dependency on MD5 for cryptographic functions
c. Complexity in configuring User-based Security Model (USM)
d. Inability to support access control using ACLs

Answer: c. Complexity in configuring User-based Security Model (USM). Explanation: USM's complexity can make deployment challenging in high-security environments. Option a is incorrect because SNMPv3 supports encryption. Option b is partially true but not a key limitation as stronger algorithms like SHA are available. Option d is wrong because SNMPv3 supports ACL-based access control.

143. In an IEEE 802.1X network, what role does Extensible Authentication Protocol (EAP) play?
a. Encrypting all traffic within the local network
b. Establishing a secure authentication framework between components

c. Managing VLAN assignments based on user roles
d. Monitoring real-time network traffic for anomalies

Answer: b. Establishing a secure authentication framework between components. Explanation: EAP provides a framework for secure authentication during 802.1X exchanges. Option a is incorrect because EAP itself does not encrypt traffic. Option c is unrelated to EAP's core function. Option d pertains to network monitoring, not authentication.

144. An organization plans to implement Mobile Device Management (MDM) to secure its fleet of mobile devices. Which feature of MDM is critical for protecting sensitive corporate data on lost or stolen devices?
a. Enforcing password policies for device access
b. Performing remote wipe of corporate data
c. Restricting access to public Wi-Fi networks
d. Blocking access to unauthorized applications

Answer: b. Performing remote wipe of corporate data. Explanation: Remote wipe ensures that sensitive data can be securely erased from a lost or stolen device, mitigating the risk of exposure. Option a enhances access security but does not address data on lost devices. Option c reduces risk from insecure networks but is unrelated to lost devices. Option d prevents unauthorized app usage but does not protect data in this scenario.

145. A financial institution is deploying an Enterprise Mobility Management (EMM) solution. Which feature is most important for ensuring compliance with regulatory requirements?
a. Geofencing to restrict device use in certain locations
b. Data encryption for both at-rest and in-transit communications
c. Blocking social media applications on corporate devices
d. Enabling secure boot for mobile operating systems

Answer: b. Data encryption for both at-rest and in-transit communications. Explanation: Encryption ensures compliance by protecting sensitive financial data from unauthorized access. Option a is useful for location-based policies but does not directly ensure compliance. Option c improves productivity but does not align with compliance goals. Option d enhances device security but is insufficient alone for regulatory adherence.

146. An organization adopts Mobile Application Management (MAM) controls for BYOD devices. Which capability best highlights the advantage of MAM over full MDM solutions?
a. Separating corporate and personal data within applications
b. Enforcing device-wide encryption policies
c. Blocking unauthorized device use outside corporate networks
d. Applying mandatory OS updates across all managed devices

Answer: a. Separating corporate and personal data within applications. Explanation: MAM allows granular control over corporate app data without managing the entire device, making it ideal for BYOD. Option b is managed by MDM, not MAM. Option c involves network policies, which are outside MAM's focus. Option d pertains to device management, not app-specific control.

147. A company implements a BYOD security framework to reduce risks. What is the primary challenge associated with BYOD policies?
a. Ensuring compatibility across diverse operating systems
b. Enforcing two-factor authentication for corporate apps
c. Preventing access to personal email accounts on devices
d. Managing physical security of personal devices

Answer: a. Ensuring compatibility across diverse operating systems. Explanation: BYOD environments often include devices with varying operating systems, requiring security policies and tools that work across platforms. Option b is a control mechanism, not a challenge specific to BYOD. Option c violates personal privacy, often avoided in BYOD frameworks. Option d is relevant but less critical than OS compatibility.

148. Which mobile threat defense strategy effectively mitigates risks associated with jailbroken or rooted devices?
a. Implementing application whitelisting for corporate apps
b. Blocking access to corporate resources for compromised devices
c. Enabling biometric authentication for all devices
d. Encrypting sensitive files stored on mobile devices

Answer: b. Blocking access to corporate resources for compromised devices. Explanation: Blocking compromised devices prevents the exploitation of security vulnerabilities introduced by jailbreaking or rooting. Option a ensures app control but does not address device compromise. Option c strengthens authentication but does not mitigate rooted risks. Option d protects data but cannot prevent rooted devices from accessing resources.

149. A healthcare organization uses MDM to enforce HIPAA compliance on mobile devices. Which policy is most critical for protecting electronic protected health information (ePHI)?
a. Enforcing screen lock and timeout settings
b. Blocking downloads from non-corporate app stores
c. Logging all incoming and outgoing calls
d. Restricting devices from connecting to public Wi-Fi

Answer: a. Enforcing screen lock and timeout settings. Explanation: Screen lock and timeout settings ensure unauthorized users cannot access ePHI if a device is left unattended, meeting HIPAA requirements. Option b is useful but secondary. Option c is unrelated to HIPAA compliance. Option d enhances security but does not directly protect ePHI.

150. An organization deploys a Mobile Threat Defense (MTD) solution. What is the primary function of MTD in enterprise security?
a. Managing mobile application permissions and access
b. Detecting and mitigating malware and network threats on devices
c. Enforcing geolocation-based security policies
d. Applying encryption to all communications on mobile devices

Answer: b. Detecting and mitigating malware and network threats on devices. Explanation: MTD focuses on identifying and addressing mobile-specific threats such as malware and insecure networks. Option a relates to MAM, not MTD. Option c is a feature of EMM, not MTD's core purpose. Option d involves encryption but is not MTD's primary function.

151. A BYOD policy mandates that employees' personal devices meet minimum security standards. Which control is most effective in verifying compliance with this policy?
a. Requiring users to install corporate antivirus software
b. Using MDM to perform device posture assessments
c. Blocking devices without the latest OS updates
d. Logging all user activity on personal devices

Answer: b. Using MDM to perform device posture assessments. Explanation: MDM can assess devices for compliance with security standards, such as encryption and OS versions. Option a is helpful but does not provide complete compliance checks. Option c is effective but may not account for other compliance factors. Option d violates privacy and is unsuitable for BYOD.

152. A retail chain allows employees to use personal devices for work but has observed increasing risks of data breaches. Which policy should the organization prioritize to address this issue?
a. Enforce data encryption for corporate email and documents.
b. Disable camera access during working hours.
c. Require employees to sign liability waivers for data misuse.
d. Implement time-based access restrictions for corporate apps.

Answer: a. Enforce data encryption for corporate email and documents. Explanation: Encrypting corporate data ensures it remains secure even if devices are lost or compromised. Option b addresses privacy concerns but is not a primary security measure. Option c is administrative, not technical. Option d improves access control but does not directly secure data.

153. During a review of Infrastructure as Code (IaC) templates for a cloud deployment, a security team identifies hardcoded credentials within the configuration files. What is the most appropriate remediation?
a. Encrypt the credentials using a symmetric key before deployment
b. Store the credentials in a secure secrets management service
c. Limit access to the configuration files using strict file permissions
d. Move the credentials to a different IaC file within the same repository

Answer: b. Store the credentials in a secure secrets management service. Explanation: Secure secrets management services ensure that sensitive data is stored securely and accessed only when necessary. Option a is incorrect because encryption alone does not prevent exposure if the key is compromised. Option c is insufficient because file permissions do not address the issue of credentials being in plaintext. Option d merely relocates the problem without solving it.

154. A Cloud Security Posture Management (CSPM) tool flags a misconfigured storage bucket as publicly accessible. What is the best course of action to mitigate this risk?
a. Encrypt all files within the bucket to prevent unauthorized access
b. Restrict access to specific IP ranges or authenticated users only
c. Enable versioning on the bucket to track changes to stored data
d. Move the bucket to a private cloud environment for added security

Answer: b. Restrict access to specific IP ranges or authenticated users only. Explanation: Restricting access prevents unauthorized users from accessing the bucket. Option a does not prevent access but protects data if compromised. Option c is unrelated to access control. Option d is impractical, as public cloud configurations can be secured without migration.

155. In a serverless environment, what is the most effective way to secure sensitive environment variables?
a. Encode the variables using Base64 encoding
b. Use a serverless-specific secrets management solution
c. Store the variables in the application's source code repository
d. Apply strict IAM policies to the serverless runtime

Answer: b. Use a serverless-specific secrets management solution. Explanation: Secrets management solutions are designed to securely store and manage sensitive environment variables. Option a is incorrect because Base64 encoding is not encryption and provides no security. Option c exposes sensitive data to potential leaks. Option d, while important, does not directly address environment variable security.

156. A container orchestration platform is configured to allow unrestricted network communication between all containers. What security risk does this pose?
a. Containers may fail to scale effectively under high loads
b. Lateral movement within the cluster becomes easier for attackers

c. Resource usage becomes unpredictable due to network congestion
d. Service discovery within the cluster is negatively impacted

Answer: b. Lateral movement within the cluster becomes easier for attackers. Explanation: Unrestricted communication enables attackers to move laterally, compromising additional containers. Option a pertains to resource management, not security. Option c, while possible, is unrelated to the primary security risk. Option d is incorrect because service discovery typically functions independently of security configurations.

157. What is a key benefit of implementing network segmentation in a cloud environment?
a. It reduces latency by streamlining routing within subnets
b. It prevents denial-of-service (DoS) attacks by isolating public-facing services
c. It limits the blast radius of a compromised workload
d. It simplifies encryption requirements across the network

Answer: c. It limits the blast radius of a compromised workload. Explanation: Network segmentation isolates workloads, reducing the impact of a breach. Option a is unrelated to segmentation's primary purpose. Option b may benefit indirectly, but segmentation alone does not stop DoS attacks. Option d is incorrect because segmentation does not inherently affect encryption.

158. Which best practice reduces the attack surface of serverless functions?
a. Deploy functions with the least privileged IAM roles
b. Enable unrestricted function-to-function communication
c. Include unused dependencies to ensure compatibility
d. Allow function logs to remain accessible to all cloud users

Answer: a. Deploy functions with the least privileged IAM roles. Explanation: Using least privilege limits an attacker's ability to exploit a compromised function. Option b increases the attack surface. Option c introduces unnecessary risk by including unused dependencies. Option d exposes logs, potentially leaking sensitive information.

159. When using Infrastructure as Code (IaC) for cloud deployments, which strategy minimizes risks associated with code changes?
a. Implementing manual reviews for all changes before deployment
b. Encrypting IaC files to protect against unauthorized access
c. Automating security scanning during the CI/CD pipeline
d. Restricting IaC usage to development environments only

Answer: c. Automating security scanning during the CI/CD pipeline. Explanation: Automated scanning identifies vulnerabilities early, reducing deployment risks. Option a slows deployment and may miss errors. Option b protects code but does not address insecure configurations. Option d limits IaC's potential, defeating its purpose.

160. A CSPM tool reports excessive permissions granted to an IAM role in a cloud environment. What is the best way to address this issue?
a. Revoke all permissions and reassign them as needed
b. Replace the role with a predefined read-only role
c. Apply the principle of least privilege by removing unnecessary permissions
d. Assign permissions at the group level rather than the individual role level

Answer: c. Apply the principle of least privilege by removing unnecessary permissions. Explanation: Least privilege minimizes access to only what is required, reducing risk. Option a disrupts operations by revoking needed permissions. Option b may not provide adequate functionality. Option d may aggregate permissions, increasing risk.

161. What is the most effective way to secure container images used in a production environment?
a. Use only official images from public registries without modifications
b. Apply patches to images directly on production systems
c. Scan container images for vulnerabilities before deployment
d. Store images in a shared public repository for easy access

Answer: c. Scan container images for vulnerabilities before deployment. Explanation: Scanning ensures that only secure images are used, reducing risks. Option a is insufficient, as official images may still contain vulnerabilities. Option b risks introducing instability in production. Option d exposes images to unauthorized access.

162. A financial services company is adopting a Secure Software Development Life Cycle (SSDLC). Which of the following is the most critical activity during the "Design" phase to minimize potential vulnerabilities?
a. Conducting static application security testing (SAST) on the codebase
b. Performing threat modeling to identify potential attack vectors
c. Deploying application patches to resolve known vulnerabilities
d. Implementing secure coding guidelines for developers

Answer: b. Performing threat modeling to identify potential attack vectors. Explanation: Threat modeling during the "Design" phase helps identify and mitigate potential vulnerabilities early in development. Option a occurs during coding or testing phases. Option c applies to post-deployment activities. Option d is part of development practices but does not directly address design-phase risks.

163. An organization is adopting the STRIDE methodology for threat modeling. Which threat category in STRIDE directly addresses unauthorized modification of data?
a. Tampering
b. Repudiation
c. Information disclosure
d. Denial of service

Answer: a. Tampering. Explanation: Tampering in STRIDE focuses on the unauthorized modification of data. Option b refers to users denying their actions. Option c involves exposing sensitive information. Option d pertains to disrupting system availability.

164. Which of the following best demonstrates the purpose of code signing in secure software development?
a. Encrypting sensitive data within the application
b. Validating the integrity and authenticity of software
c. Scanning for vulnerabilities in third-party libraries
d. Preventing unauthorized access to the application's source code

Answer: b. Validating the integrity and authenticity of software. Explanation: Code signing ensures that software is not tampered with and verifies the identity of its publisher. Option a addresses data encryption, not code signing. Option c relates to dependency scanning. Option d involves access control, not code signing.

165. A software development team uses a secure code review checklist. Which of the following practices should be included to address injection vulnerabilities?
a. Limiting the use of system-level API calls in code
b. Validating and sanitizing all user input before processing
c. Restricting access to debugging tools in production
d. Enabling application-level logging for all data transactions

Answer: b. Validating and sanitizing all user input before processing. Explanation: Input validation and sanitization are critical for preventing injection attacks like SQL injection. Option a is good practice but does not directly address injection. Option c improves security but is unrelated to input handling. Option d is useful for monitoring but does not prevent injection.

166. An e-commerce company designs an API to share order data with third-party partners. What is the most critical requirement to ensure the API is secure?
a. Using SSL/TLS to encrypt data in transit
b. Implementing IP whitelisting for partner systems
c. Adding rate-limiting to restrict API calls per minute
d. Requiring JSON formatting for all API responses

Answer: a. Using SSL/TLS to encrypt data in transit. Explanation: SSL/TLS ensures the confidentiality and integrity of data transmitted through the API. Option b adds security but does not encrypt data. Option c mitigates abuse but is not a primary security requirement. Option d is a formatting choice, not a security feature.

167. During a threat modeling exercise using the PASTA framework, what is the primary focus of the "Attack Modeling" stage?
a. Identifying organizational goals and objectives
b. Evaluating potential threat actors and their capabilities
c. Mapping business impacts to potential security events
d. Developing countermeasures to mitigate identified risks

Answer: b. Evaluating potential threat actors and their capabilities. Explanation: The "Attack Modeling" stage in PASTA focuses on understanding threat actors and their potential actions against the system. Option a occurs in earlier stages. Option c is part of the risk assessment phase. Option d happens after threats are modeled.

168. A company developing a mobile banking app conducts static application security testing (SAST). Which issue is SAST most effective at detecting?
a. Hardcoded API keys within the source code
b. Insecure API endpoints exposed during runtime
c. Misconfigured access controls in production environments
d. Unencrypted sensitive data during transmission

Answer: a. Hardcoded API keys within the source code. Explanation: SAST examines source code for vulnerabilities like hardcoded secrets. Option b requires dynamic testing. Option c pertains to deployment configuration, not code review. Option d is identified using runtime analysis tools.

169. Which practice enhances the security of APIs used in microservices architecture?
a. Using shared credentials for all services to streamline authentication
b. Applying JSON Web Tokens (JWT) for stateless authentication
c. Caching sensitive API responses to reduce server load
d. Allowing all HTTP methods to increase API flexibility

Answer: b. Applying JSON Web Tokens (JWT) for stateless authentication. Explanation: JWT enables secure, scalable authentication in microservices by maintaining a stateless authentication mechanism. Option a is insecure and violates security best practices. Option c increases the risk of exposing sensitive data. Option d introduces unnecessary risk by enabling unsupported methods.

170. A financial institution uses a secure SDLC approach and requires developers to follow secure coding practices. What is the most critical benefit of enforcing these practices?
a. Reducing the time required for penetration testing

b. Minimizing the introduction of vulnerabilities during development
c. Ensuring compliance with regulatory standards
d. Improving system performance under heavy loads

Answer: b. Minimizing the introduction of vulnerabilities during development. Explanation: Secure coding practices help developers prevent vulnerabilities before they are introduced into the codebase. Option a is incorrect because penetration testing still needs to be thorough. Option c is a secondary benefit. Option d is unrelated to secure coding.

171. An organization plans to implement FIDO2 for passwordless authentication. What is the primary security advantage of FIDO2 over traditional password-based mechanisms?
a. It uses a centralized password repository for better user management
b. It employs public key cryptography to prevent credential theft during authentication
c. It enforces multi-factor authentication by default for all users
d. It ensures compatibility with legacy authentication systems

Answer: b. It employs public key cryptography to prevent credential theft during authentication. Explanation: FIDO2 uses public key cryptography, ensuring credentials are not stored on the server or transmitted, thus mitigating credential theft risks. Option a is incorrect because FIDO2 avoids centralized storage of secrets. Option c is wrong because multi-factor authentication is optional, not default. Option d is irrelevant as FIDO2 does not guarantee legacy system compatibility.

172. In an OAuth 2.0 implementation, which grant type is most appropriate for mobile applications that cannot securely store client secrets?
a. Authorization Code Grant
b. Implicit Grant
c. Client Credentials Grant
d. Resource Owner Password Credentials Grant

Answer: b. Implicit Grant. Explanation: The Implicit Grant avoids storing client secrets by delivering access tokens directly to the application. Option a is incorrect because the Authorization Code Grant requires a secure backend. Option c is unsuitable for applications acting on behalf of users. Option d is insecure for mobile apps due to the direct handling of user credentials.

173. A Kerberos authentication process involves which component to issue a session key for secure communication between two services?
a. Ticket Granting Ticket (TGT)
b. Authentication Server (AS)
c. Ticket Granting Server (TGS)
d. Key Distribution Center (KDC)

Answer: c. Ticket Granting Server (TGS). Explanation: The TGS issues session keys to enable secure communication between services. Option a is incorrect as the TGT grants access to the TGS, not session keys. Option b refers to initial authentication. Option d encompasses the entire Kerberos infrastructure, including AS and TGS, but does not directly issue session keys.

174. When deploying certificate-based authentication in an enterprise, what is the primary advantage of using client certificates over traditional username/password authentication?
a. Reduced complexity in certificate management
b. Elimination of the need for a certificate authority (CA)
c. Resistance to phishing attacks targeting credentials
d. Simplified recovery process for lost or stolen certificates

Answer: c. Resistance to phishing attacks targeting credentials. Explanation: Client certificates do not rely on usernames or passwords, making them immune to phishing. Option a is incorrect as certificate management is typically more complex. Option b is wrong because a CA is required for issuing and validating certificates. Option d is incorrect because recovery for lost certificates is more complex than resetting passwords.

175. Biometric authentication systems must address which challenge to ensure secure user authentication?
a. Preventing cross-platform compatibility issues
b. Detecting and preventing spoofing attempts
c. Minimizing data storage requirements for biometric templates
d. Enforcing multi-factor authentication for enhanced security

Answer: b. Detecting and preventing spoofing attempts. Explanation: Anti-spoofing mechanisms ensure biometric systems can differentiate between real and fake biometric inputs. Option a is irrelevant to authentication security. Option c, while important for efficiency, is not a core security challenge. Option d is incorrect because biometric authentication is often a standalone factor.

176. A FIDO2-compliant device is used to authenticate to a web application. What ensures the device cannot be used to impersonate the user on another site?
a. The device uses a single private key for all registered applications
b. Each site generates a unique key pair during registration
c. The user's credentials are encrypted using the site's public key
d. The device requires multi-factor authentication for every session

Answer: b. Each site generates a unique key pair during registration. Explanation: FIDO2 generates unique keys for each application, preventing credential reuse across sites. Option a is incorrect because key reuse is explicitly avoided. Option c is irrelevant as FIDO2 does not encrypt user credentials. Option d, while beneficial, is not the mechanism preventing cross-site impersonation.

177. Which OAuth 2.0 flow is most appropriate for scenarios where a client application must act on its own behalf, without user interaction?
a. Authorization Code Grant
b. Implicit Grant
c. Client Credentials Grant
d. Device Authorization Flow

Answer: c. Client Credentials Grant. Explanation: The Client Credentials Grant is specifically designed for server-to-server communication where no user interaction occurs. Option a and b are user-centric. Option d is used for devices with limited input capabilities, requiring user action.

178. In Kerberos, what is the primary purpose of the Key Distribution Center (KDC)?
a. Verifying user credentials directly with resource servers
b. Storing all users' passwords securely in the authentication server
c. Issuing tickets to authenticate users and establish secure sessions
d. Encrypting all network traffic between users and services

Answer: c. Issuing tickets to authenticate users and establish secure sessions. Explanation: The KDC is responsible for ticket issuance, enabling secure and efficient authentication. Option a is incorrect as resource servers validate tickets, not credentials. Option b misrepresents the role of the authentication server. Option d refers to encryption but is not the KDC's primary function.

179. Certificate Revocation Lists (CRLs) and Online Certificate Status Protocol (OCSP) responders both address certificate validity. What is a primary limitation of using CRLs?
a. CRLs cannot identify revoked certificates
b. CRLs require manual updates to client systems
c. CRLs are less efficient due to their large size and static nature
d. CRLs cannot be used with self-signed certificates

Answer: c. CRLs are less efficient due to their large size and static nature. Explanation: CRLs grow over time, making them inefficient and less practical for real-time certificate validation compared to OCSP. Option a is incorrect because CRLs list revoked certificates. Option b is wrong; updates are automatic but periodic. Option d is irrelevant as self-signed certificates bypass CA-based validation.

180. Biometric authentication systems often store biometric data in a hashed format. What is the primary reason for this practice?
a. To ensure compatibility with encryption algorithms
b. To prevent reconstruction of the original biometric data
c. To facilitate faster authentication during high user loads
d. To enable multi-factor authentication with other methods

Answer: b. To prevent reconstruction of the original biometric data. Explanation: Hashing ensures biometric data cannot be reverse-engineered, preserving user privacy. Option a is incorrect as hashing is unrelated to encryption compatibility. Option c is irrelevant because hashing does not inherently speed up authentication. Option d is incorrect; hashing is unrelated to enabling multi-factor authentication.

181. During the implementation of a Security Orchestration, Automation, and Response (SOAR) platform, the security team wants to automate phishing email investigations. Which SOAR feature is most critical to achieving this objective?
a. Custom API integration with external email providers
b. Predefined playbooks for phishing-related incidents
c. Automated ticket creation for manual escalation
d. Real-time threat intelligence feed integration

Answer: b. Predefined playbooks for phishing-related incidents. Explanation: Playbooks allow the SOAR platform to standardize and automate phishing investigations, streamlining the process. Option a is helpful for integration but does not directly automate workflows. Option c ensures manual escalation but does not automate investigation. Option d improves context but does not handle the phishing workflow itself.

182. A SIEM has been generating a high number of false positives, overwhelming the SOC team. What is the best course of action to address this issue while maintaining detection accuracy?
a. Disable rules generating the most alerts until further notice
b. Increase the alert thresholds across all detection rules
c. Fine-tune correlation rules using historical incident data
d. Implement machine learning algorithms for automatic triaging

Answer: c. Fine-tune correlation rules using historical incident data. Explanation: Tuning rules based on historical trends helps reduce noise while preserving detection accuracy. Option a risks missing actual threats. Option b reduces noise but may lower detection sensitivity. Option d, while beneficial, requires proper training and may not yield immediate results.

183. Which of the following Indicators of Compromise (IoCs) is least likely to generate false positives in a SIEM environment?
a. IP addresses associated with malicious activity

b. File hash values of known malware
c. Domain names flagged for phishing campaigns
d. Anomalous spikes in outbound traffic volume

Answer: b. File hash values of known malware. Explanation: File hashes are specific and immutable, making them highly reliable IoCs. Option a can produce false positives as IPs may be shared or dynamic. Option c is prone to errors due to overlaps with benign domains. Option d is context-dependent and may result in noise.

184. A Network Detection and Response (NDR) system has flagged a sudden spike in DNS queries to a single external domain. What is the most appropriate next step?
a. Block all DNS traffic originating from the network
b. Perform a reverse DNS lookup to verify the domain's legitimacy
c. Investigate associated endpoint activity for additional IoCs
d. Escalate the incident to law enforcement for immediate response

Answer: c. Investigate associated endpoint activity for additional IoCs. Explanation: Endpoint investigation helps identify whether the flagged domain is part of a larger threat campaign. Option a is overly disruptive and risks blocking legitimate traffic. Option b is insufficient for comprehensive analysis. Option d is premature without confirming malicious intent.

185. In a SOC, reducing Mean Time to Detect (MTTD) is often achieved through:
a. Deploying additional threat intelligence feeds
b. Automating log analysis and anomaly detection
c. Increasing retention periods for historical logs
d. Conducting daily manual reviews of all alerts

Answer: b. Automating log analysis and anomaly detection. Explanation: Automation accelerates detection by identifying threats faster than manual methods. Option a enhances context but does not directly reduce detection time. Option c supports historical analysis but does not impact MTTD. Option d is inefficient and counterproductive.

186. An incident response playbook in a SOAR system includes a step to isolate infected endpoints. Which tool is most effective for achieving this within the SOC?
a. Endpoint Detection and Response (EDR) platform
b. Network firewall with access control lists
c. DNS filtering service
d. Cloud-based email security gateway

Answer: a. Endpoint Detection and Response (EDR) platform. Explanation: EDR solutions can quickly isolate endpoints, limiting the spread of malware. Option b is less effective for endpoint-specific isolation. Option c addresses domain access but not endpoint containment. Option d is unrelated to endpoint isolation.

187. What is the primary role of a correlation rule in a SIEM?
a. Aggregating logs from multiple data sources into a single database
b. Identifying patterns indicative of malicious behavior across events
c. Generating reports for regulatory compliance audits
d. Enabling role-based access control for SOC analysts

Answer: b. Identifying patterns indicative of malicious behavior across events. Explanation: Correlation rules detect attack patterns by linking related events. Option a pertains to log management, not correlation. Option c focuses on reporting rather than detection. Option d relates to SOC access control, not threat detection.

188. Which metric is most useful for assessing the efficiency of a SOC's response to a detected threat?
a. Mean Time to Respond (MTTR)
b. Mean Time Between Failures (MTBF)
c. First Time Fix Rate (FTFR)
d. Alert-to-Event Ratio (AER)

Answer: a. Mean Time to Respond (MTTR). Explanation: MTTR measures the time taken to mitigate threats, reflecting SOC efficiency. Option b applies to system reliability, not SOC performance. Option c is unrelated to incident response. Option d evaluates alert quality, not response effectiveness.

189. A SOAR platform is integrated with an NDR system. What capability does this integration provide to a SOC?
a. Automated response to network anomalies
b. Real-time generation of compliance reports
c. Advanced encryption of network traffic
d. Improved firewall rule management

Answer: a. Automated response to network anomalies. Explanation: Integrating SOAR with NDR enables automated detection and response to anomalous traffic. Option b is unrelated to real-time anomaly handling. Option c pertains to data security, not SOAR-NDR integration. Option d is a firewall-specific task, not NDR functionality.

190. What is the most effective method for tuning a new NDR system to avoid false positives?
a. Rely on default settings provided by the vendor
b. Customize detection thresholds based on baseline network behavior
c. Focus solely on alerts with high confidence scores
d. Disable low-priority rules to reduce alert volume

Answer: b. Customize detection thresholds based on baseline network behavior. Explanation: Baseline customization ensures that detection aligns with normal traffic patterns, reducing false positives. Option a does not address specific network requirements. Option c ignores potential threats with lower confidence. Option d may reduce noise but risks missing critical alerts.

191. An organization implements the Bell-LaPadula security model to enforce confidentiality policies. Which control best aligns with the "no-read-up" (Simple Security Property) rule in this model?
a. Restricting users from accessing files classified above their clearance level
b. Preventing users from modifying files classified below their clearance level
c. Enforcing separation of duties to limit collusion opportunities
d. Blocking unauthorized applications from reading sensitive data

Answer: a. Restricting users from accessing files classified above their clearance level. Explanation: The "no-read-up" rule ensures that users cannot access data classified at higher sensitivity levels than their clearance. Option b describes Biba's integrity controls. Option c relates to the Clark-Wilson model. Option d is a general security practice but not specific to Bell-LaPadula.

192. A manufacturing company is implementing the Biba integrity model. Which control exemplifies the "no-write-up" (Integrity Star Property) principle of this model?
a. Allowing only administrators to modify system-level files
b. Preventing low-integrity processes from altering high-integrity data
c. Requiring digital signatures on all critical configuration files
d. Logging all user access to critical databases for audit purposes

Answer: b. Preventing low-integrity processes from altering high-integrity data. Explanation: The "no-write-up" rule ensures that processes with lower integrity cannot compromise higher-integrity data. Option a reflects access control but is not directly related to the Integrity Star Property. Option c ensures authenticity, not integrity. Option d is useful for audits but does not enforce "no-write-up."

193. Which of the following scenarios illustrates the application of the Clark-Wilson integrity model?
a. Ensuring that only users with clearance levels can access classified information
b. Validating all user input in financial systems to prevent unauthorized transactions
c. Preventing users from accessing both confidential and competitor-related data
d. Encrypting all communications between systems to maintain data confidentiality

Answer: b. Validating all user input in financial systems to prevent unauthorized transactions. Explanation: The Clark-Wilson model enforces well-formed transactions and separation of duties, ensuring data integrity. Option a aligns with Bell-LaPadula. Option c describes the Brewer-Nash model. Option d addresses confidentiality, not integrity.

194. An organization applies the Brewer-Nash (Chinese Wall) model to mitigate conflicts of interest. Which scenario best demonstrates compliance with this model?
a. Restricting employees from working on data related to competing clients
b. Encrypting all client data to protect it from unauthorized access
c. Requiring multifactor authentication for all privileged accounts
d. Allowing unrestricted access to historical client records

Answer: a. Restricting employees from working on data related to competing clients. Explanation: The Brewer-Nash model prevents conflicts of interest by dynamically restricting access based on a user's previous interactions with client data. Option b relates to confidentiality, not conflicts of interest. Option c is a general security practice. Option d violates the model's principles.

195. In the context of a reference monitor, which characteristic ensures it adheres to security policies?
a. It operates in a virtualized environment to isolate sensitive processes.
b. It enforces mandatory access controls without exceptions.
c. It monitors all user activities for unauthorized behavior.
d. It requires frequent updates to reflect changing security requirements.

Answer: b. It enforces mandatory access controls without exceptions. Explanation: A reference monitor must enforce access controls consistently and without bypass to maintain security. Option a pertains to virtualization, not reference monitor functions. Option c describes general monitoring, not mandatory enforcement. Option d is unrelated to the core functionality of a reference monitor.

196. A healthcare organization uses the Bell-LaPadula model to protect patient data. How should the "no-write-down" (Star Security Property) rule be applied?
a. Prohibit users from copying sensitive patient data to a lower-classified system.
b. Allow only authenticated users to modify patient records.
c. Prevent unauthorized users from viewing patient data.
d. Encrypt patient data during transmission between systems.

Answer: a. Prohibit users from copying sensitive patient data to a lower-classified system. Explanation: The "no-write-down" rule prevents users from leaking sensitive information to lower-classified levels. Option b reflects general access controls, not Bell-LaPadula. Option c addresses "no-read-up." Option d ensures confidentiality during transmission but is unrelated to Bell-LaPadula.

197. Which control is most aligned with implementing the Clark-Wilson integrity model in a financial database?
a. Enforcing separation of duties for all transaction approvals
b. Preventing unauthorized users from reading sensitive financial data

c. Applying encryption to all stored financial records
d. Blocking all changes to the database outside of working hours

Answer: a. Enforcing separation of duties for all transaction approvals. Explanation: The Clark-Wilson model relies on well-formed transactions and separation of duties to protect data integrity. Option b addresses confidentiality, not integrity. Option c enhances security but is not specific to Clark-Wilson. Option d may improve security but is not a Clark-Wilson control.

198. In the Biba model, which principle ensures that higher-integrity processes are protected from being corrupted by lower-integrity inputs?
a. No-read-up
b. No-write-up
c. No-read-down
d. No-write-down

Answer: d. No-write-down. Explanation: The "no-write-down" rule prevents high-integrity processes from writing to lower-integrity data, protecting them from corruption. Option a applies to Bell-LaPadula. Option b protects high-integrity data from being written by low-integrity processes. Option c is not part of the Biba model.

199. A financial firm uses a reference monitor to secure access to critical systems. What is a key requirement of the reference monitor for maintaining system integrity?
a. It must be tamper-proof and verifiable.
b. It should record all failed login attempts.
c. It must allow administrators to bypass security policies for efficiency.
d. It should encrypt all communications between components.

Answer: a. It must be tamper-proof and verifiable. Explanation: A reference monitor must be tamper-proof to ensure consistent enforcement of security policies. Option b describes audit logging, not reference monitor characteristics. Option c violates the integrity of the monitor. Option d is a separate security measure unrelated to the reference monitor's core purpose.

200. During a Dynamic Application Security Testing (DAST) process, which metric is most critical for assessing the depth of security coverage?
a. Number of vulnerabilities identified during testing
b. Percentage of application endpoints actively tested
c. Time taken to complete a single scan of the application
d. False positive rate of reported vulnerabilities

Answer: b. Percentage of application endpoints actively tested. Explanation: Coverage metrics ensure that all endpoints are adequately tested for vulnerabilities. Option a indicates results but not coverage depth. Option c pertains to efficiency, not coverage. Option d measures accuracy but does not reflect endpoint coverage.

201. When using Static Application Security Testing (SAST), how does Abstract Syntax Tree (AST) analysis improve the identification of vulnerabilities?
a. By analyzing runtime behavior of the application
b. By identifying vulnerabilities in third-party dependencies
c. By evaluating the structure and logic of source code
d. By executing malicious payloads in a simulated environment

Answer: c. By evaluating the structure and logic of source code. Explanation: AST analysis examines the hierarchical structure of code to detect flaws in logic or design. Option a describes DAST. Option b refers to Software Composition Analysis (SCA), not SAST. Option d is a DAST technique, unrelated to AST analysis.

202. In a Software Composition Analysis (SCA) process, which issue poses the greatest risk if left unaddressed?
a. Licensing violations in open-source libraries
b. Slow performance due to poorly optimized code
c. Outdated coding practices in proprietary components
d. Inadequate test coverage during deployment

Answer: a. Licensing violations in open-source libraries. Explanation: SCA identifies legal risks, such as non-compliance with open-source licenses, which can have significant financial and legal consequences. Option b pertains to performance, not security or compliance. Option c is unrelated to third-party risk. Option d falls under testing, not composition analysis.

203. What is the primary advantage of deploying Interactive Application Security Testing (IAST) compared to SAST and DAST?
a. IAST identifies vulnerabilities in compiled binaries without source code access
b. IAST combines runtime analysis with code-level insights for greater accuracy
c. IAST eliminates the need for manual code reviews
d. IAST automates the creation of remediation patches for identified vulnerabilities

Answer: b. IAST combines runtime analysis with code-level insights for greater accuracy. Explanation: IAST works within the application during runtime, providing both dynamic and static insights. Option a describes DAST capabilities, not IAST. Option c is incorrect; IAST complements but does not replace manual reviews. Option d is incorrect because IAST identifies but does not fix vulnerabilities.

204. What is the most effective method for implementing Cross-Site Request Forgery (CSRF) tokens to prevent token reuse attacks?
a. Encrypting CSRF tokens with the user's session key
b. Regenerating CSRF tokens after every validated request
c. Including CSRF tokens in hidden form fields only
d. Setting a long expiration time to ensure token validity

Answer: b. Regenerating CSRF tokens after every validated request. Explanation: Regenerating tokens prevents reuse in case of token interception or misuse. Option a is insufficient without regeneration. Option c is insecure if tokens are not rotated. Option d increases the risk of token misuse due to prolonged validity.

205. During a DAST scan, a web application's login form is flagged for using weak encryption for password transmission. What is the most appropriate remediation?
a. Implement multi-factor authentication for the login process
b. Enforce strong password complexity requirements
c. Use TLS to encrypt the entire session, including login requests
d. Limit login attempts to reduce brute force risks

Answer: c. Use TLS to encrypt the entire session, including login requests. Explanation: TLS ensures that passwords are securely transmitted over the network. Option a enhances authentication but does not address encryption. Option b strengthens passwords but does not secure transmission. Option d mitigates brute force attacks but does not address encryption flaws.

206. Which deployment model is most effective for Interactive Application Security Testing (IAST) in a CI/CD pipeline?
a. Post-deployment testing in the production environment
b. Real-time monitoring of live traffic in staging environments
c. Inline testing during integration within test environments
d. Manual scanning during user acceptance testing (UAT)

Answer: c. Inline testing during integration within test environments. Explanation: IAST provides immediate feedback during integration, aligning with CI/CD processes. Option a is risky as testing in production can expose users to vulnerabilities. Option b lacks controlled conditions. Option d is too late for effective CI/CD testing.

207. What is a key limitation of SAST tools when analyzing modern web applications?
a. Inability to detect vulnerabilities in runtime dependencies
b. High false positive rates for known vulnerabilities
c. Lack of support for integration with IDEs
d. Dependency on specific programming languages for analysis

Answer: a. Inability to detect vulnerabilities in runtime dependencies. Explanation: SAST tools analyze source code but cannot inspect runtime dependencies, leaving gaps in vulnerability detection. Option b is less common in modern SAST tools. Option c is incorrect as many SAST tools support IDE integration. Option d is outdated, as most modern tools handle multiple languages.

208. How does a well-configured DAST tool handle session management during a scan?
a. It bypasses session validation to ensure comprehensive coverage
b. It maintains active sessions using automated authentication mechanisms
c. It flags session cookies as insecure without testing their behavior
d. It requires manual re-authentication after every scan phase

Answer: b. It maintains active sessions using automated authentication mechanisms. Explanation: Maintaining active sessions ensures that the DAST tool can scan authenticated areas of the application. Option a risks missing authentication-based vulnerabilities. Option c is incomplete as DAST must evaluate session behavior. Option d is inefficient and impractical.

209. An organization applies the Brewer-Nash (Chinese Wall) model to its financial analysts. What is the primary condition that must be met for this model to effectively prevent conflicts of interest?
a. Data access must be encrypted at rest and in transit.
b. Analysts must be dynamically restricted from accessing competitor-related datasets.
c. All financial transactions must be logged and reviewed regularly.
d. Analysts must only access datasets approved by their department managers.

Answer: b. Analysts must be dynamically restricted from accessing competitor-related datasets. Explanation: The Brewer-Nash model ensures that access restrictions are dynamically enforced to prevent users from accessing data associated with competing clients. Option a is a security best practice but unrelated to Brewer-Nash. Option c relates to auditing but not conflict of interest prevention. Option d introduces static controls, which are insufficient for dynamic conflicts.

210. A government agency implements the Bell-LaPadula model to protect classified data. How does this model address the risk of sensitive data leakage through writable media?
a. By enforcing the "no-write-up" rule to protect higher-classified data
b. By applying the "no-write-down" rule to prevent data leaks to lower classifications
c. By implementing mandatory encryption for all writable media
d. By requiring strict logging of all write operations for classified data

Answer: b. By applying the "no-write-down" rule to prevent data leaks to lower classifications. Explanation: The "no-write-down" rule ensures users cannot write sensitive data to lower classification levels, preventing leakage. Option a applies to the Biba model. Option c is a general security measure, not specific to Bell-LaPadula. Option d involves auditing, not mandatory controls.

211. An e-commerce company is designing an integrity model for its payment processing system using the Biba model. Which of the following controls directly implements the "no-read-down" (Simple Integrity Property) principle?
a. Restricting high-integrity users from accessing low-integrity log files
b. Limiting database writes to authorized application servers
c. Requiring dual authorization for high-value transactions
d. Encrypting all communications between users and the payment gateway

Answer: a. Restricting high-integrity users from accessing low-integrity log files. Explanation: The "no-read-down" rule prevents high-integrity users from accessing potentially corrupted or low-integrity data. Option b aligns with the "no-write-up" rule. Option c is a separation of duties control. Option d is a confidentiality measure, not integrity-focused.

212. A software development team uses the Clark-Wilson model for its order management system. Which control aligns with the Clark-Wilson principle of "well-formed transactions"?
a. Implementing input validation to ensure data integrity
b. Encrypting sensitive data during database queries
c. Logging all system access for auditing purposes
d. Restricting file access based on classification levels

Answer: a. Implementing input validation to ensure data integrity. Explanation: The Clark-Wilson model enforces well-formed transactions by requiring data to be validated and processed correctly. Option b is related to confidentiality, not transaction integrity. Option c supports accountability but does not enforce well-formed transactions. Option d reflects the Bell-LaPadula model.

213. A healthcare organization applies the Biba integrity model to protect patient data. Which policy ensures compliance with the "no-write-up" rule?
a. Preventing lower-integrity applications from modifying patient records
b. Encrypting all patient data stored in the database
c. Allowing only administrators to approve updates to critical data
d. Restricting unauthorized users from viewing patient records

Answer: a. Preventing lower-integrity applications from modifying patient records. Explanation: The "no-write-up" rule ensures lower-integrity entities cannot compromise higher-integrity data. Option b protects confidentiality, not integrity. Option c enforces access control but does not reflect the "no-write-up" rule. Option d aligns with the Bell-LaPadula model.

214. A bank implements a reference monitor to enforce access controls on its transaction processing systems. Which of the following must the reference monitor guarantee?
a. All access requests are logged and auditable.
b. Access decisions are based on dynamic risk assessments.
c. No access occurs without proper authorization checks.
d. Transactions are encrypted before being processed.

Answer: c. No access occurs without proper authorization checks. Explanation: The reference monitor ensures that all access requests are authorized according to security policies. Option a is beneficial for auditing but not a core guarantee of a reference monitor. Option b involves risk management, not reference monitor enforcement. Option d pertains to confidentiality, not access control.

215. A defense contractor enforces the Bell-LaPadula model to protect classified data. Which of the following scenarios violates the "no-read-up" rule?
a. A user with "Confidential" clearance accesses "Top Secret" documents.
b. A user copies "Confidential" data to a removable USB drive.

c. An administrator grants higher clearance to a lower-privileged user.
d. A user modifies data classified at the same clearance level.

Answer: a. A user with "Confidential" clearance accesses "Top Secret" documents. Explanation: The "no-read-up" rule prevents users from accessing information classified higher than their clearance level. Option b involves "no-write-down." Option c concerns administrative privilege management, not Bell-LaPadula rules. Option d is not a violation under Bell-LaPadula.

216. During an incident response process, a SOC analyst maps an adversary's use of PowerShell scripts to execute reconnaissance activities. Which MITRE ATT&CK tactic does this align with?
a. Credential Access
b. Execution
c. Discovery
d. Persistence

Answer: c. Discovery. Explanation: The Discovery tactic in MITRE ATT&CK includes techniques used to identify system and network information, such as PowerShell-based reconnaissance. Option a pertains to obtaining user credentials. Option b focuses on running malicious code. Option d involves maintaining access to compromised systems.

217. In a digital forensics investigation, why is hashing a disk image critical during the acquisition phase?
a. To compress the image file for storage efficiency
b. To verify that the acquired image is an exact replica of the source
c. To enable faster indexing of the acquired data
d. To encrypt the data for secure transmission

Answer: b. To verify that the acquired image is an exact replica of the source. Explanation: Hashing ensures data integrity by confirming the image matches the original without modification. Option a pertains to storage, not integrity. Option c is unrelated to the purpose of hashing. Option d addresses secure transmission but not integrity verification.

218. An organization is analyzing a ransomware attack using the Cyber Kill Chain methodology. At which phase should they focus efforts to detect and prevent the deployment of malicious payloads?
a. Weaponization
b. Delivery
c. Exploitation
d. Installation

Answer: b. Delivery. Explanation: The Delivery phase involves transmitting the malicious payload to the target, where detection and prevention can effectively block the attack. Option a occurs earlier, focusing on payload creation. Option c and d happen post-delivery, reducing preventive options.

219. What is the primary purpose of a Chain of Custody document in Digital Forensics and Incident Response (DFIR)?
a. To ensure that evidence is admissible in court
b. To prevent duplication of evidence during analysis
c. To document findings from forensic analysis
d. To expedite the processing of evidence in a legal case

Answer: a. To ensure that evidence is admissible in court. Explanation: Chain of Custody tracks who handled evidence, preserving its integrity for legal proceedings. Option b is unrelated to evidence integrity. Option c pertains to reporting, not custody. Option d does not guarantee admissibility.

220. In the Incident Command System (ICS), which role is responsible for ensuring all resources are effectively allocated during a critical cybersecurity incident?
a. Incident Commander
b. Operations Section Chief
c. Planning Section Chief
d. Logistics Section Chief

Answer: b. Operations Section Chief. Explanation: The Operations Section Chief manages tactical operations and resource allocation. Option a oversees the entire response but does not handle resource specifics. Option c focuses on planning and projections. Option d addresses logistical support, not tactical resources.

221. A SOC integrates MITRE ATT&CK techniques into its playbooks. What is the primary advantage of this approach?
a. It enhances incident response speed by automating remediation steps
b. It maps adversary tactics and techniques to improve detection and analysis
c. It standardizes incident reporting formats across the organization
d. It eliminates the need for manual correlation rules in SIEM systems

Answer: b. It maps adversary tactics and techniques to improve detection and analysis. Explanation: MITRE ATT&CK helps SOC teams identify and respond to adversary behaviors systematically. Option a is unrelated to ATT&CK's role in detection. Option c pertains to reporting, not tactical mapping. Option d overstates ATT&CK's capabilities in SIEM correlation.

222. An organization deploying the Cyber Kill Chain observes the use of legitimate administrative tools by an attacker. At which phase should they focus their mitigation efforts?
a. Reconnaissance
b. Weaponization
c. Command and Control
d. Lateral Movement

Answer: d. Lateral Movement. Explanation: The attacker uses legitimate tools to move laterally across systems, requiring mitigation at this phase. Option a and b occur before internal access. Option c involves maintaining control, not lateral spread.

223. During a ransomware investigation, which evidence must be prioritized to determine the initial attack vector?
a. Network traffic logs from the time of the attack
b. Endpoint logs from affected devices
c. System snapshots post-encryption
d. Backup files restored during recovery

Answer: b. Endpoint logs from affected devices. Explanation: Endpoint logs reveal the initial compromise, providing insight into the attack vector. Option a offers context but is secondary. Option c shows damage, not origin. Option d is unrelated to the initial vector.

224. Which of the following best describes the role of the Incident Commander in the Incident Command System (ICS)?
a. Directly managing technical response efforts during an incident
b. Coordinating communication between stakeholders and response teams
c. Ensuring all forensic evidence is securely collected and preserved
d. Evaluating post-incident reports to identify areas for improvement

Answer: b. Coordinating communication between stakeholders and response teams. Explanation: The Incident Commander oversees communication and overall response efforts. Option a falls under Operations. Option c pertains to forensic teams. Option d is part of post-incident review, not active command.

225. A Chain of Custody log shows multiple gaps in the timeline for handling a critical piece of evidence. What is the most likely consequence?
a. The evidence will require additional analysis to restore credibility
b. The evidence may be deemed inadmissible in legal proceedings
c. The incident investigation timeline will be extended
d. The evidence must be destroyed to maintain compliance

Answer: b. The evidence may be deemed inadmissible in legal proceedings. Explanation: Gaps in Chain of Custody can compromise the integrity of evidence, leading to inadmissibility. Option a does not address legal credibility. Option c delays the investigation but is not the primary issue. Option d is unnecessary and unrelated.

226. A multinational corporation has determined that its customer service platform must have a Recovery Time Objective (RTO) of 2 hours. What does this metric specifically imply for the organization's disaster recovery strategy?
a. The organization must resume full operations within 2 hours of a disruption.
b. Data loss cannot exceed 2 hours from the point of failure.
c. The system must be operational at a minimum service level within 2 hours of a disruption.
d. The recovery solution must be tested every 2 hours to ensure readiness.

Answer: c. The system must be operational at a minimum service level within 2 hours of a disruption. Explanation: RTO defines the maximum duration allowed to restore a system to a minimum service level after an outage. Option a implies complete restoration, which may not align with RTO. Option b refers to Recovery Point Objective (RPO), not RTO. Option d is unrelated to RTO and focuses on testing frequency.

227. An organization conducts a Business Impact Analysis (BIA) and identifies the Maximum Tolerable Downtime (MTD) for its payroll system as 48 hours. Which recovery site strategy best aligns with this requirement?
a. Cold site with a 72-hour setup window
b. Warm site with pre-configured servers and 24-hour data synchronization
c. Hot site with real-time data replication and automated failover
d. Co-location facility with weekly hardware checks

Answer: b. Warm site with pre-configured servers and 24-hour data synchronization. Explanation: A warm site can meet the 48-hour MTD by providing pre-configured servers and periodic synchronization. Option a exceeds the MTD. Option c provides faster recovery than needed but at higher costs. Option d lacks sufficient readiness to meet the MTD.

228. Which metric is most critical for optimizing Recovery Point Objective (RPO) in a high-frequency trading system?
a. The frequency of data backups performed
b. The number of concurrent user connections
c. The geographical location of backup servers
d. The amount of storage available for backup copies

Answer: a. The frequency of data backups performed. Explanation: RPO optimization depends on how frequently backups are performed, as this minimizes potential data loss. Option b is unrelated to RPO. Option c affects disaster recovery planning but not RPO directly. Option d supports storage capacity but does not optimize RPO.

229. During a Business Impact Analysis (BIA), which of the following metrics is the most reliable indicator of a system's criticality?
a. The system's operational cost per hour

b. The revenue lost per hour of downtime
c. The number of users dependent on the system
d. The frequency of hardware failures reported

Answer: b. The revenue lost per hour of downtime. Explanation: Revenue loss is a direct and quantifiable measure of the business impact, making it a reliable indicator of system criticality. Option a measures cost but does not account for business impact. Option c provides context but lacks financial insight. Option d pertains to reliability, not criticality.

230. An e-commerce company deploys a hot site for its disaster recovery strategy. What is the primary advantage of using a hot site compared to a warm or cold site?
a. Reduced operational costs due to shared infrastructure
b. Increased recovery speed with real-time data replication
c. Simplified testing procedures for disaster recovery plans
d. Lower bandwidth requirements for maintaining synchronization

Answer: b. Increased recovery speed with real-time data replication. Explanation: Hot sites enable immediate failover through real-time replication, ensuring minimal downtime. Option a applies more to cold sites. Option c is unrelated to recovery speed. Option d does not reflect the typical characteristics of a hot site.

231. An organization must optimize its Recovery Point Objective (RPO) to ensure minimal data loss for critical applications. Which of the following is the most effective solution?
a. Scheduling daily full backups during non-peak hours
b. Deploying asynchronous replication with a 15-minute delay
c. Implementing synchronous replication to a geographically distant site
d. Using weekly snapshots combined with differential backups

Answer: c. Implementing synchronous replication to a geographically distant site. Explanation: Synchronous replication ensures zero data loss by replicating changes in real-time, meeting stringent RPO requirements. Option a introduces longer potential data loss. Option b reduces the RPO but does not eliminate potential loss. Option d provides insufficient granularity.

232. A logistics company identifies that its supply chain management system has an MTD of 12 hours and an RTO of 6 hours. What does this indicate about its recovery requirements?
a. The system must be fully restored within 12 hours of an incident.
b. The system can operate at a reduced capacity for up to 6 hours.
c. The recovery solution must enable partial operations within 6 hours.
d. Data synchronization must occur at least every 12 hours.

Answer: c. The recovery solution must enable partial operations within 6 hours. Explanation: RTO specifies the time to achieve minimum operational functionality, while MTD sets the maximum allowable downtime for full restoration. Option a misunderstands MTD. Option b misinterprets RTO. Option d relates to RPO, not RTO or MTD.

233. During disaster recovery planning, what is the primary challenge associated with deploying a warm site compared to a cold site?
a. Higher costs for maintaining pre-configured infrastructure
b. Inconsistent synchronization between primary and backup systems
c. Greater downtime required to activate the site
d. Lack of automation in recovery processes

Answer: a. Higher costs for maintaining pre-configured infrastructure. Explanation: Warm sites require pre-configured systems and more frequent updates, increasing costs compared to cold sites. Option b applies to real-time replication in hot sites. Option c describes cold sites. Option d is unrelated to site readiness.

234. An organization conducts annual disaster recovery tests for its hot site. Which factor is most critical to validate during these tests?
a. The accuracy of data synchronization between primary and backup sites
b. The availability of sufficient bandwidth for replication processes
c. The presence of up-to-date software licenses at the hot site
d. The duration required to ship hardware components to the hot site

Answer: a. The accuracy of data synchronization between primary and backup sites. Explanation: Ensuring data synchronization is critical to validating the hot site's readiness for immediate failover. Option b supports the replication process but is not the primary validation factor. Option c ensures operational compliance but does not confirm readiness. Option d applies to cold sites, not hot sites.

235. An organization plans to implement a new customer analytics platform. To comply with GDPR, what is the primary focus of the Data Protection Impact Assessment (DPIA)?
a. Assessing the financial impact of the platform on business operations
b. Identifying risks to the rights and freedoms of data subjects
c. Ensuring that data storage complies with ISO 27001 standards
d. Verifying the encryption strength of stored customer data

Answer: b. Identifying risks to the rights and freedoms of data subjects. Explanation: The DPIA ensures risks to individuals' rights and freedoms are identified and mitigated. Option a is unrelated to GDPR compliance. Option c, while important for security, is not the primary focus of a DPIA. Option d focuses on one technical control, which is insufficient for comprehensive risk assessment.

236. Which Privacy by Design (PbD) principle ensures that privacy controls are integrated into the core architecture of an information system?
a. Full lifecycle protection
b. Privacy as the default setting
c. Embedded privacy
d. Transparency and accountability

Answer: c. Embedded privacy. Explanation: Embedded privacy ensures that privacy measures are built into the design and architecture of systems from the start. Option a relates to protecting data throughout its lifecycle. Option b ensures that privacy is the default setting, but not specifically about integration into architecture. Option d pertains to clear communication and accountability, not technical design.

237. A Data Subject Access Request (DSAR) includes a request for all third parties with whom the subject's personal data has been shared. Under GDPR, how must an organization respond?
a. Provide the names of third parties only if a formal agreement exists
b. Refuse the request if it includes commercially sensitive information
c. Disclose the list of third parties along with purposes for data sharing
d. Limit the response to internal data processing activities

Answer: c. Disclose the list of third parties along with purposes for data sharing. Explanation: GDPR requires transparency regarding third-party data sharing and its purposes. Option a is incorrect as disclosure is required regardless of agreements. Option b is invalid as GDPR mandates compliance regardless of commercial sensitivity. Option d violates GDPR's transparency requirements for external sharing.

238. What is the primary advantage of Privacy-Preserving Record Linkage (PPRL) in data sharing?
a. Ensures secure linking of data sets without revealing sensitive personal information
b. Encrypts all linked records to comply with data protection regulations
c. Simplifies compliance with cross-border data transfer laws

d. Enables full anonymization of data during linking processes

Answer: a. Ensures secure linking of data sets without revealing sensitive personal information. Explanation: PPRL allows data sets to be linked using cryptographic techniques without exposing underlying personal data. Option b conflates encryption with linkage. Option c is unrelated to PPRL's primary goal. Option d is incorrect as PPRL often uses pseudonymization, not full anonymization.

239. When transferring personal data from the EU to a US-based cloud provider using standard contractual clauses (SCCs), what additional compliance step is recommended under GDPR?
a. Registering SCCs with the European Data Protection Board
b. Performing a data transfer impact assessment (DTIA)
c. Encrypting data before transmission to the US
d. Obtaining explicit consent from data subjects

Answer: b. Performing a data transfer impact assessment (DTIA). Explanation: A DTIA ensures the receiving country provides equivalent data protection, supplementing SCCs. Option a is unnecessary as SCCs do not require registration. Option c is beneficial but not mandated for SCC compliance. Option d is only required in specific circumstances.

240. Which Privacy by Design principle aligns most closely with minimizing data retention periods?
a. Data minimization
b. Full lifecycle protection
c. Purpose limitation
d. Accountability

Answer: b. Full lifecycle protection. Explanation: Full lifecycle protection includes minimizing retention periods to reduce risks throughout data usage. Option a focuses on minimizing collected data, not retention. Option c pertains to restricting data usage to specific purposes. Option d relates to responsibility, not data retention.

241. A DSAR requests deletion of personal data, but the organization must retain the data for legal reasons. What is the correct response under GDPR?
a. Refuse the request without explanation
b. Provide a detailed justification for retaining the data
c. Anonymize the data to comply with the deletion request
d. Delete only portions of the data that are not legally required

Answer: b. Provide a detailed justification for retaining the data. Explanation: GDPR allows exceptions to deletion requests for legal reasons but requires transparent communication with the data subject. Option a violates GDPR's transparency requirements. Option c may not fulfill legal obligations. Option d risks incomplete compliance if the legal basis is unclear.

242. When implementing a cross-border data transfer mechanism, what is the primary advantage of using Binding Corporate Rules (BCRs)?
a. They eliminate the need for explicit consent from data subjects
b. They allow seamless data sharing within a multinational organization
c. They ensure compliance with local labor laws
d. They automate the encryption of all transferred data

Answer: b. They allow seamless data sharing within a multinational organization. Explanation: BCRs enable global data sharing while ensuring compliance with GDPR. Option a is incorrect because explicit consent is sometimes still required. Option c is unrelated to data transfers. Option d conflates data protection with encryption.

243. What is the purpose of a DPIA when developing a system to process sensitive health data?
a. Assessing financial costs of implementing security measures
b. Identifying and mitigating risks to individuals' privacy and data rights
c. Ensuring the system complies with local cybersecurity standards
d. Verifying the effectiveness of encryption algorithms used

Answer: b. Identifying and mitigating risks to individuals' privacy and data rights. Explanation: DPIAs focus on protecting individuals' privacy and rights. Option a pertains to budgeting, not privacy. Option c addresses standards but not privacy risks. Option d focuses on one control, not comprehensive risk assessment.

244. What is a critical limitation of Privacy-Preserving Record Linkage (PPRL)?
a. It cannot handle large-scale data sets efficiently
b. It often requires extensive pre-processing of data
c. It is incompatible with GDPR requirements for pseudonymization
d. It introduces significant data redundancy into linked records

Answer: b. It often requires extensive pre-processing of data. Explanation: PPRL techniques require cleaning and standardizing data to ensure accurate linkage. Option a is incorrect as PPRL can scale. Option c is wrong; PPRL aligns with GDPR pseudonymization principles. Option d misrepresents PPRL, which avoids redundancy.

245. An organization adopts a Software Bill of Materials (SBOM) to improve visibility into its software supply chain. What is the primary benefit of implementing an SBOM?
a. Ensuring compliance with ISO/IEC 27001 standards for third-party risk
b. Providing a detailed inventory of software components and their origins
c. Reducing the attack surface by encrypting all supply chain data
d. Enforcing contractual obligations with upstream vendors

Answer: b. Providing a detailed inventory of software components and their origins. Explanation: An SBOM offers visibility into all software components, their versions, and origins, enabling better risk management. Option a pertains to general compliance, not SBOM specifics. Option c addresses encryption, not component tracking. Option d relates to legal agreements, not the primary benefit of SBOMs.

246. A company conducts a Vendor Security Assessment Process (VSAP) for a potential supplier. Which step is critical to identify vulnerabilities in the supplier's IT infrastructure?
a. Reviewing the supplier's documented incident response plans
b. Conducting an on-site audit of the supplier's security controls
c. Verifying the supplier's compliance with GDPR requirements
d. Requiring the supplier to sign a non-disclosure agreement (NDA)

Answer: b. Conducting an on-site audit of the supplier's security controls. Explanation: An on-site audit evaluates the supplier's IT security posture and identifies vulnerabilities firsthand. Option a provides insight into processes but not infrastructure weaknesses. Option c addresses compliance but does not identify technical vulnerabilities. Option d protects confidentiality but does not assess risk.

247. Which approach in Third-Party Risk Management (TPRM) best mitigates risks associated with downstream suppliers in an N-tier supply chain?
a. Mandating comprehensive cybersecurity insurance for all direct suppliers
b. Requiring all suppliers to implement multifactor authentication (MFA)
c. Extending risk assessments to include critical third-party subcontractors
d. Limiting direct suppliers to those operating within the same region

Answer: c. Extending risk assessments to include critical third-party subcontractors. Explanation: Assessing critical subcontractors ensures visibility into risks deeper in the supply chain. Option a provides financial protection but does not mitigate operational risks. Option b is a security control, not a comprehensive TPRM approach. Option d reduces geographic risks but does not address supply chain complexity.

248. An enterprise integrates Silicon Root of Trust verification into its hardware procurement process. What does this control primarily protect against?
a. Unauthorized modifications to firmware during supply chain transit
b. Compromise of encrypted data during network transmission
c. Misconfiguration of virtualized environments in cloud systems
d. Unauthorized physical access to hardware in data centers

Answer: a. Unauthorized modifications to firmware during supply chain transit. Explanation: Silicon Root of Trust ensures that hardware components are tamper-proof by validating firmware integrity. Option b pertains to data security, not hardware. Option c addresses virtualization issues, not hardware risks. Option d is a physical security concern unrelated to firmware integrity.

249. During an N-tier supplier risk assessment, what is the most significant challenge when evaluating fourth-party suppliers?
a. Establishing enforceable security requirements with indirect suppliers
b. Determining the geographic location of fourth-party facilities
c. Ensuring timely communication of incident reports across tiers
d. Verifying the financial stability of fourth-party suppliers

Answer: a. Establishing enforceable security requirements with indirect suppliers. Explanation: Indirect suppliers often lack direct contractual obligations, making it difficult to enforce security controls. Option b provides context but is less critical. Option c relates to incident response, not assessment. Option d is a concern but secondary to security enforceability.

250. A technology company includes SBOM requirements in its procurement contracts. Which control is critical to ensure the effectiveness of this initiative?
a. Requiring SBOMs to be updated with every major software release
b. Limiting SBOM applicability to open-source components only
c. Ensuring that SBOMs are stored in an encrypted centralized database
d. Requiring annual audits to verify the accuracy of SBOM submissions

Answer: a. Requiring SBOMs to be updated with every major software release. Explanation: Updating SBOMs with every release ensures visibility into new components and vulnerabilities. Option b restricts scope unnecessarily. Option c enhances security but does not ensure effectiveness. Option d is valuable but not as critical as timely updates.

251. Which of the following scenarios illustrates a failure in Third-Party Risk Management (TPRM)?
a. A supplier's vulnerability disclosure timeline is shorter than the organization's.
b. A critical supplier suffers a data breach that exposes customer information.
c. A supplier lacks an ISO 27001 certification but passes all security audits.
d. A supplier stores data in a region with strong privacy regulations.

Answer: b. A critical supplier suffers a data breach that exposes customer information. Explanation: A data breach in a critical supplier reflects inadequate risk management or oversight. Option a may indicate better supplier processes. Option c shows that certifications are not the sole indicator of security. Option d aligns with good TPRM practices.

252. Which control best mitigates the risk of counterfeit hardware entering the supply chain?
a. Conducting regular firmware updates for procured hardware
b. Purchasing hardware exclusively from authorized distributors
c. Implementing automated intrusion detection systems (IDS)
d. Encrypting all communication with hardware vendors

Answer: b. Purchasing hardware exclusively from authorized distributors. Explanation: Sourcing from authorized distributors reduces the risk of counterfeit hardware. Option a ensures updates but does not address authenticity. Option c enhances network security, not hardware sourcing. Option d protects communication but not procurement integrity.

253. A logistics company must manage supply chain risks for software it integrates into critical systems. Which action best ensures the software's integrity?
a. Using digital signatures to verify the software's authenticity
b. Encrypting the software during transmission and storage
c. Limiting the software's execution to specific IP ranges
d. Performing penetration testing on the deployed software

Answer: a. Using digital signatures to verify the software's authenticity. Explanation: Digital signatures ensure the software is unaltered and from a trusted source. Option b secures data but does not verify integrity. Option c restricts access but does not validate software. Option d identifies vulnerabilities but does not ensure initial integrity.

254. A Configuration Management Database (CMDB) is being implemented to manage organizational assets. Which practice ensures the accuracy and reliability of the CMDB?
a. Limiting updates to the database to once per year to prevent inconsistencies
b. Automating asset discovery and reconciliation processes
c. Allowing each department to manage its own portion of the CMDB independently
d. Deleting outdated assets without prior validation to maintain currency

Answer: b. Automating asset discovery and reconciliation processes. Explanation: Automated discovery and reconciliation ensure that the CMDB is consistently updated and accurate. Option a delays updates, leading to outdated information. Option c risks inconsistency without central oversight. Option d risks deleting valid assets without verification.

255. In a Data Loss Prevention (DLP) system, which data classification scheme is most effective for protecting sensitive information in a multinational organization?
a. Uniform classification labels applied to all types of data
b. Role-based classifications tied to specific job responsibilities
c. Classification tiers based on sensitivity and regulatory requirements
d. Ad hoc classifications determined by individual data owners

Answer: c. Classification tiers based on sensitivity and regulatory requirements. Explanation: A tiered system ensures compliance with regulations while addressing varying sensitivity levels. Option a lacks granularity for diverse data types. Option b focuses on roles, not data characteristics. Option d leads to inconsistent classifications.

256. An organization performs an asset inventory reconciliation and discovers discrepancies between physical assets and records in the CMDB. What is the best first step to address this issue?
a. Update the CMDB to match the physical inventory immediately
b. Investigate the source of discrepancies and resolve errors in records
c. Remove unverified assets from the CMDB to maintain consistency
d. Conduct a new physical inventory to replace the existing records

Answer: b. Investigate the source of discrepancies and resolve errors in records. Explanation: Identifying and correcting errors ensures the accuracy of the CMDB. Option a risks propagating inaccuracies. Option c removes assets without validation. Option d is resource-intensive and unnecessary if discrepancies can be resolved.

257. When managing End-of-Life (EOL) hardware assets, which action poses the greatest risk to organizational security?
a. Decommissioning the assets without wiping stored data
b. Replacing the assets with newer models from the same vendor
c. Archiving firmware updates for future compatibility checks
d. Documenting the decommissioning process in the asset management system

Answer: a. Decommissioning the assets without wiping stored data. Explanation: Failing to wipe data exposes sensitive information to potential breaches. Option b is a routine process that does not introduce new risks. Option c is a best practice. Option d enhances traceability and poses no risk.

258. Which Hardware Asset Management (HAM) control ensures secure access to high-value IT equipment in a data center?
a. Biometric authentication at the entry point
b. Periodic audits of asset location records
c. Encryption of firmware updates for hardware devices
d. Maintaining detailed documentation of asset serial numbers

Answer: a. Biometric authentication at the entry point. Explanation: Biometric controls ensure that only authorized personnel access high-value IT equipment. Option b supports record accuracy but does not control access. Option c enhances device security but is unrelated to physical access. Option d aids in tracking but does not prevent unauthorized access.

259. A DLP policy requires monitoring of sensitive customer data across endpoints. Which control is most effective for ensuring compliance?
a. Encrypting all endpoint devices
b. Scanning files for specific keywords and patterns
c. Implementing physical security controls for endpoint devices
d. Restricting endpoint devices to internal networks only

Answer: b. Scanning files for specific keywords and patterns. Explanation: DLP tools use pattern recognition to identify and monitor sensitive data. Option a protects data but does not enable monitoring. Option c does not address data monitoring. Option d limits exposure but does not ensure compliance.

260. An organization's CMDB fails to account for shadow IT assets. What is the most effective way to address this gap?
a. Enforce stricter policies on IT procurement across departments
b. Conduct periodic audits to identify untracked assets
c. Restrict employee access to non-IT-approved resources
d. Implement stricter network access controls for unknown devices

Answer: b. Conduct periodic audits to identify untracked assets. Explanation: Regular audits uncover shadow IT, ensuring the CMDB reflects all assets. Option a prevents new shadow IT but does not address existing gaps. Option c limits employee behavior but does not track assets. Option d improves security but does not update the CMDB.

261. What is a key security consideration for managing End-of-Life (EOL) software assets?
a. Archiving source code for future feature development
b. Disabling unsupported software while keeping it installed

c. Maintaining a record of licensing agreements for compliance
d. Migrating to supported versions to mitigate vulnerabilities

Answer: d. Migrating to supported versions to mitigate vulnerabilities. Explanation: Unsupported software is prone to security risks, making migration critical. Option a supports development but does not address security. Option b retains risk by keeping outdated software. Option c aids compliance but does not mitigate vulnerabilities.

262. In a Hardware Asset Management (HAM) program, what is the most effective way to detect unauthorized hardware connected to the network?
a. Deploy network access control (NAC) solutions
b. Perform quarterly manual hardware inventories
c. Limit employee access to IT procurement processes
d. Conduct regular training on hardware security policies

Answer: a. Deploy network access control (NAC) solutions. Explanation: NAC detects and prevents unauthorized devices from connecting to the network. Option b is time-consuming and less effective. Option c restricts procurement but does not detect devices. Option d raises awareness but does not prevent unauthorized connections.

263. A Configuration Management Database (CMDB) is being implemented to manage organizational assets. Which practice ensures the accuracy and reliability of the CMDB?
a. Limiting updates to the database to once per year to prevent inconsistencies
b. Automating asset discovery and reconciliation processes
c. Allowing each department to manage its own portion of the CMDB independently
d. Deleting outdated assets without prior validation to maintain currency

Answer: b. Automating asset discovery and reconciliation processes. Explanation: Automated discovery and reconciliation ensure that the CMDB is consistently updated and accurate. Option a delays updates, leading to outdated information. Option c risks inconsistency without central oversight. Option d risks deleting valid assets without verification.

264. In a Data Loss Prevention (DLP) system, which data classification scheme is most effective for protecting sensitive information in a multinational organization?
a. Uniform classification labels applied to all types of data
b. Role-based classifications tied to specific job responsibilities
c. Classification tiers based on sensitivity and regulatory requirements
d. Ad hoc classifications determined by individual data owners

Answer: c. Classification tiers based on sensitivity and regulatory requirements. Explanation: A tiered system ensures compliance with regulations while addressing varying sensitivity levels. Option a lacks granularity for diverse data types. Option b focuses on roles, not data characteristics. Option d leads to inconsistent classifications.

265. An organization performs an asset inventory reconciliation and discovers discrepancies between physical assets and records in the CMDB. What is the best first step to address this issue?
a. Update the CMDB to match the physical inventory immediately
b. Investigate the source of discrepancies and resolve errors in records
c. Remove unverified assets from the CMDB to maintain consistency
d. Conduct a new physical inventory to replace the existing records

Answer: b. Investigate the source of discrepancies and resolve errors in records. Explanation: Identifying and correcting errors ensures the accuracy of the CMDB. Option a risks propagating inaccuracies. Option c removes assets without validation. Option d is resource-intensive and unnecessary if discrepancies can be resolved.

266. When managing End-of-Life (EOL) hardware assets, which action poses the greatest risk to organizational security?
a. Decommissioning the assets without wiping stored data
b. Replacing the assets with newer models from the same vendor
c. Archiving firmware updates for future compatibility checks
d. Documenting the decommissioning process in the asset management system

Answer: a. Decommissioning the assets without wiping stored data. Explanation: Failing to wipe data exposes sensitive information to potential breaches. Option b is a routine process that does not introduce new risks. Option c is a best practice. Option d enhances traceability and poses no risk.

267. Which Hardware Asset Management (HAM) control ensures secure access to high-value IT equipment in a data center?
a. Biometric authentication at the entry point
b. Periodic audits of asset location records
c. Encryption of firmware updates for hardware devices
d. Maintaining detailed documentation of asset serial numbers

Answer: a. Biometric authentication at the entry point. Explanation: Biometric controls ensure that only authorized personnel access high-value IT equipment. Option b supports record accuracy but does not control access. Option c enhances device security but is unrelated to physical access. Option d aids in tracking but does not prevent unauthorized access.

268. A DLP policy requires monitoring of sensitive customer data across endpoints. Which control is most effective for ensuring compliance?
a. Encrypting all endpoint devices
b. Scanning files for specific keywords and patterns
c. Implementing physical security controls for endpoint devices
d. Restricting endpoint devices to internal networks only

Answer: b. Scanning files for specific keywords and patterns. Explanation: DLP tools use pattern recognition to identify and monitor sensitive data. Option a protects data but does not enable monitoring. Option c does not address data monitoring. Option d limits exposure but does not ensure compliance.

269. An organization's CMDB fails to account for shadow IT assets. What is the most effective way to address this gap?
a. Enforce stricter policies on IT procurement across departments
b. Conduct periodic audits to identify untracked assets
c. Restrict employee access to non-IT-approved resources
d. Implement stricter network access controls for unknown devices

Answer: b. Conduct periodic audits to identify untracked assets. Explanation: Regular audits uncover shadow IT, ensuring the CMDB reflects all assets. Option a prevents new shadow IT but does not address existing gaps. Option c limits employee behavior but does not track assets. Option d improves security but does not update the CMDB.

270. What is a key security consideration for managing End-of-Life (EOL) software assets?
a. Archiving source code for future feature development
b. Disabling unsupported software while keeping it installed
c. Maintaining a record of licensing agreements for compliance
d. Migrating to supported versions to mitigate vulnerabilities

Answer: d. Migrating to supported versions to mitigate vulnerabilities. Explanation: Unsupported software is prone to security risks, making migration critical. Option a supports development but does not address security. Option b retains risk by keeping outdated software. Option c aids compliance but does not mitigate vulnerabilities.

271. In a Hardware Asset Management (HAM) program, what is the most effective way to detect unauthorized hardware connected to the network?
a. Deploy network access control (NAC) solutions
b. Perform quarterly manual hardware inventories
c. Limit employee access to IT procurement processes
d. Conduct regular training on hardware security policies

Answer: a. Deploy network access control (NAC) solutions. Explanation: NAC detects and prevents unauthorized devices from connecting to the network. Option b is time-consuming and less effective. Option c restricts procurement but does not detect devices. Option d raises awareness but does not prevent unauthorized connections.

272. A global organization identifies risks associated with fourth-party suppliers during its N-tier supplier risk assessment. What is the most effective strategy to address these risks?
a. Require direct suppliers to conduct security audits of their subcontractors.
b. Perform annual site visits for all fourth-party suppliers.
c. Include penalty clauses in contracts for non-compliance by fourth-party suppliers.
d. Limit the use of fourth-party suppliers to non-critical services.

Answer: a. Require direct suppliers to conduct security audits of their subcontractors. Explanation: Requiring direct suppliers to audit their subcontractors ensures accountability and maintains security visibility down the supply chain. Option b is impractical due to the scale of the supply chain. Option c provides recourse but does not address risk proactively. Option d limits operational flexibility and does not mitigate existing risks.

273. An enterprise uses Silicon Root of Trust to secure its supply chain hardware. What is the primary function of this technology?
a. Ensuring all hardware updates are signed by a trusted authority
b. Encrypting firmware updates for secure distribution
c. Detecting and preventing tampering at the component level during manufacturing
d. Monitoring supply chain logistics for unauthorized shipments

Answer: c. Detecting and preventing tampering at the component level during manufacturing. Explanation: Silicon Root of Trust validates hardware integrity by embedding security checks at the manufacturing level. Option a relates to update authenticity but is not exclusive to Silicon Root of Trust. Option b pertains to encryption, not tamper detection. Option d addresses logistics, not hardware security.

274. Which of the following practices best supports continuous improvement in a Vendor Security Assessment Process (VSAP)?
a. Reviewing vendor security questionnaires every five years
b. Using risk-based scoring to prioritize vendors for reassessment
c. Excluding low-risk vendors from periodic assessments
d. Standardizing assessment procedures across all vendors

Answer: b. Using risk-based scoring to prioritize vendors for reassessment. Explanation: Risk-based scoring ensures that resources are allocated to vendors with the highest potential impact, improving overall security. Option a lacks frequency for continuous improvement. Option c may exclude evolving threats. Option d ensures consistency but does not prioritize critical risks.

275. A manufacturing company requires its suppliers to provide Software Bills of Materials (SBOMs) for all delivered software. What additional control ensures these SBOMs remain actionable for managing vulnerabilities?
a. Storing SBOMs in an unencrypted local repository for quick access
b. Mandating that SBOMs include Common Vulnerabilities and Exposures (CVE) references
c. Limiting SBOM submissions to high-value applications only
d. Requiring all SBOMs to be validated by an external auditor annually

Answer: b. Mandating that SBOMs include Common Vulnerabilities and Exposures (CVE) references. Explanation: Including CVE references enables organizations to map known vulnerabilities to software components for faster remediation. Option a is insecure and risks unauthorized access. Option c limits visibility into other critical components. Option d adds validation but does not ensure real-time actionable insights.

276. During a Third-Party Risk Management (TPRM) review, a vendor is found to use outdated cryptographic protocols for data transmission. What is the most appropriate response?
a. Suspend all transactions with the vendor until protocols are updated.
b. Require the vendor to submit a remediation plan with defined timelines.
c. Terminate the vendor's contract and seek an alternative provider.
d. Provide the vendor with temporary access to your secure data transmission tools.

Answer: b. Require the vendor to submit a remediation plan with defined timelines. Explanation: A remediation plan ensures accountability and allows the vendor to address the issue without abrupt service disruption. Option a is overly disruptive and impractical. Option c is a last resort if remediation fails. Option d creates additional risk by exposing secure tools.

277. A retail organization performs penetration tests on third-party software used in its payment processing systems. Which issue, if identified, poses the greatest risk to supply chain integrity?
a. Lack of logging for non-critical API endpoints
b. Use of hardcoded credentials within the software
c. Inefficient input validation for optional form fields
d. Delayed responses during heavy transaction loads

Answer: b. Use of hardcoded credentials within the software. Explanation: Hardcoded credentials present a significant security risk, allowing attackers to exploit systems easily. Option a is a minor issue and does not compromise integrity. Option c may affect functionality but has a lower impact. Option d relates to performance, not security.

278. A technology company assesses N-tier suppliers in its supply chain and discovers multiple dependencies on a single upstream vendor. What is the most effective way to mitigate risks associated with this vendor concentration?
a. Diversify the supply chain by engaging additional upstream vendors.
b. Increase the vendor's contractual obligations for security.
c. Require the vendor to adopt ISO 27001 certification standards.
d. Limit the use of upstream vendors to low-priority services.

Answer: a. Diversify the supply chain by engaging additional upstream vendors. Explanation: Diversification reduces the risk of operational disruptions from overreliance on a single vendor. Option b strengthens contractual terms but does not address concentration risks. Option c enhances security practices but does not mitigate dependency. Option d reduces flexibility and ignores critical services.

279. A data center uses multi-factor authentication (MFA) for physical access control. Which factor provides the strongest second layer of authentication alongside a proximity card?
a. A six-digit PIN entered at a keypad
b. A biometric fingerprint scan
c. A one-time passcode delivered via email

d. An RFID badge used in sequence

Answer: b. A biometric fingerprint scan. Explanation: Biometrics are unique and non-replicable, providing strong authentication. Option a, while adding security, can be guessed or shared. Option c is less secure due to email interception risks. Option d does not add a true second factor as both layers involve possession-based elements.

280. In a high-security facility, how should a mantrap be configured to prevent tailgating?
a. Both doors should remain open during peak traffic times for efficiency
b. One door locks automatically until the other is fully closed
c. Both doors are controlled manually by security personnel
d. Doors open simultaneously to reduce wait times

Answer: b. One door locks automatically until the other is fully closed. Explanation: This configuration ensures controlled access and prevents unauthorized individuals from following authorized personnel. Option a compromises security for convenience. Option c introduces delays and is prone to human error. Option d defeats the purpose of a mantrap by allowing simultaneous entry.

281. Which HVAC consideration is most critical for maintaining physical security in a data center?
a. Preventing condensation on cooling units to avoid water damage
b. Ensuring temperature and humidity monitoring for equipment stability
c. Using HEPA filters to improve air quality for personnel health
d. Installing backup HVAC systems to reduce energy consumption

Answer: b. Ensuring temperature and humidity monitoring for equipment stability. Explanation: Monitoring ensures the environment is optimal for hardware performance and prevents failures. Option a, while important, is a secondary concern. Option c benefits personnel but does not directly affect equipment security. Option d focuses on efficiency rather than operational continuity.

282. What is the primary purpose of environmental monitoring systems in a secure facility?
a. Ensuring compliance with international building codes
b. Detecting changes in conditions that could compromise equipment
c. Monitoring personnel activities for compliance with safety policies
d. Preventing intrusion attempts through thermal imaging

Answer: b. Detecting changes in conditions that could compromise equipment. Explanation: Environmental monitoring systems track temperature, humidity, and airflow to protect equipment. Option a pertains to construction compliance, not monitoring. Option c focuses on personnel, not environmental factors. Option d describes intrusion detection, which is not the primary purpose of such systems.

283. What is the most effective way to implement physical security zones within a secure building?
a. Deploy motion detectors at every access point
b. Establish increasingly restrictive zones moving toward critical assets
c. Use transparent barriers to enhance visibility throughout the facility
d. Allow universal access to non-sensitive areas for convenience

Answer: b. Establish increasingly restrictive zones moving toward critical assets. Explanation: Layered security ensures that only authorized individuals reach sensitive areas. Option a improves detection but does not segment zones. Option c aids visibility but does not restrict access. Option d compromises security by allowing excessive access.

284. A data center lacks physical access controls for its HVAC maintenance room. What risk does this pose?
a. Unauthorized access to critical infrastructure components
b. Contamination of server rooms due to unfiltered airflow

c. Increased operational costs from inefficient HVAC usage
d. Regulatory violations due to missing inspection logs

Answer: a. Unauthorized access to critical infrastructure components. Explanation: Without access controls, attackers could tamper with systems affecting temperature and uptime. Option b is unrelated to access control. Option c is an operational issue, not a security risk. Option d pertains to compliance, not security.

285. Which security feature best enhances the effectiveness of environmental monitoring systems in critical infrastructure?
a. Integration with fire suppression systems
b. Deployment of real-time video surveillance
c. Automated alerts for abnormal environmental conditions
d. Use of biometric authentication for maintenance personnel

Answer: c. Automated alerts for abnormal environmental conditions. Explanation: Automated alerts ensure rapid response to potential threats like overheating or humidity spikes. Option a complements monitoring but does not enhance it. Option b aids situational awareness but is not specific to environmental systems. Option d controls personnel access but does not directly affect monitoring effectiveness.

286. What is a key consideration for physical security zones in environments storing classified information?
a. Regularly rotating access codes to secure areas
b. Using mantraps at every entry and exit point
c. Limiting access based on the principle of least privilege
d. Providing unrestricted access to trusted contractors

Answer: c. Limiting access based on the principle of least privilege. Explanation: Least privilege minimizes risk by restricting access to only what is necessary. Option a is insufficient as standalone security. Option b is impractical for all entry points. Option d contradicts secure access principles.

287. An environmental monitoring system flags a sudden increase in humidity levels within a server room. What should be the immediate response?
a. Power down all servers to prevent potential damage
b. Investigate the cause and deploy dehumidifiers as needed
c. Adjust airflow to increase cooling efficiency
d. Notify personnel to limit entry into the server room

Answer: b. Investigate the cause and deploy dehumidifiers as needed. Explanation: Addressing the root cause and stabilizing conditions prevents equipment damage. Option a is unnecessary unless conditions worsen. Option c addresses cooling, not humidity. Option d is insufficient for mitigating environmental changes.

288. A mantrap is designed to prevent unauthorized access in a high-security facility. What additional control can enhance its effectiveness?
a. Using one-time PIN codes for entry
b. Monitoring with real-time video surveillance
c. Installing bulletproof glass on both doors
d. Requiring dual-person authentication for access

Answer: d. Requiring dual-person authentication for access. Explanation: Dual-person authentication adds another layer of security, ensuring only authorized individuals gain access. Option a is less secure without additional factors. Option b aids monitoring but does not prevent access. Option c improves physical resilience but not access control.

289. A financial services organization implements Database Activity Monitoring (DAM) to enhance its database security. Which of the following best describes the primary function of DAM?
a. Encrypting sensitive database fields to prevent unauthorized access
b. Monitoring and logging database queries and transactions in real time
c. Scanning databases for configuration errors and known vulnerabilities
d. Restricting user access to specific rows in a database table

Answer: b. Monitoring and logging database queries and transactions in real time. Explanation: DAM tools provide real-time visibility into database activity to detect and respond to unauthorized queries or suspicious behavior. Option a describes Transparent Data Encryption (TDE). Option c pertains to security scanning, not monitoring. Option d refers to Row-Level Security (RLS).

290. A healthcare organization implements Row-Level Security (RLS) to comply with data privacy regulations. Which scenario best demonstrates a proper use of RLS?
a. Encrypting all patient data before storing it in the database
b. Restricting access to patient records based on the treating physician's ID
c. Performing periodic backups of the database to ensure recoverability
d. Blocking unauthorized users from accessing the database management console

Answer: b. Restricting access to patient records based on the treating physician's ID. Explanation: RLS applies fine-grained access controls by filtering rows based on user attributes or roles, such as a physician's ID. Option a describes encryption, not access control. Option c ensures data availability but is unrelated to RLS. Option d focuses on system access, not row-level restrictions.

291. Which of the following is a key limitation of Transparent Data Encryption (TDE) when securing databases?
a. TDE does not encrypt data during backup processes.
b. TDE only encrypts specific rows or columns instead of entire tables.
c. TDE does not protect data transmitted between database clients and servers.
d. TDE introduces significant performance overhead on query execution.

Answer: c. TDE does not protect data transmitted between database clients and servers. Explanation: TDE encrypts data at rest but does not secure data in transit, which requires network-level encryption like TLS. Option a is incorrect because TDE does encrypt backups. Option b is false, as TDE encrypts entire database files. Option d overstates performance impacts, which are minimal in most implementations.

292. During a database security scan, a misconfiguration is discovered that allows anonymous users to view schema metadata. What is the most effective immediate mitigation?
a. Enforce encryption on all database connections.
b. Implement Row-Level Security to restrict access to sensitive rows.
c. Revoke public access privileges from metadata tables.
d. Enable Transparent Data Encryption to secure metadata at rest.

Answer: c. Revoke public access privileges from metadata tables. Explanation: Revoking public access prevents unauthorized users from viewing database schema information. Option a secures data in transit but does not address the misconfiguration. Option b is unrelated to metadata visibility. Option d protects data at rest but does not limit access.

293. A retail company uses database security scanning procedures to detect vulnerabilities. Which control should be prioritized to address findings related to SQL injection risks?
a. Implementing input validation and parameterized queries in application code
b. Encrypting database tables that store sensitive customer data

c. Restricting database administrator (DBA) access to critical systems
d. Performing regular backups of the database to ensure data recovery

Answer: a. Implementing input validation and parameterized queries in application code. Explanation: Input validation and parameterized queries prevent SQL injection by ensuring that user inputs cannot manipulate database queries. Option b enhances data confidentiality but does not mitigate SQL injection. Option c addresses access control but not input handling. Option d relates to data availability, not injection prevention.

294. An organization is establishing a secure configuration baseline for its databases. Which step is most critical in preventing privilege escalation attacks?
a. Disabling unused default accounts and changing default passwords
b. Encrypting all sensitive data stored in the database
c. Configuring firewalls to block unauthorized database connections
d. Enabling database activity monitoring to detect suspicious queries

Answer: a. Disabling unused default accounts and changing default passwords. Explanation: Default accounts and credentials are common targets for privilege escalation. Disabling them reduces this risk. Option b protects data but does not address privileges. Option c enhances network security but does not mitigate privilege escalation. Option d detects issues but does not prevent them.

295. A company implements Row-Level Security (RLS) on a customer database. Which scenario would indicate a misconfiguration of RLS?
a. Sales representatives can view only customer data assigned to them.
b. Administrators have unrestricted access to all rows in the database.
c. Interns can view rows belonging to multiple sales regions.
d. External contractors are unable to access any customer data.

Answer: c. Interns can view rows belonging to multiple sales regions. Explanation: RLS misconfigurations allow users to access data beyond their intended scope. Option a describes correct RLS implementation. Option b is expected for administrative roles. Option d aligns with the principle of least privilege.

296. An e-commerce platform uses Transparent Data Encryption (TDE) for its database. What is a critical requirement for ensuring the security of TDE?
a. Regularly rotating the encryption keys stored in a hardware security module (HSM)
b. Encrypting all network traffic between the database server and clients
c. Performing full database scans to detect misconfigured permissions
d. Enabling multi-factor authentication for all database administrators

Answer: a. Regularly rotating the encryption keys stored in a hardware security module (HSM). Explanation: Key rotation reduces the risk of key compromise, ensuring TDE's effectiveness. Option b addresses data in transit, not TDE. Option c identifies vulnerabilities but does not enhance TDE. Option d secures administrator accounts but is unrelated to encryption.

297. A network administrator is implementing Transport Layer Security (TLS) 1.3 to secure communications between clients and servers. Which feature of TLS 1.3 enhances both security and performance?
a. Removal of support for forward secrecy
b. Use of RSA for key exchange during the handshake
c. Introduction of 0-RTT (Zero Round Trip Time) resumption
d. Support for compression to reduce transmission size

Answer: c. Introduction of 0-RTT (Zero Round Trip Time) resumption. Explanation: 0-RTT enables faster session resumption by eliminating the need for a full handshake, enhancing performance. Option a is incorrect because TLS 1.3 enforces forward secrecy. Option b is incorrect as TLS 1.3 removes RSA key exchange. Option d is irrelevant as TLS 1.3 prohibits compression due to security risks.

298. Which scenario justifies the use of IPSec tunnel mode over transport mode?
a. Encrypting communication between two hosts within the same LAN
b. Protecting traffic between two network gateways over the internet
c. Securing individual user sessions to a remote server
d. Providing end-to-end encryption for VoIP calls

Answer: b. Protecting traffic between two network gateways over the internet. Explanation: Tunnel mode encrypts the entire IP packet, including headers, making it ideal for gateway-to-gateway protection. Option a is better suited for transport mode. Option c describes VPN client usage, which may not require tunnel mode. Option d typically uses transport mode for efficiency.

299. Which SNMPv3 feature mitigates the risk of unauthorized access to network device configurations?
a. Use of community strings for device authentication
b. Application of AES for message encryption
c. Storing credentials in plaintext for easy retrieval
d. Relying on default security levels for simplicity

Answer: b. Application of AES for message encryption. Explanation: AES encrypts SNMPv3 messages, preventing unauthorized access during transit. Option a is outdated and less secure. Option c violates best practices. Option d increases security risks due to insufficient controls.

300. How does the Secure Remote Password (SRP) protocol ensure secure authentication?
a. By using a symmetric key for encrypting passwords during transmission
b. By generating a unique public/private key pair for each session
c. By leveraging zero-knowledge proofs to authenticate without revealing passwords
d. By requiring multi-factor authentication for every login attempt

Answer: c. By leveraging zero-knowledge proofs to authenticate without revealing passwords. Explanation: SRP ensures that passwords are never transmitted, reducing the risk of compromise. Option a does not apply as SRP avoids transmitting passwords. Option b is unrelated to SRP. Option d, while useful, is not a feature of SRP.

301. What role does the authenticator play in IEEE 802.1X port-based authentication?
a. Initiates the EAP authentication request to the supplicant
b. Acts as the certificate authority for all authentication transactions
c. Provides direct access control policies to the client
d. Validates the supplicant's identity without involving an authentication server

Answer: a. Initiates the EAP authentication request to the supplicant. Explanation: The authenticator forwards authentication requests and responses between the supplicant and the authentication server. Option b is incorrect as the authenticator is not a CA. Option c pertains to network policy enforcement, not authentication initiation. Option d misrepresents the authentication process.

302. Which advancement in TLS 1.3 enhances its resistance to cryptographic attacks?
a. Mandatory use of the RSA algorithm for key exchanges
b. Replacement of weak ciphers with secure suites like ChaCha20-Poly1305
c. Support for session persistence without key regeneration

d. Use of legacy SSL handshake protocols for backward compatibility

Answer: b. Replacement of weak ciphers with secure suites like ChaCha20-Poly1305. Explanation: TLS 1.3 removes outdated ciphers and introduces robust alternatives, enhancing security. Option a is incorrect as RSA key exchanges are removed. Option c reduces forward secrecy. Option d contradicts TLS 1.3's emphasis on removing legacy protocols.

303. Which IPSec mode is most suitable for securing communication between a user's device and a corporate VPN server?
a. Tunnel mode
b. Transport mode
c. Split-tunneling mode
d. Transparent mode

Answer: a. Tunnel mode. Explanation: Tunnel mode encrypts the entire IP packet, making it ideal for VPN connections. Option b is incorrect because it encrypts only the payload. Option c describes a routing method, not an encryption mode. Option d is unrelated to IPSec configurations.

304. What is the primary purpose of SNMPv3's User-Based Security Model (USM)?
a. To ensure that all SNMP devices use community strings for authentication
b. To provide message integrity, confidentiality, and authentication
c. To allow unencrypted management of network devices
d. To restrict SNMP usage to specific network segments

Answer: b. To provide message integrity, confidentiality, and authentication. Explanation: USM secures SNMPv3 communications using encryption and authentication. Option a is outdated. Option c violates SNMPv3's security goals. Option d pertains to access control, not USM functionality.

305. Which feature of the Secure Remote Password (SRP) protocol prevents session hijacking?
a. Mutual authentication between client and server
b. Encryption of passwords using asymmetric keys
c. Use of long-lived sessions for persistent connectivity
d. Generating static session keys for faster communication

Answer: a. Mutual authentication between client and server. Explanation: Mutual authentication ensures that both parties verify each other, preventing hijacking. Option b misrepresents SRP's reliance on zero-knowledge proofs. Option c and d weaken security by reducing session agility.

306. A global financial institution deploys a Mobile Device Management (MDM) solution to secure corporate-owned devices. Which MDM policy is most effective at protecting sensitive corporate data on lost or stolen devices?
a. Enforcing full-disk encryption on all mobile devices
b. Implementing device lockout after five failed login attempts
c. Configuring geofencing to restrict device usage to specific locations
d. Enabling remote wipe capabilities for lost or stolen devices

Answer: d. Enabling remote wipe capabilities for lost or stolen devices. Explanation: Remote wipe ensures sensitive corporate data can be erased from devices that are lost or stolen, reducing the risk of data exposure. Option a protects data at rest but does not address the issue of lost devices. Option b prevents unauthorized access but does not recover or erase data. Option c enhances security but does not resolve the data protection issue for lost devices.

307. An organization adopts Enterprise Mobility Management (EMM) to secure its mobile ecosystem. Which feature of EMM is critical for ensuring compliance with regulatory requirements for data protection?
a. Blocking access to non-corporate app stores
b. Encrypting data at rest and in transit across all managed devices
c. Enforcing time-based restrictions on device usage
d. Preventing the installation of social media applications

Answer: b. Encrypting data at rest and in transit across all managed devices. Explanation: Encryption ensures sensitive data is protected from unauthorized access, meeting regulatory requirements. Option a limits application sources but does not directly address data protection. Option c is unrelated to compliance. Option d improves productivity but does not ensure compliance.

308. A company implements Mobile Application Management (MAM) for its BYOD policy. Which capability of MAM provides the greatest benefit for securing corporate data on personal devices?
a. Enforcing device-wide encryption for all storage
b. Restricting access to corporate apps based on user roles
c. Separating corporate and personal data within managed applications
d. Requiring biometric authentication for all device logins

Answer: c. Separating corporate and personal data within managed applications. Explanation: MAM enables granular control over corporate app data while respecting user privacy, which is crucial for BYOD environments. Option a applies to MDM, not MAM. Option b enhances access control but does not address data separation. Option d secures device access but does not specifically protect corporate app data.

309. An organization implements a BYOD security framework to address risks associated with employee-owned devices. What is the primary challenge of this approach?
a. Monitoring all device activity without violating user privacy
b. Enforcing operating system updates on personal devices
c. Preventing unauthorized app downloads on personal devices
d. Implementing geolocation restrictions for remote employees

Answer: a. Monitoring all device activity without violating user privacy. Explanation: Striking a balance between security and privacy is a significant challenge in BYOD frameworks. Option b is a technical hurdle but not the primary challenge. Option c intrudes on user autonomy and may not be feasible. Option d is a control mechanism, not a core challenge.

310. A retail company deploys a Mobile Threat Defense (MTD) solution. Which feature of MTD is most effective in protecting devices from zero-day threats?
a. Real-time malware detection using behavioral analysis
b. Regular software updates delivered through MDM
c. Blocking access to public Wi-Fi networks
d. Encrypting device storage with a 256-bit key

Answer: a. Real-time malware detection using behavioral analysis. Explanation: Behavioral analysis in MTD solutions detects anomalies and mitigates zero-day threats by identifying malicious patterns. Option b ensures device security but does not target zero-day threats. Option c prevents network-based risks but is not specific to malware. Option d protects data at rest, not against threats.

311. A healthcare provider uses MDM to enforce HIPAA compliance on employee devices. Which policy best addresses the requirement to secure electronic protected health information (ePHI)?
a. Logging all file transfers to external storage devices
b. Requiring biometric authentication for accessing ePHI

c. Disabling camera and microphone functionality on all devices
d. Enforcing automatic screen lock after a period of inactivity

Answer: d. Enforcing automatic screen lock after a period of inactivity. Explanation: Screen locks prevent unauthorized access to devices left unattended, protecting ePHI. Option a aids audits but does not secure live access. Option b strengthens authentication but does not prevent physical access. Option c addresses privacy concerns but is not specific to ePHI security.

312. An organization deploys MAM for managing corporate apps on personal devices. What policy ensures that corporate data remains secure after an employee leaves the organization?
a. Performing a remote wipe of the entire device upon termination
b. Restricting app access based on predefined schedules
c. Removing corporate app access and data while preserving personal apps
d. Logging all app activity to a central database for review

Answer: c. Removing corporate app access and data while preserving personal apps. Explanation: MAM allows selective data removal, maintaining security while respecting employee privacy. Option a applies to MDM, not MAM. Option b manages app usage but does not secure data after termination. Option d supports audits but does not remove access.

313. Which mobile threat defense strategy is most effective in mitigating risks from jailbroken or rooted devices?
a. Restricting device access to corporate networks until compliance is verified
b. Encrypting all corporate communications on mobile devices
c. Deploying anti-malware apps to scan for unauthorized modifications
d. Enforcing time-based restrictions for app usage during business hours

Answer: a. Restricting device access to corporate networks until compliance is verified. Explanation: Blocking non-compliant devices prevents risks associated with jailbroken or rooted devices from impacting the corporate environment. Option b protects data in transit but does not address device compliance. Option c detects malware but does not fully mitigate risks. Option d enhances control but is unrelated to rooted devices.

314. A consulting firm uses EMM to enforce data security on contractor-owned devices. Which feature ensures that only authorized users can access sensitive corporate data?
a. Geofencing to restrict access outside specific locations
b. Integration with single sign-on (SSO) for authentication
c. Disabling external storage device connectivity
d. Logging all access attempts for forensic analysis

Answer: b. Integration with single sign-on (SSO) for authentication. Explanation: SSO ensures secure and efficient user authentication, preventing unauthorized access. Option a limits location-based risks but does not authenticate users. Option c reduces data exfiltration risks but does not control user access. Option d supports audits but does not enforce access controls.

315. An organization implements Infrastructure as Code (IaC) for cloud deployments but fails to use security scanning tools. Which risk is most likely to result from this oversight?
a. Deployment of resources without cost optimization
b. Introduction of hardcoded credentials into the environment
c. Inconsistent configuration across development and production environments
d. Increased latency due to misconfigured network settings

Answer: b. Introduction of hardcoded credentials into the environment. Explanation: IaC security scanning identifies sensitive data like hardcoded credentials, a common risk in IaC files. Option a pertains to cost management, not security. Option c describes operational inconsistencies, which security scanning does not address. Option d relates to performance issues, not security vulnerabilities.

316. A Cloud Security Posture Management (CSPM) tool flags a publicly accessible S3 bucket. What is the best immediate action to secure this resource?
a. Encrypt the bucket contents with a server-side encryption key
b. Apply a bucket policy that restricts access to specific IP ranges
c. Move the bucket to a virtual private cloud (VPC)
d. Enable versioning to track changes to bucket objects

Answer: b. Apply a bucket policy that restricts access to specific IP ranges. Explanation: Restricting access to specific IPs prevents unauthorized access while maintaining functionality. Option a protects data but does not limit access. Option c is unnecessary for S3 security. Option d aids tracking but does not enhance immediate security.

317. What is the most effective method for securing serverless functions in a cloud environment?
a. Using environment variables to store sensitive credentials
b. Applying least privilege policies to serverless execution roles
c. Allowing unrestricted function-to-function communication
d. Increasing timeout settings to support extended execution times

Answer: b. Applying least privilege policies to serverless execution roles. Explanation: Least privilege minimizes the impact of compromised serverless functions. Option a risks exposing credentials. Option c expands the attack surface. Option d focuses on performance, not security.

318. A container orchestration platform allows unrestricted pod-to-pod communication by default. What is the primary security risk of this configuration?
a. Increased risk of container image corruption
b. Easier lateral movement within the cluster for attackers
c. Inefficient resource allocation for high-traffic services
d. Inability to monitor application logs effectively

Answer: b. Easier lateral movement within the cluster for attackers. Explanation: Unrestricted communication allows attackers to exploit vulnerabilities in one pod to compromise others. Option a pertains to image integrity, not communication. Option c describes performance, not security. Option d is unrelated to network configuration.

319. Which cloud network segmentation strategy best mitigates the risk of data exfiltration?
a. Deploying firewalls at the network perimeter
b. Segmenting workloads by environment, such as development and production
c. Using public subnets for all workloads to streamline access
d. Implementing DNS filtering for outbound traffic

Answer: b. Segmenting workloads by environment, such as development and production. Explanation: Environment segmentation isolates workloads, preventing unauthorized data access. Option a is less effective without internal segmentation. Option c increases risk by exposing workloads. Option d aids detection but does not inherently isolate workloads.

320. In a CI/CD pipeline, what is the primary benefit of integrating IaC security scanning before deployment?
a. Ensuring resources are provisioned within allocated budgets
b. Identifying and mitigating misconfigurations early in the development process
c. Accelerating deployment times by automating approvals

d. Reducing the frequency of patch management for cloud workloads

Answer: b. Identifying and mitigating misconfigurations early in the development process. Explanation: Early scanning reduces the risk of deploying insecure configurations. Option a pertains to financial controls, not security. Option c improves speed but does not address security. Option d misrepresents IaC's purpose.

321. A CSPM tool reports excessive privileges for a cloud IAM role. What is the recommended approach to address this issue?
a. Delete the role and replace it with a default read-only role
b. Restrict the role to specific users and remove all permissions
c. Review and apply the principle of least privilege
d. Disable logging for the role to minimize exposure

Answer: c. Review and apply the principle of least privilege. Explanation: Least privilege ensures the role has only the permissions necessary to perform its tasks. Option a may not meet operational needs. Option b is overly restrictive and impractical. Option d reduces visibility and does not address the core issue.

322. When securing container images, what is the most effective step to minimize vulnerabilities?
a. Using base images from trusted public repositories without modification
b. Scanning images for known vulnerabilities before deploying them
c. Deploying unscanned images in isolated development environments
d. Encrypting container images to prevent unauthorized access

Answer: b. Scanning images for known vulnerabilities before deploying them. Explanation: Scanning ensures that only secure images are used, reducing risk. Option a is insufficient, as even trusted images can have vulnerabilities. Option c delays addressing security. Option d aids confidentiality but does not ensure image integrity.

323. What is a critical limitation of using serverless architecture for sensitive workloads?
a. Lack of scalability for high-demand applications
b. Limited options for applying network access controls
c. Difficulty in integrating serverless functions with IAM policies
d. Inability to encrypt data processed by serverless functions

Answer: b. Limited options for applying network access controls. Explanation: Serverless environments often abstract networking, complicating granular control. Option a misrepresents serverless capabilities. Option c is incorrect, as IAM integration is robust. Option d is incorrect because encryption is fully supported.

324. A financial application is being developed using the Secure Software Development Life Cycle (SSDLC). At which phase should threat modeling be conducted to ensure potential vulnerabilities are addressed early?
a. Implementation
b. Design
c. Testing
d. Deployment

Answer: b. Design. Explanation: Threat modeling in the Design phase allows the identification and mitigation of potential vulnerabilities before coding begins, reducing the cost and effort of remediation. Option a is too late, as code vulnerabilities have already been introduced. Option c focuses on identifying defects, not designing against threats. Option d addresses operational risks but does not mitigate design flaws.

325. A development team is adopting the STRIDE methodology for threat modeling. Which STRIDE category directly addresses the risk of unauthorized data disclosure?
a. Spoofing

b. Tampering
c. Information disclosure
d. Elevation of privilege

Answer: c. Information disclosure. Explanation: The Information disclosure category of STRIDE specifically targets risks of exposing sensitive information to unauthorized entities. Option a addresses impersonation attacks. Option b relates to data integrity, not confidentiality. Option d concerns unauthorized access escalation.

326. Which of the following demonstrates the primary purpose of code signing in secure software development?
a. Preventing reverse engineering of application code
b. Encrypting sensitive data within the software binaries
c. Ensuring the authenticity and integrity of software
d. Scanning source code for vulnerabilities before deployment

Answer: c. Ensuring the authenticity and integrity of software. Explanation: Code signing uses digital certificates to verify that software is unaltered and comes from a trusted source. Option a is unrelated to code signing. Option b focuses on data protection, not software trust. Option d relates to vulnerability detection, not authenticity.

327. During a secure code review, a team identifies several vulnerabilities related to injection attacks. Which practice should be prioritized to address these risks?
a. Enforcing secure coding standards for password storage
b. Using parameterized queries to handle user inputs
c. Encrypting database connections with SSL/TLS
d. Implementing a Web Application Firewall (WAF)

Answer: b. Using parameterized queries to handle user inputs. Explanation: Parameterized queries prevent injection attacks by ensuring user inputs are treated as data, not executable code. Option a is unrelated to injection risks. Option c secures data in transit but does not address input handling. Option d provides additional protection but is not a primary coding practice.

328. A company is developing an API for its logistics platform. Which practice best ensures the security of the API?
a. Implementing mutual TLS for client and server authentication
b. Limiting API access to specific IP ranges
c. Using HTTP for faster communication with third-party services
d. Allowing all HTTP methods to maximize flexibility

Answer: a. Implementing mutual TLS for client and server authentication. Explanation: Mutual TLS ensures that both the client and server are authenticated, securing API communication. Option b adds protection but does not authenticate endpoints. Option c introduces risks by not encrypting traffic. Option d is overly permissive and increases the attack surface.

329. Using the PASTA threat modeling framework, what is the primary focus during the Risk Analysis stage?
a. Identifying high-value business assets
b. Evaluating the likelihood and impact of potential threats
c. Implementing countermeasures for identified vulnerabilities
d. Testing the effectiveness of security controls

Answer: b. Evaluating the likelihood and impact of potential threats. Explanation: The Risk Analysis stage of PASTA assesses the probability and impact of threats to prioritize mitigation efforts. Option a occurs in earlier stages. Option c and option d take place after risks are analyzed.

330. A healthcare application undergoes regular secure code reviews. Which issue would most likely be flagged as a high-priority vulnerability?
a. Missing comments in the source code
b. Hardcoded API keys within the codebase
c. Inefficient sorting algorithms in backend queries
d. Use of third-party libraries for data parsing

Answer: b. Hardcoded API keys within the codebase. Explanation: Hardcoded API keys expose sensitive credentials, making them a critical vulnerability. Option a is a best practice issue, not a security risk. Option c affects performance, not security. Option d requires additional scrutiny but is not inherently a vulnerability.

331. An organization uses JSON Web Tokens (JWT) for stateless authentication in its APIs. Which practice enhances the security of JWT usage?
a. Signing tokens with a strong symmetric key
b. Storing tokens in a publicly accessible database
c. Allowing token expiration times of several months
d. Embedding sensitive user data directly into tokens

Answer: a. Signing tokens with a strong symmetric key. Explanation: A strong symmetric key ensures that tokens cannot be tampered with or forged. Option b compromises token confidentiality. Option c increases the risk of token compromise. Option d exposes sensitive information unnecessarily.

332. A retail company integrates static application security testing (SAST) into its SSDLC. Which type of vulnerability is SAST most effective at detecting?
a. Hardcoded passwords in the source code
b. Unpatched dependencies in third-party libraries
c. Insecure configurations in deployed systems
d. Malicious traffic targeting runtime environments

Answer: a. Hardcoded passwords in the source code. Explanation: SAST examines source code for vulnerabilities like hardcoded credentials before the application is compiled. Option b relates to dependency scanning. Option c requires configuration management tools. Option d pertains to runtime analysis.

333. A company is planning to implement FIDO2 for passwordless authentication. Which feature of FIDO2 enhances resistance to phishing attacks?
a. Use of a shared symmetric key for all relying parties
b. Generation of a unique public-private key pair for each application
c. Authentication based solely on device possession
d. Transmission of hashed passwords over encrypted channels

Answer: b. Generation of a unique public-private key pair for each application. Explanation: FIDO2 generates unique key pairs for each application, preventing credential reuse across platforms. Option a is incorrect as FIDO2 avoids shared keys. Option c lacks additional factors like public-private key cryptography. Option d is irrelevant since FIDO2 eliminates password transmission entirely.

334. In OAuth 2.0, which authorization grant type is most suitable for a mobile application that cannot securely store client secrets?
a. Client Credentials Grant
b. Resource Owner Password Credentials Grant
c. Authorization Code Grant (with PKCE)
d. Implicit Grant

Answer: c. Authorization Code Grant (with PKCE). Explanation: PKCE enhances security by eliminating the need for client secrets, making it suitable for mobile apps. Option a is for server-to-server communication. Option b is insecure for client-side applications. Option d is less secure and not recommended for new implementations.

335. What role does the Ticket Granting Ticket (TGT) play in the Kerberos authentication process?
a. Establishes a direct communication channel between the client and the resource server
b. Grants access to multiple services without requiring re-authentication
c. Validates the client's password against the authentication database
d. Encrypts all session data exchanged between the client and the resource server

Answer: b. Grants access to multiple services without requiring re-authentication. Explanation: The TGT enables access to additional services by issuing service tickets, reducing repeated authentication. Option a describes service tickets, not the TGT. Option c refers to initial authentication, handled by the Authentication Server (AS). Option d is incorrect as encryption is achieved using session keys.

336. In a certificate-based authentication system, what is the primary role of the Certificate Revocation List (CRL)?
a. To store all issued certificates in a centralized repository
b. To list certificates that have been revoked before their expiration date
c. To automate the renewal process for expiring certificates
d. To generate unique private keys for each client

Answer: b. To list certificates that have been revoked before their expiration date. Explanation: The CRL identifies invalidated certificates, preventing their use. Option a describes a certificate database, not a CRL. Option c pertains to certificate lifecycle management but is unrelated to revocation. Option d is irrelevant as private key generation is outside the CRL's scope.

337. What is a critical consideration when implementing biometric authentication systems?
a. Minimizing enrollment time by reducing the amount of stored biometric data
b. Ensuring templates are stored as plain text for easy processing
c. Implementing anti-spoofing measures to detect fraudulent biometric inputs
d. Allowing fallback to password authentication without additional controls

Answer: c. Implementing anti-spoofing measures to detect fraudulent biometric inputs. Explanation: Anti-spoofing ensures the system can distinguish between genuine and fake biometric data. Option a compromises accuracy by reducing data quality. Option b violates security best practices. Option d weakens security by enabling bypass methods.

338. An organization is deploying OAuth 2.0 for API access. Which flow is best suited for a backend service that acts on its own behalf?
a. Authorization Code Grant
b. Implicit Grant
c. Resource Owner Password Credentials Grant
d. Client Credentials Grant

Answer: d. Client Credentials Grant. Explanation: The Client Credentials Grant is designed for backend services acting independently, without user involvement. Option a requires user interaction. Option b is for single-page applications and is less secure. Option c is insecure and deprecated for such use cases.

339. What is a key advantage of FIDO2 over traditional password-based authentication systems?
a. Requires no reliance on cryptographic keys
b. Completely removes the need for user-specific credentials
c. Enables strong authentication without sharing secrets with the server

d. Allows the use of shared credentials across multiple applications

Answer: c. Enables strong authentication without sharing secrets with the server. Explanation: FIDO2 uses public-private key pairs, eliminating shared secrets and reducing attack vectors. Option a is incorrect as FIDO2 relies on cryptographic keys. Option b is wrong; user credentials are replaced with keys. Option d misrepresents FIDO2's per-application key generation.

340. In Kerberos, how is replay protection achieved during the authentication process?
a. By encrypting all messages with symmetric keys
b. By using timestamps in authentication requests
c. By requiring mutual authentication between client and server
d. By validating digital certificates for each communication

Answer: b. By using timestamps in authentication requests. Explanation: Timestamps prevent replay attacks by ensuring requests are valid only within a limited time frame. Option a is insufficient alone for replay protection. Option c is beneficial but does not directly address replay attacks. Option d is unrelated to the Kerberos mechanism.

341. What is the main purpose of an Online Certificate Status Protocol (OCSP) responder in a certificate-based authentication system?
a. Generating public-private key pairs for new certificates
b. Checking the real-time revocation status of a certificate
c. Validating the client's identity against a directory service
d. Encrypting communications between client and server

Answer: b. Checking the real-time revocation status of a certificate. Explanation: OCSP provides real-time validation of a certificate's status, complementing CRLs. Option a pertains to key management, not OCSP. Option c describes directory authentication, not certificate status. Option d is unrelated to OCSP's function.

342. An organization implements the Bell-LaPadula security model to maintain confidentiality of classified documents. How does the "no-read-up" (Simple Security Property) rule enforce confidentiality?
a. It prevents users from accessing information classified below their clearance level.
b. It restricts users from viewing information classified above their clearance level.
c. It ensures that users can only write data to higher classification levels.
d. It mandates encryption for all data at rest and in transit.

Answer: b. It restricts users from viewing information classified above their clearance level. Explanation: The "no-read-up" rule ensures that users cannot access data classified at a higher level than their clearance, protecting sensitive information. Option a misinterprets the rule. Option c aligns with the Biba model. Option d is a security control unrelated to Bell-LaPadula.

343. In the Biba integrity model, which principle prevents low-integrity processes from compromising high-integrity data?
a. No-read-down
b. No-write-up
c. No-write-down
d. No-read-up

Answer: b. No-write-up. Explanation: The "no-write-up" rule ensures that lower-integrity processes cannot alter higher-integrity data, maintaining data integrity. Option a is unrelated to data modification. Option c protects higher-integrity processes, not data. Option d pertains to Bell-LaPadula, not Biba.

344. A financial institution uses the Clark-Wilson integrity model to secure its transaction systems. Which mechanism enforces the principle of "well-formed transactions"?
a. Role-based access controls (RBAC) for privileged users
b. Input validation and predefined transaction procedures
c. Encryption of all transaction data in transit
d. Separation of data into public and confidential categories

Answer: b. Input validation and predefined transaction procedures. Explanation: The Clark-Wilson model requires transactions to follow specific rules to ensure data integrity, implemented through input validation and predefined procedures. Option a supports access control but does not define transaction rules. Option c addresses confidentiality, not integrity. Option d is unrelated to transaction structure.

345. An organization adopts the Brewer-Nash (Chinese Wall) model to manage conflicts of interest. Which scenario violates the model's principles?
a. A financial analyst accesses data for competing clients within the same industry.
b. A marketing employee is denied access to confidential product development files.
c. An administrator has unrestricted access to client data across industries.
d. A user accesses public data related to a competitor's market trends.

Answer: a. A financial analyst accesses data for competing clients within the same industry. Explanation: The Brewer-Nash model dynamically restricts access to prevent users from accessing data that could create a conflict of interest. Option b aligns with the principle of least privilege. Option c is unrelated to the model's conflict resolution purpose. Option d involves public data, which is not restricted.

346. A company integrates a reference monitor into its security architecture. What is the primary requirement for a reference monitor to be effective?
a. It must perform real-time encryption of all data.
b. It must enforce access control rules without exceptions.
c. It must log all user activities for auditing purposes.
d. It must ensure high availability during system failures.

Answer: b. It must enforce access control rules without exceptions. Explanation: A reference monitor must consistently enforce security policies to ensure the system remains secure. Option a addresses data security but is not a reference monitor requirement. Option c is beneficial but not a core requirement. Option d pertains to availability, not access control.

347. A defense contractor implements the Bell-LaPadula model to secure classified data. Which scenario demonstrates a violation of the "no-write-down" (Star Property) rule?
a. A user with "Top Secret" clearance modifies data classified as "Confidential."
b. A user accesses classified data without authentication.
c. A user copies classified data to an encrypted USB drive.
d. A user denies responsibility for accessing sensitive files.

Answer: a. A user with "Top Secret" clearance modifies data classified as "Confidential." Explanation: The "no-write-down" rule prevents higher-clearance users from writing data to lower classification levels to avoid information leakage. Option b is an access control violation but unrelated to "no-write-down." Option c pertains to data storage, not Bell-LaPadula. Option d involves repudiation, not confidentiality.

348. Which control best enforces the principles of the Biba model in a production environment?
a. Restricting users from accessing both input and output systems simultaneously
b. Preventing lower-integrity processes from writing to higher-integrity data

c. Encrypting all communications between production and development environments
d. Implementing multi-factor authentication for privileged accounts

Answer: b. Preventing lower-integrity processes from writing to higher-integrity data. Explanation: This control aligns with Biba's "no-write-up" principle, protecting the integrity of higher-classified data. Option a addresses conflict of interest, not integrity. Option c pertains to confidentiality, not integrity. Option d enhances authentication but does not implement the Biba model.

349. A pharmaceutical company uses the Clark-Wilson model for its research databases. Which scenario best demonstrates compliance with this model?
a. Researchers are required to use multi-factor authentication to access the database.
b. All research data is encrypted during transmission between labs.
c. Data modifications are only allowed through validated and logged application processes.
d. Researchers are assigned role-based access levels to limit data visibility.

Answer: c. Data modifications are only allowed through validated and logged application processes. Explanation: The Clark-Wilson model ensures data integrity through controlled modification processes and transaction logging. Option a supports authentication but is not specific to the model. Option b addresses confidentiality, not integrity. Option d aligns with access control but does not ensure transactional integrity.

350. A company plans to implement multi-factor authentication (MFA) for securing remote access to sensitive systems. Which method provides the strongest second factor for authentication?
a. A one-time passcode sent via email
b. A biometric fingerprint scan
c. A security question answer
d. A hardware token generating time-based OTPs

Answer: b. A biometric fingerprint scan. Explanation: Biometrics are highly secure as they rely on unique physical characteristics that are difficult to replicate. Option a is less secure as email can be compromised. Option c is weak because security questions are often guessable. Option d is secure but less so than biometrics due to potential token theft.

351. An organization uses Kerberos for authentication. During the process, which entity issues the Ticket Granting Ticket (TGT)?
a. Resource server
b. Authentication server (AS)
c. Ticket Granting Server (TGS)
d. Key Distribution Center (KDC)

Answer: b. Authentication server (AS). Explanation: The AS validates the user and issues the TGT, which is then used to request service tickets. Option a is incorrect as the resource server validates service tickets. Option c issues service tickets but not the TGT. Option d is a broader term encompassing both AS and TGS.

352. An enterprise deploys OAuth 2.0 for securing its APIs. Which flow is most appropriate for a single-page application (SPA) that lacks a secure backend?
a. Authorization Code Grant with PKCE
b. Client Credentials Grant
c. Implicit Grant
d. Resource Owner Password Credentials Grant

Answer: a. Authorization Code Grant with PKCE. Explanation: PKCE enhances the Authorization Code flow by securing it against interception, making it ideal for SPAs. Option b is unsuitable as it requires a backend. Option c is less secure and deprecated for SPAs. Option d involves sharing user credentials, which is discouraged.

353. A Certificate Authority (CA) issues a certificate for a web server. What role does the private key play in securing client-server communication?
a. Verifies the client's identity to the server
b. Encrypts the server's public key for distribution
c. Decrypts data encrypted with the public key
d. Signs the certificate to prove its authenticity

Answer: c. Decrypts data encrypted with the public key. Explanation: The private key decrypts data encrypted with the public key, ensuring only the intended recipient can access it. Option a describes client-side functionality. Option b misrepresents public key distribution. Option d is the CA's role, not the web server's.

354. What is the primary reason for using Online Certificate Status Protocol (OCSP) over Certificate Revocation Lists (CRLs)?
a. OCSP provides real-time certificate status updates
b. OCSP encrypts certificate details for enhanced security
c. OCSP supports self-signed certificates
d. OCSP eliminates the need for a certificate authority

Answer: a. OCSP provides real-time certificate status updates. Explanation: OCSP offers real-time responses, making it more efficient than CRLs. Option b is incorrect; OCSP does not encrypt data. Option c is unrelated to OCSP's purpose. Option d is false as OCSP relies on CAs.

355. In a certificate-based authentication system, what is the primary function of a root Certificate Authority (CA)?
a. Issuing certificates to end users directly
b. Validating intermediate CAs to maintain trust hierarchy
c. Encrypting all communication between entities
d. Generating session keys for secure transactions

Answer: b. Validating intermediate CAs to maintain trust hierarchy. Explanation: The root CA anchors the trust chain by validating intermediate CAs. Option a is typically handled by intermediates. Option c pertains to communication, not certification. Option d describes ephemeral keys, not CA functions.

356. An organization integrates biometric authentication into its security system. What is the primary advantage of biometrics over traditional passwords?
a. Biometrics are easier to reset if compromised
b. They are inherently resistant to brute-force attacks
c. Biometric systems do not require storage of user templates
d. They eliminate the need for multi-factor authentication

Answer: b. They are inherently resistant to brute-force attacks. Explanation: Biometrics rely on unique physical traits, which cannot be brute-forced. Option a is incorrect as biometric compromise is harder to recover. Option c is false since templates are required. Option d is incorrect as biometrics can complement MFA.

357. In the Kerberos authentication process, what is the purpose of the service ticket?
a. It encrypts all data exchanged between the client and server
b. It grants the client access to a specific resource
c. It authenticates the client to the Key Distribution Center (KDC)
d. It validates the server's identity to the client

Answer: b. It grants the client access to a specific resource. Explanation: Service tickets authenticate the client to access particular services. Option a refers to session encryption. Option c describes the TGT, not the service ticket. Option d is handled by mutual authentication in Kerberos.

358. What is a critical limitation of biometric authentication systems?
a. Difficulty in integrating with other authentication methods
b. High likelihood of producing false positives
c. Inability to reset credentials once compromised
d. Requirement for manual input of biometric data

Answer: c. Inability to reset credentials once compromised. Explanation: Unlike passwords, biometrics cannot be changed if compromised. Option a is false as biometrics integrate well with other methods. Option b is rare in modern systems. Option d misrepresents enrollment processes.

359. A government agency adopts the Bell-LaPadula model to protect classified data. How should the model address the risk of users inadvertently leaking sensitive information through writable media?
a. Enforce the "no-read-up" rule to restrict access to higher classification levels.
b. Apply the "no-write-down" rule to prevent data from being written to lower classifications.
c. Require users to encrypt all files before transferring them to external media.
d. Implement auditing to monitor all file transfer activities.

Answer: b. Apply the "no-write-down" rule to prevent data from being written to lower classifications. Explanation: The "no-write-down" rule ensures that sensitive information cannot be written to a lower classification, preventing leakage. Option a relates to preventing access to higher-level data, not leakage. Option c enhances confidentiality but does not align with Bell-LaPadula's core principles. Option d supports monitoring but does not directly prevent leakage.

360. An organization uses the Biba integrity model to secure critical transaction data. What would violate the "no-read-down" (Simple Integrity Property) rule?
a. A high-integrity process reads data from a lower-integrity source.
b. A user with low-integrity clearance modifies high-integrity records.
c. A system administrator views audit logs without proper access rights.
d. A low-integrity process writes data to a medium-integrity dataset.

Answer: a. A high-integrity process reads data from a lower-integrity source. Explanation: The "no-read-down" rule ensures that high-integrity processes cannot be corrupted by lower-integrity data. Option b violates "no-write-up," not "no-read-down." Option c pertains to access rights but not integrity. Option d violates data modification rules but not the "no-read-down" principle.

361. A technology firm implements the Brewer-Nash (Chinese Wall) model to prevent conflicts of interest among its consultants. Which control best aligns with the model's dynamic access restrictions?
a. Blocking access to sensitive files based on user clearance levels
b. Requiring consultants to authenticate using multi-factor authentication
c. Preventing access to data from competing clients within the same sector
d. Encrypting all data stored on consultant laptops

Answer: c. Preventing access to data from competing clients within the same sector. Explanation: The Brewer-Nash model dynamically enforces restrictions to avoid conflicts of interest by preventing access to competing clients' data. Option a relates to static access control, not dynamic restrictions. Option b strengthens authentication but does not prevent conflicts of interest. Option d protects confidentiality, not access control.

362. A defense contractor enforces the Clark-Wilson model in its manufacturing processes. How does the model ensure that only authorized processes can modify critical data?
a. By validating transactions through Transformation Procedures (TPs)
b. By encrypting all data stored in the manufacturing database
c. By applying multi-factor authentication for all access attempts
d. By segregating critical data into different classification levels

Answer: a. By validating transactions through Transformation Procedures (TPs). Explanation: Clark-Wilson requires TPs to enforce data integrity by ensuring that modifications occur only through authorized processes. Option b ensures confidentiality, not transactional integrity. Option c strengthens authentication but is not a core Clark-Wilson principle. Option d aligns with classification models like Bell-LaPadula, not Clark-Wilson.

363. An organization integrates a reference monitor into its security architecture. Which feature is most critical for the reference monitor to achieve its security goals?
a. The ability to operate independently from the operating system
b. The capacity to enforce mandatory access controls without exceptions
c. The use of advanced cryptographic methods for securing communication
d. The capability to detect and report anomalies in real-time

Answer: b. The capacity to enforce mandatory access controls without exceptions. Explanation: The reference monitor must enforce all security policies consistently, without any bypass. Option a ensures isolation but is secondary to policy enforcement. Option c relates to communication security, not access controls. Option d supports monitoring but is not a core requirement for policy enforcement.

364. A financial institution applies the Biba model to its trading systems. Which scenario complies with the "no-write-down" rule?
a. A high-integrity trading application writes data only to high-integrity databases.
b. A trader with low-integrity access reads data from a high-integrity data source.
c. A high-integrity application writes trade summaries to a lower-integrity report.
d. A system administrator modifies security settings for the trading system.

Answer: a. A high-integrity trading application writes data only to high-integrity databases. Explanation: The "no-write-down" rule ensures that high-integrity processes cannot write to lower-integrity systems to prevent corruption. Option b violates "no-read-up." Option c violates "no-write-down." Option d involves administrative actions unrelated to the rule.

365. A logistics company integrates the Bell-LaPadula model into its supply chain database. What is the primary objective of the model in this scenario?
a. To prevent unauthorized disclosure of sensitive supply chain information
b. To ensure the integrity of shipping and receiving records
c. To optimize database queries for faster data retrieval
d. To enforce encryption for all supply chain transactions

Answer: a. To prevent unauthorized disclosure of sensitive supply chain information. Explanation: The Bell-LaPadula model focuses on maintaining confidentiality by enforcing "no-read-up" and "no-write-down" rules. Option b pertains to integrity, not confidentiality. Option c relates to performance, not security. Option d enhances confidentiality but is not the primary focus of Bell-LaPadula.

366. A developer is implementing input validation for a web application. Which approach provides the strongest protection against injection attacks?
a. Using regular expressions to sanitize input before processing
b. Validating input against a whitelist of allowed values

c. Truncating input fields to a predefined maximum length
d. Filtering input to remove special characters

Answer: b. Validating input against a whitelist of allowed values. Explanation: Whitelisting ensures only explicitly permitted inputs are accepted, effectively preventing injection attacks. Option a is prone to errors and may not handle all cases. Option c limits input size but does not address content. Option d is insufficient for dynamic inputs, as some special characters may be necessary.

367. Which output encoding standard is most effective for mitigating cross-site scripting (XSS) vulnerabilities?
a. HTML encoding all dynamic content
b. UTF-8 encoding for all transmitted data
c. Escaping characters using Base64 encoding
d. Converting all text to Unicode format

Answer: a. HTML encoding all dynamic content. Explanation: HTML encoding prevents browsers from interpreting malicious scripts as executable code. Option b ensures character encoding but does not mitigate XSS. Option c obfuscates data but does not provide contextual encoding. Option d ensures compatibility but does not address XSS risks.

368. An application uses session cookies for authentication. What is the most effective control to prevent session hijacking?
a. Setting the cookie expiration to a long duration
b. Restricting the cookie to the HTTPOnly and Secure attributes
c. Using a shared secret key to sign cookies across sessions
d. Storing session tokens in local storage instead of cookies

Answer: b. Restricting the cookie to the HTTPOnly and Secure attributes. Explanation: HTTPOnly prevents client-side access, and Secure ensures cookies are transmitted only over HTTPS. Option a increases risk by prolonging session duration. Option c does not directly prevent hijacking. Option d is insecure as local storage is accessible to JavaScript.

369. An API requires robust authentication to protect sensitive user data. Which method provides the highest level of security?
a. Static API keys included in every request
b. OAuth 2.0 with client credentials and access tokens
c. Basic authentication with user credentials in the request header
d. Shared IP whitelisting for trusted clients

Answer: b. OAuth 2.0 with client credentials and access tokens. Explanation: OAuth 2.0 provides secure token-based authentication, ensuring minimal credential exposure. Option a risks key compromise due to static usage. Option c exposes credentials in transit and storage. Option d is restrictive and lacks granularity for secure access.

370. Which memory protection mechanism helps prevent buffer overflow attacks in modern operating systems?
a. Data Execution Prevention (DEP)
b. Address Space Layout Optimization (ASLO)
c. Memory Mapping Encryption (MME)
d. Code Refactoring Protection (CRP)

Answer: a. Data Execution Prevention (DEP). Explanation: DEP prevents code execution in non-executable memory regions, mitigating buffer overflow risks. Option b is a misnomer; the correct term is ASLR (Address Space Layout Randomization), which mitigates other attack vectors. Options c and d are not standard mechanisms.

371. What is the best way to enforce secure session management in a distributed microservices architecture?
a. Using a single shared session token across all services
b. Encrypting session tokens with a public-private key pair
c. Issuing stateless tokens signed with a JSON Web Token (JWT) standard
d. Storing session tokens in plaintext within each service's local cache

Answer: c. Issuing stateless tokens signed with a JSON Web Token (JWT) standard. Explanation: JWTs are secure, stateless, and portable across services, making them ideal for distributed architectures. Option a increases the risk of token compromise. Option b ensures encryption but complicates validation. Option d is insecure and violates best practices.

372. What is the most secure approach for validating user input in a RESTful API?
a. Allowing all user input and validating it at the database layer
b. Using client-side JavaScript validation exclusively
c. Validating inputs server-side against defined schema rules
d. Truncating all input fields to a fixed maximum length

Answer: c. Validating inputs server-side against defined schema rules. Explanation: Server-side validation ensures secure and consistent enforcement of input requirements. Option a risks malicious data reaching the backend. Option b is insufficient as client-side validation can be bypassed. Option d reduces size but not malicious content.

373. How can output encoding reduce the risk of command injection attacks in shell scripts?
a. By escaping special characters in user-supplied input
b. By encrypting all input values before processing
c. By truncating input to avoid overloading the command buffer
d. By converting all input to hexadecimal format

Answer: a. By escaping special characters in user-supplied input. Explanation: Escaping special characters prevents them from being interpreted as commands. Option b protects data but does not prevent command injection. Option c avoids buffer overflows but does not mitigate injection. Option d obfuscates input but does not neutralize dangerous characters.

374. Which API authentication method is least secure and should be avoided in production environments?
a. OAuth 2.0 with short-lived access tokens
b. API keys embedded in client-side code
c. Mutual TLS authentication
d. JWTs with a short expiration time

Answer: b. API keys embedded in client-side code. Explanation: Exposing API keys in client-side code risks compromise and unauthorized access. Option a is secure with proper token management. Option c offers robust security through mutual authentication. Option d ensures security with limited exposure.

375. An organization needs to map regulatory requirements to its internal security controls as part of its compliance management process. Which approach best ensures accurate and comprehensive mapping?
a. Using a control framework such as NIST CSF or ISO/IEC 27001
b. Applying automated vulnerability scanners to identify gaps
c. Assigning responsibility to individual business units for self-assessments
d. Limiting mapping to controls already implemented within the organization

Answer: a. Using a control framework such as NIST CSF or ISO/IEC 27001. Explanation: Frameworks like NIST CSF and ISO/IEC 27001 provide a structured approach to mapping requirements to controls, ensuring consistency and completeness. Option b identifies vulnerabilities but does not address regulatory mapping. Option c risks inconsistencies due to subjective assessments. Option d ignores potential gaps between regulations and existing controls.

376. A financial institution deploys compliance monitoring tools to meet regulatory obligations. Which capability is most critical for these tools?
a. Automating periodic vulnerability scans across all endpoints
b. Continuously logging and analyzing activities against policy violations
c. Encrypting compliance-related data stored in internal systems
d. Generating compliance reports on an annual basis

Answer: b. Continuously logging and analyzing activities against policy violations. Explanation: Compliance monitoring tools must identify and flag deviations from policies in real time to ensure regulatory adherence. Option a supports security but does not focus on compliance. Option c protects data confidentiality but is not central to monitoring. Option d lacks the timeliness required for continuous compliance.

377. Which practice ensures that evidence collection procedures for regulatory compliance withstand audit scrutiny?
a. Storing evidence in a centralized system with version control
b. Limiting evidence collection to the most critical controls
c. Encrypting all evidence prior to storage in any system
d. Delegating evidence collection to third-party vendors

Answer: a. Storing evidence in a centralized system with version control. Explanation: A centralized system with version control ensures evidence is organized, tamper-proof, and readily accessible for audits. Option b risks incomplete evidence collection. Option c secures evidence but does not ensure completeness or auditability. Option d introduces dependency and risks around chain of custody.

378. An organization must attest to its security controls during a compliance audit. What is the most reliable method for validating control effectiveness?
a. Conducting self-assessments based on internal documentation
b. Performing third-party assessments using independent auditors
c. Generating detailed activity logs for key security systems
d. Implementing continuous monitoring to identify emerging risks

Answer: b. Performing third-party assessments using independent auditors. Explanation: Independent assessments provide unbiased validation of control effectiveness and meet audit expectations. Option a lacks objectivity. Option c supports documentation but does not validate control performance. Option d is a proactive measure but is not sufficient for attestation.

379. During an audit, the organization must demonstrate its ability to maintain an audit trail. What is the most critical property of an effective audit trail?
a. Real-time generation of detailed system logs
b. Accessibility to all employees for operational transparency
c. Immutability to prevent unauthorized modifications
d. Automation of log deletion after 30 days to save storage

Answer: c. Immutability to prevent unauthorized modifications. Explanation: An audit trail must be immutable to ensure its integrity and reliability for audits. Option a supports log collection but does not guarantee integrity. Option b compromises confidentiality and control. Option d risks non-compliance by destroying evidence prematurely.

380. A multinational company is mapping its security policies to comply with multiple international regulations. Which tool is best suited for managing this process?
a. Governance, Risk, and Compliance (GRC) platform
b. Automated network intrusion detection systems
c. Endpoint detection and response (EDR) tools
d. Custom spreadsheets managed by compliance teams

Answer: a. Governance, Risk, and Compliance (GRC) platform. Explanation: GRC platforms provide centralized management for mapping and tracking compliance across multiple regulations. Option b focuses on network threats, not compliance mapping. Option c secures endpoints but does not manage compliance. Option d is prone to errors and inefficiencies.

381. An organization needs to monitor compliance with data retention policies. Which approach best ensures adherence to regulatory requirements?
a. Using automated tools to enforce data deletion schedules
b. Requiring manual review of data records by administrators
c. Encrypting data to protect against unauthorized access
d. Allowing users to delete records as needed for efficiency

Answer: a. Using automated tools to enforce data deletion schedules. Explanation: Automation ensures consistent application of retention policies and reduces human error. Option b is labor-intensive and prone to oversight. Option c protects data but does not enforce retention policies. Option d risks non-compliance by leaving control to users.

382. A healthcare provider must provide proof of compliance with HIPAA requirements for access control. Which evidence is most appropriate for an audit?
a. Documented user access reviews conducted quarterly
b. Encryption certificates for all stored patient data
c. Backup logs showing full recoverability of patient data
d. Network diagrams of the provider's IT infrastructure

Answer: a. Documented user access reviews conducted quarterly. Explanation: Regular access reviews demonstrate adherence to HIPAA's access control requirements. Option b relates to data confidentiality but not access control. Option c pertains to availability, not access control. Option d provides context but does not validate compliance.

383. A manufacturing facility implements the Purdue Model for Industrial Control Systems (ICS) security. What is the primary purpose of separating Level 2 (control systems) from Level 3 (site operations)?
a. To reduce latency between real-time control systems and operator consoles
b. To ensure compliance with IT network policies
c. To limit the impact of IT network breaches on operational technology (OT) systems
d. To improve data flow between SCADA systems and enterprise applications

Answer: c. To limit the impact of IT network breaches on operational technology (OT) systems. Explanation: The Purdue Model enforces strict separation to isolate IT and OT environments, reducing the risk of cross-network attacks. Option a addresses latency but is not a primary purpose. Option b focuses on compliance, which is secondary. Option d pertains to data flow optimization, not security.

384. Which control best mitigates the risk of unauthorized changes to a Programmable Logic Controller (PLC) configuration?
a. Implementing two-factor authentication for PLC access
b. Encrypting all data exchanged between PLCs and SCADA systems
c. Disabling unused ports on the PLC
d. Regularly patching PLC firmware with the latest updates

Answer: a. Implementing two-factor authentication for PLC access. Explanation: Two-factor authentication ensures only authorized users can make changes to PLC configurations. Option b protects data but does not control access. Option c is a hardening measure but does not address authentication. Option d mitigates vulnerabilities but does not prevent unauthorized changes.

385. A SCADA system uses a legacy communication protocol without built-in encryption. What is the most effective way to secure communications without replacing the protocol?
a. Segregating SCADA traffic onto a dedicated VLAN
b. Wrapping protocol traffic in an IPSec VPN tunnel
c. Using static IP addresses for all SCADA devices
d. Deploying intrusion detection systems on the SCADA network

Answer: b. Wrapping protocol traffic in an IPSec VPN tunnel. Explanation: IPSec provides encryption and integrity for SCADA communications, compensating for the lack of protocol security. Option a enhances segmentation but does not secure data in transit. Option c reduces the risk of address spoofing but does not encrypt traffic. Option d aids detection but does not secure communication.

386. What is the primary security risk of using a flat network architecture in an Operational Technology (OT) environment?
a. Increased complexity in configuring network devices
b. Limited scalability for future infrastructure growth
c. Unrestricted lateral movement by attackers across systems
d. Reduced efficiency in SCADA data collection and reporting

Answer: c. Unrestricted lateral movement by attackers across systems. Explanation: Flat networks lack segmentation, allowing attackers to move laterally once inside. Option a is irrelevant to security risks. Option b concerns scalability, not security. Option d addresses operational inefficiencies, not threats.

387. Which industrial protocol requires the most robust security hardening due to its lack of authentication features?
a. Modbus TCP
b. OPC UA
c. BACnet/IP
d. DNP3 Secure Authentication

Answer: a. Modbus TCP. Explanation: Modbus TCP lacks authentication, making it vulnerable to spoofing and command injection. Option b supports security enhancements like encryption. Option c is less commonly targeted but still needs protection. Option d incorporates secure authentication features.

388. In an ICS environment, what is the primary advantage of implementing OT network segmentation?
a. It improves the performance of time-sensitive data transmissions
b. It isolates critical systems to reduce the risk of unauthorized access
c. It simplifies compliance with industrial safety standards
d. It ensures compatibility between legacy and modern devices

Answer: b. It isolates critical systems to reduce the risk of unauthorized access. Explanation: Network segmentation limits attackers' access to sensitive ICS components. Option a is a secondary benefit. Option c pertains to compliance, not security. Option d relates to compatibility but does not address access control.

389. A PLC in a chemical processing plant is exposed to the internet for remote monitoring. What is the most critical risk associated with this setup?
a. Increased latency in control commands
b. Unauthorized access leading to process disruption

c. Higher operational costs due to bandwidth usage
d. Difficulty in troubleshooting device errors

Answer: b. Unauthorized access leading to process disruption. Explanation: Exposing PLCs to the internet without proper controls can allow attackers to manipulate processes, risking safety and operations. Option a is unrelated to security. Option c pertains to costs, not threats. Option d is irrelevant to security risks.

390. Which security control is most effective in preventing unauthorized firmware updates on SCADA devices?
a. Network-based intrusion prevention systems (IPS)
b. Secure boot mechanisms that verify firmware signatures
c. Periodic audits of device configurations
d. Using default vendor passwords for simplicity

Answer: b. Secure boot mechanisms that verify firmware signatures. Explanation: Secure boot ensures that only authorized firmware is installed. Option a detects threats but does not prevent updates. Option c identifies issues but does not actively enforce firmware security. Option d weakens security by enabling easy compromise.

391. When implementing the Purdue Model, what is the primary purpose of Level 1 (basic control) systems?
a. Providing direct data visualization to operators
b. Controlling and automating industrial processes in real time
c. Managing IT infrastructure for industrial applications
d. Securing communication between levels using encryption

Answer: b. Controlling and automating industrial processes in real time. Explanation: Level 1 focuses on real-time control and automation of industrial equipment. Option a is a Level 2 function. Option c pertains to IT infrastructure, not control systems. Option d is not a primary function of Level 1.

392. A financial organization deploys a machine learning model to detect fraudulent transactions. Which technique best mitigates the risk of model poisoning attacks during training?
a. Encrypting the training data before processing
b. Validating and filtering training data for anomalies and inconsistencies
c. Using differential privacy to limit access to the model's predictions
d. Storing the training dataset in a secure offsite location

Answer: b. Validating and filtering training data for anomalies and inconsistencies. Explanation: Validating training data prevents attackers from introducing poisoned data, which could compromise model performance. Option a protects data confidentiality but does not address poisoning. Option c mitigates information leakage, not training manipulation. Option d ensures data availability but does not prevent poisoning.

393. Which strategy best protects machine learning models from adversarial attacks?
a. Using adversarial training to enhance the model's robustness against malicious inputs
b. Encrypting the model weights to prevent unauthorized access
c. Disabling gradient-based optimization to minimize attack vectors
d. Limiting API access to authenticated users only

Answer: a. Using adversarial training to enhance the model's robustness against malicious inputs. Explanation: Adversarial training involves exposing the model to adversarial examples during training, improving its resilience. Option b protects the model from theft but not manipulation. Option c would hinder model training effectiveness. Option d reduces access risks but does not directly address adversarial inputs.

394. During a routine audit of an AI system, a security analyst discovers discrepancies in the training dataset. What is the most likely risk posed by this issue?
a. Increased model accuracy due to reduced data variation
b. Reduced trust in the model's predictions and outputs
c. Unintentional exposure of proprietary data in the training process
d. Longer training times due to inconsistencies in data structure

Answer: b. Reduced trust in the model's predictions and outputs. Explanation: Discrepancies in the training data can lead to inaccurate or biased models, undermining trust in predictions. Option a is incorrect as data discrepancies degrade, not enhance, accuracy. Option c relates to privacy, not accuracy. Option d pertains to efficiency but not trust.

395. A healthcare provider implements model integrity verification for its AI-based diagnostic tool. Which approach best ensures the integrity of the deployed model?
a. Signing the model with a digital certificate to detect unauthorized modifications
b. Encrypting the model file to prevent reverse engineering
c. Limiting the model's deployment to an isolated on-premises environment
d. Using regular backups to ensure availability of the original model

Answer: a. Signing the model with a digital certificate to detect unauthorized modifications. Explanation: Digital signatures ensure that any changes to the model are detected, maintaining integrity. Option b protects confidentiality, not integrity. Option c enhances security but does not verify integrity. Option d ensures availability, not tamper detection.

396. Which method mitigates the risk of adversarial examples targeting a machine learning model in production?
a. Encrypting all incoming data before processing
b. Applying input sanitization and feature normalization at inference
c. Training the model exclusively on publicly available datasets
d. Restricting access to the model's API to internal users only

Answer: b. Applying input sanitization and feature normalization at inference. Explanation: Input sanitization and normalization reduce the effectiveness of adversarial manipulations designed to exploit model vulnerabilities. Option a focuses on confidentiality but not robustness. Option c limits training scope and does not mitigate adversarial risks. Option d controls access but does not prevent malicious inputs.

397. An e-commerce platform uses a recommendation system powered by machine learning. What is a key risk if training data validation is not performed?
a. The system may prioritize items based on customer reviews.
b. Recommendations may favor specific products due to biased data.
c. System performance may degrade due to increased API calls.
d. Model predictions may require additional hardware resources.

Answer: b. Recommendations may favor specific products due to biased data. Explanation: Unvalidated training data may introduce bias, resulting in unfair or skewed recommendations. Option a is unrelated to data validation. Option c pertains to scalability, not bias. Option d concerns performance, not data quality.

398. What is the primary purpose of using differential privacy in machine learning?
a. Enhancing the scalability of the model during training
b. Preventing leakage of sensitive training data from model outputs
c. Accelerating the model's inference speed during production
d. Encrypting all data stored within the training environment

Answer: b. Preventing leakage of sensitive training data from model outputs. Explanation: Differential privacy ensures that individual data points cannot be inferred from the model's outputs, protecting user privacy. Option a concerns performance, not privacy. Option c pertains to inference efficiency, not privacy. Option d addresses data at rest, not privacy.

399. An AI security framework mandates periodic model retraining. What is the primary security benefit of this practice?
a. Enhancing model accuracy by incorporating recent data trends
b. Detecting and mitigating poisoning attacks introduced over time
c. Reducing storage requirements for older model versions
d. Increasing model interpretability for compliance purposes

Answer: b. Detecting and mitigating poisoning attacks introduced over time. Explanation: Regular retraining helps identify and counteract poisoned data that may have infiltrated earlier datasets. Option a improves performance but is not the primary security benefit. Option c relates to storage management, not security. Option d enhances explainability but does not address poisoning.

400. A research lab employs an ML model for image classification. Which practice ensures the model's resilience against black-box adversarial attacks?
a. Logging all API requests for anomaly detection
b. Limiting the number of queries allowed per user
c. Adding random noise to model outputs to obscure patterns
d. Regularly patching the model with updated algorithms

Answer: b. Limiting the number of queries allowed per user. Explanation: Query limitations reduce the ability of attackers to infer the model's behavior and craft adversarial inputs. Option a supports anomaly detection but does not directly prevent black-box attacks. Option c reduces transparency but risks degrading accuracy. Option d improves model updates but does not specifically target black-box attacks.

401. A DevOps team is deploying containers in production. What is the most effective way to ensure container images are free of known vulnerabilities before deployment?
a. Use a trusted public repository for all container images
b. Scan images for vulnerabilities during the CI/CD pipeline
c. Apply runtime security tools to monitor container behavior
d. Limit access to the container registry using role-based access control (RBAC)

Answer: b. Scan images for vulnerabilities during the CI/CD pipeline. Explanation: Scanning images in the CI/CD pipeline ensures that vulnerabilities are identified and addressed before deployment. Option a provides no guarantee of vulnerability-free images. Option c monitors runtime but does not prevent vulnerabilities. Option d controls access but does not address vulnerabilities in images.

402. Which runtime security control is most effective for detecting anomalous activity in containers?
a. Implementing network segmentation between container clusters
b. Deploying tools that monitor system calls and file access
c. Using a static analysis tool to evaluate container source code
d. Restricting container runtime to specific hardware nodes

Answer: b. Deploying tools that monitor system calls and file access. Explanation: Monitoring system calls and file access identifies deviations from normal container behavior. Option a isolates clusters but does not monitor activity. Option c is for pre-runtime evaluation. Option d limits deployment locations but does not monitor runtime actions.

403. A Kubernetes cluster administrator wants to secure inter-container communication. Which policy best achieves this?
a. Applying a deny-all ingress and egress network policy by default
b. Encrypting all container network traffic using TLS
c. Assigning static IP addresses to each container for traffic tracking
d. Deploying containers with privileged access for improved communication

Answer: a. Applying a deny-all ingress and egress network policy by default. Explanation: A default deny policy ensures that only explicitly permitted communications are allowed, enhancing security. Option b encrypts traffic but does not restrict flows. Option c provides tracking but not access control. Option d increases risk by enabling excessive privileges.

404. What is the primary risk of using an insecure container registry?
a. Slower image pull times during deployment
b. Potential distribution of images containing malware
c. Lack of version control for container images
d. Inefficient storage management for container layers

Answer: b. Potential distribution of images containing malware. Explanation: Insecure registries can host and distribute malicious images, compromising deployments. Option a affects performance, not security. Option c pertains to operational inefficiencies. Option d relates to storage, not registry security.

405. A container orchestration platform allows pods to run as root by default. What is the most critical risk of this configuration?
a. Increased susceptibility to denial-of-service (DoS) attacks
b. Containers can execute privileged commands on the host
c. Higher resource usage by privileged containers
d. Difficulty in logging container activity

Answer: b. Containers can execute privileged commands on the host. Explanation: Running as root allows containers to access host resources, increasing the risk of system compromise. Option a describes attack scenarios but is not directly linked to root access. Option c pertains to performance, not security. Option d is unrelated to privilege levels.

406. Which practice enhances container registry security?
a. Using public registries exclusively to streamline operations
b. Requiring signed container images before deployment
c. Allowing anonymous read access for faster image pulls
d. Storing all container images locally without validation

Answer: b. Requiring signed container images before deployment. Explanation: Signed images ensure integrity and authenticity, reducing the risk of compromised images. Option a exposes the environment to risks. Option c facilitates access but sacrifices control. Option d bypasses validation, increasing security risks.

407. A DevSecOps team notices a container attempting to access sensitive files on the host. What is the best immediate action to mitigate this behavior?
a. Disable the container and deploy a patched version
b. Move the container to a less critical node
c. Enable logging for all file access activities
d. Use a runtime security policy to restrict host file access

Answer: d. Use a runtime security policy to restrict host file access. Explanation: Runtime policies enforce restrictions on container behavior, preventing access to sensitive host files. Option a stops the issue but does not address runtime enforcement. Option b only relocates the problem. Option c provides monitoring but no enforcement.

408. In a containerized environment, why is it critical to avoid using containers with unscanned base images?
a. It increases deployment times due to unverified layers
b. Unscanned images may contain vulnerabilities exploitable at runtime
c. Such images can only be deployed on legacy orchestration platforms
d. They are incompatible with modern monitoring tools

Answer: b. Unscanned images may contain vulnerabilities exploitable at runtime. Explanation: Unscanned base images may introduce security risks that affect the entire application. Option a describes inefficiency, not security. Option c is false, as base images are platform-independent. Option d is irrelevant to scanning.

409. A Kubernetes administrator needs to enforce the principle of least privilege for containers. Which configuration is most appropriate?
a. Enable pod security policies to restrict privileged operations
b. Use host networking to simplify container communication
c. Assign all pods the same service account for resource access
d. Configure containers to run with unlimited CPU and memory quotas

Answer: a. Enable pod security policies to restrict privileged operations. Explanation: Pod security policies enforce restrictions such as disallowing privileged operations, ensuring adherence to least privilege. Option b exposes the host network. Option c increases risk by over-permissioning. Option d is unrelated to privilege.

410. A financial institution adopts a Zero Trust Architecture (ZTA). Which of the following principles ensures that access to resources is granted only when explicitly verified?
a. Network segmentation to isolate sensitive data
b. Just-in-time access controls to limit authorization duration
c. Role-based access control for predefined permissions
d. Data encryption at rest and in transit

Answer: b. Just-in-time access controls to limit authorization duration. Explanation: Just-in-time access minimizes the exposure window by granting access only when needed and revoking it promptly after use. Option a enhances network isolation but does not enforce access verification. Option c provides static access but lacks real-time verification. Option d protects data but does not govern access.

411. An organization deploys Zero Trust Network Access (ZTNA) to secure its remote workforce. What is the primary advantage of ZTNA over traditional VPN solutions?
a. Restricting access to specific IP ranges for enhanced security
b. Ensuring least privilege access to individual applications rather than the entire network
c. Enforcing multi-factor authentication (MFA) for all remote users
d. Encrypting all traffic between endpoints and corporate networks

Answer: b. Ensuring least privilege access to individual applications rather than the entire network. Explanation: ZTNA limits access to specific resources, reducing the attack surface compared to VPNs, which provide broad network access. Option a supports security but is not unique to ZTNA. Option c is a common security feature but not exclusive to ZTNA. Option d ensures confidentiality but does not address resource segmentation.

412. During a Zero Trust implementation, what is the most effective strategy for enforcing micro-perimeter controls around sensitive data?
a. Using dynamic firewalls to block unauthorized traffic

b. Implementing data encryption and tokenization across all databases
c. Deploying software-defined perimeters (SDPs) to segment resources
d. Applying role-based access controls to all data repositories

Answer: c. Deploying software-defined perimeters (SDPs) to segment resources. Explanation: SDPs create micro-perimeters by dynamically controlling access to resources based on user and device context. Option a enhances boundary security but does not provide fine-grained segmentation. Option b protects data confidentiality but does not enforce perimeters. Option d governs access but lacks the flexibility of micro-perimeterization.

413. Which practice ensures continuous trust verification in a Zero Trust Architecture?
a. Conducting quarterly security audits of user access logs
b. Implementing real-time monitoring of user and device behavior
c. Enforcing strong password policies for all employees
d. Encrypting sensitive data with public-key cryptography

Answer: b. Implementing real-time monitoring of user and device behavior. Explanation: Continuous trust verification requires dynamic monitoring to detect anomalies and reassess trustworthiness in real-time. Option a is periodic and does not ensure continuous verification. Option c strengthens authentication but does not address ongoing trust. Option d protects data but is unrelated to trust verification.

414. An organization employs an identity-centric security model as part of its Zero Trust strategy. What is the primary benefit of this approach?
a. Eliminating the need for endpoint security solutions
b. Centralizing access management through identity-based policies
c. Replacing firewalls with secure cloud-based access solutions
d. Preventing physical breaches through biometric authentication

Answer: b. Centralizing access management through identity-based policies. Explanation: Identity-centric security centralizes control by basing access decisions on user and device identities. Option a ignores complementary security layers. Option c misrepresents identity-based approaches. Option d is a specific application of identity but not a primary benefit.

415. A multinational company integrates just-in-time (JIT) access controls into its Zero Trust framework. Which use case best demonstrates JIT access in practice?
a. Temporary elevation of administrative privileges for system updates
b. Restricting access to data centers based on physical location
c. Blocking external IP addresses from accessing internal resources
d. Applying encryption to emails containing sensitive information

Answer: a. Temporary elevation of administrative privileges for system updates. Explanation: JIT access provides time-limited privileges, minimizing the exposure of high-level permissions. Option b is a static control, not JIT. Option c focuses on network security, not temporal access. Option d protects confidentiality but does not address privilege timing.

416. In a Zero Trust implementation, what is the best way to manage device compliance for accessing corporate resources?
a. Requiring endpoint detection and response (EDR) solutions on all devices
b. Enforcing device posture assessments before granting access
c. Implementing virtual private network (VPN) tunnels for secure connections
d. Conducting weekly manual inspections of device configurations

Answer: b. Enforcing device posture assessments before granting access. Explanation: Device posture assessments verify compliance with security policies before allowing resource access, aligning with Zero Trust principles. Option a enhances endpoint security but does not enforce compliance checks. Option c provides secure connections but lacks compliance validation. Option d is impractical and inefficient.

417. An organization uses Zero Trust Network Access (ZTNA) to protect its hybrid cloud environment. Which feature of ZTNA enhances security compared to traditional network controls?
a. Granting access based on geographic location
b. Providing application-level segmentation and dynamic access policies
c. Allowing unrestricted access to trusted IP addresses
d. Monitoring bandwidth usage to optimize network performance

Answer: b. Providing application-level segmentation and dynamic access policies. Explanation: ZTNA enforces granular, context-aware access controls at the application level, reducing risks inherent in broad network access. Option a is insufficient for Zero Trust. Option c contradicts the principle of least privilege. Option d focuses on performance, not security.

418. An organization plans to implement automated data labeling for a cloud storage environment. Which capability is essential for ensuring consistent and accurate labeling across all stored data?
a. Integration with existing backup and disaster recovery systems
b. Machine learning models trained to identify sensitive data patterns
c. Encryption of metadata associated with labeled files
d. Manual review of each labeled file before applying access controls

Answer: b. Machine learning models trained to identify sensitive data patterns. Explanation: Machine learning enables automated systems to identify and label sensitive data accurately based on predefined patterns. Option a supports continuity but does not aid labeling. Option c enhances security but does not improve accuracy. Option d negates automation benefits.

419. Which classification schema provides the most flexibility for aligning data handling procedures with regulatory requirements?
a. A three-tiered model with labels for public, internal, and confidential data
b. A role-based model assigning access by job responsibilities
c. A context-driven model incorporating sensitivity and usage conditions
d. A departmental model based on organizational structure

Answer: c. A context-driven model incorporating sensitivity and usage conditions. Explanation: Context-driven schemas adapt to varying regulatory and operational needs, providing flexibility. Option a is rigid and lacks granularity. Option b focuses on access control, not classification. Option d is unsuitable for cross-departmental data.

420. A company discovers unclassified sensitive data in a shared network drive. What is the most effective immediate action?
a. Encrypt the entire shared drive to prevent further access
b. Move the data to a secured location and apply appropriate classification
c. Notify all users of the drive about the sensitivity of the data
d. Restrict access to the shared drive for all non-administrative users

Answer: b. Move the data to a secured location and apply appropriate classification. Explanation: Securing and classifying the data ensures proper handling and reduces risk. Option a disrupts legitimate access. Option c increases awareness but does not mitigate risk. Option d limits access but does not address classification.

421. Which feature of Information Rights Management (IRM) ensures that sensitive data remains protected even when shared externally?
a. Encryption of files at rest and in transit
b. Dynamic revocation of access to previously shared files
c. Automated scanning of outgoing emails for sensitive content
d. Role-based access control for internal users

Answer: b. Dynamic revocation of access to previously shared files. Explanation: IRM allows revocation of permissions, ensuring control over shared data. Option a protects data but does not provide control after sharing. Option c prevents unauthorized sharing but does not secure shared data. Option d is unrelated to external sharing.

422. Which data discovery tool capability is critical for supporting compliance with GDPR?
a. Automated scanning of structured and unstructured data repositories
b. Real-time monitoring of data access patterns across the organization
c. Integration with endpoint protection platforms for unified security
d. Support for non-European languages in metadata analysis

Answer: a. Automated scanning of structured and unstructured data repositories. Explanation: Comprehensive scanning ensures identification of personal data across environments, a GDPR requirement. Option b aids security but does not ensure discovery. Option c focuses on endpoint security, not data classification. Option d supports usability but is secondary to discovery.

423. A financial institution uses a four-level classification schema: public, internal, confidential, and restricted. Which data handling procedure aligns with the "restricted" classification?
a. Requiring encryption for all internal email communications
b. Allowing access only within secure, audited environments
c. Storing data in general-purpose file servers with limited access controls
d. Permitting sharing with external partners under non-disclosure agreements

Answer: b. Allowing access only within secure, audited environments. Explanation: Restricted data requires the highest level of security, including controlled and monitored environments. Option a is suitable for lower classifications. Option c lacks sufficient controls. Option d is not restrictive enough for this classification.

424. Which automated labeling capability is most effective for preventing data spillage in a hybrid cloud environment?
a. Applying predefined labels based on file size and type
b. Enforcing labeling policies that propagate across environments
c. Assigning generic labels to all newly created files
d. Restricting labeling automation to on-premises systems

Answer: b. Enforcing labeling policies that propagate across environments. Explanation: Unified labeling prevents inconsistent application of policies in hybrid environments. Option a is insufficient for identifying sensitive data. Option c undermines classification accuracy. Option d limits automation's effectiveness in cloud systems.

425. What is a primary challenge of using manual classification methods in large organizations?
a. Lack of interoperability between classification tools
b. Inconsistency and human error in data labeling
c. Inability to support encryption for classified files
d. High resource consumption during file access audits

Answer: b. Inconsistency and human error in data labeling. Explanation: Manual processes are prone to errors, resulting in misclassified or unclassified data. Option a pertains to tool integration, not manual methods. Option c is unrelated to classification accuracy. Option d impacts operational efficiency but is not exclusive to manual methods.

426. Which IRM feature ensures that classified documents can only be accessed by authorized devices?
a. Multi-factor authentication (MFA) for document access
b. Integration with device management policies
c. Time-based expiration of document access permissions
d. Automated versioning of classified documents

Answer: b. Integration with device management policies. Explanation: Restricting access to managed devices prevents unauthorized use of classified documents. Option a authenticates users but not devices. Option c controls time-based access but not device restrictions. Option d aids tracking but does not enhance access security.

427. An enterprise deploying Zero Trust Architecture mandates multi-factor authentication (MFA) for all critical systems. Which principle of Zero Trust does this requirement support?
a. Data-centric security
b. Continuous trust verification
c. Micro-perimeter implementation
d. Network segmentation

Answer: b. Continuous trust verification. Explanation: MFA reinforces continuous trust verification by requiring additional layers of authentication to confirm user identity. Option a focuses on protecting data at the resource level. Option c deals with access segmentation, not trust validation. Option d addresses network-level isolation.

428. In a Zero Trust model, which strategy is most effective for securing workloads in a hybrid cloud environment?
a. Applying role-based access control (RBAC) to all cloud resources
b. Encrypting data in transit using IPsec tunnels
c. Implementing identity-aware proxies to broker access to resources
d. Disabling public IP addresses for all cloud workloads

Answer: c. Implementing identity-aware proxies to broker access to resources. Explanation: Identity-aware proxies enforce Zero Trust principles by validating user and device context before granting access to workloads. Option a provides static access but lacks dynamic verification. Option b secures data in transit but does not control access. Option d reduces exposure but does not enable granular security.

429. An organization leverages machine learning to analyze user behavior in a Zero Trust environment. What is the primary advantage of this approach?
a. Automating incident response workflows
b. Reducing the need for periodic user access reviews
c. Detecting anomalies indicative of insider threats
d. Encrypting sensitive data before it leaves the network

Answer: c. Detecting anomalies indicative of insider threats. Explanation: Machine learning models identify deviations in user behavior, helping detect insider threats and enhancing Zero Trust capabilities. Option a addresses response, not detection. Option b overlooks the importance of regular reviews. Option d protects data but does not identify anomalies.

430. Which practice aligns with the principle of least privilege in a Zero Trust Architecture?
a. Granting blanket access to all resources for administrators
b. Assigning users access only to applications necessary for their roles

c. Configuring access based solely on IP address location
d. Allowing unrestricted API access for trusted third parties

Answer: b. Assigning users access only to applications necessary for their roles. Explanation: The least privilege principle limits user access to what is required, reducing the attack surface. Option a violates this principle. Option c is insufficient for role-based controls. Option d risks over-permissive access.

431. A Zero Trust Architecture requires organizations to secure east-west traffic within a data center. What is the most effective strategy to achieve this?
a. Enforcing firewalls at the perimeter of the data center
b. Applying micro-segmentation to isolate workloads
c. Disabling lateral movement through hardware-based VLANs
d. Encrypting north-south traffic entering and exiting the data center

Answer: b. Applying micro-segmentation to isolate workloads. Explanation: Micro-segmentation restricts lateral movement within the data center by creating security boundaries around workloads. Option a focuses on the perimeter, not internal traffic. Option c offers basic isolation but lacks granularity. Option d addresses external traffic, not internal.

432. An organization deploys a Zero Trust identity solution. What is a critical factor for ensuring its effectiveness?
a. Frequent rotation of cryptographic keys used for user authentication
b. Integration with endpoint compliance checks before granting access
c. Implementation of time-based one-time passwords (TOTP)
d. Centralization of logging for all authentication attempts

Answer: b. Integration with endpoint compliance checks before granting access. Explanation: Ensuring devices meet compliance requirements is essential to a Zero Trust identity solution, as access depends on both identity and device posture. Option a secures credentials but does not verify endpoints. Option c enhances MFA but is not comprehensive. Option d aids monitoring but does not control access.

433. Which of the following best demonstrates Zero Trust principles in API security?
a. Securing API endpoints with a web application firewall (WAF)
b. Authenticating API requests using OAuth 2.0 and mutual TLS
c. Restricting API access to traffic from known geographic locations
d. Allowing unauthenticated API requests for faster performance

Answer: b. Authenticating API requests using OAuth 2.0 and mutual TLS. Explanation: OAuth 2.0 and mutual TLS enforce strong authentication and encryption, aligning with Zero Trust principles. Option a protects applications but does not govern API authentication. Option c lacks comprehensive security. Option d violates access control principles.

434. A financial organization implements Security Orchestration, Automation, and Response (SOAR) to enhance its incident response capabilities. Which feature of SOAR is most critical for enabling automated containment of a ransomware attack?
a. Automated quarantine of infected endpoints based on predefined playbooks
b. Real-time monitoring of network traffic for anomalies
c. Integration with threat intelligence feeds for malware identification
d. Generating detailed incident reports for post-attack analysis

Answer: a. Automated quarantine of infected endpoints based on predefined playbooks. Explanation: Automated containment relies on predefined playbooks to isolate infected systems and prevent the spread of ransomware. Option b detects anomalies but does not contain incidents. Option c identifies threats but does not address containment. Option d is valuable post-incident but does not mitigate the active attack.

435. An enterprise automates its incident scoring mechanism using machine learning. What is the primary advantage of this approach?
a. Eliminating the need for human oversight in critical incidents
b. Accurately prioritizing incidents based on contextual factors
c. Generating compliance reports with reduced manual effort
d. Detecting zero-day vulnerabilities in real time

Answer: b. Accurately prioritizing incidents based on contextual factors. Explanation: Machine learning improves incident scoring by considering multiple contextual factors, enabling better prioritization. Option a is incorrect because human oversight remains essential. Option c addresses reporting, not scoring. Option d pertains to threat detection, not incident prioritization.

436. Which scenario best illustrates the use of playbook automation in incident response?
a. Automatically disabling compromised user accounts after a phishing attack
b. Conducting a forensic analysis of logs to identify attack vectors
c. Implementing firewalls to block incoming traffic from specific IP ranges
d. Manually correlating alerts from different security tools

Answer: a. Automatically disabling compromised user accounts after a phishing attack. Explanation: Playbook automation involves predefined responses to specific incidents, such as disabling compromised accounts. Option b supports investigation but is not automated. Option c is a proactive control, not an incident-specific response. Option d is manual and contradicts automation.

437. A cybersecurity team integrates automated response workflows into their Security Information and Event Management (SIEM) system. Which feature ensures that responses are not triggered by false positives?
a. Correlating multiple alerts to validate an incident before triggering a response
b. Requiring manual approval for all containment actions
c. Using anomaly detection to identify unusual patterns
d. Logging all responses for post-incident review

Answer: a. Correlating multiple alerts to validate an incident before triggering a response. Explanation: Alert correlation minimizes the risk of acting on false positives by confirming the validity of incidents. Option b reduces automation benefits. Option c supports detection but does not validate actions. Option d aids reviews but does not prevent false positives.

438. What is the primary benefit of using SOAR to optimize incident response workflows?
a. Reducing the overall time to detect threats within the network
b. Streamlining coordination between security tools and team members
c. Enhancing encryption standards for sensitive communications
d. Automating software updates for all security appliances

Answer: b. Streamlining coordination between security tools and team members. Explanation: SOAR optimizes workflows by integrating tools and automating communication, improving response efficiency. Option a relates to detection, not workflow optimization. Option c enhances confidentiality but is unrelated to workflows. Option d addresses maintenance, not response.

439. Which automated containment procedure is most effective against a distributed denial-of-service (DDoS) attack?
a. Blocking malicious traffic using network-layer access controls
b. Generating alerts for excessive bandwidth consumption
c. Encrypting all inbound and outbound traffic during the attack
d. Limiting access to critical systems through manual intervention

Answer: a. Blocking malicious traffic using network-layer access controls. Explanation: Automated network-layer controls can immediately block malicious DDoS traffic, minimizing impact. Option b aids detection but does not contain the attack. Option c ensures confidentiality but does not mitigate the attack. Option d is manual, not automated.

440. A SOC deploys machine learning-based tools to refine incident scoring mechanisms. Which challenge is most likely to arise from this approach?
a. Difficulty in integrating the tools with existing threat intelligence feeds
b. Increased false positives due to lack of adequate training data
c. Delayed incident detection caused by computational overhead
d. Reduced visibility into low-severity incidents

Answer: b. Increased false positives due to lack of adequate training data. Explanation: Insufficient training data may lead to inaccurate scoring, increasing false positives. Option a relates to integration but is less common. Option c is not a typical issue with incident scoring. Option d misunderstands how incidents are scored.

441. What is a key consideration when automating incident response workflows for cloud environments?
a. Ensuring that all responses are aligned with shared responsibility models
b. Restricting automation to prevent modification of cloud configurations
c. Prioritizing encryption of all communications with cloud service providers
d. Limiting workflow automation to public cloud environments only

Answer: a. Ensuring that all responses are aligned with shared responsibility models. Explanation: Automated workflows must respect the shared responsibility model to avoid conflicts with the cloud provider's domain. Option b reduces the effectiveness of automation. Option c enhances security but does not address workflow alignment. Option d unnecessarily limits automation scope.

442. An organization is conducting phishing simulation campaigns as part of its security awareness training. What is the most important metric to evaluate the effectiveness of these campaigns?
a. The number of phishing emails sent during the campaign
b. The click-through rate on simulated phishing links
c. The total time spent on employee training sessions
d. The number of employees reporting simulated phishing emails

Answer: d. The number of employees reporting simulated phishing emails. Explanation: Reporting indicates employees recognize phishing attempts and take appropriate action. Option a tracks volume but not behavior. Option b identifies susceptibility but not improvement. Option c measures effort, not outcomes.

443. Which method is most effective for enhancing employees' resistance to social engineering attacks?
a. Providing annual compliance training sessions
b. Implementing a security champion program in each department
c. Distributing monthly newsletters with social engineering examples
d. Enforcing strict penalties for falling victim to social engineering attempts

Answer: b. Implementing a security champion program in each department. Explanation: Security champions create a culture of vigilance and provide peer guidance. Option a lacks regular engagement. Option c raises awareness but lacks depth. Option d discourages reporting and undermines training goals.

444. A security awareness program requires employees to complete compliance training annually. What is the most effective way to track completion rates across the organization?
a. Using a Learning Management System (LMS) with automated tracking
b. Maintaining a manual spreadsheet updated by department heads
c. Requiring employees to submit email confirmations upon completion
d. Conducting quarterly surveys to assess training participation

Answer: a. Using a Learning Management System (LMS) with automated tracking. Explanation: An LMS centralizes training data and automates tracking for scalability. Option b is prone to errors and inefficiencies. Option c lacks centralization and may not capture all data. Option d assesses perceptions, not completion rates.

445. What is a primary advantage of conducting live social engineering awareness workshops over online training modules?
a. They require fewer organizational resources to implement
b. Participants can practice identifying real-time social engineering tactics
c. Workshop content is more consistent across multiple sessions
d. Online training cannot be customized to address specific threats

Answer: b. Participants can practice identifying real-time social engineering tactics. Explanation: Workshops enable interactive, scenario-based learning to build practical skills. Option a is false as workshops often require more resources. Option c favors online modules for consistency. Option d underestimates the customizability of online training.

446. What is the most significant limitation of phishing simulation campaigns as a sole measure of security awareness effectiveness?
a. They cannot simulate sophisticated spear-phishing attacks
b. They fail to address broader cybersecurity threats beyond phishing
c. They often generate high operational costs for organizations
d. They require advanced technical skills to design and execute

Answer: b. They fail to address broader cybersecurity threats beyond phishing. Explanation: Phishing simulations focus on specific threats, overlooking issues like password hygiene or physical security. Option a is false; sophisticated simulations can be designed. Option c is minor compared to the benefits. Option d is mitigated by third-party tools.

447. An organization launches a security champion program to promote cybersecurity awareness. What is the most important criterion for selecting security champions?
a. Technical expertise in IT security practices
b. Strong communication and leadership skills
c. Experience with compliance auditing processes
d. Familiarity with advanced cybersecurity tools

Answer: b. Strong communication and leadership skills. Explanation: Security champions must effectively communicate and influence peers. Option a is useful but not critical for champions. Option c applies to auditors, not champions. Option d is secondary to advocacy skills.

448. How should the effectiveness of a security awareness program be measured?
a. The number of training sessions completed annually
b. The percentage decrease in security incidents caused by human error

c. The level of engagement in post-training surveys
d. The total cost of the program compared to its initial budget

Answer: b. The percentage decrease in security incidents caused by human error. Explanation: A reduction in incidents reflects real behavioral changes from the program. Option a measures effort, not outcomes. Option c gauges satisfaction but not effectiveness. Option d evaluates cost, not impact.

449. What is a key consideration when designing phishing simulation emails for a global workforce?
a. Using culturally relevant examples to increase realism
b. Ensuring all emails are identical for fairness
c. Including technical jargon to challenge employees' knowledge
d. Repeating the same simulation content to reinforce learning

Answer: a. Using culturally relevant examples to increase realism. Explanation: Tailoring emails improves relatability and training effectiveness. Option b reduces realism. Option c risks alienating non-technical employees. Option d leads to desensitization.

450. Which action demonstrates a failure in security awareness training despite high completion rates?
a. Employees frequently report simulated phishing emails
b. Employees continue to use weak passwords across systems
c. Employees request additional cybersecurity resources
d. Employees challenge suspicious behavior in physical environments

Answer: b. Employees continue to use weak passwords across systems. Explanation: Weak passwords indicate poor retention or application of training content. Option a reflects positive outcomes. Option c shows engagement. Option d demonstrates program success.

451. A company uses Kubernetes to manage its cloud-native applications. Which security control best prevents unauthorized access to sensitive workloads within a Kubernetes cluster?
a. Configuring role-based access control (RBAC) to limit user permissions
b. Using network segmentation to isolate Kubernetes nodes from the public internet
c. Encrypting all application data stored in the cluster
d. Enabling Kubernetes audit logs for detailed activity monitoring

Answer: a. Configuring role-based access control (RBAC) to limit user permissions. Explanation: RBAC ensures that users and services only have the permissions required for their roles, reducing the risk of unauthorized access. Option b enhances network security but does not govern workload permissions. Option c protects data confidentiality but not access control. Option d supports monitoring but does not restrict access.

452. A financial institution uses a service mesh to secure communication between microservices. What is the most critical feature of a service mesh for ensuring secure communication?
a. Encrypting inter-service communication using mTLS
b. Routing traffic dynamically to optimize performance
c. Implementing centralized logging for all service interactions
d. Providing APIs for easy integration with third-party tools

Answer: a. Encrypting inter-service communication using mTLS. Explanation: Mutual TLS (mTLS) ensures encrypted communication and authenticates services, preventing unauthorized access and eavesdropping. Option b focuses on performance, not security. Option c aids visibility but does not secure communication. Option d supports extensibility but is not critical for security.

453. Which strategy best mitigates the risks associated with serverless architectures in a cloud-native environment?
a. Limiting function execution to a predefined runtime duration
b. Deploying the serverless functions in private subnets
c. Using IAM roles to define fine-grained permissions for each function
d. Implementing a Web Application Firewall (WAF) at the cloud perimeter

Answer: c. Using IAM roles to define fine-grained permissions for each function. Explanation: Fine-grained IAM roles enforce the principle of least privilege, reducing the attack surface for serverless functions. Option a minimizes resource usage but does not address permissions. Option b provides isolation but does not mitigate risks from over-permissive access. Option d protects against external threats but does not secure function execution.

454. An e-commerce company implements a cloud-native firewall to protect its workloads. What is the primary advantage of using a cloud-native firewall over a traditional firewall?
a. Enhancing encryption for data in transit
b. Integrating directly with cloud services for granular traffic control
c. Blocking all inbound and outbound traffic by default
d. Simplifying firewall rule management through a command-line interface

Answer: b. Integrating directly with cloud services for granular traffic control. Explanation: Cloud-native firewalls offer integration with cloud platforms, enabling context-aware rules based on service metadata. Option a addresses encryption but is unrelated to firewall capabilities. Option c is a baseline security practice, not unique to cloud-native firewalls. Option d simplifies management but is not the primary advantage.

455. A security team uses a container runtime security tool to detect and mitigate risks in their production environment. Which threat is the tool best suited to address?
a. Network-based attacks from external actors
b. Unauthorized privilege escalation within containers
c. Distributed denial-of-service (DDoS) attacks on cloud resources
d. Loss of data due to insufficient backup policies

Answer: b. Unauthorized privilege escalation within containers. Explanation: Container runtime security focuses on detecting anomalous behaviors, such as privilege escalation, to protect the runtime environment. Option a addresses network security, not runtime risks. Option c pertains to availability, not runtime security. Option d is unrelated to runtime operations.

456. A Kubernetes cluster is configured to deploy applications with minimal security. What is the most immediate step to improve container security?
a. Enforcing image scanning before deployment to detect vulnerabilities
b. Implementing a service mesh to encrypt all inter-service traffic
c. Running all containerized applications with root privileges disabled
d. Setting up monitoring tools to detect resource consumption spikes

Answer: a. Enforcing image scanning before deployment to detect vulnerabilities. Explanation: Image scanning prevents the deployment of containers with known vulnerabilities, addressing risks early in the pipeline. Option b focuses on communication security. Option c is essential but does not mitigate issues originating from unscanned images. Option d improves monitoring but does not directly enhance security.

457. What is the primary function of pod security policies (PSPs) in a Kubernetes environment?
a. Restricting which users can deploy applications within the cluster
b. Defining constraints on how pods can operate, such as disabling privileged escalation
c. Monitoring pod activity for anomalous behaviors in real time
d. Automatically scaling pods to meet application demand

Answer: b. Defining constraints on how pods can operate, such as disabling privileged escalation. Explanation: PSPs enforce security best practices by restricting operational behaviors of pods. Option a pertains to user access, not pod configurations. Option c aligns with monitoring but not operational constraints. Option d relates to scalability, not security.

458. A cloud-native application uses containers to deploy its services. What is the best practice for securely managing container secrets?
a. Storing secrets in environment variables within the container
b. Encrypting secrets and embedding them in container images
c. Using a secrets management tool to dynamically inject secrets at runtime
d. Configuring a single shared secret across all containerized applications

Answer: c. Using a secrets management tool to dynamically inject secrets at runtime. Explanation: Secrets management tools ensure secure, dynamic delivery of secrets without embedding them in the container, reducing risk. Option a risks accidental exposure. Option b makes secrets difficult to update securely. Option d violates the principle of least privilege.

459. A security architect is performing a threat modeling exercise using STRIDE. Which type of threat does the "S" in STRIDE represent?
a. Spoofing
b. Structured query injection
c. Session hijacking
d. System misconfiguration

Answer: a. Spoofing. Explanation: The "S" in STRIDE refers to spoofing, which involves impersonation of an entity to gain unauthorized access. Option b is a specific injection attack, not a STRIDE category. Option c is related to information disclosure, not spoofing. Option d pertains to configuration issues, not authentication threats.

460. During an architecture risk assessment, which factor should be prioritized for evaluation?
a. The compatibility of legacy systems with new applications
b. The likelihood and impact of identified security threats
c. The alignment of system architecture with organizational goals
d. The cost of implementing new infrastructure components

Answer: b. The likelihood and impact of identified security threats. Explanation: Risk assessment focuses on quantifying potential threats and their effects. Option a relates to system integration but is secondary to security risks. Option c addresses strategic alignment, not risk. Option d is important for budgeting but not the primary focus of risk assessment.

461. Which security design pattern is best suited for isolating untrusted code execution in a web application?
a. Secure session management
b. Privilege separation
c. Input validation
d. Sandboxing

Answer: d. Sandboxing. Explanation: Sandboxing isolates code execution, preventing untrusted code from affecting the system. Option a ensures session integrity but does not isolate code. Option b separates user roles, not code. Option c validates inputs but does not address execution isolation.

462. What is the primary purpose of a secure baseline architecture in a cloud environment?
a. Optimizing resource allocation to reduce operational costs
b. Ensuring consistent security configurations across deployments

c. Enhancing compatibility with third-party software providers
d. Improving scalability for high-demand applications

Answer: b. Ensuring consistent security configurations across deployments. Explanation: A secure baseline ensures uniform security controls, reducing the risk of misconfiguration. Option a focuses on cost, not security. Option c enhances integration but does not address baseline security. Option d pertains to performance, not secure configurations.

463. Which methodology best aligns with identifying risks in a system during its design phase?
a. Red team testing
b. Architectural risk analysis
c. Security Information and Event Management (SIEM) deployment
d. Continuous vulnerability scanning

Answer: b. Architectural risk analysis. Explanation: Architectural risk analysis identifies vulnerabilities during design, enabling early mitigation. Option a focuses on live system testing. Option c aids detection but does not address design risks. Option d is useful for deployed systems, not early-phase assessments.

464. A critical component in a secure baseline architecture is misconfigured, leaving administrative ports exposed. What is the best immediate remediation?
a. Enable logging to monitor administrative port activity
b. Restrict port access using network security group rules
c. Notify the system administrator of the misconfiguration
d. Perform a complete rebuild of the baseline architecture

Answer: b. Restrict port access using network security group rules. Explanation: Applying network security controls mitigates the exposure immediately. Option a monitors activity but does not secure the ports. Option c raises awareness but does not resolve the issue. Option d is unnecessary and time-intensive.

465. Which threat modeling methodology uses data flow diagrams (DFDs) to identify potential risks?
a. PASTA (Process for Attack Simulation and Threat Analysis)
b. STRIDE
c. OCTAVE (Operationally Critical Threat, Asset, and Vulnerability Evaluation)
d. FAIR (Factor Analysis of Information Risk)

Answer: b. STRIDE. Explanation: STRIDE often employs DFDs to visualize data flows and identify threats. Option a is focused on attack simulation but not specific to DFDs. Option c uses a risk-driven approach without visual modeling. Option d emphasizes quantifying risks, not modeling data flows.

466. What is the most critical factor when reviewing the security of a new software component in an enterprise architecture?
a. Its licensing and cost structure
b. Its compatibility with existing infrastructure
c. Its adherence to secure coding standards
d. Its availability in open-source and proprietary formats

Answer: c. Its adherence to secure coding standards. Explanation: Adhering to secure coding standards ensures the component minimizes vulnerabilities. Option a affects cost, not security. Option b addresses integration but not risk. Option d considers formats but does not ensure security.

467. A secure baseline architecture specifies encryption for all sensitive data. Which encryption standard provides the strongest protection for data at rest?
a. AES-256
b. RSA-1024
c. DES (Data Encryption Standard)
d. MD5

Answer: a. AES-256. Explanation: AES-256 offers strong, efficient encryption for data at rest. Option b, RSA-1024, is used for key exchanges but is less secure for data storage. Option c is outdated and insecure. Option d is a hashing algorithm, not an encryption standard.

468. An enterprise implements just-in-time privileged access for its IT administrators. What is the primary benefit of this approach in a Privileged Access Management (PAM) strategy?
a. Preventing privilege escalation by enforcing time-based restrictions
b. Reducing the number of privileged accounts within the organization
c. Encrypting all administrative session logs for compliance purposes
d. Automatically rotating privileged account passwords after use

Answer: a. Preventing privilege escalation by enforcing time-based restrictions. Explanation: Just-in-time privileged access minimizes the risk of privilege misuse by granting temporary permissions only when needed. Option b addresses account minimization but is not specific to JIT access. Option c enhances log security but is unrelated to access control. Option d pertains to password management, not JIT access.

469. A company deploys privileged session monitoring tools to enhance its security posture. Which feature is most critical for detecting suspicious activity during a privileged session?
a. Real-time behavioral analysis of user actions
b. Logging all session activities for future audits
c. Encrypting session data to prevent eavesdropping
d. Blocking access from untrusted IP addresses

Answer: a. Real-time behavioral analysis of user actions. Explanation: Behavioral analysis identifies anomalous activities as they occur, enabling immediate responses to potential threats. Option b supports forensic investigations but does not detect threats in real time. Option c ensures confidentiality but does not monitor behavior. Option d restricts access but does not monitor ongoing sessions.

470. Which step in privileged account discovery ensures comprehensive identification of all privileged accounts in a hybrid cloud environment?
a. Reviewing Active Directory logs for failed login attempts
b. Scanning both on-premises and cloud environments for privileged account usage
c. Analyzing application logs for hardcoded administrative credentials
d. Conducting interviews with department heads to identify shared accounts

Answer: b. Scanning both on-premises and cloud environments for privileged account usage. Explanation: A thorough scan of all environments ensures that privileged accounts are identified, regardless of their location. Option a focuses on login issues, not discovery. Option c targets a specific vulnerability but is not comprehensive. Option d relies on manual input, which can be incomplete.

471. A financial institution implements a password vault for privileged account management. What is the key advantage of using a password vault?
a. Preventing unauthorized users from guessing complex passwords
b. Enforcing automatic password rotation for all stored credentials

c. Encrypting passwords to meet regulatory compliance requirements
d. Limiting privileged account usage to a single administrator

Answer: b. Enforcing automatic password rotation for all stored credentials. Explanation: Password vaults ensure secure storage and automatic rotation of passwords, reducing the risk of credential theft. Option a supports password strength but is unrelated to vault functionality. Option c pertains to encryption, a secondary benefit. Option d restricts usage but does not reflect vault functionality.

472. Which control best supports emergency access procedures in a Privileged Access Management framework?
a. Creating a separate superuser account for emergency situations
b. Logging all actions performed during emergency access sessions
c. Requiring biometric authentication for all privileged accounts
d. Implementing a default-deny policy for all privileged access attempts

Answer: b. Logging all actions performed during emergency access sessions. Explanation: Comprehensive logging ensures accountability and supports post-incident reviews for emergency access. Option a introduces risk if the account is not secured. Option c enhances authentication but does not address emergency access. Option d hinders legitimate emergency access.

473. During a security audit, a privileged account is discovered with no recent activity. What is the most appropriate action to mitigate potential risks?
a. Delete the account immediately to prevent misuse
b. Lock the account and review its necessity with stakeholders
c. Change the account's password and monitor it for future activity
d. Assign the account to a different administrator for better oversight

Answer: b. Lock the account and review its necessity with stakeholders. Explanation: Locking the account prevents misuse while allowing stakeholders to determine whether it is still required. Option a risks removing legitimate functionality. Option c secures the account but does not address necessity. Option d introduces potential misuse without justification.

474. An organization integrates PAM with its Security Information and Event Management (SIEM) system. What is the primary benefit of this integration?
a. Centralizing access management for all privileged accounts
b. Enhancing visibility into privileged account activities for threat detection
c. Automating password changes for all privileged accounts
d. Encrypting all privileged session logs for compliance purposes

Answer: b. Enhancing visibility into privileged account activities for threat detection. Explanation: Integrating PAM with SIEM provides comprehensive monitoring and correlation of privileged account activities, improving security insights. Option a pertains to access management, not SIEM integration. Option c supports password management but is unrelated to visibility. Option d focuses on log security but not visibility.

475. A company is deploying a Data Loss Prevention (DLP) solution to monitor outbound emails. Which content inspection rule is most effective for identifying sensitive data in attachments?
a. Scanning for keywords like "confidential" in email subject lines
b. Detecting file extensions commonly used for documents, such as .docx or .pdf
c. Using regular expressions to identify patterns like Social Security numbers
d. Blocking all attachments larger than 5 MB to prevent data exfiltration

Answer: c. Using regular expressions to identify patterns like Social Security numbers. Explanation: Regular expressions allow precise detection of sensitive data formats, such as Social Security numbers. Option a does not inspect attachment content. Option b only identifies file types but not data within. Option d is overly restrictive and not context-sensitive.

476. Which factor is critical for the successful implementation of a DLP policy across an organization?
a. Centralizing DLP policy creation within the IT department
b. Aligning DLP policies with existing data classification schemes
c. Limiting DLP monitoring to high-level executives' communications
d. Applying identical DLP policies across all departments to ensure consistency

Answer: b. Aligning DLP policies with existing data classification schemes. Explanation: Integrating data classification ensures that DLP policies apply to relevant data based on its sensitivity. Option a limits stakeholder involvement, reducing effectiveness. Option c neglects non-executive risks. Option d ignores department-specific requirements.

477. What is the primary advantage of endpoint DLP controls compared to network DLP solutions?
a. Detecting and preventing data exfiltration via encrypted traffic
b. Monitoring user activity on devices even when offline
c. Identifying sensitive data in cloud storage applications
d. Enforcing stricter access control policies for internal servers

Answer: b. Monitoring user activity on devices even when offline. Explanation: Endpoint DLP controls protect data on devices regardless of network connectivity. Option a pertains to network DLP solutions. Option c applies to cloud DLP, not endpoints. Option d is unrelated to endpoint-specific protections.

478. A DLP system in a hybrid cloud environment needs to identify and protect sensitive data stored in multiple cloud services. What is the best approach to achieve this?
a. Encrypting all data before uploading to the cloud
b. Deploying a cloud-native DLP solution with API integrations
c. Restricting cloud usage to approved vendors only
d. Scanning all cloud data using on-premises DLP appliances

Answer: b. Deploying a cloud-native DLP solution with API integrations. Explanation: Cloud-native DLP solutions integrate directly with cloud platforms, providing efficient data protection across services. Option a is preventive but does not identify sensitive data. Option c limits flexibility. Option d is inefficient and incompatible with cloud-scale operations.

479. Which method is most effective for ensuring that DLP policies are applied consistently across an organization's global workforce?
a. Implementing separate DLP solutions tailored to regional regulations
b. Using a centralized management console for global policy enforcement
c. Allowing regional IT teams to define their own DLP policies
d. Restricting DLP policies to employees working with classified data

Answer: b. Using a centralized management console for global policy enforcement. Explanation: Centralized management ensures uniform application of policies while allowing regional customization if needed. Option a increases complexity and fragmentation. Option c risks inconsistency. Option d narrows the policy scope unnecessarily.

480. A company's DLP system frequently generates false positives when detecting sensitive data in outbound communications. What is the best way to reduce these false positives?
a. Disabling content inspection for low-risk departments

b. Increasing the sensitivity level of detection rules
c. Refining detection rules to include context-aware analysis
d. Reducing the scope of monitored communication channels

Answer: c. Refining detection rules to include context-aware analysis. Explanation: Context-aware analysis reduces false positives by considering data use and intent. Option a decreases monitoring effectiveness. Option b exacerbates false positives. Option d limits overall protection.

481. What is the primary challenge of integrating data classification with a DLP solution?
a. Ensuring consistent labeling across unstructured data sets
b. Encrypting classified data during transmission
c. Limiting user access to classified data in real time
d. Applying classification labels retroactively to archived data

Answer: a. Ensuring consistent labeling across unstructured data sets. Explanation: Unstructured data is difficult to classify consistently, complicating DLP enforcement. Option b pertains to data protection, not classification. Option c relates to access control, not integration. Option d addresses archiving but is secondary to labeling.

482. How can a DLP system effectively protect sensitive data from being transferred via removable storage devices?
a. Blocking all USB ports on employee devices
b. Encrypting data stored on removable storage devices
c. Applying endpoint DLP controls to monitor and block unauthorized transfers
d. Allowing transfers only during predefined time windows

Answer: c. Applying endpoint DLP controls to monitor and block unauthorized transfers. Explanation: Endpoint DLP controls enable granular monitoring and enforcement of removable storage usage. Option a is overly restrictive. Option b secures data but does not prevent unauthorized transfers. Option d offers limited protection.

483. A DLP policy blocks emails containing sensitive data. However, legitimate business communications are also being blocked. What is the best solution to address this issue?
a. Whitelist specific email domains to bypass the DLP policy
b. Implement a data encryption solution instead of DLP
c. Create an exception workflow for legitimate business needs
d. Disable the DLP policy for all outbound emails

Answer: c. Create an exception workflow for legitimate business needs. Explanation: Exception workflows allow business-critical communications while maintaining security controls. Option a weakens security. Option b complements DLP but does not replace it. Option d removes protection entirely.

484. An enterprise develops a security scorecard to track its risk posture. Which metric is most appropriate for assessing the effectiveness of its access control policies?
a. Percentage of privileged accounts with multi-factor authentication enabled
b. Total number of security incidents reported in the past year
c. Mean time to detect (MTTD) and remediate access-related breaches
d. Percentage of employees who have completed security awareness training

Answer: a. Percentage of privileged accounts with multi-factor authentication enabled. Explanation: This metric directly measures the implementation of access controls, a critical aspect of security posture. Option b is broader and not specific to access control. Option c focuses on detection and response but not policy effectiveness. Option d pertains to user awareness, not access controls.

485. An organization uses a risk metrics framework to evaluate its security risks. Which metric provides the most actionable insight into risk mitigation efforts?
a. Number of open vulnerabilities in high-priority systems
b. Percentage of endpoints running outdated antivirus software
c. Frequency of penetration tests conducted per quarter
d. Volume of phishing emails reported by employees

Answer: a. Number of open vulnerabilities in high-priority systems. Explanation: Tracking open vulnerabilities in critical systems highlights areas requiring immediate mitigation efforts. Option b is useful but less focused on high-priority systems. Option c assesses testing frequency, not risk mitigation. Option d relates to awareness, not direct risk reduction.

486. Which measure best evaluates the effectiveness of implemented security controls?
a. Reduction in the average number of security incidents year over year
b. Number of users accessing security awareness portals monthly
c. Average time spent on compliance audits across departments
d. Percentage of automated responses to detected threats

Answer: a. Reduction in the average number of security incidents year over year. Explanation: Fewer incidents indicate that controls are effectively preventing threats. Option b measures awareness efforts, not control effectiveness. Option c pertains to efficiency in audits, not security performance. Option d measures response automation but not control quality.

487. A security maturity assessment reveals a lack of incident response planning. Which maturity metric best tracks progress in addressing this gap?
a. Percentage of employees trained in incident response annually
b. Number of incidents successfully mitigated through documented procedures
c. Total investment in security training programs over a fiscal year
d. Frequency of updates to the organization's disaster recovery plan

Answer: b. Number of incidents successfully mitigated through documented procedures. Explanation: This metric measures the practical application of incident response planning, directly reflecting maturity improvement. Option a is general and not specific to incident response. Option c measures investment but not effectiveness. Option d tracks planning but not operational maturity.

488. Which operational metric is most relevant for tracking the efficiency of a Security Operations Center (SOC)?
a. Mean time to detect (MTTD) and respond to threats
b. Percentage of SOC personnel holding advanced certifications
c. Total number of alerts generated by intrusion detection systems
d. Frequency of SOC technology upgrades

Answer: a. Mean time to detect (MTTD) and respond to threats. Explanation: MTTD and response times directly measure the SOC's ability to efficiently address security incidents. Option b measures personnel qualifications, not efficiency. Option c tracks alert volume, not SOC performance. Option d relates to technology, not operational efficiency.

489. An organization integrates automated tracking of control effectiveness into its security dashboard. Which metric is most critical to include for evaluating endpoint security?
a. Percentage of endpoints with encryption enabled
b. Number of endpoints infected by malware in the past month
c. Total storage capacity used by endpoint backup solutions
d. Average cost of endpoint replacement during breaches

Answer: a. Percentage of endpoints with encryption enabled. Explanation: This metric directly reflects the effectiveness of endpoint security controls in protecting sensitive data. Option b measures impact but not control effectiveness. Option c pertains to storage management, not security. Option d relates to cost, not control quality.

490. A security team uses security scorecards to report progress to the board. Which high-level metric is most suitable for demonstrating organizational security improvements?
a. Reduction in risk exposure for critical assets
b. Number of phishing emails blocked by security filters
c. Total hours spent on employee security training
d. Frequency of password resets across departments

Answer: a. Reduction in risk exposure for critical assets. Explanation: Risk reduction aligns with board-level priorities and reflects meaningful security improvements. Option b is tactical and less strategic. Option c shows effort but not outcomes. Option d lacks relevance to overall improvements.

491. An organization adopts a risk metrics framework for vendor security assessments. What is the most relevant metric to assess third-party risk?
a. Number of third-party vendors audited annually
b. Percentage of vendors compliant with cybersecurity standards
c. Average time to onboard new vendors into security systems
d. Total cost of vendor security breach incidents

Answer: b. Percentage of vendors compliant with cybersecurity standards. Explanation: Vendor compliance reflects the security posture of third-party partners and their risk to the organization. Option a tracks audit frequency, not compliance. Option c focuses on onboarding efficiency, not risk. Option d measures impact but not current posture.

492. A company is implementing 802.1X for network access control. Which component acts as the intermediary between the supplicant and the authentication server during the authentication process?
a. RADIUS server
b. Authenticator
c. Supplicant
d. Network switch

Answer: b. Authenticator. Explanation: The authenticator (often a switch or wireless access point) forwards authentication messages between the supplicant and the RADIUS server (authentication server). Option a validates credentials but does not forward them. Option c is the client device seeking authentication. Option d is too generic and does not clarify its role.

493. MAC address filtering is used to secure a wireless network. What is the most significant limitation of this method?
a. It requires frequent software updates to function correctly
b. It cannot block unauthorized devices with dynamic IP addresses
c. MAC addresses can be easily spoofed by attackers
d. It is incompatible with WPA3 encryption standards

Answer: c. MAC addresses can be easily spoofed by attackers. Explanation: MAC address filtering is ineffective against attackers who can spoof authorized addresses. Option a is false; no updates are required. Option b conflates IP and MAC functionalities. Option d is incorrect as MAC filtering operates independently of encryption protocols.

494. Which posture assessment feature best ensures that endpoint devices comply with security policies before gaining network access?
a. Scanning for unpatched operating systems during authentication

b. Verifying the endpoint's MAC address against a trusted list
c. Requiring multifactor authentication for user access
d. Logging user activity after network connection

Answer: a. Scanning for unpatched operating systems during authentication. Explanation: Posture assessment checks compliance with security policies like patch management. Option b is part of basic access control, not posture assessment. Option c ensures identity verification but does not evaluate device compliance. Option d monitors activity but does not enforce policy before access.

495. A company provides a guest Wi-Fi network for visitors. What is the best practice to ensure security on the guest network?
a. Enabling SSID broadcast to simplify connectivity
b. Using WPA2-Enterprise encryption with guest accounts
c. Segregating the guest network from internal networks
d. Requiring guests to install security certificates on their devices

Answer: c. Segregating the guest network from internal networks. Explanation: Segmentation prevents guest users from accessing sensitive internal resources. Option a simplifies usability but does not enhance security. Option b is unnecessarily complex for guests. Option d creates a poor user experience without providing significant security benefits.

496. In a Network Admission Control (NAC) system, which factor is most critical for allowing or denying access?
a. User's geographical location during login attempts
b. Device compliance with security policies
c. User's session duration on the network
d. Type of applications used after authentication

Answer: b. Device compliance with security policies. Explanation: NAC ensures only compliant devices gain network access, reducing risk. Option a is secondary to device compliance. Option c does not impact admission decisions. Option d pertains to post-access monitoring, not admission control.

497. What is the primary security advantage of using 802.1X over MAC address filtering?
a. It supports dynamic VLAN assignment for authenticated users
b. It prevents spoofing of IP addresses on the network
c. It simplifies access control by bypassing the authentication process
d. It requires manual configuration for every connected device

Answer: a. It supports dynamic VLAN assignment for authenticated users. Explanation: 802.1X allows dynamic VLAN assignment, enhancing flexibility and security. Option b is unrelated; 802.1X focuses on authentication. Option c is false as 802.1X requires robust authentication. Option d is incorrect; manual configuration is needed in MAC filtering, not 802.1X.

498. A company implements posture assessment to check for endpoint compliance. Which tool is most effective for assessing endpoints before granting access?
a. Intrusion detection system (IDS)
b. Endpoint detection and response (EDR) platform
c. Network access control (NAC) solution
d. Security Information and Event Management (SIEM)

Answer: c. Network access control (NAC) solution. Explanation: NAC solutions assess endpoint compliance with policies before allowing network access. Option a detects intrusions but does not enforce compliance. Option b protects endpoints but does not evaluate posture pre-access. Option d aggregates logs but does not control admission.

499. Why is a posture assessment critical in bring-your-own-device (BYOD) environments?
a. To verify the user's identity before granting access
b. To ensure that personal devices meet security standards
c. To reduce bandwidth usage by limiting device connections
d. To enforce static IP address allocation for each device

Answer: b. To ensure that personal devices meet security standards. Explanation: Posture assessment verifies BYOD compliance, reducing the risk of insecure devices accessing the network. Option a focuses on identity, not device posture. Option c is unrelated to security posture. Option d pertains to networking, not compliance.

500. What is a key limitation of guest network security when using a shared passphrase for all visitors?
a. It increases administrative overhead for onboarding guests
b. It exposes internal network resources to all connected guests
c. It allows unauthorized individuals to reuse the passphrase
d. It requires guests to authenticate multiple times during a session

Answer: c. It allows unauthorized individuals to reuse the passphrase. Explanation: Shared passphrases can be shared, compromising network security. Option a is false; shared passphrases reduce administrative effort. Option b is incorrect if segmentation is applied. Option d is unrelated; guests authenticate once per session.

501. A healthcare organization uses operational metrics to track the effectiveness of its data loss prevention (DLP) program. Which metric best reflects the program's success in protecting sensitive data?
a. Number of attempted data exfiltration incidents blocked by DLP controls
b. Percentage of employees trained on data classification policies
c. Volume of encrypted files stored on the corporate network
d. Frequency of DLP policy updates applied to endpoint systems

Answer: a. Number of attempted data exfiltration incidents blocked by DLP controls. Explanation: This metric measures the program's ability to prevent unauthorized data movement, a direct indicator of DLP effectiveness. Option b pertains to awareness, not effectiveness. Option c tracks encryption usage but not data loss prevention. Option d supports policy updates but does not measure success in preventing incidents.

502. A security maturity assessment reveals inconsistencies in vulnerability management. Which maturity metric best tracks progress in addressing this gap?
a. Percentage of critical vulnerabilities patched within SLA timelines
b. Total number of system vulnerabilities detected across all assets
c. Average time spent on patch management for critical systems
d. Number of vulnerability scans conducted per month

Answer: a. Percentage of critical vulnerabilities patched within SLA timelines. Explanation: Tracking SLA adherence ensures timely resolution of high-risk vulnerabilities, demonstrating improved maturity. Option b measures volume, not effectiveness. Option c focuses on time efficiency, not outcomes. Option d relates to scanning frequency, not vulnerability management.

503. An organization implements control effectiveness measures for its identity and access management (IAM) program. Which metric is most appropriate for evaluating its impact?
a. Percentage of failed login attempts flagged as suspicious

b. Number of access requests processed per month
c. Percentage of dormant accounts deactivated within 30 days
d. Frequency of role-based access policy updates

Answer: c. Percentage of dormant accounts deactivated within 30 days. Explanation: Deactivating dormant accounts reduces the attack surface and ensures IAM controls are effective. Option a pertains to detection, not control effectiveness. Option b measures operational workload, not impact. Option d supports policy updates but not direct control outcomes.

504. Which security performance metric best demonstrates an organization's preparedness for a ransomware attack?
a. Average recovery time for encrypted systems during simulated attacks
b. Percentage of endpoints running real-time antivirus protection
c. Total bandwidth consumed by data backups across the network
d. Frequency of employee phishing simulation exercises

Answer: a. Average recovery time for encrypted systems during simulated attacks. Explanation: Recovery time reflects the organization's ability to respond to ransomware, demonstrating preparedness. Option b measures prevention, not recovery. Option c pertains to backup infrastructure, not attack preparedness. Option d supports awareness but not operational readiness.

505. A global enterprise uses security scorecards to prioritize investments. Which metric is most effective for identifying areas requiring immediate attention?
a. Number of high-severity incidents reported in the past quarter
b. Total cost of security technology investments for the year
c. Percentage of compliance audit findings marked as resolved
d. Average time to respond to low-severity security events

Answer: a. Number of high-severity incidents reported in the past quarter. Explanation: High-severity incidents indicate critical risks and highlight areas needing immediate attention. Option b tracks spending but does not identify gaps. Option c measures compliance, not risk prioritization. Option d focuses on low-severity events, which are less urgent.

506. An organization tracks security maturity using operational metrics. Which metric best reflects improvements in security awareness among employees?
a. Increase in phishing emails reported by employees
b. Reduction in the number of security incidents per quarter
c. Total hours spent on security awareness training
d. Frequency of compliance audit pass rates

Answer: a. Increase in phishing emails reported by employees. Explanation: Reporting phishing attempts demonstrates employee engagement and heightened awareness. Option b reflects overall security but not awareness. Option c tracks training effort, not outcomes. Option d relates to compliance, not awareness.

507. A manufacturing company deploys IoT sensors to monitor production lines. Which authentication method provides the most secure mechanism for IoT devices in this environment?
a. Pre-shared keys (PSKs) for all devices
b. Public key infrastructure (PKI) using device certificates
c. Basic username and password authentication
d. MAC address whitelisting on the network

Answer: b. Public key infrastructure (PKI) using device certificates. Explanation: PKI ensures secure, scalable, and unique authentication for IoT devices using cryptographic certificates. Option a is less secure as PSKs can be shared or exposed. Option c is unsuitable due to weak credentials. Option d is vulnerable to MAC address spoofing.

508. An organization uses IoT devices on the same network as critical business systems. What is the most effective way to mitigate risks associated with this setup?
a. Deploy IoT devices on a dedicated VLAN with strict access controls
b. Configure static IP addresses for all IoT devices
c. Enable encryption for all IoT traffic over the existing network
d. Use intrusion detection systems to monitor IoT traffic for anomalies

Answer: a. Deploy IoT devices on a dedicated VLAN with strict access controls. Explanation: Segmentation isolates IoT devices from critical systems, reducing the risk of lateral movement by attackers. Option b aids identification but does not isolate devices. Option c protects data but not access. Option d detects threats but does not prevent unauthorized access.

509. Which firmware security control is critical to prevent malicious updates on IoT devices?
a. Encrypting firmware images during distribution
b. Restricting firmware updates to internal devices only
c. Validating firmware signatures before installation
d. Storing firmware updates on secure local servers

Answer: c. Validating firmware signatures before installation. Explanation: Signature validation ensures only trusted and unaltered firmware is applied to devices. Option a protects images in transit but does not verify their integrity. Option b restricts access but does not validate updates. Option d secures storage but not firmware integrity.

510. What is the most significant challenge when protecting IoT data at rest on resource-constrained devices?
a. Limited support for strong encryption algorithms
b. High costs of integrating encryption into device designs
c. Increased latency in accessing encrypted data
d. Complexity in managing encryption keys across devices

Answer: a. Limited support for strong encryption algorithms. Explanation: IoT devices often lack the processing power to implement robust encryption, making data protection challenging. Option b is secondary to technical constraints. Option c is more relevant to data in transit. Option d is a key management issue but not specific to encryption on constrained devices.

511. How can device lifecycle management minimize security risks in an IoT deployment?
a. By ensuring all devices are replaced after a fixed period of time
b. By applying firmware updates and revoking access for decommissioned devices
c. By limiting the number of devices connected to the network
d. By enabling remote access for troubleshooting during device failures

Answer: b. By applying firmware updates and revoking access for decommissioned devices. Explanation: Lifecycle management ensures devices are updated and access is removed when they are retired. Option a is costly and impractical. Option c does not address lifecycle security. Option d introduces risks without addressing end-of-life management.

512. What is a common vulnerability associated with IoT device boot processes, and how can it be mitigated?
a. Unsecured debug interfaces; mitigated by disabling unused ports
b. Lack of encrypted boot loaders; mitigated by enabling secure boot
c. Hardcoded credentials; mitigated by enforcing complex password policies

d. Insecure wireless protocols; mitigated by restricting access to local networks

Answer: b. Lack of encrypted boot loaders; mitigated by enabling secure boot. Explanation: Secure boot ensures the integrity of the boot process by validating signed firmware. Option a addresses a separate issue not specific to boot processes. Option c is unrelated to boot security. Option d addresses network security, not boot vulnerabilities.

513. In an IoT environment, what is the primary goal of implementing data minimization practices?
a. To reduce the volume of data transmitted over the network
b. To ensure compliance with data privacy regulations
c. To minimize the storage requirements on IoT devices
d. To limit the risk of exposing unnecessary sensitive information

Answer: d. To limit the risk of exposing unnecessary sensitive information. Explanation: Data minimization reduces the attack surface by collecting only essential data. Option a is a secondary benefit. Option b is an outcome, not the primary goal. Option c addresses resource constraints, not security.

514. Which feature is essential for ensuring secure decommissioning of IoT devices?
a. Secure erasure of stored data
b. Manual logging of decommissioned devices
c. Recycling of device components
d. Retaining device configurations for future reuse

Answer: a. Secure erasure of stored data. Explanation: Securely wiping data prevents sensitive information from being recovered after decommissioning. Option b aids tracking but does not secure data. Option c is environmentally friendly but not a security measure. Option d risks exposing outdated configurations.

515. How can a lightweight encryption protocol like DTLS improve IoT data protection?
a. By providing a transport-layer alternative to TLS for resource-constrained devices
b. By encrypting device firmware images to prevent tampering
c. By replacing public key cryptography with symmetric encryption
d. By increasing device compatibility with legacy IoT systems

Answer: a. By providing a transport-layer alternative to TLS for resource-constrained devices. Explanation: DTLS is optimized for constrained environments, enabling secure communication. Option b is unrelated to runtime communication. Option c misrepresents DTLS, which supports both key types. Option d does not describe DTLS functionality.

516. A multinational corporation uses Remote Desktop Protocol (RDP) for remote administrative access. Which control best mitigates the risk of brute-force attacks on RDP?
a. Configuring account lockout policies after a predefined number of failed attempts
b. Restricting RDP access to a specific geographic region using firewall rules
c. Encrypting RDP traffic using TLS to prevent eavesdropping
d. Enforcing multi-factor authentication for all RDP users

Answer: a. Configuring account lockout policies after a predefined number of failed attempts. Explanation: Account lockout policies effectively limit brute-force attempts by disabling accounts after multiple failed logins. Option b reduces exposure but does not directly mitigate brute-force risks. Option c ensures confidentiality but does not prevent brute-force attempts. Option d strengthens authentication but does not address repetitive failed attempts.

517. An organization uses a Virtual Private Network (VPN) for secure remote access. What is the most effective way to prevent unauthorized access to the VPN?
a. Using pre-shared keys for authentication

b. Enforcing multi-factor authentication for VPN logins
c. Restricting VPN access to non-business hours
d. Monitoring VPN activity for unusual login patterns

Answer: b. Enforcing multi-factor authentication for VPN logins. Explanation: Multi-factor authentication adds a strong layer of security by requiring a second form of verification, significantly reducing the risk of unauthorized access. Option a is less secure than MFA. Option c restricts access but does not verify identity. Option d helps detect threats but does not prevent them.

518. A company implements split tunneling for its VPN users. What is the primary security risk associated with this configuration?
a. Increased latency for critical business applications
b. Exposure of corporate traffic to unsecured networks
c. Reduced visibility into user activity for security teams
d. Overloading of VPN servers due to non-business traffic

Answer: b. Exposure of corporate traffic to unsecured networks. Explanation: Split tunneling allows non-business traffic to bypass the VPN, potentially exposing corporate resources to risks from unsecured networks. Option a is unrelated to security. Option c impacts monitoring but is not the primary risk. Option d concerns performance, not security.

519. An enterprise enforces remote access policies for employees working from home. Which policy most effectively reduces the risk of data breaches?
a. Requiring employees to connect through a VPN before accessing sensitive data
b. Mandating the use of personal devices for non-critical tasks
c. Disabling automatic software updates to reduce system disruptions
d. Allowing unrestricted access to corporate applications for all employees

Answer: a. Requiring employees to connect through a VPN before accessing sensitive data. Explanation: VPNs encrypt data in transit, ensuring secure communication with corporate resources. Option b increases risk by using less secure personal devices. Option c compromises security by leaving systems unpatched. Option d contradicts the principle of least privilege.

520. An organization uses Virtual Desktop Infrastructure (VDI) to secure remote work. Which VDI feature provides the strongest defense against data exfiltration?
a. Centralizing all data storage on corporate servers
b. Requiring users to log in using complex passwords
c. Blocking file transfers between the VDI environment and local devices
d. Encrypting VDI sessions to prevent interception

Answer: c. Blocking file transfers between the VDI environment and local devices. Explanation: Restricting file transfers prevents sensitive data from being moved out of the controlled VDI environment. Option a centralizes data but does not prevent exfiltration. Option b strengthens authentication but does not address data movement. Option d protects data in transit but not exfiltration.

521. A security team implements monitoring for remote access sessions. Which metric is most useful for identifying potential insider threats?
a. Duration of remote sessions exceeding normal working hours
b. Total bandwidth consumed by remote users during sessions
c. Number of support tickets submitted for remote access issues
d. Frequency of connection timeouts during active sessions

Answer: a. Duration of remote sessions exceeding normal working hours. Explanation: Unusual session durations can indicate unauthorized activity, helping identify insider threats. Option b tracks usage but not threat behaviors. Option c pertains to support issues, not threats. Option d indicates technical problems, not malicious intent.

522. A cloud services company requires its employees to use a secure remote desktop solution. What is the most critical factor for ensuring its security?
a. Limiting the number of users with remote desktop access
b. Regularly updating remote desktop software to patch vulnerabilities
c. Using network address translation (NAT) for all remote desktop connections
d. Allowing connections only during predefined business hours

Answer: b. Regularly updating remote desktop software to patch vulnerabilities. Explanation: Updating software ensures known vulnerabilities are mitigated, reducing the risk of exploitation. Option a limits access but does not address vulnerabilities. Option c obscures endpoints but is not a primary security control. Option d improves operational control but is insufficient for security.

523. A development team is implementing OAuth 2.0 for securing an API. What is the primary function of the "authorization server" in this framework?
a. To authenticate API requests based on client credentials
b. To issue access tokens to clients after user authentication
c. To enforce rate limiting policies for API consumers
d. To store user data for identity validation

Answer: b. To issue access tokens to clients after user authentication. Explanation: The authorization server issues tokens that grant access to protected resources. Option a describes authentication, not token issuance. Option c pertains to API gateway functions. Option d relates to identity providers, not the authorization server's role.

524. Which API gateway security feature is most effective for protecting against distributed denial-of-service (DDoS) attacks?
a. Enforcing rate limiting and throttling policies
b. Using static API keys for client authentication
c. Implementing IP whitelisting for trusted clients
d. Encrypting traffic between the gateway and backend services

Answer: a. Enforcing rate limiting and throttling policies. Explanation: Rate limiting and throttling mitigate DDoS by capping the number of requests from a client or IP address. Option b provides basic authentication but does not mitigate DDoS. Option c restricts access but is not dynamic. Option d secures communication but does not address request volumes.

525. An API requires rate limiting to prevent abuse. Which configuration best balances security and user experience?
a. Allowing unlimited requests for authenticated users
b. Setting a global limit of 1,000 requests per second for all users
c. Configuring per-user rate limits based on subscription tiers
d. Rejecting all requests once the global rate limit is reached

Answer: c. Configuring per-user rate limits based on subscription tiers. Explanation: Per-user limits tailored to subscription levels provide security without impacting legitimate users. Option a risks abuse. Option b may penalize legitimate users during high traffic. Option d disrupts service for all users.

526. What is the most significant risk of embedding API keys in client-side code?
a. API keys may become invalid if the client application is updated
b. API keys are not compatible with secure REST API designs

c. API keys can be extracted and reused by unauthorized users
d. API keys increase the complexity of client-side authentication

Answer: c. API keys can be extracted and reused by unauthorized users. Explanation: Exposed API keys in client-side code are vulnerable to theft and misuse. Option a is unrelated to security risks. Option b is incorrect; keys can be used securely if properly managed. Option d pertains to operational complexity, not security.

527. During REST API security testing, a tester identifies that sensitive data is being exposed in error messages. What is the best remediation to address this issue?
a. Encrypt all error messages before returning them to clients
b. Implement detailed error logging on the client side
c. Replace verbose error messages with generic ones
d. Require authentication before returning error messages

Answer: c. Replace verbose error messages with generic ones. Explanation: Generic error messages prevent attackers from gaining insights into system vulnerabilities. Option a is unnecessary; sensitive data should not be included in messages. Option b improves logging but does not secure API responses. Option d adds authentication but does not address the exposure.

528. What is the primary role of OpenID Connect (OIDC) in API security?
a. Providing user identity information through an ID token
b. Managing API keys and secret rotation
c. Enforcing rate limiting based on user behavior
d. Securing backend services with mutual TLS

Answer: a. Providing user identity information through an ID token. Explanation: OIDC extends OAuth 2.0 by including identity tokens to share user identity with the client. Option b pertains to API key management, not OIDC. Option c is unrelated to OIDC's purpose. Option d describes transport security, not identity management.

529. Which API gateway feature enhances security by ensuring only authorized clients access the API?
a. Static IP whitelisting for backend servers
b. JSON Web Token (JWT) validation
c. Enabling cross-origin resource sharing (CORS)
d. Using plaintext traffic between the gateway and clients

Answer: b. JSON Web Token (JWT) validation. Explanation: JWT validation ensures that clients present valid, tamper-proof tokens for API access. Option a restricts server communication but does not validate clients. Option c addresses cross-domain requests but not authentication. Option d weakens security.

530. What is the primary purpose of using HMAC (Hash-based Message Authentication Code) in API key security?
a. To encrypt API keys stored on client devices
b. To validate the integrity and authenticity of API requests
c. To generate unique keys for each client application
d. To replace tokens in secure API communication

Answer: b. To validate the integrity and authenticity of API requests. Explanation: HMAC ensures that API requests have not been tampered with during transmission. Option a pertains to key storage, not HMAC. Option c describes key generation, not HMAC's role. Option d misrepresents HMAC's functionality.

531. A tester identifies a Cross-Origin Resource Sharing (CORS) misconfiguration in an API. What is the primary risk associated with this issue?
a. Exposure of backend API endpoints to unauthorized domains

b. Denial-of-service (DoS) attacks against the API
c. Unencrypted data transmission between the client and server
d. Misuse of rate limiting mechanisms by attackers

Answer: a. Exposure of backend API endpoints to unauthorized domains. Explanation: CORS misconfigurations allow unauthorized domains to access API resources, bypassing security controls. Option b is unrelated to CORS. Option c pertains to encryption, not CORS. Option d involves rate limiting, not CORS policy.

532. A financial organization develops a new security policy template. What is the most critical element to include for ensuring compliance with industry regulations?
a. A list of penalties for non-compliance with the policy
b. References to applicable regulatory requirements and standards
c. Detailed technical instructions for policy enforcement
d. A section on the history and revisions of the policy

Answer: b. References to applicable regulatory requirements and standards. Explanation: Including references to regulatory requirements ensures the policy aligns with industry and legal obligations. Option a provides accountability but does not ensure compliance. Option c supports enforcement but is less critical for compliance. Option d aids version control but is not mandatory for regulatory alignment.

533. Which practice ensures that Standard Operating Procedures (SOPs) are effective and actionable during a security incident?
a. Writing SOPs in technical jargon for accuracy
b. Including roles and responsibilities for each procedural step
c. Limiting SOP distribution to senior security team members
d. Updating SOPs annually, regardless of new risks or technologies

Answer: b. Including roles and responsibilities for each procedural step. Explanation: Clearly defining roles ensures accountability and coordination during incidents. Option a risks alienating non-technical stakeholders. Option c limits accessibility, hindering effectiveness. Option d overlooks the need for timely updates in response to emerging risks.

534. An organization updates its incident response playbooks. Which element is most critical for ensuring their effectiveness during a ransomware attack?
a. A flowchart of the communication escalation process
b. A detailed timeline of previous ransomware incidents
c. An exhaustive list of antivirus software compatible with the organization
d. A section assigning penalties for failing to follow the playbook

Answer: a. A flowchart of the communication escalation process. Explanation: Communication flowcharts facilitate quick decision-making and response coordination, which is critical in a ransomware incident. Option b provides context but does not guide action. Option c is overly specific and not universally applicable. Option d focuses on enforcement rather than response effectiveness.

535. During a change management process, what documentation is most critical for minimizing security risks associated with system updates?
a. A detailed log of all previous changes to the affected system
b. A risk assessment outlining potential impacts of the change
c. A checklist of team members involved in the approval process
d. A summary of training materials provided to IT staff

Answer: b. A risk assessment outlining potential impacts of the change. Explanation: Risk assessments identify potential security risks, ensuring changes are implemented securely. Option a aids tracking but does not minimize risks. Option c ensures accountability but does not address security. Option d supports staff readiness but is less critical during the change process.

536. A multinational company designs security architecture diagrams for its cloud infrastructure. Which feature of these diagrams is essential for ensuring their utility?
a. Highlighting high-traffic network segments in the architecture
b. Annotating all security controls and their respective enforcement points
c. Including data transfer speeds for each network link
d. Providing a detailed history of previous architecture versions

Answer: b. Annotating all security controls and their respective enforcement points. Explanation: Annotation of controls ensures that stakeholders can identify and assess security measures across the architecture. Option a pertains to network performance, not security. Option c focuses on speed, not architecture utility. Option d supports version control but does not directly enhance security.

537. Which practice best ensures that security documentation remains relevant over time?
a. Reviewing and updating all documents on a quarterly basis
b. Assigning a dedicated team to manage and approve updates
c. Archiving older versions of documents in an encrypted repository
d. Including expiration dates for each document to prompt periodic review

Answer: d. Including expiration dates for each document to prompt periodic review. Explanation: Expiration dates ensure timely reviews and updates, maintaining relevance. Option a lacks adaptability to urgent changes. Option b provides oversight but not proactive updating. Option c aids recordkeeping but does not ensure relevance.

538. An organization distributes its incident response playbooks to all employees. What is the best way to ensure employees understand their responsibilities?
a. Requiring employees to acknowledge receipt of the playbooks
b. Conducting regular tabletop exercises using the playbooks
c. Including a glossary of technical terms in the playbooks
d. Making the playbooks available as a download on the intranet

Answer: b. Conducting regular tabletop exercises using the playbooks. Explanation: Tabletop exercises test understanding and ensure employees are prepared to execute their responsibilities during an incident. Option a ensures receipt but not comprehension. Option c aids understanding but does not confirm readiness. Option d ensures access but does not measure understanding.

539. A financial institution is implementing an encryption solution for protecting customer data. Which key management procedure is most critical to prevent unauthorized decryption of sensitive data?
a. Storing encryption keys in an encrypted database alongside the data
b. Rotating encryption keys periodically and securely deleting old keys
c. Using symmetric encryption to reduce the complexity of key management
d. Sharing encryption keys with trusted third-party vendors for redundancy

Answer: b. Rotating encryption keys periodically and securely deleting old keys. Explanation: Key rotation limits the impact of a compromised key, while secure deletion ensures old keys cannot be reused. Option a risks exposure if the database is breached. Option c simplifies management but does not address secure practices. Option d increases risk by involving external parties.

540. Which encryption algorithm is most suitable for securing communication between web clients and servers?
a. Advanced Encryption Standard (AES)
b. RSA (Rivest-Shamir-Adleman)
c. Elliptic Curve Diffie-Hellman (ECDH)
d. Secure Hash Algorithm (SHA-256)

Answer: c. Elliptic Curve Diffie-Hellman (ECDH). Explanation: ECDH provides efficient key exchange for secure communication. Option a is for data encryption, not key exchange. Option b offers encryption but is less efficient than ECDH. Option d is a hashing algorithm, not encryption.

541. What is the primary function of a digital signature in securing electronic documents?
a. Encrypting the document to ensure confidentiality
b. Validating the document's authenticity and integrity
c. Securing the document against unauthorized deletion
d. Ensuring the document is accessible only to authorized users

Answer: b. Validating the document's authenticity and integrity. Explanation: Digital signatures verify the sender and ensure the document has not been altered. Option a pertains to confidentiality, not authenticity. Option c is unrelated to signature functions. Option d describes access control, not signature validation.

542. During certificate lifecycle management, what is the most important action when a certificate is revoked?
a. Archiving the revoked certificate for compliance audits
b. Publishing the certificate in a Certificate Revocation List (CRL)
c. Updating all systems using the revoked certificate with new certificates
d. Informing users that the certificate is no longer valid

Answer: b. Publishing the certificate in a Certificate Revocation List (CRL). Explanation: CRLs notify systems to reject revoked certificates, maintaining trust. Option a ensures recordkeeping but does not prevent misuse. Option c is part of renewal, not revocation. Option d informs users but does not address technical enforcement.

543. Which hardware encryption module feature is most critical for securing cryptographic keys?
a. Remote key management capabilities
b. FIPS 140-2 Level 3 compliance
c. High-speed encryption performance
d. Integration with cloud storage platforms

Answer: b. FIPS 140-2 Level 3 compliance. Explanation: FIPS 140-2 Level 3 ensures keys are tamper-resistant and securely managed. Option a supports management but does not guarantee security. Option c focuses on speed, not security. Option d facilitates usage but is not critical for key protection.

544. An organization needs to select an encryption algorithm for encrypting large amounts of data at rest. What is the most appropriate choice?
a. AES-256 in CBC mode
b. RSA-2048
c. Triple DES (3DES)
d. SHA-3

Answer: a. AES-256 in CBC mode. Explanation: AES-256 in Cipher Block Chaining (CBC) mode is efficient and secure for bulk data encryption. Option b is computationally expensive and better suited for small data or key exchange. Option c is outdated and less secure. Option d is a hashing algorithm, not encryption.

545. What is the primary risk of implementing symmetric encryption without proper key distribution procedures?
a. Increased likelihood of encryption algorithm obsolescence
b. Higher susceptibility to cryptanalysis attacks
c. Potential exposure of keys during transfer
d. Reduced encryption speed due to key management complexity

Answer: c. Potential exposure of keys during transfer. Explanation: Symmetric encryption relies on secure key distribution to prevent compromise. Option a concerns algorithm choice, not key management. Option b relates to algorithm strength, not distribution. Option d misrepresents the effect of key distribution on encryption speed.

546. A company plans to use digital signatures for document workflows. What is the most critical requirement for implementing this solution?
a. Using a secure hashing algorithm like SHA-512
b. Encrypting the entire document with a private key
c. Ensuring signatures are created using symmetric keys
d. Applying expiration dates to all signed documents

Answer: a. Using a secure hashing algorithm like SHA-512. Explanation: Secure hashing ensures the integrity of the document being signed. Option b misrepresents signature creation, which uses hashes. Option c is incorrect as digital signatures use asymmetric keys. Option d is optional and not critical for signing.

547. When securing certificates used in Transport Layer Security (TLS), which aspect of certificate lifecycle management is most critical?
a. Using self-signed certificates for internal applications
b. Regularly renewing certificates before their expiration date
c. Generating certificates with a validity period of 10 years
d. Storing certificates in plaintext for easy access

Answer: b. Regularly renewing certificates before their expiration date. Explanation: Renewing certificates ensures uninterrupted security and trust. Option a lacks third-party validation. Option c increases the risk of compromise over time. Option d exposes certificates to unauthorized access.

548. An organization maintains change management documentation for its IT systems. Which element is most critical for ensuring that security impacts are properly addressed during a proposed change?
a. A security approval checklist signed by all stakeholders
b. Documentation of rollback procedures for failed changes
c. A description of the proposed change's business justification
d. An inventory of all affected hardware and software components

Answer: b. Documentation of rollback procedures for failed changes. Explanation: Rollback procedures ensure the organization can quickly revert changes that introduce security vulnerabilities, minimizing risk. Option a supports accountability but does not address mitigation. Option c focuses on business needs, not security. Option d aids planning but does not directly reduce risk.

549. A global enterprise uses security policy templates to standardize its documentation. What is the most effective way to ensure the templates are adaptable across various business units?
a. Writing all templates in technical terms to ensure precision
b. Including customizable sections for unit-specific policies and controls
c. Using the same template for all units to maintain uniformity
d. Limiting the scope of policies to high-level guidelines

Answer: b. Including customizable sections for unit-specific policies and controls. Explanation: Customizable sections allow business units to address unique requirements while maintaining overall consistency. Option a risks excluding non-technical stakeholders. Option c overlooks the diversity of needs across units. Option d sacrifices detail, reducing policy effectiveness.

550. Which approach is most effective for ensuring that security architecture diagrams are actionable during an incident response?
a. Including real-time monitoring tool integrations in the diagrams
b. Designing the diagrams with a focus on aesthetic simplicity
c. Limiting distribution to senior-level engineers for confidentiality
d. Including a section that tracks architecture review meeting minutes

Answer: a. Including real-time monitoring tool integrations in the diagrams. Explanation: Real-time monitoring tools provide actionable insights during incidents, enabling faster responses. Option b prioritizes aesthetics over utility. Option c restricts accessibility unnecessarily. Option d supports recordkeeping but does not aid incident response.

551. During a security audit, outdated Standard Operating Procedures (SOPs) are identified. What is the most effective corrective action to ensure SOPs remain current?
a. Assigning SOP ownership to individual department heads
b. Establishing a centralized repository with version control for all SOPs
c. Scheduling automated reminders for periodic SOP reviews
d. Providing incentives to employees for reporting outdated SOPs

Answer: c. Scheduling automated reminders for periodic SOP reviews. Explanation: Automated reminders ensure consistent review cycles, preventing SOPs from becoming outdated. Option a supports accountability but may not ensure updates. Option b aids organization but does not enforce reviews. Option d encourages feedback but lacks consistency.

552. An organization's incident response playbooks lack clear metrics for success. Which addition best ensures measurable outcomes during an incident?
a. A section detailing the roles and responsibilities of all stakeholders
b. Metrics such as mean time to detect (MTTD) and mean time to respond (MTTR)
c. A checklist of all tools and systems required for effective response
d. A timeline of previous incidents and their resolutions

Answer: b. Metrics such as mean time to detect (MTTD) and mean time to respond (MTTR). Explanation: MTTD and MTTR provide quantifiable benchmarks for assessing the effectiveness of incident response efforts. Option a supports coordination but lacks measurability. Option c is operationally useful but does not measure success. Option d provides historical context but no actionable metrics.

553. A healthcare organization designs a security policy template for its compliance program. Which feature ensures the policy aligns with healthcare-specific regulatory requirements?
a. Detailed examples of non-compliance penalties under GDPR
b. A mapping of policy requirements to HIPAA and HITECH standards
c. References to ISO/IEC 27001 controls for general security best practices
d. An appendix summarizing international privacy regulations

Answer: b. A mapping of policy requirements to HIPAA and HITECH standards. Explanation: Mapping to healthcare-specific regulations ensures the policy directly addresses compliance requirements. Option a focuses on GDPR, which is less relevant in healthcare-specific contexts. Option c provides general guidance but lacks specificity. Option d is too broad for healthcare compliance.

554. An organization plans to conduct a penetration test on its production environment. What is the first step to ensure the test is effective and minimizes operational risks?
a. Executing reconnaissance activities to identify potential targets
b. Obtaining written approval from stakeholders and defining the scope
c. Deploying automated tools to identify vulnerabilities
d. Simulating a denial-of-service attack to assess system resilience

Answer: b. Obtaining written approval from stakeholders and defining the scope. Explanation: Scope definition and stakeholder approval establish boundaries and ensure the test aligns with organizational objectives. Option a is part of the testing phase, not preparation. Option c is a tool-based activity, not a preparatory step. Option d is highly disruptive and typically excluded from most penetration tests.

555. During a vulnerability assessment, a security analyst identifies unpatched software on critical servers. What is the next best step to address this finding?
a. Remove the affected software from production servers immediately
b. Report the issue to the compliance team for documentation
c. Prioritize patch deployment based on risk assessment results
d. Perform a full system reboot to mitigate the vulnerabilities

Answer: c. Prioritize patch deployment based on risk assessment results. Explanation: Risk-based prioritization ensures critical vulnerabilities are addressed first, minimizing potential impact. Option a disrupts operations unnecessarily. Option b delays mitigation without addressing the risk. Option d does not resolve the vulnerabilities.

556. What is the primary goal of a red team exercise?
a. To validate the effectiveness of defensive controls
b. To assess compliance with regulatory frameworks
c. To identify gaps in user training and awareness
d. To demonstrate the organization's incident response capability

Answer: a. To validate the effectiveness of defensive controls. Explanation: Red team exercises simulate real-world attacks to evaluate the efficacy of security measures. Option b is secondary to the exercise's goal. Option c is typically covered by awareness training. Option d is the focus of blue team activities.

557. In a purple team engagement, what is the primary role of the blue team?
a. To actively support and learn from red team activities
b. To execute offensive tactics against the organization's defenses
c. To identify vulnerabilities and suggest remediation steps
d. To audit security policies and ensure regulatory compliance

Answer: a. To actively support and learn from red team activities. Explanation: Purple team engagements foster collaboration between offensive (red) and defensive (blue) teams to improve overall security. Option b describes the red team's role. Option c is the focus of vulnerability assessments. Option d pertains to compliance, not defense activities.

558. Which activity best validates the implementation of security controls during a system upgrade?
a. Running automated vulnerability scans post-upgrade
b. Conducting a pre-deployment penetration test
c. Reviewing change management documentation
d. Applying patches to all components after the upgrade

Answer: b. Conducting a pre-deployment penetration test. Explanation: Penetration testing identifies weaknesses in upgraded systems before deployment. Option a identifies vulnerabilities but lacks the depth of penetration testing. Option c reviews processes but does not test controls. Option d focuses on patch management, not control validation.

559. What is a key limitation of automated vulnerability assessment tools?
a. Inability to detect outdated encryption protocols
b. Excessive resource consumption during scans
c. High false-positive rates requiring manual verification
d. Lack of compliance reporting features

Answer: c. High false-positive rates requiring manual verification. Explanation: Automated tools often flag false positives, necessitating manual validation. Option a is incorrect; most tools detect weak encryption. Option b can occur but is not a key limitation. Option d is false as many tools include compliance reporting.

560. A security team plans to test how employees react to phishing attacks. What methodology should be used?
a. Penetration testing with email spoofing techniques
b. Social engineering simulations as part of red team exercises
c. Automated vulnerability scanning for email servers
d. Incident response tabletop exercises with phishing scenarios

Answer: b. Social engineering simulations as part of red team exercises. Explanation: Red team exercises simulate phishing attacks to test user awareness and security defenses. Option a focuses on technical vulnerabilities, not user behavior. Option c is unrelated to phishing simulations. Option d addresses response planning, not testing.

561. What is the primary benefit of including a purple team exercise in a security testing program?
a. Improved collaboration between offensive and defensive teams
b. Increased automation of vulnerability management processes
c. Reduced costs of penetration testing services
d. Enhanced focus on regulatory compliance requirements

Answer: a. Improved collaboration between offensive and defensive teams. Explanation: Purple team exercises ensure that red and blue teams share insights, improving security posture. Option b is not the focus of purple teaming. Option c pertains to cost management, not collaboration. Option d is unrelated to the exercise's purpose.

562. Which vulnerability assessment scope ensures maximum coverage with minimal operational risk?
a. Scanning only external-facing systems for vulnerabilities
b. Including all systems but excluding active exploitation tests
c. Performing deep scans on high-priority systems only
d. Focusing exclusively on recently deployed applications

Answer: b. Including all systems but excluding active exploitation tests. Explanation: This approach ensures broad coverage while minimizing disruptions. Option a is narrow and excludes internal systems. Option c provides depth but sacrifices breadth. Option d neglects older systems that may still pose risks.

563. A financial organization implements Database Activity Monitoring (DAM) to secure its customer database. Which query analysis technique best detects suspicious activity without prior knowledge of attack patterns?
a. Comparing query execution times against historical averages
b. Identifying queries containing anomalous combinations of SQL commands
c. Logging all queries executed by privileged accounts
d. Monitoring for queries that fail due to syntax errors

Answer: b. Identifying queries containing anomalous combinations of SQL commands. Explanation: Analyzing unusual SQL command combinations helps detect potential threats, such as SQL injection, without relying on predefined patterns. Option a focuses on performance metrics, not security. Option c supports audit trails but does not actively detect threats. Option d identifies errors but does not address malicious queries.

564. Which scenario best illustrates the use of privilege escalation detection in a Database Activity Monitoring system?
a. Alerting on a database user executing administrative queries outside of business hours
b. Blocking queries that attempt to access tables in high-traffic schemas
c. Notifying administrators when a user connects from an unregistered IP address
d. Tracking changes to the database schema during routine maintenance

Answer: a. Alerting on a database user executing administrative queries outside of business hours. Explanation: Privilege escalation detection identifies actions that deviate from a user's normal behavior, such as running administrative commands without authorization. Option b relates to performance, not privilege escalation. Option c pertains to connection monitoring, not privilege misuse. Option d focuses on schema changes, not privilege activity.

565. An e-commerce platform configures anomaly detection rules for its DAM solution. Which rule is most effective for detecting potential insider threats?
a. Identifying excessive SELECT queries executed by a single user in a short time
b. Blocking all UPDATE statements during peak business hours
c. Alerting on failed login attempts across multiple user accounts
d. Monitoring for changes to the database encryption configuration

Answer: a. Identifying excessive SELECT queries executed by a single user in a short time. Explanation: Excessive SELECT queries may indicate data exfiltration attempts, a common insider threat indicator. Option b is overly restrictive and operationally disruptive. Option c addresses authentication issues, not insider threats. Option d pertains to configuration monitoring, not behavioral anomalies.

566. A manufacturing company configures its audit log settings for regulatory compliance. Which configuration is most critical for ensuring complete and actionable logs?
a. Enabling logging of all data modification queries, including INSERT, UPDATE, and DELETE
b. Capturing execution times for all queries to optimize database performance
c. Disabling logging for low-priority queries to save storage space
d. Storing audit logs on the same server as the production database for easy access

Answer: a. Enabling logging of all data modification queries, including INSERT, UPDATE, and DELETE. Explanation: Logging data modification queries ensures traceability and supports compliance by identifying who changed data and when. Option b focuses on performance, not compliance. Option c risks incomplete logs. Option d introduces a single point of failure.

567. An organization uses access pattern monitoring to enhance its database security. Which scenario is most likely to trigger an alert in a well-configured DAM system?
a. A user accessing the same table repeatedly during an 8-hour work shift
b. A user querying a sensitive table for the first time outside their normal job scope
c. A query failing due to exceeding memory allocation limits
d. A database administrator reviewing user permissions during a routine audit

Answer: b. A user querying a sensitive table for the first time outside their normal job scope. Explanation: Access pattern monitoring detects deviations from normal behavior, such as unauthorized access to sensitive tables. Option a reflects routine activity. Option c pertains to resource management, not access. Option d aligns with legitimate administrative tasks.

568. Which audit log configuration best supports forensic analysis following a data breach?
a. Logging only administrative account activity to reduce log volume
b. Capturing query text, user identity, and timestamps for all queries
c. Retaining logs for 30 days to comply with standard practices
d. Encrypting logs without implementing access controls

Answer: b. Capturing query text, user identity, and timestamps for all queries. Explanation: Comprehensive logs provide critical details needed to trace actions and identify breach sources. Option a limits scope and risks missing relevant details. Option c may not provide sufficient historical data. Option d ensures confidentiality but not accessibility for forensic purposes.

569. An organization's DAM system flags a sudden spike in failed queries against a critical table. What is the most likely explanation for this alert?
a. A distributed denial-of-service (DDoS) attack targeting the database server
b. A SQL injection attempt exploiting improperly sanitized inputs
c. Routine maintenance causing temporary query failures
d. Increased user demand for the table during peak hours

Answer: b. A SQL injection attempt exploiting improperly sanitized inputs. Explanation: Multiple failed queries often indicate an attacker probing the database for vulnerabilities, such as SQL injection flaws. Option a relates to network-level threats, not database-specific issues. Option c is predictable and should be preemptively accounted for. Option d reflects normal activity, not malicious behavior.

570. A financial institution integrates privilege escalation detection into its Database Activity Monitoring (DAM) system. Which of the following activities should most likely trigger an alert?
a. A user with read-only access executes a CREATE TABLE statement
b. A database administrator queries sensitive customer data during routine maintenance
c. A scheduled job fails to run due to a permission issue
d. A user accesses the same table multiple times during business hours

Answer: a. A user with read-only access executes a CREATE TABLE statement. Explanation: Privilege escalation detection flags activities that exceed a user's granted permissions, such as executing a CREATE TABLE command with read-only access. Option b is typical administrative activity. Option c indicates an error, not a privilege issue. Option d reflects routine behavior.

571. An e-commerce organization configures query analysis in its DAM system. What query characteristic is most likely to indicate a potential data exfiltration attempt?
a. Use of nested SELECT statements to retrieve data
b. Execution of a query that retrieves an unusually large volume of data
c. Queries that include a JOIN clause spanning multiple tables
d. Queries that fail due to syntax errors

Answer: b. Execution of a query that retrieves an unusually large volume of data. Explanation: Large-volume data queries can indicate exfiltration attempts, especially when performed by users without a clear need. Option a is common and not inherently suspicious. Option c is typical for relational database usage. Option d indicates user error, not malicious intent.

572. A healthcare organization uses anomaly detection rules in its DAM system. Which scenario is most indicative of an insider threat?
a. A user queries the same database table daily as part of their role
b. A user executes SELECT queries on tables unrelated to their job responsibilities

c. A database administrator runs a script to update schema definitions
d. A backup system accesses tables at scheduled intervals

Answer: b. A user executes SELECT queries on tables unrelated to their job responsibilities. Explanation: Anomalous access to unrelated tables can indicate unauthorized or malicious activity. Option a reflects expected behavior. Option c is routine administrative activity. Option d is predictable system behavior.

573. An enterprise designs its audit log configuration to support legal investigations. Which setting best ensures compliance with chain-of-custody requirements?
a. Automatically encrypting logs and limiting access to authorized personnel
b. Deleting logs older than 90 days to conserve storage space
c. Storing logs in plain text for easier search and analysis
d. Configuring logs to overwrite older entries when storage capacity is exceeded

Answer: a. Automatically encrypting logs and limiting access to authorized personnel. Explanation: Encryption and access controls maintain log integrity and confidentiality, ensuring compliance with chain-of-custody standards. Option b risks losing evidence. Option c compromises security. Option d risks destroying critical evidence.

574. Which DAM feature best supports real-time detection of suspicious access patterns in a multi-tenant database environment?
a. Role-based access controls (RBAC) to limit user permissions
b. Threshold-based alerts triggered by unusual query frequencies
c. Data encryption to secure sensitive information at rest
d. Scheduled vulnerability scans to identify misconfigurations

Answer: b. Threshold-based alerts triggered by unusual query frequencies. Explanation: Real-time alerts on anomalous query patterns help identify suspicious behavior in multi-tenant environments. Option a enforces access controls but does not provide real-time detection. Option c secures data but does not monitor activity. Option d is periodic and not real-time.

575. An IT services company configures access pattern monitoring for its database. Which scenario is most likely to result in an actionable alert?
a. A user queries tables in a schema they rarely access
b. A query joins two large tables and takes longer than expected
c. A database backup job fails due to network connectivity issues
d. A query is executed outside of the organization's normal business hours

Answer: a. A user queries tables in a schema they rarely access. Explanation: Accessing rarely used schemas can indicate unauthorized activity or privilege misuse. Option b pertains to performance, not security. Option c indicates a technical issue, not a security incident. Option d may or may not be suspicious without additional context.

576. A security analyst identifies multiple failed login attempts from a single IP address across multiple systems. Which log correlation technique is most effective in determining if this activity is malicious?
a. Performing IP address geolocation analysis
b. Identifying patterns of similar failed attempts across logs
c. Filtering for critical events in the system logs
d. Monitoring the network traffic for bandwidth usage spikes

Answer: b. Identifying patterns of similar failed attempts across logs. Explanation: Correlating failed login attempts across systems helps detect brute-force attacks or malicious patterns. Option a is useful but does not establish intent. Option c may overlook important patterns. Option d focuses on traffic volume, not authentication attempts.

577. An analyst receives a high-priority alert for unusual outbound traffic. What is the first step in triaging this alert?
a. Quarantine the affected device immediately
b. Validate the alert by comparing it with baseline network behavior
c. Notify the incident response team to initiate containment measures
d. Update the SIEM rules to reduce similar alerts in the future

Answer: b. Validate the alert by comparing it with baseline network behavior. Explanation: Validating the alert ensures that it represents a genuine threat before taking action. Option a may cause unnecessary disruptions. Option c is premature without validation. Option d does not address the immediate alert.

578. What is the primary reason for reducing false positives in a security event management system?
a. To lower the cost of managing the system
b. To decrease the workload on the security operations team
c. To ensure critical alerts receive prompt attention
d. To improve compliance reporting accuracy

Answer: c. To ensure critical alerts receive prompt attention. Explanation: Reducing false positives ensures that analysts focus on real threats. Option a is secondary to the main goal. Option b is a benefit but not the primary reason. Option d pertains to reporting, not alert management.

579. A security team categorizes an incident as a "data breach" after discovering sensitive information exfiltration. Which factor was likely critical in this categorization?
a. The volume of data transmitted outside the network
b. The confirmation of unauthorized access to sensitive data
c. The use of encryption during the data transfer
d. The type of malware used to exfiltrate the data

Answer: b. The confirmation of unauthorized access to sensitive data. Explanation: Unauthorized access to sensitive data is the defining characteristic of a data breach. Option a could be normal activity without confirmation of sensitivity. Option c relates to transmission security, not incident categorization. Option d focuses on the method, not the breach itself.

580. During root cause analysis of a malware infection, the analyst identifies a vulnerable web application as the entry point. What is the most effective long-term solution?
a. Isolating the affected systems from the network
b. Applying patches to the vulnerable web application
c. Enhancing monitoring for similar attacks
d. Blocking all incoming traffic to the application

Answer: b. Applying patches to the vulnerable web application. Explanation: Patching addresses the root cause, preventing future exploitation. Option a is a containment measure, not a long-term fix. Option c improves detection but does not resolve the vulnerability. Option d disrupts legitimate usage of the application.

581. Which type of event is most likely to generate false positives in a SIEM?
a. Failed login attempts from a single source
b. Traffic flagged by anomaly-based intrusion detection systems
c. Port scans originating from external IP addresses
d. Antivirus alerts for known malicious signatures

Answer: b. Traffic flagged by anomaly-based intrusion detection systems. Explanation: Anomaly detection often generates false positives due to variations in legitimate activity. Option a is less prone to false positives if thresholds are tuned. Option c is typically accurate but may include benign scans. Option d has low false positive rates due to signature reliability.

582. What is the best approach to determine whether an alert represents a true positive?
a. Reviewing historical logs for similar activities
b. Escalating the alert to the incident response team
c. Investigating the alert against known threat intelligence
d. Suppressing the alert if it matches a previously seen pattern

Answer: c. Investigating the alert against known threat intelligence. Explanation: Threat intelligence helps validate whether the alert aligns with known malicious activity. Option a aids context but does not confirm threat validity. Option b is unnecessary for low-confidence alerts. Option d risks ignoring evolving threats.

583. A SOC analyst categorizes an alert as a "medium-priority event." What should primarily influence this decision?
a. The severity of the potential impact on business operations
b. The number of systems reporting similar alerts
c. The presence of similar alerts in threat intelligence feeds
d. The frequency of the alert within the past 24 hours

Answer: a. The severity of the potential impact on business operations. Explanation: Categorization prioritizes alerts based on their potential effect on operations. Option b may inflate importance without context. Option c provides supporting evidence but is not definitive. Option d indicates volume, not criticality.

584. A SIEM generates multiple alerts for unusual activity on an endpoint. What is the best way to determine whether this endpoint is compromised?
a. Running a full antivirus scan on the endpoint
b. Performing a forensic analysis to identify signs of compromise
c. Quarantining the endpoint to prevent further damage
d. Notifying the affected user to check for suspicious activity

Answer: b. Performing a forensic analysis to identify signs of compromise. Explanation: Forensic analysis provides detailed insights into the activity and confirms compromise. Option a may miss sophisticated threats. Option c is useful but does not confirm compromise. Option d is ineffective for in-depth investigation.

585. A multinational organization implements a formal change management process. Which step is most critical for ensuring the security impact of a proposed change is fully understood?
a. Documenting the business justification for the change
b. Conducting a security impact assessment during the approval phase
c. Scheduling the change during a maintenance window to minimize disruptions
d. Notifying all affected users about the change prior to implementation

Answer: b. Conducting a security impact assessment during the approval phase. Explanation: A security impact assessment identifies potential vulnerabilities introduced by a change and ensures appropriate mitigation strategies are implemented. Option a supports transparency but does not address security. Option c reduces operational disruptions but does not assess security impacts. Option d aids communication but is not critical for security evaluation.

586. The Change Advisory Board (CAB) is reviewing a proposed network architecture update. What is the primary role of the CAB in this context?
a. Conducting penetration testing to identify security vulnerabilities

b. Approving or rejecting changes based on business and security impacts
c. Implementing the approved change in the production environment
d. Assigning roles and responsibilities for post-change validation

Answer: b. Approving or rejecting changes based on business and security impacts. Explanation: The CAB evaluates proposed changes to ensure they align with organizational goals and security policies. Option a pertains to vulnerability assessment but is not a CAB responsibility. Option c relates to implementation, which is performed by technical teams. Option d focuses on validation but is not the CAB's primary role.

587. An organization uses emergency change controls to address a critical system vulnerability. What is the most important step to ensure the emergency change does not introduce additional risks?
a. Implementing the change as quickly as possible to minimize exposure
b. Documenting the change after implementation to maintain compliance
c. Conducting a post-implementation review to evaluate security impacts
d. Limiting the change to systems deemed high priority

Answer: c. Conducting a post-implementation review to evaluate security impacts. Explanation: A post-implementation review ensures the emergency change did not create new vulnerabilities or misconfigurations. Option a prioritizes speed but overlooks security validation. Option b maintains documentation but does not mitigate risks. Option d narrows the scope but does not evaluate the overall impact.

588. During release management, what is the most effective way to validate that a software update complies with security requirements?
a. Performing automated regression testing on all system functions
b. Conducting security-specific tests as part of the staging environment
c. Requiring developers to submit a self-assessment of the update
d. Notifying end users to report issues after deployment

Answer: b. Conducting security-specific tests as part of the staging environment. Explanation: Testing in a controlled environment ensures updates meet security standards before deployment. Option a addresses functionality, not security. Option c lacks objectivity. Option d supports feedback but does not validate security compliance proactively.

589. A company implements configuration validation as part of its change management process. Which tool or practice is most effective for detecting unauthorized changes to configurations?
a. Periodic manual inspections of system configurations
b. Using a configuration management database (CMDB) with automated monitoring
c. Storing configuration baselines in encrypted files for reference
d. Assigning dedicated personnel to review change logs weekly

Answer: b. Using a configuration management database (CMDB) with automated monitoring. Explanation: A CMDB with automated monitoring detects unauthorized changes in real time, ensuring configurations align with baselines. Option a is error-prone and inefficient. Option c provides a reference but does not monitor changes. Option d delays detection and response.

590. What is the primary purpose of a rollback plan in a change management security process?
a. To minimize downtime in case of a failed change implementation
b. To document the original configuration for audit purposes
c. To train staff on alternative methods of handling failed changes
d. To provide evidence of compliance with regulatory requirements

Answer: a. To minimize downtime in case of a failed change implementation. Explanation: Rollback plans allow organizations to quickly revert to a known good state if a change introduces issues, reducing operational disruptions. Option b supports audits but does not address downtime. Option c pertains to training, not recovery. Option d ensures compliance but is not the primary purpose of a rollback plan.

591. An IT team deploys a high-priority security patch to address a critical vulnerability. Which release management practice best ensures the patch does not introduce new vulnerabilities?
a. Releasing the patch during business hours for immediate feedback
b. Requiring all deployments to be approved by the security team
c. Testing the patch in a sandbox environment before deployment
d. Applying the patch only to systems confirmed as affected by the vulnerability

Answer: c. Testing the patch in a sandbox environment before deployment. Explanation: Testing in a sandbox ensures the patch functions as intended and does not introduce additional risks. Option a provides feedback but risks immediate disruptions. Option b supports governance but is not sufficient on its own. Option d narrows scope but does not address unintended effects.

592. A data center implements a multi-factor authentication (MFA) system for physical access. Which combination of factors best aligns with the concept of MFA?
a. A proximity card and a passphrase
b. A biometric fingerprint scan and a retinal scan
c. A one-time PIN and a smartphone proximity check
d. A smart card and a PIN

Answer: d. A smart card and a PIN. Explanation: MFA requires two different factors from distinct categories: something you have (smart card) and something you know (PIN). Option a uses two similar factors (knowledge). Option b uses two biometrics, violating MFA's diversity principle. Option c involves only possession-based factors.

593. An organization deploys biometric access controls at its secure facility. What is the primary limitation of biometric systems?
a. Biometric systems cannot handle multiple user enrollments simultaneously
b. Biometric systems are more prone to false negatives than false positives
c. Biometric data, if compromised, cannot be reset like passwords
d. Biometric systems are ineffective in preventing tailgating

Answer: c. Biometric data, if compromised, cannot be reset like passwords. Explanation: Biometric traits are permanent, making them irreplaceable if breached. Option a is false as systems handle many enrollments. Option b incorrectly characterizes false negatives versus false positives. Option d pertains to physical security design, not biometrics.

594. A company uses visitor management software to track individuals entering secure zones. Which feature is most critical for ensuring compliance with audit requirements?
a. Real-time alerts for unauthorized visitor access attempts
b. Integration with building management systems for seamless operation
c. Automatic logging of visitor check-ins, check-outs, and zones accessed
d. Customizable visitor badges for identification

Answer: c. Automatic logging of visitor check-ins, check-outs, and zones accessed. Explanation: Logging ensures an auditable trail of visitor activities. Option a provides proactive security but not compliance evidence. Option b enhances convenience but does not ensure compliance. Option d aids visibility but is secondary to logging.

595. Which configuration is critical for implementing security zones within a high-security facility?
a. Using cameras to monitor all access points within the facility
b. Configuring mantraps to separate each security zone
c. Deploying motion detectors to cover open spaces in each zone
d. Installing uniform access controls across all zones

Answer: b. Configuring mantraps to separate each security zone. Explanation: Mantraps enforce controlled transitions between zones, preventing unauthorized movement. Option a aids monitoring but not separation. Option c complements security but does not create zones. Option d contradicts the concept of tiered security levels.

596. What is the primary advantage of integrating environmental monitoring systems with physical access controls in a data center?
a. Simplifying the overall infrastructure management
b. Enhancing protection against unauthorized access during environmental incidents
c. Providing real-time alerts for critical temperature fluctuations
d. Improving compliance with energy efficiency standards

Answer: b. Enhancing protection against unauthorized access during environmental incidents. Explanation: Integration ensures access restrictions during emergencies like fires or floods. Option a addresses management but not security. Option c pertains to environment monitoring alone. Option d is unrelated to access controls.

597. During a security audit, it is discovered that employees regularly hold doors open for others in secure areas. What is the best control to mitigate this issue?
a. Installing badge readers on all entrances
b. Deploying security guards to monitor access points
c. Installing anti-tailgating mechanisms such as optical turnstiles
d. Requiring employees to sign agreements prohibiting tailgating

Answer: c. Installing anti-tailgating mechanisms such as optical turnstiles. Explanation: Physical controls prevent tailgating without relying on employee behavior. Option a enables logging but does not prevent tailgating. Option b is resource-intensive and less effective. Option d addresses policy but not enforcement.

598. What is the most significant risk of relying solely on proximity cards for physical access control?
a. Proximity cards are prone to signal interference in high-density environments
b. Lost or stolen cards can be easily used by unauthorized individuals
c. Proximity cards cannot be integrated with other security systems
d. The physical wear and tear of cards reduces their lifespan

Answer: b. Lost or stolen cards can be easily used by unauthorized individuals. Explanation: Without additional authentication, stolen cards allow easy access. Option a rarely impacts security. Option c is false; cards are highly integrable. Option d is operational, not security-related.

599. A security administrator needs to ensure that only authorized personnel can access high-security zones after hours. What is the most effective solution?
a. Restricting access through time-based policies in the access control system
b. Requiring manual approval by security staff for after-hours entry
c. Deploying motion-activated cameras to monitor high-security zones
d. Setting up biometric access controls for all zones

Answer: a. Restricting access through time-based policies in the access control system. Explanation: Time-based policies automatically enforce restrictions, ensuring compliance. Option b delays operations and is error-prone. Option c is reactive, not preventive. Option d increases security but does not address time restrictions.

600. An e-commerce company conducts load testing for its web application. Which practice best ensures the security of sensitive data during the testing process?
a. Using production databases to simulate real-world traffic patterns
b. Sanitizing sensitive data in test environments before running the tests
c. Conducting the tests during non-business hours to minimize customer impact
d. Running the load tests on external third-party platforms for scalability

Answer: b. Sanitizing sensitive data in test environments before running the tests. Explanation: Sanitizing sensitive data ensures no real customer information is exposed during load testing. Option a risks exposing live data. Option c minimizes disruptions but does not secure sensitive data. Option d introduces risks by involving external platforms without adequate controls.

601. Which DoS protection measure is most effective for maintaining application performance during a volumetric attack?
a. Deploying rate-limiting rules at the application layer
b. Using intrusion detection systems to identify malicious IP addresses
c. Configuring a web application firewall (WAF) to block known attack signatures
d. Scaling up application resources to handle increased traffic

Answer: a. Deploying rate-limiting rules at the application layer. Explanation: Rate-limiting helps control traffic at the application layer, mitigating the impact of volumetric attacks without overloading resources. Option b identifies malicious traffic but does not actively mitigate the attack. Option c protects against specific threats but may not address all volumetric attacks. Option d can be costly and only delays the impact.

602. An organization implements resource limitation controls for its cloud-hosted application. What is the primary benefit of these controls?
a. Preventing a single user from monopolizing shared resources
b. Reducing costs by optimizing resource utilization
c. Blocking unauthorized access to critical application components
d. Enhancing application availability during peak usage periods

Answer: a. Preventing a single user from monopolizing shared resources. Explanation: Resource limitation controls prevent resource exhaustion by restricting excessive usage by individual users or processes. Option b is a secondary benefit, not the primary goal. Option c addresses access control, not resource management. Option d pertains to scalability, not resource limitations.

603. Which metric is most critical when establishing a performance baseline for application security monitoring?
a. Average response time under normal traffic conditions
b. Peak bandwidth usage during heavy traffic periods
c. Number of concurrent users supported by the application
d. Total number of daily transactions processed by the application

Answer: a. Average response time under normal traffic conditions. Explanation: Response time under normal conditions serves as a baseline for detecting performance anomalies caused by potential security incidents. Option b provides insight into capacity but not baseline performance. Option c reflects usage but does not establish a baseline. Option d relates to volume, not performance.

604. An application monitoring system flags a sudden spike in CPU usage on a server hosting critical workloads. Which scenario is most indicative of a security issue?
a. A scheduled batch process running longer than expected
b. An unoptimized query causing increased database load

c. A brute-force attack targeting application login endpoints
d. Routine software updates being applied during peak hours

Answer: c. A brute-force attack targeting application login endpoints. Explanation: A brute-force attack can cause a spike in CPU usage due to repeated authentication attempts. Option a reflects operational inefficiencies, not security issues. Option b pertains to performance tuning. Option d relates to scheduling, not security.

605. During performance testing, an application fails to scale under high traffic loads. Which security risk is most likely to result from this failure?
a. Exposure of sensitive data due to unencrypted traffic
b. Resource exhaustion leading to a denial-of-service (DoS) condition
c. Unauthorized access caused by weak authentication mechanisms
d. Injection attacks exploiting poorly validated inputs

Answer: b. Resource exhaustion leading to a denial-of-service (DoS) condition. Explanation: Failure to scale can cause resource exhaustion, making the application unavailable to legitimate users. Option a pertains to data confidentiality, not performance. Option c relates to access control, not resource management. Option d is unrelated to scaling issues.

606. An organization integrates application monitoring tools with its security information and event management (SIEM) system. What is the primary advantage of this integration?
a. Automating the patching of application vulnerabilities
b. Correlating performance anomalies with potential security incidents
c. Enhancing compliance with regulatory requirements
d. Reducing the number of false-positive alerts in the SIEM system

Answer: b. Correlating performance anomalies with potential security incidents. Explanation: Integration allows the SIEM to identify security incidents linked to abnormal application performance. Option a focuses on vulnerability management, not monitoring. Option c pertains to compliance but is not the primary advantage. Option d supports alerting but is not directly related to integration.

607. An organization is pursuing ISO 27001 certification. Which of the following actions is most critical during the implementation phase?
a. Identifying all data processors and ensuring compliance with GDPR
b. Establishing an information security management system (ISMS)
c. Conducting annual penetration tests to validate security controls
d. Assigning roles and responsibilities for the incident response team

Answer: b. Establishing an information security management system (ISMS). Explanation: ISO 27001 certification revolves around implementing an ISMS, which forms the framework for managing security. Option a relates to GDPR compliance, not ISO 27001. Option c is a control validation measure but not foundational for certification. Option d is important for incident handling but is secondary in ISO 27001 implementation.

608. A SaaS provider wants to achieve SOC 2 compliance to assure customers of its security practices. Which trust service category is mandatory for all SOC 2 reports?
a. Privacy
b. Security
c. Availability
d. Confidentiality

Answer: b. Security. Explanation: Security is the only mandatory trust service category for SOC 2 compliance, ensuring baseline protection. Option a focuses on personal data but is optional. Option c and d are critical but also optional depending on business needs.

609. A payment processing company is preparing for a PCI DSS audit. What is the minimum frequency for conducting internal vulnerability scans on systems handling cardholder data?
a. Monthly
b. Quarterly
c. Semi-annually
d. Annually

Answer: b. Quarterly. Explanation: PCI DSS requires quarterly vulnerability scans to identify and address security weaknesses. Option a exceeds the standard requirement. Option c and d fall short of the compliance standard.

610. Under HIPAA's Security Rule, what is a primary requirement for securing electronic protected health information (ePHI)?
a. Encrypting all ePHI both at rest and in transit
b. Implementing technical safeguards to control access to ePHI
c. Performing annual penetration testing on systems storing ePHI
d. Auditing all ePHI access attempts in real time

Answer: b. Implementing technical safeguards to control access to ePHI. Explanation: HIPAA requires technical safeguards such as access controls to secure ePHI. Option a is not strictly required in all cases under HIPAA. Option c is recommended but not mandatory. Option d is unrealistic for many organizations and not a specific HIPAA requirement.

611. What is the most critical step in achieving GDPR compliance for processing personal data?
a. Encrypting all personal data to ensure confidentiality
b. Appointing a Data Protection Officer (DPO) for the organization
c. Establishing a legal basis for data processing activities
d. Conducting annual training for all employees on GDPR principles

Answer: c. Establishing a legal basis for data processing activities. Explanation: GDPR mandates a valid legal basis for data processing, such as consent or legitimate interest. Option a is a control but not foundational for compliance. Option b is required only for specific organizations. Option d supports compliance but is not central to GDPR requirements.

612. Which control is a unique requirement of PCI DSS that distinguishes it from other frameworks?
a. Developing an incident response plan
b. Implementing a web application firewall (WAF)
c. Encrypting sensitive data at rest
d. Conducting regular security awareness training

Answer: b. Implementing a web application firewall (WAF). Explanation: PCI DSS uniquely requires a WAF to protect web-facing applications. Options a, c, and d are shared requirements across many security frameworks.

613. A healthcare organization is preparing for a HIPAA compliance audit. Which activity best demonstrates adherence to the Security Rule's risk management requirement?
a. Performing a gap analysis against the HIPAA Privacy Rule
b. Documenting periodic risk assessments and implementing mitigations
c. Conducting annual HIPAA training for employees
d. Encrypting all mobile devices used for accessing ePHI

Answer: b. Documenting periodic risk assessments and implementing mitigations. Explanation: Risk management under HIPAA requires organizations to assess and address risks to ePHI. Option a addresses a different rule. Option c is not directly tied to risk management. Option d is a safeguard, not a risk management process.

614. What is the purpose of GDPR's Data Protection Impact Assessment (DPIA)?
a. To document all personal data processing activities within the organization
b. To evaluate the risks associated with high-risk data processing activities
c. To ensure compliance with cross-border data transfer regulations
d. To notify supervisory authorities of a data breach

Answer: b. To evaluate the risks associated with high-risk data processing activities. Explanation: DPIAs are used to identify and mitigate risks for high-risk processing under GDPR. Option a describes data mapping, not DPIAs. Option c is addressed by standard contractual clauses or adequacy decisions. Option d pertains to breach reporting, not risk assessment.

615. Which framework explicitly requires organizations to maintain a documented risk treatment plan?
a. PCI DSS
b. SOC 2
c. ISO 27001
d. HIPAA

Answer: c. ISO 27001. Explanation: ISO 27001 requires a risk treatment plan detailing how identified risks will be managed. Option a focuses on controls for payment data. Option b is focused on reporting, not risk treatment plans. Option d addresses risk but does not mandate a specific treatment plan.

616. An application hosting provider deploys resource limitation controls to prevent abuse of its services. Which configuration best prevents resource exhaustion caused by malicious activity?
a. Setting maximum query execution time for database queries
b. Blocking all traffic from non-whitelisted IP addresses
c. Requiring CAPTCHAs for all login attempts during high traffic periods
d. Restricting API requests to a fixed number per second per user

Answer: d. Restricting API requests to a fixed number per second per user. Explanation: API rate-limiting effectively prevents resource exhaustion by limiting the impact of excessive requests from a single user. Option a focuses on database performance, not broader resource exhaustion. Option b is overly restrictive and impacts legitimate users. Option c reduces spam but does not control resource usage.

617. An online retail company detects a sudden drop in application performance during peak shopping hours. What is the most likely security-related cause?
a. Increased customer traffic exceeding server capacity
b. A distributed denial-of-service (DDoS) attack targeting application endpoints
c. An unoptimized query being executed on the backend database
d. Routine server maintenance scheduled during business hours

Answer: b. A distributed denial-of-service (DDoS) attack targeting application endpoints. Explanation: DDoS attacks aim to overwhelm application resources, causing performance degradation. Option a is operational, not security-related. Option c pertains to performance tuning, not malicious activity. Option d reflects poor scheduling, not an external attack.

618. Which practice best ensures secure load testing in a production-like environment?
a. Using real customer data to simulate accurate traffic patterns
b. Isolating the testing environment from external networks

c. Running load tests during business hours for immediate feedback
d. Integrating load testing tools with live production systems

Answer: b. Isolating the testing environment from external networks. Explanation: Isolation prevents unauthorized access or accidental data leaks during testing. Option a risks exposing customer data. Option c prioritizes operational convenience over security. Option d jeopardizes the integrity of production systems.

619. An organization establishes a performance baseline for its web application. Which security advantage does this baseline provide?
a. Detecting anomalous traffic patterns that may indicate an attack
b. Reducing the likelihood of insider threats by tracking user activity
c. Preventing the deployment of untested application updates
d. Enhancing encryption protocols for sensitive data transmission

Answer: a. Detecting anomalous traffic patterns that may indicate an attack. Explanation: A performance baseline helps identify deviations caused by potential security incidents, such as DDoS attacks. Option b pertains to access control, not performance baselines. Option c focuses on testing processes. Option d relates to data confidentiality, not baselines.

620. During application monitoring, an alert is triggered due to a sudden increase in failed login attempts. What is the most likely cause of this security event?
a. A system administrator performing a routine login audit
b. A brute-force attack targeting user accounts
c. A misconfiguration in the application's authentication module
d. A scheduled database backup conflicting with user authentication

Answer: b. A brute-force attack targeting user accounts. Explanation: A spike in failed login attempts typically indicates a brute-force attack. Option a is routine and not likely to cause such activity. Option c reflects a technical error, not malicious intent. Option d is unrelated to login attempts.

621. An organization deploys a web application firewall (WAF) as part of its performance security strategy. Which attack type is most effectively mitigated by the WAF?
a. Resource exhaustion due to excessive API requests
b. SQL injection attacks targeting backend databases
c. Unauthorized access through stolen credentials
d. Insider threats exploiting privileged user accounts

Answer: b. SQL injection attacks targeting backend databases. Explanation: WAFs analyze and block malicious traffic, such as SQL injection payloads, that target web applications. Option a is better addressed by rate-limiting. Option c involves authentication, not a WAF's primary function. Option d relates to internal misuse, not external threats.

622. A company experiencing intermittent application slowdowns integrates performance and security monitoring. What is the most effective first step to determine if these issues are security-related?
a. Increasing the server's processing capacity during peak usage times
b. Analyzing performance logs for correlations with unusual traffic patterns
c. Disabling unnecessary application features to reduce resource consumption
d. Conducting penetration testing to identify vulnerabilities

Answer: b. Analyzing performance logs for correlations with unusual traffic patterns. Explanation: Reviewing performance logs can reveal security-related anomalies, such as DDoS attacks or malicious traffic. Option a temporarily alleviates slowdowns but does not address security. Option c improves efficiency but does not investigate the root cause. Option d is comprehensive but not the most immediate action.

623. A development team integrates static code analysis into their secure software development lifecycle. What is the primary advantage of static code analysis?
a. It identifies runtime vulnerabilities during application execution
b. It automates the process of applying secure coding guidelines
c. It detects vulnerabilities in the source code without executing it
d. It eliminates the need for manual code reviews by developers

Answer: c. It detects vulnerabilities in the source code without executing it. Explanation: Static code analysis scans code for flaws and security issues before execution, improving early detection. Option a describes dynamic analysis, not static analysis. Option b mischaracterizes static tools; they do not apply guidelines but enforce them. Option d is incorrect; static analysis complements manual reviews, not replaces them.

624. A secure code review reveals an input validation flaw in a web application. Which issue is most likely associated with this finding?
a. Cross-Site Scripting (XSS)
b. Privilege escalation
c. Hardcoded credentials
d. Insecure cryptographic storage

Answer: a. Cross-Site Scripting (XSS). Explanation: XSS vulnerabilities commonly stem from improper input validation, allowing malicious scripts to execute. Option b is unrelated to input validation. Option c pertains to authentication, not input validation. Option d concerns data protection, not user inputs.

625. What is the purpose of a code review checklist in a secure development process?
a. To define development timelines for secure coding projects
b. To standardize the evaluation criteria for detecting security flaws
c. To automate vulnerability detection during code compilation
d. To ensure compatibility with third-party libraries

Answer: b. To standardize the evaluation criteria for detecting security flaws. Explanation: A checklist ensures consistency and thoroughness in identifying issues during reviews. Option a focuses on project management, not code quality. Option c describes static analysis tools, not manual reviews. Option d is unrelated to the purpose of a checklist.

626. During a secure code review, the reviewer identifies a use of predictable session IDs in the application. What is the potential security impact of this issue?
a. It enables unauthorized access through session hijacking
b. It allows attackers to inject malicious scripts into the application
c. It increases the risk of brute-force attacks on the login system
d. It exposes sensitive data during transmission

Answer: a. It enables unauthorized access through session hijacking. Explanation: Predictable session IDs allow attackers to guess or reuse them, leading to unauthorized access. Option b pertains to XSS, not session management. Option c involves authentication, not session handling. Option d concerns data encryption, not session IDs.

627. Which security bug classification is associated with improper error handling in code?
a. Information disclosure
b. Race condition
c. SQL injection
d. Denial of service (DoS)

Answer: a. Information disclosure. Explanation: Improper error handling can expose sensitive information, leading to unintended data leaks. Option b involves concurrent processing issues. Option c concerns input sanitization flaws. Option d relates to resource exhaustion, not error handling.

628. What is the most effective way to ensure compliance with secure coding guidelines during code development?
a. Conducting security awareness training for developers annually
b. Using Integrated Development Environment (IDE) plugins to enforce rules
c. Reviewing code only at the end of the development cycle
d. Outsourcing secure code reviews to third-party vendors

Answer: b. Using Integrated Development Environment (IDE) plugins to enforce rules. Explanation: IDE plugins provide real-time feedback and enforce coding standards during development. Option a supports awareness but does not enforce guidelines. Option c delays issue detection. Option d can be helpful but is not the most effective internal control.

629. A static code analysis tool reports a potential buffer overflow vulnerability in a function. What is the most effective remediation for this issue?
a. Replace static memory allocation with dynamic memory allocation
b. Validate input lengths before processing user-provided data
c. Encrypt all data passing through the affected function
d. Add logging to track usage of the vulnerable function

Answer: b. Validate input lengths before processing user-provided data. Explanation: Input validation prevents buffer overflows by ensuring data fits within allocated memory. Option a may reduce but not eliminate risks. Option c is unrelated to memory management. Option d aids monitoring but does not prevent the issue.

630. Which metric is most useful for measuring code quality in a secure development process?
a. Lines of code per developer
b. Defect density per 1,000 lines of code
c. Code deployment frequency
d. Number of features delivered per release

Answer: b. Defect density per 1,000 lines of code. Explanation: Defect density measures the number of issues relative to code volume, highlighting quality. Option a measures productivity, not quality. Option c relates to deployment, not security. Option d focuses on features, not quality.

631. What is the main reason for classifying bugs into categories during secure code reviews?
a. To prioritize remediation based on severity and risk
b. To ensure compliance with organizational coding standards
c. To track developer productivity across teams
d. To standardize formatting across the codebase

Answer: a. To prioritize remediation based on severity and risk. Explanation: Bug classification helps focus resources on critical vulnerabilities that pose the greatest risk. Option b addresses standardization, not prioritization. Option c is unrelated to security bugs. Option d pertains to code style, not security.

632. A multinational corporation implements SAML for identity federation. Which SAML component is responsible for authenticating users and issuing assertions to service providers?
a. Service provider
b. Identity provider
c. Relying party
d. Metadata repository

Answer: b. Identity provider. Explanation: The identity provider (IdP) authenticates users and issues SAML assertions, which service providers rely on to grant access. Option a consumes assertions but does not issue them. Option c is a term used interchangeably with service provider but is less specific. Option d stores configuration information but does not authenticate users.

633. An organization is selecting an identity provider for its federation system. Which feature is most critical for ensuring secure integration with multiple service providers?
a. Support for JSON Web Tokens (JWT) in all transactions
b. Compatibility with service provider metadata files
c. Built-in multi-factor authentication mechanisms
d. High availability and load balancing

Answer: b. Compatibility with service provider metadata files. Explanation: Service provider metadata ensures proper communication and trust between the IdP and service providers in a federated setup. Option a pertains to token standards, which are not specific to SAML. Option c enhances authentication but is not critical for integration. Option d is operationally important but unrelated to federation security.

634. An e-commerce company configures its service provider for a SAML-based identity federation system. Which step is essential to establish trust with an identity provider?
a. Encrypting SAML responses using the service provider's private key
b. Importing the identity provider's public certificate into the service provider
c. Enabling single logout functionality for all federated sessions
d. Synchronizing system clocks to within 5 minutes of each other

Answer: b. Importing the identity provider's public certificate into the service provider. Explanation: Importing the IdP's public certificate establishes trust, allowing the service provider to verify SAML assertions. Option a involves encryption but does not establish trust. Option c enhances session management but is not foundational for trust. Option d is important for avoiding assertion expiration issues but is not trust-specific.

635. Which federation trust model provides the most scalability for managing a large number of federated entities?
a. Hub-and-spoke model
b. Direct trust model
c. Mesh trust model
d. Third-party broker model

Answer: a. Hub-and-spoke model. Explanation: The hub-and-spoke model centralizes trust management, making it scalable for numerous entities. Option b requires individual trust relationships, which can become unmanageable at scale. Option c involves direct relationships between entities, adding complexity. Option d uses a third party, which introduces potential dependency risks.

636. An organization implements Single Sign-On (SSO) using SAML. What is the primary security benefit of SSO in a federated environment?
a. Reducing password reuse across multiple applications
b. Ensuring end-to-end encryption of all user sessions
c. Providing centralized logging of user activity for audits
d. Eliminating the need for session timeouts on service providers

Answer: a. Reducing password reuse across multiple applications. Explanation: SSO minimizes the need for users to manage multiple credentials, reducing the likelihood of password reuse and related risks. Option b pertains to encryption, not SSO specifically. Option c supports monitoring but is a secondary benefit. Option d compromises security by ignoring timeout policies.

637. During a SAML-based SSO session, a user encounters an error stating "Assertion signature invalid." What is the most likely cause of this issue?
a. The service provider's metadata file is missing required attributes
b. The identity provider's public key has not been imported into the service provider
c. The SAML assertion has exceeded its expiration timestamp
d. The user's browser session cookies have been cleared prematurely

Answer: b. The identity provider's public key has not been imported into the service provider. Explanation: Without the IdP's public key, the service provider cannot verify the signature on SAML assertions. Option a pertains to metadata configuration but is unrelated to signature validation. Option c causes assertion expiration errors, not invalid signatures. Option d relates to session management, not assertion verification.

638. An organization uses a mesh trust model for federated identity. What is the primary drawback of this approach compared to other trust models?
a. Increased latency during authentication requests
b. Lack of support for multi-factor authentication mechanisms
c. Complex trust relationship management between entities
d. Dependency on a third-party trust broker for coordination

Answer: c. Complex trust relationship management between entities. Explanation: In a mesh model, each entity establishes and maintains direct trust with every other entity, leading to complexity. Option a is unrelated to the trust model. Option b pertains to authentication, not trust. Option d describes the third-party broker model, not mesh.

639. A security analyst is collecting digital evidence during an incident investigation. What is the primary reason for maintaining a strict chain of custody?
a. To ensure evidence integrity is not altered during analysis
b. To comply with the organization's internal security policy
c. To reduce the time required for legal proceedings
d. To document the financial impact of the incident

Answer: a. To ensure evidence integrity is not altered during analysis. Explanation: A chain of custody maintains the integrity of evidence, ensuring it is admissible in court and has not been tampered with. Option b focuses on internal policy, not evidence handling. Option c pertains to legal efficiency but is not the purpose of the chain of custody. Option d is unrelated to evidence procedures.

640. During a memory forensics analysis, which artifact is most likely to reveal active network connections on a compromised system?
a. Volatile data from process memory
b. The system's master boot record (MBR)
c. Persistent logs stored in the registry
d. Deleted file fragments in unallocated disk space

Answer: a. Volatile data from process memory. Explanation: Process memory contains information about active network connections, such as IPs and ports. Option b relates to boot processes, not memory. Option c pertains to system configurations, not network connections. Option d is unrelated to active memory or connections.

641. Which network traffic analysis technique is most effective for detecting data exfiltration using encrypted communications?
a. Monitoring for large outbound data transfers to unknown IPs
b. Analyzing the content of outbound packets for sensitive keywords
c. Using deep packet inspection (DPI) to decrypt SSL/TLS traffic
d. Reviewing DNS query logs for unusual domain requests

Answer: a. Monitoring for large outbound data transfers to unknown IPs. Explanation: Unusual data volumes can indicate exfiltration, even with encryption in place. Option b is ineffective with encrypted communications. Option c often requires SSL key access, which is impractical. Option d detects domain abuse but not data exfiltration.

642. What is the primary goal of static malware analysis during an investigation?
a. To identify dynamic behavior patterns of the malware
b. To extract indicators of compromise (IOCs) from the malware binary
c. To monitor real-time interactions between the malware and the operating system
d. To evaluate the malware's impact on system resources

Answer: b. To extract indicators of compromise (IOCs) from the malware binary. Explanation: Static analysis identifies IOCs like hashes, file names, and embedded URLs without executing the malware. Option a describes dynamic analysis. Option c involves monitoring execution, not static analysis. Option d is unrelated to static analysis.

643. A forensic investigator is reconstructing a timeline of events from an incident. What data source is most useful for determining the sequence of file modifications?
a. Process memory dumps
b. System event logs
c. File system metadata timestamps
d. Network packet captures

Answer: c. File system metadata timestamps. Explanation: Timestamps reveal creation, modification, and access times, helping reconstruct a timeline. Option a captures transient data but lacks chronological structure. Option b supports event correlation but not file-level detail. Option d focuses on network activity, not file modifications.

644. When handling digital evidence stored on a hard drive, what is the most critical first step?
a. Creating a bit-by-bit forensic image of the drive
b. Performing a quick scan for malware indicators
c. Isolating the drive from the compromised system
d. Notifying the legal team of the discovery

Answer: a. Creating a bit-by-bit forensic image of the drive. Explanation: Imaging preserves evidence integrity and allows analysis without altering the original. Option b risks modifying the evidence. Option c is useful but secondary to imaging. Option d supports compliance but is not the initial technical step.

645. During network traffic analysis, the investigator identifies unexpected traffic to port 4444 on an internal server. What is the most likely explanation for this finding?
a. Port 4444 is commonly used for secure file transfers
b. The traffic indicates possible backdoor activity
c. The port is associated with database management services
d. The activity suggests an attempted denial-of-service attack

Answer: b. The traffic indicates possible backdoor activity. Explanation: Port 4444 is frequently used by malware for backdoor access. Option a is incorrect; file transfers typically use ports like 21 or 22. Option c is unrelated to port 4444. Option d does not align with the observed behavior.

646. What is the primary challenge of analyzing volatile memory in incident investigations?
a. Volatile memory is difficult to access on virtualized systems
b. The data in volatile memory is overwritten when power is lost
c. Memory dumps cannot be acquired without disrupting active processes
d. Analysis tools cannot distinguish legitimate processes from malicious ones

Answer: b. The data in volatile memory is overwritten when power is lost. Explanation: Volatile memory is transient and lost upon shutdown, requiring immediate acquisition. Option a is less common with modern tools. Option c is untrue for non-intrusive acquisition methods. Option d is mitigated by skilled analysis and threat intelligence.

647. A security team identifies suspicious activity involving unauthorized remote access. Which artifact is most valuable for correlating the attacker's actions?
a. VPN authentication logs
b. Local application error logs
c. Packet captures from the network perimeter
d. Temporary files in the user's profile directory

Answer: a. VPN authentication logs. Explanation: VPN logs provide details on unauthorized access attempts, including timestamps and user IDs. Option b contains unrelated application issues. Option c aids analysis but lacks user-specific correlation. Option d is rarely relevant to remote access.

648. A financial institution is performing a business continuity test to validate its recovery procedures. Which action best ensures the recovery process meets the required recovery time objective (RTO)?
a. Simulating a power outage to test the failover of critical systems
b. Reviewing the incident response plan with senior leadership
c. Documenting lessons learned from previous recovery attempts
d. Conducting a tabletop exercise to evaluate team readiness

Answer: a. Simulating a power outage to test the failover of critical systems. Explanation: A simulated power outage provides a realistic scenario to measure the actual recovery time and ensure it aligns with the RTO. Option b enhances strategic planning but does not validate RTO. Option c supports continuous improvement but is not a test. Option d evaluates readiness but does not measure recovery time.

649. An organization conducts business process testing as part of its continuity plan. Which approach best ensures that dependencies between processes are identified and addressed?
a. Isolating individual processes to assess their standalone recovery capabilities
b. Simulating end-to-end workflows involving multiple dependent processes
c. Testing only the most critical processes to streamline resource usage
d. Verifying process documentation against the continuity plan requirements

Answer: b. Simulating end-to-end workflows involving multiple dependent processes. Explanation: Testing workflows ensures that interdependencies are understood and addressed, supporting seamless recovery. Option a ignores dependencies. Option c is insufficient for comprehensive validation. Option d improves documentation but does not test dependencies.

650. During a business continuity communication plan test, what metric is most critical for evaluating the plan's effectiveness?
a. The percentage of employees who acknowledge receipt of the test notification
b. The average time taken to disseminate critical information across the organization
c. The number of communication channels included in the plan
d. The total cost of conducting the communication plan test

Answer: b. The average time taken to disseminate critical information across the organization. Explanation: Timely communication is essential during incidents, making the time metric crucial for evaluating the plan. Option a measures acknowledgment but not speed. Option c focuses on quantity, not effectiveness. Option d pertains to cost, not efficiency.

651. A global enterprise is testing the readiness of its alternate site for disaster recovery. Which factor is most critical to assess during the test?
a. The geographic distance between the alternate site and the primary site
b. The ability of the alternate site to operate without access to the primary site
c. The physical security controls in place at the alternate site
d. The cost of maintaining the alternate site for extended periods

Answer: b. The ability of the alternate site to operate without access to the primary site. Explanation: Alternate site readiness depends on its capability to function independently during a disaster. Option a affects risk but is less critical during testing. Option c ensures security but does not test operational readiness. Option d relates to budget, not functionality.

652. An IT team performs a critical system recovery test. Which outcome best demonstrates the test's success?
a. Recovery logs showing zero errors during the test
b. Restoration of the system within the established RTO
c. Identification of previously undocumented recovery dependencies
d. No user complaints reported during the recovery process

Answer: b. Restoration of the system within the established RTO. Explanation: Meeting the RTO ensures the recovery aligns with business continuity objectives. Option a focuses on technical execution but not timing. Option c aids improvement but is not a measure of success. Option d may indicate success but is not definitive without validating RTO.

653. A manufacturing company tests its ability to recover from a ransomware attack. What scenario best validates the organization's recovery readiness?
a. Conducting a full system restore from an offline backup
b. Simulating an attack using penetration testing tools
c. Reviewing the encryption keys used to secure data backups
d. Training employees on recognizing phishing emails

Answer: a. Conducting a full system restore from an offline backup. Explanation: A full restore validates the organization's ability to recover data and resume operations after a ransomware attack. Option b focuses on attack simulation, not recovery. Option c pertains to backup security, not testing. Option d supports prevention but not recovery.

654. Which test scenario best validates the scalability of a business continuity plan during a widespread disaster?
a. Simulating a localized incident affecting a single department
b. Testing simultaneous failures of multiple critical systems
c. Conducting a tabletop exercise with senior leadership
d. Reviewing alternate supplier agreements for supply chain continuity

Answer: b. Testing simultaneous failures of multiple critical systems. Explanation: A widespread disaster involves cascading failures, making simultaneous system testing crucial for validating scalability. Option a tests localized issues. Option c enhances coordination but does not test scalability. Option d evaluates supply chain readiness, not systemic failures.

655. An organization adopts a microservices architecture. What is the best approach to secure inter-service communication in this environment?
a. Using API keys shared among all microservices
b. Implementing mutual TLS (mTLS) for service-to-service authentication
c. Encrypting all internal traffic using AES-256 without authentication
d. Deploying a web application firewall (WAF) to monitor service traffic

Answer: b. Implementing mutual TLS (mTLS) for service-to-service authentication. Explanation: mTLS ensures that both client and server authenticate each other, securing inter-service communication. Option a lacks dynamic security and revocation capabilities. Option c encrypts traffic but does not verify identities. Option d monitors traffic but is not designed for inter-service authentication.

656. A company uses an event-driven architecture for real-time data processing. Which security measure is most effective for ensuring the integrity of messages between producers and consumers?
a. Encrypting messages using symmetric cryptography
b. Signing messages with a digital signature
c. Enforcing access control at the message queue level
d. Using obfuscation techniques to mask message content

Answer: b. Signing messages with a digital signature. Explanation: Digital signatures ensure the authenticity and integrity of messages, preventing tampering. Option a encrypts messages but does not verify their origin. Option c restricts access but does not address message integrity. Option d hides content but provides no guarantees of authenticity.

657. In a service mesh architecture, what is the primary role of a sidecar proxy?
a. Managing distributed denial-of-service (DDoS) protection
b. Offloading security policies and traffic control from application code
c. Detecting and blocking malware in service communications
d. Ensuring scalability by balancing loads across services

Answer: b. Offloading security policies and traffic control from application code. Explanation: Sidecar proxies centralize security and networking policies, reducing the burden on application developers. Option a is incorrect; DDoS protection typically involves external tools. Option c is not the primary function of a sidecar. Option d relates to load balancers, not service mesh.

658. Which pattern is most effective for enforcing security in APIs exposed to external clients?
a. Directly exposing microservices to external consumers
b. Implementing an API gateway with rate limiting and authentication
c. Using a reverse proxy to log incoming requests
d. Encrypting API responses with asymmetric cryptography

Answer: b. Implementing an API gateway with rate limiting and authentication. Explanation: API gateways centralize access control, throttling, and monitoring for external APIs. Option a exposes microservices directly, increasing risk. Option c provides logging but lacks access control. Option d secures responses but does not enforce access policies.

659. What is the most significant risk of failing to decompose security responsibilities in a monolithic architecture?
a. Increased attack surface for distributed systems
b. Difficulty in auditing centralized security configurations
c. Over-reliance on runtime security tools to mitigate vulnerabilities
d. Lack of scalability due to tightly coupled services

Answer: b. Difficulty in auditing centralized security configurations. Explanation: In monolithic architectures, centralized security leads to complex, error-prone audits. Option a pertains to distributed systems, not monoliths. Option c involves operational tools, not architectural design. Option d relates to performance, not security responsibilities.

660. An organization uses mutual TLS (mTLS) for securing its microservices. What is the biggest challenge in managing this solution?
a. Ensuring encryption algorithms remain up to date

b. Rotating certificates without causing service downtime
c. Implementing traffic monitoring in encrypted channels
d. Authenticating external users accessing microservices

Answer: b. Rotating certificates without causing service downtime. Explanation: Certificate rotation in mTLS must be carefully managed to avoid disrupting service communication. Option a is routine and less challenging. Option c involves visibility, not mTLS management. Option d pertains to external users, not inter-service communication.

661. Which mechanism ensures secure, scalable access control in an event-driven architecture?
a. Embedding hardcoded credentials in each service
b. Using OAuth 2.0 tokens to authorize event consumers
c. Encrypting message headers with the sender's private key
d. Establishing IP whitelists for producers and consumers

Answer: b. Using OAuth 2.0 tokens to authorize event consumers. Explanation: OAuth 2.0 tokens provide scalable, context-aware access control in event-driven systems. Option a is insecure and unscalable. Option c ensures message integrity but not access control. Option d lacks dynamic scalability.

662. What is the primary advantage of implementing a zero-trust model in a microservices architecture?
a. Eliminating the need for traditional perimeter firewalls
b. Simplifying compliance audits for distributed services
c. Verifying every request regardless of origin or location
d. Ensuring faster deployment of new microservices

Answer: c. Verifying every request regardless of origin or location. Explanation: Zero-trust ensures that access is continuously verified, minimizing insider and external threats. Option a mischaracterizes zero-trust, which complements firewalls. Option b is a secondary benefit. Option d pertains to operational efficiency, not zero-trust.

663. A team is designing a secure API gateway. What is the best method to protect APIs from automated abuse?
a. Requiring multi-factor authentication for all API consumers
b. Implementing CAPTCHA challenges for high-volume requests
c. Using rate limiting and dynamic throttling policies
d. Encrypting all API requests with AES-256

Answer: c. Using rate limiting and dynamic throttling policies. Explanation: Rate limiting and throttling effectively deter automated abuse by restricting request rates. Option a is impractical for automated systems. Option b disrupts legitimate API consumers. Option d secures data but does not prevent abuse.

664. A healthcare organization performs a cloud configuration review. Which misconfiguration poses the highest risk to compliance under HIPAA?
a. An inactive storage bucket containing PHI is publicly accessible
b. Database backups are stored in the same region as production databases
c. An S3 bucket is encrypted using a default AWS-managed key
d. A multi-factor authentication policy is enforced for all administrative accounts

Answer: a. An inactive storage bucket containing PHI is publicly accessible. Explanation: Publicly accessible buckets containing protected health information (PHI) directly violate HIPAA's privacy and security rules. Option b risks regional dependency but is not a compliance violation. Option c uses adequate encryption, albeit with default keys. Option d enhances security and aligns with compliance.

665. An organization maps its cloud security controls to a regulatory framework. What is the most critical step to ensure completeness in the mapping process?
a. Using a checklist of all cloud-native security features
b. Identifying and prioritizing high-risk services and data types
c. Mapping controls to specific requirements in the framework
d. Auditing third-party vendor compliance reports for alignment

Answer: c. Mapping controls to specific requirements in the framework. Explanation: Mapping controls directly to requirements ensures that the organization addresses all compliance obligations. Option a supports mapping but lacks specificity. Option b focuses on risk but does not ensure comprehensive mapping. Option d assesses vendors but not the organization's controls.

666. During a cloud compliance validation, which evidence is most relevant to demonstrate adherence to GDPR requirements?
a. Logs of data subject access requests and their resolutions
b. Encrypted backups of user data stored in the cloud
c. Documentation of role-based access controls for cloud resources
d. A penetration test report of the cloud environment

Answer: a. Logs of data subject access requests and their resolutions. Explanation: GDPR requires organizations to respond to data subject access requests (DSARs), making this evidence critical for validation. Option b supports data protection but is not specific to DSAR compliance. Option c pertains to access control, not DSARs. Option d verifies security but is not GDPR-specific.

667. A financial institution performs a cloud data protection assessment. Which practice best ensures the confidentiality of sensitive customer data stored in the cloud?
a. Encrypting all data in transit using TLS 1.2 or higher
b. Using access logs to track administrative activity on sensitive data
c. Enforcing geofencing for storage locations within specific jurisdictions
d. Configuring automated alerts for anomalous data access patterns

Answer: a. Encrypting all data in transit using TLS 1.2 or higher. Explanation: TLS encryption protects sensitive data from interception during transmission, ensuring confidentiality. Option b supports monitoring but does not directly protect data. Option c ensures compliance with jurisdictional requirements but is less critical for confidentiality. Option d aids detection but not prevention.

668. An organization conducts an access control review for its cloud environment. What finding poses the greatest security risk?
a. A service account with wide permissions that is shared across multiple applications
b. An expired user account that has not been removed from the environment
c. A privileged account that has not logged in for more than 90 days
d. A group policy that enforces password rotation every 30 days

Answer: a. A service account with wide permissions that is shared across multiple applications. Explanation: Shared service accounts with extensive permissions increase the attack surface and risk of privilege misuse. Option b represents hygiene but is less risky. Option c is inactive but does not actively pose a threat. Option d enhances security by enforcing best practices.

669. During a cloud configuration review, which control most effectively limits the blast radius of a compromised cloud resource?
a. Enforcing network segmentation between cloud subnets
b. Deploying endpoint detection and response (EDR) tools

c. Encrypting data using customer-managed keys (CMK)
d. Configuring automated backups for critical cloud resources

Answer: a. Enforcing network segmentation between cloud subnets. Explanation: Network segmentation limits the spread of an attack by isolating resources. Option b focuses on endpoint security, not network isolation. Option c enhances encryption but does not mitigate lateral movement. Option d supports data recovery, not containment.

670. An organization assesses compliance with its cloud provider's shared responsibility model. Which activity falls under the customer's responsibility in the model?
a. Ensuring the availability of physical infrastructure hosting cloud resources
b. Configuring role-based access control for cloud-native applications
c. Conducting background checks for cloud provider personnel
d. Monitoring and patching the hypervisor for virtualization security

Answer: b. Configuring role-based access control for cloud-native applications. Explanation: Under the shared responsibility model, customers manage access controls for their data and applications. Option a is the provider's responsibility. Option c pertains to personnel management, not the customer's domain. Option d is handled by the cloud provider.

671. An organization is implementing a security metrics program. What is the most important consideration when selecting key performance indicators (KPIs)?
a. Ensuring KPIs align with the organization's strategic goals
b. Selecting metrics that are easy to measure and report
c. Choosing a large number of KPIs to cover all security areas
d. Defining KPIs that focus on compliance with external frameworks

Answer: a. Ensuring KPIs align with the organization's strategic goals. Explanation: Effective KPIs support strategic objectives, ensuring security aligns with business priorities. Option b sacrifices meaningfulness for simplicity. Option c dilutes focus and adds complexity. Option d focuses narrowly on compliance, ignoring broader goals.

672. A security team uses automated tools for metric collection. What is the primary advantage of automation in this context?
a. It eliminates the need for human involvement in data analysis
b. It ensures consistent and accurate data collection across systems
c. It allows for the integration of compliance requirements into metrics
d. It identifies new security vulnerabilities in real-time

Answer: b. It ensures consistent and accurate data collection across systems. Explanation: Automation reduces human error and ensures uniformity in metric collection. Option a is incorrect; analysis still requires human oversight. Option c pertains to compliance but is not the primary advantage. Option d is unrelated to metric collection.

673. Which dashboard design principle best supports effective decision-making for security leaders?
a. Including detailed technical logs for every monitored system
b. Focusing on metrics that highlight trends and deviations from baselines
c. Presenting data in raw numerical form to avoid bias
d. Using static charts that remain unchanged between reporting cycles

Answer: b. Focusing on metrics that highlight trends and deviations from baselines. Explanation: Dashboards should emphasize actionable insights by showing trends and anomalies. Option a overwhelms users with unnecessary detail. Option c sacrifices clarity for perceived objectivity. Option d lacks adaptability to current events.

674. A security operations center (SOC) uses trend analysis to track incident response times. Which metric best supports this analysis?
a. Number of incidents detected per month
b. Average time to detect (MTTD) incidents
c. Percentage of incidents escalated to management
d. Number of false positives generated by monitoring tools

Answer: b. Average time to detect (MTTD) incidents. Explanation: MTTD tracks how quickly threats are identified, highlighting performance trends over time. Option a tracks volume, not response efficiency. Option c focuses on escalation, not detection. Option d measures tool accuracy, not SOC performance.

675. What is the greatest risk of using lagging indicators as primary security metrics?
a. They are difficult to collect consistently across systems
b. They require advanced tools for accurate measurement
c. They provide limited insights into current vulnerabilities or risks
d. They often conflict with external compliance requirements

Answer: c. They provide limited insights into current vulnerabilities or risks. Explanation: Lagging indicators focus on past events, offering little predictive value for proactive security. Option a is false; lagging metrics are often easier to collect. Option b pertains to advanced metrics, not lagging indicators. Option d is unrelated to metric selection.

676. What is the primary purpose of security performance reporting to executive stakeholders?
a. To demonstrate compliance with regulatory requirements
b. To highlight areas of poor performance for disciplinary action
c. To show how security investments align with organizational objectives
d. To provide detailed technical insights into security operations

Answer: c. To show how security investments align with organizational objectives. Explanation: Reporting should link security efforts to business goals, justifying investments. Option a is secondary and does not address strategic alignment. Option b undermines the collaborative nature of reporting. Option d provides unnecessary detail for executives.

677. How can organizations ensure their metrics program remains effective over time?
a. By updating KPIs annually based on changing regulations
b. By eliminating underperforming security controls
c. By periodically reviewing metrics for relevance and alignment
d. By implementing new tools to collect additional data

Answer: c. By periodically reviewing metrics for relevance and alignment. Explanation: Metrics must evolve to reflect current goals, threats, and business contexts. Option a overemphasizes compliance. Option b confuses control management with metric evaluation. Option d risks adding complexity without improving effectiveness.

678. A SOC manager notices an increase in false positives from an automated monitoring system. What is the most effective way to address this issue?
a. Disabling the rules generating the most false positives
b. Refining detection thresholds and tuning rules
c. Escalating all alerts for manual review
d. Reducing the frequency of metric collection to minimize noise

Answer: b. Refining detection thresholds and tuning rules. Explanation: Tuning reduces false positives while maintaining effective monitoring. Option a risks missing true positives. Option c is inefficient and resource-intensive. Option d sacrifices metric quality and frequency for simplicity.

679. When presenting security metrics to non-technical stakeholders, what is the most effective approach?
a. Using simple visualizations and avoiding technical jargon
b. Providing detailed descriptions of metric calculation methods
c. Presenting raw data for stakeholders to interpret independently
d. Limiting reports to compliance-related metrics

Answer: a. Using simple visualizations and avoiding technical jargon. Explanation: Clear visuals and plain language ensure metrics are accessible to non-technical audiences. Option b adds unnecessary detail. Option c shifts the burden of interpretation. Option d narrows the focus, missing other critical insights.

680. An organization discovers that several cloud storage buckets are configured without encryption. What is the most immediate action to secure these resources while minimizing operational disruptions?
a. Enable server-side encryption on the affected storage buckets immediately
b. Move the unencrypted data to new, encrypted storage buckets
c. Delete the storage buckets and notify users to re-upload their data
d. Implement network-based controls to restrict access to the storage buckets

Answer: a. Enable server-side encryption on the affected storage buckets immediately. Explanation: Enabling server-side encryption secures the data with minimal disruption and ensures compliance with security best practices. Option b involves unnecessary data migration. Option c is disruptive and impractical. Option d restricts access but does not secure the data.

681. During a cloud security control mapping exercise, an auditor identifies gaps in monitoring for privileged account activities. Which control best mitigates this issue?
a. Enabling session recording for privileged users in the cloud management console
b. Requiring multi-factor authentication for privileged account logins
c. Restricting privileged accounts to specific IP ranges
d. Performing quarterly access reviews for all privileged accounts

Answer: a. Enabling session recording for privileged users in the cloud management console. Explanation: Session recording provides detailed logs of privileged activities, enhancing accountability and visibility. Option b improves authentication but does not monitor activity. Option c restricts access but does not provide detailed insights. Option d supports periodic reviews but lacks real-time monitoring.

682. A cloud service provider offers compliance certifications such as SOC 2 and ISO/IEC 27001. How should a customer use these certifications when assessing cloud security?
a. As evidence that the provider fully meets the customer's compliance requirements
b. To verify that the provider's infrastructure adheres to recognized security standards
c. As proof that the customer's data will remain secure without additional controls
d. To eliminate the need for independent audits of the cloud environment

Answer: b. To verify that the provider's infrastructure adheres to recognized security standards. Explanation: Certifications demonstrate that the provider follows specific security practices but do not guarantee compliance with the customer's unique requirements. Option a overstates the scope of certifications. Option c assumes compliance without customer controls. Option d ignores the value of independent audits.

683. A retail company performs a data protection assessment in its multi-cloud environment. Which practice best addresses data sovereignty requirements?
a. Encrypting all data using the strongest available encryption algorithm
b. Storing sensitive data only in regions that comply with local regulations
c. Implementing an access control list (ACL) for each storage bucket
d. Performing regular data integrity checks on stored files

Answer: b. Storing sensitive data only in regions that comply with local regulations. Explanation: Data sovereignty requires that sensitive data remain in jurisdictions with appropriate regulations. Option a supports confidentiality but does not ensure sovereignty. Option c provides access control but does not address location-specific requirements. Option d validates data integrity but is unrelated to sovereignty.

684. During an access control review, an organization finds that several inactive user accounts still have access to sensitive cloud resources. What is the most effective remediation step?
a. Reset the passwords for all inactive accounts and require reauthentication
b. Disable or delete the inactive accounts after verifying their activity
c. Add the inactive accounts to a low-privilege group for monitoring
d. Notify the account owners and request immediate action

Answer: b. Disable or delete the inactive accounts after verifying their activity. Explanation: Removing inactive accounts reduces the risk of unauthorized access while maintaining a clean access control environment. Option a addresses authentication but retains unnecessary accounts. Option c reduces privileges but does not resolve the issue. Option d is slow and relies on user compliance.

685. An organization performs a cloud compliance validation. Which approach best ensures ongoing adherence to regulatory requirements?
a. Conducting annual compliance audits with external consultants
b. Implementing automated compliance monitoring tools with real-time alerts
c. Training employees on regulatory updates during biannual workshops
d. Documenting all compliance-related incidents in a centralized repository

Answer: b. Implementing automated compliance monitoring tools with real-time alerts. Explanation: Automated monitoring ensures continuous validation and prompt detection of non-compliance. Option a is periodic and not real-time. Option c supports awareness but does not enforce compliance. Option d aids tracking but does not ensure adherence.

686. A company is assessing a third-party vendor for data processing services. Which aspect of the vendor's operations is most critical to evaluate during the initial risk assessment?
a. The vendor's compliance with ISO 9001 standards
b. The vendor's implementation of secure coding practices
c. The vendor's data breach history and response measures
d. The vendor's financial stability and profitability

Answer: c. The vendor's data breach history and response measures. Explanation: Evaluating breach history and response readiness ensures the vendor can handle security incidents effectively. Option a focuses on quality management, not security. Option b is important but less relevant unless the vendor develops software. Option d addresses business continuity but not directly security risks.

687. Which supply chain security measure is most effective for mitigating risks from compromised components?
a. Conducting regular penetration testing on the supplier's environment
b. Verifying the integrity of components using a digital signature
c. Auditing the supplier's compliance with regulatory frameworks
d. Requiring suppliers to provide vulnerability scans of their systems

Answer: b. Verifying the integrity of components using a digital signature. Explanation: Digital signatures validate that components are untampered and authentic. Option a does not directly secure delivered components. Option c supports compliance but does not guarantee security. Option d helps identify risks but doesn't mitigate them proactively.

688. What is the most critical security requirement to include in third-party contracts to minimize risk exposure?
a. A confidentiality clause specifying penalties for data breaches
b. A clause requiring annual security awareness training for vendor employees
c. A requirement for incident notification within a defined timeframe
d. A provision allowing on-site audits of the vendor's facilities

Answer: c. A requirement for incident notification within a defined timeframe. Explanation: Timely notification enables the organization to mitigate risks associated with third-party incidents. Option a is important but secondary to incident response. Option b enhances security culture but does not address immediate risk. Option d is useful but less critical than notification.

689. A vendor has been approved after an initial risk assessment. What is the best approach to ensure ongoing monitoring of the vendor's security posture?
a. Conducting periodic vulnerability scans on the vendor's network
b. Requiring the vendor to submit regular security audit reports
c. Monitoring the vendor's public reputation through media channels
d. Requesting annual updates to the vendor's security policies

Answer: b. Requiring the vendor to submit regular security audit reports. Explanation: Regular audits provide insight into the vendor's current security posture and compliance. Option a is intrusive and may not be feasible. Option c offers limited actionable information. Option d ensures policy updates but not operational security.

690. What is the primary challenge when coordinating incident response with a third-party vendor?
a. Verifying the authenticity of the vendor's incident reports
b. Ensuring alignment of the vendor's response plans with organizational policies
c. Determining whether the vendor's actions violated contract terms
d. Identifying which organization holds liability for the incident

Answer: b. Ensuring alignment of the vendor's response plans with organizational policies. Explanation: Incident response coordination requires harmonized policies to ensure effective resolution. Option a is part of validation, not coordination. Option c pertains to contract enforcement, not immediate response. Option d is important but secondary to operational alignment.

691. Which tool is most effective for assessing the cybersecurity maturity of potential third-party vendors?
a. Self-assessment questionnaires completed by the vendor
b. Automated threat intelligence tools monitoring vendor activities
c. The NIST Cybersecurity Framework (CSF) applied to vendor practices
d. A scorecard system based on regulatory compliance metrics

Answer: c. The NIST Cybersecurity Framework (CSF) applied to vendor practices. Explanation: The CSF provides a standardized approach to evaluate cybersecurity maturity. Option a is subjective and prone to inaccuracies. Option b offers insight but not comprehensive maturity assessment. Option d focuses on compliance, not overall security posture.

692. What is the most significant risk of relying solely on vendor-provided documentation during risk assessments?
a. The documentation may be incomplete or outdated
b. It may conflict with internal security policies
c. It often omits technical details about the vendor's systems
d. The documentation does not include specific threat scenarios

Answer: a. The documentation may be incomplete or outdated. Explanation: Vendor documentation can fail to reflect current practices or risks, making assessments less reliable. Option b pertains to policy alignment, not the reliability of documentation. Option c may occur but is less critical. Option d is typically outside the scope of standard assessments.

693. What is the most effective supply chain security practice for organizations procuring hardware from international vendors?
a. Requiring vendors to use encrypted communication for all orders
b. Ensuring components include tamper-evident seals
c. Maintaining a detailed log of all vendor transactions
d. Conducting on-site inspections of international production facilities

Answer: b. Ensuring components include tamper-evident seals. Explanation: Tamper-evident seals protect against hardware alterations during transit. Option a secures communication but not the product. Option c tracks transactions but does not verify security. Option d is costly and impractical for most organizations.

694. A third-party risk management program identifies a high-risk vendor due to its access to sensitive data. What is the best mitigation strategy?
a. Restricting the vendor's access to sensitive data until the risk is resolved
b. Terminating the vendor's contract and seeking an alternative provider
c. Conducting additional audits to monitor the vendor more frequently
d. Encrypting all sensitive data before providing it to the vendor

Answer: d. Encrypting all sensitive data before providing it to the vendor. Explanation: Encryption limits the impact of vendor compromise by securing data at rest and in transit. Option a delays operations. Option b may be premature without addressing the risk. Option c adds oversight but does not mitigate the risk directly.

695. A financial organization performs a vendor assessment for a cloud service provider. Which criterion is most critical for evaluating the provider's security posture?
a. The provider's adherence to ISO/IEC 27001 standards
b. The provider's use of a dedicated support team for enterprise accounts
c. The provider's pricing structure for long-term contracts
d. The provider's geographic location relative to the organization

Answer: a. The provider's adherence to ISO/IEC 27001 standards. Explanation: ISO/IEC 27001 ensures the provider follows a recognized information security management system, addressing critical risks. Option b focuses on support, not security. Option c pertains to cost, not security posture. Option d impacts jurisdictional concerns but not overall security.

696. An organization evaluates its supply chain security. Which control best ensures the integrity of software components sourced from third parties?
a. Implementing a software bill of materials (SBOM) for all suppliers
b. Requiring suppliers to sign non-disclosure agreements (NDAs)
c. Using geofencing to limit supplier access to corporate systems
d. Performing annual performance reviews with all key suppliers

Answer: a. Implementing a software bill of materials (SBOM) for all suppliers. Explanation: An SBOM provides transparency into software components, helping to identify vulnerabilities and ensure integrity. Option b protects confidentiality but does not validate software integrity. Option c supports access control, not software integrity. Option d evaluates performance, not security.

697. A manufacturing company includes security requirements in contracts with its vendors. Which clause is most effective for ensuring compliance with cybersecurity standards?
a. Vendors must encrypt all data shared with the company using AES-256

b. Vendors must provide 24/7 technical support for critical systems
c. Vendors must allow the company to conduct periodic security audits
d. Vendors must agree to fixed timelines for contract renewals

Answer: c. Vendors must allow the company to conduct periodic security audits. Explanation: Audit rights enable the company to verify compliance with cybersecurity requirements. Option a enforces encryption but does not address broader security practices. Option b focuses on support, not compliance. Option d relates to contract management, not security.

698. During ongoing monitoring of a third-party vendor, an organization detects multiple failed login attempts from the vendor's account. What is the most appropriate immediate response?
a. Disabling the vendor's account and initiating a security review
b. Notifying the vendor and requesting an explanation for the failed attempts
c. Increasing the frequency of the vendor's activity audits
d. Requiring the vendor to reset all user passwords immediately

Answer: a. Disabling the vendor's account and initiating a security review. Explanation: Disabling the account prevents further unauthorized attempts while a review identifies potential issues. Option b delays remediation and increases risk. Option c is reactive and insufficient for an immediate threat. Option d addresses credentials but does not investigate the root cause.

699. An organization collaborates with a vendor for incident response coordination. Which step best ensures effective communication during a joint response effort?
a. Establishing a predefined incident escalation matrix with contact points
b. Requiring vendors to share their proprietary incident response playbooks
c. Conducting biannual tabletop exercises focused on shared risks
d. Documenting incidents in a centralized repository for post-incident analysis

Answer: a. Establishing a predefined incident escalation matrix with contact points. Explanation: An escalation matrix ensures clear communication pathways and responsibilities during an incident. Option b is unrealistic, as vendors may not share proprietary details. Option c enhances preparation but is not an immediate communication control. Option d supports post-incident review, not real-time coordination.

700. A supply chain security audit identifies that a key supplier lacks multi-factor authentication (MFA) for accessing sensitive systems. What is the most effective mitigation action?
a. Requiring the supplier to implement MFA within a set timeline
b. Restricting the supplier's access to sensitive systems
c. Terminating the supplier's contract immediately
d. Conducting awareness training for the supplier's employees

Answer: a. Requiring the supplier to implement MFA within a set timeline. Explanation: Mandating MFA enhances access security without severing the relationship. Option b reduces access but does not address the root cause. Option c is extreme and disrupts operations. Option d improves awareness but does not enforce controls.

701. A security team is tasked with developing KPIs for a new security metrics program. Which KPI is most effective for measuring the efficiency of the organization's incident response process?
a. Percentage of false positive alerts generated by monitoring systems
b. Average time to detect and contain a security incident
c. Number of security incidents reported to regulatory authorities annually
d. Percentage of security patches applied within 30 days of release

Answer: b. Average time to detect and contain a security incident. Explanation: This KPI directly evaluates the efficiency and effectiveness of the incident response process. Option a measures detection system performance, not response efficiency. Option c focuses on regulatory reporting, not operational performance. Option d relates to vulnerability management, not incident response.

702. What is the greatest advantage of automating the collection of security metrics in a large organization?
a. Reducing the likelihood of errors in metric calculation
b. Allowing real-time adjustments to security controls
c. Eliminating the need for manual security assessments
d. Ensuring compliance with regulatory requirements

Answer: a. Reducing the likelihood of errors in metric calculation. Explanation: Automation ensures accuracy and consistency in metric collection, minimizing human error. Option b relates to operational controls, not metrics collection. Option c is incorrect because manual assessments may still be required for context. Option d is a benefit but not the primary advantage.

703. Which element is most critical for an effective security metrics dashboard aimed at executive stakeholders?
a. Detailed logs of all network activity
b. Summary metrics aligned with business objectives
c. Real-time alerts for critical vulnerabilities
d. Technical graphs showing system performance

Answer: b. Summary metrics aligned with business objectives. Explanation: Executives need high-level, actionable insights to align security performance with organizational goals. Option a provides excessive detail. Option c is operationally useful but not appropriate for a dashboard aimed at executives. Option d includes technical information that may not be relevant.

704. A SOC manager uses trend analysis to assess the effectiveness of phishing email detection. Which metric would provide the best insight?
a. Number of phishing emails reported by employees
b. Percentage of phishing emails blocked by security controls
c. Average time to investigate phishing-related incidents
d. Volume of email traffic scanned by the system daily

Answer: b. Percentage of phishing emails blocked by security controls. Explanation: This metric evaluates the system's ability to detect and prevent phishing attacks. Option a measures awareness, not control performance. Option c assesses investigation efficiency, not detection. Option d is unrelated to phishing prevention effectiveness.

705. What is the primary limitation of using lagging indicators for measuring security performance?
a. They are difficult to communicate to non-technical stakeholders
b. They do not provide predictive insights into emerging threats
c. They require significant computational resources for analysis
d. They are more expensive to collect than leading indicators

Answer: b. They do not provide predictive insights into emerging threats. Explanation: Lagging indicators focus on past events and cannot predict future risks. Option a relates to communication, not the limitation of lagging indicators. Option c is false; lagging indicators are computationally simpler. Option d mischaracterizes the cost comparison.

706. Which action best supports accurate trend analysis in security metrics reporting?
a. Collecting data manually to ensure it is validated before analysis
b. Establishing consistent data collection intervals and methodologies

c. Aggregating all metrics into a single report for simplicity
d. Avoiding comparisons between data from different departments

Answer: b. Establishing consistent data collection intervals and methodologies. Explanation: Consistency ensures comparability over time, enabling meaningful trend analysis. Option a sacrifices efficiency for manual validation. Option c simplifies reporting but can obscure specific trends. Option d unnecessarily limits insight into organizational performance.

707. A CISO wants to demonstrate the effectiveness of recent investments in a security awareness program. Which metric is most appropriate?
a. Number of employees completing annual security training
b. Reduction in the click-through rate on phishing simulations
c. Percentage of employees using complex passwords
d. Average time to respond to phishing emails reported by employees

Answer: b. Reduction in the click-through rate on phishing simulations. Explanation: This metric directly measures the program's impact on employee behavior. Option a shows participation, not effectiveness. Option c measures password practices, unrelated to awareness training. Option d relates to response time, not training outcomes.

708. What is the best way to ensure the relevance of a security metrics program over time?
a. Reviewing metrics annually to align with evolving business goals
b. Increasing the number of metrics to cover all areas of security
c. Standardizing metrics to match industry benchmarks
d. Outsourcing the metrics program to a third-party vendor

Answer: a. Reviewing metrics annually to align with evolving business goals. Explanation: Regular reviews ensure metrics remain aligned with organizational priorities. Option b risks diluting focus. Option c standardizes but does not ensure relevance. Option d delegates responsibility but may not maintain alignment with internal goals.

709. Which trend analysis technique best helps identify areas for improvement in vulnerability management?
a. Calculating the average time to patch critical vulnerabilities
b. Tracking the total number of vulnerabilities identified per quarter
c. Comparing patch deployment rates with industry averages
d. Counting the number of vulnerabilities discovered during penetration tests

Answer: a. Calculating the average time to patch critical vulnerabilities. Explanation: This metric identifies gaps in patch management by highlighting delays in addressing critical issues. Option b tracks volume, not performance. Option c benchmarks but does not indicate specific areas for improvement. Option d provides isolated findings, not trends.

710. A healthcare organization performs a cloud configuration review. Which misconfiguration poses the greatest risk to patient data under HIPAA?
a. Allowing unrestricted inbound traffic to a storage bucket containing electronic health records (EHRs)
b. Using default encryption keys provided by the cloud provider for sensitive data
c. Storing backup data in a different geographic region than the primary storage location
d. Granting read-only permissions to external auditors on shared cloud storage

Answer: a. Allowing unrestricted inbound traffic to a storage bucket containing electronic health records (EHRs). Explanation: Unrestricted access exposes sensitive EHRs to unauthorized users, violating HIPAA regulations. Option b provides basic encryption but does not present as critical a risk. Option c impacts data sovereignty but not confidentiality. Option d supports auditing with minimal risk if properly managed.

711. An organization maps its cloud security controls to the NIST Cybersecurity Framework. What is the most critical step in this process?
a. Documenting control implementation details for each framework function
b. Reviewing the framework's applicability to the organization's industry
c. Aligning security controls with the framework's identified risk categories
d. Conducting regular audits to verify the effectiveness of mapped controls

Answer: c. Aligning security controls with the framework's identified risk categories. Explanation: Aligning controls with risk categories ensures they address relevant threats systematically. Option a improves documentation but is not the critical step. Option b is preliminary and does not guarantee proper mapping. Option d focuses on validation, not initial mapping.

712. A cloud compliance validation identifies that a company's encryption policies do not align with GDPR requirements. Which remediation best ensures compliance?
a. Encrypting all personal data with AES-256 in transit and at rest
b. Implementing mandatory encryption for backups stored in non-EU regions
c. Replacing legacy encryption algorithms with SHA-1 for compatibility
d. Requiring all encryption keys to be managed by the cloud service provider

Answer: a. Encrypting all personal data with AES-256 in transit and at rest. Explanation: GDPR requires strong encryption for personal data to ensure its confidentiality, and AES-256 meets this standard. Option b addresses jurisdictional concerns but is narrower. Option c uses an outdated algorithm and is non-compliant. Option d reduces customer control over encryption keys.

713. An organization conducts a data protection assessment for its SaaS applications. Which measure best ensures the integrity of data stored in the cloud?
a. Configuring checksum validation for data uploads and downloads
b. Using geofencing to restrict data access based on location
c. Enabling read-only permissions for external consultants
d. Conducting vulnerability scans on the cloud service provider's infrastructure

Answer: a. Configuring checksum validation for data uploads and downloads. Explanation: Checksum validation ensures data is not corrupted or tampered with during transit or storage. Option b supports access control, not integrity. Option c limits access but does not verify integrity. Option d focuses on vulnerabilities, not data validation.

714. During an access control review, an organization discovers that temporary contractors have administrator-level access to sensitive cloud resources. What is the most effective remediation step?
a. Removing administrator access from contractor accounts and assigning least privilege
b. Extending the contractors' access period to complete current projects
c. Disabling the accounts and creating shared administrator credentials for temporary use
d. Configuring a single sign-on (SSO) solution to manage all contractor accounts

Answer: a. Removing administrator access from contractor accounts and assigning least privilege. Explanation: Implementing least privilege minimizes the risk of misuse or compromise of sensitive resources. Option b prolongs risk exposure. Option c introduces shared credentials, violating best practices. Option d aids management but does not reduce access risks.

715. A retail company performs a cloud security control mapping exercise. Which step ensures the mapped controls remain effective over time?
a. Reviewing the mapping quarterly to account for new threats and requirements
b. Limiting control updates to avoid unnecessary operational disruptions

c. Using static mapping templates provided by the cloud service provider
d. Delegating responsibility for the controls to the service provider

Answer: a. Reviewing the mapping quarterly to account for new threats and requirements. Explanation: Regular reviews ensure controls adapt to evolving threats and compliance standards. Option b prioritizes stability over security. Option c is static and cannot account for changes. Option d misunderstands the shared responsibility model.

716. An IT team conducts a cloud configuration review. Which finding poses the highest risk to data confidentiality?
a. Misconfigured IAM policies allowing public access to sensitive resources
b. Disabled logging on storage buckets used for archiving
c. Use of customer-managed encryption keys for data protection
d. Inconsistent naming conventions for cloud resource identifiers

Answer: a. Misconfigured IAM policies allowing public access to sensitive resources. Explanation: Public access to sensitive resources significantly compromises confidentiality. Option b impacts auditability, not confidentiality. Option c enhances data protection. Option d relates to organization, not security.

717. An organization adopts a microservices architecture for its core business applications. Which security practice is most effective in mitigating risks associated with unauthorized service communication?
a. Deploying a network-based firewall to control inter-service traffic
b. Implementing mutual TLS (mTLS) between services
c. Restricting access to microservices using IP whitelists
d. Configuring rate limiting on external-facing APIs

Answer: b. Implementing mutual TLS (mTLS) between services. Explanation: mTLS provides robust service-to-service authentication and encryption, ensuring secure communication. Option a lacks granularity and dynamic adaptability for microservices. Option c is difficult to manage at scale in dynamic environments. Option d mitigates external abuse but does not address inter-service communication.

718. A company implements an event-driven architecture to process real-time transactions. What is the best approach to ensure the integrity of messages between producers and consumers?
a. Encrypting messages using symmetric encryption
b. Signing messages with a secure digital signature
c. Storing all messages in a centralized database for audit purposes
d. Using a secure VPN for message delivery

Answer: b. Signing messages with a secure digital signature. Explanation: Digital signatures ensure both integrity and authenticity of messages. Option a protects confidentiality but not integrity. Option c supports auditing but does not guarantee integrity during transit. Option d secures transport but not message validation.

719. In a service mesh architecture, what is the primary purpose of a sidecar proxy?
a. To handle service discovery and routing
b. To enforce security policies and monitor service communication
c. To detect and block malicious traffic at the network perimeter
d. To balance loads across services in the mesh

Answer: b. To enforce security policies and monitor service communication. Explanation: Sidecar proxies manage traffic, enforce security policies, and monitor service-to-service interactions. Option a is a function of service discovery tools, not proxies. Option c pertains to network-based firewalls. Option d refers to load balancing, not sidecar functionality.

720. What is the primary security challenge in an API gateway architecture?
a. Monitoring API performance and uptime
b. Enforcing consistent authentication and authorization mechanisms
c. Encrypting all data transmitted between APIs and clients
d. Configuring API request throttling to prevent service abuse

Answer: b. Enforcing consistent authentication and authorization mechanisms. Explanation: API gateways centralize and enforce access controls, ensuring uniform security across services. Option a relates to performance monitoring, not security. Option c ensures confidentiality but not access control. Option d prevents abuse but does not address authentication and authorization.

721. Which security pattern is best suited for decomposing a monolithic application into a secure microservices architecture?
a. Zero-trust security with granular access controls
b. Flat network segmentation for simplified communication
c. Static rule-based firewall configurations
d. Encryption-only approach to protect data in transit

Answer: a. Zero-trust security with granular access controls. Explanation: Zero-trust ensures that access is continuously verified at a granular level, fitting the microservices model. Option b lacks the necessary segmentation granularity. Option c is rigid and insufficient for dynamic services. Option d focuses only on data security, neglecting authentication and access control.

722. What is the most effective way to prevent privilege escalation in a service mesh?
a. Using role-based access control (RBAC) for each service
b. Isolating services into different physical servers
c. Implementing mutual authentication between the client and server
d. Logging all access attempts to critical services

Answer: a. Using role-based access control (RBAC) for each service. Explanation: RBAC limits permissions based on roles, preventing unauthorized privilege escalation. Option b is costly and not scalable for microservices. Option c ensures communication security but does not control permissions. Option d supports monitoring but does not prevent escalation.

723. In an event-driven security model, what is the primary advantage of using a publish/subscribe pattern for real-time alerts?
a. It ensures that all systems process the alerts sequentially
b. It allows multiple subscribers to receive alerts simultaneously
c. It provides end-to-end encryption for all alert messages
d. It guarantees that all alert messages are stored for future reference

Answer: b. It allows multiple subscribers to receive alerts simultaneously. Explanation: The publish/subscribe pattern ensures real-time distribution to multiple systems. Option a is inaccurate; processing is often asynchronous. Option c depends on implementation but is not the pattern's primary advantage. Option d pertains to message durability, not real-time distribution.

724. An organization deploys an API gateway to manage access to its microservices. What feature is most critical for detecting and blocking automated attacks?
a. Static IP filtering for incoming requests
b. Dynamic rate limiting and behavioral analytics
c. Encryption of all request and response data
d. Manual review of suspicious traffic patterns

Answer: b. Dynamic rate limiting and behavioral analytics. Explanation: These features identify and mitigate automated abuse effectively. Option a lacks adaptability to dynamic attacks. Option c protects data but not against abuse. Option d is slow and resource-intensive for real-time protection.

725. What is the primary reason for implementing security decomposition in a microservices environment?
a. To simplify application performance monitoring
b. To distribute security responsibilities among smaller components
c. To reduce costs associated with centralized security tools
d. To streamline compliance reporting for external auditors

Answer: b. To distribute security responsibilities among smaller components. Explanation: Decomposition ensures that each service independently manages its security, reducing attack surface and simplifying scalability. Option a focuses on monitoring, not security. Option c is unrelated to decomposition. Option d is an indirect benefit, not the primary reason.

726. A global financial organization conducts a recovery procedure validation for its core banking system. Which approach best ensures the procedure aligns with the established Recovery Time Objective (RTO)?
a. Conducting a tabletop exercise to discuss the recovery steps with the IT team
b. Simulating a complete system outage and measuring recovery time
c. Reviewing the recovery documentation for accuracy and completeness
d. Performing daily backups to reduce recovery complexity

Answer: b. Simulating a complete system outage and measuring recovery time. Explanation: Simulating an outage validates the procedure's ability to meet the RTO under realistic conditions. Option a provides awareness but lacks practical validation. Option c enhances documentation but does not test recovery. Option d supports data protection but does not address RTO alignment.

727. An organization performs business process testing for its manufacturing operations. Which scenario best evaluates the resilience of interdependent processes?
a. Testing the recovery of individual processes in isolation
b. Simulating a disruption to upstream processes and assessing downstream impacts
c. Using historical incident data to predict potential process failures
d. Conducting surveys to gather employee feedback on process priorities

Answer: b. Simulating a disruption to upstream processes and assessing downstream impacts. Explanation: Simulating disruptions evaluates how interdependencies affect overall resilience. Option a fails to account for dependencies. Option c provides insights but does not test resilience. Option d gathers opinions but lacks practical testing.

728. A healthcare provider tests its communication plan for disaster response. Which metric is most critical for evaluating the plan's effectiveness?
a. Percentage of staff who acknowledged receipt of notifications
b. Average time to disseminate critical information to all stakeholders
c. Number of communication channels included in the plan
d. Cost of maintaining the communication infrastructure

Answer: b. Average time to disseminate critical information to all stakeholders. Explanation: Speed of communication ensures timely responses during emergencies. Option a measures acknowledgment but not timeliness. Option c focuses on diversity, not efficiency. Option d pertains to budget, not effectiveness.

729. During alternate site readiness testing, what factor is most critical for ensuring the site can support critical operations?
a. The proximity of the alternate site to the primary location
b. The availability of physical security measures at the alternate site
c. The alternate site's ability to operate independently of the primary site
d. The cost of maintaining the alternate site for extended periods

Answer: c. The alternate site's ability to operate independently of the primary site. Explanation: Alternate site readiness depends on its ability to function autonomously during disruptions. Option a impacts disaster risk but not readiness. Option b ensures security but not operational independence. Option d relates to cost, not functionality.

730. An IT team conducts critical system recovery testing. Which result best demonstrates that the system meets business continuity requirements?
a. The system is restored within the defined RTO with no data loss
b. The system shows no errors during the recovery process
c. The recovery process identifies previously undocumented dependencies
d. Users experience no noticeable disruption during recovery testing

Answer: a. The system is restored within the defined RTO with no data loss. Explanation: Meeting RTO and data integrity requirements ensures the system aligns with continuity objectives. Option b reflects technical execution but not timing. Option c supports improvement but is not a success measure. Option d indicates minimal disruption but does not guarantee objectives are met.

731. A retail company performs business continuity testing for a ransomware attack scenario. Which action best validates the company's ability to recover critical operations?
a. Simulating an attack and restoring systems using isolated backups
b. Conducting a tabletop exercise focused on ransomware response
c. Reviewing the incident response playbook with senior leadership
d. Enforcing strict data retention policies across all systems

Answer: a. Simulating an attack and restoring systems using isolated backups. Explanation: Simulating recovery with isolated backups ensures ransomware cannot affect recovery efforts. Option b enhances preparedness but does not validate recovery. Option c supports planning but lacks practical testing. Option d reduces data risk but does not test recovery.

732. A business continuity test involves simulating simultaneous disruptions to multiple systems. What is the primary objective of this test?
a. To evaluate the scalability of the business continuity plan
b. To measure the financial impact of potential system failures
c. To assess employee readiness for disaster scenarios
d. To document lessons learned for future plan updates
Answer: a. To evaluate the scalability of the business continuity plan. Explanation: Testing simultaneous disruptions assesses the plan's ability to handle widespread incidents. Option b focuses on cost, not scalability. Option c measures awareness, not the plan itself. Option d supports improvement but is not the primary objective.

733. A forensic investigator is tasked with collecting digital evidence from a compromised system. What is the most critical first step to ensure the integrity of the evidence?
a. Perform a live analysis of the system to capture volatile data
b. Create a forensic image of the system using write-blocking tools
c. Disconnect the system from the network to prevent further compromise
d. Perform a full malware scan before collecting the evidence

Answer: b. Create a forensic image of the system using write-blocking tools. Explanation: Creating a forensic image ensures an exact copy of the data is preserved without altering the original evidence. Option a may lead to evidence contamination. Option c is useful but not the first step for preserving evidence integrity. Option d risks altering or deleting evidence.

734. During memory forensics, which artifact is most likely to provide insights into malware persistence mechanisms?
a. Network session details captured in volatile memory
b. The loaded kernel modules and process handles
c. The system's ARP cache entries
d. Deleted files recovered from the hard drive

Answer: b. The loaded kernel modules and process handles. Explanation: Kernel modules and process handles often reveal how malware persists in memory or interacts with the OS. Option a highlights network activity, not persistence. Option c shows network mappings but not malware mechanisms. Option d pertains to disk-based artifacts, not memory.

735. While reconstructing a timeline for an incident, which data source provides the most accurate sequence of system activities?
a. Application logs stored on the compromised system
b. File system metadata such as MAC (Modified, Accessed, Created) times
c. Network traffic captures from the perimeter firewall
d. User activity reports from the SIEM

Answer: b. File system metadata such as MAC (Modified, Accessed, Created) times. Explanation: MAC times provide granular details on file activity, essential for reconstructing events. Option a may be altered by the attacker. Option c provides external activity, not internal events. Option d summarizes activity but lacks granular timestamps.

736. What is the most effective technique to analyze a newly discovered malware sample in a secure environment?
a. Perform static analysis to extract indicators of compromise (IOCs)
b. Deploy the malware on a production system to observe behavior
c. Use a packet sniffer to monitor all communications from the infected system
d. Reverse engineer the malware code to identify all vulnerabilities exploited

Answer: a. Perform static analysis to extract indicators of compromise (IOCs). Explanation: Static analysis safely identifies IOCs without executing the malware. Option b risks spreading infection. Option c supports analysis but requires execution. Option d is resource-intensive and not the initial step.

737. Which network traffic pattern is most indicative of data exfiltration during an investigation?
a. High volumes of outbound traffic to a single foreign IP address
b. Frequent DNS queries to well-known domain names
c. Repeated failed authentication attempts across multiple endpoints
d. Elevated HTTP POST requests to internal servers

Answer: a. High volumes of outbound traffic to a single foreign IP address. Explanation: Unusual outbound traffic to foreign IPs is a common indicator of data exfiltration. Option b suggests domain reconnaissance. Option c indicates potential brute-force attempts. Option d could indicate lateral movement but not exfiltration.

738. What is the primary challenge when handling evidence collected from cloud environments?
a. Inability to capture full packet data from cloud services
b. Verifying the chain of custody for shared infrastructure
c. Performing a forensic analysis without disrupting cloud services
d. Extracting data encrypted by cloud providers

Answer: b. Verifying the chain of custody for shared infrastructure. Explanation: Shared infrastructure in the cloud complicates establishing a clear chain of custody. Option a is incorrect; metadata is often more critical than packet captures. Option c is a secondary challenge but manageable. Option d pertains to encryption, not evidence handling.

739. An investigator discovers a suspicious executable on an endpoint. What should be prioritized during static malware analysis?
a. Analyzing the executable's behavior in a sandbox environment
b. Identifying embedded URLs or IP addresses in the code
c. Tracking the system changes made by the executable
d. Observing the executable's interactions with network services

Answer: b. Identifying embedded URLs or IP addresses in the code. Explanation: Static analysis focuses on extracting hardcoded IOCs for detection and prevention. Option a is dynamic analysis. Options c and d pertain to behavior monitoring, not static analysis.

740. What is the main advantage of using timeline reconstruction in an incident investigation?
a. It highlights anomalies in system logs automatically
b. It organizes events chronologically to identify the attack sequence
c. It eliminates the need for manual log analysis
d. It ensures all user activities are captured in real-time

Answer: b. It organizes events chronologically to identify the attack sequence. Explanation: Timeline reconstruction provides a clear view of the attack's progression, aiding analysis. Option a describes automated tools but is not exclusive to timelines. Option c is inaccurate; manual verification is still required. Option d pertains to monitoring, not forensic timelines.

741. A multinational corporation implements SAML-based identity federation. Which SAML component is responsible for issuing authentication assertions to the service provider?
a. Relying party
b. Identity provider
c. Metadata repository
d. Assertion consumer service

Answer: b. Identity provider. Explanation: The identity provider (IdP) authenticates users and issues SAML assertions to the service provider, enabling federated authentication. Option a, relying party, refers to the service provider that consumes assertions. Option c, metadata repository, stores configuration details but does not authenticate. Option d, assertion consumer service, processes assertions but does not issue them.

742. An organization selects an identity provider for its federation system. Which criterion is most critical for ensuring secure integration with multiple service providers?
a. Support for federated logout across all sessions
b. Compatibility with service provider metadata exchange protocols
c. Availability of dedicated support for account recovery
d. Inclusion of a customizable user interface for authentication portals

Answer: b. Compatibility with service provider metadata exchange protocols. Explanation: Metadata exchange ensures secure and seamless integration between the identity provider and service providers. Option a improves session management but is not essential for integration. Option c addresses support, not security. Option d pertains to usability, not integration.

743. A global retailer configures its service provider for SAML-based federation. Which step is critical to establish trust with the identity provider?
a. Importing the service provider's private key into the identity provider
b. Configuring the identity provider to accept unsigned assertions
c. Exchanging public certificates between the service provider and identity provider
d. Enforcing session timeout policies on the identity provider

Answer: c. Exchanging public certificates between the service provider and identity provider. Explanation: Public certificate exchange allows the service provider to verify the authenticity of SAML assertions issued by the identity provider. Option a introduces unnecessary risk. Option b reduces security by accepting unsigned assertions. Option d is unrelated to trust establishment.

744. Which federation trust model provides the most scalable solution for managing trust relationships across hundreds of organizations?
a. Peer-to-peer trust model
b. Hub-and-spoke model
c. Web of trust model
d. Direct trust model

Answer: b. Hub-and-spoke model. Explanation: The hub-and-spoke model centralizes trust relationships at a central hub, simplifying management across many entities. Option a requires individual relationships, which is not scalable. Option c, web of trust, is more decentralized and complex. Option d involves direct relationships, making it inefficient at scale.

745. An organization implements Single Sign-On (SSO) using identity federation. What is the primary security benefit of SSO in this context?
a. Enhanced end-to-end encryption for user sessions
b. Reduced attack surface by limiting the number of user accounts
c. Minimized password fatigue and credential reuse risks
d. Faster session termination across all federated applications

Answer: c. Minimized password fatigue and credential reuse risks. Explanation: SSO reduces the number of credentials users need to remember, lowering the risk of weak or reused passwords. Option a relates to encryption, not SSO. Option b oversimplifies the risk reduction. Option d addresses session management, not credential security.

746. A financial institution using SAML-based SSO reports errors stating, "Assertion expired." What is the most likely root cause?
a. The service provider's public certificate has expired
b. The identity provider and service provider clocks are not synchronized
c. The user's browser is blocking cookies required for session tracking
d. The assertion signing algorithm is not supported by the service provider

Answer: b. The identity provider and service provider clocks are not synchronized. Explanation: SAML assertions include timestamps, and clock discrepancies between entities can cause assertions to be deemed expired. Option a would cause signature validation failures. Option c affects session persistence but not assertion expiration. Option d causes incompatibility but does not affect expiration.

747. Which practice best ensures the integrity of metadata exchanged between federated entities?
a. Encrypting metadata files with the service provider's private key
b. Signing metadata with a certificate issued by a trusted certificate authority
c. Hosting metadata on secure, internal-only servers to restrict access
d. Including metadata in emails to ensure authenticity via sender verification

Answer: b. Signing metadata with a certificate issued by a trusted certificate authority. Explanation: Signed metadata ensures that it has not been tampered with and is from a trusted source. Option a encrypts metadata but does not confirm authenticity. Option c restricts access but does not validate integrity. Option d risks phishing and lacks strong verification.

748. A development team uses static code analysis during their secure coding process. What is the primary advantage of this approach?
a. It ensures runtime vulnerabilities are detected and prevented
b. It identifies vulnerabilities in code before it is executed
c. It reduces the need for manual code review by automating best practices
d. It automatically fixes discovered vulnerabilities

Answer: b. It identifies vulnerabilities in code before it is executed. Explanation: Static code analysis examines code for security flaws without executing it, catching issues early in the development cycle. Option a describes dynamic analysis. Option c partially automates the process but doesn't replace manual reviews. Option d is false; most tools highlight issues but do not resolve them.

749. During a secure code review, a developer discovers improper error handling. What is the primary risk associated with this issue?
a. Unauthorized escalation of privileges
b. Leakage of sensitive information to attackers
c. Increased risk of denial-of-service attacks
d. Insecure random number generation

Answer: b. Leakage of sensitive information to attackers. Explanation: Poor error handling often exposes sensitive details, such as stack traces or database information, useful to attackers. Option a relates to access control issues. Option c concerns resource exhaustion, not error handling. Option d pertains to cryptographic flaws, not error management.

750. What is the primary purpose of a code review checklist in a secure development lifecycle?
a. To ensure consistent evaluation of security best practices
b. To automatically detect all vulnerabilities during reviews
c. To enforce compliance with external regulatory standards
d. To reduce the time required to deploy code to production

Answer: a. To ensure consistent evaluation of security best practices. Explanation: A checklist standardizes the review process, ensuring that key areas are not overlooked. Option b misrepresents manual code reviews. Option c may be a secondary benefit but isn't the main purpose. Option d relates to operational efficiency, not code review focus.
751. A static code analysis tool flags a possible SQL injection vulnerability. What is the most effective remediation?
a. Using input validation to sanitize all user inputs
b. Encrypting database queries with a secure algorithm
c. Restricting database access based on IP addresses
d. Performing regular backups of the database

Answer: a. Using input validation to sanitize all user inputs. Explanation: Proper input validation and parameterized queries prevent SQL injection attacks. Option b ensures data confidentiality but doesn't prevent injection. Option c adds a layer of security but doesn't address the root issue. Option d protects data but doesn't stop injection.

752. Which metric is most useful for measuring the effectiveness of secure coding practices?
a. Number of lines of code reviewed per week
b. Average defect density per thousand lines of code

c. Total vulnerabilities detected during penetration testing
d. Developer productivity in terms of features delivered

Answer: b. Average defect density per thousand lines of code. Explanation: Defect density indicates code quality and the impact of secure coding practices. Option a measures activity, not quality. Option c focuses on testing outcomes, not coding effectiveness. Option d is unrelated to security.

753. A secure coding guideline recommends avoiding the use of hardcoded credentials. What is the primary risk of violating this guideline?
a. Increased susceptibility to cross-site scripting (XSS) attacks
b. Reduced performance due to inefficient code execution
c. Exposure of sensitive credentials if source code is compromised
d. Inability to implement role-based access controls effectively

Answer: c. Exposure of sensitive credentials if source code is compromised. Explanation: Hardcoded credentials are easily accessible if the code is exposed, leading to potential breaches. Option a is unrelated to credential storage. Option b is false; performance is unaffected by hardcoding credentials. Option d relates to access control implementation, not credential storage.

754. What is the best approach to classify and prioritize security bugs discovered during a code review?
a. Sorting bugs by the time required for remediation
b. Categorizing bugs by their potential business impact
c. Grouping bugs based on the affected modules
d. Prioritizing bugs reported most frequently by developers

Answer: b. Categorizing bugs by their potential business impact. Explanation: Classifying bugs by business impact ensures critical vulnerabilities are addressed first. Option a may delay critical fixes. Option c helps organization but doesn't prioritize risks. Option d is based on frequency, not severity.

755. A code review identifies the use of an insecure random number generator. What is the primary consequence of this vulnerability?
a. Increased exposure to timing attacks
b. Predictable values that compromise cryptographic operations
c. Elevated risk of buffer overflow vulnerabilities
d. Difficulty in maintaining code readability

Answer: b. Predictable values that compromise cryptographic operations. Explanation: Insecure random number generators produce predictable outputs, undermining cryptography. Option a concerns timing issues, not RNG flaws. Option c is unrelated. Option d is a coding style issue, not a security risk.

756. A security bug is discovered in a third-party library used in the application. What is the most effective mitigation?
a. Removing the library entirely from the application
b. Updating the library to the latest secure version
c. Writing custom code to replace the library functionality
d. Scanning the application weekly for related vulnerabilities

Answer: b. Updating the library to the latest secure version. Explanation: Patching to the latest secure version addresses vulnerabilities without additional complexity. Option a sacrifices functionality unnecessarily. Option c is resource-intensive and less efficient. Option d monitors but doesn't fix the issue.

757. An organization implements ISO 27001. Which element is essential to demonstrate compliance with the framework during a certification audit?
a. Conducting a penetration test of all externally facing systems
b. Documenting and maintaining an information security management system (ISMS)
c. Implementing multi-factor authentication for privileged user accounts
d. Training employees on secure software development practices

Answer: b. Documenting and maintaining an information security management system (ISMS). Explanation: ISO 27001 requires the establishment and continuous maintenance of an ISMS as a central component of compliance. Option a supports security but is not a mandatory ISO 27001 element. Option c enhances access control but is not specifically required. Option d pertains to training but is not central to certification.

758. A cloud service provider seeks SOC 2 certification. Which principle of the SOC 2 Trust Services Criteria (TSC) focuses on preventing unauthorized disclosure of information?
a. Availability
b. Security
c. Confidentiality
d. Processing Integrity

Answer: c. Confidentiality. Explanation: The confidentiality principle addresses the protection of sensitive information from unauthorized disclosure. Option a pertains to system availability. Option b relates to overall system security, not specifically to information protection. Option d ensures accurate and authorized processing of data.

759. An e-commerce company processes credit card payments and must comply with PCI DSS. Which control is mandatory to meet requirement 10 of PCI DSS regarding log management?
a. Retaining logs for at least one year and ensuring three months are readily available
b. Encrypting all stored log files using AES-256 encryption
c. Performing real-time monitoring of network traffic for anomalies
d. Requiring a quarterly review of access control logs by a third party

Answer: a. Retaining logs for at least one year and ensuring three months are readily available. Explanation: PCI DSS requires specific log retention periods to ensure accountability and traceability. Option b enhances log security but is not mandated by requirement 10. Option c pertains to network monitoring, not log retention. Option d is an operational best practice but not a requirement.

760. A healthcare provider must comply with HIPAA security rules. Which practice best ensures compliance with the Security Rule's technical safeguards?
a. Encrypting ePHI at rest and in transit using industry-standard protocols
b. Conducting regular training sessions for staff on HIPAA policies
c. Signing business associate agreements with all third-party vendors
d. Storing ePHI only on-premises to minimize exposure to external threats

Answer: a. Encrypting ePHI at rest and in transit using industry-standard protocols. Explanation: HIPAA's technical safeguards include ensuring the confidentiality of ePHI through encryption. Option b is part of the administrative safeguards. Option c pertains to legal agreements, not technical safeguards. Option d is a strategy but not specifically required.

761. During a GDPR compliance review, an organization identifies gaps in handling data subject access requests (DSARs). What is the most effective remediation step?
a. Implementing an automated tool for tracking and responding to DSARs
b. Encrypting all data subject information stored in the organization's systems

c. Reducing the amount of personal data collected to limit exposure
d. Updating the organization's privacy policy to reflect DSAR procedures

Answer: a. Implementing an automated tool for tracking and responding to DSARs. Explanation: Automation ensures timely and accurate handling of DSARs, which is a critical GDPR requirement. Option b enhances security but does not address DSARs. Option c supports data minimization but does not improve DSAR handling. Option d is necessary but not as effective for addressing gaps.

762. An organization pursuing ISO 27001 certification conducts a risk assessment. Which action best demonstrates compliance with the risk treatment process?
a. Applying compensating controls to address identified high-risk areas
b. Documenting a risk treatment plan and obtaining management approval
c. Purchasing cyber insurance to transfer all identified risks
d. Encrypting all network traffic to reduce risk of data breaches

Answer: b. Documenting a risk treatment plan and obtaining management approval. Explanation: ISO 27001 mandates that risks be formally addressed in a treatment plan approved by management. Option a applies controls but does not cover documentation. Option c transfers risks but does not satisfy documentation requirements. Option d reduces risks but is not comprehensive.

763. A retail company seeks to meet SOC 2 criteria for availability. Which test is most relevant to demonstrate compliance?
a. Simulating a DDoS attack and verifying system uptime during the test
b. Conducting penetration tests on external-facing systems
c. Reviewing employee training records on availability best practices
d. Encrypting all backups stored in off-site locations

Answer: a. Simulating a DDoS attack and verifying system uptime during the test. Explanation: SOC 2's availability principle focuses on ensuring systems remain accessible under stress or attack conditions. Option b supports security but not availability testing. Option c relates to training, not system availability. Option d pertains to data protection, not uptime.

764. An application undergoes load testing to simulate high user traffic. What is the primary security risk if proper controls are not in place during load testing?
a. Exposure of sensitive user data in test logs
b. Compromise of the production environment due to weak authentication
c. Generation of false positives in application monitoring systems
d. Overloading application components, leading to a denial-of-service (DoS) condition

Answer: d. Overloading application components, leading to a denial-of-service (DoS) condition. Explanation: Uncontrolled load testing can mimic a DoS attack, disrupting application availability. Option a concerns data privacy but is not specific to load testing. Option b pertains to deployment, not testing. Option c relates to monitoring anomalies but not critical risks during load testing.

765. Which control is most effective in mitigating the risk of resource exhaustion from malicious traffic?
a. Implementing multi-threading in application code
b. Using rate limiting and throttling mechanisms
c. Increasing system memory and CPU capacity
d. Deploying a dedicated logging server for monitoring

Answer: b. Using rate limiting and throttling mechanisms. Explanation: Rate limiting ensures traffic does not exceed application capacity, preventing resource exhaustion. Option a improves performance but does not control malicious traffic. Option c is a temporary fix, not a preventive control. Option d supports monitoring but does not mitigate the risk.

766. A web application experiences periodic performance degradation during peak usage. Which baseline metric is most useful for diagnosing security-related performance issues?
a. Average response time under normal conditions
b. Number of concurrent users accessing the application
c. CPU and memory utilization thresholds for backend servers
d. Peak load capacity during stress testing

Answer: a. Average response time under normal conditions. Explanation: Comparing current performance to the baseline response time identifies deviations indicating potential security issues, such as resource abuse. Option b tracks usage but does not explain degradation. Option c monitors resources but not response time. Option d focuses on load testing, not normal operation.

767. What is the primary advantage of deploying a web application firewall (WAF) to protect application performance?
a. Detecting and blocking malicious traffic in real-time
b. Encrypting all application traffic to prevent data breaches
c. Improving the speed of legitimate traffic processing
d. Performing deep packet inspection for all network layers

Answer: a. Detecting and blocking malicious traffic in real-time. Explanation: A WAF safeguards application performance by filtering malicious requests, preserving resources for legitimate users. Option b focuses on data protection, not performance. Option c is not a primary function of a WAF. Option d refers to network firewalls, not application-level security.

768. A financial application is prone to resource-intensive requests. What is the best mitigation to maintain performance under attack?
a. Partitioning database queries across multiple servers
b. Rewriting application code to improve efficiency
c. Enforcing client-side request validation
d. Setting hard limits on per-session resource usage

Answer: d. Setting hard limits on per-session resource usage. Explanation: Resource limits prevent individual sessions from monopolizing system resources, maintaining performance. Option a optimizes database performance but does not address resource hogging. Option b improves efficiency but may not address targeted abuse. Option c is insufficient against resource-intensive requests.

769. Which security measure is most effective against a distributed denial-of-service (DDoS) attack targeting application performance?
a. Configuring stateful firewalls to monitor inbound traffic
b. Deploying a content delivery network (CDN) with traffic filtering capabilities
c. Restricting access to the application using IP whitelisting
d. Increasing server capacity to handle higher traffic volumes

Answer: b. Deploying a content delivery network (CDN) with traffic filtering capabilities. Explanation: A CDN can absorb and filter DDoS traffic, protecting application performance. Option a lacks scalability for distributed attacks. Option c is impractical for dynamic environments. Option d addresses capacity but not malicious traffic.

770. What is the primary reason to monitor application performance during security testing?
a. To ensure compliance with regulatory performance benchmarks

b. To identify vulnerabilities that impact user experience
c. To detect configuration errors in the testing environment
d. To validate encryption mechanisms for secure communication

Answer: b. To identify vulnerabilities that impact user experience. Explanation: Security issues such as resource abuse or poor input handling can degrade performance, harming user experience. Option a focuses on compliance, not testing outcomes. Option c relates to setup, not application vulnerabilities. Option d is unrelated to performance monitoring.

771. Which metric best measures the effectiveness of DoS protection mechanisms in an application?
a. Number of blocked IP addresses during an attack
b. Application uptime percentage during sustained traffic spikes
c. Average time to mitigate an ongoing DoS attack
d. Total data throughput handled by the application

Answer: b. Application uptime percentage during sustained traffic spikes. Explanation: Uptime reflects the ability of DoS protection mechanisms to maintain availability. Option a tracks blocking efforts but not performance. Option c measures response speed, not effectiveness. Option d focuses on throughput, not availability.

772. A load-balanced application experiences uneven traffic distribution across servers. What is the most likely cause of this issue?
a. Misconfigured rate-limiting rules in the WAF
b. Asymmetric session stickiness settings in the load balancer
c. Insufficient encryption of application requests
d. High latency caused by inefficient server routing

Answer: b. Asymmetric session stickiness settings in the load balancer. Explanation: Session stickiness can lead to uneven load distribution if misconfigured. Option a impacts request filtering, not traffic distribution. Option c pertains to data protection, not load balancing. Option d results from routing, not load balancing configurations.

773. An organization aiming for PCI DSS compliance reviews its cardholder data environment (CDE). Which action best aligns with PCI DSS requirement 1 for network security?
a. Installing and maintaining a firewall to segment the CDE from other networks
b. Implementing role-based access controls for all payment processing systems
c. Encrypting all stored cardholder data with strong encryption algorithms
d. Monitoring CDE user activity through centralized logging

Answer: a. Installing and maintaining a firewall to segment the CDE from other networks. Explanation: PCI DSS requirement 1 mandates firewalls to protect the CDE from unauthorized access. Option b aligns with access controls but falls under a different requirement. Option c addresses data protection but is not relevant to network segmentation. Option d pertains to monitoring but not firewall implementation.

774. A global enterprise integrates GDPR compliance measures into its cloud storage system. Which action best ensures compliance with data transfer regulations?
a. Encrypting all data transfers between the EU and non-EU regions
b. Ensuring cloud providers implement standard contractual clauses (SCCs)
c. Limiting data storage to servers within the EU
d. Regularly conducting penetration tests on the cloud provider's infrastructure

Answer: b. Ensuring cloud providers implement standard contractual clauses (SCCs). Explanation: SCCs are a GDPR-compliant mechanism for transferring data outside the EU. Option a secures data but does not address legal transfer requirements. Option c ensures location compliance but limits flexibility. Option d enhances security but is unrelated to transfer regulations.

775. During an ISO 27001 audit, an organization identifies a lack of documentation for incident response. What is the most effective immediate action to address this non-conformity?
a. Conducting an incident response tabletop exercise with key stakeholders
b. Developing a formal incident response policy and incorporating it into the ISMS
c. Implementing an automated incident detection tool across all systems
d. Providing employees with training on recognizing security incidents

Answer: b. Developing a formal incident response policy and incorporating it into the ISMS. Explanation: ISO 27001 requires documented processes for incident response as part of the ISMS. Option a aids preparedness but does not address documentation gaps. Option c improves detection but not compliance. Option d supports awareness but is not sufficient to meet audit requirements.

776. A company pursuing SOC 2 certification for security reviews its access management practices. Which practice best demonstrates compliance with the security principle?
a. Requiring multi-factor authentication for all administrative accounts
b. Encrypting data at rest with AES-256
c. Monitoring server uptime to ensure high availability
d. Implementing redundant backups for disaster recovery

Answer: a. Requiring multi-factor authentication for all administrative accounts. Explanation: Multi-factor authentication directly addresses the security principle by mitigating unauthorized access risks. Option b enhances data protection but is not an access control. Option c pertains to availability, not security. Option d focuses on recovery, not access management.

777. A healthcare organization reviews its HIPAA compliance with a focus on the administrative safeguards. Which action is most critical to meet compliance?
a. Conducting a formal risk analysis of potential threats to ePHI
b. Encrypting email communications containing ePHI
c. Limiting physical access to areas storing ePHI servers
d. Retaining audit logs of ePHI access for a minimum of six years

Answer: a. Conducting a formal risk analysis of potential threats to ePHI. Explanation: Risk analysis is a cornerstone of HIPAA administrative safeguards, helping to identify and mitigate risks to ePHI. Option b pertains to technical safeguards. Option c relates to physical safeguards. Option d addresses logging requirements but falls under technical safeguards.

778. A retail company undergoing a PCI DSS audit discovers that some wireless networks in its environment lack proper segmentation. What is the most effective remediation to ensure compliance?
a. Implementing WPA3 encryption for all wireless networks
b. Disabling all wireless networks within the cardholder data environment
c. Deploying network segmentation to isolate wireless traffic from the CDE
d. Requiring all employees to use a VPN when accessing wireless networks

Answer: c. Deploying network segmentation to isolate wireless traffic from the CDE. Explanation: Network segmentation ensures that unauthorized access through wireless networks does not compromise the CDE. Option a secures wireless traffic but does not address segmentation. Option b is impractical for many operations. Option d enhances security but does not meet segmentation requirements.

779. A data center implements biometric access controls to secure critical areas. What is the primary limitation of biometric systems that should be addressed in the security plan?
a. High cost of hardware installation and maintenance
b. False rejection rates (FRR) during user authentication
c. Lack of integration with other physical security systems
d. Risk of biometric data theft leading to identity compromise

Answer: d. Risk of biometric data theft leading to identity compromise. Explanation: If biometric data is stolen, it cannot be reset like a password, creating long-term risks. Option a is a valid concern but secondary to data security. Option b affects usability but can be mitigated with tuning. Option c pertains to operational efficiency, not core risks.

780. A financial institution uses multi-factor authentication (MFA) for physical access to secure areas. Which factor combination best enhances security?
a. Proximity card and PIN
b. Biometric scan and PIN
c. Biometric scan and proximity card
d. PIN and knowledge-based answers

Answer: c. Biometric scan and proximity card. Explanation: Combining biometrics (something you are) with a proximity card (something you have) ensures strong, layered security. Option a uses two factors but lacks the uniqueness of biometrics. Option b is weaker than combining physical and biometric factors. Option d relies entirely on knowledge-based factors, reducing effectiveness.

781. Which visitor management procedure minimizes the risk of unauthorized access in a multi-tenant building?
a. Requiring visitors to sign a paper logbook at the reception
b. Issuing temporary access badges with restricted permissions
c. Assigning security personnel to escort all visitors
d. Recording video surveillance footage of entry points

Answer: b. Issuing temporary access badges with restricted permissions. Explanation: Temporary badges with limited access prevent unauthorized entry while maintaining operational efficiency. Option a is outdated and prone to errors. Option c is resource-intensive and not scalable. Option d enhances monitoring but does not restrict access.

782. A company uses a tiered security zone model. Which factor is most critical for defining access restrictions between zones?
a. The operational role of employees in each zone
b. The value and sensitivity of the assets within each zone
c. The number of personnel requiring access to each zone
d. The physical layout of the building and facilities

Answer: b. The value and sensitivity of the assets within each zone. Explanation: Security zones should be defined by asset value and sensitivity to ensure proper protection. Option a supports role-based access but isn't the primary determinant. Option c addresses traffic but not security needs. Option d affects zone design but not access restrictions.

783. Which environmental monitoring system component is most critical for maintaining security in a data center?
a. Smoke and fire detection sensors
b. Humidity and temperature control systems
c. Water leak detection devices
d. Integrated alerting and reporting mechanisms

Answer: a. Smoke and fire detection sensors. Explanation: Fire is a critical threat to data centers, making detection and prevention systems essential. Option b affects equipment performance but is secondary. Option c mitigates water damage risks but is less common. Option d enhances response but relies on primary detection systems.

784. What is the most effective way to enforce security in a high-traffic lobby without impeding operations?
a. Installing a full-height turnstile system
b. Deploying an automated visitor management kiosk
c. Assigning additional security guards to monitor the lobby
d. Placing surveillance cameras to deter unauthorized entry

Answer: b. Deploying an automated visitor management kiosk. Explanation: Automated kiosks improve access control while maintaining throughput. Option a causes delays in high-traffic areas. Option c increases operational costs. Option d enhances monitoring but doesn't actively control access.

785. What is the primary benefit of using biometric authentication for securing high-value physical assets?
a. Eliminates the need for additional physical security controls
b. Prevents unauthorized access by ensuring user uniqueness
c. Reduces the cost of managing access control systems
d. Simplifies the process of resetting compromised credentials

Answer: b. Prevents unauthorized access by ensuring user uniqueness. Explanation: Biometric systems verify identity based on unique physical characteristics, reducing unauthorized access risks. Option a overstates biometrics' capabilities. Option c is incorrect; biometrics often increase costs. Option d is false since biometric credentials cannot be reset.

786. An environmental monitoring system detects rising temperatures in a server room. What is the first response to minimize damage?
a. Notify the IT and security teams to investigate the cause
b. Shut down all systems in the server room immediately
c. Activate the room's fire suppression system as a precaution
d. Increase the cooling output of HVAC systems to stabilize temperature

Answer: a. Notify the IT and security teams to investigate the cause. Explanation: Identifying the root cause prevents unnecessary downtime or damage. Option b disrupts operations unnecessarily. Option c is premature without identifying a fire. Option d may address the symptom but not the underlying issue.

787. A data center uses mantraps to control access to secure areas. What is the primary weakness of this control if improperly implemented?
a. Delays in entry during peak traffic hours
b. High costs associated with maintenance
c. Inability to verify identities inside the mantrap
d. Potential for tailgating if doors are not properly synchronized

Answer: d. Potential for tailgating if doors are not properly synchronized. Explanation: Tailgating undermines mantrap effectiveness by allowing unauthorized access. Option a affects usability, not security. Option b is a concern but unrelated to security effectiveness. Option c is mitigated by integrating authentication systems.

788. A multinational corporation performs a security impact assessment for a planned software upgrade. Which action is most critical to identify potential vulnerabilities introduced by the change?
a. Conducting a vulnerability scan on the upgraded software in a test environment
b. Documenting all changes in the release notes for stakeholder review

c. Reviewing the change proposal with the legal and compliance teams
d. Scheduling the change during non-business hours to minimize disruptions

Answer: a. Conducting a vulnerability scan on the upgraded software in a test environment. Explanation: A vulnerability scan identifies security weaknesses introduced by the upgrade before deployment. Option b enhances documentation but does not identify vulnerabilities. Option c ensures compliance but does not address security risks directly. Option d reduces operational impact but does not assess vulnerabilities.

789. An organization's Change Advisory Board (CAB) evaluates a major system change. What is the CAB's primary responsibility in this context?
a. Conducting penetration tests to validate the change's security impact
b. Reviewing the proposed change to assess risks and approve implementation
c. Implementing the approved change in the production environment
d. Providing post-implementation user training for the new system

Answer: b. Reviewing the proposed change to assess risks and approve implementation. Explanation: The CAB ensures that risks are identified, mitigated, and documented before approving a change. Option a involves security testing, which is performed by technical teams. Option c pertains to implementation, not CAB duties. Option d focuses on training, not change review.

790. An IT team implements an emergency change to address a critical zero-day vulnerability. Which post-implementation action best ensures security compliance?
a. Updating the incident response plan to include the vulnerability details
b. Conducting a retrospective review of the change's impact on security controls
c. Notifying all affected users about the emergency change via email
d. Performing a full network scan to identify other vulnerabilities

Answer: b. Conducting a retrospective review of the change's impact on security controls. Explanation: A post-implementation review ensures the emergency change did not compromise existing security controls. Option a supports future preparedness but does not validate the change. Option c ensures communication but does not address compliance. Option d identifies unrelated vulnerabilities but does not validate the emergency change.

791. During release management, which control is most effective in preventing unauthorized changes to the production environment?
a. Requiring peer code reviews for all changes before deployment
b. Using an automated CI/CD pipeline with integrated security checks
c. Configuring role-based access control for production systems
d. Scheduling weekly audits of deployed changes

Answer: c. Configuring role-based access control for production systems. Explanation: Role-based access control restricts unauthorized users from making changes to production systems. Option a ensures code quality but does not prevent unauthorized changes. Option b automates deployment but relies on proper configuration. Option d identifies unauthorized changes after the fact.

792. An organization discovers discrepancies during configuration validation for its cloud-based services. What action is most effective for addressing these discrepancies?
a. Reverting the configurations to a previous known-good state
b. Notifying the cloud service provider to investigate the discrepancies
c. Documenting the discrepancies and scheduling a follow-up review
d. Performing a root cause analysis to identify why discrepancies occurred

Answer: d. Performing a root cause analysis to identify why discrepancies occurred. Explanation: Root cause analysis ensures the underlying issue is resolved, preventing future discrepancies. Option a restores functionality temporarily but does not resolve the root cause. Option b shifts responsibility without internal investigation. Option c delays corrective action.

793. A company's change management policy includes a requirement for pre-change testing. What is the primary objective of this requirement?
a. Ensuring the change meets performance expectations under realistic conditions
b. Identifying users who will be affected by the change during implementation
c. Reducing the cost of implementing the change across the organization
d. Validating the completeness of the change's documentation

Answer: a. Ensuring the change meets performance expectations under realistic conditions. Explanation: Pre-change testing verifies that the change functions as intended and minimizes the risk of failure. Option b aids communication but does not validate performance. Option c focuses on cost, not testing. Option d improves documentation but does not test functionality.

794. A security operations team is overwhelmed by a high volume of alerts from their SIEM. What is the most effective initial step to reduce the noise and improve efficiency?
a. Increase logging levels across all critical systems to gather more detailed information
b. Adjust correlation rules to filter out low-priority events automatically
c. Disable alerts from non-critical systems to reduce the total volume
d. Implement a policy requiring manual review of all alerts

Answer: b. Adjust correlation rules to filter out low-priority events automatically. Explanation: Correlation rules allow the team to focus on high-priority events by eliminating irrelevant noise. Option a increases data volume, exacerbating the issue. Option c risks missing relevant alerts from non-critical systems. Option d is impractical and inefficient.

795. During an investigation, an analyst correlates logs from a firewall, endpoint detection system, and email gateway. What is the primary purpose of log correlation in this context?
a. To identify vulnerabilities in each system's configuration
b. To detect patterns that indicate coordinated malicious activity
c. To ensure compliance with logging and retention policies
d. To improve the speed of system log retrieval during audits

Answer: b. To detect patterns that indicate coordinated malicious activity. Explanation: Log correlation identifies patterns across multiple systems, revealing potential attacks. Option a pertains to configuration management, not correlation. Option c ensures compliance but doesn't detect threats. Option d focuses on operational efficiency, not security analysis.

796. What is the primary goal of alert triage in a security operations center (SOC)?
a. To escalate all alerts to incident responders for detailed investigation
b. To categorize alerts based on severity and prioritize response actions
c. To automatically resolve low-severity alerts without human intervention
d. To generate reports for stakeholders on daily alert volumes

Answer: b. To categorize alerts based on severity and prioritize response actions. Explanation: Triage ensures that critical alerts are addressed promptly while minimizing resource waste on false positives. Option a overloads responders. Option c eliminates useful context. Option d provides reporting but does not address immediate response needs.

797. Which approach is most effective for reducing false positives in a SIEM environment?
a. Lowering alert thresholds to capture all potential threats
b. Fine-tuning rules based on historical alert patterns
c. Disabling correlation rules with low match rates
d. Increasing the number of sources feeding into the SIEM

Answer: b. Fine-tuning rules based on historical alert patterns. Explanation: Fine-tuning rules reduces false positives by aligning thresholds and conditions with real-world activity. Option a increases noise. Option c may remove valid rules. Option d adds more data but doesn't address false positives.

798. An incident responder is tasked with categorizing an event involving unauthorized access to sensitive data. Which category is most appropriate under standard incident classification?
a. Reconnaissance
b. Privilege escalation
c. Data exfiltration
d. Denial of service

Answer: c. Data exfiltration. Explanation: The unauthorized access and removal of sensitive data align with the definition of data exfiltration. Option a refers to pre-attack information gathering. Option b involves gaining higher privileges but not data removal. Option d focuses on disrupting services, not data theft.

799. A SOC analyst identifies repeated failed login attempts from a single IP address across multiple systems. What is the most likely root cause?
a. Credential stuffing attack
b. Insider misuse of privileges
c. Man-in-the-middle attack
d. Misconfigured authentication protocols

Answer: a. Credential stuffing attack. Explanation: Repeated failed login attempts indicate automated testing of stolen credentials. Option b involves authorized users, not external attacks. Option c focuses on interception, not login attempts. Option d affects access reliability, not behavior.

800. What is the best method to identify the root cause of an incident where a previously trusted certificate was flagged as invalid?
a. Reviewing certificate expiration dates across the environment
b. Verifying the certificate's chain of trust and revocation status
c. Increasing the log verbosity of all certificate-related processes
d. Reissuing the certificate to restore its validity

Answer: b. Verifying the certificate's chain of trust and revocation status. Explanation: Checking the chain of trust and revocation determines whether the certificate was compromised or invalidated. Option a addresses expiration but not revocation. Option c may assist later but isn't the first step. Option d risks reinstating a potentially compromised certificate.

801. Which incident categorization best describes a scenario where a web application firewall blocks SQL injection attempts?
a. Precursor
b. Reconnaissance
c. Containment
d. Exploitation attempt

Answer: d. Exploitation attempt. Explanation: SQL injection is an attempt to exploit a vulnerability in the application. Option a refers to early signs of an attack. Option b involves gathering information, not exploiting a system. Option c is a response phase, not a categorization of the event.

802. A SOC team implements automated alert suppression for low-severity events. What is the greatest risk of this approach?
a. Missing critical threats hidden within suppressed alerts
b. Overloading incident responders with unnecessary alerts
c. Slowing down the processing speed of high-priority events
d. Violating regulatory requirements for alert retention

Answer: a. Missing critical threats hidden within suppressed alerts. Explanation: Suppression risks discarding alerts that may indicate larger patterns of attack. Option b describes suppression's intended benefit. Option c is unlikely due to prioritization mechanisms. Option d is unrelated to suppression.

803. An organization deploys a critical security patch as part of its emergency change management process. What is the most effective method to validate that the patch has been successfully applied across all affected systems?
a. Reviewing system logs for evidence of the patch installation
b. Conducting an automated vulnerability scan targeting the patched vulnerability
c. Notifying system administrators to manually verify patch deployment
d. Comparing system uptime before and after the patch installation

Answer: b. Conducting an automated vulnerability scan targeting the patched vulnerability. Explanation: A vulnerability scan ensures that the specific security issue addressed by the patch has been mitigated across all systems. Option a confirms patching but does not validate its effectiveness. Option c is time-consuming and prone to human error. Option d is unrelated to patch validation.

804. A software company introduces a new feature that significantly alters the behavior of its application. What is the most critical consideration for the Change Advisory Board (CAB) when reviewing the change?
a. Verifying that the feature has been tested for usability
b. Assessing the impact of the feature on existing security controls
c. Confirming that the marketing team has been informed of the release
d. Ensuring that training materials are updated to reflect the new feature

Answer: b. Assessing the impact of the feature on existing security controls. Explanation: The CAB's primary role is to evaluate the risks and impacts of changes, including how they affect security controls. Option a focuses on usability, which is outside the CAB's core responsibilities. Option c pertains to communication, not risk assessment. Option d supports training but is not the CAB's primary focus.

805. During an audit of the release management process, an organization finds that undocumented changes were deployed to production. What is the most effective way to address this issue?
a. Implementing a strict policy that prohibits emergency changes
b. Requiring all changes to be tracked in a centralized change management system
c. Increasing the frequency of audits to detect undocumented changes sooner
d. Limiting access to the production environment to senior IT staff only

Answer: b. Requiring all changes to be tracked in a centralized change management system. Explanation: Centralized tracking ensures accountability and prevents undocumented changes. Option a is impractical for emergency scenarios. Option c improves detection but does not prevent the issue. Option d limits access but does not guarantee proper documentation.

806. An IT team implements a change to upgrade a database server. Shortly after deployment, users report performance issues. Which action best addresses the situation?
a. Rolling back the change to the previous database version
b. Increasing server resources to handle the additional load
c. Reviewing post-implementation monitoring data to identify performance bottlenecks
d. Conducting a root cause analysis after notifying users of the delay

Answer: c. Reviewing post-implementation monitoring data to identify performance bottlenecks. Explanation: Analyzing monitoring data helps identify the specific cause of performance issues, enabling targeted remediation. Option a may be premature without identifying the issue. Option b mitigates symptoms but does not resolve the root cause. Option d delays resolution without addressing the immediate impact.

807. An organization conducts a post-implementation review of a major system upgrade. Which finding would most likely indicate a failure in the pre-change testing process?
a. Unanticipated performance degradation under heavy user loads
b. Users reporting difficulty navigating the updated system interface
c. Delayed communication of the change to key stakeholders
d. Security controls requiring manual reconfiguration post-upgrade

Answer: a. Unanticipated performance degradation under heavy user loads. Explanation: Performance issues under load suggest that pre-change testing did not adequately simulate real-world conditions. Option b indicates usability issues but not a testing failure. Option c reflects a communication lapse, not a testing problem. Option d pertains to configuration management, not pre-change testing.

808. A financial services organization integrates configuration validation into its change management process. What is the most effective approach to ensure that validation identifies unauthorized changes?
a. Automating configuration checks using a baseline comparison tool
b. Conducting monthly reviews of all implemented changes
c. Requiring dual approval for every change in the configuration
d. Storing configuration snapshots in an encrypted archive

Answer: a. Automating configuration checks using a baseline comparison tool. Explanation: Automated checks quickly identify deviations from approved configurations. Option b delays detection and increases risk exposure. Option c enhances governance but does not directly identify unauthorized changes. Option d supports security but does not actively monitor for changes.

809. A database administrator implements database activity monitoring (DAM) to identify potential privilege escalation attempts. Which activity would most likely indicate a privilege escalation event?
a. Multiple failed login attempts from a single user account
b. Execution of administrative queries by a non-administrative account
c. High-volume read queries from a privileged account
d. Repeated connections from an unfamiliar IP address

Answer: b. Execution of administrative queries by a non-administrative account. Explanation: A non-administrative account executing administrative queries suggests a privilege escalation attempt. Option a indicates brute force or credential testing. Option c may reflect legitimate high-volume access. Option d could signal reconnaissance but not privilege escalation.

810. What is the primary advantage of using query analysis in database activity monitoring?
a. It detects and prevents unauthorized access attempts in real time
b. It identifies anomalous query patterns that deviate from normal activity
c. It improves database performance by optimizing query execution plans

d. It ensures compliance with regulatory logging requirements

Answer: b. It identifies anomalous query patterns that deviate from normal activity. Explanation: Query analysis detects abnormal patterns, such as unexpected data access or malicious queries. Option a focuses on real-time prevention, not analysis. Option c addresses performance, not security. Option d relates to compliance, not query analysis.

811. Which anomaly detection rule is most effective in identifying a potential data exfiltration attempt?
a. Alerting on any SELECT query executed outside business hours
b. Flagging queries that retrieve a higher-than-usual volume of rows
c. Monitoring for failed queries due to syntax errors
d. Detecting multiple users accessing the same table simultaneously

Answer: b. Flagging queries that retrieve a higher-than-usual volume of rows. Explanation: High-volume queries are a common indicator of data exfiltration. Option a may generate too many false positives. Option c identifies poorly constructed queries, not exfiltration. Option d is more indicative of shared usage patterns than a security threat.

812. A security team configures audit logs for a critical database. What is the most important consideration to ensure the effectiveness of the logs?
a. Using a secure, tamper-evident storage mechanism for logs
b. Including all SQL statements executed by privileged accounts
c. Retaining logs for at least one year to comply with regulations
d. Storing logs on the same server as the database for quick access

Answer: a. Using a secure, tamper-evident storage mechanism for logs. Explanation: Tamper-evident storage ensures logs remain trustworthy and admissible as evidence. Option b is critical but secondary to ensuring log integrity. Option c supports compliance but doesn't enhance security. Option d risks log loss in case of server compromise.

813. Which access pattern would most likely trigger an alert in a database activity monitoring system?
a. A developer running multiple SELECT queries on a test database
b. A user account accessing tables that they do not normally access
c. A series of UPDATE statements executed by an administrative account
d. A query involving multiple JOIN statements on large tables

Answer: b. A user account accessing tables that they do not normally access. Explanation: Deviating from usual access patterns is a strong indicator of suspicious activity. Option a reflects legitimate testing. Option c aligns with routine administrative activity. Option d indicates complex queries but not anomalous behavior.

814. What is the most effective way to detect lateral movement attempts within a database environment?
a. Correlating database activity with endpoint detection logs
b. Monitoring for excessive login attempts across multiple accounts
c. Identifying sequential access to different databases by the same user
d. Configuring alerts for failed queries with syntax errors

Answer: c. Identifying sequential access to different databases by the same user. Explanation: Sequential access to multiple databases by the same user is a common tactic in lateral movement. Option a adds context but is not specific to lateral movement. Option b suggests brute force, not lateral movement. Option d relates to query construction, not movement detection.

815. Which configuration error in audit logs would most likely reduce their effectiveness in detecting insider threats?
a. Excluding failed login attempts from logging
b. Setting logs to overwrite after a specific size limit is reached

c. Not logging queries executed by privileged accounts
d. Logging only changes to schema objects

Answer: c. Not logging queries executed by privileged accounts. Explanation: Privileged accounts often perform malicious actions during insider threats, so excluding them undermines monitoring. Option a reduces visibility but is less critical. Option b risks losing older logs but doesn't prevent threat detection. Option d focuses too narrowly on schema changes.

816. A query analysis tool flags a single, rarely accessed table being queried at a high frequency. What is the most likely explanation?
a. An attacker attempting a brute-force attack on table data
b. A data migration process temporarily increasing access frequency
c. A poorly optimized query causing redundant table scans
d. A legitimate user performing business analytics

Answer: b. A data migration process temporarily increasing access frequency. Explanation: Data migrations often access tables at a high rate, deviating from normal patterns. Option a would involve multiple tables or repeated attempts. Option c causes performance issues, not access frequency. Option d typically involves multiple tables or queries.

817. What is the best strategy to mitigate the impact of a successful SQL injection attack detected through database monitoring?
a. Disabling all database user accounts immediately
b. Rolling back transactions initiated by the attacker
c. Replacing vulnerable application code with secure versions
d. Enforcing parameterized queries for all database interactions

Answer: d. Enforcing parameterized queries for all database interactions. Explanation: Parameterized queries prevent SQL injection attacks by ensuring input is treated as data, not executable code. Option a disrupts operations unnecessarily. Option b mitigates data impact but doesn't prevent recurrence. Option c is long-term but doesn't address root causes.

818. A financial institution schedules a penetration test on its external-facing applications. Which step is most critical to ensure the test adheres to organizational policies?
a. Using automated tools to scan for vulnerabilities in real-time
b. Defining the test scope and obtaining written authorization from management
c. Engaging a red team to simulate real-world attack scenarios
d. Performing the test during non-business hours to reduce user disruption

Answer: b. Defining the test scope and obtaining written authorization from management. Explanation: Clearly defined scope and authorization are essential to ensure the test aligns with policies and avoids unintended consequences. Option a supports the test but does not address policy adherence. Option c describes an advanced approach but does not focus on scope and authorization. Option d minimizes disruption but is secondary to policy compliance.

819. An organization conducts a vulnerability assessment of its cloud environment. Which activity ensures comprehensive coverage of potential risks?
a. Scanning only production environments to identify high-priority vulnerabilities
b. Reviewing system configurations against a predefined security baseline
c. Limiting the assessment to externally exposed systems to prioritize impact
d. Excluding third-party managed services from the assessment scope

Answer: b. Reviewing system configurations against a predefined security baseline. Explanation: Comparing configurations to a security baseline ensures a comprehensive understanding of potential risks, including misconfigurations. Option a narrows the focus to production, which might miss other vulnerabilities. Option c overlooks internal risks. Option d neglects third-party services, leaving potential gaps.

820. A red team exercise is planned to test the resilience of an organization's security controls. Which step is critical to the success of this exercise?
a. Pre-approving attack vectors with the organization's IT team
b. Defining clear objectives and desired outcomes for the exercise
c. Limiting the duration of the exercise to prevent extended exposure
d. Informing all employees to ensure they do not mistake the exercise for a real attack

Answer: b. Defining clear objectives and desired outcomes for the exercise. Explanation: Establishing objectives ensures that the red team's activities are focused on testing specific controls and improving security posture. Option a limits the realism of the exercise. Option c prevents prolonged efforts but is secondary to objective setting. Option d reduces realism and impacts test efficacy.

821. During a purple team engagement, what is the primary role of the blue team?
a. Simulating attacks on critical systems to identify gaps in defenses
b. Assisting the red team in creating realistic attack scenarios
c. Defending against simulated attacks and analyzing detection capabilities
d. Performing a post-mortem review of security incidents

Answer: c. Defending against simulated attacks and analyzing detection capabilities. Explanation: The blue team focuses on defending and improving security measures during a purple team engagement. Option a describes the red team's role. Option b is a collaborative activity but not the blue team's primary function. Option d occurs post-exercise and is not exclusive to the blue team.

822. An organization validates the effectiveness of its security controls by conducting periodic testing. Which approach best demonstrates the ability of controls to mitigate advanced persistent threats (APTs)?
a. Performing a vulnerability scan to identify common misconfigurations
b. Conducting threat intelligence-based penetration testing
c. Reviewing historical incidents involving similar threat actors
d. Running a tabletop exercise focused on executive decision-making

Answer: b. Conducting threat intelligence-based penetration testing. Explanation: Penetration tests informed by threat intelligence simulate APT tactics, techniques, and procedures (TTPs) to evaluate control effectiveness. Option a identifies vulnerabilities but does not test APT resilience. Option c provides historical insights but not real-time validation. Option d enhances decision-making but does not test controls.
823. A healthcare organization requires security testing for systems that process protected health information (PHI). Which testing approach best ensures compliance with HIPAA?
a. Black-box penetration testing to simulate external attacks on PHI systems
b. White-box testing with a focus on access controls and data encryption mechanisms
c. Red team exercises targeting the organization's physical security
d. Automated scanning of public-facing applications for known vulnerabilities

Answer: b. White-box testing with a focus on access controls and data encryption mechanisms. Explanation: White-box testing evaluates the internal workings of systems to ensure compliance with HIPAA's technical safeguards, such as encryption and access control. Option a tests external risks but lacks compliance focus. Option c is unrelated to PHI system testing. Option d provides limited insights into internal controls.

824. An organization plans to implement encryption for sensitive customer data. Which encryption algorithm is most appropriate to achieve both high performance and security for large volumes of data?
a. RSA-2048
b. AES-256
c. ECC-384
d. SHA-256

Answer: b. AES-256. Explanation: AES-256 is a symmetric encryption algorithm ideal for securing large volumes of data due to its high performance and strong encryption. Option a (RSA-2048) is used for asymmetric encryption and is computationally slower. Option c (ECC-384) provides secure key exchange, not bulk encryption. Option d (SHA-256) is a hashing algorithm, not encryption.

825. A security administrator is tasked with implementing a digital signature to ensure message integrity and authentication. Which element is required for this implementation?
a. Symmetric key shared between sender and recipient
b. Private key of the signer to create the signature
c. Certificate Revocation List (CRL) to validate signatures
d. Secure Hash Algorithm (SHA) for encrypting the message

Answer: b. Private key of the signer to create the signature. Explanation: The signer uses their private key to generate the digital signature, ensuring authenticity. Option a applies to symmetric encryption, not digital signatures. Option c is used to verify the certificate, not create the signature. Option d is incorrect because SHA creates a hash, not a signature.

826. What is the most significant risk of using self-signed certificates in a production environment?
a. They cannot be revoked if compromised
b. They are incompatible with most encryption algorithms
c. They lack validation from a trusted certificate authority (CA)
d. They require frequent renewal compared to CA-signed certificates

Answer: c. They lack validation from a trusted certificate authority (CA). Explanation: Self-signed certificates do not provide third-party trust validation, making them less secure for public-facing systems. Option a is incorrect; self-signed certificates can be revoked manually. Option b is unrelated to compatibility. Option d is false; renewal requirements depend on configuration.

827. During certificate lifecycle management, what is the primary purpose of a Certificate Revocation List (CRL)?
a. To monitor the expiration dates of certificates
b. To maintain a list of revoked certificates for validation checks
c. To manage the issuance of certificates by the CA
d. To store public keys for certificate verification
Answer: b. To maintain a list of revoked certificates for validation checks. Explanation: A CRL provides a centralized way to track and validate revoked certificates. Option a pertains to expiration tracking, not revocation. Option c relates to issuance, not revocation. Option d involves key storage, not revocation status.

828. What is the primary benefit of using hardware security modules (HSMs) for encryption key management?
a. They provide faster encryption compared to software solutions
b. They ensure keys never leave the secure hardware environment
c. They allow secure key sharing across multiple devices
d. They eliminate the need for certificate-based encryption

Answer: b. They ensure keys never leave the secure hardware environment. Explanation: HSMs securely generate, store, and manage keys within a tamper-proof environment. Option a is partially true but secondary to security. Option c is incorrect; HSMs focus on security, not sharing. Option d is irrelevant; HSMs complement certificate-based encryption.

829. A company needs to ensure that encrypted data remains secure for at least 20 years. Which encryption algorithm is most appropriate for this use case?
a. DES
b. Blowfish
c. RSA-4096
d. AES-128

Answer: c. RSA-4096. Explanation: RSA-4096 provides strong encryption suitable for long-term security. Option a (DES) is obsolete and insecure. Option b (Blowfish) is outdated and less commonly used. Option d (AES-128) is strong but less resistant to future cryptographic attacks compared to RSA-4096.

830. Which method ensures secure key exchange in asymmetric encryption systems?
a. Diffie-Hellman key exchange protocol
b. Secure Hash Algorithm (SHA)
c. Symmetric key pre-distribution
d. Certificate signing by a trusted CA

Answer: a. Diffie-Hellman key exchange protocol. Explanation: Diffie-Hellman securely exchanges keys over an insecure channel. Option b is unrelated to key exchange. Option c applies to symmetric systems, not asymmetric encryption. Option d supports key authenticity, not exchange.

Wow. Take a moment to appreciate how far you've come. From those early chapters where we tackled the foundations of security principles, through the complex maze of cryptography, all the way to the nitty-gritty of network security and beyond - you've absorbed an incredible amount of knowledge.

You know what? This journey reminds me of building a house. We started with the foundation (those core security concepts), added the framework (risk management and security architecture), put up the walls (access control and identity management), and finally topped it off with all the essential systems that make it functional (network security, software development security, and business continuity). Now you're standing back, looking at this impressive structure of knowledge you've built.

Here's the thing about the CISSP exam - it's not just about memorizing facts. It's about understanding how all these pieces fit together in the real world. Through our practice questions, case studies, and detailed explanations, you've developed something more valuable than just test answers - you've gained the mindset of a security professional.

Remember those moments when concepts finally clicked? When you connected the dots between different domains? That's the kind of thinking that will serve you well not just on the exam, but throughout your career in information security.

Looking ahead to your exam day, trust in your preparation. You've put in the hours, wrestled with complex concepts, and worked through countless practice questions. Yes, the exam is challenging - that's exactly why the CISSP certification carries so much weight in our industry.

Some practical advice for the big day: Get a good night's sleep. Arrive early. Take deep breaths. Read each question carefully, and trust your instincts - they've been shaped by all this preparation.

You might encounter questions that seem ambiguous or tricky. That's normal. Remember our discussions about thinking like a manager and always considering the bigger picture of business impact and risk management.

Beyond the exam, these concepts you've mastered will guide you throughout your career in information security. This field keeps evolving, and you're now equipped with the foundational knowledge to grow and adapt with it.

I genuinely believe in your ability to succeed. Whether this is your first attempt or you're returning to conquer this challenge, you've given yourself the tools you need. You've done the work. You understand the material. Now it's time to show what you know.

Go forward with confidence. The information security community needs professionals like you who take the time to truly understand these concepts and their real-world applications.

Best of luck on your exam. You've got this.

Stay curious, stay secure, and never stop learning.

Made in the USA
Middletown, DE
13 March 2025